# SPANISH AMERICA
# AFTER INDEPENDENCE,
### *c.* 1820 – *c.* 1870

The complete *Cambridge History of Latin America* presents a large-scale, authoritative survey of Latin America's unique historical experience from the first contacts between the native American Indians and Europeans to the present day. *Spanish America after Independence* c. *1820* – c. *1870* is a selection of chapters from volume III brought together to provide a continuous history of Spanish America during the first half century following independence from Spain. The first two chapters form a general survey of economy and society, politics and ideology for Spanish America as a whole; the remaining chapters provide a more detailed history of individual countries or groups of countries: Mexico; Central America; Venezuela, Colombia and Ecuador; Peru and Bolivia; Chile; and the River Plate Republics. Bibliographical essays are included for all chapters. The book will be a valuable text for both teachers and students of Latin American history.

# SPANISH AMERICA
# AFTER
# INDEPENDENCE,
## c. 1820 – c. 1870

*edited by*

## LESLIE BETHELL

*Professor of Latin American History*
*University of London*

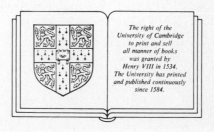

The right of the
University of Cambridge
to print and sell
all manner of books
was granted by
Henry VIII in 1534.
The University has printed
and published continuously
since 1584.

## CAMBRIDGE UNIVERSITY PRESS

*Cambridge*

*London   New York   New Rochelle*
*Melbourne   Sydney*

Published by the Press Syndicate of the University of Cambridge
The Pitt Building, Trumpington Street, Cambridge CB2 1RP
32 East 57th Street, New York, NY 10022, USA
10 Stamford Road, Oakleigh, Melbourne 3166, Australia

First published 1987

Printed in Great Britain by Woolnough Bookbinding, Irthlingborough

*British Library cataloguing in publication data*

The Cambridge history of Latin America. Vol. 3 *Selections*
Spanish America
after independence, *c.* 1820.
*c.*1870.
1. Latin America – History – To 1830
2. Latin America – History – 1830–1898
I. Bethell, Leslie
980'.031    F1413

*Library of Congress cataloguing in publication data*

Spanish America after independence, c. 1820–c. 1870.
"Previously published as part of volume III of the
Cambridge history of Latin America"
Includes bibliographies and index.
1. Latin America – History – 1830–1898.   I. Bethell, Leslie.
F1413.S72    1987    980'.031    87-31047

ISBN 0 521 34128 0 hard covers
ISBN 0 521 34926 5 paperback

# CONTENTS

*List of maps*        *page* vii
*Preface*        ix

1   Economy and society       1
     TULIO HALPERÍN DONGHI, *Professor of History,*
     *University of California at Berkeley*

2   Politics, ideology and society       48
     FRANK SAFFORD, *Professor of History, Northwestern*
     *University*

3   Mexico       123
     JAN BAZANT, *Professor, El Colegio de México*

4   Central America       171
     R. L. WOODWARD, Jr, *Professor of History, Tulane*
     *University*

5   Venezuela, Colombia and Ecuador       207
     MALCOLM DEAS, *Fellow of St Antony's College, Oxford*

6   Peru and Bolivia       239
     HERACLIO BONILLA, *Professor of Latin American*
     *History, University of California, San Diego* and *Instituto de*
     *Estudios Peruanos, Lima*

7   Chile       283
     SIMON COLLIER, *Reader in Latin American History,*
     *University of Essex*

8 The River Plate Republics 314
JOHN LYNCH, *Director of the Institute of Latin American
Studies and Professor of Latin American History, University
of London*

*Bibliographical essays* 376
*Index* 413

# MAPS

Spanish America in 1830                                          *page* x
Mexican territories ceded to the United States                  140
Central America in 1855                                          173
Colombia, Venezuela and Ecuador in 1830                         209
Peru and Bolivia after Independence                             242
Nineteenth-century Chile                                        287
The River Plate Republics, 1820–70                              318

# PREFACE

*The Cambridge History of Latin America (CHLA)* is an authoritative survey of Latin America's unique historical experience during the five centuries from the first contacts between the native peoples of the Americas and Europeans in the late fifteenth and early sixteenth centuries to the present day.

*Spanish America after Independence,* c. *1820* – c. *1870* brings together the eight chapters of Part Three of volume III of *The Cambridge History of Latin America* in a separate volume which, it is hoped, will be useful for both teachers and students of Latin American history. The first two chapters offer general surveys of economy and society and politics and ideology in Spanish America during the first half-century following independence from Spain; the six remaining chapters provide detailed histories of individual countries or groups of countries: Mexico; Central America (Guatemala, El Salvador, Honduras, Nicaragua and Costa Rica); Venezuela, Colombia and Ecuador; Peru and Bolivia; Chile; and the River Plate Republics (Argentina, Uruguay and Paraguay). Each chapter is accompanied by a bibliographical essay.

MEXICO

Mexico • • Veracruz

CUBA
(Spanish)

HAITI

SANTO DOMINGO
(occupied by Haiti 1822–44)

PUERTO RICO (Spanish)

JAMAICA
(British)

UNITED PROVINCES
of CENTRAL AMERICA

TRINIDAD (British)

Caracas
VENEZUELA

NEW GRANADA

• Bogotá

Quito
ECUADOR

R. Amazon

EMPIRE of
BRAZIL

Lima
PERU

La Paz
BOLIVIA

Sucre

Salvador
(Bahia)

PARAGUAY

Asunción

Rio de Janeiro

ARGENTINE
CONFEDERATION

Santiago

CHILE

Buenos
Aires

URUGUAY

Montevideo

0          2000 km

0        1000 miles

Spanish America in 1830

x

# 1

## ECONOMY AND SOCIETY

In the years between 1808 and 1825 a new relationship was established between the Spanish American economies and the world economy. In comparison with their much fuller incorporation into the expanding international economy which began around the middle of the century and became more pronounced from the 1870s, the changes which accompanied the achievement of political independence may well appear superficial and limited; nevertheless, they constitute a decisive turning-point in the relations between Spanish America and the rest of the world.

The old colonial commercial system had been breaking down since the end of the eighteenth century, but it was only after 1808 that Spain was finally eliminated as the commercial intermediary between Spanish America and the rest of Europe, especially Britain. The special circumstances prevailing both in Europe and the Atlantic economy as a whole at the time had important consequences for Spanish America's future commercial relations. The advance of the French armies into the Iberian peninsula, which triggered off the separation of the American colonies from Spain and Portugal, was intended to complete the closure of continental Europe to British trade. Increasingly isolated from its European markets, Britain was trying, with an urgency bordering on desperation, to replace them. Thus, the opportunity provided by the transfer of the Portuguese court to Rio de Janeiro to trade directly with Brazil for the first time was eagerly accepted. And as, following the overthrow of the Spanish crown in Madrid, the first political upheavals in Spanish America occurred, Rio de Janeiro became not only the entrepôt for an aggressive British commercial drive in Brazil itself but also in Spanish America, especially the Río de la Plata area and the Pacific coast of South America.

[1] Translated from the Spanish by Dr Richard Southern; translation revised by the Editor.

The Río de la Plata was opened to British trade as early as 1809 – by the last Spanish viceroy. The subsequent British expansion into Spanish South America was, however, to depend on the fortunes of revolutionary arms; for even though Royalist administrators eventually showed themselves prepared, as an exceptional measure, to open up their territories to direct trade with Britain, the activities of patriot corsairs made such trade very unattractive. Chile was finally opened up in 1818, Lima not until 1821 – and the rest of Peru even later. In the countries bordering the Caribbean progress was slow and less complete. Venezuela's war of independence lasted for ten years, as did New Granada's. Mexico, with more than half the population and wealth of the Spanish Indies, achieved its independence late (in 1821). Even then it was several years before the Royalists in San Juan de Ulua were eliminated, and this affected Veracruz, the chief Mexican port in the Caribbean. The islands of Cuba and Puerto Rico remained Spanish possessions, but were open to direct trade with foreign countries from 1817, although that trade suffered restrictions aimed at preserving this last colonial market for Spanish products, from textiles to flour. Santo Domingo remained under Haitian occupation until 1844.

The Atlantic coast of South America was therefore the first zone to be incorporated into the new commercial system and the circumstances which impelled Britain rapidly to expand its overseas markets had their earliest and greatest impact there. British merchant adventurers arrived in Rio de Janeiro, Buenos Aires and Montevideo in considerable numbers during the years 1808–12. A few years later Valparaiso became the main port on the Pacific coast of South America, the centre from which British goods were trans-shipped to ports along the coast from La Serena to Guayaquil. The merchant adventurers engaged in the exploration and exploitation of the Latin American market were acting directly for merchants and industrialists in Britain: their task was to find a market as rapidly as possible for the surplus goods which threatened the growth of the British economy. From the outset, they were less concerned with price than with a quick sale and an equally quick return (of which precious metals were easily the most preferred form). To achieve this commercial penetration British goods had often to be offered at prices even lower than had been planned. For example, in 1810, after hearing the news of the liberalization of trade and the outbreak of the revolution in Buenos Aires, many merchant adventurers left London hoping to sell British goods in South America; however, when they arrived in Buenos

Aires, they not only found that there were too many of them, but that they had to face unexpected competition from the shipments of British merchants in Rio de Janeiro. The result was that they had to sell at a loss, thereby hastening the victory of overseas products over those tradition-ally supplied to the Buenos Aires market from the foothills of the Andes or from Peru and Upper Peru. Another consequence was the expansion of the existing consumer market through the inclusion of social groups which had not previously formed part of it.

The opening of Latin American trade to the outside world and the arrival of the British in large numbers also dealt a severe blow to the old style commercial practices which, in Spanish America at least, had been based on a rigid hierarchy. The merchant-exporter in Spain was linked to the Spanish merchant at the Spanish American ports and centres of distribution, and thence to the smaller merchants in the minor centres, and from them to the itinerant peddlers. The system was essentially maintained by *avío* (Mexico) or *habilitación* (Spanish South America), that is to say, the provision of capital by those in the higher levels of the hierarchy to those at the lower level of entrepreneurial activity, and by credit. Very high profit margins were guaranteed at each of these stages, although the profits derived from the provision of credit are not always easily distinguished from commercial activity in the strict sense of the term. The entry of the British, impelled by desperation to make their presence felt, albeit sporadically, at ever lower levels of this commercial system, had a devastating effect. Their preference for quick sales at lower prices, and for the use of cash rather than credit, began to offer at all levels an alternative to a system which conferred its greatest benefits on those at the top.

The peaceful British invasion of Spanish America was facilitated by the long period of political, social and military instability during the wars of independence in which potential local rivals were weakened. The merchant adventurers soon perceived opportunities for excellent profits in the unstable conditions prevailing. Rather than make any attempt to establish regular commercial relations, they employed an opportunistic style of trading. For example, on the Paraná river the Robertson brothers hurried to Santa Fe, to sell Paraguayan *yerba maté*, which scarcity had made much more expensive.[2] Again, in 1821 when San Martín in Chile was preparing his campaign to capture Lima, Basil Hall was secretly

[2] J. P. and W. P. Robertson, *Letters on Paraguay* (London, 1838) 1, 358–9.

commissioned by London merchants to take a shipment of goods there before competitors reached it; he was able to 'skim the cream' off that long-isolated market which was the capital of the viceroyalty of Peru.[3]

Although this trade was fatal for local competitors, it was not without risk for British merchant adventurers. They were obliged to be increasingly audacious and very few survived to the end of this phase of exploration and conquest unharmed. This was perhaps inevitable, given the conditions of the period. The needs of the British economy forced the merchants constantly to expand markets whose limits were only apparent when local demand failed to materialize; a process of trial and error ensured that each attempt at expansion ended in failure (because only such failure could bring it to an end); understandably, the embittered reports of the victims accumulated. However, no victim actually reversed the overall advance to which he himself had contributed. Even those who assess the results from a British, rather than a Latin American, point of view find it difficult to argue that the events of this period did not leave a significant legacy for the future. Although British exports to Latin America as a whole no longer accounted for 35 per cent of total British exports, as they had done in 1809 and 1811, nevertheless, with an annual average of around £5 million in the period 1820–50 (roughly half of which went to Spanish America and half to Brazil), they had doubled the averages of the second half of the eighteenth century in terms of value (and multiplied them several times in terms of volume).[4]

During the second quarter of the nineteenth century Britain gradually lost the commercial quasi-monopoly which she had acquired during the wars of independence. This predominance had for a while been threatened by United States competition. Supported by an excellent merchant navy, American merchants spearheaded a more flexible system of trade and navigation. Because they were not serving the needs of an industrial economy like their British competitors, they brought not only United States, but also European, African and Oriental goods to the markets of Latin America (and particularly to those worst supplied by the British, who tended to imitate their Spanish and Portuguese predecessors'

[3] Samuel Haigh, *Sketches of Buenos Aires, Chile and Peru* (London, 1831), vii.
[4] For the figures on British exports to Latin America, 1820–50, see D. C. M. Platt, *Latin America and British trade, 1806–1914* (London, 1973), 31. Whether one concludes, with Professor Platt, that the figures for the three decades following independence are not 'totally out of line' with 'what estimates survive of the colonial trade' depends on whether a doubling of trade is considered to be a significant change. Of course, this change may appear insignificant if it is compared with that which was to occur in the second half of the nineteenth century.

preference for the richest and most densely populated zones). However, an essential element in American exports were 'domestics', a rougher and cheaper cloth than that of Manchester. When the long-term fall in prices caused by the advance of the Industrial Revolution nullified the price advantage, it eliminated an irreplaceable element of the challenge to British predominance. Thereafter, even though American trade was able to obtain local advantages (in Venezuela, for example, it rivalled British trade in the middle of the century), it did not cause London and Liverpool any alarm.

In addition to the North American trade, there was increasingly intensive trade with France, the German states, Sardinia and the old mother countries. However, this appears to have complemented British trade rather than rivalled it. France led in the market for luxury goods, and Germany (as it had before Independence) in semi-luxury goods; this did not affect British dominance in the much wider range of industrial products for popular consumption. France, Sardinia, Spain, Portugal as well as the United States became once again the countries of origin for the growing exports to Latin America of agricultural products (wine, oil and wheat). It could hardly be expected that Britain would preserve the pre-eminence it had achieved through Gibraltar in the export of these products because of the highly exceptional political and military circumstances of the wars of independence.

Britain, then, preserved its leading position as an exporter to Latin America. It was at the same time the principal market for Latin American exports, although there were some important exceptions (like Brazilian coffee) and Britain's position declined more rapidly than in the case of exports to Latin America. This mercantile connection was reinforced by the dominant role of the 'bill on London' in financial transactions between Latin America and the rest of the world.

The increase in British exports to Spanish America after 1808 had a profound impact on the region's balance of trade. Throughout the colonial period (and despite the effects of the so-called Imperial Free Trade established in 1778–82), the value of Spanish American exports had been consistently higher than the value of imports. This was now reversed. Most of the trade gap was, of course, filled by exports of precious metals, which in colonial times had always been the principal item in Spanish American exports – and which dominated Brazilian exports during the first two-thirds of the eighteenth century. However, the Brazilian gold boom now belonged to an irrecoverable past, and although in Spanish America – apart from Upper Peru, the only significant exception – gold and silver mining did not suffer substantial falls in production until the very eve of the crisis of Independence, production fell precipitately during the period of the wars. The substantial export of metal coinage from Spanish America during the second and third decades of the nineteenth century is, therefore, rightly considered as a loss (and even flight) of capital rather than the continuation or renewal of a traditional line of exports.

No doubt there were many causes of this flight of capital. Political instability, which led to the departure of many Spaniards, was one. Certainly the commercial habits of the British conquerors of the Latin American market caused an outflow of precious metals. However, as early as 1813–17, the drive that characterized the first British commercial offensive slackened. And from the early 1820s a more regular system was established throughout most of Latin America underpinned by a series of commercial treaties with the new states which guaranteed freedom of trade and which were imposed (with no possibility of negotiation) as the precondition for British recognition. British merchants began to adopt patterns of trading similar to those of their Spanish predecessors, including the use of credit. Nevertheless, even when at the same time British exports to Latin America declined, the imbalance of trade continued. The fundamental reason appears to be, therefore, the stagnation of Latin American exports. In some spheres of particular significance in international trade (especially mining) these were considerably lower than in the last decades of the colonial period. At the same time, the characteristics of the new commercial system did not favour local capital accumulation. On the contrary, quantities of precious metals accumulated during several decades were actually lost, just at the time when a greater access to the world economy offered opportunities for their investment. Instead they were squandered on imports of consumer goods at a level which Latin America was not able to afford on the basis of its normal flow of exports. Even the reduced level of international trade prevailing in the early 1820s could not be maintained without an increase in production for export, which required massive investment far in excess of the available local capital. It seemed to some at the time (as it did a century later) that if Britain wished to retain and indeed expand its links with the newly independent Latin American states, the commercial relationship would have to be accompanied by a financial relationship which would provide government loans and private investment. This was the proposal for the future of Mexico proposed in 1827 by Sir H. G. Ward, the British chargé d'affaires, a perceptive but by no means disinterested observer: according to him, the first and foremost responsibility of British investors was the outfitting of the mining industry, which in the long term would create the capital necessary for the exploitation of crops in the neglected and depopulated tropical lowlands, thus giving a new impulse to Mexico's exports. In the short term, however, the outfitting of the mining industry was to allow Mexico to continue to pay for its increased imports. It is not surprising that Ward vehemently rejected the alternative solution: to achieve equilibrium by restricting imports and encouraging local production (of textiles, for example).[5]

The investment of capital in Latin America was not the main concern of British merchants anxious as they were to support a reciprocal flow of trade. It appealed more to investors in search of high and quick profits. However, they suffered a swift and harsh disappointment: although the bonds of the new states and the shares of the companies organized in London to exploit the mines of various Latin American countries at first rode easily on the crest of the London stock exchange boom of 1823–5, by 1827 every state except Brazil had ceased to pay interest and amortization on its bonds, and only a few Mexican mining companies had avoided bankruptcy.

For the next quarter of a century (1825–50), the economic relationship between Latin America and the outside world was largely a commercial one; of the financial connection there survived only some mining firms organized as joint-stock companies (whose failure to prosper did not encourage imitators) and a number of committees of disappointed and discontented bondholders, who watched anxiously for a sign of improvement in the Latin American economies in order to press their claims. Even Brazil, which had managed to avoid cessation of payments, would not for many years again have recourse to external credit.

Since the trade imbalance did not disappear immediately, it must, however, be assumed that there was in this period a volume of credit and investment from outside at least sufficient (in the absence of any more effectively institutionalized mechanisms) to maintain some kind of equilibrium. To begin with, from 1820 there was the investment needed to establish the more regular mercantile system which now prevailed

---

[5] H. G. Ward, *Mexico in 1827* (London, 1828), I, 328.

(warehouses, means of transport, etc.), and then there was the investment which was at least partly sumptuary; even in the minor commercial centres, foreign merchants generally owned the best houses. Other investment resulted from these merchants managing industrial undertakings or, more often, agricultural properties. However, these investments were only capable of offsetting the trade imbalance between the Latin American economies and the outside world if it is assumed that, during this period of consolidation and regularization, the resident foreign merchants continued to act as agents or partners of merchants or capitalists in the metropolitan countries. It is not easy to be sure on this point, but there are examples of this relationship to be found from Mexico to the Río de la Plata.

For Latin America, independence had redefined the connection with the metropolis on more favourable terms than in the past. It was not simply that the commercial connection was no longer accompanied by direct political domination; this eliminated a fiscal dimension that had been one of the most onerous elements of the former colonial relationship. The new commercial metropolis had an industrial economy far more dynamic than that of the former colonial powers and, at least in the short term, its agents were prepared to sacrifice profit margins to obtain a greater volume of sales in the new markets. Even when, from the 1820s, Latin America's trade with Britain came to resemble rather more that of the late colonial period, the steady advance of the Industrial Revolution guaranteed that Latin America would benefit in the long term, despite fluctuations caused by temporary circumstances, from a fall in the price of British exports. By 1850 the price of the most popular grades of cotton cloth (which was still the most important article exported to Latin America) had fallen by three-quarters from its level during the 1810–20 period. The price of other products fell less sharply: woollen cloth, which did not undergo its technological transformation until around 1850, declined in price by about one-third. Comparison is less easy in the case of other products – china, porcelain and glass, for example – owing to changes in the British customs system of classification, but they appear to have suffered a similar decline and, in any case, they represented a much smaller proportion of total exports than did textiles. Taking the picture as a whole, around the middle of the century the price of British exports, the composition of which was remarkably similar to that prevailing in the early years of liberalization of trade, appears to have fallen to about half the level of the period 1810–20.

During these decades the price of primary products also tended to fall, but less markedly. Silver suffered a fall of 6 per cent as against gold, leather from the Río de la Plata region a fall of around 30 per cent, and coffee and sugar a similar decline. Only tobacco suffered a fall of around 50 per cent.[6] It was not until the middle of the nineteenth century that the first signs became evident of a change in Latin America's favourable terms of trade.

Paradoxically, as a result of these favourable terms, the opening up of Latin America to world trade had less profound consequences than had been expected before 1810. Since the level of prices of exportable products did not seem immediately threatened, the effect was more to encourage an increase in the volume of exports than to promote any technological advances in production leading to a reduction of costs. In any case, attempts to develop the export sector were severely restricted by a scarcity of local capital which was aggravated by the war and, as we have seen, by the imbalance in trade in the independence period.

However, the limitations of the transforming impact of the new external connection were principally due to the almost exclusively commercial character of that connection; as we have seen, only exceptionally (during the brief period of optimism that accompanied the boom of 1823–5) was consideration given to capital investment from the metropolis designed to expand and modernize production of goods for export; and we have also observed how the subsequent fortunes of those undertakings were to ensure that they would retain their exceptional character for several decades.

The scarcity of local capital and the reluctance of foreign capitalists to invest in the area were not seen by contemporaries as the principal reasons for the slow growth of the Latin American export economies in the period after independence. Contemporary observers usually drew attention above all to the destruction caused by the wars. In order to appreciate the validity of this point of view, it must be recalled that it was not only resources which were destroyed – that is to say, livestock consumed by the warring armies, mines flooded, money seized from public or private coffers – but also an entire system of economic, juridical and social relationships. Thus, one might include in the inventory of damage the way planters and miners lost control of their slaves in

---

[6] British export prices are based on the real values declared for exports to Buenos Aires, in Public Record Office, London, Customs, Series 6, for the years concerned. For those of leather from the Río de la Plata region, see T. Halperín-Donghi, 'La expansión ganadera en la campaña de Buenos Aires', *Desarrollo económico* (Buenos Aires), (1963), 65. For the prices of Venezuelan coffee, see Miguel Izard, *Series estadísticas para la historia de Venezuela* (Mérida, 1970), 161–3. For those of sugar and tobacco, see M. G. Mulhall, *Dictionary of statistics* (London, 1892), 471–4.

Venezuela, the Upper Cauca in Colombia, or the coast of Peru; the ending of the *mita* system which forcibly recruited workers in the highlands of Peru for work in the mines of Upper Peru and the impossibility of re-establishing this system because of the subsequent political separation of the two areas; the fluctuations in Chilean wheat exports to what had become a Peruvian market; the disruption of the complicated traffic in mules, foodstuffs, liquor and handwoven textiles throughout the Andes. One might even include the indirect consequences of the wars; besides the destruction of mines in the battle areas the fall in production of mines elsewhere whose owners, because of the war, for years neglected to make the necessary investment. Looked at in this way, the legacy of the war may indeed appear overwhelming, although difficult to evaluate precisely. Even the actual damage has never been adequately assessed. Moreover, like the impact of the opening up of Latin America to world trade, the effects of the war were very unequally distributed over the different regions and sectors of production.

Opinion in both Spanish America and Europe predicted that mining products would be most likely to take rapid advantage of the opportunities offered by the opening up of trade, but optimism gradually faded. Only in Chile would mining production, in the middle of the century, exceed the volume (in this case small) achieved during the colonial period. In the rest of Spanish America the most successful mining areas were those where, after a serious decline, production recovered its pre-revolutionary level; in many areas, such as New Granada or Bolivia, this was not to be regained until later, and in some others never.

The reasons for this disappointing performance are complex. In order to understand them more fully, we must emphasize that the disappointment may be explained in part by the perhaps excessively high hopes raised, somewhat artificially, in Europe and, by extension, in Spanish America during the short-lived investment boom which came to an abrupt end in the crisis of 1825. When considered in the context of the entire history of mining in Spanish America from its beginning in the sixteenth century, developments between 1810 and 1850 do not appear to us to be a consequence of the new socio-economic conditions in which mining found itself as clearly as they did to contemporary observers. Whatever the prevailing circumstances, mining went through cycles of discovery, exploitation and exhaustion. Thus, it is not entirely surprising that Mexico, or even Peru, which had reached their highest levels of production in the last decades of the colonial period, should have required a quarter of a century after the return of peace to recover. Similarly it is easier to understand why Chile enjoyed the earliest period of post-independence mining prosperity if it is remembered that its centre was the mine of Chañarcillo, which was only discovered after independence. The recovery of mining in Mexico, as in Bolivia even later, was due not so much to a return to former levels of production in the old mining centres as to the emergence of new centres in Zacatecas and other states. Nevertheless, the disappointment over mining production and exports in the post-independence period still appears justified. It was reasonable to expect that the commercial revolution by stimulating a rise in the volume and value of imports would lend an added urgency to the need for more exports, especially of precious metals. The sluggish response of the mining industry, therefore, requires an explanation that takes into account more than the cycle of bonanza and crisis as determined by the discovery or exhaustion of the richest veins of ore.

Cultural and institutional explanations were for the most part, not surprisingly, proposed by foreigners who had been attracted by the apparently brilliant prospects before 1825: the immorality or frivolity of the ruling classes; the difficulty of finding mine workers with the necessary qualities; the surprising leniency displayed by the ruling classes towards workers during episodes of industrial indiscipline involving foreign entrepreneurs; the rigid character of the laws governing the mining industry; and so on. We will not attempt here to examine the mass of accusations, which reflected above all the profound differences between Spanish Americans and those who were trying to insert themselves into the Spanish American economies. These differences were naturally much sharper where foreigners no longer confined themselves to commerce and moved into productive activities.

Other obstacles to progress in the mining sector were more strictly economic, i.e. the shortage of labour and capital. Both factors were present in varying degrees in all the mining areas of Spanish America. Nevertheless, it seems possible to conclude that the difficulties of recruiting labour have everywhere been exaggerated. There is no doubt that war damage in Mexico, the richest mining zone in the late colonial period, severely hampered post-war reconstruction; however, there is no evidence of a labour shortage as such. After independence, mineworkers received higher monetary wages than the agricultural workers, but this was nothing new, and in any case did not necessarily signify any difference in real wages. Moreover, even though the ending of the *mita* system in mining, referred to above, deprived independent Bolivia of an important source of labour, it is not without significance that the wages of the free workers during the first decades after independence were closer to the wages received by the *mita* workers than to those of the free workers during the colonial period;[7] this does not suggest any shortage of labour. Furthermore, the new mining zones, or those demonstrating the most rapid expansion, do not appear to have found it more difficult than did the older, stagnant zones to recruit the necessary labour; for example, no shortage appears to have impeded the expansion of Chilean mining.

The problem created by the shortage of capital appears to have been more serious. In this sphere, the damage caused by the war seemed less easy to repair. The destruction of the mines and processing plants by actual military operations was very limited even where the mining zone concerned was the theatre of war. The suspension of investment in expansion and maintenance had a more lasting effect, and a concentrated investment of capital became necessary before mining in Spanish America could recover. However, from this point of view, the development of mining up to 1850 does not appear too unsatisfactory: thanks to British and local capital in Mexico and Bolivia, and almost exclusively local capital in Chile and Peru, there was in fact a modest recovery. Nevertheless, we may ask why investment was not more intensive and results more impressive. From the point of view of those responsible for taking the decision to invest, the reasons why this did not occur are quite understandable. Except in Chile, the yield from mining investment was non-existent or very low. In Mexico, for example, there was absolutely no return on the investment made by the British company of Real del Monte, the most important established during the boom which ended in 1825. This was not due to any lack of measures designed to bring the mine out of its stagnation: on the contrary, the company made several costly attempts at improvement; it continued, with even less success, the efforts of the former proprietors to pump water out of the lower levels of the mine, and built an access road for vehicles in an area previously served only by mules. The Real del Monte Company certainly had good reason to complain of its ill fortune: when, after a quarter of a century of investing at a loss, the rights of exploitation were transferred to local

7 Luis Peñaloza, *Historia económica de Bolivia* (La Paz, 1953–4), I, 208; II, 101.

entrepreneurs, the latter quickly began to make profits, partly as a result of the very same investments.[8] However, contemporary observers seemed prepared to draw a more precise moral from this experience: H. G. Ward, by no means a disinterested apologist for the British companies established in Mexico, willingly admitted that the decision to invest vast sums in improving production, exploitation and transport had been imprudent. At the other end of Spanish America, John Miers drew a similar conclusion from his experience as an unsuccessful producer of copper in Chile: in his opinion, too, it was necessary to examine carefully the economic impact to be expected from each of the proposed technical improvements; and even investment designed to increase the volume of production without introducing technological innovation ran the risk of being counter-productive.[9] Thus, a conservatism, which reflected the prevailing atmosphere during a period in which there was no technical progress comparable to what was to take place in the second half of the century, led to greater caution where new investment in mining was concerned, except when, as in the case of Chile, exceptionally rich veins of ore guaranteed quick and large profits.

The post-war reconstruction did not lead to the introduction of decisive innovations in the organization of mining operations. In the case of labour there is no doubt that wage-labour now played a dominant role even where it had not done so in the colonial period. This was certainly the case in Bolivia; the picture was slightly different in the gold-mining zone of New Granada, though even there the decline in the importance of slave-labour was clear. However, in the mining areas that had enjoyed the most rapid development during the last years of the colonial period, wage-labour was already dominant. This, of course, concealed even then very different real conditions in the different parts of Spanish America ranging from Mexico, where Humboldt found wage-levels to be higher than those prevailing in Saxony, to the Norte Chico of Chile, where it has been denied, more convincingly than in the case of other zones, that a true wage-labour force existed. These variations continued to exist after the transition to independence, although there is no doubt that the change from stagnation to rapid expansion must have affected the situation of the workers in the Chilean mines.

In colonial times there were similar variations in the way mining itself

---

[8] Robert W. Randall, *Real del Monte, a British mining venture in Mexico* (Austin, Texas, 1972), 81, 100–8, 54–6.
[9] John Miers, *Travels in Chile and la Plata* (London, 1826), II, 382–5.

was organized. In Mexico large productive units which financed their expansion from their own profits predominated; they were sometimes even able to invest their profits in the acquisition of agricultural properties which were economically integrated with the mines. In Peru, Bolivia and Chile productive units were smaller and lacked real independence from their suppliers and those who advanced the capital to enable them to continue their activities.[10] (In the case of Upper Peru, the situation of the mining entrepreneurs was further aggravated by the fact that frequently they had to pay high rents to the absentee holders of exploitation rights.) After independence the contrast between Mexico and Peru in this respect continued. As late as 1879, Maurice du Chatenet observed that the majority of the mining entrepreneurs of Cerro de Pasco were not 'rich people, who have capital available . . . [but] have to borrow money from others'. They had to sell their products to their creditors for less than the normal price.[11] Miers had described similar conditions in the Chilean copper-mining zone in the 1820s. However, the prosperity of silver-mining in Chile after 1831 led to the rise of a class of mining entrepreneurs who were not only independent but successful enough for significant amounts of capital to be invested after the middle of the century; the richest entrepreneurs emerged as the proprietors of large urban and rural properties in central Chile. In Bolivia during the same period there were radical changes in the legal framework within which mining activities operated. The newly independent nation cancelled the privileges of the absentee concessionaires and, by granting new concessions, encouraged the rise of larger mining undertakings than those of the colonial period. However, as Bolivian silver mining stagnated in the post-independence period the consequences of these changes were not felt until the last thirty years of the nineteenth century.

The expansion of mining in Spanish America was, therefore, limited almost everywhere by the need for capital, which was never more than partially satisfied. However, another factor limiting the expansion of the Latin American export economies, the level of demand, did not on the whole affect the mining sector. There was, it is true, in the 1820s a boom and a slump in Chilean copper production, which was largely a result of the growth and subsequent catastrophic decline in the demand for

---

[10] John Fisher, *Minas y mineras en el Perú Colonial, 1776–1824* (Lima, 1977), 101.

[11] Maurice du Chatenet, 'Estado actual de la industria minera en el Cerro de Pasco', *Anales de la Escuela de Construcciones Civiles y de Minas*, First Series, 1 (Lima, 1880), 119.

copper in British India.[12] But throughout the region silver was far more important than any other mineral and the demand for Spanish American silver for coinage was so vast that it was impossible to imagine any limit to the expansion of production. The agricultural sector could not depend on such a steady demand. On the other hand, depending on the commodity concerned, this sector could count on one advantage. This was that it was not so necessary to make a considerable investment before profits could be realized as in the case of a mining industry shattered during the struggle for independence.

The sector of production offering the greatest advantages from minimal investment was stockraising. It was, moreover, influenced, perhaps more than any other sector, by the availability of external markets. From the very beginning of the colonization of Latin America, cattleraising became the way by which land resources could be utilized when other more profitable methods became impossible. The areas over which it spread, without at that time being able to count on satisfactory external markets, were eventually extremely wide: from the north of Mexico to the north-east of Brazil (and, within Brazil, to Minas Gerais once its mining prosperity had ended); from the highlands of New Granada, to the plains of Venezuela and immense areas in Central America to a large part of the Central Valley of Chile as well as the whole of the Río de la Plata region and southern Brazil. In the first half of the nineteenth century a system of exploitation that was still technologically very backward meant it was not necessary (as it was to be later) to limit cattleraising to the most suitable land in these vast areas. The reason why only some of these areas were probably incorporated into the new export economy has less to do, therefore, with production methods than with commerce: it was the ability to channel production into both pre- and post-independence commercial circuits that explains the success of cattleraising in the Río de la Plata area, Venezuela and southern Brazil.

In view of the absence or extreme scarcity of capital and in view of the fact that these were very thinly populated areas in which social discipline was, in several cases, further affected by the disturbed times, the expansion of cattle production was based on extending the available land. However, the difference is striking between the growing prosper-

[12] Report of the British Consul in Valparaiso, Charles R. Nugent, 17 March 1825, in R. A. Humphreys (ed.), *British consular reports on the trade and politics of Latin America* (London, 1940), 96ff.

ity of the cattleraisers of Buenos Aires and the impoverishment of those on the Pacific coast of Central America, as John L. Stephens noted in the middle of the nineteenth century: the reason was, of course, that owners of properties in Central America comparable in area to a European principality had no way to sell their useless wealth, while landowners in the Río de la Plata had free access to the European market.[13] This was because the expansion of imports from abroad consequent upon the liberalization of trade had occurred in the Río de la Plata region earlier and with greater intensity than elsewhere, and it had created the need for a flow of exports which would make a continuing flow of imports possible. In Chile, despite the absence of natural conditions comparable to those of the Río de la Plata region, there was also an expansion of cattleraising for export, although the volume concerned was much smaller. Importers in Buenos Aires, Montevideo and Valparaiso needed goods to send to Europe; their ships needed cargoes for the return journey. They sometimes themselves assumed responsibility for exporting livestock products. What hindered the expansion of exports in other areas less affected by the opening up of trade, therefore, was the absence of a flow of imports and this was especially true, around the middle of the century, of the Pacific coast between Guayaquil and California.

The opening up of trade gave Latin American stockraisers access to a European market which had been from earlier times, and was still, dominated by Russia. This limited the possibilities of Latin American expansion which occurred largely thanks to the extreme abundance and cheapness of land. The long-term decline in the price of leather in the European market dangerously ate into landowners' profit-margins. Hides, of course, maintained their position as the leading export but breeding was maintained and expanded through the diversification of livestock products. Exports of salted meat, which had commenced before the wars of independence, had by 1820 already recovered their prewar level and continued to increase until the middle of the century. Slaves constituted the main market for salted meat (above all, in Cuba and Brazil). Tallow began to make up a higher proportion of exports to Europe from 1830 and, in contrast to leather, enjoyed an almost constant rise in price. Much of the tallow exported was no longer raw but, strictly speaking, grease concentrated by steam; landowners and merchants in the rural areas of the Río de la Plata, for example, had installed 'steam-

---

[13] John L. Stephens, *Incidents of travel in Central America, Chiapas and Yucatan* (New Brunswick, N.J., 1949), I, 300–1.

plants'. Its production, therefore, included a manufacturing stage, although this made but modest demands on numbers and specialization of the labour force or the investment of capital. The production of beef required a much more important manufacturing dimension. The salting-plant, established in or near the port, normally concentrated at least fifty and, in the bigger plants, sometimes several hundred workers, who specialized in widely differentiated tasks, covering the various stages of processing from the slaughter of the animal to the salting and drying of the pieces of meat. In the south of Brazil, these manufacturing enterprises, characterized by many capitalistic traits, used mostly slave-labour, whereas in the Río de la Plata area and in Chile the labourers in the salting-plants were wage-earners who benefited from the high levels of remuneration enjoyed by specialized workers in the Latin American cities at that time.[14]

The labour force required for cattle breeding was also composed of wage-earners; the worker received his wages in money and was not obliged by non-economic pressures or by isolation to spend his wages exclusively on goods acquired from his employer, or from the merchant who owed to that employer his ability to trade on the estancia. This was true of the temporary and specialized workers like horse-breakers, farriers and muleteers, whose wages were in any case higher than those of the permanent workers. However, even though the latter might not have had direct access to the market as consumers (and this is far from evident in all cases), and were the victims of legislative measures that obliged them to be constantly employed, under pain of imprisonment, forced labour or recruitment into the army, this entire apparatus of economic and political control – according to the evidence from all the cattleraising zones – served only to ensure the physical presence of the labour force on the cattle estate; its discipline continued to be less than complete, partly because of the very nature of cattlebreeding and partly because of the scarcity of labour.

Of the various types of livestock raising cattleraising (especially in the half empty areas of Latin America) was by far the most affected by the consequences of the liberalization of trade at the beginning of the nineteenth century. The breeding of sheep, goats and animals native to the Americas was well established in the older, more densely populated

[14] For southern Brazil, see Fernando H. Cardoso, *Capitalismo e escravidão no Brasil meridional: o negro na sociedade escravocrata do Rio Grande do Sul* (São Paulo, 1962). For the Río de la Plata region, see Alfredo J. Montoya, *Historia de los saladeros argentinos* (Buenos Aires, 1956).

and traditional areas, but its transformation did not occur until the second half of the century, when the new commercial pressures had become more intense and spread more evenly over the whole of Spanish America. In the period immediately after independence only Peru experienced a significant expansion in wool exports, both from sheep and Andean camelids. There is no evidence, however, that this was due to an increase in the number of head of wool-bearing animals; it was rather the result of a reorientation towards export overseas of fibres previously utilized by the Andean weaving industry.[15]

Some sectors of agriculture succeeded in taking advantage of the opportunities offered by the liberalization of trade, although none adapted to the prevailing economic conditions as completely as did cattleraising. Temperate crops (cereals, vines and olives) had only limited possibilities for growth because of the lack of additional demand in the European market and high transport costs. Tobacco (which can be produced in both tropical and temperate climates) did not show any significant increase in exports until the middle of the century; and only in Colombia did this process commence as early as the late 1840s. Spain continued to be the chief market for cacao and therefore the change in the structure of foreign trade did not have such a favourable effect on cacao production as it did on other agricultural exports; nevertheless, there was a continued increase in production on the coast of Ecuador, and even in Venezuela, which had been the leading cacao producer in the last years of the colonial period, there was a slight increase in the absolute value of cacao exports, even though its relative proportion of exports declined.

In Venezuela, and to a lesser extent in Ecuador, cacao had been produced by slave labour. It appears that in Ecuador, from the beginning of the post-independence economic reconstruction, the shortage of labour, brought about by manumission and forced recruitment of slaves during the war, though rather less significant here than elsewhere, was filled by Indians from the coast and the highlands. The latter were not organized for production in a unit like the traditional hacienda: they settled on lands belonging to the *hacendado*, to whom they delivered part of their crops and, it seems, also paid rent in the form of labour.[16] In Venezuela the development was more complex: because of the previous

[15] Jean Piel, 'The place of the peasantry in the national life of Peru in the nineteenth century', *Past and Present* 46 (1970), 108–36.

[16] For Venezuela, see John V. Lombardi, *The decline and abolition of Negro slavery in Venezuela, 1820–1854* (Westport, Conn., 1971), *passim*. For Ecuador, see Michael T. Hamerly, *Historia social y económica de la antigua provincia de Guayaquil, 1763–1842* (Guayaquil, 1973), 106ff.

predominance of slave labour, the war had had a more disruptive effect on the labour force in Venezuela than in Ecuador, and during the post-war period there was a sustained and not entirely unsuccessful effort to return some of those slaves to their masters, and to place the emancipated blacks in conditions in many ways comparable to slavery. Nevertheless, the proportion of both slaves and ex-slaves in the labour force declined steadily. In Venezuela they seem to have been replaced by wage-earners more often than by peasants working their lords' lands in return for plots on which they could cultivate their own crops.

That cacao lost its relative importance in Venezuelan agriculture was due, above all, to the expansion of coffee cultivation. Coffee had been grown in Venezuela during the colonial period. It spread rapidly in the post-war period, and reached its highest level of activity in the 1830s. Coffee cultivation, when it spread to new lands, required a delay of three years between the planting of the bushes and the first harvest and therefore the first profits. Expansion was undertaken by landowners who lacked capital, and they were, therefore, obliged to raise money on the market. The law of 10 April 1834, which eliminated the restrictions on contractual freedom imposed by the anti-usury legislation inherited from the colonial period, had as its purpose the creation of a more broadly based money market, and it was, perhaps, too successful. The prosperity of the coffee sector encouraged landowners to raise loans at very high rates of interest, and when that prosperity ended in 1842 they had good reason to regret it. The tension between a chronically indebted landowning class and a mercantile and financial sector intent on collecting its debts was to be a principal factor in the turbulent political history of Venezuela for several decades to come. However, the ending of the coffee boom, following a fall in coffee prices, did not remove coffee from its central place in the export economy of Venezuela. The volume of exports rose by about 40 per cent in the five-year period after the crisis of 1842, compared with the five years before, and this new level was to be maintained until, in 1870, a new and very marked expansion commenced. In the middle of the century coffee accounted for more than 40 per cent of Venezuela's exports, and in the 1870s for over 60 per cent.[17] Unlike Brazil where the expansion of coffee cultivation in this period was almost totally dependent on slave labour, coffee producers in Venezuela generally employed free labour. The increasing financial penury of the

---

[17] Izard, *Series estadísticas*, 191–3.

landowners, however, led to a decline in the use of wage-labour; arrangements between coffee producer and *conuqueros*, who in return for grants of land worked on the coffee plantations, now became more frequent, and finally became the dominant labour system in the coffee regions of Venezuela.

Thus, despite its need for capital and labour, coffee cultivation in Venezuela found a way of surviving and expanding during the period after independence when plantations worked by slave labour no longer seemed a viable long-term solution. On the other hand, the cultivation of sugar-cane everywhere in Spanish America had been confined within the framework of the plantation employing slave labour (the small sugar-growing areas of Mexico were only partially an exception), and it proved difficult to escape from this system. In the coastal areas of Peru, sugar cultivation in the period after independence depended on the use of slave labour as it had throughout the colonial period. And sugar planters always pointed to the impossibility of increasing the number of slaves as the principal reason for the stagnation of production (until the 1860s). A more satisfactory explanation, however, would seem to be lack of markets.

The one region of Spanish America where tropical agriculture in the form of sugar-cane cultivation enjoyed a spectacular advance was, paradoxically, Cuba which, together with Puerto Rico, remained subject to Spain throughout this period. The brief British occupation of Havana in 1762 is generally considered as the starting-point for a phase of expansion which, despite fluctuations, was to continue for over a century. In the late eighteenth century the Cuban economy, until then diversified but poorly developed, began to be slowly reoriented towards the predominance of sugar, though tobacco and coffee also expanded, and cattleraising by no means disappeared. The Spanish crown partly encouraged this process by liberalizing the laws governing the acquisition and utilization of land. More directly influential, however, were other external changes, notably the end of French rule in Saint-Domingue, which eliminated from the market the biggest sugar producer in the world and caused the migration to Cuba of some of its landowners – with their capital and their slaves.

At the beginning of the nineteenth century the centre of gravity of sugar production shifted from Oriente Province to Havana. The unit of production, the sugar-mill, however, remained relatively small for several decades. The reasons for this were high transport costs and the mill's fuel requirements. There were some big producers who owned several mills, but even they for the most part were dependent on the merchants who had advanced them their initial capital and who continued to provide them with goods and, above all, with slaves. It was, in fact, the continued supply of slaves, most of them directly imported from Africa, which made possible the expansion of Cuban sugar production. In the first decade of the nineteenth century, Britain and the United States had closed their territories to the import of slaves and had forbidden their citizens to engage in the international slave trade. Despite intense international (and especially British) pressure, however, Spain consistently failed to fulfil an early commitment – and later commitments – to terminate the trade. The protection afforded to the slave trade was not the least important motive for the Cuban sugar barons' acceptance of Spanish rule over the island, since an independent Cuba would have been even less able than the decadent Spanish monarchy to resist British demands. In the course of the nineteenth century before the ending of the slave trade in the 1860s – ten years after the final suppression of the Brazilian slave trade in 1850–1 – Cuba was to import hundreds of thousands of slaves. The traffic reached its highest intensity between 1835 and 1840; during those six years, 165,000 Africans were brought to the island, the majority of them destined for the sugar plantations. The slave population grew from under 40,000 in 1774 to almost 300,000 in 1827, when the white population for a time ceased to constitute a majority of the population, to almost 450,000 in 1841.[18]

From the 1840s there was a decline in the import of slaves as British control over the slave trade became more effective. Yet the expansion of sugar cultivation continued for another two decades. It was, in fact, no longer so dependent on vast increases in the size of the slave labour force. The first railway construction began in Cuba as early as 1834, and the first stretch of track was inaugurated in 1838 when neither Spain itself nor independent Spanish America had any railways. The railway not only facilitated communications between the sugar estates and the port, but also made possible the expansion of sugar cultivation which high transport costs had previously prevented; it also freed the estate from its dependence on nearby sources of fuel thus making it possible to grow cane on a much greater proportion of the land of the estate. Later, the

---

[18] Franklin W. Knight, *Slave society in Cuba during the nineteenth century* (Madison, 1970), 22 (Table 1), 86 (Table 8). For further discussion on the Cuban sugar industry and slavery in Cuba, see Thomas, *CHLA* III, chap. 7.

railway was introduced into the estate itself, where it made internal communications cheaper and more efficient, and thus contributed decisively to overcoming the limitations which previously existed on the size of each individual estate.[19]

At the same time the increasing difficulty experienced in renovating the stock of slaves facilitated a parallel transformation in the sugar industry: the more widespread use of steam-driven machinery. This, in turn, made more inevitable the transition from the estate employing a hundred slaves and producing a hundred tons a year to the much bigger estate and the replacement of a significant part of the landowning class. Typically, those who best took advantage of the new opportunities came not from the landowning but from the commercial sector. It was not only a question of a difference of mentality, but of a disparity of resources: few among the old sugar barons were able to make the investments that modernization required. Nevertheless, the expansion of Cuban sugar-cane production, still based as it was on slavery, is the greatest economic success story of the first half of the nineteenth century in Latin America.

Moreover, apart from the small amount of British capital invested in the railways, this success was not due to a fuller incorporation of the Cuban economy into the expanding capital market of Europe. The capital needed for the expansion of sugar production came either from the island itself (with mercantile capital, as we have observed, enjoying a predominant position) or from Spain, or even from the Spaniards who left the continent after independence. (Cuba appears to have been the principal refuge of those fleeing, for example, from Mexico in the 1820s.) In Cuba, as on the mainland, there was an almost total absence of capital from new overseas sources. In contrast to independent Spanish America, Cuba nevertheless achieved an impressive rate of growth during this period.

The exceptional success of the Cuban export economy was the principal factor stimulating the far-reaching transformation of Cuban society, not least the change in the ethnic composition of the population. In continental Spanish America the export economy, which even in the most favoured areas did not expand as quickly as in Cuba, was much less important an influence on social change during the period following

[19] For an excellent analysis of this process, see Manuel Moreno Fraginals, *El ingenio: el complejo económico social cubano del azúcar. Vol. I, 1760–1860* (Havana, 1964).

independence. Indeed, for most contemporary observers social change on the contrary created obstacles and limitations to which the export economies had to adapt.

This does not mean that there are no examples of regions in which changes in the texture of society were induced by the growth of production for export. Take, for example, the Norte Chico, in Chile, where a society less rigidly structured than that of central Chile emerged. However, there are few examples as convincing as this and, even here, its impact on Chilean society as a whole was comparatively slight. The other examples of export sector growth, from the considerable success of hides in the Río de la Plata region and Venezuelan coffee to the much more modest success of wool in southern Peru, tend to confirm the view that the effort to expand exports could only achieve success if its protagonists learned to adapt themselves to a social framework which was slowly changing but on which their own influence was marginal. Since throughout most of continental Spanish America, from Mexico to Central America, from New Granada (Colombia) to the Peruvian coast and Bolivia, export sector growth was unexpectedly weak in this period, it is necessary to look to other factors influencing the direction of social change, notably the crisis of the old colonial order (and not only the administrative structure but the set of patterns regulating the relations between social and ethnic groups) and the opening up of Spanish America to world trade, with all that it signified (and not only in the field of commerce).

The Wars of Independence, of course, did a great deal to undermine the *ancien régime* in Spanish America. They were the first wars since the Conquest to affect directly almost all continental Spanish America. They not only led to the destruction of assets, as we have seen, but also to changes in the relations between the different sectors of Spanish American society. The fragmentation of political power, the militarization of society, the mobilization for war of resources and, above all, men meant that the old social order and especially social control of the subordinate classes would never be completely restored on, for example, the plains and in the Oriente region of Venezuela, in the highlands of Peru and Bolivia, and on the plains of Uruguay.

Social relations during and after the Spanish American Wars of Independence were also profoundly affected by a new liberal and egalitarian ideology which rejected the hierarchical society characteristic of the colonial period, and aspired to integrate the different social and ethnic groups into a national society in order to reinforce the political unity of the new states.

Three features of Spanish American society in particular were in conflict with the more liberal and egalitarian tendencies of the early nineteenth century: they were black slavery; legal discrimination, both public and private, against those of mixed race; and the division of society as old as the Conquest itself, into a *república de españoles* and a *república de indios*, the barriers between which, though in fact very easy to cross, were to some extent still in place in 1810.

Slavery was nowhere as central to the relations of production in continental Spanish America at the beginning of the nineteenth century as in Cuba – and, of course, Brazil. Most revolutionary governments had ended the slave trade, in many cases as early as 1810–12. Laws freeing children born to slaves had been introduced in, for example, Chile (1811), Argentina (1813), Gran Colombia (1821), Peru (1821), although these were partly offset by regulations for a period of apprenticeship or forced labour to pay for the costs of upbringing. Laws of free birth were rarely implemented effectively and in any case, except in the long run, did not constitute an attack on the institution of slavery itself. We have already observed that the requirements of war led to the recruitment of slaves, some manumitted, some not. After independence a few countries with only a small number of slaves abolished slavery: Chile (1823), Central America (1824), Mexico (1829). At the same time efforts were also made to revitalize the institution, particularly in areas where it had some importance in production for export. These efforts were frustrated by, above all, the exhaustion of external sources of slaves. The African slave trade was necessary for the maintenance of the slave system, and in continental Spanish America only the Río de la Plata region imported slaves in significant numbers after independence – and then only during the 1820s and 1830s. This led inexorably to the decline, in terms of both quantity and quality, of African slavery, and explains why abolition was eventually decreed in Venezuela, Colombia, Peru and the Argentine provinces in the 1850s without causing significant social and economic disruption.

Less hesitant, and on the whole more successful, was the onslaught on the legal discrimination under which those of mixed race suffered. Its abolition was, it is true, less complete and immediate than the measures announced during the revolutionary period might lead one to suppose;

to cite only one example, in the Río de la Plata region, where egalitarian rhetoric and legislation were very much in evidence during the decade following the Revolution of 1810, *mestizos* and *pardos* were not admitted to the University of Córdoba until the 1850s. Furthermore, when a new state had a financial interest in the maintenance of differential standards, inequalities were more likely to continue: in Peru, for example, the tax paid by the *mestizos* (*contribución de castas*), which brought in considerable revenue, was abolished for a brief period, but then reimposed and survived until the 1850s. However, the system of ethnic castes was undermined nearly everywhere at its very roots when from early in the national period it was no longer obligatory to record a child's racial origin at birth. Even Peru abolished separate registers of baptisms and marriages for *mestizos* and Indians.

The successful abolition of the legal differentiation between the ethnic groups, though not necessarily the ending of inequality in the payment of taxes, becomes more understandable when it is recalled that, in the last years of the colonial period, from Caracas to Buenos Aires, the rise of prosperity at least in urban areas of some people of mixed ethnic origin, even though only an infinitesimal minority, began to affect the ethnic composition of the propertied classes. The war then enabled people of mixed ethnic origin to rise to positions of military and, rather less often, political influence. The Creole elite, still proudly conscious of its own ethnic purity, was nevertheless persuaded that any attempt to embody its prejudices in legal or political discrimination was no longer possible.

The fiscal needs of the new states also contributed to the slowness with which the legal position on the Indians was modified in the half-century following independence. Spain had abolished Indian tribute in 1810. Among the newly independent countries with large Indian populations, it was never reimposed in Mexico, but in Peru and Bolivia, and to a lesser extent in New Granada and Ecuador, despite its legal abolition (in some cases reiterated as, for example, at the Congress of Cúcuta in 1821), tribute continued to be an important source of government revenue, either under its traditional name or disguised by transparent euphemisms.[20]

Relatively little is known of the impact on the Indians of the changes that accompanied the ending of colonial rule. What research there is reveals a picture basically stable but rich in variety and contrasts. This is

---

[20] Nicolás Sánchez-Albornoz, 'Tributo abolido, tributo impuesto. Invariantes socioeconómicas en la época republicana', *Indios y tributos en el Alto Perú* (Lima, 1978), 187–218.

not surprising in view of the great variety of situations already prevailing before the final crisis of the colonial order: cultural Hispanicization and economic and social integration had of course progressed much further in some areas than in others. The contrast between the centre-north and south in Mexico, a subject which has only recently begun to be investigated, is now as clear as that between the coastal region and highlands of Peru and Ecuador. These differences determined the effect the crisis of independence had on the Indians. And it was the more general changes in the political, social and economic order which accompanied the crisis of emancipation rather than specific changes in the law itself which had the greatest impact. The wave of Indian rebellions in Mexico in the period after independence, for example, was the consequence of the general relaxation of traditional political and social discipline in rural Mexico.

Although the new regimes introduced almost everywhere substantial modifications in the legal status of the Indians, and adopted a concept of the place of the Indian in society substantially different from that prevailing under the *ancien régime*, these specific innovations seem to have had less effect than the general crisis of the old order. The very notion of a separate and parallel *república de indios* was repugnant to the new order and it rejected any alternative method of recognizing, legally and politically, a separate way of life for the Indians. Moreover, the basic institution of the *república de indios*, the Indian community endowed with rights over land, was now considered as an aberration in legal terms, detrimental in economic terms (since it impeded the incorporation of land and labour into a market economy) and disastrous in social and political terms, since it was seen as a formidable obstacle to the assimiliation of the Indian into the new political order. Nevertheless, the Indian community, which had suffered a slow process of erosion even during the colonial period, survived remarkably well in Mexico, Central America and the Andean republics during the first half-century after independence. Its legal dissolution (which would have transformed its members into individual proprietors) had been proposed, for example, by Bolívar in Peru, but it was enacted only occasionally and even then does not appear to have affected the actual functioning of community life. Nor was there any significant erosion on the territorial patrimony which the communities had managed to preserve from the colonial period, in spite of the more favourable ideological climate. This was, no doubt, delayed by the temporary fragility of the new political order and the absence of demographic pressures in this period. Even more decisive was the failure of commercial agriculture to expand significantly. In short, the delayed impact of the new external connection on the complex and loose structures of the Spanish American economies – the effective economic isolation of, for example, the Andean region – is probably the principal explanation for the social stability of those areas inhabited overwhelmingly by Indians.

In vast areas of Spanish America the lack of the stimulus that might have been provided by an expansion of the market weakened the pressures towards further land concentration and the advance of the hacienda at the expense of the Indian communities. Landownership outside the communities remained highly concentrated, of course, though existing landholdings changed hands more frequently in a period of civil war and political upheaval than during the colonial period, and sometimes the largest units were divided. A study of an area near Mexico City shows how a great territorial holding was transformed into the scarcely disguised booty of political and military victory; the first new proprietor was the ephemeral Emperor Agustín de Iturbide, then the estate passed into the hands of Vicente Riva Palacio, who was connected with the liberal faction which emerged for the first time in the following decade. In the long run, however, this booty became less attractive, partly because the weakening of the traditional system of rural labour made the exploitation of these lands less profitable than in the past.[21] In Jiquetepeque on the northern coast of Peru, this period witnessed the consolidation of a class of Creole big landowners, partly recruited from those holding in emphyteusis lands that were formerly ecclesiastical, and partly from among the civilian and military officials of the new republic.[22] In Venezuela, General Páez, among many others, entered into the propertied classes with which he had identified himself politically. In the region of Buenos Aires, so much land was available for cattleraising that it could be divided into huge estates and shared out without much dispute among old and new landowners. Any general conclusion about landholding in the aftermath of independence is, however, highly dangerous in view of the size and diversity of Spanish America and the limited amount of research which has so far been done.

In the cities, the Creole elites were the main beneficiaries of political

---

[21] John M. Tutino, 'Hacienda social relations in Mexico: the Chalco region in the era of Independence', *Hispanic American Historical Review*, 55/3 (1975), 496–528.

[22] Manuel Burga, *De la encomienda a la hacienda capitalista. El valle de Jiquetepeque del siglo XVI al XX* (Lima, 1976), 148ff.

emancipation; they achieved their aim of displacing the Spanish in the top bureaucratic and commercial positions, and at the same time the establishment of independent republican governments increased the opportunities for careers in government and politics. Compared with the pre-revolutionary period the urban elite was, however, weakened by several factors: the elimination of the patrimony and prestige of the Spaniards themselves who had formed such an important part of it; the entry, but not the full integration, of groups of foreign merchants who so often replaced the Spaniards; the upward mobility of individual *mestizos*; and, most important, the replacement of a system of power based on the metropolis and exercised through the cities as political and administrative centres by another system, more locally based, more rural, in which power was exercised by *hacendados* – and caudillos. The urban elites were deprived of part of the material basis of their pre-eminence and also of a large part of its ideological justification. They enjoyed much less of a monopoly of wealth than in the past at a time when wealth was becoming, in comparison with the past, the chief criterion of social differentiation. This led them to regard themselves, even more than in the past, as an educated class, but the justification of a pre-eminent position in society on the basis of education was less and less universally accepted. Its rejection provided an opening – no doubt exaggerated by the urban elites – for an understanding between rural (or urban) political leaders of conservative inclination and an urban popular sector, more numerous, more prosperous and affected to a greater or lesser degree by the egalitarian ideologies diffused by the revolutions for independence.

This leads us to consider a problem which is central to an understanding of what was happening in this phase of the evolution of urban society, in particular in the cities most directly affected by the liberalization of foreign trade. It is usually asserted that this liberalization, by making possible the importation of large quantities of the products of the new industries of Britain and Europe, must have had detrimental effects on those who had hitherto produced these goods locally by craft methods; that is to say, the pauperization of the urban popular sectors was the inevitable consequence of free trade. The counter-argument is that even before 1810 the import of 'luxury' goods (Castilian cloth, metallurgical products, wine) and the inter-regional trade both in these products and in goods for popular consumption had already imposed limitations on the expansion of urban craft industries and that, moreover, the expansion of foreign trade led to a growth of the internal market, which created fresh opportunities for local artisans. Both effects were doubtless felt, and their point of equilibrium was obviously not the same in all Spanish American cities.[23] A more easily defined consequence of the expansion of trade – and the increasing complexity of urban society – was the rise of a more numerous group of retail traders. The increase in the volume of imports did not necessarily lead to the abandonment by the big foreign importers of the Spanish practice of selling direct to the public. However, they were obliged to channel a growing quantity of their retail business towards an increasing number of small shopkeepers. The increase in the consumption of wheat bread led to the replacement of various kinds of maize bread which had been produced in the home by a product often acquired in the shops. And the increased movement of people led to the opening of more inns. Moreover, although the increase in the volume of imported cloth may have adversely affected local producers (who were in fact rarely to be found in the important urban centres), it created a demand for more dressmakers and tailors in the cities where its consumption was concentrated. In general, although it was not universal, there was a growth rather than a decline of the more prosperous sector of the lower classes in the cities of Spanish America in the period following independence. This partly explains the urban elite's often expressed concern for social order which was thought to be threatened, but which nevertheless does not appear to have faced any overt challenge.

There were, nevertheless, few opportunities available to the non-primary sectors of the Spanish American economies for autonomous development in the new post-independence international economic order. Economic dependence – understood, with regard to this period, as above all the acceptance of a place in the international division of labour as defined by the new economic metropolis – imposed rigid limitations on the possibilities for economic diversification in the areas thus incorporated more closely into the world market. Until the end of the period under consideration, the only part of Spanish America that was to create a textile industry capable of transforming its productive processes and competing with overseas imports was, in fact, Mexico. When the causes of Mexico's comparative success are examined, it appears that perhaps the most important factors were the dimensions of

[23] For a suggestive examination of these changes in Santiago, Chile, see Luis Alberto Romero, *La Sociedad de la Igualdad. Los artesanos de Santiago de Chile y sus primeras experiencias políticas, 1820–1851* (Buenos Aires, 1978), 11–29.

the market and the existence since the colonial period of an active internal trade, which made production on the scale required by the new technology economically possible. Moreover, in its early stages, there was a mass of skilled artisans concentrated in one urban centre, Puebla, available for employment in the new, more decidedly industrial, phase of textile production in Mexico.[24] Elsewhere the internal market was much more limited – fewer people, often with lower incomes than in Mexico – and it was captured by the foreign merchants, as in the Río de la Plata region, or the market remained small, unintegrated and largely isolated from the outside world, as was the case in almost the entire Andean region. There, the traditional system of textile production – and much else – survived.

In this necessarily brief examination of continuity and change in Spanish American society during the period immediately following independence no mention has so far been made of one factor which might be considered fundamental, that is to say, demographic trends. This omission is partly because very little is known about population trends during this period, but above all because what is known leads to the conclusion that they were not as decisive a factor in the evolution of society as they had been in the colonial period or as they were to be after 1870. In Mexico, following an increase in population in the eighteenth century, the early decades of the nineteenth appear to show a decline in some areas and an overall stagnation. In the rest of Spanish America the trend was clearly upwards, though certainly subject to marked variations from one region to another. Nicolás Sánchez-Albornoz considers it possible to distinguish a more rapid population growth in the regions of more recent Spanish settlement (Cuba, the Antioquia-Cauca region in New Granada, the Río de la Plata area and Venezuela, where the population more than doubled), whether or not these areas were affected by the opening up of overseas trade after independence, and a slower growth in the regions from Mexico through Central America to the Andean backbone of South America populated predominantly by Indians. In the case of Cochabamba (Bolivia), a comparison of the figures for 1793 and 1854 confirms these general conclusions: there was a more rapid growth in the valleys (which expanded their agriculture and attracted immigrants) than in the highlands.[25]

---

[24] Jan Bazant, 'Evolución de la industria textil poblana', *Historia Mexicana* (Mexico), 13 (1964), 4.
[25] Nicolás Sánchez-Albornoz, *La población de América Latina desde los tiempos precolombinos al año 2000* (2nd edn, Madrid, 1977), 127ff.

The overall increase in the population was based above all on the advance of the agricultural frontier. This advance, although in New Granada or the Río de la Plata region it might take the form of the incorporation of new territories beyond the limits of those previously subject to the political domination of Spain, was almost everywhere based on an expansion into the vast territories which lay between areas of settlement during the colonial period. Cuba and Venezuela offer perhaps the best examples of this process. The connection between the expansion of the frontier and the growth of the agricultural export sector is evident in the case of Cuba, Venezuela or the Río de la Plata region, but less so in New Granada, Chile or – in the minor example just quoted – the valleys of remote Cochabamba. The major urban centres, despite the contrary impressions of contemporary observers, local and foreign, either grew at a slower rate than that of the population as a whole (e.g. Havana or Buenos Aires) or, where the initial urban population was small, at only a slightly higher rate (e.g. Santiago in Chile, or Medellín in Antioquia, Colombia). Some cities remained substantially static during the first half of the nineteenth century, because the slow post-war recovery did not suffice to offset the decline in population caused by the Wars of Independence and their indirect consequences (e.g. Lima and Caracas). Thus, the proportion of the total population of Spanish America living in major cities did not increase, and the opening up of trade appears not to have especially stimulated their growth. Havana, Caracas and Buenos Aires, which were the centres of regions most affected by a vigorous expansion of exports, evinced a relative growth that appears to be lower than the average for Spanish America.

This comparatively slow urban growth, and also the similarity of the rate of growth of the population in the regions which were and which were not incorporated into an expanding economy based on the export of agricultural produce, provide yet another measure of the limited impact of the insertion of Spanish America into the new international economic system, whose nucleus was Britain rather than the old imperial metropolis. From the middle of the nineteenth century, however, there was a gradual transition to a closer and more complex relationship between Spanish America and the outside world than that prevailing in the period immediately after independence.

The third quarter of the nineteenth century was a transition in the economic history of Spanish America between the period of economic stagnation after independence (except in Cuba) and the period of export-led growth from the 1870s or 1880s until the World Depression of the 1930s. The relations between the Spanish American economies and the metropolitan economies were gradually redefined. New opportunities for the export sectors of some continental Spanish American economies, notably Argentina, Peru and Chile, were opened up.

The middle years of the nineteenth century marked, for the economy of Europe, the ending of a period of decline which, after reaching its lowest point in the crisis of 1846, aggravated by the political storms of 1848, yielded place to an impressive wave of expansion destined to last (despite the crisis of 1857 and 1865) until the Great Depression of 1873. During this period the continent of Europe closed the gap with the island that had initiated the Industrial Revolution. Industrial growth continued, in both Britain and Europe, at a faster pace than in the immediate past, and the leading continental European countries introduced, in a more decisive manner than Britain, institutional and organizational innovations: for example, deposit and investment banks, and businesses no longer based on the family, particularly in banking and transport. There was increasing European (and North American) demand for Latin American primary products. The progress of steam navigation was much slower in the South Atlantic and the Pacific than in the North Atlantic, but the establishment of mail-packets was sufficient to ensure a new regularity in the movement of people – and in the flow of information. (South America was linked to the outside world by telegraph only from the 1870s: the submarine cable reached Rio de Janeiro in 1874.)

Even more important for the future was the re-establishment on a more solid basis of the financial connection which had made only an ephemeral appearance in the early 1820s. A surplus of capital in Europe created a more favourable climate for Latin American loans and investment. It is true that the expansion of external credit was far from achieving the volume that it was to attain in the 1880s, and was channelled in a most uneven manner towards the various Latin American states, which only exceptionally succeeded in establishing the close connections with banking houses of solid repute that would make it possible for investors to enter the Latin American market with greater confidence than in the past (a confidence that was not always well-founded). During the period 1850–73, credits granted to Spanish American states were highly speculative in character, and more than one episode before the crisis of 1873 – for example, concerning loans to

Honduras and Paraguay[26] – recalled events of half a century before. Nevertheless, there were signs of the future pattern of financial relations with the metropolis. In some cases (like Peru, as we shall see) credit was linked to the control of the peripheral country's external trade. In others (such as the loans to Argentina and Chile) the granting of credit facilitated the export to the periphery of non-consumer goods. In the 1860s the first foreign private banks specializing in credit for overseas trade and the remittance of funds between Spanish America and Europe were established: the British banks which eventually were to be amalgamated as the Bank of London, Mexico and South America. Of course, bankers from continental Europe also moved into Spanish America, but they did not challenge British hegemony in this field until the 1880s.

Finally, the role of the groups of British merchants established in the ports and commercial centres of Spanish America at the time of the opening up to world trade, and linked to major commercial firms in Britain, began to decline, as did their autonomy. Both the local state and local capitalists became more involved in the growth of the Spanish American economies during this period, but more important for the future was the increasing influence of a new type of business concern, of which the railway company is the best example, metropolitan not only in its origins (even though its capital might not be exclusively metropolitan) but in the headquarters of its management and, above all, in the close connections which it preserved with the metropolitan economy. The new railway company was not only an instrument of mercantile integration between the metropolitan and the neo-colonial economies, which facilitated the concentration of the latter on the sector exporting primary products; from the metropolitan point of view, it fulfilled a more immediately useful function by offering an outlet for metallurgical and engineering products during the construction phase and, in smaller but regular quantities, for those products, and for coal, once the operation of the railways had begun.

The beginnings of railway expansion in continental Spanish America, and especially Argentina, in this period reflects the new relationship between the metropolitan and the peripheral area. In Buenos Aires province the Western railway was begun in 1857 by local capitalists to facilitate the transport of wool. However, this source of capital was soon

[26] For Honduras, see D. C. M. Platt, 'British bondholders in nineteenth-century Latin America. Injury and remedy', *Inter-American Economic Affairs*, 14/3 (1960). For Paraguay, see H. G. Warren, *Paraguay and the Triple Alliance. The post-war decade, 1869–1878* (Austin, 1978), 129ff.

found to be insufficient, and eventually the provincial treasury took over the extension of the line before looking to the alternative of handing over the building and operation of the railways to foreign companies. A decade later, local producers and merchants of British origin played an important role in the promotion of the second important railway in Buenos Aires province, the Southern (like the Western at this stage a railway for the transportation of wool) and some of them were to become members of the board of directors of the private company which undertook its management. However, this company was established in London and was responsive from the outset to metropolitan interests; in a few decades the connection, which at first had been so close, between the Southern railway and the economic interests dominant in the region it served had disappeared almost entirely. The line from Rosario to Córdoba, the axis of the future network of the Argentine Central railway, was from the beginning a very different concern. Unlike both the Western and the Southern which served the needs of a productive region already being exploited, this was a line aimed at development, the encouragement of rural industry and commerce; it could not offer quick profits. It was, in fact, built thanks to a state guarantee of minimum earnings by means of a subsidy (in addition to grants of land) paid to the British company which undertook its construction and operation. The metropolitan connection was established, even more overwhelmingly than in the case of the Southern railway, with interests connected to railway building. Connections with local agrarian and commercial interests were developed largely after, and as a consequence of, the building of the railway. These connections were not only less close than in the case of the Southern, but were characterized by an almost permanent antagonism. One reason for this was the conditions offered for the establishment of the line; the guarantee was in proportion to its extension and, even though this encouraged investment, it discouraged those whose objective was an improvement of the service. A second reason was that the railway between Córdoba and Rosario was constructed for the transport of cereals, and from the special characteristics of their storage and transport there arose more serious conflicts of interest between producers and transporters than in the case of wool.[27] Finally, as a consequence of the depression of 1873, the effects of which were felt in Argentina in 1874, the British railway company refused to extend the track, which had

[27] Later studies have not superseded H. S. Ferns, *Britain and Argentina in the XIXth Century* (Oxford, 1960), 342ff.

reached, in 1870, as far as Córdoba. The state assumed responsibility for the undertaking, but this decision, which would appear to make the expansion of the railways independent of the metropolis, modified but did not put an end to the external connection. The building of the line was undertaken by a British entrepreneur, Telfener, who had invested his capital in materials for railway construction and who, in this period of economic depression, agreed to advance the necessary funds to the Argentine state.

Argentina, however, though it anticipated future trends in the financial relations between Spanish America and the metropolis, was not typical of the pattern of railway building during this period. In Chile, even though the first railway, in the mining zone of the Norte Chico, was due to the initiative of William Wheelwright, the capital seems to have been raised from local mining entrepreneurs and from the Anglo-Chilean merchants of Valparaíso. In Central Chile, the state played a decisive role from the outset and, although railway building was largely financed through foreign loans, the construction itself was undertaken by an entrepreneur who was certainly foreign (namely the American, Henry Meiggs), but who did not belong to the closely-knit community of entrepreneurs and technicians that was carrying the railway from Britain to South America and the world in general. It was Meiggs who dominated even more completely railway construction in Peru. Here, too, foreign credit provided the basis for the expansion of the railways, not because of any ambition on the part of the metropolis to share in the undertaking, but as an indirect consequence of the monopoly enjoyed by Peru in the guano market. Even in Mexico, which was hampered during this phase of its development by civil war and foreign intervention, the role played by companies based on the metropolis was a secondary one; the main line from Mexico City to Veracruz, inaugurated in 1873, was built and brought into operation by a Mexican private company, with funds in part advanced by the French occupation forces, who needed to expedite its construction for military purposes.[28]

The increasing participation of the metropolitan economies in the peripheral economies through, for example, the incipient banking system and the railway companies, was not only necessary for the expansion of the volume of production in the Spanish American export sectors; it

---

[28] Margarita Urias Hermosillo, 'Manuel Escandón, de las diligencias al ferrocarril, 1833–1862', in Ciro F. S. Cardoso (ed.), *Formación y desarrollo de la burguesía en México. Siglo XIX* (Mexico, 1978), 52.

was no less necessary to enable Spanish America to produce at competitive prices. The advantages as regards the terms of trade which the Spanish American economies had possessed in the preceding period (1808–50) began to become less evident, and by the end of the transitional period (1850–73) they had disappeared or at least sharply declined. The peripheral economies were now no longer growing more slowly than the metropolitan economies, despite the geographical expansion of the metropolitan area in continental western Europe and North America. Within the periphery the Spanish American economies were now competing not only among themselves, or with the old peripheral economies of Eastern Europe, but with new areas, ranging from Canada to Africa and Australia. Without a transfer of capital and technology it was even more difficult to achieve a sustained export boom than in the period immediately after independence.

One obstacle to economic growth in the Spanish American countries during the third quarter of the nineteenth century, and therefore one explanation for the increasing divergence of economic performance between the Spanish American economies, was the continuation, indeed intensification, of political – and military – conflict which destroyed assets and absorbed resources which should have been employed in productive purposes and frightened off foreign capital. Throughout almost the whole of this period, Mexico and, to a somewhat lesser extent, Venezuela, for example, were to be profoundly disturbed by civil wars, the worst since the Wars of Independence. The Mexican civil war was complicated by foreign intervention. Even in Argentina, the minister of finance calculated in 1876 that the cost of the civil wars of the 1850s and 1860s together with the Paraguayan war (1865–70) equalled the total foreign credits received by the Argentine state during this period.

The most highly developed export economy in Spanish America in the two decades after 1850 was the Spanish colony of Cuba; in 1861–4 her exports reached an annual average value of 57 million pesos, and they were not to decline from this level even in the first phase of the Ten Years' War, which began in 1868. At the beginning of the 1870s, therefore, Cuba's exports were almost double those of the independent Spanish American republics that had been most successful in increasing their exports. Argentina, Chile and Peru each had exports of around 30 million pesos, higher than Mexico (with exports worth 24 million pesos in 1870) whose economic stagnation was a reflection both of the effects of the political and military conflicts of the 1850s and 1860s and the decline of its mining sector. There were also significant realignments among the smaller exporters: Uruguay, whose exports were valued at 12½ million pesos, had double the exports of Bolivia and Venezuela (both with around 6 million pesos in value), partly because Montevideo was also the port of shipment for some of Argentina's produce.[29] Bolivia still suffered from the collapse of its mining economy, Venezuela from the social and economic costs of civil war and the gradual fall in the price of coffee, its major export.

The Cuban sugar industry continued its impressive growth in the middle decades of the nineteenth century, but there were problems on the horizon. The decline in the price of sugar, though not so pronounced as it was to be later, had already begun, and expectation of the final abolition of the transatlantic slave trade (it was finally ended in 1865–6) had already led to a marked increase in the price of imported slaves. As a result of this pincer movement there was growing pessimism about the future of the plantation economy: it was now realized that in order to survive sugar cultivation needed to be able to count on alternative sources of labour and capital that would make possible the modernization of the industrial sector. It was doubtful whether both these could be found, and it was increasingly evident that the majority of Cuban planters, even those who had most recently entered the industry and were largely responsible for the recent expansion, could not maintain their dominant position in the face of the introduction of changes that were necessary for the very survival of the sugar-growing sector. The Ten Years' War (1868–78) revealed and aggravated the strains within Cuba's sugar industry, and made it even more certain that the ending of slavery (in the 1880s) and the modernization of the sugar mills would signify the end of the domination of Cuban sugar cultivation by the Cuban and Spanish planters.

The prosperity of the Peruvian export economy, like that of Cuba, was continually accompanied by gloomy forecasts. But this was the only characteristic the two economies had in common. The expansion of Peruvian exports was based on guano; only in the final stage of the guano boom did other products, some of them traditional like sugar and cotton, others new like nitrate, begin to rival guano. And the role played by guano in the Peruvian economy was very different from that played by sugar in Cuba. In the first place, the characteristics of the international guano trade were different: in a context of increasing demand for guano, arising out of the needs of European agriculture, Peru enjoyed through-

[29] For Spanish American exports in this period, see F. Martin, *The Statesman's Yearbook* (London, 1874), *passim*.

out this period a virtual monopoly of supplies. The impact of guano on the Peruvian economy was different too: to export it, all that was needed was collection, which did not require complex techniques and which absorbed above all unskilled labour; furthermore, from the point of view of shipment, its volume was much less than that of sugar of comparable value. Finally, there was a difference in the geographical relationship between the guano-producing area and the core of the Peruvian economy; guano came from a marginal and very small area, consisting of a group of islands a relatively long distance from the coast. All these factors influenced the impact made by the expansion of guano on the Peruvian economy. Its capacity to effect directly transformations in the other sectors, by means of forward and backward linkages, was extremely limited. However, thanks to Peru's monopoly of the supply of guano the Peruvian state was uniquely able to retain a very considerable part of the profits from the export sector, in excess of fifty per cent it appears,[30] a proportion only equalled by Venezuela in the case of petroleum during the Second World War.

Until 1860, the guano trade was in the hands of foreign business concerns, among which the British firm of Antony Gibbs & Sons enjoyed a dominant position. But the royalties obtained by the treasury (in addition to the income derived from the fact that, due to its solvency, Peru again had access to internal and foreign credit) were soon reflected in an increase in public expenditure which was principally channelled into increases in the remuneration of the bureaucracy and the military. Moderate amounts of guano revenue were used for public works and even arms purchases, and the consolidation of the internal debt, which transferred vast resources to private individuals (often with very dubious claims) was, in terms of its political and social impact, an essential aspect of this first phase of the Peruvian guano boom.

The second phase was characterized by the granting of a monopoly of the Peruvian guano trade with the most important market, Britain, to a group of Peruvian concessionaries. The period of expansion had come to an end and the treasury, accustomed to a constant increase in its revenues, began to feel impoverished. It now increasingly had recourse to credits obtained from the guano concessionaries, who had a growing influence in the financial and political life of Peru. In 1869, a government

---

[30] According to the figures given by Shane Hunt in Heraclio Bonilla, *Guano y burguesía en el Perú* (Lima, 1974), 144. For further discussion of the impact of guano on the Peruvian economy, see ch. 6 below.

of conservative tendencies led by General Balta, with more support in the army and the south of Peru than in Lima, broke this financial nexus by transferring the concession for the guano trade to Auguste Dreyfus, a French businessman. Once the concession was obtained, he found no difficulty in obtaining the necessary financial backing in Europe. There was a further increase in both government revenue from guano and credit, and these fresh resources were channelled into an ambitious programme of railway construction, designed to link the southern and central highlands with the Pacific ports. Meanwhile, even though the guano boom had undoubtedly contributed to the recovery of sugar and cotton cultivation in the coastal areas of Peru, it had not succeeded in creating a vigorous group of native capitalists. This was partly, it seems, because the Peruvian group active in the export of guano had only limited financial independence; from the beginning it was dependent on Chilean and British credit. In particular, Peruvian participation in the exploitation of nitrate, which in the far south of Peru and the Bolivian littoral offered an alternative less expensive than guano and which hastened the decline of the latter, was extremely small. From 1874, the end of the guano boom made some painful readjustments necessary and Peru was not well prepared for the very severe trial which the War of the Pacific (1879–83) represented.

Paradoxically, even though the exhaustion of this first cycle of the export trade after independence decisively weakened Peru as it was about to face the challenge of Chile, it was partly the simultaneous exhaustion of their own first export cycle which persuaded Chilean leaders of the urgency of mounting that challenge in order to conquer, along the nitrate-producing coast, a new base for Chile's own exporting capacity and to broaden the fiscal basis of the Chilean state. The expansion of Chilean exports had taken place on a much broader front than that of Peru. In the mining sector the rise of silver was followed by that of copper; in the early 1860s Chile was the biggest exporter of copper in the world. The expansion of mining in Coquimbo and Copiapó, in the Norte Chico, was the result above all of local entrepreneurial activity and investment efforts (though with the usual connections to British mercantile capital, through the Anglo-Chilean firms in Valparaíso). The labour force, though swollen by immigrants from western Argentina, was also predominantly Chilean. This expansion of the northern mining sector was complemented by that of commercial agriculture in the Central Valley, of which the most important export product continued to be, as it had been since colonial times, wheat. From the late 1840s wheat was exported far beyond the traditional, and limited, Peruvian market, to the new markets in the Pacific, namely California and Australia. When the latter quickly became self-sufficient in cereals, the bulk of Chilean exports of flour and wheat were shipped to Argentina, which was to achieve self-sufficiency only in 1870, and to Europe.

The expansion of cereal-growing southwards in Chile began before the building of the longitudinal railway, thanks to the establishment of minor ports such as Constitución and Tomé, which offered an outlet for areas still isolated by land from the nucleus formed by Santiago and Valparaíso. This geographical expansion led to the eviction of the mass of squatters who, as long as the effective ownership of these lands was of no economic interest to the landowning class, had been free to occupy both state-owned and private land. The latter were now claimed more vigorously, and the former soon passed into private hands. Although in the far south there was a significant effort at agricultural colonization, carried out by German immigrants who eventually became proprietors, on the whole this transfer to private ownership benefited the old-established landowners or new owners recruited from the urban upper classes. At the same time this solved the problem of finding a rural labour force; even though the landowners complained at the threat to rural discipline posed by the opening up of new possibilities of employment in mines, public works and the urban areas, there was in fact an increase in the supply of labour. This was reflected in the progressive deterioration of the position of the *inquilinos*, tenant-labourers, whose numbers grew but who had to offer an increased quantity of labour in return for ever-decreasing plots of land.

The existence of an abundant and cheap labour force provided Chilean agriculture with a refuge in the face of increased competition from Argentina, which had more abundant land, and from the United States and Canada which, thanks to mechanization and selection of seeds, were to produce crops at lower costs and also achieve higher quality. This refuge took the form of an archaic system of production, which employed a great deal of labour but which attracted little capital investment, except in irrigation works. However, it was not a very secure refuge: the first casualty was the flour industry, which was complementary to cereal-growing. Chile soon lost the battle with the European and North American producing centres that used the new mills with steel cylinders; thereafter Chilean agriculturists declined to produce the hard wheat these mills required and, as a result, within twenty years Chilean wheat was to be driven out of the international market.

In the mid-1870s this process of involution was only just beginning and was reflected above all in a decline in the volume of agricultural exports and more especially in profits. Not everybody realized this was not merely due to temporary circumstances. In mining, however, there was a complete collapse; at the end of the 1870s Chile, which had enjoyed as a copper producer a position that the country had never attained as a producer of cereals, had been completely driven out of the world market. The reason for this was that the United States, with a new system of mining incorporating new technological processes, began to produce copper at a much lower cost than Chile; the mining entrepreneurs of the Norte Chico had neither the capital nor the access to technological innovations to allow them to compete. There was to be a resurgence of Chilean copper mining in the twentieth century, with the help of those who had indirectly destroyed it in the nineteenth century.

Thus Chile learned that the new world economic climate, even though it opened up fresh opportunities to the peripheral economies, subjected them to a harsher environment, and prosperity did not always survive its rigours. The decline of copper coincided with a resurgence of silver, but the latter, though produced by Chilean mining entrepreneurs, came from the northern littoral which was still Bolivian territory. It was, above all, accompanied by an expansion in the production of nitrate in the Peruvian and Bolivian coastal regions. Paradoxically, however, the War of the Pacific, which gave Chile political control over this area, weakened the predominance of the Chilean and Anglo-Chilean exploiters over the new northern nitrate regions. The victory did not, therefore, bring about the extension to the new territory of the system which had given Chile an ephemeral prosperity in the third quarter of the nineteenth century, and in which the protagonists had been a landowning, mercantile and entrepreneurial class which, though partly foreign in origin, was essentially local. On the contrary, the outcome was to be similar to that of Peru in the case of guano: the principal connection between the nitrate-exporting sector, increasingly controlled from abroad, and the Chilean economy was provided by the state, which received from the taxes on the export of nitrates a very considerable proportion of its increased revenues.[31]

In Argentina a more pronounced tendency towards expansion ensured

[31] For further discussion of the Chilean economy before the War of the Pacific, see ch. 7 below.

less abrupt transitions between one phase and another of her export sector growth; nevertheless, it is possible to detect in Argentina the same tendencies that we have observed in Chile. In the middle of the nineteenth century the old cattleraising sector, oriented towards the production of hides, tallow and salted beef, appears to have reached its limit owing to the saturation of the European markets. After the middle of the 1850s renewed expansion became possible, firstly as a consequence of the Crimean War which isolated Russian suppliers from western markets, and also in a more permanent way by the progress of the footwear industry, in which mass-production led to an increase in the demand for leather. Nevertheless, the brief period of stagnation was enough to offer decisive encouragement to the expansion of sheepraising; very soon, and until the end of the century, wool was to become the most important livestock product among Argentina's exports.

The expansion of sheepraising which, until the mid-1860s, occurred in a context of rising prices, was facilitated firstly by the extension of the railway, but above all by the increase in immigration (in this case from Ireland and the Basque country). The growing number of immigrants obliged them to accept increasingly unfavourable conditions and it was the sharp decline in agricultural wages which made it possible to maintain and even expand pastoral activity in the hard years that began in 1867. The two most important markets, France and the United States, imposed high duties on the import of wool, while Australian competition depressed the price of Argentine wool, which was of inferior quality owing to the primitive conditions of production and, above all, of storage and marketing.

In these circumstances the pasturing of sheep could no longer provide the main impetus for the expansion of the Argentine export economy. The following decade saw a resurgence of cattleraising in the peripheral lands in the south of Buenos Aires province, where sheep had driven out cattle; and there was a final period of prosperity for the archaic salted beef industry, which still retained its old Cuban market and part of the Brazilian market. Above all, there was also an increase in the production of cereals. In Buenos Aires province this occurred, even in this late period, within the context of the traditional large estate, but in Sante Fe, which became the principal cereal-growing province, it was based on centres of agricultural colonization, once again with immigrant farmers. As has been mentioned above, in the mid-1870s, stimulated by rising demand, due to the growth of the cities and the presence in them of an increasing number of immigrants, Argentina expanded wheat production to the point where it became self-sufficient in cereals.

Also in the 1870s there was a final offensive against the Indians in the Pampa zone which, by offering fresh booty in land, gave a new lease of life to the economic formula on which Argentine expansion had been based: that is, abundant and cheap land, which made it possible to produce at competitive prices with techniques that required little capital and comparatively little labour. Labour was scarce in Argentina, and immigrant labour was never to be as cheap as that available to landowners in rural Chile. Even within the frame of this formula, investment of capital began to increase, for example in wire fencing and the beginning of cross-breeding of livestock, which in the 1870s chiefly affected sheep. However, the Argentine export economy was not to reveal its new orientation decisively until the 1890s, when cereals and meat were to become the principal exports, as a result of a transformation no less profound, albeit less traumatic, than those undergone by the economies of Peru and Chile.

The redefinition of Spanish America's commercial and financial relations with the European metropolis was one factor promoting social transformation during the period 1850–70, but it was by no means the only factor and what social change there was came slowly. In the first place, there continued the gradual elimination of slavery throughout Spanish America. Although in some countries, where there was only a comparatively small number of slaves – Chile, Central America, Mexico – slavery had been abolished immediately after independence; in the countries where there was an economically more significant number of slaves, abolition did not occur until the middle of the century. Slavery was abolished in 1846 in Uruguay and in 1853 in the Argentine republic (except in the province of Buenos Aires, which abolished it only when it became part of the republic in 1860). It was abolished in Colombia in 1850 and in Peru and Venezuela in 1854. And in 1870 Paraguay became the last country in continental Spanish America to abolish slavery. Almost everywhere slavery had been losing its economic significance principally because the gradual abolition of the Atlantic slave trade and the various laws of free birth made it increasingly difficult even to maintain the relatively small existing slave population.

Only Cuba, along with Brazil the last remaining slave society in the New World, still regarded slavery as essential to agriculture, that is to say, the sugar industry. And even there, following the ending of the

Cuban slave trade in the mid-1860s, slavery came under threat and among Cuban planters the discussion of possible alternatives became more common. Whereas the alternative preferred by many of them was the immigration of Spanish peasants, which would involve the replacement of the plantation as a productive unit by smaller units worked by tenant farmers or by sharecroppers, the alternative most often adopted in practice was the importation of Chinese coolies, as in Peru, where they were employed in the guano-producing areas and in agriculture in the coastal region. However, Chinese immigration, which was finally ended by British pressure, never contributed a mass of workers comparable in number to those supplied by the African slave-trade.

During the first war of independence in Cuba (1868–78), both sides tried to gain the support of the slaves by offering freedom to those who fought: as the experience of the Wars of Independence in continental Spanish America had demonstrated, slaves were an attractive source of recruits. And in 1870 the Moret Law, passed by the Spanish Cortes, proclaimed the freedom of children born to slaves. Even though these measures did not lead to a very large number of slaves securing their liberty, they helped to consolidate the consensus of opinion with regard to the inevitable and imminent end of slavery. The end came in the 1880s and, along with other factors, forced some painful readjustments on the Cuban sugar industry.

There was during the period 1850–70 further encroachment on the land of the Indian communities, as there had been ever since independence – indeed before. Moreover, legal reforms undermined the juridical basis of the existence of those communities, either by imposing the division of their territorial patrimony among their members, who became proprietors with the right to alienate their property (a right which was not always recognized legally but which could nevertheless be exercised), or by making the usufruct of communal land revert to the state (which could then sell it, along with the other public land, to private owners). Nowhere, however, did these reforms result in a sudden social cataclysm. In Mexico, for example, the effects of the *Ley Lerdo* (1856) and the other laws of the *Reforma* did not come into full effect until the era of Porfirio Díaz (1876–1911); while in the large areas of the Peruvian highlands the legal abolition of the communities was not followed by their effective liquidation until the twentieth century. The reason was that, as always, such liquidations took place above all when the more general transformation of the economy made it profitable to channel the production of the communal lands towards expanding markets, internal or external, and even in such cases it did not always happen. In Guatemala and northern Peru, for example, the economic sector based on the export of agricultural and livestock products required a labour force recruited from the communities, but expanded into land not held by the communities themselves (as in Guatemala), or expanded into a very small area of the communal lands (as in Peru). The consequence was an actual strengthening of the communities since their economic viability was maintained by the labour of those who had migrated. Thus, there did not always occur a linear development from communal to private individual landholding, to the benefit of the hacienda, and where it did take place it was a comparatively slow process: during the period under consideration here the expansion of agriculture for export scarcely affected the communal lands, and thus did not succeed in undermining decisively their social organization.

The beginning of the transformation of Spanish America's external commercial and financial relations and the consequent improvement in the finances of the state in this period contributed to the growth as well as the increased political and social influence of the cities, especially the capitals. There is no doubt that urban growth in the last analysis depended on the expansion of the export sector. In 1870, it is true, Mexico City with about 220,000 inhabitants remained, as it had been at the beginning of the century, the biggest city in Spanish America. But Havana and Buenos Aires had over 200,000 and Buenos Aires was growing much more rapidly than either and was soon to overtake them both. Lima, whose population had just reached 100,000, was now smaller than Montevideo (with an estimated population in 1870 of 125,000) and Santiago (130,000). Bogotá and Caracas, on the other hand, remained stagnant with 50,000 inhabitants each. There were, of course, cases in which urban expansion took place, not in the political centres, but in the centres of the export trade; thus, in Colombia Barranquilla grew faster than Bogotá, and in Ecuador Guayaquil overtook Quito, though the rate of growth of all these cities was small. In Chile, on the other hand, Santiago overtook Valparaíso in this period.[32]

Foreign trade could not directly give employment to a significant number of people; its influence on urban growth was felt through the expansion of the state and the numbers it employed, and the moderniza-

---

[32] For the figures on the populations of cities in this period, see Richard M. Morse, *Las ciudades latinoamericanas. II Desarrollo histórico* (Mexico, 1973), *passim.*

tion of transport which, although it diminished the actual number of people employed, tended to urbanize them; thus, railway and tramway workers replaced carters and muleteers. At the same time the process of modernization did not affect other aspects of the life of the cities: the retail trade and domestic service continued to absorb a disproportionate share of the growing number of those employed in cities. Modernization was perhaps superficial, but evident in, for example, the adoption of such innovations as street-lighting by gas and, as a result of growing public and private prosperity, the building of theatres and performances by artists of international repute. As the cities grew, the residential separation of different social groups increased; although in the past there had been no lack of quarters characterized by poverty and crime, the reasons for which rich and poor found it mutually convenient to live close together had weighed more heavily than was now the case in the expanded and renovated cities. The major cities, indeed, grew sufficiently for property speculation to occur. In the 1850s Mexico City witnessed its earliest urban 'colonies'; in Buenos Aires speculative division into lots did not begin until nearly two decades later, but then it grew very swiftly.[33] Simultaneously there occurred the beginnings of public transport; its earliest significant manifestation was the horse-drawn tramcar. Urban growth, by creating a larger potential market, also encouraged the growth of craft industries, and some factories employing a concentrated labour force, such as breweries and cigarette factories. The population attracted to the tertiary sector was, however, more numerous than that employed in the secondary, and the beginnings of a modern proletariat were more often to be found in transport and public services than in industry.

These growing 'bureaucratic-commercial' cities depended for their prosperity on the expansion of the primary exporting sector. Their social structure became more complex, but at the same time more vulnerable to the effects of developments outside Spanish America. Until the mid-1870s, however, this basic fragility and the possible political consequences of the instability of the economic basis of urban expansion did not constitute a cause for alarm. One reason for this was that, through the expansion of the bureaucracy and of public works, the state could indirectly control wider sectors of the urban population than in the past.

[33] María Dolores Morales, 'El primer fraccionamiento de la ciudad de México, 1840–1899', in Cardoso, *Formación y desarrollo*; James R. Scobie, *Buenos Aires, plaza to suburb, 1870–1910* (New York, 1974).

Another factor was the high proportion of foreigners in the urban economy, and no longer only at the upper levels. Although cases such as Buenos Aires and Montevideo, where in the middle of the century the majority of the economically active population was foreign born (and the proportion was to increase subsequently), were far from being typical, in most of the rapidly growing cities the proportion of foreigners in the retail trade and in light industry was considerable.

Quite apart from the peculiar characteristics of this expanding urban society, the reason for the growing weakness of any specifically urban political expression was the peculiar position of the city in the economic and fiscal system consolidated by the steady progress of the sector based on the export of agricultural and livestock products. The prosperity and stability of both the state and the cities were now dependent on the continued growth of the primary export sector of the Spanish American economies.

# 2

## POLITICS, IDEOLOGY AND SOCIETY

To develop valid general statements about Spanish American politics in the half century that followed independence is a formidable task. The countries were diverse in ethnic composition. Bolivia, Peru, Ecuador, Guatemala and (to a lesser degree) Mexico possessed large Indian populations that were only partially assimilated into the dominant Hispanic culture. Elsewhere the *mestizo* was more clearly predominant numerically and almost all of the population was culturally integrated into Hispanic society. These differences had implications for political behaviour. In those societies in which the lower class was largely composed of people culturally distinct from the Hispanic elite, that class was less likely to become actively involved in politics.

The countries also vary greatly geographically. Much of the population of Mexico, Guatemala and the Andean countries was locked into interior highlands, while in Venezuela, Chile and much of the Río de la Plata significant proportions of the population were located in coastal regions. This difference had important implications for the economies, and hence the politics, of these countries. The earlier onset of intensive trade relations with western Europe in the countries with coastal populations and resources enabled their governments, through customs collections, to develop firmer financial bases, and therefore somewhat greater stability, than was often the case in the landlocked countries. Even here, however, there are not simply two patterns. In the 1830s and 1840s Chile's relative stability encompassed the entire area of the republic, while in the Plata region there were only pockets of order. In Venezuela a period of equilibrium in the prosperous 1830s was followed by one of instability with the decline of coffee prices in the 1840s.

The colonial heritage of these countries also varied in important ways. All shared Spanish language and institutions; all had been governed under the same colonial system. Yet the system and its institutions, while recognizably Spanish, were not precisely the same everywhere at the beginning of the republican era. Because of Mexico's political and economic importance throughout almost three centuries of Spanish rule, the Church there had developed an institutional and economic preponderance that was not matched in more recently developed regions such as Venezuela and the Río de la Plata. Generations of wealthy Spaniards and creoles in Mexico had endowed convents and pious foundations with economic resources that made them a major factor in the national economy. Partly for this reason, in Mexico the power and wealth of the Church became a major issue considerably before it developed much significance elsewhere. And the struggle to dismantle church power in Mexico endured for decades and took on a life-and-death intensity. In the Río de la Plata region and Venezuela, on the other hand, the Church had much shallower roots and the powers and privileges of the colonial church were trimmed with relative ease.

Similarly, the Wars of Independence affected these countries in different ways. In Mexico and, to a lesser degree, Peru, a creole officer corps that had been trained and socialized into military careers by the Spanish on the eve of independence remained substantially intact after independence. As a consequence, in Mexico and Peru the professional military tended to play an important part in politics as a self-conscious, more or less coherent interest group. Military leaders in Mexico frequently intervened in the political process to defend the special privileges (*fueros*) that the military had enjoyed under Spanish rule. In Peru the military *fuero* was less an issue. Yet the politics of the military as a corporate group also left an imprint upon the general politics of the nation, while individual military leaders ruled Peru for most of the nineteenth century. Elsewhere the late colonial military was shattered in the Wars of Independence, but with varied results. The substantial group of revolutionary creole officers who emerged to win the independence of Venezuela (and played an important role in liberating New Granada, Ecuador, Peru and Bolivia as well) attempted to assert for the heroes of independence a privileged place like that enjoyed by the Spanish-trained professionals in Mexico. In Venezuela, however, the independence heroes were never able to act effectively as a corporate interest group, though, as in Peru, individual leaders emerged as dominant figures in politics. In New Granada and Chile, the military leaders of independence quickly became subordinated to the interests of a civilian political elite and after 1830 rarely acted as a corporate group. In Argentina the professional military in effect was destroyed in conflict with local militia groups. It is thus difficult to sustain a single simple generalization about the role of the military in politics.

Beyond the problems inherent in the heterogeneity of the countries of Spanish America, generalization is impeded by the paucity of systematic research into the politics of the period after independence. Aside from some notable contributions in the histories of Mexico and Argentina, there has been little analytical work conforming to current canons of historical research. Some of the best work is still at the first stratum of historical research: the analysis of ideas expressed by the elite in printed materials. There is still little analysis of the actual functioning of the political process or of its social connections. And most existing work attempts to deal with politics entirely at the national level, describing primarily the activities of political actors in the national capital. Apart from scattered work in Argentina and Mexico, there are few studies of the political process at the local level, of the groups and interests in play there, or of their connections to national politics. Thus, we have a distorted view of the political process, as we see it primarily through the eyes of a few articulate members of the political elite struggling for possession of the national state. It is well to remember, however, that in this period most of the national states were extremely weak. They could command very limited revenues. And in many cases the national armies were hardly stronger than the forces that could be rallied on an ad hoc basis in the various provinces. In most countries the provinces were effectively controlled by local landowners and merchants, who were often somewhat removed from national politics. Most of the participants in politics were from the upper sectors, but not all members of the upper classes were participants in national politics.

Perhaps the most important theme in the political history of Spanish America in this period is the difficulty encountered in establishing viable new states after the separation from Spain. Most Spanish American states were unable fully to re-establish the legitimacy of authority enjoyed by the Spanish crown before 1808. Formal constitutional systems were enacted, most of which provided for the transfer of power through elections and guaranteed individual liberties. But these formal constitutional provisions frequently proved a dead letter. No political group believed its adversaries would abide by them. Those who held power bent constitutional principles and often harshly repressed those in opposition in order to retain the government. Those out of power believed, generally correctly, that they could not gain possession of the state by means formally prescribed by the constitution, because those who held the government controlled the elections. Opposition politicians, both military and civilian, therefore waited for, and took advantage of, moments of government weakness in order to overthrow the ruling group. Governments were frequently unable to resist these rebellions, often because they were too weak financially to maintain dominant military force or to provide sufficient patronage to buy the allegiance of potential rebels. In few cases were the political elites sufficiently united to enable their countries to escape frequent *coups d'état*, rebellions and civil wars.

A second, related set of themes has to do with the disintegration – in some respects gradual, in others rapid – of Spanish colonial political, social and economic institutions. In political terms, the movement was not merely from monarchy to republic but also from centralized structures of control to the collapse or loosening of these structures, often in the form of federal systems. Along with the weakening of the central state there occurred a sapping of the strength of corporate groups and the caste distinctions that had dominated colonial society and had played important roles in social governance.

This disruption and disintegration of colonial structures was the result not only of the Wars of Independence and subsequent civil conflicts but also of the dominant liberal ideology. Although elements in the political elites strongly disagreed on some issues, there was, broadly speaking, a general acceptance of many aspects of liberal individualist conceptions of society and economy and (to a lesser degree) of liberal ideals of legal equality. Liberal social and economic ideas were associated with the most powerful and economically advanced western nations. Most of Spanish America's political elite ascribed the economic achievements of Great Britain and the United States to their adherence to liberal principles and attributed the economic backwardness of Spanish America to the dominance of illiberal Spanish institutions and policies. In addition, the French Revolution, despite the violence that attended it, had served at least partially to legitimize the liberal ideal of legal equality. Accordingly, the political elites proceeded, with some interruptions and retrogressions, to abolish or weaken the colonial corporate and caste structures most offensive to liberal principles.

In the first decades of the independence era distinctions among castes were abolished in law, if not always in fact. Simultaneously, the first steps were taken toward the abolition of black slavery, a process brought substantially to its conclusion by the middle of the 1850s. Early on in the independence era the elites also proposed, though they did not immediately bring into effect, the division of communally held Indian lands into individual holdings. Such communal holdings were considered inimical to liberal individualist conceptions of society, as well as to liberal economic principles, which held that only an individual property interest and the free play of economic factors (like Indian land and labour) in the marketplace could bring about greater productivity.

Although Spanish American elites often asserted that the division of Indian lands was in the best interests of the Indians themselves, they were also more than dimly aware that Indian lands once divided were likely to fall into the hands of creole landowners. In some places the appropriation of Indian lands resulted from the necessity, or hope, of more effectively mobilizing land and labour for the production of raw materials for export. Although the first steps toward the destruction of Indian communities were taken at the beginning of the period, the process did not reach its culmination until after 1850 when the Spanish American economies were much more closely integrated into the expanding international economy.

Through the interplay of liberal ideologies and economic realities, some corporate groups that had dominated colonial society, notably the colonial guilds of merchants, mining entrepreneurs and artisans, for the most part disappeared. The merchants' and miners' guilds undoubtedly were affected by the collapse of the Spanish state upon which they depended, by the emigration of their Spanish members, and by the fact that to a considerable extent British and other foreign capital and entrepreneurship replaced Spanish capital and enterprise. Artisans' guilds may have been weakened by the gradual decline of handicrafts under the impact of imported manufactures as much as by ideological aversion to guild organization.

The two largest corporate groups of the colonial period, the Church and the military, remained important, if not dominant, even though their structures were also shaken during the independence period. The Church was weakened temporarily by the fact that part of the clergy, particularly among the clerical hierarchy, had defended the royalist cause and by continuing conflict between the new states and the papacy over the right to appoint bishops. Over the longer term it also suffered from seizures of economic resources by the new governments and from the declining attractiveness of ecclesiastical vocations as alternative careers opened up for the creole upper sectors. The professional military also declined in some places because of the inability of the republican governments to support large military establishments, as well as from civilian opposition to large standing armies. Nevertheless, both the Church and the military remained formidable institutions with which the new states had to contend.

Church and military *fueros*, the special juridical privileges enjoyed by clergy and military officers, flew in the face of the liberal ideal of legal equality and also tended to abridge the authority of the state. Furthermore, in various ways the Church obstructed the realization of the liberal economy: Church holidays impeded productivity, and, indeed, the clergy themselves were held to be unproductive. The tithe, collected upon agricultural products, cut farm profits and thus obstructed agricultural development. *Censos* (quitrents) held by the Church on privately-owned property were believed to impede its free circulation in the marketplace. Similarly, Church properties held in mortmain were thought to obstruct the free circulation of property and, according to liberal assumptions, were not worked productively – in these respects being similar to the Indian communal lands. Many civilian politicians therefore came to view Church power and privilege as an important obstacle to economic growth. Finally, many considered the entrenched power of both the Church and the military as a threat to civilian control of the secular state.

Attempts to implant republican systems politically and individualist conceptions juridically and economically were complemented by efforts to create broad-based and practically oriented educational systems. Political elites were worried that the ignorance of the mass of the people, as well as their lack of experience in self-government, might make impossible the foundation of republican governments. It was imperative to establish primary schools in all communities so that the people might be prepared to exercise their functions as citizens. At the same time, though this intention was less explicitly enunciated, primary education under the control of the state (rather than the Church) would serve to inculcate loyalty to the new polities, whose legitimacy was at best uncertain. In addition, basic education was necessary for each person to behave responsibly in an individualistic social system and to maximize his potential in a free economy. Some leaders in all political groups also sought to transform the higher education of the sons of the elite, turning them from the study of useless scholastic formulas and encouraging experimental instruction in the natural sciences, in the hope of creating a new, more practically oriented, economically enterprising elite.

A number of these ideological and institutional changes had their roots in the colonial period, particularly in the period of the so called Bourbon reforms. The decentralization of political structures in the early republican era has been linked by some scholars to the introduction of the intendancy system in the late colonial period. Similarly, under the late Bourbons there occurred some significant alterations of the caste system, with some tendency to increasing incorporation of castes previously discriminated against. Some Bourbon administrators had also advocated the abandonment of the Habsburg policy of holding Indian communities in isolation from Spanish society and had encouraged the integration of the Indians into the society at large. The late Bourbon period also witnessed the undermining of many Indian communities. Under the Bourbons a series of measures attacked the juridical privileges of the Church and attempted to reduce its drag upon the economy. Finally, the first steps to establish public primary schools and to implant practical, scientific instruction at the secondary level had also been taken during the years after 1780.

But if the nineteenth-century liberalization of Spanish America had some roots in the eighteenth century, the process accelerated and broadened with independence. The process fell roughly into three phases. At the dawn of independence, the Spanish American elites, moved by a spirit of optimism about the political and economic possibilities of their new nations, initiated a considerable array of political, juridical, social, economic, fiscal and educational reforms. In some regions, most notably the Río de la Plata, New Granada and Venezuela, this reformist period fell between 1810 and 1827; in Bolivia it was concentrated in the 1820s; in Mexico and Guatemala its zenith occurred in the early 1830s. This reformist burst was followed almost everywhere, however, by a period of pessimism and conservatism, because of deepening economic crisis, early bouts of political instability, and (in some places) social reactions against reforms. This conservative mood, bringing a pause in efforts at institutional change, dominated Spanish America until the middle of the 1840s. Finally, in a number of countries, from the middle of the 1840s to the 1860s, a new generation, charged with a new optimism, encouraged by more favourable economic circumstances, resumed the liberalization process with renewed vigor.

In many respects the institutional changes of the period were more of form than of substance. The new republics, as indicated, often failed to conform to constitutionalist ideals. While upholding the fiction of an individualist society of putatively equal atoms, the elite, as well as others, in fact lived according to the norms established by traditional patron-client relationships in societies marked by great economic and social inequality. Attacks upon ecclesiastical and military privilege hardly dented the political influence of the Church or the power of the military. Many more schools were envisioned by legislators than were actually constructed by villages, and the practical reorientation of the sons of the elite proved a will-o'-the-wisp. Nevertheless, the new forms were believed in, and did not fail to have some influence upon attitudes and behaviour.

Finally the political effects of the region's economic engagement with, and dependence upon, the more developed Atlantic world in the period 1810–70 are too important to go unmentioned. At first, the severe trade imbalances, and consequent monetary and economic constriction, endured by the new Spanish American nations, as well as the mounting external debts of their governments, played an important part in destabilizing these new polities. These problems worked together to create the atmosphere of conservatism that dominated from the end of the 1820s to the middle of the 1840s. The growth of the export economies and the expansion of trade that set in after the middle of the 1840s encouraged a new burst of liberal enthusiasm in many countries. The political effects of increased integration into the international economy varied from country to country. Chile, through its exports and the notable pre-eminence of the port of Valparaiso on the Pacific coast, achieved a prosperity that aided the creation of national unity and a stable state as early as the 1830s. Elsewhere economies that were more or less integrated in the colonial era shattered under the impact of external economic forces. For example, in the late colonial period much of present day Argentina was knitted together economically by the silver trade between Potosí and Buenos Aires. In the independence era this vital economic link disappeared, as Potosí both was cut off from Buenos Aires and declined as a mining centre. Further, as Buenos Aires became an effective exporter of pastoral products and an importer of foreign manufactures, it became politically disengaged from the interior provinces, which were barred from effective exporting by transportation costs and which could offer little of value to Buenos Aires in competition with foreign manufactures. Similarly, in New Granada after independence the improvement of communications with more advanced Atlantic nations, while internal transportation remained backward, encouraged the fragmentation of an inter-regional economy that had flourished in the colonial period. Trade of cotton textiles from Socorro in the eastern part of the country to gold-producing Antioquia in the west diminished as Antioquia's gold increasingly was used to purchase foreign cloth. In a number of Spanish American countries, some regions traded more with the outside world than with other provinces, and political ties were weakened as a consequence.

A deep and abiding problem faced by Spanish American elites was that of constructing political systems that could command effective and enduring authority. In constructing new states, Spanish American leaders were influenced by, and tried somehow to make compatible, a number of conflicting elements. No matter how hostile they had become to Spanish rule during the struggle for independence, they could hardly escape the Spanish political tradition in which they had been nurtured; no matter how much they might formally disavow tradition, it lived on, often in formal institutions and, in any case, informally in modes of political behaviour. But, inevitably, they were strongly influenced by French and British political examples, both directly and through the medium of Spanish liberalism, as well as by North American models. Major political events, particularly in France, from the French Revolution to the Revolutions of 1830 and 1848, clearly affected elite conceptions about proper political modes. Salient European political thinkers, from Montesquieu and Rousseau to Constant and Bentham to Tocqueville, deeply influenced their ideas about the structure of political institutions and the functioning of the political process. One problem confronted by the elite was how to reconcile Spanish political culture with British, French and North American political models. Further, this problem had to be worked out in an economic context that in many places was extremely unfavourable to the maintenance of stable states of any kind.

The first, and most enduring problem was that of reconstructing legitimate authority in the absence of the king. With the removal of the Spanish crown as symbol of authority, could an adequate substitute be found? Furthermore, there was the manner in which the authority of the

Spanish king was conceived. Since the beginning of the sixteenth century, the Spanish monarchs had thoroughly dominated the Cortes, the nobility, the Church and the other potential power-holders in Spanish society. Consequently the concepts of representative government and, even more, of popular sovereignty were, at best, weakly developed in Spain, and power was concentrated in the hands of the monarch. The king's power was conceived to be virtually absolute and unrestricted. Could or should the new Spanish American governments be constructed along these traditional Spanish authoritarian lines? Or should the Spanish American elite abandon its political tradition in favour of the liberal constitutional models manifested in England, English America and (very briefly) in the French Revolution? Finally, there was the question of controlling the strongest corporate groups in Spanish American society, the Church and the military. Under the Spanish system, it was the king alone, ultimately, who could command the loyalty and obedience of these corporate bodies. In the absence of the king, would the new states be able to exert equally effective authority over them?

None of these issues was resolved in the first stage of the independence period. The earliest governments (1810–13) appealed to conceptions of popular sovereignty, but also recognized the authority of the captive Ferdinand VII. The problem of adequately symbolizing authority had to be confronted only when the final break with Ferdinand VII came. In any case, in the first stage of independence, despite their formal allegiance to Ferdinand VII, the authority of the various juntas and provisional governments was incomplete at best. In Buenos Aires and Santiago contending groups resorted to *coups d'état*, while in the Río de la Plata, New Granada and Venezuela inter-regional civil wars broke out over the efforts of the colonial capitals to control the provinces.

In this early period of disorder, the problem of controlling the established corporate groups emerged almost immediately. In Buenos Aires in particular, but also to a lesser degree in Caracas, Bogotá and Santiago, the militia had played an important role in deposing Spanish administrators. The militia continued to be an important political force, making and unmaking governments, a role by no means diminished as its ranks expanded in the struggle against Spanish centres of power. In this period the question at issue was the control of the military in a very direct sense; the question of military *fueros* (privileges) had not yet been raised.

Control of, and support by, the Church was equally critical to the survival of the new governments. The earliest creole leaders were solicitous of the Church, generally making few alterations in its status as the official religion. Although the newly constituted governments almost invariably abolished the Inquisition, this was not viewed as an attack upon the Church *per se*, but simply as the elimination of an institution whose excesses were out of keeping with post-Enlightenment western states. In maintaining traditional state protection of the Church creole leaders at the same time claimed the powers of patronage, most particularly the right to present (in effect, to appoint) clergymen for ecclesiastical offices. The new governments claimed this right enjoyed by the Spanish monarchs, on the ground that it was inherent in sovereignty. Papal authorities and the local church hierarchies just as steadfastly denied this claim, arguing that the patronage was granted solely to the Spanish crown. In general, the new governments were only partially successful in controlling the Church and in using its influence to sustain the state. While many in the lower clergy were sympathetic to the new autonomous governments, the Church hierarchy, with certain exceptions, was hostile to the new Spanish American republics. In Venezuela, clerical attacks upon the new republic played a part in its downfall in 1812. Elsewhere, the creole elite was more successful in harnessing the Church to the cause of independence even though the question of state control of ecclesiastical appointments remained unresolved.

While the earliest creole leaders sought to maintain continuity by recognizing Ferdinand VII as the symbolic head of government and by attempting to perpetuate the traditional relationship of state and Church, the political conceptions embodied in the new governments represented clear ruptures with the past. All of the new governments were stamped by the influence of Enlightenment rationalism and most were constructed along the lines of the republican models of the United States and the French Revolution. With the exception of those in the Río de la Plata, almost all of the revolutionary leaders moved quickly to write constitutions, thus expressing the belief that the state must be subject to a written constitution. Implicitly or explicitly these constitutions were based upon the concept of the social contract. The first constitutions (in Venezuela, New Granada and Chile, 1811–12) were proclaimed to be founded upon popular sovereignty, with the law considered the expression of the 'general will' – though usually the 'general will' was interpreted to mean the vote of the majority. The general will was to be exercised, of course, through representative government. Almost all of these earliest constitutions proclaimed the existence of inalienable natural rights (liberty, legal equality, security, property); many provided for freedom of the press; and some attempted to establish jury trials. Almost all sought to protect these rights through the separation of powers and by making the executive branch relatively weaker than the legislature.[1]

The early experiments in liberal constitutionalism in Venezuela, New Granada and Chile collapsed, destroyed by struggles among elite factions and between rival regions, in the process of which power gravitated into the hands of a single Supreme Director. Soon afterward creole government itself was annihilated by Spanish forces in all three places. Later critics, echoing Simón Bolívar in 1819, have tended to emphasize that the early creole leaders were undone in part by the Enlightenment assumptions that guided them: an excessive optimism about human nature, an excessive trust in the capacity of laws and constitutions to mould the behaviour of men, a failure to consider the weight of Spanish tradition and Spanish colonial history in influencing real political behaviour. Liberal constitutional principles, including most particularly the separation of powers and constitutional checks upon the power of the executive, flew in the face of Spanish political traditions, in which authority was concentrated in the hands of the crown, and the realities of Spanish America at the time. By adopting institutions inspired by Enlightenment ideas and foreign models, according to this view, creole leaders assured their own political failure. Such alien institutions were inevitably doomed to a speedy collapse.

While there is merit in this view, the creation of these institutions may have been influenced by more than foreign models. The establishment of constitutionally restricted, weak executives, while taking foreign-inspired forms, may also be seen as expressing a local reaction against the dominance of colonial governors. Similarly, the adoption of the federal structure, which generally has been attributed to the influence of the United States' constitution, was also a response to political realities. In New Granada and Venezuela in 1810–11 and in Mexico in 1822–4, the various provinces had developed autonomous governments that were extremely resistant to centralized rule.[2] And in Chile federalism emerged

---

[1] Simon Collier, *Ideas and politics of Chilean independence, 1808–1833* (Cambridge, 1967), 140, 154, 177–8, *passim*; Antonio Pombo and José Joaquín Guerra, *Constituciones de Colombia* (4 vols., Bogotá, 1951), I, 122–9, 144–7, 151–7, 189–90, 246–50, 261–2, 273, 294–303; II, 97–106; Ulises Picon Rivas, *Indice constitucional de Venezuela* (Caracas, 1944), 9–15.

[2] On Mexico, see in particular Nettie Lee Benson, *La diputación provincial y el federalismo mexicano* (Mexico, 1955), 85ff.

temporarily in 1826 in part because of the collapse of the central government in 1824–5.

After 1815 there was a general tendency towards creating governments with strong executives and centralized control of provincial administration. In part this phenomenon was fostered by the mobilization required to defeat the Spanish royalist forces on the battlefield. Many creole leaders also believed stronger, more centralized governments would be necessary to gain the confidence of the European powers, to obtain loans as well as diplomatic recognition. There also was some fear that, even after independence from Spain had been achieved, Spanish American governments would have to be strong if they were to resist intervention by other foreign powers. The reactionary, anti-republican atmosphere of Restoration Europe both reinforced these fears and also subjected Spanish American leaders to more conservative ideological influences than they had known before 1815.

But the tendency to increasing executive power and centralization continued after the Wars of Independence were over, after Spanish American independence had been recognized by the major powers, after the Revolution of 1830 in France. In fact, the tendency to centralization became particularly pronounced between 1826 and 1845. Local conditions, existing before 1825 and continuing through to the 1840s, therefore, played an important role in the centralizing process. At the dawn of independence there had existed a political atmosphere of optimism which had encouraged the utopian constitutional formulations of 1811–12. After 1825, however, continuing political disorder and the onset of economic crisis created an atmosphere of greater pessimism about the social order and the economic and political prospects of Spanish America. During the period from 1820 to 1845 political leaders frequently expressed their fears of the imminence (or the actuality) of anarchy. The great preoccupation of these decades then was the pursuit of political order.

There was, however, some disagreement about how that order was to be achieved. Some, particularly the university educated, looked to various sorts of European constitutional forms as keys to stability. Others, for the most part among the military and the less well educated, preferred to dispense with such constitutional frippery and looked to the use of force, if not terror, as a means of maintaining order.

The desire to establish a stronger constitutional state after 1815 is observable in, for example, the effort, relatively transitory, to erect constitutional monarchies headed by European princes, a pattern most visible in Argentina (1814–18) and Chile (1818). In many cases proponents of monarchy sought to reach accomodation with the reactionary monarchies of post-Napoleonic Europe. In both Argentina and Chile gestures towards monarchy were made in the hope of gaining recognition of their independence and, if possible, protection from external attack. The monarchist schemes of 1814–19 also reflected the conviction of at least some leaders that constitutional monarchy would bolster internal stability. General Manuel Belgrano, in arguing for constitutional monarchy in the 1816 Congress at Tucumán, emphasized both the internal disorder in the Plata region and the dominant political atmosphere in Europe; the adoption of monarchy would be politically advisable as well as diplomatically prudent.

After 1819, when the idea of constitutional monarchy lost its reputability in the Río de la Plata, constitutional monarchy as a means of achieving political stability had important support only in Mexico. There, as early as 1830, Lucas Alamán gave the British envoy to understand that because of Mexico's chronic disorder the idea of importing a European prince was gaining adherents. Such a proposal was publicly discussed in the 1840s, though its proponents probably still were quite few. Finally, between 1864 and 1867 the only actual experiment with rule by a European prince was attempted when Mexican conservatives, in league with Napoleon III, imported Archduke Maximilian of Austria as emperor of Mexico. As in the earlier cases, however, internal political stability was not the only goal in view. For Mexican conservatives the French-backed monarchy was a last gasp effort to recoup declining political strength. For both Mexican conservatives and Napoleon III the experiment ended in ignominious defeat; when Maximilian was executed in 1867, Mexican conservatism as a political movement died with him.

Constitutional monarchy was never a success in Spanish America. In the early stages (1810–30) it was hard to find a generally acceptable European candidate. Because of the intransigence of Ferdinand VII, a candidate closely linked to the Spanish monarchy proved impossible. On the other hand, it was hard to find anyone else acceptable to both England and France – a prerequisite for the success of the measure as a diplomatic gambit. Even if a candidate acceptable to the European powers were found, he would have been an artificial graft (as Maximilian later proved to be), lacking the legitimacy that was supposed to be the key to the success of monarchy. Attempts at homegrown monarchy failed for similar reasons. Belgrano's proposal to enthrone a descendant of the Inca might offer some colour of legitimacy, but was, given creole contempt for the Indian, inherently absurd. Nor would a creole monarch do, as General Agustín Iturbide discovered in Mexico in 1821–2. The elite could hardly accept monarchical or imperial rule by someone already known close at hand as a man of no finer clay than the rest. Most important, perhaps, after the American and French Revolutions the idea of monarchy lost much of its appeal. While the solidity of the British constitutional monarchy was admired everywhere in Spanish America, monarchy as a system represented a remnant of the past. In the optimism of the first years of independence, most in the creole elite preferred to associate themselves with republicanism, a system that seemed to represent the wave of the future. Also, in the early phases, the erection of republics helped to justify the break with Spain. Later, after the early optimism and revolutionary enthusiasm had begun to fade, the now-established republican mode had begun to develop an institutional momentum. After 1820, therefore, most efforts at consolidating central control were at least formally republican in character.

Two basic constitutional formulas stand out in the period from 1819 to 1845: that of centralized republics similar in form to the Spanish Constitution of Cádiz of 1812, and that of the Napoleonic state as advocated by Simón Bolívar. The first type, by far the most common, tended to have broad support among civilian elites, and in particular among lawyers and the university-educated, while the Napoleonic–Bolivarian model tended to have more adherents in the military.

The mark of the Constitution of Cádiz is evident in most of the constitutions of the 1820s and 1830s: in those of Gran Colombia (1821), of New Granada (1830, 1832) and Venezuela (1830); in those of Peru of 1823 and 1828; in the Argentine constitution of 1826, that of Uruguay in 1830, and the Chilean constitution of 1828. The Mexican constitution of 1824 also was heavily influenced by the Spanish constitution but diverged importantly in having a federal structure. Most of these charters created councils of state to advise the president; most provided the executive with only a suspensive veto; most asserted the principle of ministerial responsibility at least by requiring ministers to co-sign all decrees. Many followed the Constitution of Cádiz in attempting to bolster the power of the legislature by instituting a permanent committee of the Congress to act for the legislature when it was out of session. All, with the exception of the Mexican constitution, provided for centrally-appointed provincial officers (variously called intendants, prefects or governors), though in many cases the president had to choose these from panels nominated by provincial bodies. Finally, almost all of these charters created variants of the Spanish *diputación provincial*, an elected body that was to aid the intendant or governor in promoting education and economic development and in assessing and collecting taxes. As in Spain, the presumed functions of these bodies was essentially advisory and administrative, not legislative. In Mexico, however, these *diputaciones provinciales* quickly evolved into full-scale provincial legislatures. In New Granada this evolution was slower and more stunted: until the 1840s their decrees had to be approved by the national legislature. Elsewhere, as in Peru and Uruguay, these bodies either died or never became significant. Thus, following the model of the Spanish constitution of 1812, the creole elite in many places attempted to establish a centralist system, bedizened with the ornaments of constitutionalism.

Spanish American elites were probably attracted to the 1812 Constitution because it represented an effort to do essentially the same thing that they were trying to do: to introduce Anglo-French liberal constitutional ideals into a Spanish political structure. There was, however, one significant difference between the tasks of the constitution-writers of Cádiz and those of the authors of the Spanish American charters of later years. In Cádiz the Spanish liberals were preoccupied with circumscribing the power of an absolutist king, turning him into a constitutional monarch. In Spanish America, however, the same constitutional model was used in an attempt to strengthen, rather than to weaken, central authority as previously constituted in the earliest Spanish American charters. Furthermore, most of the Spanish American constitutions made a significant addition to the Cádiz model, permitting their presidents the use of extraordinary powers in time of external threat or internal disturbance. This escape hatch from the formal constraints of constitutionalism was put to considerable use throughout Spanish America and frequently served to nullify in fact the liberties solemnly proclaimed in the constitutions.

In some countries which opted for the Cádiz model support for centralized authority was not unanimous; elements in the political elite continued to argue for federal structures. In Colombia in 1821, in Chile through the end of the 1820s, and in Mexico and Argentina throughout the period, important political figures supported the federal system, because of regional antagonisms or provincial distrust of the capital but also because they considered the federal structure a barrier against tyranny. In many countries, however, federalists were overwhelmed by those who feared that the federal system would lead (or had led) to anarchy. Usually those who advocated a centralist state were willing to admit the theoretical desirability of federalism from the point of view of liberal constitutionalist principles, but in the same breath they contended the system was 'too perfect', impracticable for Spanish America. The centralist litany held that Spanish rule, by keeping the people ignorant and denying them political experience, had left them unprepared for so extreme a version of democratic republican government. The populace as a whole lacked sufficient enlightenment and civic responsibility (civic virtue) to be able to make wise choices at the local level. Further, there were not enough competent men to fill all of the provincial offices that would be required. Finally, the system, with its multiplication of offices, implied costs which the Spanish American republics could not sustain. Rather than risk the anarchy that surely would follow upon the adoption of the federal system, centralists argued, a little bit of liberty must be sacrificed in order to obtain order. Civic liberties, they contended, would be adequately protected by the division of powers, alternation in office, and other constitutional restraints at the national level, which each of the Cádiz model charters prescribed.

Distrust of the political capacity of the mass of the people was reflected in the property qualifications established in almost all of the centralist constitutions of the 1820s and 1830s. However, as in other cases, it is difficult to discern the degree to which the establishment of property restrictions on suffrage expressed a current of conservatism within Spanish America and to what extent these restrictions were adopted in imitation of European models. European constitutional example, as well as the theories of leading European constitutionalists like Benjamin Constant, provided ample sanction for strict property qualifications of the sort adopted throughout Spanish America.

There were some exceptions to the general tendency to centralization in Spanish America that marked the 1820s and 1830s. But these exceptions were in some cases more or less temporary aberrations, as in the case of the Chilean federalist constitution of 1826–8. And in other cases they were produced by the peculiarities of local political history. For example, as independence from Spain came rather late to Mexico (1821) and to

Peru (1824), they began the sequence of constitutional evolution later than some other regions. Thus, the first Peruvian constitution (1823) corresponded to the earlier constitutions of Venezuela, New Granada and Chile (1811) in establishing a weak, legislature-dominated, plural executive, while the Mexican constitution of 1824 created the federal structure of the 1811 constitutions of Venezuela and New Granada. But both Peru and Mexico rather quickly followed the general tendency to increasing executive power and centralization. The Peruvian constitution of 1823, with its plural executive, was overthrown almost immediately and from that time onward Peru was in the hands of military caudillos operating through a strong presidential regime. In Mexico the federal constitution suffered *de facto* abridgements in 1830–2 and was formally replaced by a centralized system from 1836 through to 1846. The greatest exception to the pattern, Argentina, reflects another kind of local peculiarity. In the Río de la Plata attempts to establish a centralized system culminated in the constitution of 1826. However, the centralist system broke down almost immediately as provincial caudillos and their local backers asserted their independence from Buenos Aires, an independence ratified in the Federal Pact of 1831. During the 1830s and 1840s Juan Manuel de Rosas in Buenos Aires proved able to influence the political direction of the other provinces, but such powers as he had over them were exercised informally and were not recognized in a constitutional system.

While approximations of the Cádiz constitution were most favoured among university-educated politicians between 1820 and 1845, some important elements in the political elite – most notably in the military – believed even this model was not strong enough to provide stable government in Spanish America. Men of this persuasion, of whom Simón Bolívar was the most prominent, shared many of the same assumptions as the proponents of the Cádiz model. They agreed on the danger of anarchy and on the fact that the Spanish American populace lacked the political experience and civic virtue required to sustain a full-blown liberal republic. Yet they differed on the conclusions they drew from these premises. The civilian exponents of the Cádiz constitutions assumed that, while the people could not be trusted, there existed an elite large enough and enlightened enough to run centralized republics. As Fernando de Peñalver, a Venezuelan centralist, explained to his fellow delegates at the Colombian constitutional convention of 1821, 'I do not see virtues in the people, although I see enlightenment in the Congress.'[3] In particular, these centralist republicans believed, along with their federalist peers, in the importance of the principle of alternation in power as a protection against tyranny. Bolívar and other military leaders, on the other hand, did not entirely trust even the elite to conduct politics in an orderly and enlightened manner. They therefore sought to establish a more paternalistic republic, in effect, a constitutional monarchy in republican dress. While Bolívar's constitutional proposals provided for popular elections, much of the power was to be held by men who, once in office, were not subject to elections – most notably a life-president and a hereditary or life-senate. Bolívar hoped that these would provide elements of permanence and continuity that would help to stabilize the new republics.

For Bolívar and others of his inclination, the most appealing constitutional models were those of the British constitutional monarchy and the Napoleonic Consular Constitutions of 1799 and 1802 (which were in part derived from the British model). Generally, the constitutional solutions they supported provided for presidents with long terms of office (eight or ten years, or, in the case of Bolívar's last constitutional schemes, life) and for multiple legislative bodies, one of which would have lifetime or hereditary membership. An early example of a constitutional plan following this model was a proposed outline by Bolívar in 1819 at the Congress of Angostura, which called for a hereditary senate modelled on the British House of Lords and for a strong president. While Bolívar's Angostura plan had a British model, his Bolivian constitution of 1826 was more influenced by the Napoleonic constitutions. The president in effect would be a life consul, with power to designate the vice-president, his successor, as well as the secretaries of state. The president could not be held responsible for the acts of his administration; only the vice-president and the secretaries of state could be impeached. Beyond his extensive appointment powers, the president had the authority freely to adjourn and convoke the legislative bodies. The system was further to be anchored by a chamber of censors (one of three legislative bodies), to be appointed for life, whose duties primarily were to promote and protect the exercise of civic virtue (safeguarding freedom of the press and vigilance against the abuse of authority were two of its jobs).

[3] Colombia, Congreso General, 1821, *Congreso de Cúcuta, 1821: libro de actas* (Bogotá, 1971), 60.

During the 1830s and 1840s the Napoleonic–Bolivarian model was resurrected by several generals who had served under Bolívar and clearly were influenced by him. In 1837 General Andrés Santa Cruz, having temporarily unified Peru and Bolivia in a confederation, promulgated a constitution in which the executive was headed by a protector, with a ten-year term, and in which there was a lifetime senate, whose members were appointed by the protector. In 1843 a similar constitution was proclaimed in Ecuador by another former subordinate of Bolívar, General Juan José Flores, in this case with an eight-year president and the familiar lifetime senate. A modified version of the same constitutional model was implanted by conservative elements in Mexico in 1836.

The constitutions based on the Napoleonic–Bolivarian model were short-lived. In Bolivia and Peru, Bolívar actually succeeded temporarily in imposing his constitution in 1826; but the governments he erected collapsed, and his constitutions were abandoned practically as soon as he removed himself from the scene. When Bolívar attempted to impose his ideas on the Republic of Colombia between 1826 and 1830, he encountered such opposition among the civilian elite that he found it necessary to establish dictatorial rule; the dictatorship in turn provoked an attempt upon his life (September 1828) by younger members of the civilian elite in Bogotá, and Bolívar soon had to admit failure, resigning his office as his enterprise dissolved about him. The Santa Cruz and Flores variations on the Bolivarian constitutions also were short-lived, in each case lasting no more than two years – though that of Santa Cruz was defeated by external intervention from Chile as well as by internal revolt.

The Bolivarian model failed everywhere in part because to many in the civilian elite it smacked too much of monarchy. In addition, by prescribing a life-president and life-censors, Bolívar's scheme violated one of the constitutional principles that university-educated liberals held dear: the principle of alternation in office as a protection against tyranny. Civilians also feared that military leaders would monopolize the presidency. Whether from principle or self-interest, the Bolivarian constitutions were vigorously fought by educated liberals, led in Peru by the priest, Francisco Javier Luna Pizarro, and in Colombia by General Francisco de Paula Santander and a clutch of young lawyers.

Although Bolívar and many among the university-educated were mortal antagonists in the years 1826–30, their differing governmental prescriptions drew on the same body of political thought, most particularly on the doctrines of Benjamin Constant, which were widely circulated in a Spanish translation published in Spain at the time of the liberal revolution of 1820. But liberals tended to emphasize more than Bolívar the individual liberties side of Constant (jury trials, freedom of the press, inviolability of property, restrictions upon the military). Bolívar, on the other hand, stressed the stabilizing elements in Constant, in particular in his conception of the division of powers. Constant conceived of the constitutional monarch as a neutral balance wheel, moderating conflicts among the executive, the representative and judicial powers. Bolívar followed this scheme both in distinguishing the president (constitutional monarch) and the actions of his ministers and in placing the moderating power in the hands of the censors. This Constantian conception of a moderating power was also found in the Mexican centralist constitution of 1836, known as the Seven Laws.

The universal influence of Constant in the 1820s and 1830s is only one indication of the hegemony of moderate European constitutional ideas among Spanish American intellectuals. Whether in Chilean newspapers of the 1820s, the Uruguayan constitutional convention of 1830, or the libraries of New Granadan politicians in the 1840s, the three authors most frequently encountered were Montesquieu, Constant and Bentham. Rousseau, of great help in justifying the establishment of revolutionary governments between 1810 and 1815, was decreasingly relevant to Spanish American concerns after 1820. What most interested the political elite were those works on the practical arts of government, rather than abstract, theoretical treatises on the foundations of sovereignty. Machiavelli figured prominently in libraries of the period. But constitutionalist authors were also consulted as helpful guides. The civilian elite turned to Constant's *Curso de política* for its usefulness in constitution-writing. Of Bentham they read less the philosophical early writings than those works that seemed to offer some guidance in legislation and jurisprudence (the treatises on civil and penal legislation, on judicial evidence, on penal law and the essays on political tactics and parliamentary fallacies). Many other works to which the elites were attracted also were viewed as manuals for the conduct of constitutional government: for example, Cottu on the administration of criminal justice in England and the spirit of English government, Filangieri on legislation, Beccaria and Dumont on criminal punishments, Guizot on the death penalty, Say on political economy. After 1835, Alexis de Tocqueville's *Democracy in America* joined Montesquieu, Constant and Bentham as universally-read authority on the practice of constitutional government. For those of conservative disposition a list of the 1830s or 1840s might also include Chateaubriand, Burke, and Cousin.[4]

Notably missing from the intellectual armature of politicians active between 1820 and 1845 were the extremes of European political thought of the time. In their libraries and public discussions the absolutist royalists, de Maistre and de Bonald, rarely appeared. At the same time, French socialist writings left little imprint on those who dominated politics before 1845. The most notable case of socialist influence in the 1830s is that of the Argentine Esteban Echeverría, who was especially current with Saint-Simonian writings. But Echeverría was really a man of a younger generation not yet contending for power.

Between 1820 and 1845 liberal-to-moderate European constitutionalism thus formed the intellectual stock of educated leaders of all political factions, whether 'extremist' (*exaltado*), moderate, or conservative. There was, of course, some disagreement about aspects of this early nineteenth-century list of political authorities. Bentham and Destutt de Tracy were more widely read than they were accepted. Both were bitterly attacked by political conservatives for their 'materialist' (i.e. sensationalist) philosophies. Yet those conservatives who most objected to Bentham's materialism were nevertheless orthodox liberal constitutionalists. Joaquín Mosquera, a notable anti-Benthamite in New Granada, attacked the English utilitarian partly on the ground that he denied the doctrine of natural rights. Another strong anti-utilitarian, the Peruvian, José María de Pando, was one of the few political intellectuals in Spanish America somewhat influenced by the arch-conservatism of de Bonald and de Maistre. Yet in his constitutional prescriptions even Pando argued not for absolutism but for a decorous, Constantian constitutional monarchy, with guarantees of liberty of the press and trial by jury.[5] Thus, even in a period of marked social and political conservatism, liberal constitutional ideals continued to dominate among the university-educated elite.

Despite an at least intellectual acceptance of constitutionalist ideas by

4 Collier, *Ideas and politics*, 171–6; Juan E. Pivel Devoto, *Historia de los partidos y de las ideas políticas en el Uruguay*, II. *La definición de los bandos (1829–1838)* [the only volume published] (Montevideo, 1956), 53; lists of books in mortuaria, Archivo Nacional de Colombia, Sección República, Notaría 2a, 1840, tomo 43, fos. 57r–58r; 1851, tomo 264, fos. 759r–763v; 1852, tomo 269, fos. 26r–29v; Notaría 3a, 1848, tomo 435, fos. 534v–6r. See also Charles A. Hale, *Mexican liberalism in the age of Mora, 1821–1853* (New Haven, 1968), 55–60, 76, 149–54, *passim*. For sources favoured by an extreme conservative in the 1840s, see Bartolomé Herrera, *Escritos y discursos* (2 vols., Lima, 1929), I, 95–6.
5 José María de Pando, *Pensamientos y apuntes sobre moral y política* (Cádiz, 1837), 3–5, 14–22, 62, 110–11.

the university-educated, constitutionalist precepts often were not observed in fact. Not everyone active in politics was committed to these ideas. University men predominantly wrote the constitutions and laws, filled most of the seats of the legislatures and held the cabinet posts. But they were not the only political actors, even though they generally had the most to do with the formal aspects of statecraft. Important political roles, as holders of ultimate power, were also played by others – professional military officers, regional caudillos, merchants and landowners – who often knew little of liberal constitutional ideas and cared less. For intellectual politicians the forms of politics, the ideas embodied in laws and constitutions were important. They cared about these ideas and their presumed social consequences, and also these ideas and institutions signified political respectability, in their own eyes as well as in those of civilized Europe. But for those not socialized to European political modes through travel or university education, this sort of consideration had much less weight. Professional military officers were often motivated in politics by concern to protect their reputations, sometimes by a desire to protect the military as an interest group and on occasion by a concern to represent broader social interests. Regional caudillos had to take care to satisfy the local landed oligarchies who often formed the bases of their power. The primary concern of large landowners was to have the support or benevolent neutrality of local officials in their disputes over land tenure. Merchants worried less about the form of government than about whether commercial regulations would be favourable, or at least predictable. Thus, while political ideologies and the institutions they embodied stirred the emotions of educated politicians, to many others they were of little significance.

This lack of concern for constitutional principles was piquantly expressed by Diego Portales, a merchant and dominant political figure in Chile in the 1830s. In 1834 Portales, then governor of Valparaiso, vented his outrage at the opinion of a conservative jurist, Mariano Egaña, that he could not have a dissident arrested without a court order. (Egaña had further enraged Portales by sending along a book on habeas corpus.)[6]

In sum, to follow the opinion of the jurist Egaña, confronting a threat to overthrow authority, the Government ought to cross its arms, unless the suspect was caught in the act. . . . With the men of the law one cannot come to an understanding; and if it's that way, what [expletive] purpose do Constitutions and papers serve, if they are incapable of providing a remedy to an evil that is

---

[6] Raúl Silva Castro (ed.), *Ideas y confesiones de Portales* (Santiago de Chile, 1954), 57–8.

known to exist. . . . In Chile the law doesn't serve for anything but to produce anarchy, the lack of sanctions, licentiousness, eternal law suits. . . . If I, for example, imprison an individual who is conspiring, I violate the law. Damned law, then, if it does not allow the Government to proceed freely in the opportune moment.

University-educated politicians who were nurtured in constitutionalist principles also found themselves betraying these principles in the exercise of power. Vicente Rocafuerte, for example, a leader of the liberal opposition in Mexico in the 1820s and in Ecuador until 1834, once in power and facing armed rebellion in Ecuador in 1835, declared that 'only terror' could reduce the rebels to order and 'conserve the first of all laws which is that of public tranquillity'.

The only course that I have is that they tremble before me. If it were necessary, I will know how to convert myself into a Sylla [Sulla] to save my country from the anarchy that is trying to devour it. A true lover of enlightenment and civilization, I consent to pass for a tyrant.[7]

And, as good as his word, he had dozens of rebels shot.

The frequent breach of proclaimed constitutionalist principles in nineteenth century Spanish America has been the subject of various interpretations. One view is that constitutionalism was necessarily a dead letter because it was completely out of keeping with Spanish political traditions.[8] It may also be suggested, however, that, at least in some cases, the violation of constitutional principles was inherent in the task of the educated elite. Their effort to overthrow Spanish social, economic and political institutions and to implant new ones based on British, French and other foreign models was, in effect, revolutionary.[9] Consequently, it is not surprising that in attempting to introduce these changes they frequently resorted to violent measures.

To a considerable degree authority was not successfully embodied in the formal institutions envisioned in Spanish America's many constitutions;

---

[7] Quoted in Richard Pattee, *Gabriel García Moreno y el Ecuador de su tiempo* (Quito, 1941), 56.

[8] Glen Dealy, 'La tradición de la democracia monista en América Latina', *Estudios Andinos*, 4/1 (1974–5), 159–201.

[9] See Ralph Lee Woodward, 'Social revolution in Guatemala: the Carrera revolt', in *Applied enlightenment: 19th century liberalism* (Middle American Research Institute, Publication 23, Tulane University, New Orleans, 1972), 49–53, *passim*. See also Charles Hale's discussion of the contradiction between the liberals' goal of constitutionalism, which implied limited governmental powers, and their desire to break down corporate barriers to individualism, which required a strong state, 'José María Luis Mora and the structure of Mexican liberalism', *Hispanic American Historical Review*, 45/2 (1965), 196–227.

rather it was incarnated in persons. Authority gravitated into the hands of strong leaders, who tended to stand above laws or constitutions. These leaders often were and are thought of as caudillos – men whose force of character enabled them to command the personal loyalty of a substantial band of followers, and who mobilized their adherents to challenge constituted authority or to seize power by violence or the threat of violence.

The term caudillo refers to any kind of pre-eminent leader, and it was used in this sense between 1810 and 1870. Most caudillos, particularly in the first decades of the period, were specifically military leaders who had gained stature during the Wars of Independence. But the term was also applied in these years to other kinds of leaders. In the 1820s, the Peruvian General Agustín Gamarra, himself clearly a caudillo, used the word with reference to the political leadership of a bishop.[10] In current scholarship regarding the nineteenth century the term tends to be used somewhat more narrowly than it was by contemporaries. The caudillo is now generally thought of as one who used violence or the threat of violence for political ends – whether as a professional officer commanding regular army units, or as a militia officer or civilian-on-horseback leading militia or irregular forces into political battle, or (more broadly) as an essentially civilian leader who engaged in violent repression (as in the cases of Dr Francia in Paraguay or Diego Portales in Chile).

Before 1840, most of the men whom we currently think of as caudillos were individuals with some kind of military attainment before their political careers began – soldiers of the independence or provincial militia leaders like Juan Manuel de Rosas, who gained fame as a fighter of Indians. After the 1840s, as the generals of the independence passed from the scene, their roles as military leaders in internal political warfare were partially assumed by men who began their political careers as civilians – by lawyers, journalists, merchants and landowners who were drawn into military leadership by the exigencies of the violent politics of the time.

The caudillo and his band of followers were held together by a network of personal loyalties. What was the basis of these personal attachments? Why did people follow the caudillo? Nineteenth-century writings on this phenomenon, and much of the literature of the twentieth century also, have stressed the personality of the caudillo himself. According to the stereotype, he was a man of great personal magnetism,

10 Gran Mariscal Agustín Gamarra, *Epistolario*, ed. Alberto Tauro (Lima, 1952), 47, 148, 209.

who dominated lesser men by force of will. In the classic nineteenth-century portrait of the caudillo, Domingo Faustino Sarmiento's depiction in 1845 of the Argentine provincial leader Facundo Quiroga, the caudillo is described as saying, 'If I should go into the street and say to the first man I met, "Follow me!", he would follow me without hesitation.' The caudillo's followers responded to him both because they found him attractive and because he intimidated them. The caudillo, again according to the stereotype, was courageous, a man who could command others to perform feats of valour because he himself set the example of bravery and boldness. He also is frequently described as 'telluric', earthy; even if a member of the upper class, he often cultivated a popular style in order to encourage his followers to identify with him personally. Both to demonstrate their virility and to establish their identity with their followers, José Antonio Páez in Venezuela and Juan Manuel de Rosas in Buenos Aires are alleged to have matched their cowboy retinues in feats of horsemanship. While many caudillos affected a common touch, others celebrated themselves with pomp, which may have served to overawe the populace as well as to gratify the leader himself. The caudillo characteristically had an authoritarian personality. Because of his ruthlessness and, even more perhaps, his unpredictability, the caudillo often frightened his followers and his enemies alike.

Many recent treatments, while not denying the personality characteristics of the caudillo, tend to focus instead upon the network of relations between the leader and his adherents. *Caudillismo*, in these accounts, is viewed as a social system, a system structured upon the mutual dependence of the chief and his band. Various kinds of patron–client relationships have been posited. Commonly the caudillo is viewed as handing out largesse to his followers as a reward for faithful service.[11] But more sophisticated interpretations have also noted another kind of patron–client relationship, one in which the caudillo himself was the client of wealthy patrons who 'created and controlled' him as an investment for their own political and/or economic designs.[12] Even in this latter case, of course, one must assume a relationship of mutual dependence, in which neither the caudillo-client nor his wealthy patrons completely controlled the relationship. Most treatments of *caudillismo* as a

[11] Eric R. Wolf and Edward C. Hansen, 'Caudillo politics: a structural analysis', *Comparative Studies in Society and History*, 9/2 (1967), 168–79.

[12] Roger M. Haigh, 'The creation and control of a caudillo', *Hispanic American Historical Review*, 44/4 (1964), 481–90. See also Robert L. Gilmore, *Caudillism and militarism in Venezuela, 1810–1910* (Athens, Ohio, 1964), for a well-informed discussion.

patron–client relationship focus on the caudillo as a figure emanating from some regional backwater and assume the network supporting him to be an alliance of local landowners. But not all caudillos emerged from provincial obscurity. Many had as their base of power the support of officers in the national army, or of certain cliques of such officers. Some of the most powerful caudillos, such as General Antonio López de Santa Anna in Mexico, combined the support both of regional oligarchies and of the officers' corps. Finally, one should note that caudillistic patron–client networks often formed elaborate pyramids – in which local *caciques*, with their personal followings, pledged loyalty to regional chieftains, who in turn gave at least temporary and conditional support to caudillos, or other political leaders operating at the national level.

In terms of social classes, the caudillo is frequently thought of as being socially emergent, a man of relatively humble origins whose ambitions for power were prompted in part by a hunger for wealth and social status. Such a conception, of course, nicely fits the idea of a caudillo who is both client to wealthy patrons and patron to followers. One can find many cases of caudillos who fit this description in some degree. But many caudillos, such as Simón Bolívar and General Tomás Cipriano de Mosquera in Colombia, were born to the upper class. Such men were less easily controlled and were viewed as especially unpredictable and therefore intimidating by the upper sectors.

As the caudillo came to power through violence, the legitimacy of his rule was always in question. Consequently he often ruled his domain, local or national, with a sense of insecurity of tenure, knowing that he too might be overthrown by some competing chieftain. Because his *de facto* regime lacked constitutional legitimacy and often met resistance from other caudillos, he often found himself compelled to rule by violence, with little or no attention to constitutional niceties. Not infrequently he seemed to be arbitrary in his political acts. The caudillo's unpredictability was increased by the fact that he ruled according to personal consider-ations. For the caudillo, the primary question was personal loyalty. Those thought to be loyal could depend upon support; those suspected of disloyalty could expect terrible vengeance. On the other hand, the caudillo might make surprising alliances, again often on the basis of personal relations. As ideology was of little concern to most caudillos, they found no difficulty in supporting quite diverse and contradictory causes. In the Río de la Plata caudillos identified themselves variously as unitarians or federalists, often with little sense of the meaning of these terms except as a way of identifying friends and enemies. In Mexico, General Santa Anna threw his weight variously behind liberals or conservatives, depending upon his estimate of the relative strength of their forces. In New Granada, General José María Obando in 1840 waved the banner of federalism in a rebellion launched to defend himself from prosecution (or, in his eyes, persecution) by the national government; in 1853 he considered it impossible to govern as president of a federalist government. Obando's arch-rival, General Tomás Cipriano de Mosquera, on the other hand, moved rather easily from a vigorous centralism in the 1840s to an equally vigorous federalism in the 1850s, following the dictates of his ambition.

Often the personalist leadership of caudillos found expression in rebellion against constituted governments. But in a number of cases a dominant caudillo used his authority to shore up fledgling governmental structures. In Chile caudillistic rebellion and seizure of power characterized the period of the Patria Vieja (1810–14) and the 1820s. But after 1830 a government established through the personal authority of General Joaquín Prieto and his minister Diego Portales ultimately developed institutional strength. By 1851 the Chilean governments were able to sustain their authority without benefit of charismatic leadership. In New Granada the personal authority of General Francisco de Paula Santander in the 1830s and of General Tomás Cipriano de Mosquera in the 1840s helped to support constitutional government which in these years was threatened by only one major caudillistic rebellion. Similarly, in Venezuela the authority of General José Antonio Páez (1830–48) and in the province of Buenos Aires of Juan Manuel de Rosas (1829–52) served to maintain a substantial public order. In much of Spanish America, during much of the time, however, no single caudillo was able to dominate the scene and seemingly interminable series of civil wars or *coups d'état* were staged to determine who should rule. This pattern is most notable in Bolivia, in Peru (1823–45), and in much of the pre-1860 history of the Río de la Plata region.

The sources of *caudillismo* have been the subject of much speculation, but of rather little systematic research. While the full array of hypotheses about the caudillo cannot be presented here, some of the principal explanations can be sketched. Many interpretations emphasize the impact of the Wars of Independence. According to one, the struggle for independence raised military heroes to status and power while the civilian elites and the governing institutions they controlled were correspondingly weakened. The emergence of the caudillo thus can be seen as the result of a 'militarization' of politics between 1810 and 1825.[13] This interpretation has merit for those regions that suffered prolonged periods of violent conflict in the struggle for independence – most notably Venezuela, New Granada, the Río de la Plata and Mexico. But in some regions, such as Central America, there was relatively little military conflict in the process of winning independence, yet caudillos nonetheless emerged in the post-independence period. This fact and the continuation of caudillesque politics for decades after the independence struggle suggest that it is necessary to look beyond the independence period militarization for the sources of caudillismo. The independence wars undoubtedly affected the *forms* that personalist leadership took. But *caudillismo* itself had deeper roots, was the work of more enduring forces.[14]

The most notable beneficiary of independence in Spanish America was the creole upper class. At the end of the colonial period most of its members owned landed property, many could be found in the priesthood, a few engaged in large-scale international commerce. Some also held government positions, but primarily in lesser posts – as lawyers, revenue agents or secondary provincial administrators. With independence, opportunities for careers in government and politics for creoles multiplied, not only because they displaced Spaniards in the highest positions but also because of the very nature of the republican governments that they came to establish. Whereas the colonial system had required only a relatively small corps of judges, provincial administrators, military officers and revenue agents, the new republics demanded all of these and much more: more elaborate systems of appeals courts were established; national legislators, usually in two chambers, and frequently also provincial legislators had to be found; finally, at the highest level there were cabinet and sub-cabinet positions, councils of state, and at least a few diplomatic posts to be distributed.

New political opportunities led to considerable territorial mobility among elements in the creole group. Provincials who came to the capital as legislators often stayed on to educate their families, to enjoy the

---

[13] For example, Asher Christensen, *The evolution of Latin American government* (New York, 1951), and, in a much more sophisticated version, Tulio Halperín Donghi, *The aftermath of revolution in Latin America* (New York, 1973), 1–43.

[14] For further discussion on this point, see below pp. 114–21, section on interpretations of political instability in Spanish America during the post-independence period.

cultural ambience and to further their political careers. Provincial families also sent their sons to the capital cities to be educated in the principal secondary schools and universities, not necessarily intending political careers for them – though passage through those institutions provided both the educational certification and the contacts required for such careers. Those who went to be educated in the capital rarely returned to the provinces. One unintended effect of this tendency to converge upon the capital cities was to undermine the development of the provinces by draining off their educated elites.

While ambitious men from the provinces, or from otherwise relatively obscure locations in the upper sectors, entered politics, in some places the richest and traditionally most prestigious families were notably absent from political life. In some cases this was not a matter of choice: men of wealth and social position sometimes were simply displaced by military men who commanded instruments of violence. In other cases the wealthiest men voluntarily removed themselves from the political arena – perhaps as a matter of prudence, perhaps because disorder had brought political careers into discredit, perhaps in distaste for the new social elements that were active in politics. Often, however, men of wealth moved discreetly behind the scenes, directing, or at least influencing, the military caudillos who so much appeared to dominate political life.[15] The withdrawal from overt participation in political office by the richest members of the upper class was perhaps most evident in Argentina and, to a lesser degree, in Mexico. It was, however, far from a universal phenomenon. In Chile, Colombia and Venezuela the wealthiest and most established families were quite prominent in politics through most of the period.

Outside the creole group the political rewards of independence were limited. The creoles were loath to share power with the *mestizos* and others in the nether regions of the colonial social order. Some individual *mestizos* and mulattos did emerge to political prominence during the struggle for independence, largely on the basis of their prowess as leaders of guerrilla or other military forces. But the emergence of these few individuals worried the creoles. Simón Bolívar, for example, was much given to expressing anxiety about a looming 'pardocracy' (rule by the dark-skinned). And the creole elite almost systematically (it now seems in

---

[15] Haigh, 'Creation of a caudillo', 481–90. Haigh's case deals with the northern interior province of Salta in Argentina. A similar argument could be made for the influence of Tomás Manuel de Anchorena and other landed magnates on Juan Manuel de Rosas in Buenos Aires.

retrospect) eliminated from high positions these lower-caste individuals, particularly the mulattos. The two highest-ranking mulatto officers in Venezuela and New Granada, Generals Manuel Piar and José Padilla, were shot for offences that might well have been pardoned in whites. In Mexico the dark-hued insurgent leader, Vicente Guerrero, was detested by the upper classes as uncouth, ignorant and generally unfit; overthrown as president, he was shot by his opponents.

Although the few prominent mulatto officers were eliminated with some dispatch, the elite faced a much more troublesome problem in the distribution of power between civilian and military creoles. Tulio Halperín Donghi has emphasized that the fight for independence, and in the Río de la Plata for national consolidation, brought the military so much to the fore that the civilian elites who had dominated the colonial regime (civil bureaucrats and ecclesiastical hierarchies) suffered a relative decline in power. Not only were the ranks of the military swollen by the exigencies of war but the structure of civil administration was weakened as the governments lacked revenues. The situation was symbolized by the fact that in many places governments gave first priority to paying the troops, putting civilian bureaucrats on reduced pay. The Church was also debilitated by papal opposition to Spanish American independence, which compromised the Church hierarchy politically, and by conflict over whether appointment of bishops belonged to the nations or reverted to the pope. No new bishops were appointed until 1827. Over the long term the Church also suffered the loss of financial resources that were requisitioned in time of war. Paralleling the decline of the civil and ecclesiastical bureaucracies, in Halperín's view, there occurred a relative loss of power and position by urban merchants, particularly insofar as commerce fell under the domination of foreigners, and a corresponding gain in the power of landowners. Thus, according to Halperín, there occurred both a militarization and a ruralization of power in this period.[16] The following discussion will suggest that this militarization and ruralization thesis, while substantially correct, must be seen not as an absolute but as a change in degree, relative to the colonial order.

For civilian politicians between 1810 and 1830, and in many places long after that, the militarization of politics was an inescapable fact. At the outset the civilian elite was disposed to accept the necessity of military governance, particularly while independence remained

----

[16] Halperín, *Aftermath of revolution*, 1–43.

insecure. At the end of the 1820s, however, independence now seemed a fact and civilians everywhere in Spanish America began to chafe at military domination and at the excessive size of the armies. The late 1820s and early 1830s, therefore, were marked by civilian efforts both to reduce the numbers of military officers on active duty and to counterbalance the standing army through the creation of provincial militias. These years also were characterized, not surprisingly, by a strong mutual hostility between military men and civilian politicians.

Efforts at civilian control of the military were notably successful in Chile, where Diego Portales, strongly backed by the Santiago aristocracy, created militias with upper-class officers as a counterpoise to the standing army and then encouraged young men of good family to take up professional careers in the regular army itself. In Venezuela in the 1830s some of the heroes of the independence movement rebelled against the loss of military privileges and reduction of the size of the army, but these rebellions were quickly put down by the Venezuelan president, General José Antonio Páez, again with backing from the civilian upper classes. In Argentina, militia forces under Juan Manuel de Rosas succeeded in dismantling the remains of an army of independence already weakened by efforts to dominate the Banda Oriental. In New Granada the problem of managing the military was partly resolved by the breakup of the republic of Gran Colombia, for many of the most troublesome officers were Venezuelans, most of whom returned to their homeland after 1831. Many of the highest New Granadan officers remaining were closely tied to the civilian elite. While some military officers followed General José María Obando into a rebellion that wracked the country from 1839 through 1841, they took up arms on behalf of a general political movement, with both civilian and military adherents, and not in defence of the interests of the military as a corporate group. In all of these countries the reduction of the standing armies was facilitated by the fact that they were substantially *ad hoc* creations, established for the purpose of winning independence, and many of the highest officers were members of landed, upper class families whose social position derived only partly from their military careers and who, therefore, were not averse to retirement from active duty. For others, who were not originally of the upper class, retirement was made attractive through the acquisition of large landholdings granted to them in compensation for their services.

In Mexico, however, the officers who headed the regular army were professional soldiers, men who had been recruited into the Spanish army in the last years of the colonial period. Because of the peculiarities of Mexico's independence, with the royalist army leading the ultimate break with Spain rather than being defeated by insurgent forces, the Spanish-recruited creole professional military hierarchy had remained intact and powerful. And more of them than in some other countries identified strongly with the military career as a source of status and with the army as a corporate group. Consequently, in Mexico the national army retained a strong sense of its corporate interests and acted decisively to defend them until the 1850s. But the political activities of Mexican military officers were hardly confined to the defence of army privileges; in most cases their interventions were acts of political enterprise, reflecting concerns of particular groups but not of army officers as a whole. In Peru and Bolivia remnants of the Spanish-recruited colonial officer class remained in the republican armies and there was a similar identification with the military career as a source of status. In these countries also military officers played a dominant role in politics, rarely, however, acting in defence of corporate interests, usually pursuing individual ambitions.

Cutting back the power of the regular army, even where it proved possible, did not necessarily take the military out of politics. Even where civilian elites were able to establish dominançe over the military, almost everywhere they employed generals as the formal heads of state. Civilian politicans felt that only a prestigious general would be sufficiently intimidating to prevent barrack revolts or regional challenges to national authority. Thus, in Chile, where a fortunate combination of upper-class unity and economic prosperity enabled the civilian elite to construct a strong state and to dominate the standing army, two generals presided over the critical first two decades of relatively stable government. In Venezuela also the government of the civilian 'oligarchy' of the 1830s and 1840s was either headed or enforced by General José Antonio Páez and his lieutenant and successor General Soublette. In these countries relations between the civilian elite and the military were relatively untroubled. Elsewhere, where civilian control was much less certain, elites found it necessary to make use of military leaders whom they distrusted, in the knowledge that their countries were not yet ready for outright civilian rule. Thus, in Mexico a succession of civilians of all political persuasions attempted to turn the mercurial General Santa Anna to their uses, with only partial success. In Peru the leader of the liberal faction, Francisco Javier Luna Pizarro, deeply disliked the pre-eminence of military leaders in politics but, recognizing their indispensability, managed the elections of several he thought he could control.

Military leaders were equally important as implements of order in cases where the national state became so weak that political power was fragmented and decentralized. In Argentina the destruction of the national army left the field to local caudillos, whom provincial civilian elites attempted to use as instruments of control but who were themselves not always completely controllable. In Venezuela also locally based caudillos came to the fore, particularly at the end of the 1840s after the demise of the establishment over which General Páez presided. And in Mexico, even though the national army retained ultimate military superiority until its annihilation in the war of 1846, some provincial caudillos, like Juan Alvarez in the region of present-day Guerrero state, were locally dominant. As in Venezuela, the numbers and power of these regional bosses in Mexico increased in the 1850s with the weakening of the war-torn central government. In New Granada, the adoption of federalist government in the 1850s also had the effect of shifting relatively more power into the hands of regional caudillos.

The militarization of politics thus took two basic forms. In Mexico and Peru the dominant caudillos had their bases of support in regular army units, and they attempted to seize control of the national government, acting out of various combinations of individual ambition, corporate interest and upper-class civilian inspiration. At the other extreme, for which the fragmented provinces of Río de la Plata provide the best example, the dominant mode was the caudillo whose base of support was the local militia unit and the backing of the landowners and merchants in the region. In this case the primary function of the caudillo, in the eyes of his upper-class backers, was to keep order in the region and to defend the province from external disruption. Not infrequently, however, the region would serve the caudillo and his backers as a base for an attempt to seize national power. In most countries there were varying combinations of these army-based and regionally based caudillos, their relative importance depending partly on the extent to which the central state could sustain a national army strong enough to dominate the provinces.

Although armed force, either in the hands of national armies or local caudillos, often determined who possessed national or provincial governments, this does not necessarily mean that military figures, national or provincial, determined the direction of politics or of policy, even in those countries where their activities were most evident. Military caudillos, whether ranking generals in the regular army or local figures, often seized power at the behest of civilians or in alliance with them, and, even more commonly, once in power depended upon civilians for political advice and delegated to them the actual work of government. Only exceptionally did a man like New Granada's General Tomás Cipriano de Mosquera make his own policy decisions and actively operate the levers of government.

Caudillos are often depicted as either in alliance with, or created and controlled by, large landowners, whose economic resources and peones provided the essential bases of caudillistic military action. Certainly this was a common pattern, particularly at the provincial level – though one should add that merchants also formed part of these local power elites. But these economic elites were not the only civilian elements linked to caudillos. Often caudillos were allied with the same university-educated lawyer–politicians who so frequently complained of caudillistic military interventions in politics. Both at the local and the national levels university men attached themselves to promising military leaders, and then proceeded to manipulate them. Often these educated men served as secretaries upon whom the caudillos leaned heavily for advice. Sometimes the manipulation occurred at long distance, with intellectual politicians in the capital cities influencing both provincial and national caudillos with a steady flow of newspaper articles and epistolary advice.[17] Finally, once a caudillo was in power, it was to the university men that he must turn to carry on the actual work of government, as well as to defend it in the press. Thus, the caudillos and civilian politicians were linked in a symbiotic relationship marked by mutual suspicion and mutual dependence.[18] The university men often needed the caudillos to carry them to power; the caudillos needed the intellectual and administrative skills of the educated civilians. The character of the relationship between caudillos and intellectual politicians varied a good deal, of course, depending on the relative social position and economic means of both. A wealthy and respected Lucas Alamán might well lecture in a schoolmasterly manner even so powerful a caudillo as General Santa Anna (or an Egaña might so behave toward a Portales); needier and more

[17] Gilmore, *Caudillism*, 54–6; Flora Tristán y Moscozo, *Peregrinaciones de una paría* (Lima, 1946), 261–2; Venezuela, Presidencia, *Pensamiento político venezolano del siglo xix: textos para su estudio* (15 vols., Caracas, 1960–2), XI, 320–33.

[18] Pivel Devoto, *Historia de los partidos y de las ideas políticas*, 9–21, 67; idem, *Historia de los partidos políticos en el Uruguay* (2 vols., Montevideo, 1942), I, 57–9.

obscure men might well adopt a more obsequious posture and bend their political principles more than a little.

Thus, while caudillos in many places determined who would exercise power, it would be misleading to conceive of them as monopolizing power or of the urban elites as completely helpless before them. It would be similarly misleading to suggest that great landowners overwhelmingly dominated the politics of the period. It is true that some *hacendados* could sway elections in their areas or mobilize support for provincial or national caudillos. But this does not mean that landowners always used this power; much less can it be assumed that landowners as a class used this potential in a co-ordinated way. Most *hacendados* simply wanted to be left alone. Generally they did not need the services of the state; if they needed help from provincial authorities, perhaps in a dispute over land, they usually could obtain it by virtue of their own local prominence, without recourse to the national capital. In general, for most landowners, national politics simply meant trouble – seizures of their cattle and forced loans in time of civil war, and rhetoric, agitation and insecurity at other times. Even those landowners who were interested in national politics influenced its course rather little. Insofar as they lived on their haciendas, they were removed from the centre of public events and their relationship to them was necessarily passive. Information on events in the capital was sparse and infrequent. And landowners, in any case, usually had to depend for political instruction and direction on the newspapers and correspondence of professional politicians resident in the capital. By contrast, urban politicians may have lacked the landowners' local influence, and often were in tight financial straits. But as they lived in the nation's nerve centre and their livelihood often depended heavily upon influence with the government, they were both well placed for, and had an interest in, shaping the course of national politics. Thus, the intellectual elite in various ways – as influence-peddlers, journalists, teachers of the sons of the elite and government employees – despite their relative poverty probably had more effective power at the national level than landowners.

The validity of such generalizations, however, varies considerably depending upon the country. In Buenos Aires, in some sense at once a province and a nation in these years, large landowers were sufficiently concentrated regionally to make their influence felt decisively, while their agent, Rosas, effectively removed the intellectual elite from the scene. In a much more geographically fragmented political system, like

that of New Granada, landowners were regionally dispersed and most
were extremely isolated. The intellectual elite therefore played a much
more important role in political organization and mobilization at the
national level. To a considerable degree this also seems to have been true
of Mexico and Venezuela.

Although in many places the urban elites exercised predominant
influence over national politics, it may, nevertheless, be questioned how
much effective power this gave them. The national governments were
weak and their control over the provinces was incomplete at best. The
urban elites therefore directed an apparatus whose actions might often be
thwarted at the provincial level by locally dominant landowners and
merchants. And, of course, many issues of local importance were settled
by provincial elites, without significant involvement of the national
government. In this sense one may say that power was ruralized.

Many, if not most, of the political conflicts in Spanish America in the
period after independence were fought simply to determine who would
control the state and its resources. Nevertheless, there were important
political issues which varied in character and significance from country
to country. Between 1810 and 1845 the issue of whether the state should
have a centralist or federalist structure brought violent conflict to
Mexico, Central America and the River Plate region. In Chile and New
Granada it was only of temporary significance – in the 1820s in Chile,
between 1838 and 1842 in New Granada. Furthermore, where it appeared, the conflict of centralism versus federalism did not always have
the same nature or origins. In the Río de la Plata the federalist cause was
in some places linked to regional economic interests. In Mexico and
Chile, on the other hand, regional economic interests, at least in this
period, seem to have been less important in the emergence and growth of
federalism. Rather, in these countries, federalism reflected both regional
desires for political autonomy and an ideological conviction that the
federal system was the best means of protecting individual liberties from
state power. In New Granada in the late 1830s federalism was simply a
banner raised at an opportune moment by the party out of power to
justify its attempt to reconquer control of the state by force of arms. In
Peru and Bolivia, also the principal issue may have been less regional
interests than who would possess the state. And in the Río de la Plata,
while federalism at times may have expressed regional economic interests, the federalist–unitarian struggle also may be described as a series of

local battles to determine which caudillos (and segments of local oligar-chies) would control particular provinces.

The federalist–centralist conflict tended to be submerged in many places between 1835 and 1845. The forces of centralism had triumphed, definitively in Chile in 1831, temporarily in Mexico (1836–46) and in New Granada (1841–9). In the Río de la Plata, while federalism remained formally triumphant after 1831, Juan Manuel de Rosas moved to centralize power within the federalist framework. Thus, whether through repression or some other resolution of the issue, federalism tended to recede into the background for a time.

Between 1845 and 1870, however, there occurred a second wave of federalism in Mexico, New Granada, Venezuela and, more weakly, Peru. But in this period federalism was much less a source of heated conflict than was the status of the Church. In New Granada and Venezuela an interparty consensus developed in favour of federalism during the 1850s and 1860s. In New Granada liberals of the 1850s supported federalism out of conviction, while conservatives, formerly centralist in inclination, embraced federalism from opportunism. Having lost control of the central government, they concluded that a federal system would best enable them to protect their dominance of regions where conservative strength was greatest. In contrast to the strong emotions and deep commitments generated by questions relating to the Church, positions on the centralist–federalist issue tended to be more rhetorical and tactical.

While there was some variation in the form of political issues, as the federalist question indicates, there was a more or less common theme underlying much political conflict. This theme was the desire of some politicians, university-educated men for the most part, to modernize Spanish America. Particularly among intellectual politicians there was a general belief that Spanish institutions and values were responsible for Spanish American backwardness; they wanted to remodel their societies as much as possible along British, French and North American lines.

As previously indicated, aspects of the modernization process had roots in the Bourbon programme of administrative, economic, fiscal and educational rationalization. In carrying out this programme of rationalization the Bourbons asserted the supremacy of the secular over the ecclesiastical, in particular attempting to reduce the clergy's juridical privileges and tax exemptions and to place church economic resources in the service of the state. The Bourbons also sought to turn university instruction away from scholastic teachings and toward those natural sciences that were thought to be of practical utility.

In addition to pursuing the reform goals associated with the Bourbons, republican politicians of the nineteenth century also sought something that was at most a minor theme under the Spanish Bourbons – the implantation of English and French liberal individualism in social, economic and political institutions and behaviour. The creation of a liberal individualist society meant, in political terms, the establishment of legal equality and the supremacy of the secular state. It also meant guaranteeing freedom of thought. All of these goals – the supremacy of the state, legal equality and freedom of thought – required breaking down the corporate organizations that had dominated colonial society, most particularly the Church and the military. These two institutions challenged the supremacy of the state; their privileges negated legal equality; and their control over their members made impossible the exercise of free thought. The creation of a liberal individualist society meant, in economic terms, the establishment of a free market. To achieve a free market it was necessary to abolish the monopoly privileges stemming from the colonial period, whether those of the government or those that were privately held. For the same reason it was necessary to break up Indian community lands in order to force Indian peasants to operate as individual entrepreneurs under the discipline of market forces. And, it came to be argued, for the nation's economic resources to become fully productive it was necessary to remove the enormous resources held in mortmain by the Church and to free private properties from the burden of perpetual quitrents so that they might circulate freely in the market.

Many aspects of this reform programme had rather generalized support among the educated elite, though there were differences of opinion over the pace at which the reforms should occur. With the exception of the Río de la Plata region and, for a time, Venezuela, there usually tended to be a consensus on economic policy. Between 1820 and 1845 most of those who later became known as conservatives and liberals alike professed Manchesterian liberal economic principles and both varied actual policy from these principles as the occasion demanded. During the late 1820s and early 1830s, when the deluge of British imports had produced heavy trade imbalances, scarcity of circulating media and consequent economic contraction, protection of local manufacturing had adherents among both liberals, like the Mexican Lorenzo Zavala, and men later known as conservatives, like Lucas Alamán in Mexico and Alejandro Osorio in New Granada. At the same time, some men of both political tendencies remained resolutely committed to free trade principles.

This tendency to inter-factional agreement on economic policy, evident between 1825 and 1845, became even more marked after 1845, as most of Spanish America became more fully incorporated into the Atlantic trade system. During the 1830s there had been reason for disagreement: the fact of serious trade imbalances with England and France supported the argument for the protection of native industry, while the hegemony of liberal economic theory encouraged heroic (if misguided) adherence to free trade principles. After 1845, however, fact and theory were no longer so clearly in conflict and tended rather to be mutually reinforcing. Increasing European and North American demand for Spanish America's raw materials enabled more of the countries in the region to bring their external trade into balance, thus seeming to justify the liberal economic faith in free trade. Consequently, during the years 1845 to 1870, in most countries there was a near unanimity on at least the free trade aspects of economic liberalism. (Mexico, where established industrial interests pressed for protection, was an exception to the general pattern.)

Venezuela was one place where disagreement over economic principles for a time became a source of serious political conflict. There coffee planters who had indebted themselves to expand production during years of high prices in the 1830s found themselves unable to repay their creditors when the market declined at the end of the decade. Throughout the 1840s coffee planters campaigned fervently against liberal legislation of 1834 which had freed interest rates from colonial restrictions upon usury and against later laws facilitating the sale of debtors' property. The planters also strayed from liberal economic principles by calling for active government aid for the distressed agricultural sector. Interestingly, this planters' reaction against the effects of economic liberalism provided much of the impetus for the formation of Venezuela's Liberal Party, which in almost every other respect was conventionally liberal. The predictable obverse side of this was that the 'conservative' establishment presided over by Generals Páez and Soublette adhered rigorously to liberal economic principles in defence of the creditor interest.

Like economic policy, fiscal policy generally was not a party or factional issue. Men in all political groups agreed in condemning the tax system inherited from the Spanish as unliberal and irrational, and moved to reform it during the optimism of the early 1820s. When direct taxes introduced during the 1820s and the early 1830s met popular resistance and failed to produce much revenue, almost everyone in the political elite agreed to put them on the shelf. In an atmosphere of fiscal crisis men of all parties agreed to postpone reform to a more favourable occasion. In the period of optimism after 1845, when renewed efforts were made to abolish traditionally established taxes that conflicted with liberal economic principles, such reforms evoked no major conflict.

If elite political groups generally agreed upon economic principles, the same was also true of social policy regarding slavery and Indian communities. In the 1820s, the elites in most countries, in a burst of revolutionary enthusiasm, moved with more or less unanimity to make legislative commitments to the eventual abolition of slavery. But subsequently, through the 1830s and into the 1840s, all parties prudently refrained from hastening the demise of slavery and even took steps to slow its end. While conservative establishments generally presided over attempts to maintain slavery, they faced no serious criticism from liberals. Indeed, Tomás Lander, Venezuela's leading liberal ideologist of the 1830s and 1840s, was an outspoken defender of slavery.

In the latter part of the 1840s attitudes toward slavery changed as some in the younger generation emerging on the political scene at this time attacked the institution as part of their general commitment to ideals of social equality. This new political generation played a prominent role in the abolition of slavery in New Granada in 1850, in Ecuador in 1852, in Argentina in 1853 and in Venezuela and Peru in 1854. However, all political groups apparently recognized that this was an idea whose time had come. Once the young liberals had raised the question forcefully, conservatives made little resistance to abolition and indeed many of them supported it.[19]

A similar tendency to consensus is observable in attitudes toward communal landholding in Indian communities. From the 1820s onward there was a general agreement that communal holdings should be divided among the Indians. Almost all members of the elite considered communal property-holding contrary to liberal economic principles, in that they presumably did not engage the interest of the individual. It was also felt that Indians should be more fully integrated into the dominant

[19] See ch. 1 above.

society on at least a theoretical or formal basis of equality, something which could not be done as long as they lived apart in communities governed by different principles from the rest of the society. The elite implicitly recognized the unlikelihood that such incorporation would occur on a basis of equality: during the 1820s and 1830s laws breaking up Indian lands placed some checks upon the freedom of the Indians to sell their property, in order to protect them from exploitation. Nevertheless, there was a general belief that the goal of converting Indians to individual property-holders and integrating them into the dominant society was a desirable one. During the initial process of incorporation few voices were raised against it. Only toward the end of the 1840s did a few members of the elite – some conservatives, some liberals – express alarm about potential injury to the Indian peasantry. Only in the 1860s did a somewhat greater number of both liberals and conservatives recognize the devastating results of this reform in depriving the Indians of their land and reducing them to an ever more miserable poverty.[20]

Thus, many aspects of attempts to rebuild Spanish American society and economy in the liberal image did not provoke conflict among the educated political elites. These efforts at liberal reform divided the political elite principally when they impinged upon the power and privileges of the Church. This, of course, they frequently did. For doctrinaire liberals the Church became the principal obstacle to economic, social and political modernization. Its control of substantial properties denied wealth to the state, which desperately needed revenues. Its claims to income from quitrents upon private properties depressed agricultural enterprise. Its juridical privileges both undermined the authority of the state and made a mockery of the principle of legal equality. Its status as a special corporate group encouraged the clergy to identify primarily with the Church, not with the nation. Church discipline denied freedom of thought to the clergy, and the clergy in turn, in the liberal view, attempted to impose thought control on the population at large, condemning books thought to be prejudicial to morals and the faith. Church control of educational institutions also threatened freedom of thought and hampered the introduction of new scientific knowledge. Church opposition to religious toleration hindered the immigration of non-Catholic Europeans, whose skills and capital were desperately needed to build a modern economy.[21]

[20] See ch. 1 above.
[21] See, for example, José María Luis Mora, *El clero, la educación y la libertad* (Mexico, 1949), 43–61; idem, *El clero, el estado y la economía nacional* (Mexico, 1959), 22, 27–34.

Confronting liberal efforts to weaken its powers and trim its privileges, the Church could count on various allies. The clergy was able to mobilize elements of the urban lower classes against both religious toleration and the foreign immigrants it was meant to protect. If liberals attempted to end ecclesiastical juridical privileges (*fueros*), the clergy could often depend upon the support of the professional military, whose own special privileges usually were in jeopardy at the same time. Efforts to seize Church economic resources often provoked elements in the upper classes, who viewed such measures as assaults upon property in general. It has been argued that, at least in the early decades of the republican period, large landowners tended to support the Church in political conflicts because they were beholden to ecclesiastical institutions for loans.[22] Whether this was the case or not, it is clear that a substantial proportion of the upper class defended the Church against liberal attack primarily because they viewed the Church as an indispensable instrument of social control.

It would be misleading to give the impression that the issue of the status and power of the Church emerged everywhere simultaneously. On this, as on other issues, each country had its own particular rhythm. In Buenos Aires in the 1820s and Montevideo in the 1830s liberal secularist politicians were able substantially to reduce the powers and privileges of the Church without effective resistance from the clergy. In Mexico and Guatemala, on the other hand, when liberals carried out a frontal assuault upon Church interests in the 1830s, major conflict ensued in both countries, the liberal reformers were defeated, and many of the changes they sought were delayed for decades. Elsewhere the conflict was less dramatic in the early years. In New Granada, the use of Bentham and de Tracy as university texts provoked vigorous denunciations from the clergy and its political supporters in the 1820s and 1830s, but a frontal conflict over the powers and status of the Church was avoided until the 1850s. In Peru and Chile, where liberal forces were weak, liberals even more assiduously avoided confrontation with the Church in the early years of the republican era, deferring serious efforts to trim Church powers and privileges until the 1850s.

Between 1830 and 1845 a relative political stability had prevailed in some parts of Spanish America – most notably in Chile, Venezuela and Buenos Aires, but also to a somewhat lesser degree in New Granada and

---

22 Michael P. Costeloe, *Church wealth in Mexico: a study of the 'Juzgado de Capellanías' in the archbishopric of Mexico, 1800–1856* (Cambridge, 1967), 28.

Ecuador, where national authority was challenged by only occasional violence. After 1845, however, elite consensus in these countries began to fracture. In the 1840s a new generation of politicians emerged, challenging the persons and policies of those who had held power since the end of the 1820s. Most Spanish American countries had been ruled by the same generation that had made independence. In Mexico, Peru, Venezuela and New Granada presidential power seemed to be the monopoly of the military heroes of Independence, with civilian elites of the same generation collaborating in the organization of politics and the management of government. Men born at the eve of independence, particularly civilians, had cause to wonder when their time might come. Tulio Halperín Donghi has suggested that the fiscal penury endured by almost all Spanish American governments limited their capacity to absorb the younger generations into public posts.[23] Whatever the reason the fact is that in the 1840s the younger generation began, in many places quite consciously, to challenge the existing political establishment which in some places, it should be said, had lost its will or ability to dominate. In Venezuela, by 1844, General Carlos Soublette, who currently governed for the Venezuelan oligarchy, calmly tolerated the mobilization of university students (including two of his sons) in opposition, making little effort to generate support for the established system. In Mexico, disastrous defeat in war with the United States (1846–8) undermined the authority of established politicians in all the major factions and filled the new generation with a sense of the urgency of taking radical measures in order to form a strong, modern state. In New Granada in 1848–9, the government party split, thus opening the way for challenge by a new generation. In Chile, the Portalean system also began to show signs of wear as elements in the governing party began to break away in opposition to President Manuel Montt, thus encouraging a series of liberal rebellions in the 1850s.

Although the political dynamic of the period may be seen as a challenge from a new age-group within the upper social sectors, the struggle also had a class aspect in some places. Historians of the Reforma period in Mexico (1855–76) consider many of the liberal protagonists of this struggle to have been a 'new' generation not merely in the sense of age but also in that of social origin. The new liberal generation that emerged in the 1840s is described as typically composed of mostly ambitious

---

[23] Halperín, *Aftermath of revolution*, 127–9.

provincials whose social mobility was made possible by the expansion of secondary education during the early independence period.[24] A similiar generalization might be made about New Granada and, to a lesser degree, Peru and Chile. Young men of such social origins had particular reason to challenge the monopoly of power by established groups and to wish to destroy those remnants of colonial institutions that tended to block social mobility.

Along with young educated provincials, another social group that began to figure prominently between 1845 and 1860 consisted of urban artisans. In New Granada, and to a lesser degree in Mexico, Peru and Chile, this group came into temporary alliance with young upper-sector politicians. Although they collaborated for a time, the two groups seem to have been mobilized for quite different, and even contradictory, reasons. One factor tending from the mid-1840s to energize upper-sector young men was the expansion of Spanish America's external trade. Expanding European demand for Spanish America's tropical products and raw materials created a new ambience of optimism among the upper classes, encouraging a spirit of political regeneration and institutional experimentation. For urban artisans, however, it meant a wave of imported consumer goods that threatened to engulf them. Distressed by increased imports between 1845 and 1855, they briefly found themselves in a paradoxical alliance with young upper-sector politicians, almost all of whom were devout believers in free trade and the expansion of external commerce.

The emerging generation of upper-sector politicians, seeking to develop its own sense of political identity as against the older generation, was receptive to new European influences that had little appeal to the already-formed, established politicians. The impact of these new external influences, along with the dynamic of inter-generational tensions, helped to polarize politics from the middle of the 1840s until 1870, by which time the new generation was thoroughly dominant.

The European political events and ideological currents influencing the new generation varied depending upon local political conditions. In much of Spanish America the powers and privileges of the Church remained a central, and unresolved, problem. Consequently, agitation in France over ecclesiastical issues in the 1830s and 1840s influenced some of these countries after 1845, most particularly Mexico, New Granada,

---

[24] Justo Sierra, *The political evolution of the Mexican people* (Austin, Texas, 1969), 204; Moisés González Navarro, *Anatomía del poder en México, 1848–1853* (Mexico, 1977), 442–3.

Chile and Peru. The attacks of Michelet and Quinet on the role of the Church in higher education in the 1840s and their book assailing the Jesuits had an impact upon young democrats like Francisco Bilbao (1823–65) in Chile and also served to inflame antagonism toward the Jesuits among the younger generation in New Granada.

In Buenos Aires and Montevideo, where many of the Church's powers and privileges had already been stripped away before 1835, religio-political controversies in Europe were of relatively little concern to young intellectuals. Mazzini's Young Italy, however, had a notable influence among the dissident youth of the Río de la Plata region; one of their intellectual leaders, Esteban Echeverría, for example, proclaimed a Young Argentina. Echeverría and his associates also found some interest in French Socialism, particularly in Saint-Simonian currents. This was much less true in other parts of Spanish America, at least until the European Revolution of 1848.

The inflammation of Church–State issues between 1845 and 1870 in some Spanish American republics, and the new, more fervent spirit with which civilian politicians approached these issues, derived in part from the influence of Lamennais. His criticism of the Church as a political establishment concerned primarily with money, power, and dignities, and his advocacy of a primitive, popular, extra-ecclesiastical Christianity, inspired many in the new generation. He provided them with a rhetoric with which to attack the established Church as part of the old, oppressive order, while claiming adherence to a purer, democratic Christianity. His insistence upon the separation of religion and politics, and therefore upon the separation of Church and State, found echo in Mexico, New Granada, Peru, and Chile. His strongly democratic spirit, with his support of a wide extension of the suffrage, also encouraged the democratic enthusiasms of the new generation, just as his call for administrative decentralization reinforced the federalist political currents in Spanish America. Lamennais's influence, perhaps more than any other, demarcates the generation of the 1840s from its predecessors, who for the most part ignored him. Undoubtedly, Lamennais, like Mazzini, had a special appeal for the younger generation in symbolizing rebellion against established authority.

The European Revolution of 1848 both drew attention to, and crystallized the influence of, utopian Socialist ideas in Spanish America. Shortly after the European revolutions began, aspiring young politicians, influenced by European example, began to reach out to elements in the urban underclasses – principally to the artisan class, not to the very poorest – in an effort to mobilize them politically. In some places such mobilization already had begun to occur even before the Revolution of 1848, most notably perhaps in the agitation carried out in Venezuela by Antonio Leocadio Guzmán in the middle of the 1840s. There were also some precedents in New Granada in the 1830s. But there can be no doubt that the 1848 revolutions stimulated further efforts to mobilize the urban working class. In New Granada an artisans' society formed in 1848 to protest the lowering of tariffs on finishing goods was taken over as a political arm by ambitious liberal university students and young professionals. Reconstituted as the Democratic Society, the artisans' organization helped the liberals gain power in 1849, after which branch societies were established throughout the country to mobilize support for the new government. The New Granadan liberal government made a gesture at socialist forms by decreeing artisans' training shops inspired by the French National Workshops, and young liberals indulged in associational and Christian democratic rhetoric.

In general, however, the new generation was more individualist and liberal than socialist in ideology.[25] Their principal contribution to the artisans' society was a series of unwelcome lectures on the virtues of liberal political economy. The inherent incompatibility between the young upper-class radicals and Bogotá's artisans became evident when the new liberal government failed to provide tariff protection for the artisans' products. A joint military–artisan revolution in 1854 overthrew the liberal government, forcing the young radicals to seek alliance with conservatives in order to suppress the now far-too-popular government established in behalf of the artisans in Bogotá. Although many of their leaders were banished to almost certain death in the jungles of Panama, the artisans remained an element to be contended with in later decades.

Similar efforts to mobilize the urban workers were made by young political aspirants in Peru, where the Progressive Society was established in 1849, and in Chile, where the Society of Equality was formed in 1850. Like the one in New Granada, the Peruvian and Chilean societies attempted rather paternalistically to enlighten the masses in order to mobilize them. Characteristic of this process was the publication by the Chilean society of a periodical, *El amigo del pueblo* (The Friend of the People), in which the *Paroles d'un croyant* of Lamennais was serialized. In

---

[25] See Robert L. Gilmore, 'Nueva Granada's Socialist Mirage', *Hispanic American Historical Review*, 36/2 (1956), 190–211.

both Peru and Chile youthful agitators stimulated popular uprisings during the 1850s. As much as they preached identification with the masses, the young members of the upper class who created these societies could never move beyond their imported rhetoric to a real comprehension of working-class interests. While they attempted to appeal to artisans by supporting model shops patterned after those of France in 1848, in other respects their programmes reflected the concerns of young university graduates anxious to create a political environment favourable to their own emergence. The Peruvian society, for example, like its New Granadan counterpart, particularly emphasized the need for political reforms making possible civilian-controlled government, including reduction of the size of the army and strengthening of the locally based national guard. The Peruvian society also called for the encouragement of immigration, something which could hardly have appealed to its working-class constituency.

The Revolution of 1848 was greeted enthusiastically in New Granada, Peru and Chile, where the new generation had to contend with established government groups that could be viewed as essentially elitist and where, consequently, democratic revolution appealed as a means of political change. In the Río de la Plata, however, the dictatorship of Juan Manuel Rosas in Buenos Aires, like the regimes of lesser caudillos in the provinces, had enjoyed widespread support from the popular classes. In the Plata, therefore, younger intellectual politicians tended to take a more negative view of democratic revolution. In exile in Chile in the 1840s, Domingo Faustino Sarmiento and Juan Bautista Alberdi, even before the European revolutions, expressed the belief that popular sovereignty, in the hands of an ignorant mass, would inevitably lead to dictatorship. While Francisco Bilbao and others in the new generation of Chileans attacked their government as elitist, their Argentine contemporaries resident in Chile defended the Portalean regime as the rule of an enlightened minority, far preferable to the tyranny produced in Argentina by a barbarous majority. The Revolution of 1848, with the subsequent election of Louis Napoleon, served to confirm Sarmiento and Alberdi in their distrust of democracy, at least in countries where the large majority was illiterate. Thus, whereas in parts of Spanish America the new generations tended to a democratic rhetoric (not necessarily democratic practice) even after they became ascendant between 1850 and 1870, in Argentina after the overthrow of Rosas in 1852 the newly dominant intellectual elite tended to a more conservative view of political democracy.

The new generation of liberal politicians that emerged in the 1840s in many respects pursued the same tendencies as their political progenitors, the liberal reformers of the 1820s. But they did so with a new spirit and intensity, in the belief that the earlier generation had failed in its mission to liberalize Spanish American society. Like the liberals of the 1820s, the reformers of 1845–70 affirmed essentially individualist conceptions of state, society and economy. Like their predecessors, they were libertarian constitutionalists, in belief if not in behaviour. But they tended to be more absolute in their individualism, more fervent in their libertarian rhetoric. They called not merely for individual freedoms but for an absolute freedom of conscience, of the press, of education and of commerce – in New Granada even to the extent of sanctioning an absolute freedom of commerce in arms. They called not merely for trial by jury and the abolition of the death penalty but also for constitutional recognition of the right to insurrection. To safeguard these individual freedoms liberals in Mexico, New Granada and Venezuela re-committed themselves to the ideal of federalism looking to the United States as a model, and they resurrected plans of 1825–35 to limit the size of the army and to establish citizens' national guards.

In economic and social policy also the mid-century reformers rededicated themselves to liberal individualism and the ideal of legal equality, both of which they felt had been compromised by their predecessors. They sought to rationalize their countries' economies in accord with nineteenth-century liberal conceptions. This meant abolishing enterprise-constricting taxes that had been allowed to hang on from the colonial period, such as the *alcabala* (sales tax), the tithe and government monopolies. At least during the 1850s they rather dogmatically opposed government intervention in the economy, whether in the form of public enterprise, the extension of monopoly privileges to private enterprise, or protectionist tariffs. Their affirmation of the ideal of legal equality meant the elimination of the juridical privileges of the Church and the military. They also sought the fulfilment of legal equality, as well as of individualist social conceptions, through the abolition of slavery and the incorporation of Indian communities into the dominant, capitalistic, European society. The new generation of reformists recognized that these were themes pursued by the earlier liberals of the 1820s. But they believed that the earlier generation had taken only the first tentative steps toward a necessary elimination of colonial structures. They saw themselves as carrying out a political, economic and social revolution that would bring to completion the movement that had begun in 1810, but had been betrayed during the 1830s.

While the liberals of 1845–70 saw themselves as continuing the work of the reformers of 1810–25, the content and spirit of their enterprise was in some respects different. First, the power and the privileges of the Church came to the fore much more sharply as an issue. The question of the relationship of Church to State had been at issue in the earlier period, but, except in Mexico and Guatemala, it had been a relatively muted one. Between 1845 and 1870 the conflict over the power and privileges of the Church broke into full-scale war, particularly in Mexico and New Granada, and in Ecuador, Peru and Chile, the Church for the first time became a central political issue. Second, in the generation of 1845–70 liberal individualism was in some places – such as New Granada and Chile – combined with an element of French socialist associational rhetoric, though this tendency did not outlast the 1850s. Third, also because of the influence of French socialism and the Revolution of 1848, there was – except in Argentina – a much greater emphasis on the ideal of social democracy than had existed in earlier generations. And along with the emphasis on social democracy, there was a kind of revolutionary fervour that had not been characteristic of the earlier period of reform. One might characterize the reformers of 1810 to 1825 as trying to rationalize the system that they had inherited, in a cool Benthamite spirit. The generation of 1845–70, on the other hand – at least in New Granada, Peru and Chile – conceived themselves more as carrying out a revolution. Or, as Echeverría in the Plata preferred to think of it, a 'regeneration'.

Just as liberalism developed more fervour in the middle of the 1840s, there was a parallel development of a more articulated conservatism. In the 1830s conservative political forces in Spanish America had operated essentially without doctrine. Three of the most successful architects of a conservative order in this decade – Rosas in Buenos Aires, Portales in Chile and General José Antonio Páez in Venezuela – had acted without the aid of any intellectual rationale. In some sense, having the united support of the social establishment and no significant political opposition, they did not need a doctrine. For Portales, statecraft was essentially a practical matter of counterbalancing, if not repressing, threatening forces, in which he felt no need to appeal to broader social or political theories.

In the 1830s the conservatism of the Mexican, Lucas Alamán, resided essentially in a defence of his class: he viewed the political wars of that decade as a battle between 'men of property and respectability', whose social position guaranteed responsible use of power, on the one hand, and a clutch of ambitious social inferiors, who wanted to benefit themselves 'at the nation's cost'. During the 1840s, however, Alamán was sustaining a more explicit conservatism similar to and influenced by Edmund Burke. Alamán now argued explicitly against the liberal tendency to base political thought and action on abstract first principles, emphasizing that political institutions had to be the result of the long historical experience of a given people. The construction of an effective polity could not be the work of a single conception, nor could it 'proceed from theories of speculative legislators, who pretended to subject the human race to imaginary principles that they want to make pass as oracles of incomparable truth'. It had to be 'the result of the knowledge and experience' of centuries. Authority, in effect, had to be based upon tradition. Liberal theories, by destroying the traditional bases of respect for authority, left governmental authorities no 'other means than force to make themselves obeyed'. Alamán, like many other Mexican conservatives, ended by committing himself to the cause of constitutional monarchy.[26]

While Alamán looked to a Burkean tradition and to men of substance as the basis of the political order, the cleric, Bartolomé Herrera, the leading conservative theoretician in Peru, turned to traditional Spanish political thought in making a much more systematic effort to advance a conservative theory of authority. Following sixteenth- and seventeenth-century Spanish scholastic doctrines, Herrera denied the liberal theory of popular sovereignty based upon a social contract, holding that the origin of sovereignty lay in 'divine reason', acting through natural law. Sovereignty had to emanate from eternal principles and therefore could not be based upon the popular will, which is variable and thus often wrong. In Herrera's view the people had neither 'the capacity nor the right to make laws'. The principles upon which laws must be based could be perceived only by 'intellects habituated to conquer the difficulties of mental work'.[27]

---

[26] José C. Valadés, *Alamán: Estadista e historiador* (Mexico, 1938), 367; Moisés González Navarro, *El pensamiento político de Lucas Alamán* (Mexico, 1952), 59, 86, 116–17, 123–8.

[27] Herrera, *Escritos y discursos*, I, 63–150; quotations on 131, 137. Similar arguments were made in Mexico by the cleric, Clemente de Jesús Munguía, in his *Del derecho natural* (1849), and by J. J. Pesado in 1857. See González Navarro, *Anatomía del poder*, 374–5; Walter V. Scholes, *Mexican politics during the Juárez regime, 1855–1872* (Columbia, Missouri, 1969), 18–19.

Alamán and Herrera were early and extreme exponents of conservatism. At the end of the 1840s they were joined in political alliance by men who had thought of themselves as moderate liberals, but now began to redefine themselves as conservatives. The European Revolution of 1848 strongly influenced this process. The European revolution was at first greeted with enthusiasm not only by young men but also by moderate liberals of an older generation, who viewed it at first merely as a triumph of the republican ideal. However, as the revolution in France began to take on the character of a socialist revolution, Spanish American moderates recoiled, fearing the impact that European insurrection might have in deranging the lower elements in their own societies. In Mexico, where Indian peasant rebellion already was a concern, Luis Gonzaga Cuevas, a characteristic moderate who evolved into an extreme conservatism, condemned the European revolution as an attack upon property, the very foundation of society. If Mexico were carried along by the 'absurd doctrines' of 1848, Cuevas feared, its small educated class might not be able to repress the ensuing popular disorders. In the context of imminent upheaval, Cuevas, Bernardo Couto and other Mexican moderates were particularly concerned by the intensification of anti-clericalism in Mexico as the Church more than ever appeared indispensable as a bulwark against social disorder. After 1848, therefore, many Mexican moderates joined the country's small group of monarchists in a militant, pro-clerical conservatism.[28]

In other Spanish American countries the ingredients of conservatism were not quite the same. In New Granada conservatives feared not the possibility of peasant rebellion but rather the mobilization of artisans in Bogotá and, after a time, of popular elements in Cali. In Peru and Chile also urban insurrection was more of a threat than the peasantry. Also, outside of Mexico there existed no monarchist movement to serve as the backbone of conservative parties. Nevertheless, with these variations, mid-century conservatism in other parts of Spanish America bore many of the same marks as the Mexican movement. Conservatives for the most part were men who formerly had identified themselves as moderates, who reacted with horror not only at the excesses of Paris but even more at the mouthing of socialist rhetoric by youths in their own countries, and who identified with the Church as the most solid foundation for the defence of the social order.

---

[28] González Navarro, *Anatomía del poder*, 29–35; Guillermo Prieto, *Memorias de mis tiempos* (Paris–Mexico, 1906), 55, 166–7, 174, 287–9, 332.

In general, conservatives, often with the Spanish clerical writer Jaime Balmes as inspiration, conceived of the Church as central to the stability of society, as well as to the authority of the state. However, conservatives varied in the ways in which they viewed their political ties to the Church. The Church was integral to Herrera's conception of state and society. Many other conservative leaders, however, seem to have thought of the Church in a somewhat more instrumental way, as an institution that was useful as a cohesive social bond, or as a means of political mobilization. Alamán, whose piety cannot be questioned, hinted at this kind of social utility concept of the Church in 1853 when he wrote Santa Anna that 'the Catholic religion [is] . . . the only link that binds all Mexicans when all others have been broken.'[29] An even more clearly instrumental approach to the Church can be seen in one of the founders of New Granada's Conservative Party, Mariano Ospina Rodríguez, who viewed religion as a force for political mobilization. Writing to his fellow conservative, José Eusebio Caro, in 1852, Ospina clinically surveyed the options of conservatives in the choice of 'banners' under which they might organize resistance to a radical-liberal government. Political liberty, he said, was a theme in which intelligent conservatives believed, but it would not serve as a rallying point because the conservative masses did not understand it. Security of person and property were also important to conservatives, but, unfortunately, people motivated only by concern for security would act prudentially and not fight. 'The only conservative banner that has life, and shows resolution and vigor', he concluded, 'is that which acts because of religious sentiments.'[30]

Because of their tendency to use religion as a source of political support, if not as a political weapon, conservatives thrust the Church into the centre of political controversy quite as much as the liberals who sought to reduce ecclesiastical powers and privileges. This occurred at a relatively early point in Mexico, when the government of Anastasio Bustamante (1830–2), in order to shore up a fragile political position, adopted a markedly pro-clerical posture. As a consequence, questions of Church power and privilege, which had played a minor role in Mexican politics up to that point, now came to the fore in opposition politics. Almost immediately after the overthrow of Bustamante those formerly

---

[29] As quoted in Hale, *Mexican liberalism*, 32. A similarly instrumental view of religion as protector of property was also espoused by the conservative journal *Omnibus* in 1852. (González Navarro, *Anatomía del poder*, 110.)

[30] Mariano Ospina Rodríguez to José Eusebio Caro, Medellín, 22 June 1852, in José Eusebio Caro, *Epistolario* (Bogotá, 1953), 348–52; quotation on p.350.

in opposition carried out a frontal attack on ecclesiastical privilege. Similarly, in New Granada ecclesiastical questions remained more or less dormant after the 1820s until the conservatives in 1842–4 imported the Jesuit order to serve as educational disciplinarians of a potentially rebellious younger generation. The obvious political purpose of this move was not lost upon the student generation of the 1840s, who, once in power in 1849, quickly pressed for and obtained the expulsion of the Jesuits in 1850, which led to a general confrontation with New Granada's clerical hierarchy.

This is not to say that conservative use of the Church as a political ally was the only source of attacks upon ecclesiastical power. In Mexico, in particular, the fiscal penury of the state governments in the 1820s and of the national government in subsequent decades induced both civilian and military politicians to cast an envious eye upon the considerable wealth of the Church. Financial exactions and seizures of church property, particularly in time of internal conflict or foreign war, served to inflame the purely political issue of ecclesiastical privileges in Mexico. In New Granada, seizures of church property also occurred in time of civil war, in 1861. In still other places church property never became a major issue.

Although conservatives and the church hierarchy, as their political positions weakened, tended naturally to reach out to each other, the interests of the ecclesiastical establishment and conservative politicians were by no means identical. Occasionally church leaders found themselves attempting futilely to disengage themselves from the conservative embrace, precisely because this political linkage sometimes brought down upon the Church political attacks that it might otherwise have avoided.

While the conservatives' instrumental use of the Church as a political weapon was partly responsible for attacks upon church powers and privileges at mid-century, attitudes within the Church itself also had an important effect upon the outcome. Under Pius IX the Roman Catholic Church after 1848 became increasingly obdurate in its opposition to liberalism and the pope encouraged (sometimes commanded) a similar intransigence in prelates in Spanish America. In Mexico, in the heat of Puebla's clergy-led rebellion against the government (1855), the archbishop of Mexico reproved the rebels and attempted to conciliate the government; when the pope denounced the liberal constitution of 1857, however, the archbishop accordingly adopted an intransigent position, expelling from the Church all those who adhered to the new constitution. Partly because of the hard line taken by the pope and curia, in countries where issues affecting the status of the Church were raised between 1845 and 1870, as in Mexico and New Granada, the outcome was dramatic and violent confrontation. (Where liberalism was too weak a force to raise these issues until after 1870, as in Bolivia, the process of liberalization, when ultimately undertaken, was relatively smooth and peaceful.)

The intensity of Church–State conflict also depended, however, on the personalities of civilian and clerical leaders. In Mexico, stiff resistance to civil authority on the part of Bishop Munguía of Michoacán in 1851 played an important part in setting off the intense civil–ecclesiastical struggle of the 1850s. In New Granada, Archbishop Mosquera adopted similarly unbending attitudes, thus encouraging polarization. In Peru, on the other hand, Archbishop Goyeneche adopted a conciliatory stance and was able to avoid major conflict. It should be added, however, that the Peruvian prelate did not really face the same kind of challenge as the hierarchies in Mexico and New Granada. In these two countries a broad political movement backed the liberal opposition: in Peru, liberal forces were much weaker and could be controlled by the strong, moderate-centrist leadership of General Ramón Castilla.

In Mexico and New Granada, issues affecting the status of the Church were of central importance between 1845 and 1870; in each the abolition of its juridical privileges, the seizure and sale of its properties, the prohibition of religious orders, the secularization of birth, marriage and death became the foci of political contention. Elsewhere, however, the conflict was less dramatic or the issue was fought over and/or settled at other times. In Peru ecclesiastical privileges were abolished in 1851, but liberals were not able to carry out a total assault like those in Mexico and New Granada. In Central America the liberal attack had begun earlier (1829–38) and had been defeated at least in Guatemala, where conservative, pro-clerical governments dominated until 1870. In Ecuador the Church did not become a source of dramatic conflict until the end of the 1860s, when Gabriel García Moreno instituted a system so extremely pro-clerical as finally to goad liberals into action. In Bolivia and also (with some exceptions) Chile, church issues were kept more or less in abeyance until after 1870. In Buenos Aires, Uruguay and Venezuela, on the other hand, the Church was weaker, and secularizing influences were stronger, so that ecclesiastical privilege and religious orders were removed or reduced easily and early (before 1840).

Apart from the question of the Church, which was an important source of division in Mexico, Guatemala, New Granada, Ecuador and, to a lesser degree, Peru, on many issues there was, among the contending political groups, as much a shifting consensus as conflict. Nevertheless, political elites divided into factions with more or less clear identities. The extent to which these factions could be called political parties prior to 1870 varied from region to region. In countries dominated by violent caudillistic politics, such as the United Provinces of the Río de la Plata, Bolivia, or Peru, there was no place for the development of parties whose purpose was the winning of elections. Elsewhere it is a question of definition.

Certainly there were no political organizations mobilizing large masses of people anywhere in Spanish America before the 1850s – and only rarely then. Throughout the period only a very small number of people were actively engaged in politics. If the existence of parties requires a general consistency of political allegiance over long periods of time, then only a few countries possessed parties before the 1840s. In Chile, despite the shifting commitments of individuals, two general political constellations are observable by the end of the 1820s (the conservative *pelucones, estanqueros* and O'Higginists *versus* the liberal *pipiolos*, federalists and *populares*), though neither existed as a coherent, organized and disciplined group. In New Granada and Uruguay, more or less consistent group loyalties had developed by the end of the 1830s, even though they lacked ideological definition.

In those republics where elections played a significant role in politics, parties in the sense of political groups organized for the purpose of winning elections developed from an early date. Because most national political offices were filled by indirect election, it was crucial to marshal support for certain previously selected electors. Therefore, it was common to distribute printed lists of electors to mobilize the voters of one band or another. This was done in New Granada as early as 1825, in Mexico in 1826 and in Uruguay's first national election in 1830. In New Granada in 1836–8 the names on the lists were being determined by informal, but publicly acknowledged, juntas in both parties.[31] Newspapers were also an important means of mobilizing political forces and

[31] 'El sufragante parroquial', (Bogotá, 1825); Michael P. Costeloe, *La primera república federal de México (1824–1835)* (Mexico, 1975), 73–8; Pivel Devoto, *Historia de los partidos políticos*, I, 37; 'Presidente para 1837. El Jeneral Ciudadano José María Obando', *Constitucional de Cundinamarca*, 15 May 1836; *El Argos*, Bogotá, 15 April 1838; *La Bandera Nacional*, Bogotá, 6 May 1838.

achieving a certain measure of coherence. Through newspapers published in the capital cities, political leaders were able to establish for their adherents in the provinces the political line to be followed. In Venezuela during the 1840s, newspapers, as well as political agents sent out from Caracas, played an important part in mobilizing provincial support.[32] Throughout the 1840s party directorates remained informal, often developing from congressional caucuses or among journalists and others active in politics in the national capital. But, even if informal, they did exist as a means of unifying party action. Not until the beginning of the 1870s, however, were candidates for national office in some countries being selected by party conventions with delegates formally representing all the provinces.

Whether the political groupings be considered as parties or simply as factions, what was the basis of their formation, and how did individuals come to adhere to one group or another? A cynical, and not unreasonable, answer to the first question would be that factions or parties were formed primarily to seize control of the government and the jobs at its disposal. Sustaining this view would not necessarily imply that party choices were accidental. Individuals would attach themselves to political leaders or groups that were more likely to reward them. Often this would mean adhering to leaders and groups with whom they shared regional origin or other personal associations. This way of looking at Spanish American politics in the period has much to recommend it, for there are many instances of political groupings which seem to have at their centre this sort of personal association rather than any ideological consistency. It is particularly true of those groups that formed around caudillos or other dominant individual political leaders (e.g., in Mexico the *jalapeños* and *veracruzanos* who followed Santa Anna, irrespective of ideology, and in New Granada the *caucanos* who formed around General Mosquera, etc.). Such regional or other associational networks clearly also played an important role in cementing political groups otherwise bound by ideological convictions. In New Granada, for example, the Radicals of 1850–80 shared not only standard liberal ideas but also a common generation experience (university students together in the 1840s) and regional background (coming predominantly from the eastern part of the country).

[32] *Pensamiento político venezolano*, XI, 320–33.

In the past most attempts at sociological analysis of the divisions among political elites have viewed the matter in terms of class and economic function. Many appear to have taken Mexico as a model from which to extrapolate. Most sources on Mexican politics, including many more or less contemporary to the events (for example Alamán's history), have described the political battles of 1820–50 as pitting large landowners, the ecclesiastical hierarchy and high-ranking professional military officers against less respectable, socially-emergent elements. The descriptions vary somewhat, depending upon the analyst and the political moment being described. Sometimes government bureaucrats and wealthy merchants and financiers are placed in the conservative alliance. Among those that various authors include in liberal coalitions are young professionals and intellectuals, particularly from the provinces; lower-level military officers; small merchants, artisans, and the petit bourgeoisie in general. With individual variations among these categories, there has been a general agreement upon the validity of a class analysis of Mexican politics in the period, though the most sophisticated descriptions have also introduced regional variables.[33]

In general accounts of Spanish American politics in the nineteenth century the nuances of these statements about Mexico are often stripped away. The usual formulation groups together landowners, military and clergy in a conservative coalition, while professionals and merchants are cast into a liberal bloc. Possibly merchants and professionals have been lumped together, as against landowners and clergy, because of a tendency to apply European categories of bourgeoisie and aristocracy to Spanish America. The idea of a split between an urban bourgeoisie and a rural landowning class has also been reinforced by the fact that in the Río de la Plata region most analysts, following the powerful example of Domingo Faustino Sarmiento's dichotomy between civilization and barbarity, have emphasized a conflict between city and country.

This kind of formulation is increasingly being brought into question.[34] First, insofar as it implies a virtual unanimity within each of these social groups, it is almost certainly wrong. There are, however, a number

[33] Lucas Alamán, *Historia de Méjico* (5 vols., Mexico, 1849–52), v, 823–4, 850–1; Sierra, *Political evolution*, 185–6, 203–5, 226; Costeloe, *La primera república federal*, 74, 85, 169, 185–7, 276, 342; François Chevalier, 'Conservateurs et libéraux au Mexique: essai de sociologie et géographie politiques de l'Indépendance à l'intervention français', *Cahiers d'Histoire Mondiale*, 8 (1964), 457–74.

[34] The following argument is presented at greater length in Frank Safford, 'Bases of political alignment in early republican Spanish America', in Richard Graham and Peter H. Smith (eds.), *New approaches to Latin American history* (Austin, 1974), 71–111.

of other reasons for rejecting *prima facie* this type of general description. The use of such categories as landowner, merchant and professional as ways of dividing social interest groups is implausible, because the upper classes in nineteenth-century Spanish America lacked the specificity of function that this description implies. A single individual was likely to be a large landowner, a merchant and possibly also a university-educated professional or military officer. And if one individual did not fulfil all of these functions, someone else in his immediate family generally supplied the lack. Therefore it is often artificial to divide people politically according to occupation.

Furthermore, even if members of the upper sectors could be divided neatly into economic functional groups, it still would be implausible to see them as in conflict along economic interest group lines. In economies based upon the exportation of agriculturally produced raw materials and the importation of consumer goods for the use of those producing the raw materials, there was a natural identity of interest among the land-owner-producer, the merchant-conveyer and the lawyer who, whether in private practice or public office, attended to the needs of both landowners and merchants. In such a system, of course, there would be temporary conflicts between individual landowners and merchant-creditors. But, except in Venezuela in the 1840s, these disputes did not take on the character of systemic conflict required for them to become political issues. In general an urban-rural upper-class solidarity prevailed. This seems even to have been true in the Río de la Plata, all of the talk of city–country conflict there notwithstanding, for in Buenos Aires the interests of merchants and producers of hides and salted meat were closely meshed, and they often were the same individuals.

Recent studies of various parts of Spanish America have concluded that landowners, merchants and professionals are to be found prominently figuring in almost all political groups. What then can one say about the social characteristics differentiating the contending political groups? First, it cannot be expected that a single principle, or set of principles, of differentiation can be found that will apply accurately to all of the various Spanish American countries, with their differing geographies, ethnic configurations, economic characteristics and colonial traditions. However, several patterns may be posited that are applicable at least to some countries.

If a division between economic functional groups does not hold up well, one can perceive in several countries political divisions in which the distribution of power and status (across occupational lines) played an important role. In Mexico, New Granada and Peru there is a tendency for the affiliations of members of the political elite to correspond roughly to their social location, that is, to their relationship to the structures of economic and political power and of social prestige. This relationship generally was determined in part by regional origins as well as by accidents of birth and social connection within given regions.

Men tended to become conservatives if, in social terms, they were centrally located. This central location might be institutional. Often conservatives were born and raised in towns that had been administratively prominent and/or were educational centres in the colonial period. These places were characterized by a more aristocratic ethos, a more rigid social hierarchy, than the less significant provincial towns. Often the conservative atmosphere of these colonial administrative centres was reinforced by the fact that they were in a state of economic stagnation or decline during the first half of the nineteenth century. Nevertheless, the young men who grew up in them had distinct advantages in entering the political elite, both because of social ties to the hierarchies of civil and ecclesiastical administration and because of access to institutions of higher education that served as conduits to positions of power. Central social location might also be economic. Conservatives also tended to come from towns where there was concentrated economic power. Or their own families were important property owners or were in other ways economically powerful as large merchants or entrepreneurs.

Liberals tended to have more peripheral social locations. They often came from provincial towns that were less significant economically, administratively, or culturally in the colonial period, and where social stratification was less pronounced. They frequently had more limited access to the institutions of higher education that provided channels for entry into the political elite, both through formal training and through social contacts. As young men who journeyed from the provinces to the established cultural centres, often virtually penniless, they suffered a partial or difficult social incorporation into the political elite. Individuals of this sort, who entered the political elite through demonstrated talent, pluck and luck, rather than by birth, were likely to be most sensitive to liberal ideologies of legal equality and individual opportunity and to have no vested interest in the protection of colonial structures of power, privilege and prestige.

There also were peripheral merchants and landowners in the liberal ranks – though they were generally less visible than the professionals because a pronounced political identity could make economic enterprise more hazardous. Typical peripheral merchants might be provincial retailers who possessed limited capital, confronted limited markets and depended upon large merchants in the commercial centres for their supplies of goods and credit. Such men might see themselves as fighting to break through an established commercial structure of oligopoly-controlled trade and credit. However, the motivations of their liberalism might be associated with social opportunity as much as with economic role. Often these provincial merchants were even less privileged versions of the provincials who journeyed to the cultural centres to study law; they were men whose families' economic circumstances did not permit this luxury; thus they too identified strongly with the ideal of equality of opportunity. Many such marginal merchants, however, might be conservative or hostile to all political activity. Peripheral landowners were those holding properties that were relatively marginal either because of modest size or distance from urban markets and that, by the same token, conferred less social distinction than more favourably situated properties. Alternatively, they may have been engaged in export agriculture and thus were more exposed to fluctuations in world markets. Such men, like the peripheral merchants, *might* be, but were not necessarily, attached to liberal political forces.

Many men behaved contrary to the pattern which has been outlined. In particular, socially emergent professionals, whether from the capital city or the provinces, often were co-opted into conservative ranks where they served as political agents (journalists, legislators, etc.). It also should be noted that liberalism was strongest in those provinces that, while less important colonial centres, were not completely marginal in the scheme of republican national politics. They were provinces that could aspire to contend for political influence and power, not regions that were insignificant demographically and economically. Thus, in Mexico, liberalism was a dominant force in such states as Zacatecas, Michoacán, or Jalisco; it was less characteristic of the sparsely populated far north of Mexico which was more removed from national politics and where a few large landowners could dominate politics. Similarly, in New Granada, liberalism was strong in Socorro, which could challenge Bogotá; provinces such as Pasto, the Chocó, or Riohacha, which remained largely outside of the arena of national politics, were ruled by a few entrenched families and remained conservative rather than liberal in inclination.

In Mexico in the 1830s and 1840s it is hard to establish hard-and-fast social identifications of political alignments in part because there were so many political cross-currents, changing individual commitments, shifting factional alliances. Nevertheless it is possible to identify in these years four tendencies whose strength waxed and waned at various moments. At one extreme of the political spectrum were those who after 1830 assumed a centralist and pro-clerical stance and who became identified as conservatives at the end of the 1840s. A large proportion of those publicly identified as conservatives came from the centre of the country – from the upper sectors of Mexico City, the centre of all things; from Puebla, a city of importance as an industrial centre as well as in ecclesiastical administration and education; from Orizaba, closely associated with Puebla. Another city that spawned significant members of the conservative political elite was Campeche in Yucatán, not geographically central, but a town of local importance in the colonial period that was suffering stagnation in the early nineteenth century. Lucas Alamán, widely recognized as the central figure of Mexican conservatism, was the son of a rich mine-owner in Guanajuato, whose family was also closely linked to Spanish administrators there. Other prominent conservatives, like Antonio de Haro y Tamariz and Estevan de Antuñano, were connected with the industrial development of Puebla. Often allied with these civilian conservatives were a number of high-ranking officers in the professional army, particularly those whose military careers began in the Spanish army. While the civilian conservatives were attached to a centralist political system because they thought it more likely to produce order, for the professional military a centralist system was a prerequisite for the budgetary support of a large national army and for the military dominance of that army.

At the other political extreme were the federalists of the 1820s and 1830s or *puros* of the 1840s, who were most firmly committed to a programme of legal equality and the destruction of clerical and military privilege. The leadership of these liberals came predominantly from men with legal or medical professional education, though through the exigencies of civil war some developed military careers. They hailed particularly from provinces encircling the conservative, centralist core area, in an arc running from San Luis Potosí in the north, through Guanajuato and Zacatecas in the north-west to Jalisco and Michoacán in the west to Guerrero and Oaxaca in the south. The provincials' position outside the central structures of power and privilege inherited from the colonial period generally disposed them to the destruction or weakening of these

structures. Particularly in provinces to the north and west of Mexico
City a class of small farmers created an atmosphere of relative social
egaliterianism contrasting with the seigneurial style of the aristocracy
of the centre, and provided a substantial base of support for the
liberal provincial elites' attacks upon centralist control and clerical
privilege.[35]

Between the two poles of the Mexican political spectrum were two
mediating groups that often came to power in coalition with one of the
extremes. Moderate liberals gathered around Manuel Gómez Pedraza
formed one of these intermediary or swing groups. Liberals in principle,
they shared the conservatives' distaste for anything smacking too much
of the rabble. They alternated between alliances with the conservatives,
whose authoritarian centralism they distrusted, and the extreme liberals,
whose populist tendencies they disliked. During the 1840s a number of
these moderate liberals gravitated into the conservative camp, rallying
behind the Church in opposition to *puro* anti-clericalism. The social
origins of the moderates tended to be more heterogeneous than those of
either extreme, drawing both from the same provincial element that
formed the backbone of *puro* liberalism and from the aristocracy of the
centre that characterized centralist, pro-clerical conservatism. The other
intermediary group was that headed by General Antonio López de Santa
Anna, which drew principally upon three clienteles – local supporters
from his territorial base in Jalapa and Veracruz, the *agiotistas* (speculators
in government bonds), and his following among the professional army,
whose interests he often represented.

In New Granada the pattern of political division was sociologically
similar to that in Mexico, though somewhat simpler. By the end of the
1830s two parties had emerged, in conflict less over ideology than over
control of the government. The party that came to be called conservative
at the end of the 1840s had particular strength in the cities of Bogotá,
Popayán, Cartagena, and Tunja. All were centres of civil and ecclesiastical administration in the colonial period. In these cities also resided
creoles enriched by gold-mining or commerce, or holding large properties worked by Indian peasants or black slaves. All consequently were
dominated by social hierarchies headed by civilian and clerical administrators and supported by large property-owners. As centres of concentrated wealth and prestige, they were well endowed with conventual
establishments and pious foundations. This meant that they possessed

[35] David A. Brading, *Los orígenes del nacionalismo mexicano* (Mexico, 1973), 207–21; Chevalier.
'Conservateurs et libéraux', 457–74.

the most important secondary schools, for in 1821 the properties of understaffed conventual establishments were used to finance *colegios* and universities in these localities. Until mid-century Bogotá, Cartagena and Popayán were the sites of the nation's three universities, and Tunja possessed the best-endowed secondary school. The political establishment ruling from 1837 through the 1840s (ultimately known as conservatives), reinforced the educational advantages of these cities by creating regulations making it impossible for other towns to grant degrees in medicine or law. Consequently, youths growing up in these favoured cities could obtain their university certificate for statecraft much more easily than those from smaller, less educationally endowed towns. The governing elite justified these restriction on the ground that a surplus of young, under-employed lawyers would increase demand for public office and thus create instability.[36]

Liberal strength was most evident in the region of Socorro, in the Caribbean port of Santa Marta and parts of the Upper Magdalena Valley. The Socorro region in the late colonial period was economically of some importance as a supplier of cottage-woven textiles to other parts of the viceroyalty. But Socorro was not an important centre of civil or ecclesiastical administration, and consequently lacked an elaborate social hierarchy or extensive conventional foundations. It was a society of small, independent farmers whose incomes were supplemented by the household weaving of their women, and it was much less aristocratic in social spirit than the administrative centres. The port of Santa Marta was relatively unimportant in the colonial period, for overseas trade was held as the monopoly of Cartagena, the administrative, military and ecclesiastical centre of the Caribbean coast. After 1820, however, under a system of free trade, Santa Marta emerged as New Granada's principal conduit for imported goods, displacing a declining Cartagena. Santa Marta was the seat of a group of emergent, energetic merchants fully committed to the benefits of free enterprise. The Upper Magdalena Valley, producer of tobacco, cinchona bark and cacao, was similarly linked to the expansion of international trade. In the Magdalena Valley as in Socorro small merchants and farmers called for the abolition of the government tobacco monopoly, which constricted individual opportunity and limited production of a potentially important export product but which those established in the government defended on grounds of fiscal

[36] Frank Safford, *The ideal of the practical: Colombia's struggle to form a technical elite* (Austin, Texas, 1976), 107–35.

necessity. In all of these provinces and others, secondary schools were either nonexistent or did not meet government requirements; young men who sought law degrees had, if their parents could afford it, to journey to the established centres, usually to the capital, to make their way. The abolition of restrictions on secondary education was one of the first concerns of the emergent liberal elite after it gained power in 1849.

One region in New Granada, however, fails to conform to the dichotomy of conservative administrative centres *versus* liberal provinces – the gold-mining province of Antioquia. Antioquia, like Socorro and the other liberal provinces, lacked an elaborate ecclesiastical establishment and hence a conventual endowment for secondary education. Like Socorro also, it was characterized by a relatively egalitarian society, compared with Bogotá or Popayán. Yet Antioquia during the 1840s became a bastion of conservatism. Apparently, while not favoured by a colonial institutional inheritance, it became identified with conservatism because of its substantial economic power. Through its gold-mining, it produced the majority of New Granada's foreign exchange in the late colonial period and through the first half of the nineteenth century. Antioqueño merchants, therefore, had a prospering economy to protect, unlike the elites in many other provinces. Thus, they enlisted themselves on the side of order, whatever political form that might take. Like other conservatives they supported the Roman Catholic Church, both out of piety and because it helped to shore up the social order.

The social-location analytical model may be extended to Peru, where a division may be perceived between the conservative Pandos, Pardos and Herreras of Lima and emergent liberals from the provinces, such as Luna Pizarro from Arequipa, Benito Laso from Puno and the Gálvez brothers from Cajamarca. The model works less well in some other places, however. In Buenos Aires it is possible to identify economic power, in the persons of the cattle and salt-meat entrepreneurs, with conservative political forces in the 1820s and 1830s. But the political conservatives who gathered around Juan Manuel de Rosas were no more closely linked to colonial institutional structures than their opponents. In Buenos Aires the conflict seems to have been essentially a struggle between these dominant economic interests, who preferred to do without the nuisance of politics and stood behind Rosas as an agent of order, and a group of educated men who aspired to western liberal political standards. In this sense it was a struggle between 'barbarism' and 'civilization'. A similar struggle between an urban literary elite, attempting to impose something like European political norms, and caudillos with rural ties and little sense of constitutionalism, also marked the politics of Uruguay in the period.

Whatever the political persuasion of members of the Spanish American elite, it is striking how little confidence they showed in their new countries. The largely Spanish-descended elites in no way identified with the *mestizos*, Indians and blacks who formed the lower classes in their countries, and in their own minds they associated themselves more with the European bourgeoisie. Judging the majority of the people in their societies to be backward and ignorant, the elite believed it would be hard to forge a nation from such elements. Partly for this reason almost everywhere in Spanish America the elites enthusiastically encouraged European immigration; they believed immigrants would bring not merely skills and capital but also a more European cast to society. In addition to their distrust of the general population, confidence was further undermined by the chronic political instability of the period, with its attendant insecurity of property in time of civil war. This loss of confidence was reflected in various ways. Some members of the elite emigrated to Europe, and a few more attempted to emigrate without leaving home, seeking to protect their property by becoming recognized as citizens of the United States or of some European power.

Loss of confidence in the new nations was augmented by pressure from foreign powers. Mexico, the Río de la Plata region, New Granada and other areas felt the weight of British and French blockades in the 1830s. Mexico and Central America had to cope with the additional problem of North American aggression. These external forces at once intimidated and seduced the elites. Factions in the elite were often tempted to compromise national independence in order to obtain the aid of an external power. Such was the case of the Uruguayan gentlemen who sought aid from Portuguese Brazil between 1817 and 1825 and of the Argentine *unitarios* exiled in Montevideo who in the late 1830s could not resist alliance with the French against their enemy Rosas in Buenos Aires. (Political factions almost everywhere, of course, also had recourse to aid from neighbouring Spanish American countries.)

On occasion the collapse of confidence in the nation reached such a pitch that elites were willing, in one way or another, to abandon national independence altogether. Lorenzo Zavala in Mexico was so impressed by the economic strength and dynamism of the United States that by 1831 he welcomed North American penetration of Texas as the prelude to a general triumph of liberty in Mexico through the agency of Yankee colonization. Not long afterward Zavala cast his lot with the Yankee state of Texas in its assertion of independence from Mexico. In the following decade the elites in Yucatán, unable to obtain effective help from a collapsed Mexican government in their efforts to dominate Indian rebellion, attempted to annex their province to the United States. More startling and less well known, when in 1857 the United States was pressing New Granada for compensation for the deaths of American citizens in riots in Panama and New Granadan leaders despaired of obtaining British protection, President Mariano Ospina Rodríguez proposed to Washington the annexation of the entire republic of New Granada by the United States. Ospina reasoned that in view of the United States' inexorable expansion, as demonstrated in war with Mexico in 1846–8 and in the filibuster adventures in Nicaragua of the 1850s, New Granada would inevitably be swallowed up sooner or later. Better to get it over with quickly, without unnecessary bloodshed, particularly considering the probability that rule by the United States would bring stability and security of property. A different sort of abdication of independence, but for the same ends, was pursued in the same period by Mexican conservatives who sought to introduce a European monarch to their country.

This fragile sense of the nation was probably greatest in Mexico, most threatened by the United States, and in the Río de la Plata, where the so-called United Provinces could hardly be said to have constituted a nation at all before 1861. A sense of nationhood was probably strongest, on the other hand, in Chile, where national pride was bolstered by triumph in the war against the Peruvian–Bolivian Confederation in 1839, combined with a notable economic prosperity and substantial political order between 1830 and 1850.

Political instability in Spanish America between 1810 and 1870 has invited many explanations. These can be broken down into two general categories, though there are numerous subdivisions within each category. One line of interpretation, taking an extremely long view, tends to emphasize the role of deep-rooted cultural and institutional patterns. Other approaches, which tend to look more closely at events in time, stress the effects of economic and social variables.

Cultural explanations of Spanish American instability have several variants. Earlier in the twentieth century interpretations tended to stress psycho-cultural elements somewhat more than institutions. The Peruvian Francisco García Calderón, under the influence of Miguel de Unamuno and other turn-of-the-century Spanish writers, attributed Spanish American instability to an anarchic, intolerant and exclusivist individualism that was embedded in Spanish culture. At the same time García Calderón noted a seemingly contrary monarchical tradition that, in the republican era, was conducive to presidential dictatorship, which in turn provoked rebellion.[37]

Another exploration of psycho-cultural elements in political instability, a brilliant *tour de force* by the British scholar, Cecil Jane, drew upon the same Spanish sources as García Calderón, but emphasized more the contradictions within Spanish culture. Jane viewed Spaniards and Spanish Americans as idealistic extremists who sought both order and individual liberty in such perfect forms that Spanish American politics swung from one extreme (despotism) to the other (anarchy), rather than finding stability in constitutional compromise between the two contending principles. In the sixteenth and seventeenth centuries, according to Jane, the Hapsburg monarchy managed to embody both of these extreme tendencies, holding them in contradictory, but effective, co-existence. (The Hapsburg monarch proclaimed absolute order but in effect, through inefficiency, permitted much freedom.) Once the king was removed, the extremes found no effective resolution. In the nineteenth century, when conservatives, who embodied the principle of order, were in power, they carried the pursuit of order to such extremes that they inevitably provoked a violent reaction in behalf of liberty. Similarly, when liberals enacted standard western liberal protections of the individual, Spanish Americans did not use these liberties with the responsibility expected by the Englishmen who had developed these liberties, but rather carried them to the extreme of anarchy. The lack of dictatorial restraint brought individualistic chaos, which in turn provoked the resumption of dictatorship.[38]

More recently the cultural mode of explanation has been reformulated in still another way by Richard Morse. Morse, like García Calderón,

[37] Francisco García Calderón, *Latin America: its rise and progress* (New York, 1913). Recently an American scholar, Glen Dealy, has not only exhumed the theme of Spanish anarchic individualism to explain the phenomenon of *caudillismo* but has argued that liberal constitutionalism, with its emphasis on tolerance of dissent, was doomed in Spanish America because it was in conflict with the Spanish Catholic 'monist' tradition, which assumes a unified, not a pluralist, society. Dealey, 'La tradición de la democracia monista', 159–201, and idem, *The public man: an interpretation of Latin American and other Catholic countries* (Amherst, Mass., 1977).

[38] Lionel Cecil Jane, *Liberty and despotism in Spanish America* (London, 1929).

is concerned with explaining the tendency to both personalist authoritarianism and anarchy in nineteenth-century Spanish America. Morse sees these characteristics both as being inherent in the Spanish legacy itself and also as being reinforced by the conflict between Spanish traditions and the imported Western liberal constitutional ideals that came into play in Spanish America at the time of independence.

For Morse the key to understanding Spanish American politics lies in the Spanish patrimonial state. He points out that in Spain, as contrasted with other parts of Europe, feudal institutions were weak; the various interest groups (nobility, Church, merchants, etc.) rather than constituting relatively autonomous power centres were heavily dependent upon the state. The state was embodied in the patrimonial power of the king, who was not only the source of all patronage but also the ultimate arbiter of all disputes. The patrimonial ruler (in accord with the Weberian typology):

is reluctant to bind himself by 'law', his rule takes the form of a series of directives, each subject to supersession. . . . Legal remedies are frequently regarded not as applications of 'law', but as a gift of grace or a privilege awarded on the merits of a case and not binding as precedent.[39]

He thus governs in a personalist, potentially arbitrary, manner rather than according to a rule of law.

Thus the organization of power in the system ultimately depended upon the king. Without the presence of the king, the system shattered. Because of the lack of a feudal tradition, Spanish America did not possess the 'underpinning of contractual vassalic relationships that capacitate the component parts of a *feudal* regime for autonomous life'. Most importantly perhaps, the weakness of Spanish feudalism contributed to the weakness of parliamentary traditions. Thus, with the disappearance of the king,

the collapse of the supreme authority activated the latent forces of local oligarchies, municipalities, and extended-family systems in a struggle for power and prestige in the new, arbitrarily defined republics . . . In the absence of developed and interacting economic interest groups having a stake in constitutional process, the new countries were plunged into alternating regimes of anarchy and personalist tyranny. The contest to seize a patrimonial state apparatus, fragmented from the original imperial one, became the driving force of public life in each new country.[40]

---

[39] Richard M. Morse, 'The heritage of Latin America', in Louis Hartz, *The founding of new societies* (New York, 1964), 157.
[40] *Ibid.*, 162.

In Morse's view, Spanish American political leaders in the nineteenth century were constantly trying to reconstruct the patrimonial authority of the Spanish Crown. But the personalist political leaders (caudillos), while in a number of cases able to establish a temporary charismatic authority, were not able to institutionalize their rule in a generally-accepted 'super-personal legitimacy'. The great exception proving Morse's rule was nineteenth-century Chile, where a unified landowning and commercial elite, under the charismatic leadership of Diego Portales, was able to legitimate a system in which a strong executive could successfully exercise patrimonial power approximating that of the Spanish crown.

One important factor impeding the reconstruction of patrimonial authority along traditional Spanish lines, according to Morse, was the intromission of Western constitutional ideas during the independence era. Anglo-French liberal constitutionalism – with its emphasis on the rule of law, the division and separation of powers, constitutional checks on authority and the efficacy of elections – stood as a contradiction to those traditional attitudes and modes of behaviour which lived in the marrow of Spanish Americans. Because liberal constitutionalism was ill-adapted to traditional Spanish political culture, attempts to erect and maintain states according to liberal principles invariably failed. On the other hand, the authority of imported liberal constitutional ideas, while insufficient to provide a viable alternative to the traditional political model, was often sufficient to undermine the legitimacy of governments operating according to the traditional model. Thus, Spanish America's political instability between 1810 and 1870 was, in Morse's view, aggravated by the tension between traditional political models, to which Spanish American leaders gravitated instinctively, and constitutional principles, which served as a constant criticism of those who used power in the traditional manner. In Morse's interpretation stability could be achieved only when a synthesis could be achieved in which traditional models dominated and constitutional principles became mere window-dressing. This, he contends, was the pattern in the exceptional case of Chile, where the 'structure of the Spanish patrimonial state was re-created, with only those minimum concessions to Anglo-French constitutionalism that were necessary for a nineteenth-century republic which had just rejected monarchical rule'.[41]

----

[41] *Ibid.*, 163–4.

Morse's cultural analysis is in many ways compelling. Reviewing the political history of Spanish America in the fifty years after independence, one can find many examples of behaviour that fit well into his conceptions. On the other hand, the approach has some evident weaknesses. First, like many analyses that emphasize culture as a determining variable, Morse's interpretations, and those that follow him, treat culture in an excessively static manner – as if Spanish culture, once crystallized at some point in the distant past, never underwent significant change afterward. In particular, there is a tendency to underestimate the degree to which imported liberal constitutional ideas came not only to be sincerely believed by the university-educated but even to attain a substantial legitimacy. Liberal constitutionalist ideals failed to achieve the hegemony they enjoyed in British cultures, but they did have a significant effect on modes of political thought and became at least partially incorporated into the political rules. The constitutionalist idea of 'no re-election', for example, was violated frequently, yet the idea had sufficient power to serve as a means of discrediting those who sought to continue themselves in office. And in a number of countries by the end of the period it had become an effective part of the living constitution.

Second, the cultural interpretations of Morse and others in their concentration on concepts of legitimacy and political and social values tend to disregard the role of geographic, economic, and social structural factors in destabilizing political systems, and in permitting their stabilization. For example, Chile's unique stability in the 1830s and 1840s was aided by the singular geographical concentration of its landed and commercial elite. Chile in these years was also enjoying a prosperity that was exceptional by comparison with other Spanish American countries. This prosperity generated funds that enabled the Chilean government to sustain itself against attempted rebellions. In this light, the success of the Portalean system of presidential authoritarianism which after Portales' death became institutionalized may not so much be attributable to its harmony with traditional values and expectations[42] as to the fact that it had the wherewithal to suppress dissidents, something that other, fiscally weakened republics were less able to do. In some circumstances, may not a government be considered 'legitimate' largely because it has the power to maintain itself?

---

[42] See Francisco Antonio Moreno's application of Morse's interpretations to Portalean Chile in *Legitimacy and stability in Latin America: a study of Chilean political culture* (New York, 1969), 91–127.

In contrast with the cultural interpretations, other analyses emphasize the economic causes of political instability in Spanish America. One variant of such analyses, now of some vintage, stresses conflicts among different regions or social groups that were generated by their differing interests in relation to the international economy. An interpretation of this sort, although unstructured, is implied in the work of Justo Sierra, who contends that several of the rebellions in pre-1850 Mexico were produced by the machinations of coastal merchants who objected to changes in government tariff policies. A much clearer example is Miron Burgin's analysis of Argentine politics in the period, which stresses the conflict of regional economic interests.[43]

Recently there has developed some scepticism about interpretations emphasizing conflicting group or regional interests. While individual merchants or landowners might have civil or private disputes over loans or contracts, almost never were there political conflicts between merchants and landowners as groups, because, in an export economy, their long-term interests tended to coincide. The case of Venezuela in the 1840s is, in this respect, exceptional. Conflicting regional economic interests, while possibly discernible in some cases, were also unlikely to generate major political conflict. In most Spanish American countries transportation was so backward and expensive that the various regions hardly formed part of the same economy and there was little opportunity for their interests to come sharply into conflict. Minor intra-regional conflicts did occur, as different towns in the same region competed for supremacy as ports or political centres. But these intra-regional conflicts were unlikely to cause national government to become unstrung.

In fact, in these unintegrated economies instability was more likely to be caused by *lack* of economic interest than by conflicting economic interests. In a number of countries the regions that most frequently initiated rebellions against the national government were those whose location made it difficult or impossible to participate effectively in the export trade. In these regions the local elites, for lack of economic opportunities in which to invest their energies, turned to politico-military enterprise. In New Granada, the Cauca region, trapped between two looming mountain-ranges and thus unable to export its product effectively, was a seedbed of rebellion throughout the period. Economic stagnation undoubtedly also played a part in the frequent rebellions of Arequipa and Cuzco against authorities in Lima. And parts of the

[43] Sierra, *Political evolution of the Mexican people*, 213, 218–19, 222, 229–30; Miron Burgin, *Economic aspects of Argentine federalism* (Cambridge, Mass., 1946).

Argentine interior probably also fit this pattern. In contrast, those regions that were most effectively integrated into the export economy tended to be the most stable politically. In Argentina, the possibility of profiting from external trade undoubtedly played an important part in unifying the merchants and ranchers of Buenos Aires behind the stern, no-nonsense government of Juan Manuel de Rosas. Realization that the progress of their province lay in international trade and that efforts to dominate the rest of the country had only served to check this economic progress encouraged them to support Rosas in a policy of attending to the province and forgoing political grandeur.

Several interpretations argue that before 1870 limited integration into the international economy and the lack of an integrated national economy delayed the emergence of dominant bourgeoisies that could, in alliance with foreign interests, act effectively to guarantee political order and stability in Spanish America. Because of the character of the hacienda economy, landowners were not cohesive enough to form political alliances that could control the politics of their countries. Consequently, ambitious, socially-emergent caudillos stepped into the power vacuum. However, these caudillos as political entrepreneurs were not able to satisfy more than temporarily the armed bands that followed them, so that their periods of dominance generally were short-lived.[44]

Interpretations of instability that emphasize the lack of a strong, united class committed to sustain the state are complemented by treatments that stress the financial weakness of the new governments. Lack of funds made it difficult for them to retain the loyalty of the armies as well as to co-opt potentially dissident civilian elites through patronage. Like other Spanish American countries, Mexico, for example, was burdened with heavy foreign debts acquired originally in the 1820s. Mexican governments, according to Jan Bazant, faced a choice of either collecting taxes to make payments on the debts, thus courting internal rebellion, or of not paying the foreign creditors, thus inviting the intervention of foreign powers. Hoping to rescue the state from its chronic near-bankruptcy, Mexican leaders were tempted to lay their hands on the great wealth of the Church; but attacks upon Church property also brought rebellion, and, on occasion, the overthrow of the government.[45]

Both the fiscal approach to political instability and the analysis

[44] Wolf and Hansen, 'Caudillo politics', 168–79. For further discussion of *caudillismo*, see above, pp. 71–6.
[45] Jan Bazant, *Alienation of church wealth in Mexico* (Cambridge, 1971), as elaborated upon by Stephen R. Niblo and Laurens B. Perry, 'Recent additions to nineteenth-century Mexican historiography', in *Latin American Research Review*, 13/3 (1978), 13–15.

pointing to the lack of strong supporting classes are brought together in the interpretation of Tulio Halperín Donghi. Halperín ascribes the financial weakness of the new states partly to the effects of Spanish America's engagement with the Atlantic economy. Acute trade imbalances created currency stringencies and economic contraction, weakening the economic underpinnings of their governments. At the same time their social underpinnings, most particularly the urban bourgeoisie, were weakened by the invasion of foreign merchants and the inability of the state to pay its civilian employees.[46] Possibly Halperín, on the basis of Argentine experience, exaggerates the extent to which Spanish American merchants were undermined, for in some places foreign merchants' control of the markets was only temporary. But an interpretation stressing the commercial situation of the new countries has the advantage of helping to explain not merely the instability of the 1810–70 period when the trade positions of most of them were relatively weak but also the relatively greater political stability of the post-1870 period, when increasing European demand greatly augmented the volume of their exports as well as improving their trade balances.

By contrast with the political instability that characterized most of Spanish America between 1810 and 1870, the decades from 1870 to 1910 were years of political consolidation and centralization, generally under governments of a secular and modernizing but more or less authoritarian and undemocratic cast. In Mexico, the liberal hegemony established by Benito Juárez with the overthrow of Maximilian's imperial government in 1867 evolved into the dictatorship of Porfirio Díaz (1876–1911). In Guatemala the regime of Justo Rufino Barrios (1871–85) provided a similar combination of formal liberalism and authoritarian rule. In Venezuela the comparable anti-clerical, liberal, modernizing dictator was Antonio Guzmán Blanco (1870–88). In Colombia the establishment of authoritarian order was attempted in the 1880s by Rafael Núñez, a man of liberal antecedents who sustained his centralist regime through alliance with the Church and ardently pro-clerical Conservatives. Argentina presented another variation on the same theme, as, under an oligarchy rather than a dictator, it became consolidated politically as a unified nation in the 1870s and enjoyed economic growth unparalleled in Latin America during subsequent decades.

[46] Halperín, *Aftermath of revolution*, 1–43.

From the point of view of the intellectual and cultural historian the Porfiriato and other authoritarian liberal regimes are notable for their abandonment of all but the external trappings of liberal ideology and for the adoption of a more hardheaded, authoritarian political style. These regimes may thus be considered as having returned to something more closely approximating the governing mode of Spanish tradition. Most interpreters of the era of political consolidation after 1870, however, tend to emphasize the economic foundations of the new order. Growing European and North American demand for Latin American raw materials brought a flow of foreign loans and investments in railroads, mines and export agriculture and, in the case of Argentina and Uruguay, European immigrants as well. These foreign inputs, as well as greatly increased returns from exports and customs collections on imports, gave some regimes in the 1870–1910 period the wherewithal to co-opt potential dissidents into government jobs, and placate them with concessions or contracts, and to maintain modernized national armies with which to repress those opponents who could not be bought. Not only were these central governments now fiscally stronger and therefore more able to contain dissent, but the economic opportunities of the era also tended so to absorb the attention of the upper sectors that their interest in politics as a form of economic enterprise greatly subsided. The new era was, for the upper sectors, one of moneymaking more than political conflict, of businesslike practicality rather more than ideological crusading. It was an era of 'order and progress'.

# 3

## MEXICO

The royalist brigadier, Agustín de Iturbide, proclaimed the independence of Mexico on 24 February 1821 at Iguala, a small town in the heart of the southern, tropical *tierra caliente* or 'hot country'. In his manifesto, the Plan of Iguala, Iturbide called for independence, the union of Mexicans and Spaniards and respect for the Roman Catholic Church. The form of government was to be a constitutional monarchy in which the emperor would be chosen from a European, preferably Spanish, dynasty 'so as to give us a monarch already made and save us from fatal acts of ambition', and the national constitution was to be drawn up by a congress. With this the first of his so-called 'three guarantees', Iturbide won the support of the old guerrilla fighters for independence, particularly General Vicente Guerrero who at this time was operating not far from Iguala. The second guarantee offered security to Spanish-born residents of Mexico, and with the third he sought to attract the clerical establishment by promising to preserve ecclesiastical privileges, recently under attack in Spain by the liberal, revolutionary regime. The army would take upon itself the task of 'protecting' the guarantees.

Iturbide's appeal proved remarkably successful. In less than six months, he was master of the country, except for the capital city and the ports of Acapulco and Veracruz. It was at Veracruz that the newly appointed Spanish captain-general, Juan O'Donojú, disembarked on 30 July. He had been instructed to introduce liberal reforms in New Spain but at the same time to ensure that the colony remained within the Spanish empire. His instructions, however, were based on information received in Madrid about events which had taken place in the colony some four or five months previously, and he at once recognized that the

---

[1] The Author and the Editor wish to acknowledge the help of Professor Michael P. Costeloe, University of Bristol, in the final preparation of this chapter.

situation had changed significantly since then. Mexican independence appeared to him already a fact and, wanting to depart as quickly as possible from the yellow fever infested port, he decided to seek a meeting with Iturbide. They met on 24 August in Córdoba, at the foot of the snow-capped Citlaltepetl volcano, and they signed a treaty which recognized 'The Mexican Empire' as a sovereign and independent nation. The treaty paraphrased the Iguala manifesto, but there were several modifications. According to the manifesto, the throne was to be offered to Ferdinand VII, or, in case of his refusal, to a prince of a reigning dynasty. It was assumed that there would be at least one prince willing to accept. The text signed in Córdoba, however, named four specific candidates, all of the Spanish dynasty, and no reference was made to other European royal families. If the four Spaniards were to refuse the throne, the future emperor was to be selected by the Mexican congress. This change is unlikely to have been fortuitous, and it was to have important consequences, especially in the career of the ambitious Iturbide. As the meeting at Córdoba lasted only a few hours, it seems certain that Iturbide had already carefully prepared the long text in advance and was well aware of the implications of the changes made to the original Iguala declaration. O'Donojú, on the other hand, who must have been tired following his long journey from Spain and was possibly ill, overlooked the modification. He signed the document with his constitutional title of Captain General and Superior Political Chief, although to the present day he remains known in Mexico as the last Spanish viceroy. Brigadier Iturbide signed as First Chief of the Imperial Army. Within a few months he was to be Generalísimo.

The acceptance of independence by O'Donojú facilitated the transfer of power in the capital. Having delayed his entrance so that it coincided with his thirty-eighth birthday, Iturbide rode into Mexico City on 27 September. On the next morning, he chose the thirty-eight members of the governing junta stipulated in both the Iguala manifesto and the treaty of Córdoba. In a formal act, this junta then declared the independence of Mexico. With Iturbide acting as its president, the junta consisted of well-known ecclesiastics, lawyers, judges, members of the Mexican nobility and a few army officers, among them Colonel Anastasio Bustamante who, like Iturbide, was a former royalist officer. Old fighters for independence such as Nicolás Bravo, Guadalupe Victoria and Guerrero were not members, but O'Donojú was included in accordance with the agreement reached at Córdoba. It was expected that he would give

Iturbide a helping hand in the transition between the viceroyalty and a future empire under a Spanish prince. In fact, O'Donojú fell ill and died ten days later before being able to appoint the commissioners who were to have gone to Madrid to negotiate a settlement, again as envisaged in the Córdoba agreement. As president of the junta and regent of the empire, Generalísimo Iturbide could still have sent envoys to Madrid but he did not do so.

Not surprisingly, the Spanish attitude towards Mexican independence was hostile from the beginning. Although the greater part of the Spanish army stationed in Mexico swore allegiance to the new nation, a group of royalist diehards withdrew to San Juan de Ulúa, an island fortress in front of Veracruz harbour, and waited there for reinforcements with which to reconquer the country. They were not disavowed by the Madrid government and on 13 February 1822 the Spanish Cortes rejected the Córdoba treaty. The news of this refusal by the mother country to accept Mexico's independence reached Mexico City several months later.

Independence in 1821 did not bring any immediate revolutionary change in the social or economic structure of the country. The first and principal effect was that the political power formerly exercised by the royal bureaucracy was transferred to the army, that is to say, to a coalition of Iturbide's royalist and Guerrero's republican armies.

The second pillar of the new nation was the Roman Catholic Church. Like all the established colonial institutions, it had suffered significant losses in its manpower and material possessions during the decade of war. By 1822 there were ten dioceses but only four had bishops, and from a total of 4,229 in 1810 the secular clergy had decreased to 3,487. The male regulars had decreased from 3,112 in 1810 to approximately 2,000 by the end of 1821 and the number of monasteries from 208 to 153. In sum, the total number of clergy fell from 9,439 to 7,500 and the number of parishes also declined. Church revenues, particularly from tithes, showed a substantial fall. In the archbishopric of Mexico, the tithe income was reduced from 510,081 pesos in 1810 to 232,948 pesos in 1821 and in the dioceses of Michoacán, from 500,000 pesos to 200,000 pesos by 1826.

The tithe figures reflect the general economic decline which had taken place. The statistics provided by the amount of coinage minted indicate that mining decreased by more than a half from a yearly average of $22\frac{1}{2}$ million pesos in 1800–9 to approximately 10 million pesos in 1820 and 1822. (In 1821 only about 6 million pesos were minted.) There is no reliable information available on agriculture and manufacturing. Cereal production may have recovered by 1820, but sugar cane and other farming sectors remained depressed. Manufacturing output may have declined by as much as a half and public finances were reduced by a similar proportion. Government revenues in 1822 amounted to over 9 million pesos but expenditure rose to 13 million pesos, leaving a deficit of 4 million pesos. The public or national debt had shown a marked increase from 20 million pesos in 1808 to 35 million pesos in 1814 and 45 million pesos by 1822.

It was against this background of economic recession and budget deficit that the constitutional congress assembled in the capital on 24 February 1822. To Iturbide's unpleasant surprise, most of the deputies were either 'bourbonists', that is, pro-Spanish monarchists, or republicans. They were in dispute with him over several matters from the very first day and it was against a background of rapidly deteriorating relations between Iturbide and the deputies that the Spanish rejection of the Córdoba agreement became known. Until that moment, Spain, the mother country with which the bonds of kinship and religion remained strong, had still been venerated by almost everyone. Now Spain denied freedom to her daughter country. The ensuing resentment and disappointment quickly gave rise to the feeling that there was no reason why Mexico should not have a monarch of its own choosing. Spain, by its refusal to accept the reality of independence and its rejection of the opportunity to keep Mexico within the Bourbon dynasty, played into the hands of Iturbide. On the night of 18 May 1822, the local army garrison proclaimed him Emperor Agustín I and on the next morning, under considerable military and popular pressure, congress accepted the situation and acknowledged its new monarch. Since Spain had rejected the Córdoba treaty, said deputy Valentín Gómez Farías, a physician and future liberal leader, Mexico was free to determine its own destiny. In the absence of the archbishop who declined to anoint the new ruler, Iturbide was crowned by the president of the congress on 21 July in the capital's magnificent cathedral.

Iturbide's empire was not to last. From the outset, there were basic obstacles to its survival. The Mexican nobility yearned for a European prince and looked with disdain on Iturbide, the son of a merchant; *hacendados* and traders, most of whom were Spanish born, hoped for a European prince to deliver them from forced loans and other fiscal burdens; and finally there was a strong body of republicans which included some prominent journalists, lawyers and progressive clergy. One such cleric was Servando Teresa de Mier who, after an adventurous life in Europe and the United States, had been imprisoned in the dungeons of the San Juan de Ulúa fortress. Its shrewd Spanish commander released him at the end of May and Servando soon occupied a seat in congress. Both within that assembly and in the public arena outside, he was to propagate his republican ideas with great vigour.

It is not surprising, therefore, that Iturbide's fall was even faster than his elevation. The bourbonists charged him with having violated his promise to offer the throne to a European prince. Iturbide's own arbitrary acts encouraged the spread of republican ideas which until then had by and large been restricted to intellectuals. Ambitious army officers were also discontented; while a foreign prince might be tolerable, they found it difficult to accept one of their own kind; if an imported prince was not to be had, then the solution was a republic, which was at least a system in which they could become presidents. Opposition to Iturbide grew and in an atmosphere of restricted freedom of expression, conspiracies mushroomed. By 26 August, just five weeks after his coronation, Iturbide had already imprisoned nineteen members of congress and several army officers. On 31 October, he dissolved the troublesome congress altogether. He weakened his position even further by a series of confiscatory fiscal measures and the merchants who suffered, for the most part Spanish, turned to the bourbonists for support.

The port of Veracruz was especially important to Iturbide's security. It was situated opposite the island fortress of San Juan de Ulúa which remained in Spanish hands.[2] A rebellion might be started there, with Spanish acquiescence if not support, and in the event of failure, rebel leaders could take refuge in the fortress. Distrusting the ambitious young military commander of Veracruz, a twenty-eight-year old colonel, Antonio López de Santa Anna, Iturbide summoned him to Jalapa, a town in the mountains over a hundred kilometres from the port, where he relieved him of his command and ordered him to report to Mexico City. Santa Anna had not the slightest intention of obeying the emperor. After galloping all night, he returned to his barracks the following morning and, before news of his removal reached Veracruz, on the afternoon of the same day, 2 December 1822, he publicly accused Iturbide of tyranny. He proclaimed a republic, calling for the reinstallation of congress and

[2] The Spaniards in San Juan de Ulúa did not capitulate until 1825.

the formation of a constitution based on 'Religion, Independence and Union', that is, the same three guarantees of the Iguala manifesto which he claimed had been infringed by the emperor. He also made a bid for the support of influential local Spanish merchants at Veracruz by calling for peace and commerce with the mother country.[3]

Within a few days, however, Santa Anna had changed his mind about his hasty profession of republican faith. In 1822, Mexican republicans did not often use the term 'republic' in their propaganda; instead, they spoke of Liberty, Nation and the Sovereignty of Congress. A decade previously, Hidalgo had not formally proclaimed independence and it had taken several years for the idea of a Mexico not subject to the king of Spain to take root. Now, similarly, the word republic also sounded too revolutionary. Hence Santa Anna revised his position and, four days later, he issued a more moderate and detailed manifesto. This document was probably drawn up by the former minister of the newly independent republic of Colombia to Mexico, Miguel Santa María (a native of Veracruz), who had been expelled by Iturbide for participating in a republican conspiracy and was at that time in Veracruz awaiting a ship to take him home. Without mentioning a republic, the manifesto called for the removal of the emperor. 'The true liberty of the fatherland' meant a republic to the republicans and a constitutional monarchy to bourbonists and Spaniards. Thus both factions were urged to unite against Iturbide. The insistence on the Iguala guarantees had the same purpose: 'independence' was essential to Mexicans, 'union' to Spaniards, and 'religion' to both. It is not known whether Santa Anna was sincere about the republic or whether he had imperial ambitions of his own.

A fortuitous circumstance helped Santa Anna: the inveterate guerrilla fighter, Guadalupe Victoria, who had recently escaped from prison, chanced to be in Veracruz and he signed Santa Anna's manifesto of 6 December 1822. Thus Santa Anna, who had been a royalist officer during the war of independence and until now a supporter of Iturbide, secured the aid of a famous insurgent general who was already suspected of republican inclinations. A few weeks later, Generals Bravo and Guerrero, former comrades-in-arms of Morelos, escaped from Mexico City and once back in their own region of the *tierra caliente*, they declared their support for the Veracruz uprising. 'We are not against the established system of government', they declared: 'we do not intend to

---

[3] The proclamation is reproduced in C. M. Bustamante, *Diario Histórico de México, I, 1822–1823* (Zacatecas, 1896), 16–17.

become republicans; far from that, we only seek our liberty.' Such denials, however, seem to confirm the impression that they were indeed republicans, but their own support was among Indian peasants who were held to be not only religious but also monarchist. Finally, the majority of the army in which the officers – many of them Spaniards by birth – had been royalists and later supporters of Iturbide succumbed to the influence of two former Mexican liberal deputies to the Spanish Cortes, the priest Miguel Ramos Arizpe and José Mariano Michelena. The army 'pronounced' itself against Iturbide. The emperor abdicated on 19 March 1823, and the reassembled congress promptly appointed a provisional triumvirate consisting of Generals Victoria, Bravo and Negrete, the first two of whom were generally thought to be republicans. On 8 April, congress nullified the Iguala manifesto as well as the Córdoba treaty and decreed that Mexico was henceforth free to adopt whatever constitutional system it wished. The republic was a fact.

Thus Santa Anna had unleashed a movement which brought down Iturbide's empire and ended with the establishment of a republic. Even if the new political system was conceived by intellectuals, it was the army which had converted it into reality and at the same time become its master. The speed with which it succeeded pointed the way to future uprisings by dissatisfied military officers.

Bearing in mind Iturbide's past services to the nation's independence, congress did not at first deal with him harshly. He was offered a generous allowance provided that he resided in Italy. But the former emperor was not happy in exile. Misled by rumours of support, he returned in July 1824, landing near Tampico on the Gulf Coast, and unaware that, during his absence, congress had declared him a traitor. He was arrested and executed within a few days of his arrival.

Iturbide's inability to introduce some measure of order into the Treasury had been an important cause of his downfall. The triumvirate applied itself at once to the task of restoring public confidence and the improved atmosphere made it possible to obtain two loans on the London market: 16 million pesos were borrowed at the beginning of 1824 with Goldschmitt and Company and a similar amount with Barclay and Company a few months later.[4] Mexico thereby assumed a burden of 32 million pesos in foreign debt, but because of a low contract price and bankers' deductions, only about 10 million pesos was in fact received.

[4] Throughout the period examined in this chapter one peso equalled one U.S. dollar.

The government originally expected to use this money for long-term improvements, but when it finally arrived it was quickly absorbed by current expenses such as salaries of public employees, notably the military. Nevertheless, the proceeds of these loans seem to have been a stabilizing factor in the first years of the republic and in 1823–4 the foreign debt which they entailed did not seem excessive.[5] With British interest in the mineral resources of the country very evident, Mexico was optimistic about its future. During the years 1823 to 1827 the British invested more than 12 million pesos in Mexican mining ventures, especially silver-mining companies. Thus a total of well over 20 million pesos were injected into the ailing economy.

The person who was most instrumental in bringing British capital to Mexico was Lucas Alamán, who from April 1823 was Minister of the Interior and of Foreign Affairs (one of four Cabinet members). The brilliant son of a Mexican mining family which had acquired a Spanish title of nobility, Alamán had returned from a prolonged stay in Europe shortly after Iturbide's fall from power. As Marquis of San Clemente, he had perhaps dreamt of becoming a minister in the court of a Mexican Bourbon monarch, but the end of Iturbide's empire was not followed by any renewal of attempts to offer the throne to a European prince. On the contrary, it meant the end of serious monarchist plans for many years to come. Alamán entered, therefore, into the service of a republican government.

With the republic now taken for granted and monarchism being viewed almost as treason, new labels began to be adopted. Former supporters of a Mexican empire with a European prince at its head became centralist republicans, advocating a strong, centralized régime, reminiscent of the viceroyalty. Most of the republican opponents of Iturbide became federalists, supporting a federation of states on the United States model. The old destructive struggle between royalists and independents, who had in 1821 become bourbonists and republicans respectively and then temporary allies against Iturbide, re-emerged in 1823 under different slogans. After Iturbide's abdication power fell briefly into the hands of the bourbonist faction, but then a perhaps unexpected turn of events had helped the republican cause. Blaming the bourbonists for having overthrown Iturbide, the former emperor's supporters now joined the republicans and the elections for the new constitutional congress produced a majority for the federalists.

[5] There was at this time an internal public debt of 45 million pesos.

The constitutional congress met in November 1823 and almost a year later adopted a federal constitution which closely resembled that of the United States. The Mexican constitution of 1824 divided the country into nineteen states which were to elect their own governors and legislatures, and four territories which were to be under the jurisdiction of the national congress. The usual division of powers – executive, legislative and judicial – was retained but in one important respect the Mexican constitution differed from its northern model: it solemnly proclaimed that: 'The religion of the Mexican nation is and shall be perpetually the Catholic, Apostolic, Roman religion. The nation protects it with wise and just laws and prohibits the exercise of any other.'[6] Of the three guarantees in the Iguala manifesto only two remained; independence and religion. The third, union with Spaniards which implied a monarchy with a European prince, had been replaced by the federal republic.

In contrast to the insurgent constitution of Apatzingán in 1814 which specified that the law should be the same for everyone, the 1824 charter did not mention equality before the law. This omission was certainly not intended to safeguard the interests of the small, if not insignificant, Mexican nobility which only comprised a few dozen families. Its significance was much greater because it permitted the continuation of the *fueros* or legal immunities and exemptions from civil courts enjoyed by the clergy and the military. These privileges had, of course, existed before independence but then both the Church and the army had been subject to royal authority on which civil obedience to laws depended and which had not been seriously questioned for three centuries. With the supreme regal authority gone, and in the absence of a strong nobility or bourgeoisie, the vacuum was at once filled by the popular heroes of the victorious army. Freed of royal restraint, the army became the arbiter of power in the new nation. Federalist or centralist, a general was to be president of the republic.

Mexico also adopted the United States practice of electing a president and a vice-president. The two leading executives could be men of different or opposing political parties with the obvious danger of rivalry continuing between them while in office. Indeed, the first president was a liberal federalist, General Guadalupe Victoria, a man of obscure origins, and the vice-president a conservative centralist, General Nicolás Bravo, a wealthy landowner. Both men had been

[6] Felipe Tena Ramírez, *Leyes fundamentales de México, 1808–1973* (Mexico, 1973), 168.

guerrilla fighters for independence but by 1824 they belonged to two hostile factions. Political parties were as yet unknown but the two groups used the masonic movement as a focal point for their activities and propaganda. The centralists tended to become masons of the Scottish Rite while the federalists, with the help of the United States minister to the new republic, Joel R. Poinsett, became members of the York Rite. The lodges provided the base from which the conservative and liberal parties would arise almost a quarter of a century later.

President Victoria sought to maintain in his cabinet a balance between the centralists and the federalists in the hope of keeping some semblance of unity in the national government. Nevertheless, the most able of the pro-centralist ministers, Lucas Alamán, was, as early as 1825, quickly forced out of office by federalist attacks. In the following year, after a long and bitterly fought electoral campaign, the federalists gained a significant majority in Congress, particularly in the chamber of deputies. Tension increased in January 1827 with the discovery of a conspiracy to restore Spanish rule. Spain was the only important country not to have recognized Mexican independence and with many wealthy Spanish merchants still resident in the new republic, as well as others who retained their posts in the government bureaucracy, it was not difficult to incite popular hatred against everything Spanish. Mexican nationalism became a convenient and effective weapon used by the federalists to attack the centralists who were widely believed to favour Spain. Fighting on the defensive and using religion as a counter to nationalism, the centralists took revenge for Alamán's dismissal in a campaign against the American minister Poinsett who was a Protestant. As the well-intentional but ineffectual President Victoria was unable to control the ever more aggressive federalists, the centralist leader and vice-president, Bravo, finally resorted to rebellion against the government. Bravo was promptly defeated by his former comrade-in-arms, General Guerrero, and sent into exile. Both had fought the Spaniards side by side under the command of Morelos, but Guerrero had chosen the federalist cause which allowed him to keep control of his native *tierra caliente*.

The main political issue was the forthcoming presidential election, scheduled for 1828. Bravo's revolt spoiled the chances of the centralists who were unable even to present a candidate. Then the federalists split into moderates and radicals. The centralists or conservatives chose to rally behind the moderate candidate, General Manuel Gómez Pedraza, the Minister of War in Victoria's cabinet and a former royalist officer and then supporter of Iturbide. His opponent was General Guerrero, nominally the leader of the federalists but believed by many to be little more than a figurehead controlled by the liberal journalist and former senator for Yucatán, Lorenzo Zavala. Gómez Pedraza was elected president and General Anastasio Bustamante vice-president, but Guerrero refused to recognize the result and, on his behalf, Zavala organized a successful revolution in the capital in December 1828. Mere formalities followed. Guerrero was duly 'elected' in January 1829 and received the office from Victoria on 1 April. Constitutional order had collapsed after only four years.

Guerrero, a popular hero of the war against Spain, was a symbol of Mexican resistance to everything Spanish. The expulsion of Spaniards still living in the republic was quickly decreed[7] and preparations to resist a long-expected Spanish invasion force were begun. Guerrero's minister of finance, Zavala, found the Treasury almost empty and set about raising revenue. Obtaining some funds by selling Church property nationalized by the colonial authorities, he also decreed a progressive income tax, a unique attempt of its kind in this period of Mexico's history. His moves against ecclesiastical property and his well-known friendship with Poinsett made him unpopular with the Church and his attempts at social reform and at seeking support among the lower classes made him hated by all the propertied groups.

The long-awaited invasion by Spanish troops came at the end of July 1829, and it served to cause a temporary lull in the factional political conflict as the nation rallied to the call for unity. General Santa Anna hurried from his Veracruz headquarters to Tampico where the invading force had landed, and he promptly defeated it. He became an instant war hero and the country enjoyed the exhilaration of victory. But the euphoria was brief and with the external threat overcome, the Catholic and conservative faction soon renewed their campaign against the Guerrero administration. It did not yet dare to touch the president, still the hero of independence and now the saviour of the nation from Spanish aggression. Instead, the targets became the Protestant Poinsett and the democrat Zavala. The attacks on them became so fierce that Zavala was obliged to resign on 2 November and Poinsett, an easy, expendable scapegoat, left Mexico soon afterwards.

Deprived of the support of Zavala and Poinsett, Guerrero lost his

---

[7] The expulsion of certain groups of Spaniards had already been decreed in 1827.

office the following month when Vice-president Bustamante led a revolt with the support of General Bravo, already returned from his recent exile. Guerrero retired, unmolested, to his hacienda in the south, far from the central government's control. On 1 January 1830, Bustamante, acting as president, formed his cabinet. In contrast with the governments of 1823–7, which had tried to keep an uneasy balance of federalists and centralists, and with the populist inclined Guerrero régime, the new administration was openly conservative. The leading cabinet member was Alamán, once again occupying the key post of Minister of Internal and Foreign Affairs. He began to implement his political programme at once: opposition was suppressed after years of complete freedom; for the first time since Iturbide's fall, the central government sought to curb the states in several of which new, liberal ideas were rampant; property rights which in the last analysis could be traced to the Spanish conquest were safeguarded, and the Church's privileges were reaffirmed. Alamán evidently had in mind a settlement with Spain and with the Holy See.

Some of these and other developments were not to Guerrero's liking and he again revolted in the south at the head of a band of guerrilla fighters. General Bravo chose to remain loyal to Bustamante and Alamán, and he was appointed to lead the army against Guerrero who was captured in January 1831 and executed by order of the central government a few weeks later.

The cruel treatment of Guerrero requires an explanation. Bravo had been defeated in 1827 but was merely exiled and there were other similar cases. It is reasonable to ask, therefore, why in the case of Guerrero the government resorted to the ultimate penalty. The clue is provided by Zavala who, writing several years later, noted that Guerrero was of mixed blood and that the opposition to his presidency came from the great landowners, generals, clerics and Spaniards resident in Mexico. These people could not forget the war of independence with its threat of social and racial subversion. Despite his revolutionary past, the wealthy creole Bravo belonged to this 'gentleman's club', as did the cultured creole, Zavala, even with his radicalism. Hence Guerrero's execution was perhaps a warning to men considered as socially and ethnically inferior not to dare to dream of becoming president.

The conservative government of Bustamante was not negative and reactionary in everything it did. The country's economy and finances were improved as a result of a variety of measures. Since the end of 1827 when the civil conflict had begun to emerge Mexico had been unable to pay interest on the two foreign loans contracted in London. Now it was agreed with bondholders that the debt arrears, amounting to more than 4 million pesos, should be capitalized. Confidence was thus restored at the price of increasing the capital debt, but there was probably no other solution. Silver-mining remained in a depressed condition as a result of the overexpansion of previous years, and of military and civil disturbances. There was not much that could be done at the time to revive the industry and Alamán turned his attention to other spheres of economic activity. For example, he established a government bank which was to finance the introduction of cotton spinning and weaving machines and he prohibited the import of English cottons. The bank's funds were to come from high protectionist tariffs. Money was lent to Mexican and foreign merchants and financiers interested in becoming manufacturers. Machines were ordered in the United States and the first cotton-spinning mills began to operate in 1833. By this time, the Bustamante–Alamán government was no longer in power, but Alamán had laid the foundations of a revolution in the textile industry which, once started, continued to grow while the governments around it changed. As a result of his initiatives, a decade later Mexico had some fifty factories which could reasonably supply the mass of the population with cheap cotton cloth. The industry was especially prominent in the traditional textile city of Puebla and in the cotton-growing state of Veracruz where water power was abundant. The rate of growth can be seen in the following figures: in 1838, the factories spun 63,000 lb of yarn and in 1844 over 10,000,000 lb: in 1837 they wove 45,000 bolts of cloth and in 1845, 656,500. Thereafter the growth was slow. Alamán did not restrict his attention to textiles but he failed to accomplish any such spectacular results in, for example, agriculture which, although a devout Roman Catholic himself, he had to acknowledge was severely hampered by the ecclesiastical tithe.

Bustamante was not strong enough to impose a permanent centralized republic and rival political groups soon emerged. Francisco García, governor of the silver-mining state of Zacatecas, had carefully developed a powerful civilian militia, and he decided to challenge the pro-clerical regime in the capital. His friend, the senator and former supporter of Iturbide, Valentín Gómez Farías, suggested that the state sponsor an essay competition on the respective rights of Church and State in relation to property. The winning entry, submitted in December 1831 by an impecunious professor of theology, José María Luis Mora, justified the disentailment of ecclesiastical property and thus provided a theoretical basis for an anti-clerical, liberal ideology and movement. The timing was propitious. With the defeat of Guerrero and Zavala, the rights of private property had been definitively safeguarded. Hence there was no real danger that an attack on Church property might develop into a radical assault on property in general. The essence of liberalism lay precisely in the destruction of Church property combined with a strengthening of private property.

Mora was a theoretician rather than a man of action and it fell to Gómez Farías to organize the opposition against Bustamante. Since the Zacatecas militia of volunteers was merely a local force, he needed an ally in the professional army. General Santa Anna had been in revolt against Bustamante since January 1832. His personal ideology was obscure, but in the public mind he was widely associated with Guerrero whom he had consistently supported. Here, therefore, was an opportunity for him to benefit from the unpopularity of Guerrero's execution. Furthermore, as he was still a national hero, having reaped the glory from the defeat of the Spanish invasion of 1829, he could seek to take Guerrero's place as the popular favourite. The combination of Gómez Farías's liberal campaign and Santa Anna's military revolt forced Bustamante to dismiss Alamán and his Minister of War, José Antonio Facio, the two men who were widely held to have been responsible for Guerrero's death. Such cabinet changes were not sufficient and by the end of 1832, Bustamante was obliged to admit defeat. As the new Minister of Finance in the interim administration, Gómez Farías took control of the government in the capital. Zavala, who had returned to Mexico after more than two years in the United States, was not offered a cabinet post; his brand of populism was now replaced by a middle class anti-clericalism and he had to be satisfied with the governorship of the state of Mexico. In March 1833, Santa Anna was elected president and Gómez Farías, vice-president, with their term of office beginning formally on 1 April. Gómez Farías was eager to introduce liberal reforms and Santa Anna, for the time being, preferred to leave the exercise of power to his vice-president while remaining on his Veracruz estate and awaiting the reaction of public opinion.

Freed of presidential restraint, Gómez Farías initiated a broad reform programme, particularly in respect of the Church. The obligation under civil law to pay tithes was removed and payment became entirely voluntary. Then civil enforcement of monastic vows was removed and friars and nuns were permitted to leave the monastery or nunnery at their convenience. All transfers of property belonging to the regular orders since independence were also declared null and void. While the first law affected mainly the bishops and canons, whose income came mostly from the tithe revenues, the last two decrees were intended to bring about the eventual disappearance of the regular orders. The disposal of monastic real estate was already under discussion in congress and the sale of such property was declared illegal to prevent the Church from selling to trusted persons and thus evade the disentailment. Even so, the liberals were not to see the disentailment implemented for many years to come.

Gómez Farías, his cabinet and the liberal congress also attempted to reduce the size of the army and it was not long before senior military officers and the higher clergy were imploring Santa Anna to intervene. At last, when several army officers and their troops revolted in May 1834 and when the rebellion spread, he chose to leave his hacienda and assume his presidential authority in the capital. The consequences were soon apparent. The reforms were repealed and, in January 1835, Gómez Farías was stripped of his vice-presidential office. Two months later, a new congress approved a motion to amend the 1824 constitution with a view to introducing a centralist republic. Well aware that the bastion of federalism was Zacatecas, Santa Anna invaded the state, defeated its militia and deposed Governor García. On 23 October 1835 Congress delivered a provisional centralist constitution which replaced the states by departments, the governors of which would henceforth be appointed by the president of the republic.

Santa Anna was not, however, to complete the establishment of a strong, centralized régime. Not long after the defeat of Zacatecas, an unforeseen and, for Mexico as well as for Santa Anna, a most unwelcome complication arose in the north. The province of Texas resisted the move towards centralism and finally resorted to arms. After colonists had driven out the northern Mexican forces Santa Anna decided to lead in person what he regarded as a mere punitive expedition. Before leaving Mexico City, he told the French and British ministers that if he found that the United States government was aiding the rebels, 'he could continue the march of his army to Washington and place upon its Capitol the Mexican flag'.[8] Santa Anna succeeded in capturing San Antonio at the beginning of March 1836, but was decisively defeated and taken prisoner

[8] W. H. Callcott, *Santa Anna, the story of an enigma who once was Mexico* (Hamden, Conn., 1964), 126.

the following month. By this time, the Texans had already declared their independence. The vice-president of the new Texan republic was none other than the liberal from Yucatán, Lorenzo Zavala, but he died six months later. In the hands of the Texans as a prisoner of war, Santa Anna signed a treaty granting Texas its independence and recognizing the Rio Grande as the boundary between the two countries. He was subsequently released and in February 1837 he returned to Mexico in disgrace, for the Mexican government had meanwhile repudiated the treaty and refused to relinquish its claim to the former province.

To some extent, Mexico managed to balance its defeat in the north with a success on the European diplomatic front: Spain and the Holy See finally recognized the nation's independence at the end of 1836. At about the same time, Congress approved a detailed centralist constitution. In the hope of giving the country much needed stability, this increased the presidential term from four to eight years, and it seemed for a time that a period of peace could be anticipated. The hopes were premature. Bustamante was returned to office as the new president, but those conservatives who remembered his strong régime of 1830–2 were disappointed. The two leading centralists, Santa Anna and Alamán, had been discredited, and without their support or pressure Bustamante showed an increasing inclination to lean towards the federalists who agitated for the return of the 1824 constitution. A conservative politician warned the president that the clergy and the wealthy classes might feel compelled to 'deliver themselves into the hands of General Santa Anna'.

It was a French invasion of Veracruz in 1838, undertaken to exact compensation for damages to French-owned property, which gave Santa Anna the opportunity to regain popular esteem. He marched to Veracruz and his brave conduct once again made him a national hero. The following year, he was appointed interim president while Bustamante left the capital to fight federalist rebels. A few months later, however, he returned the office to its legitimate holder and retired to his rural retreat to wait for favourable developments. He did not have long to wait. Bustamante's popular support was dwindling, and in July 1840 he was captured by federalist army units. They summoned Gómez Farías – who on his return from exile had been in and out of prison – and proclaimed a federal republic. The uprising was suppressed after several days' street fighting and Bustamante was released. In a reaction against the growing chaos, the writer José María Gutiérrez Estrada advocated a monarchy with a European prince as the solution for the ills of Mexico. Gutiérrez Estrada, like Zavala, was a native of Yucatán, although he took the opposite road. While Yucatán, encouraged by the success of Texas, was fighting its own battle against Mexican centralism, he concluded that the centralist republic was too weak to impose order. Although few shared Gutiérrez Estrada's monarchist opinions, Bustamante had clearly lost the support of both radical federalists and extreme conservatives. Santa Anna was also unhappy with the 1836 constitution which had introduced a curious 'supreme conservative power' as a restraint on the power of the president. Finally, Yucatán declared its independence and Bustamante proved unable to bring it back into the republic, either by negotiation or by force of arms. An increase in taxes, tariffs and prices served only to spread the mood of discontent even wider. The country was ripe for another revolution.

Thus, in August 1841, General Mariano Paredes Arrillaga, commander of Guadalajara, called for the removal of Bustamante and amendments to the 1836 constitution to be enacted by a new constitutional congress. He was promptly supported by the army, and Santa Anna stepped in as an intermediary, becoming provisional president in October 1841. Another former royalist officer, General Paredes was known as a conservative and the new situation constituted, in effect, a centralist revolt against centralism. Santa Anna was, however, too shrewd to let himself be tied to any one party. He needed funds for the reconquest of Texas and Yucatán, as well as for his own ostentatious behaviour, and only the Church could provide them. As a way of putting pressure on the clergy, he offered the portfolio of finance to Francisco García, the former liberal governor of Zacatecas whom he himself had deposed in 1835. The elections to the new congress were sufficiently free to produce a majority of federalist or liberal deputies many of whom were young and were to achieve prominence years later. In 1842 they were obliged to labour on the new constitution in the shadow of Santa Anna's presidency. Nevertheless they managed to produce two drafts. Both still recognized the Roman Catholic faith as the only permitted religion and, in order not to annoy Santa Anna, they spoke of departments rather than states. The distinctive feature of the second draft, however, was the inclusion of a declaration of human rights, or 'guarantees'; in particular, it specified that the law should be the same for all and that no special law courts should exist. In other words, immunities from civil law should be abolished and all government monopolies were to end. Moreover, education was to be free.

In December 1842 the army disbanded Congress while it was discussing the constitutional reforms and, in the absence of Santa Anna, acting

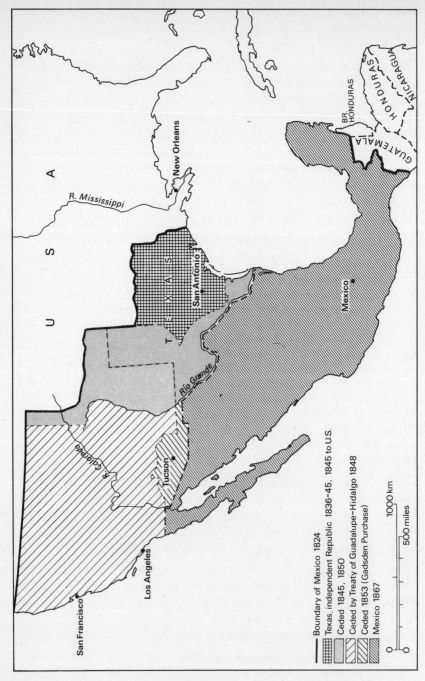

R. Mississippi

New Orleans

U S A

TEXAS

San Antonio

Rio Grande

R. Colorado

Tucson

Los Angeles

San Francisco

Mexico

BR. HONDURAS

HONDURAS

NICARAGUA

GUATEMALA

Boundary of Mexico 1824

Texas, independent Republic 1836–45, 1845 to U.S.

Ceded 1845, 1850

Ceded by Treaty of Guadalupe–Hidalgo 1848

Ceded 1853 (Gadsden Purchase)

Mexico 1867

1000 km

500 miles

Mexican territories ceded to the United States

President Bravo appointed a committee of leading conservative land-owners, clerics, army officers and lawyers which a few months later had devised a constitution acceptable to Santa Anna. The document was centralist and conservative, and human rights, especially equality, were not mentioned. Presidential powers, however, were enhanced by the omission of the 'supreme conservative power' introduced in the 1836 constitution. The president's power was not to be absolute, for although the authors of the new charter wanted a strong head of state, they did not want a despot.

The new Congress proved little more tractable than the disbanded one and when Santa Anna's fiscal extortions became unbearable, General Paredes, known for his honesty in financial matters, rebelled in Guadala-jara. The Chamber of Deputies in the capital showed sympathy with his movement and other army units soon declared their support. Santa Anna was overthrown at the end of 1844, imprisoned and then exiled for life. Congress elected General José Joaquín Herrera, reputed to be a moderate, to the presidency.

This latest round of political upheavals in the capital had taken place against the background of deteriorating relations between Mexico and the United States. In 1843 Great Britain and France had arranged a truce between Mexico and Texas, but the truce did not lead to recognition of Texan independence by the Mexicans. On the contrary, insisting that Texas was still part of Mexico, Santa Anna announced that its annexation by the United States, which was favoured by many Americans, would be tantamount to a declaration of war.

Annexation was in fact approved by the United States Congress in February 1845, and thereafter the pace of events quickened. Mexican public opinion, both conservative and liberal, was inflamed against the aggressive politicians in Washington, but the new president, General Herrera, soon found that the financial and military state of the country made resistance hopeless and that help from Europe would not be forthcoming. Hence he attempted to negotiate a settlement. In the atmosphere of the time such a move was seen as treasonable by the Mexican people. In December 1845 General Paredes rebelled again on the pretext that 'territory of the Republic was to be alienated, staining forever national honour with an everlasting infamy in consenting to deal with the perfidious cabinet of the United States'.[9] He demanded the

[9] T. E. Cotner, *The military and political career of José Joaquín Herrera, 1792–1854* (Austin, Texas, 1949), 146.

removal of Herrera and another extraordinary congress to produce a new constitution. The army units in the capital obeyed the call, Herrera resigned and Paredes became president at the beginning of January 1846. At that time, the 1843 conservative constitution was in force and in seeking to change it, Paredes, a Catholic conservative, was clearly not looking towards a liberal republic. He gave an inkling of his views when he proclaimed: 'We seek a strong, stable power which can protect society; but to govern that society, we do not want either the despotic dictatorship of a soldier or the degrading yoke of the orator.'[10] It soon became apparent that he meant monarchy and, under his protection, Lucas Alamán publicly revived the central idea of Iturbide's Plan of Iguala, that of setting up a Mexican monarchy with a European prince on the throne. Given the international situation, such a monarchy could have been a bulwark against United States expansion, but it should by then have been clear to every educated Mexican that a monarchy had to stand on the shoulders of a strong and numerous nobility. A member of one of the few Mexican noble families, Alamán had overlooked this pre-condition of a monarchy, although it is possible that he expected it to be supported by European armies. He also seemed to have ignored the fact that the ruling group in Mexico, the army, was republican.

In any event, there was simply no time to import a European prince and thus obtain help against the United States. Hostilities broke out in April 1846 and in two or three months the United States army had defeated the Mexican forces and occupied parts of northern Mexico. Paredes' inability to defend the country and his monarchist sympathies swayed public opinion to the other extreme; perhaps, it was thought, the old federalist Gómez Farías and the once-national-hero Santa Anna, both known to hate the United States, might be more effective. Santa Anna, in his Cuban exile, had foreseen this possible reaction as early as April when he wrote to Gómez Farías, then in exile in New Orleans. As if nothing had happened between them, Santa Anna suggested in his customary verbose style that they should work together; that the army and the people should unite; and that he now accepted the principles of freedom. Possibly thinking that the army needed Santa Anna and that he could get rid of him later, Gómez Farías agreed. It was tacitly understood that Santa Anna would again become president and Gómez Farías vice-president.

---

[10] J. F. Ramírez, *Mexico during the war with the United States*, ed., W. V. Scholes, trans., E. B. Scherr (Columbia, Missouri, 1950), 38.

Gómez Farías departed for Mexico and at the beginning of August, aided by army units headed by General José Mariano Salas, the capital was taken and the constitution of 1824 restored. The United States government then permitted Santa Anna to pass through the blockade and land at Veracruz – in the belief, perhaps, that with the fall of the extreme anti-American Paredes the war might be stopped or that Santa Anna would make peace on terms favourable to the United States, or that he would simply bring more chaos into the already chaotic Mexico. On 16 September 1846, the two contrasting heroes, Santa Anna and Gómez Farías, rode together through the capital in an open carriage, and their relationship was formalized in December when congress appointed Santa Anna president and Gómez Farías, vice-president.

Santa Anna soon left to lead the army, and Gómez Farías, to satisfy the pressing needs of the army, nationalized ecclesiastical properties to the value of 15 million pesos, approximately one-tenth of the Church's total wealth. As there was no time for their valuation, he then ordered the immediate confiscation and sale of Church assets estimated at 10 million pesos. The Church, of course, protested and a reactionary military revolt began in the capital towards the end of February 1847. Santa Anna returned on 21 March and a week later he repealed both confiscatory decrees but not without first receiving a promise from the Church authorities that they would guarantee a loan of a million and a half pesos. Santa Anna had evidently learned to use the liberals to blackmail the Church. The clergy complied, knowing that the loan would probably never be repaid. They did not have the ready cash, however, and the money was raised by the government selling short-term bonds at a discount to financiers with the guarantee that the Church would redeem them. As Gómez Farías resisted dismissal the vice-presidency was abolished on 1 April. This second partnership of the two leading politicians of the period was to be their last.

On 9 March, while the capital city was the theatre of civil war, the United States forces, under the command of General Winfield Scott, landed near Veracruz, and the port surrendered on 29 March. The invading forces took Puebla in May, and despite many acts of heroism by the city's inhabitants, the capital was occupied on 15 September. The following day, Santa Anna resigned as president (but not as commander-in-chief) and eventually left the country. Mexican resistance ended and the United States army did not proceed further inland. It set up a municipal council in the capital, consisting of prominent liberals, among them Miguel Lerdo who would achieve fame some years later, while it awaited the emergence of a Mexican government with which the peace negotiations could begin. With General Herrera holding together the remnants of the army, a new government was formed in non-occupied Toluca and later Querétaro under the presidency of Manuel de la Peña y Peña, the non-political chief justice of the Supreme Court. Anti-American liberals like Gómez Farías and, among the rising new generation, Melchor Ocampo, also to become famous in later years, would have no part in the new administration. Defeat was generally attributed to the incompetence and treason of Santa Anna. Some Mexicans blamed the 'colossus of the north'. Fifteen prominent men wrote thus in 1848: 'The Mexican Republic, to whom nature has been prodigal, and full of those elements which make a great and happy nation, had among other misfortunes of less account, the great one of being in the vicinity of a strong and energetic people.'[11] Not everybody looked for a scapegoat. One writer complained of 'the iniquitous and shameful rule the Americans have imposed on us', but he added, 'the sad thing about it is that the punishment has been deserved.'[12]

The United States army did its best to shorten the suffering and the humiliation of the Mexican people. The new government was contacted and a peace treaty negotiated and finally signed on 2 February 1848. Mexico forfeited what was already in fact lost: Texas, New Mexico and California. The Mexican negotiators, however, did obtain the return of much that the United States believed it had occupied on a permanent basis, like, for example, Lower California. Even so, the lost provinces amounted to about half of Mexico's territory, although they only contained between one and two per cent of its total population and had then few known natural resources. Hence their loss did not disrupt the Mexican economy, and Mexico was to receive an indemnity of 15 million dollars. Understandably, sections of Mexican society viewed the treaty as ignominious and its signatories as traitors, and some wished to wage a guerrilla war against the invaders. But reason prevailed. A reluctant congress finally ratified the treaty on 30 May and the occupation forces left shortly afterwards, to the mixed joy of the Mexican landed class which was by this time threatened by a social revolution.

---

[11] Ramón Alcaráz *et al.*, *Apuntes para la historia de la guerra entre México y los Estados Unidos* (Mexico, .848); Eng. trans., *The other side: or notes for the history of the war between Mexico and the United States* (New York, 1850), 1.
[12] Ramírez, *Mexico during the war*, 161.

In 1829, the United States' diplomat, Poinsett, had summed up the situation in the Mexican countryside with the following words:

Here therefore is wanting that portion of a community which forms the strength of every nation, a free peasantry. The Indians cannot as yet be regarded in that light. They are laborious, patient and submissive, but are lamentably ignorant. They are emerging slowly from the wretched state to which they had been reduced . . . At present seven-eighths of the population live in wretched hovels destitute of the most ordinary conveniences. Their only furniture a few coarse mats to sit and sleep on, their food Indian corn, pepper and pulse, and their clothing miserably coarse and scanty. It is not that the low price of labour prevents them from earning a more comfortable subsistence in spite of the numerous festivals in each year but they either gamble away their money or employ it in pageants of the Catholic Church . . . All these evils would be greatly mitigated by education.[13]

The condition of Indian peasants in Mexico remained the same in 1847. The rural areas consisted of haciendas, which may be described as large farming enterprises, settlements or estates, and Indian villages with communal lands. On the hacienda labourers were often bound to the estate by peonage or debt-servitude – a legacy of the colonial period. The peon in debt was not permitted to leave until he had paid it, or unless another *hacendado* paid it for him. In other words, rural labourers were bought and sold for the price of their debt. If a peon in debt fled, he could be hunted down, brought back and punished. This *de facto* peonage was typical of central Mexico. In the isolated Yucatán peninsula and in the thinly populated north legalized servitude still existed.

Melchor Ocampo was the first liberal *hacendado* to write on the sensitive subject of the Mexican rural labour system. In a short article published in 1844, he condemned peonage not only as immoral but as not conducive to progress. Ocampo wrote that he had cancelled the full debt of all his peons four times. If one of his labourers in debt fled from his farm, perhaps to find work with another *hacendado* offering higher wages, he claimed him only if he was guilty of a criminal offence. He ended by exhorting peons not to borrow money and employers to lend only in cases of emergency.

Recent research has shown that not all rural labourers owed money to their employers. On some haciendas, at least, a considerable number of workers owed nothing and there were even some to whom the hacienda owed money. The peons would usually withdraw this from what

[13] *Diplomatic correspondence of the United States concerning the Independence of the Latin-American Nations*, William R. Manning (ed.) (New York, 1925), III, 1673–6; reproduced in Lewis Hanke (ed.), *History of Latin American civilization*, II *The modern age* (London, 1967), 22–6.

amounted to a savings account to make purchases at the hacienda store. Finally, some *hacendados* either did not bother to denounce indebted fugitives to the authorities or were not successful in bringing them back.[14] Even if they owed nothing, the peons were not entirely free to leave their employment at will. Vagrancy laws, also inherited from the colonial period, made it difficult for landless peons to wander around the country looking for another or better job. It was safer to attach oneself to a hacienda and stay there permanently. Curiously, it was to the peon's advantage to borrow as much and work as little as possible because then he could never be dismissed. This was another feature of the system specifically criticized by Ocampo.

Indians in the villages were better off because they could work as seasonal labourers on the neighbouring hacienda. This was a convenient arrangement because few peasants had enough land to support themselves throughout the year. They were free men, but, on the other hand, if their harvest failed they starved. One advantage of peonage was that the peons could always borrow maize from the *hacendado*.

There were several other rural groups who must be distinguished from peons and village peasants. These were squatters, renters, tenants, or sharecroppers who lived within the bounds of the hacienda, usually in small settlements. Rarely able to pay rent in cash, they were often forced to pay with their own or their sons' labour, and, if they resisted, their animals, perhaps a few head of cattle, might be confiscated. They could also, of course, be evicted although this was probably rare because it was to the landowner's convenience to have them there as potential peons. The *hacendado* was obviously a lord on his territory. The social and ethnic inequalities were accepted by all and peons, peasants and tenants do not seem to have resented their inferior status. Their protests were restricted to the abuses of the powerful against which it was difficult, if not impossible, to find redress through normal channels.

Special conditions prevailed in Yucatán. The local *hacendados* were successfully growing *henequén* – sisal, a fibre-producing agave – for export and had few ties with central Mexico.[15] Quite naturally, Yucatán

---

14 See J. Bazant, *Cinco haciendas mexicanas. Tres siglos de vida rural en San Luis Potosí, 1600–1910* (Mexico, 1975), 103–8; *idem, A concise history of Mexico from Hidalgo to Cárdenas 1805–1940* (Cambridge, 1977), 64–6, 88–9; *idem,* 'Landlord, labourer and tenant in San Luis Potosí, northern Mexico, 1822–1910', in *Land and labour in Latin America,* Kenneth Duncan and Ian Rutledge (eds.) (Cambridge, 1977), 59–82.

15 Howard Cline, 'The henequén episode in Yucatán', *Interamerican Economic Affairs,* 2/2 (1948), 30–51.

embraced federalism and in 1839 rebelled against Mexico with the help of Mayan soldiers, becoming for all practical purposes an independent state. In 1840, the American traveller, John L. Stephens, found the Indian peons submissive and humble. Two years later, after his second visit, he warned:

What the consequences may be of finding themselves, after ages of servitude, once more in the possession of arms and in increasing knowledge of their physical strength is a question of momentous import to the people of that country, the solution of which no man can foretell.[16]

Stephen's forebodings were borne out five years later. In return for the service of Indian peasants as soldiers, the whites had promised to abolish or at least reduce parochial fees, to abolish the capitation tax payable by all Indian adults, and to give them free use of public and communal lands. None of these promises were fulfilled and the Mayas rebelled in the summer of 1847 with the aim of exterminating or at least expelling the white population. The revolt soon developed into full-scale war, known ever since as the War of the Castes. Mexico had just been defeated by the United States and, even had it wished to do so, was unable to send an army to Yucatán to suppress the revolt. In the cruel war which followed, the Indians almost succeeded in driving their enemies into the sea. In their despair, the whites went as far as to offer Yucatán to Great Britain, the United States, or, indeed, any country willing to protect them.

While Yucatán was in the throes of this race war, Indian tribes, forced southward by the expansion of the United States, invaded the sparsely populated regions of northern Mexico, burning haciendas, villages and mining settlements, and indiscriminately killing their inhabitants. Again, the Mexican government was too weak to prevent these incursions.

Social and ethnic revolt took a different form in central Mexico. Here the Indians did not form a compact, linguistic group and nor were they in a clear majority, as were the Mayas in Yucatán. However, deserters from the army, fugitives from justice, vagrants and similar elements, taking advantage of Mexico's military defeat and the chaos which followed, formed armed bands which began to terrorize the countryside. In at least one district, in the mountains of the states of Guanajuato, Querétaro and San Luis Potosí, a revolutionary agrarian movement developed. This so-called Sierra Gorda rebellion sought to give free land to hacienda tenants and peons, but the rebels were not strong enough to attack cities, and

[16] John Lloyd Stephens, *Incidents of travel in Yucatán* (Norman, Oklahoma, 1962), II, 214.

they had to be satisfied with the burning of haciendas. The Mexican ruling class, demoralized, embittered and divided, watched helplessly as the remnants of their once great country were beginning to fall apart.

But then the situation began slowly to improve. The United States military historian, R. S. Ripley, commented in 1849:

The effect of the war upon Mexico has been and will continue to be greatly beneficial. The first great apparent good is that the prestige of the army . . . has been entirely swept away. That this has been the case is demonstrated by the comparative quietude which has existed in Mexico since the conclusion of peace, and the at least apparent stability of a government administered upon republican principles.[17]

The main explanation for the improvement, however, was the war indemnity. President Herrera's government of moderate liberals had no revenues and no doubt would have collapsed had it not received at the outset 3 million pesos of the indemnity on account. With this money it was able to purchase surplus military equipment from the United States army, re-establish social order in central Mexico and send reinforcements to the north and to Yucatán. After several years of fighting in Yucatán, in which the local landowners had enlisted the support of their peons and also hired United States mercenaries, the insurrection of the Mayan Indians was gradually quelled. The Yucatán creoles saved their skins and their property, but lost forever their hope of becoming independent of Mexico. Moreover, the population of Yucatán had been reduced by almost half.[18]

Payments on account of the indemnity continued, and Mexico was able to put its public finances in order. In 1846, the principal of the foreign public debt was fixed, after protracted negotiations in London, at 51 million pesos. Then the war intervened, and interest on the new principal was not paid, but in a friendly gesture towards Mexico, the London committee of bondholders sacrificed the arrears and agreed to a reduction of the annual interest rate from 5 per cent to 3 per cent. Thereafter, the fairly reasonable payments were met until 1854. The economy as a whole also seems to have improved. On the evidence of coinage figures, silver and gold-mining, the most important industry, showed some recovery. From a yearly average production of over 20 million pesos before the war of independence which fell to 10 million

---

[17] R. S. Ripley, *The war with Mexico* (1849; New York, 1970), II, 645.
[18] The population in 1837 was 582,173; in 1862, 320,212.

pesos in 1822, there was a gradual increase thereafter, reaching almost 20 million pesos a year again in 1848–50, the three years in which the indemnity payments were available. This was followed by a decline to 16 million pesos in 1854 and a rise in the decade 1858–67 to 17,800,000 pesos.

The final months of 1850 saw presidential elections once more in Mexico. Herrera's favourite was his own minister of war, General Mariano Arista, a moderate liberal. Other groups backed their own candidates and although Arista did not receive an absolute majority, he secured a commanding lead. Early in January 1851, the Chamber of Deputies elected him president with the delegations of eight states voting for him as against five who preferred General Bravo. This was the first time since independence that a president had been able not only to complete his term, although not a full one, but also to hand over office to a legally elected successor. The constitutional process was, however, soon to break down once again.

As long as social subversion threatened the established order, liberals and conservatives were willing to unite in mutual self-defence. The conservative, anti-American Alamán had even deplored the withdrawal of the hated Protestant army of occupation which had protected his and everybody else's property against bandits and rebels. The liberal oracle, Mora, had written from Europe to his friends in Mexico that Indian rebellions should be rigorously suppressed. But once the immediate danger was swept away, conservative opposition to the moderate liberal regime had intensified once more. More than one-third of the votes in the elections at the beginning of 1851 went to the conservative Bravo. Moreover, the financial outlook for the new government was far from promising; the funds of the United States indemnity were almost exhausted; government revenues had fallen because of increased contraband made easier by the closer proximity of the United States border; the size of the army had been reduced, but military expenditure was still enormous because of renewed Indian invasions of northern Mexico (and dismissed officers joined the ranks of the opposition). The budget deficit exceeded 13 million pesos in 1851.[19] The government of General Arista soon came under attack from conservatives, radical liberals and supporters of Santa Anna. It did not matter that some leading conservatives were tarnished by their past monarchist views, some radical liberals by their

---

[19] In the period 1821–67 government expenditure averaged $17.5 million, revenue only $10 million a year.

collaboration with the occupation authorities and, of course, Santa Anna by his ineptitude bordering on treason. The tide was moving against the moderate liberals who, in the popular mind, had betrayed the nation by signing the peace treaty and by 'selling' one-half of its territory; they were responsible for the present disaster.

In July 1852, in Guadalajara, José M. Blancarte, a former colonel in the national guard, deposed the state governor, Jesús López Portillo, a moderate liberal, and yet another military revolt spread to other states. It was not immediately clear who was in revolt, whether conservatives or liberals, or both, nor for what purpose. When the dust settled a few months later, it appeared that everybody wanted the return of Santa Anna. Arista resigned and the generals, believing themselves unable to rule, agreed to summon the former dictator, then living in Colombia. On 17 March 1853, Congress duly elected Santa Anna to be president and the government sent for him to return.

In a letter to Santa Anna Alamán explained the conservative programme: full support for the Church; a strong army; the abolition of federalism; and a strong executive subject to certain principles and responsibilities. He did not make clear, however, who was to watch over Santa Anna. Perhaps he viewed Santa Anna's next presidency as a stepping stone to a Bourbon monarchy. The conservatives were not alone in their renewed activity. When Santa Anna landed at Veracruz, he was greeted by Miguel Lerdo de Tejada, who had been sent there as a representative of the radical liberals. As early as 1848, Lerdo had accused the army and the Church of being the cause of Mexico's ruin. Santa Anna asked him to submit his ideas in writing and Lerdo complied with a long letter in which he reiterated his earlier criticisms and ended by proposing various material improvements which the republic badly needed.

Santa Anna took possession of the presidency on 20 April 1853. On this occasion his support was broader than it had been in 1846 when the radical liberals alone of organized political groups had called for his return. Now both conservatives and liberals were bowing to his leadership, each convinced that they could bring him to their side. He formed a mixed cabinet with the conservative Alamán in the Ministry of Internal and Foreign Affairs and the independent liberal, Antonio de Haro y Tamariz, as Minister of Finance. The latter was a particularly important appointment in view of Santa Anna's previous use of liberals to blackmail the Church. Lerdo de Tejada became Under-Secretary of the new Ministry of Development and did much to promote the building of telegraph lines, essential for progress in the mountainous terrain of

Mexico. The 1824 constitution was suspended but nothing was proclaimed in its place. Santa Anna could have reinstated the 1843 centralist constitution but, conservative though it was, it did put severe limits on the power of the president. Among other things, for example, it prohibited the president from selling, giving away, exchanging, or mortgaging any part of the national territory. For reasons known at the time only to himself, such restrictions were not to his liking. He governed, therefore, without a constitution.

During the first months of his government, Santa Anna lost his two most able Ministers: Alamán died in June and Haro resigned in August, after failing in his attempt to cover the budget deficit of 17 million pesos with the issue of bonds guaranteed by Church property. The clergy had protested vehemently against Haro's policy and Santa Anna had to devise another means of finding the money. In March, just a few weeks before he became president, the United States had seized what is now part of southern Arizona. Mexico was powerless to expel the invaders and was strongly invited to sell it to the United States. An agreement was reached towards the end of 1853. From the sale price of 10 million pesos, Mexico was to receive immediately 7 million pesos.[20]

Santa Anna's regime became increasingly reactionary and autocratic. He loved the pageantry and pomp of office but despised the daily work of administration. During his several earlier periods as head of state, he had resolved the problem by leaving the presidential work to a civilian vice-president while reserving affairs of the army and the glory to himself. In 1853, with the country split into two hostile parties and on the brink once more of disintegration, he found that he had to accept the full burden of the presidency. He embellished it, however, with such a variety of titles and prerogatives that he became a monarch in all but name. Iturbide's execution meant that he could never assume the title of emperor but instead he acquired more real power than Iturbide had even imagined. In December 1853, he was granted the right to name his successor and when the sealed envelope was later opened, it was found to contain the name of Iturbide's son. To bolster his authority and prestige, and perhaps also to ease his conscience, Santa Anna did everything he could to appear as heir of the man to whose downfall he had so much contributed. For example, in November 1853 he announced the posthumous award to Iturbide of the title of liberator and had his portrait placed in government buildings.

[20] The territory in question is called, in Mexico, La Mesilla; in the United States, the transaction is known as the Gadsden purchase.

In accordance with his reactionary posture, he also granted many concessions to the Church, allowing the reinstatement of the Jesuits and repealing the 1833 law which had removed the civil enforcement of monastic vows. He restricted the press and sent many liberals to gaol and exile. Eventually he went too far. In February 1854, several army officers in the south, led by Colonel F. Villareal, rose in arms and on 1 March, at Ayutla, the revolution was provided with a programme, which was amended ten days later at Acapulco. Its main points were as follows: the removal of Santa Anna; the election of a provisional president by representatives appointed by the commander-in-chief of the revolutionary army; and, finally, a demand for an extraordinary congress to produce a new constitution. Similar appeals had been proclaimed earlier and elsewhere but with little impact. This Ayutla–Acapulco manifesto made no mention of the well-known liberal demands and nobody could have suspected that out of this army uprising with limited objectives liberal Mexico would be born. In Acapulco, the obscure colonel who had launched the revolt at Ayutla was replaced by a retired colonel, Ignacio Comonfort, a wealthy merchant and landowner and a friend of General Juan Alvarez, the *cacique* of the ever rebellious south.

Alvarez had inherited control of the *tierra caliente* from Guerrero who had himself inherited the prestige of Morelos. They had all fought together in the War of Independence. The power of Alvarez, himself a *hacendado*, was based on the support of Indian peasants whose lands he protected. His army was drawn from the Indians and their support was sufficient to keep him in power on the Pacific coast for more than a generation. Eventually, the area under his control was separated from the state of Mexico to form the new state of Guerrero. He had no higher ambition and as long as central governments, liberal or conservative, did not meddle in his domain, his relations with them were good. Certainly, Santa Anna had displeased him when he appointed Alamán to the cabinet because Alamán was widely regarded as the author of Guerrero's execution, but, as the able conservative minister died soon after being appointed, relations between Santa Anna and Alvarez improved.

Then the ageing dictator made a mistake. Perhaps he no longer trusted Alvarez or perhaps he simply wished to pursue his plan to centralize the administration. Whatever the case, he removed some army officers and government officials on the Pacific coast, whereupon they flocked to Alvarez. It was on his hacienda that the revolution was planned. The strategy was to unite the nation against Santa Anna and hence the programme was restricted to generalities. The only indication that the revolution might be liberal in character was the presence of Comonfort, a moderate liberal. Alvarez assumed the leadership but, as had been the case with Guerrero, his views on basic national issues were unknown. The revolt spread irresistibly and in August 1855 Santa Anna relinquished the presidency and sailed into exile. The revolutionary government confiscated his property which had once been worth the enormous sum of one million pesos.[21] Soon a forgotten man, he was not permitted to re-enter the country until 1874 when the then president, Sebastián Lerdo, allowed him to return to Mexico City where he died two years later.

As the capital was in the hands of Alvarez's Indian soldiers it was not surprising that he was elected president by the representatives he had chosen from among the leaders of the revolt and the liberal intellectuals returned from prison and exile. Bravo had recently died leaving him as the sole surviving hero of the War of Independence, and his election thus symbolized the revolutionary tradition of Hidalgo, Morelos and Guerrero. Yet Alvarez had not sought the presidency – he was sixty-five years old – and he did not feel at home in the capital. He must also have resented the way in which he and his Indians were treated by both conservatives and moderate liberals who feared a renewal of race and class war. Instinctively perhaps, they recalled the democratic undercurrent in Morelos's rebellion and Guerrero's association with the radical Zavala. Alvarez now had the opportunity to punish the ruling groups and avenge Guerrero's death but his objective may have been limited to strengthening his hold on the south by enlarging the state of Guerrero and moving its boundaries closer to the capital. Whatever his aims, he ignored Comonfort's advice and, with one exception, appointed to the cabinet radical liberals, or *puros* as they were known. Leaving the Ministry of War to Comonfort himself who, as a moderate, could be expected to hold the army together, Alvarez entrusted the portfolio of Foreign Affairs to Melchor Ocampo and appointed Benito Juárez to the Ministry of Justice, Guillermo Prieto to the Treasury, Miguel Lerdo de Tejada to the Ministry of Development and Ponciano Arriaga to the Ministry of the Interior.

These five ministers belonged to a new generation, untainted by the failures of previous liberal governments. All except one had been born

[21] Robert A. Potash; 'Testamentos de Santa Anna', *Historia Mexicana*, 13/3 (1964), 428–40.

during the War of Independence and they only remembered an independent Mexico with its perpetual disorders. Although they dreamed of an orderly regime based on the rule of law, none of them was a systematic thinker or theoretician. This was not perhaps a serious weakness, for Mora had worked out the liberal programme many years before. Apart from Lerdo, they shared one other thing in common; they had all been persecuted by Santa Anna.

Ocampo and Lerdo have already been mentioned above. Both as governor of the state of Michoacán and as a private citizen, Ocampo had acquired a reputation for his attacks on high parochial fees which were one of the main causes of the indebtedness of hacienda peons. Because both birthrate and infant mortality were high, hacienda labourers spent a great deal of their money on baptisms and funerals. In most cases, it was the *hacendado* who paid the actual fees and then charged them to their peons' accounts. Marriage fees were also so high that many couples did not marry. In striking at the root of the problem Ocampo inevitably attracted the hatred of thousands of parish priests whose livelihood depended on the fees, in contrast to the higher clergy, bishops and canons, who lived mainly from the tithe revenues (the payment of which had been voluntary since 1833). Not surprisingly, Ocampo had been exiled from Mexico soon after Santa Anna's rise to his last presidency. In New Orleans, where the liberal exiles gathered, Ocampo befriended the former governor of the state of Oaxaca, Benito Juárez, the only Indian in the group, who had been exiled by Santa Anna for having opposed him in the Mexican–American war. Under Ocampo's influence, Juárez became a radical liberal.

In November 1855 Juárez, the Minister of Justice, produced a law which abolished clerical immunities by restricting the jurisdiction of ecclesiastical courts to ecclesiastical cases. It also proposed to divest the army of some of its privileges. Perhaps thinking that he had done enough to create irreversible changes, or perhaps compelled by the storm of protest raised by the so-called 'Juárez Law', Alvarez appointed Comonfort as substitute president at the beginning of December and resigned a few days later. Short as his presidency had been – only two months – it was decisive for the future of the country.

Comonfort appointed a cabinet of moderate liberals, but it was already too late. In several parts of the country, groups of laymen, army officers and priests had rebelled with the cry of *religión y fueros* (religion and immunities). One armed band called for the repeal of the Juárez Law, the removal of Comonfort and the return to the 1843 conservative constitution. In January 1856, it managed to seize the city of Puebla and establish a government there. Moderate though he was, Comonfort had to suppress the uprising and he forced the surrender of Puebla at the end of March. The local bishop, Labastida, took pains to disassociate himself from the rebels, but Comonfort put the blame on the Church and decreed the attachment of ecclesiastical property in the diocese until the cost of his campaign had been covered. Feeling that the Church should not be blamed for the insurrection, Labastida refused to pay the indemnity with the result that the government expelled him and confiscated the clerical property. In one way or another, Church property was being used to finance rebellion against the government and the answer seemed to be confiscation. But in view of the violent reaction unleashed by the Puebla confiscatory decree, it seemed prudent to try a different, indirect approach which would appear less anti-clerical. This was probably the reasoning behind the disentailment law enacted at the end of June 1856 by Lerdo de Tejada, now Minister of Finance.

Lerdo de Tejada has already been mentioned as the radical liberal who had 'collaborated' with the United States' occupation army in the municipal council of the capital and then with the reactionary Santa Anna in the Ministry of Development. He had been pessimistic about Mexico's ability to carry out a liberal revolution; he believed it would have to be imposed from above or from abroad. But finally, in 1856, he had the opportunity to carry out a programme of radical anti-clericalism. The main feature of the so-called 'Lerdo Law' was that the Church must sell all its urban and rural real estate to the respective tenants and lessees at a discount which would make the transaction attractive to buyers. Should buyers refuse to purchase, the property would be sold by government officials at public auction. The ecclesiastical corporations most affected by the law were the regular orders. The monasteries owned large country estates as well as town houses and the convents possessed the best real estate in the cities. The higher clergy were not to suffer much because its wealth was of a different kind and parish priests were not affected directly because parishes did not generally own any property except the parish house itself.[22] In the villages, however, there were brotherhoods or confraternities devoted to religious purposes, and many of them owned land or property which was now to be disentailed, much to the

[22] Parish priests might, of course, have property of their own; but that would not be affected by the law.

grief of villagers and priests alike. At first sight, the law did not look confiscatory: the Church was to be paid either in instalments equal to former rents or in a lump sum equal to the capitalized rent. But there was a loophole. According to the law, the Church in the future would not be able to acquire or own properties. The Church would therefore have no safeguards and hence would face a gradual despoilment. Consequently, the Church authorities protested and refused to comply.

As believers in private property, the liberals also sought the liquidation of the property of civil corporations. This affected in particular the Indian villages, most of which were still large landholders. These villages possessed various types of property including communal pastures, or *ejidos*, which were exempted from disentailment because Lerdo considered them essential for the village. Nevertheless, in actual practice, parts of the *ejidos* began to be sold, despite protests by the peasants.

The Lerdo Law was put into effect at once. As the Church in most cases refused to sell, government officials signed the deeds of sale to the former tenants or lessees and now house or landowners. Many pious tenants refrained from claiming the property which was then purchased by wealthy speculators, some of whom were well-known financiers who specialized in loans to the government and had thus become important holders of government bonds. Whereas they might have been previously connected with conservative regimes, their investments in the disentailed clerical properties tended to make them allies of the liberals. Tenants loyal to the Church ignored the new landlords, continuing to pay their rent to the former ecclesiastical owner, awaiting the day when the house would be returned to the Church. This confused and complex situation regarding the disentailed properties was evident within a few months of the law's implementation and it was clear that it could not be permitted to last indefinitely.

While Lerdo was dealing with Church property, his colleague, José María Iglesias, the new Minister of Justice, was working on a law to limit parochial fees. In general, the 'Iglesias Law' of 11 April 1857 declared as valid the fees charged in the colonial period or at the beginning of independent Mexico and which were evidently low. It then prohibited the collection of parochial fees from the poor who were defined as persons earning the minimum amount necessary for survival. As most parishioners were poor, this meant the end of wealthy curates. The law prescribed severe penalties for those priests who charged the poor for their services or refused to baptize, marry or bury them free of charge.

Again, the Church condemned the law as illegal and immoral, and refused to comply.

In the meantime, approximately 150 deputies in congress, most of whom were young liberals drawn from the professional classes – lawyers, government officials or journalists – were debating the new constitution. Among the older generation there was Valentín Gómez Farías, after Mora's death in Paris in 1850 the patriarch of Mexican liberalism and now seventy-five years old. The issues and problems in 1856 were different from those which Ocampo had faced in 1842 and even more so than those confronting Gómez Farías in 1833. The war with the United States had inevitably left a mark on the mind of most liberals. For example, in 1848 Ocampo described the struggle between the states and the central, federal government, as 'systematic anarchy'.[23] He came to the conclusion that federation, as it had existed in Mexico since the adoption of the 1824 constitution, had made easier the separation of Texas and the temporary secession of Yucatán, and had subsequently been a cause of the defeat and dismemberment of the country. He must have recalled Servando Teresa de Mier's opinion that Mexico needed a strong central government in the first phase of its independence. Perhaps centralism was the right course after all, though not if it meant the domination of the army and the Church. Now that the government was a liberal one, it was advisable to strengthen it, especially since the proximity of the American border weakened the hold of central Mexico on the states to the north, making a further dismemberment of the country possible in the future. Liberals, therefore, became just as centralist as their conservative rivals, although they continued to pay lip service to the federalism with which liberalism had been identified for so many years. The new constitution, approved on 5 February 1857 following almost a year of discussion, kept the federal structure but, characteristically, while the official title of the 1824 document had been the Federal Constitution of the United Mexican States, the new charter was named the Political Constitution of the Mexican Republic.

Now that federalism had lost its meaning, the Church took its place as the main issue between liberals and conservatives. In a radical departure from the 1842 constitutional projects, and even more from the 1824 constitution, the liberals in 1856 wished to introduce full freedom of worship for all religions; in other words, religious toleration. The

---

[23] Moisés González Navarro, *Anatomía del poder en México (1848–1853)* (Mexico, 1977), 378.

proposal turned out to be too advanced. Mexico's population consisted mostly of peasants loyal to their Church, and although the educated classes may have been as liberal as their European counterparts, they could not antagonize the mass of villagers, already stirred by their priests. The Minister of the Interior warned Congress: 'the Indians are excited and for this reason it is very dangerous to introduce a new element which will be exaggerated by the enemies of progress in order to drown us in a truly frightening anarchy'.[24] The proposal was dropped, but, at the same time, the traditional assertion that Mexico was a Roman Catholic nation was also omitted, thus leaving a curious gap in the constitution. Not daring to touch the image, sacred to the common people, of a Catholic Mexico, the delegates nevertheless included in the constitution all the other anti-clerical demands, especially the basic concepts of the 'Juárez Law' (1855) and the 'Lerdo Law'(1856).

The liberals were as anti-militaristic as they were anti-clerical. In this respect, however, they realized that they had to tread carefully because General Comonfort, president and commander-in-chief of the army, was already showing signs of impatience with Congress. Hence the liberal deputies restricted themselves to the abolition of the judicial privileges of the army, thereby confirming what had already been enacted in the Juárez Law.

Finally, the new constitution affirmed complete freedom for all citizens. For the first time since the 1814 Apatzingán constitution, every Mexican, however poor (but excluding vagrants and criminals), was given the right to vote and to be elected, and a declaration of human rights, including the inviolability of private property, was also specified. With its ban on the corporate ownership of real estate, the constitution was more sweeping than the Lerdo Law. Lerdo had exempted village *ejidos* or communal pastures, but the constitution did not mention them, the implication being that they could be disentailed. Their disentailment was, in fact, attempted on the basis of the new constitution, but it had to be halted because of Indian opposition. The liberals could not afford to wage war on two fronts, against the Church and against the Indian peasants. As far as the Church was concerned, they sought to isolate it by gaining allies among all social strata. They succeeded in doing so in urban centres where the middle and some of the upper classes profited by the disentailment of corporate property. In the rural areas where the Church was traditionally strong, they were unable to isolate it, but they

24 Francisco Zarco, *Historia del Congreso Constituyente (1856–1857)* (2nd edn, Mexico, 1956), 630.

did drive a wedge into the hitherto solidly conservative countryside by letting large landowners purchase former ecclesiastical haciendas. Ironically, it was the rural rich, not the rural poor, who tended to support the liberals.

Most liberals saw in the adoption of the constitution of 1857 a realization of their life-long dreams. They were now able to assume a more conciliatory attitude in some respects. For example, a subtle change in public opinion caused the government to reopen the Franciscan monastery in the capital which had been closed some months previously because an alleged conspiracy had taken place within its walls. Moreover, with the resignation of Lerdo at the beginning of the year, the disentailment of property slowed down. The government was ready to negotiate and on 1 May 1857, Comonfort sent his Minister of Justice to Rome. The Holy See appeared ready to accept the disentailment transactions so far implemented, but it demanded that the legal right to acquire and own property should be restored to the Church. Even the conservative Mexican press suggested in August that the disentailment should be legalized through an agreement with Rome.

It seemed obvious that a compromise with both the Church and the conservatives would require the repeal of the more extreme articles of the constitution. Comonfort, elected constitutional president in September with only reluctant support from the radicals who preferred Lerdo, was believed to favour such a course as the only way of avoiding civil war. But compromise was not to prevail. The liberals saw in Comonfort a conservative and the conservatives a liberal, and he was left without support. In the civil war which followed it was the conservatives who took the initiative. Reactionary army units in the capital, led by General Félix Zuloaga, rebelled in December 1857 with the avowed aim of annulling the constitution. While upholding Comonfort's authority, the army took control of the city, dissolved Congress and arrested, among others, the new president of the Supreme Court, Benito Juárez. After some hesitation, Comonfort approved Zuloaga's programme. A month later, Zuloaga took the second step: he removed Comonfort and assumed the presidency himself. Perhaps out of revenge against ungrateful conservatives, Comonfort, in the final moments of his power, managed to release Juárez from prison before leaving the country, unmolested by conservatives and ignored by liberals. Yet his decision to free Juárez rendered an immense service to the liberal cause, as future events were to show.

Juárez fled to Querétaro. From there, he proceeded to Guanajuato and, arguing that the constitutional order had been destroyed, he proclaimed himself president of the republic and appointed a cabinet with Ocampo as its most distinguished member. As head of the Supreme Court – the office of vice-president not having been adopted by the 1857 constitution – he had the constitutional right to the presidential succession in the absence of the legally elected president. Shortly after his arrival at Guanajuato, a resident wrote to a friend in Mexico City: 'An Indian by the name of Juárez, who calls himself president of the republic, has arrived in this city.'[25]

Thus, with a conservative president in Mexico City and a liberal president in Guanajuato, the Three Years War began. In earlier decades, when faced by a counter-revolution, the liberals had submitted to the army virtually without resistance. Now, they still did not have an army of consequence, but they had mass support in cities and parts of the rural areas which made it possible for them gradually to create a new army with former liberal lawyers and journalists as officers. In contrast, since Alamán's death, there had been a curious lack of educated civilians among the conservatives. Events were to reveal that the regular army and the Church were not by themselves strong enough to resist the liberal movement. This was not to be a walkover, as Santa Anna's counter-revolutionary coups had once been.

Following Zuloaga's second coup, some state governors acknowledged him as president, others declared their opposition and some reversed their original stance. Amidst this confusion, Juárez was able to escape to Veracruz, the governor of which had invited him to establish his administration in the port. The country as a whole soon divided into two sections of approximately equal strength. The states bordering on the Gulf of Mexico were under liberal control, with the exception of the exhausted Yucatán which chose to remain neutral. The far northern states were also liberal. The central core of the country was conservative, except for the states of Michoacán and Zacatecas.

From the start, both factions had to find ways of financing their war efforts. Zuloaga, fulfilling a promise to the Church, declared the Lerdo Law null and void: the Church was to regain ownership of its disentailed property. In exchange for this, the metropolitan chapter was obliged to promise him a loan of one and a half million pesos, but as the ecclesiastical corporations had little ready cash, nine-tenths of the amount was paid in

[25] Ralph Roeder, *Juárez and his Mexico* (2 vols., New York, 1947), I, 161.

bills guaranteed by clerical property. The conservative government sold these bills at a discount to financiers who in due course acquired the clerical real estate because the Church was unable to redeem them. A discount was necessary because the liberal government had declared illegal all acts and transactions of the conservative regime. Hence the price was lowered in proportion to the risk. Other similar loans followed, including one granted by the House of Rothschild. In this way, moneylenders financed Zuloaga at the expense of the Church which was obliged to watch its wealth dispersed. Arguing that the Church was voluntarily financing Zuloaga, liberal governors and military commanders of relatively isolated areas such as Michoacán and the north decreed forced loans on the clergy which for all practical purposes amounted to confiscation of Church property. At Veracruz, the conditions were rather different. Soon after Juárez's arrival in May 1858, a shipload of rifles, consigned to a French captain, José Yves Limantour, reached the port. Of course, the constitutional government promptly requisitioned the weapons. As it could not pay for them with the limited amount of Church property left in the Gulf states, and as it had no cash available, payment was made in the form of clerical real estate in Mexico City. With the capital held by Zuloaga, all the liberal regime could do was to promise to hand over the property in the event of a liberal victory. Again, the price set for the weapons was proportional to the risk of this credit arrangement and thus Limantour, and other foreign importers, were to acquire urban property in Mexico City at a fraction of its real value.

Juárez faced a critical situation in February–March 1859 when the new conservative president and military commander, Miguel Miramón, attempted to capture Veracruz. The attempt failed, but, at almost the same time, the liberal commander of western Mexico, Santos Degollado, also failed in his attempt to seize Mexico City. After Degollado's defeat, more than a dozen liberal officers, including seven army surgeons, were taken prisoner and executed in a suburb of the capital. The conflict was becoming increasingly cruel and destructive with almost the entire country now a theatre of war. No end was in sight. The nation was divided into irreconcilable camps.

The moment had arrived for the liberals to put their aims before the nation. Thus, the constitutional government in Veracruz issued a manifesto on 7 July 1859. The document, signed by President Juárez and the two most prominent cabinet members, Ocampo and Lerdo, put all the blame for the war on the Church and a series of reforms was announced:

the confiscation of all Church wealth, both real estate and capital; the voluntary payments of parochial fees; the complete separation of Church and State; the suppression of all monasteries and abolition of novitiates in nunneries. Full freedom of worship was not proclaimed. The manifesto also recognized the need for a division of landed property, but it added that such a redistribution would take place in the future as a natural consequence of economic progress. For the moment, it promised only a law which would remove legal obstacles to the voluntary division of rural estates.

The specific laws to enact these reforms were issued during the following four weeks. The confiscated, 'nationalized' wealth, both real estate and mortgages, were to be sold to buyers of clerical properties under the Lerdo Law. Lerdo, who as Minister of Finance in the Veracruz government had drafted the confiscatory law, insisted on the continuity between the earlier disentailment and the present nationalization. The buyers who had returned the properties to the Church in areas occupied by the conservatives would, in the event of a liberal victory, recover them and then pay the government for them either in instalments extending for long periods of time or in cash at a fraction of their value. The measure was bound to attract both former and potential buyers to the liberal cause, particularly in conservative occupied central Mexico where the most valuable clerical properties were concentrated. In the areas under liberal control, most of the Church property had already been disposed of and in some states, like Veracruz, the Church had always been poor. Hence the liberal government itself obtained only a small immediate revenue from the sale of the confiscated wealth.

But the die had been cast. Now it was a life-and-death struggle of the Church and the old army against the middle class professionals, of the old world against the new. The revolutionary 'reform' laws of July 1859 drove political passions to their highest pitch, fighting increased and the demands of the Treasury became ever greater. In desperation, the constitutional government granted the United States, in exchange for 2 million dollars, transits and right of way across the Isthmus of Tehuantepec and from the Rio Grande and Arizona to the Gulf of California, as well as the right to employ its own military forces for the protection of persons and property passing through these areas. This so-called McLane–Ocampo treaty was negotiated by Melchor Ocampo who was certainly no friend of the United States, and it was signed on 14 December 1859. A liberal newspaper commented: 'Does not Señor

Juárez know that the liberal party prefers to fall anew under the double despotism of the army and the clergy before committing itself to a foreign yoke?'[26] We do not know if the liberal government was sincere in its proposed treaty or whether it was playing for time. Whatever the case, the United States Senate repudiated the treaty a few months later, thus freeing the liberals from the embarrassing position into which their extreme penury had placed them. In fact, the 2 million dollars were not needed. The war of propaganda was bearing fruit, and after the failure of Miramón's second attempt to capture Veracruz in the spring of 1860, the fortunes of the conservative armies began to decline. They began to retreat towards the capital where Miramón was trying to raise money. He now did, with the archbishop's permission, what the liberals had done against the will of the Church; in August he confiscated wrought silver from churches for coinage as well as gold and other jewels which were pawned to moneylenders. Then, in November, without either credit or funds, he confiscated 660,000 pesos which had been entrusted to the British legation on behalf of English bondholders who were going to receive part of the interest due to them for the first time since 1854. It was too late: the liberal armies were closing in on the capital.

Early in December 1860, victory was so certain that the liberal government at Veracruz finally decreed complete religious toleration. It no longer mattered what priest-led Indians might think. The liberals had won the war. On 22 December, the liberal commander, General Jesús González Ortega, a former journalist from Zacatecas, defeated Miramón in the battle for possession of Mexico City and he occupied it three days later, on Christmas day. President Juárez arrived from Veracruz three weeks later. With the cities taken by the liberals and the conservative armies scattered into rural guerrilla groups, Mexico was free to enjoy a political campaign, and the presidential contest began almost with the arrival of the president and his cabinet.

Among the liberal leaders there were four possible presidents: Melchor Ocampo, Miguel Lerdo, Benito Juárez and González Ortega. Ocampo did not seek the presidency. Considered as heir to Mora, he was satisfied with being the prophet of liberalism and hence he helped his protégé, Juárez, against Lerdo in whom he sensed a rival. Juárez may have needed such help for, even though president, he was viewed by many as second rate in comparison with Ocampo and Lerdo. Reserved and

[26] Walter V. Scholes, *Mexican politics during the Juárez regime, 1855–1872* (2nd edn, Columbia, Missouri, 1969), 36.

unassuming, he was described later as 'not a leader who conceived and gave impulse to programmes, reforms, or ideas. That task reverted to the men who surrounded him, and he acquiesced in or rejected their leadership'.[27] As author of the revolutionary laws affecting Church wealth, Lerdo had prestige and authority, and he was popular with radical liberals. González Ortega in turn was a national hero – the man who had defeated the conservative army. These three man – Juárez, Lerdo and González Ortega – were candidates for the highest office.

At the end of January 1861, it seemed that six states favoured Juárez, six were for Lerdo and five for González Ortega; there was no information about the remaining seven states. Lerdo won in the capital and two states, only to die on 22 March. The protracted system of indirect elections had to continue with the two remaining candidates, Juárez against González Ortega, and in the final count, Juárez obtained 57 per cent of the vote, Lerdo almost 22 per cent and González Ortega over 20 per cent. It would seem that in the districts where after Lerdo's death the elections were still in progress, his supporters had given their votes to Juárez. One obvious explanation was liberal mistrust of the military. The most distinguished liberal politicians had been civilians: Zavala, Mora, Gómez Farías, Ocampo, Lerdo, Otero and de la Rosa. None of them had become president. The army, by nature conservative, was unwilling to share power with them. Excepting the transitional presidency of de la Peña, there had been no civilian head of state before Juárez. Although González Ortega was a good liberal, he was a general and therefore not to be trusted.

In June 1861, Congress declared Juárez to be president of Mexico. He was to bear the whole burden of office alone, for Ocampo had recently been captured and executed by conservative guerrillas, thus surviving his rival, Lerdo, by just over two months. Nor would Juárez ever get rid of the shadow of the army, even though it was a liberal, revolutionary force. While González Ortega was in the field fighting the conservatives, he was elected by Congress (unconstitutionally, since he should have been directly elected) president of the Supreme Court and thus next in line for the presidency. The anti-Juárez faction felt that as the president of the republic was a presumably weak civilian, some provision should be made for any possible emergency. To González Ortega's credit, it must be said that he did not attempt a military takeover

The problems facing Juárez were staggering. The sale of confiscated

27 Frank Averill Knapp, Jr., *The life of Sebastián de Tejada, 1823–1889* (Austin, Texas, 1951), 157.

Church wealth valued at around 150 million pesos – perhaps one-fifth of the total national wealth – had begun in January 1861. To attract Mexican buyers who, as good Roman Catholics, were opposed to the confiscation, and to create a broad social base for itself, the liberal government had been accepting all kinds of paper, credits, promissory notes and depreciated internal debt bonds in payment for, or at least in part payment for, the clerical properties. Consequently, from the sale in 1861 of confiscated properties in the Federal District, worth 16 million pesos which was already a depreciated value, the government received only one million pesos in actual cash. Moreover, Veracruz financiers, like Limantour and others, had already paid for their properties in kind or cash. Finally, the government recognized as valid the purchases of ecclesiastical properties made by the powerful House of Rothschild during the conservative regime. The fact that the properties had been purchased at a fraction of their value and that many had been paid for in advance explains the extremely low revenue from the confiscation in 1861. The English bondholders, who expected some of their arrears of interest from the proceeds of the sale, received nothing. Similarly, France was pressing her claims for the Jecker bonds issued by the conservative government and recently acquired by influential politicians in France. There were all sorts of other claims for damages allegedly or actually suffered during the civil war by foreign nationals. Juárez, however, refused to accept responsibility for the acts of the conservative regime: he simply had no money. His government was obliged to suspend all payments in July. European creditors felt cheated and pressed their governments to obtain redress. On 31 October 1861, France, Great Britain and Spain signed in London a Tripartite Convention in favour of military intervention in Mexico. Their troops landed at Veracruz shortly afterwards. It soon became clear, however, that Napoleon III had ulterior motives and designs for Mexico. Hence Britain and Spain withdrew their forces, leaving the enterprise to the French.

These developments provided Mexican monarchists living in Europe, like Gutiérrez Estrada, for example, with the opportunity they had been looking for. A French occupation of Mexico would make it possible to realize their life-long dream of establishing a Mexican empire under European – this time, French – protection. And a suitable candidate for the monarchy was found in the person of the Austrian Archduke Maximilian.

Meanwhile, the French armies were advancing in Mexico. The invasion aroused genuine patriotic feelings in the country, not only among the liberals. It was not known at this point whether France was seeking to help conservatives against liberals, or in fact trying to subjugate the country. The two former conservative presidents, Zuloaga and Miramón, hesitated. As generals and former presidents, they were not enthusiastic about an empire with a foreign prince. Furthermore, they distrusted France and were devoted to their country's independence. Miramón finally offered his sword to Juárez. The issue was not liberalism against conservatism, as it had been in 1858–60, but Mexican independence against conquest by a foreign power. Certainly, in their hatred of Juárez most conservatives did accept the French as liberators from the liberal yoke, but some also found their way into the army which was fighting the invaders. For example, Manuel González (future president of Mexico 1880–4), who had been an officer in the conservative army in 1858–60, volunteered and was accepted to fight the French. Comonfort was also accepted by Juárez and he was to die on the battlefield in 1863

Temporarily repulsed by General Zaragoza in the battle of Puebla in May 1862, the French forces were reorganized and, under Marshall Forey, they embarked on a more powerful campaign. Zaragoza died and Juárez had to appoint González Ortega, whom he had kept without military assignment, to the command of the eastern armies. He surrendered in Puebla in May 1863, after a two months' siege of the city. The French were free to take the capital and from there extended their domination to other parts of the country. Aiming to continue the fight from the north, Juárez left Mexico City on 31 May, and ten days later he established his government in San Luis Potosí. He was joined by González Ortega who had managed to escape from the French while being taken to Veracruz.

The conservatives in the capital, especially the former bishop of Puebla and now archbishop of Mexico, Labastida, expected the French to do as Zuloaga had done in 1858, that is, repeal all the confiscatory laws and return the nationalized wealth to the Church. Napoleon, however, had decided to adopt the liberal programme and to the dismay of Church dignitaries, Marshal Forey recognized the validity of the nationalization and sale of ecclesiastical property. On accepting the crown of Mexico at Miramar, his castle near Trieste, on 10 April 1864, Maximilian, whose liberal background was well known, had undertaken to follow French policy in respect of the Church and the nationalization of its property. On his arrival in Mexico City in June, he found the republican government of Juárez still in control of northern Mexico and the republican guerrillas fighting the occupation forces. He attempted to bring Juárez to his side and to persuade him to submit to his empire but, of course, he failed. Nevertheless, he did succeed in winning over some of those liberals who had chosen to remain in the capital under the French occupation. He rejected the support of the conservatives and sent their best-known leader, General Miramón, abroad. Thus, he was able to form a cabinet consisting almost entirely of liberals, among them two former deputies to the constituent congress of 1856–7, Pedro Escudero y Echánove and José M. Cortés y Esparza. Escudero became Minister of Justice and Ecclesiastical Affairs and Cortés, Minister of the Interior. Foreign Affairs, Development and the new Ministry of Public Education were also in the hands of liberals. The Treasury was managed directly by the French.

Maximilian even went so far as to draft a liberal constitution. Known as the Provisional Statute of the Mexican Empire, it was signed by the emperor on the first anniversary of his acceptance of the Mexican crown. Together with a 'moderate hereditary monarchy with a Catholic prince', it proclaimed freedom of worship as one of the rights of men. As the first and foremost of these rights, 'the Government of the Emperor' guaranteed equality under the law 'to all inhabitants of the Empire',[28] a right which had only been implied in the 1857 constitution. Freedom of labour was also established. While the liberal regime had never enacted a law expressly prohibiting debt peonage, Maximilian did so on 1 November 1865. Labourers were granted the right to leave their employment at will, independently of whether or not they were in debt to their employer: all debts over ten pesos were cancelled; hours of work and child labour were restricted; corporal punishment of labourers was forbidden; and to allow competition with hacienda stores, peddlers were permitted to enter haciendas and offer their wares to peons. Finally, in a departure from the 1857 constitution, Maximilian restored to Indian villages the right to own property and granted communal lands to those villages which did not have them.

It is possible that Maximilian was seeking support among the Mexican poor – the overwhelming majority of the nation – because his authority depended so far entirely on the strength of a foreign army of occupation. But this in the eyes of most Mexicans was more important than the question of his liberal or conservative convictions. In 1858–60 the

[28] Ramírez, *Leyes fundamentales de México*, 670–80

struggle had been between Mexican liberals and Mexican conservatives. Now the issue was between Mexico and France, between the Mexican republic and a foreign monarchy. The liberal government of Juárez came to represent Mexico and the empire was seen as an instrument of a foreign power.

The conquest and the empire almost succeeded. In the final months of 1865, the advancing French armies pushed Juárez to Paso del Norte, a town on the Rio Grande across the United States border. At the same time, Juárez faced a serious internal crisis. His four-year term as president was due to expire on 1 December 1865 and it was impossible to hold elections with the French occupying most of the country. Basing himself on the extraordinary powers previously granted to him by Congress, Juárez extended his own term of office until such time as new elections again became possible. This action was no doubt unconstitutional and General González Ortega, the (also) unconstitutional president of the Supreme Court, claimed the presidency of the republic. It seemed that the days of Juárez, and even the republic, were numbered, but the general had neither the nerve nor the strength to attempt a military takeover. Juárez arrested and imprisoned him. For the moment, he weathered the storm.

In 1866 the military situation turned against the empire as a result of Napoleon's decision to withdraw his troops. They began to leave, exposing the weakness of Maximilian's position. For two years he had tried to lure the liberals into his camp and many of them had become imperial civil servants, but with the French expeditionary force about to depart he had to replace it with a Mexican army. Unable to find liberals willing to fight and, if necessary, die for his empire, he turned to the conservatives. After the departure of the French, it would once again be a war of Mexican conservatives against Mexican liberals. Maximilian appointed a conservative cabinet and welcomed the best conservative commander, Miramón, back to Mexico. Without knowing it, the conservatives and the Austrian archduke had sealed a death pact.

Republican armies closed the circle around the tottering empire which retained control of central Mexico. The eastern army moved against Puebla, and the northern army against Querétaro and it was there that Maximilian decided to make what was to be his last stand. He was defeated and became a prisoner of war, together with Generals Miramón and Mejía, the latter a conservative of Indian origins. Executions of military and civilian prisoners had been common both in the civil war of

1858–60 and during the French invasion of 1862–6. If Ocampo had been shot, why should Maximilian be spared? His royal blood made no difference. He had to come to the same end as Iturbide. Juárez intended to warn the world that an attempted conquest of Mexico, for whatever aim, did not pay. The execution of Maximilian, Miramón and Mejía was, therefore, a foregone conclusion. They were court-martialled, convicted of war crimes and faced the firing squad on 19 June 1867. After an absence of more than four years, President Juárez returned to his capital city on 15 July 1867.

In retrospect, the second Mexican empire appears to have been a tragi-comedy of errors. The conservatives had picked the wrong man. They needed a strong, conservative monarch to bolster their cause, not someone who put only obstacles in their way. They might have done better had they obtained an ultra Catholic Spanish prince. As it was, Maximilian's attempt to graft a liberal, European monarchy on a Church-dominated Latin American republic was a forlorn enterprise. He quarrelled with Miramón without winning over Juárez. His social reforms brought him into conflict with the ruling classes, particularly the large landowners. His reforms came too late to earn him popularity with the poor. In the end, he was in a country which did not want him, especially not as a gift from an invading army. In sum, the emperor who had sought to bring together liberals and conservatives, rich and poor, Mexicans and Europeans, ended by being repudiated and abandoned by almost all.

And yet, at the beginning, in 1863–4, some Mexicans did see in an empire an answer to their problems and a reasonable, even desirable alternative to the almost fifty years of anarchy and civil war that had gone before. They had lost faith in the ability of their nation to govern itself. Only a European of royal blood could command the respect of all, restrain individual ambition and be an impartial judge of their disputes. Did not the empire fulfil the Plan of Iguala of 1821 which had insisted on a European prince as the only force capable of holding the nation together? The answer, of course, is that it did, but it had come too late. Had it come immediately after independence, it might have given some stability to the new country. But now Mexico had a group of men capable of ruling, as they were soon to show, and it was these men who fought and defeated the empire.

Restored by Juárez in 1867, the liberal republic lasted until 1876 when General Porfirio Díaz, a hero of the patriotic war against the French, overthrew the civilian president, Sebastián Lerdo, a younger brother of

Miguel Lerdo and successor to Juárez after his death in 1872. Using parts of his predecessor's political machine, Díaz built one of his own which helped him to retain power for thirty-five years. He was to bring considerable stability to Mexico, making possible unprecedented economic development, but his absolute control of political offices and what to most younger contemporaries appeared to be the regime's mounting tyranny finally brought his downfall in 1911 in the first stage of the Mexican Revolution.

# 4

## CENTRAL AMERICA

The first half century of national independence was an unhappy time for the provinces formerly comprising the kingdom of Guatemala: Guatemala, El Salvador, Honduras, Nicaragua and Costa Rica.[1] Tensions in the economic and social structures of the late colonial period led to bitter political struggles and civil war, and the high expectations expressed by Central American leaders at the beginning of the period were soon dashed on the hard rock of reality. Economic stagnation, class antagonism, political tyranny and anarchy replaced the relative tranquillity and stability of the Hispanic era. Instead of a united and prosperous independent isthmian nation, a fragmented and feuding cluster of city states calling themselves 'republics' had emerged by 1870. Nevertheless, however disappointing the rate of economic and social change, some important and necessary steps had been taken in the transition from colonialism to modern capitalist dependency.

Historians of Latin America often pass rapidly over Central American independence with the suggestion that it came about merely as a natural consequence of Mexican independence. It is true that Central America was spared the bloody wars that characterized the struggles for independence in Mexico and Spanish South America. Central American creoles did not seize control of the government following Napoleon's invasion of Spain in 1808. Peninsular rule continued in Guatemala City until 1821. And independence when it came was the result of an act of an assembly of notables who on 15 September 1821 accepted the *fait accompli* of Agustín de Iturbide's Plan of Iguala. However, during the first two decades of the nineteenth century the kingdom of Guatemala had experienced severe

---

[1] Chiapas, a province of the kingdom of Guatemala, joined Mexico at independence. Panama was a province of the viceroyalty of New Granada and became part of the republic of Gran Colombia.

economic stress and social dislocation, and significant political activity. The conflicts of the years immediately preceding independence bear directly on the issues that disrupted the Central American union during the half century after 1821.

The period 1810–14, in particular, witnessed the beginnings of the political struggles in Central America that were to last for decades. There were creole conspiracies and rebellions in El Salvador, Nicaragua and Honduras as early as 1811 and 1812 and, towards the end of 1813, in the capital itself, but the strong and efficient government of José de Bustamante y Guerra, captain general and president of the *audiencia* of Guatemala (1811–18), denied success to these movements. Meanwhile, the Cortes of Cádiz and the Constitution that it promulgated in 1812 provided political definition and substance for the emerging creole liberals who had already begun to articulate economic and social grievances. The Constitution of 1812 established freedom of the press, elections not only for city councils but new provincial bodies (*diputaciones provinciales*) and colonial representation in Spain; it pointed the way towards more representative government and more democratic procedures; it encouraged freer trade and threatened traditional *fueros* and monopolies. The political foundation of the Liberal Party in Central America and of much of its programme for the remainder of the century was laid.[2] Bustamante abhorred the 'Cádiz Constitution and did his best to prevent or delay its implementation. Finally, the restoration of Ferdinand VII in 1814 justified Bustamante's authoritarian dictatorship and his repression of the liberals. But his successor in 1818, Carlos Urrutia y Montoya, feeble with age and illness, first relaxed the strong-arm rule and then accepted the re-establishment of the 1812 Constitution following the Revolution of 1820 in Spain.

The 1812 Constitution had not only encouraged and strengthened liberal political arguments in Central America, but also emphasized the function of local and provincial governments in making decisions for themselves and in standing up against the traditional domination of the metropoli – Spain, Mexico or Guatemala. This regional resentment and the emergence of separatism in Central America can be documented in all of the provinces, but nowhere was it so obvious as in El Salvador. Long an integral part of the province of Guatemala, El Salvador had grown in importance in the eighteenth century as the principal producer of indigo, the kingdom's leading export. Following the destruction of Santiago de

[2] Mario Rodríguez, *The Cádiz experiment in Central America, 1808–1826* (Berkeley, 1978).

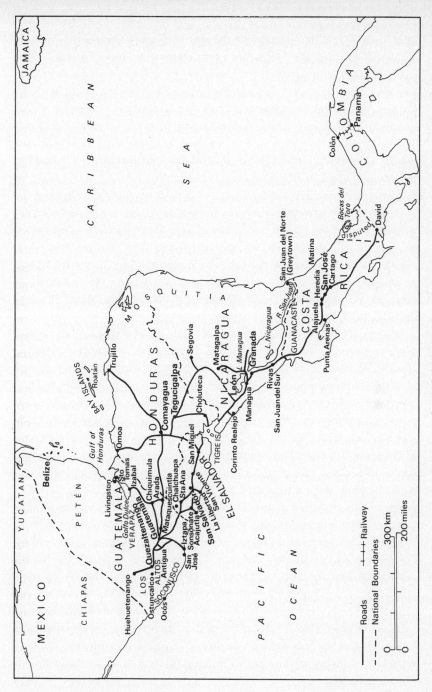

Central America in 1855

Guatemala in 1773 and its move to a new site about 40 kilometres away in 1776, San Salvador became the largest city in Central America and remained so until well after the establishment of independence. The creation of an intendancy in San Salvador in 1786 provided a degree of administrative autonomy for the first time and can be seen as the first step toward Salvadoran nationalism. Calls for ecclesiastical autonomy followed, as Salvadorans demanded their own bishop and separation from the diocese of Guatemala. The Cádiz reforms offered the Salvadoran creoles an opportunity for self-rule, and, understandably, San Salvador became a hotbed of liberal thought and action.

The resentment Salvadoran liberals felt towards what they termed the 'aristocracy' in Guatemala City, the conservative families (mostly creole) who controlled the land, the *consulado* and the *ayuntamiento*, was echoed in other provincial centres from Chiapas to Costa Rica. The restoration of the 1812 Constitution and the call for elections for the *ayuntamientos* and *diputaciones provinciales* in 1820 stimulated an increase in the level of political activity and a renewal of the political debate of 1811–14 throughout Central America.

Within the capital itself, the dialogue was between liberals and moderates and it was made public in the pages of two newspapers. *El Editor Constitucional,* directed by the fiery Pedro Molina, a physician of illegitimate parentage, without close ties to the principal families and representing the creole *letrados*, now for the first time challenged traditional institutions and the continuation of Spanish rule. Answering him was *El Amigo de la Patria*, edited by José Cecilio del Valle, who had come to the capital from a Honduran ranching family for an education and stayed to become one of the colony's leading intellectuals and a prominent attorney, widely respected among the creole elite. He had risen in position and importance during the Bustamante years as a loyal servant of that government, and his government connections caused him to counsel moderation and caution regarding independence. The leading creole families, led by the Aycinena clan, however, supported Molina's rabble-rousers, for they were now uneasy with the threats to their positions of prestige and monopoly that the return to power of the Spanish liberals promised. José del Valle, on the other hand, had the support of the colonial government, the Europeans, the opponents of free trade and the less wealthy creoles. The elections at the end of 1820 were not decisive, although Valle himself won election as *alcalde* of Guatemala City.

In February 1821 Iturbide began his rebellion in Mexico and news of his Plan of Iguala in favour of an independent monarchy spread southward. The new emphasis on local decision-making came into play, as the *ayuntamientos* in each city took it upon themselves to decide how they should react to events in Mexico. In Chiapas, the *ayuntamientos* of Comitán, Ciudad Real and Tuxtla each declared separately for the Plan respectively on 28 August and 3 and 5 September 1821 and joined independent Mexico. In Guatemala the acting Captain General, Gabino Gaínza, agreed on 14 September to the Diputación Provincial's request for a general meeting of the representatives of the principal institutions. In a stormy session the next day, creole and peninsular leaders debated the issues while a crowd outside clamoured for independence. In the end, the delegates, including most of the moderates led by José del Valle, voted in favour of independence. Virtually nothing else changed. The Spanish bureaucracy, headed by Gaínza, remained. The Guatemalan aristocracy were left in control of the government and the economy. Having escaped from the Spanish liberal regime, the creole elite no longer needed its alliance with Molina and the more radical of the local liberals; the Conservative Party was born.

It was intended that the decision taken in Guatemala City in favour of independence should apply to the entire kingdom, but the idea of local participation was now so powerful that each municipality voted separately as news travelled southward. All accepted independence from Spain, but there were variations in their approaches to the future. In San Salvador on 29 September a junta under the liberal leadership of Father José Matías Delgado proclaimed the independence of El Salvador and forced those who favoured union with Guatemala or Mexico to leave the city. Other Salvadoran towns responded differently and trouble broke out. Meanwhile, in Honduras Tegucigalpa accepted Guatemalan leadership while Comayagua insisted on independence from Guatemala as well as from Spain. Similarly, in Nicaragua conservative Granada promised to support the central government in Guatemala while León declared independence from Spain and Guatemala, although it was apparently willing to unite with Mexico! Costa Rica, remote and generally aloof from activities in the captaincy general, seceded from Spain on 27 October, leaving its position with respect to Guatemala and Mexico ambiguous while it established a provisional government completely independent of that in Nicaragua. But almost immediately its four major towns began to quarrel, as San José, Heredia and Alajuela vied for equality with Cartago, the colonial seat of power. As the national period opened, then, Central America was politically fragmented and caught up in a wave of regional and local acts of separation.

Annexation to Mexico became the first real issue clearly dividing conservatives and liberals. In general, conservatives all across Central America endorsed annexation, while liberals called for an independent republican federation. Because they controlled the apparatus of government in Guatemala and most of the other states, the conservatives succeeded in thwarting liberal efforts to resist annexation. Iturbide's dispatch of a Mexican army at the end of November furthered the annexationist cause. Violence flared in Guatemala and Nicaragua, but only in El Salvador did the republicans gain the upper hand. By the end of December 1821, 115 (104 unconditionally and 11 with certain stipulations) *ayuntamientos* had declared for incorporation into the Mexican empire. Another 32 left the matter to the provisional government while 21 declared that only a general congress could decide the issue. Only two *ayuntamientos* had opposed union absolutely, while 67 remained to be heard from. Also on the side of annexation was the powerful influence of Archbishop Ramón Casáus, who had only reluctantly accepted independence. On 5 January 1822 the provisional government declared that annexation was the overwhelming will of the country – as expressed through the *ayuntamientos* – and a few days later Gaínza, who remained titular head of state, prohibited further opposition to the decision. The provisional junta dissolved itself and Gaínza supervised a speedy election of delegates to the new congress in Mexico.

Only San Salvador and Granada rejected annexation outright, although division on the question continued in Costa Rica, where there was also sentiment for union with Colombia, and in Honduras, where the rivalry between Comayagua and Tegucigalpa continued. Led by Delgado, San Salvador turned to arms to maintain its position. Its forces, under the command of Manuel José de Arce, defeated Gaínza's Guatemalan army near Sonsonate, touching off a bloody war which was to continue intermittently for decades and was to poison chances for a successful Central American union. The arrival of a new captain-general, Vicente Filísola, with 600 Mexican troops proved decisive. Filísola took office on 22 June 1822 and immediately sought to reach a negotiated settlement. San Salvador entered into these talks apparently to buy time, for by November it was clear that the city would not submit peaceably to Mexican rule. Late that month Filísola invaded El Salvador with a force of two thousand. Frantically San Salvador sought a way out of its predicament, including a declaration of annexation to the United States. All failed, and the city capitulated on 10 February 1823. In the meantime, however, Granada continued to hold out against the annexationists in Nicaragua and in April in Costa Rica anti-Mexican troops from San José and Alajuela subdued the pro-imperial forces in Cartago.

Iturbide's empire, of course, was already doomed. While Filísola had subdued the liberals in El Salvador, liberals in Mexico had pronounced against the empire with the Plan of Casa Mata. After news arrived of the emperor's abdication, Filísola told the Guatemalan Diputación Provincial on 29 March that Mexico was in a state of anarchy. The provinces responded enthusiastically to his call for a Central American congress in accordance with the plan of 15 September 1821. Elections followed and the body which began its sessions on 24 June 1823 represented all of the states except Chiapas, which chose to remain with Mexico. Perhaps the most representative ever assembled by a Central American authority, this congress was decidedly more liberal than the previous government. Many of the conservatives were still in Mexico, and they had in any case been discredited by the collapse of the monarchy. Under the presidency of Father Delgado of El Salvador, on 1 July 1823 congress declared Central America free and independent and adopted the name *Provincias Unidas del Centro de América*, 'The United Provinces of the Centre of America'. The next day the congress became a National Constituent Assembly and set to work writing a republican constitution. Mexico recognized the United Provinces in August as Filísola and his army withdrew.

The new Central American republic began with rather naïve expressions of unity and optimism for the future after nearly two years of disunion and chaos which were now blamed on Spain, Mexico and their 'servile supporters'. Despite the sudden turn of political events in favour of the liberals, the real situation in Central America was not conducive to the success of the sort of modern, progressive nation that the framers of the 1824 Constitution envisioned. Serious economic and social problems and divisions stood in the way.

The United Provinces, even with the loss of Chiapas and excluding Belize, had a population of more than a million persons.[3] (See Table 1)

---

[3] Contemporary estimates of the population vary widely and are of doubtful reliability. The estimates in Table 1 reflect an analysis of these estimates together with colonial and late nineteenth-century demographic data and an estimated growth rate of about 1.3% during the first fifty years of independence, taking into consideration some variations caused by local disasters, epidemics and other circumstances.

Table 1  *Estimated Population of Central America, 1820–70*
(Thousands of inhabitants)

| State | 1820 | 1830 | 1840 | 1850 | 1860 | 1870 |
|---|---|---|---|---|---|---|
| Costa Rica | 63 | 72 | 86 | 101 | 115 | 137 |
| El Salvador | 248 | 271 | 315 | 366 | 424 | 493 |
| Guatemala | 595 | 670 | 751 | 847 | 951 | 1080 |
| Honduras | 135 | 152 | 178 | 203 | 230 | 265 |
| Nicaragua | 186 | 220 | 242 | 274 | 278 | 337 |
| Central America | 1227 | 1385 | 1572 | 1791 | 1998 | 2312 |

Most were illiterate peasants or peons with little voice in the future of the country. About 65 per cent of the population of Central America were Indian, 31 per cent *ladino* (*mestizo* and mulatto) and only about 4 per cent white. Individual states varied considerably from these estimates, of course. Guatemala had a larger percentage of Indians than any other state, while Costa Rica's tiny population was predominantly white. El Salvador, Nicaragua and Honduras had substantial *ladino* populations. There were some blacks, principally along the Honduran and Nicaraguan coasts, but they were for the most part outside Central American society.[4]

The economy of Central America had experienced considerable change in the two decades prior to independence, which placed additional burdens on the new republic. Briefly, in the late eighteenth century the kingdom of Guatemala had become an important exporter of Salvadoran and Guatemalan indigo. Exports beyond the isthmus from the other provinces were not very great, but Honduras and Nicaragua, and to a lesser extent Costa Rica, were important suppliers of livestock and agricultural foodstuffs to the indigo-producing regions and administrative centre of the kingdom. Growing evidence suggests that the late colonial economy was, therefore, very much tied to the international

[4] Reliable statistics on the racial composition of the population do not exist, but for the whole region, see the estimates of Severo Martínez Peláez, *La patria del criollo, ensayo de interpretación de la realidad colonial guatemalteca* (Guatemala, 1971), 397–8. Martínez Peláez says that Nicaragua was 84% *ladino* at the close of the colonial period. Alejandro Marroquín, *Apreciación sociológica de la independencia* (San Salvador, 1964), 25–8, has calculated the following percentages for El Salvador in 1807 (not including Sonsonate and Ahuachapán, which were still part of Guatemala): Spaniards 0.86%; creoles 2%; *ladinos* 53.07%; negroes and mulattos 0.1%; Indians 43.07%. It is probable that the racial composition of the Central American population did not greatly change during the period, although the process of *mestizaje* certainly continued. It is also probable that, owing to European immigration, the percentage of whites in Central America very slightly increased during the period 1821–70.

economy and that there was significant integration of the economy within the kingdom.[5]

The rapid decline of Salvadoran indigo production during the first two decades of the nineteenth century, however, brought serious economic dislocation throughout Central America. Locust plagues, attacks on Spanish shipping and competition from other indigo-producing areas with better access to European markets contributed to this significant reduction of exports and forced planters in Salvador and Guatemala to shift to producing foodstuffs, in turn cutting back purchases of livestock and grain from Honduras, Nicaragua and Costa Rica. Thus, as the colonial period closed, the kingdom was becoming less interdependent and less tied to the international market. This meant reduced living standards at a time when heavy taxes and loan demands by the Spanish government during the Napoleonic Wars were additional burdens on the Central American elites.[6]

The Guatemalan aristocracy, understandably, looked towards expanding trade, the removal of economic restrictions and new exports, notably of cochineal, as a means out of their difficult straits. Some had already turned to contraband trade, principally through British Honduras, compounding their difficulties with the Bustamante regime. At the same time they opposed economic advancement for other elements of the society and after independence the basic conservatism of the dominant class became manifest. Opposing them, especially in the provinces, were representatives of the professions and middle sectors and government bureaucrats who saw in liberalism the opportunity for greater advancement and economic opportunity. Both factions represented only a tiny percentage of the total population; the mass of Indians and *ladinos* were outside the political debates. But the economic hard times were felt not only by the elites. Indeed, the spread of poverty among the urban poor increased social tensions at the time of independence and helped to provide soldiers for the armies of both sides in the conflicts that followed.

The issues that divided liberals from conservatives at the outset of the national period were not very different from those which divided

[5] See Alberto Lanuza Matamoros, 'Estructuras socioeconómicas, poder y estado en Nicaragua (1821–1875)', (unpublished thesis, University of Costa Rica at San José, 1976), 83–9.

[6] R. L. Woodward, Jr, *Class privilege and economic development: the Consulado de Comercio of Guatemala, 1793–1871* (Chapel Hill, N.C., 1966), 39–41; R. S. Smith, 'Indigo production and trade in colonial Guatemala', *Hispanic American Historical Review*, 39/2 (1959), 183; Miles Wortman, 'Government revenue and economic trends in Central America, 1787–1819', *loc. cit.*, 55/2 (1975), 262–4.

Spaniards at the same time, and they had largely been delineated in debates over the Cádiz Constitution of 1812. Conservatives felt more secure with a monarchy while the liberals were republican. The Spanish Bourbons had not endeared themselves to either group sufficiently to allow monarchy to remain an institution long cherished by the conservatives, but even after the issue of monarchy *versus* republic was apparently settled in 1824, Central American conservatives retained serious scepticism about the ability of any but the educated and proper-tied to govern. A more important institution in the liberal–conservative struggle was the Church. The liberals sought to disestablish it and remove it from political and economic power, while the conservatives cherished it as a defender of their privileges and a vital element in both controlling and securing the support of the masses. Liberals sought to destroy monopolistic control of the economy and to eliminate the *fueros* of the conservatives – ecclesiastical, commercial, university, etc. Educa-tion was an issue closely related to the Church controversy, for the liberals favoured secular education with mass education as the ultimate goal, while conservatives defended an elitist educational system under the supervision of the Church. Leaders in both parties recognized the need for modernization and a rational approach to economic problems, as the utilitarian influence of Jeremy Bentham on both sides illustrates. Although the leading families of Central America were connected across the region by ties of family and marriage, differing economic and political circumstances at the local level tended to divide them along conservative or liberal lines. At the outset, there was considerable political manoeuvring, but the bitter struggles that wracked Central America after independence removed much of the middle ground and crystallized the two parties into warring camps that would characterize Central American politics for the remainder of the century.

After the declaration of independence from Mexico (1 July 1823) the liberals at first dominated the National Constituent Assembly. They moved quickly to remove class privileges. On 23 July all titles of distinction, royalty or nobility, including even the use of 'don', were abolished. The same decree included anticlerical reforms; bishops and archbishops, for example, were stripped of any title except 'padre'.[7]

---

[7] Colonial terminology was also rejected: *audiencias* and *ayuntamientos* became, respectively, *cortes territoriales* and *municipalidades*. Later, other ceremonial forms, symbols and aristocratic vestiges were abolished (21 August 1823). 'Dios, Union, Libertad', replaced 'Dios guarde a Ud. muchos

Annulment of all acts of the imperial Mexican government and peremptory dismissal of Spanish and Mexican officials soon contributed to resentment against the liberals. The first violence flared in mid-September, when Captain Rafael Ariza y Torres led a revolt, ostensibly demanding backpay for the military. It resulted in a reshuffling of the government towards more conservative interests, but then liberal troops from El Salvador arrived to support the government. Civil war was averted, but Guatemalan residents resented strongly the presence of the Salvadorans and ill-feeling persisted even after the troops left. This uprising – and a pro-Spanish revolt which the army also quicky suppressed – revealed the unsettled conditions in Guatemala and the growing hostility to the liberal assembly. Inevitably, therefore, the balance of power in the assembly began to shift as debate over the proposed constitution continued. The document that finally emerged in November 1824 was a compromise between radicals and conservatives, and José del Valle played an important part in its formulation. It blended elements of the Spanish Constitution of 1812 with the U.S. Constitution of 1789. Dedicated to the protection of 'liberty, equality, security and property' (art. 2), the 1824 Constitution guaranteed Roman Catholicism as the religion of the state 'to the exclusion of the public exercise of any other' (art. 11), outlawed slavery (art. 13), and provided extensive guarantees of individual liberties (arts. 152–76). A complex system of indirect election provided for a unicameral federal congress (arts. 23–54). All legislation had to be approved by a senate composed of two senators from each state, no more than one of whom could be an ecclesiastic (art. 92), although the congress could override senate vetoes with a two-thirds vote, except in cases concerning taxation, which required a three-fourths majority (arts. 76–86). The president had no veto and was required to execute the law once it had passed the senate (arts. 87–8). The president, who also was commander-in-chief of the armed forces, and vice president were indirectly elected for four-year terms. A supreme court, also elected indirectly, had from five to seven justices serving two-year, staggered terms (arts. 132–40). The Constitution provided for a federation of five autonomous states with state assemblies, state executives and state judicial officers, whose first duty would be to form state

años' as the official compliment closing all correspondence (4 August 1823). Alejandro Marure, *Efemérides de los hechos notables acaecidos en la República de Centro-América desde el año de 1821 hasta el de 1842* (2nd edn, Guatemala, 1895), 11–12; Isidro Menéndez, comp., *Recopilación de las leyes del Salvador en Centro América* (2nd edn, San Salvador, 1956), I, 20, 126.

constitutions consistent with the federal charter. Each state was also to have a representative council, analogous to the federal senate, to approve legislative acts and advise state governors (arts. 177–95). The Constitution went into effect immediately, even before it was ratified by the first elected congress in August 1825.[8]

The first national elections were dominated by a spirited campaign between Salvadoran liberal Manuel José de Arce and moderate José del Valle, both members of the interim governing junta. Violence erupted in several places, and the government threatened those who opposed the new constitutional system with death. When the new congress convened in February 1825, presided over by Guatemalan Dr Mariano Gálvez, liberals appeared to have triumphed, yet the election for president in April favoured the more moderate José del Valle. Receiving 41 of the 79 electoral votes actually cast, he nevertheless lacked by one vote a majority of the 82 votes authorized, and thus the election was thrown into the Congress. Arce intrigued not only to win the presidency, but also to form a broadly-based coalition which, he believed, would allow the federal government to govern successfully. To this end he gained support from conservative members with assurances that he would not insist on a separate bishop for El Salvador. The congress elected Arce by a vote of 22–5. Valle refused to accept the vice-presidency, as did the liberal radical, José Francisco Barrundia, the position finally going to the Guatemalan conservative Mariano Beltranena. The new republic began its existence, therefore, under the cloud of suspicion of betrayal of the wishes of the electorate and with the extreme liberals (the Barrundia faction) already disenchanted with the liberal president, who they believed had sold out to the hated '*serviles*' (conservatives).

President Arce's government never really had effective control of any of the five states which made up the federation. Each continued to go its own way. State governments organized themselves in accordance with the Constitution, but in several there was serious disagreement between liberal and conservative factions. Arce had personally led the troops in pacifying Nicaragua early in 1825, but the peace he established there was but a brief interlude in the struggle between Granada and León. Costa Rica, under the firm hand of Juan Mora, remained aloof from the federal government and achieved a degree of order and progress. Serious trouble loomed in El Salvador, where the installation of Father Delgado

---

[8] 'Constitución Federal de 1824' in Ricardo Gallardo, *Las constituciones de la República Federal de Centro-América* (Madrid, 1958), II, 103–38.

as bishop faced opposition from Archbishop Casáus and Arce's coalition federal government in Guatemala City. This was a symbolic issue, representing the powerful Salvadoran urge for independence from Guatemala. The most urgent problem faced by Arce, however, was the Guatemalan state government, dominated by the liberal '*Fiebres*' and led by Juan Barrundia. That government proceeded along radical lines, repeatedly offending the more conservative elements in the federal government with whom Arce had allied. During Arce's first year in office the rift between the two governments widened. In April 1826 Arce deposed Barrundia and in September he placed him under arrest. The remainder of the Guatemalan state government, under Lieut. Governor Cirilio Flores, fled first to San Martín Jilotepeque and later to Quezaltenango, where the state legislature enacted inflamatory liberal laws, declaring children of the clergy legal inheritors of Church property, abolishing the merchant guild (*Consulado*), and cutting the *diezmo* in half. These laws were unenforceable, but they served as a basis for much liberal legislation after 1829. The liberals' tenure in Quezaltenango was short-lived, for in October a mob attacked Flores, tearing him literally limb from limb, and the liberal government collapsed.

A new Guatemalan state government under the conservative Mariano Aycinena now co-operated with President Arce in driving the remaining liberals from the state. But Salvadoran liberals now rose to challenge the pro-Arce government in San Salvador, touching off a bloody three-year civil war. Arce commanded the federal forces, but his government depended so heavily on the state of Guatemala that Aycinena soon supplanted him in importance. Bitterness and atrocities characterized both sides in this vicious struggle that spread over much of Guatemala, El Salvador and Honduras. In the latter state, Francisco Morazán rallied the liberals and, following his defeat of federal forces at La Trinidad, Honduras (10 November 1827), emerged as the leading liberal military figure. Arce now sought conciliation, and when that failed he resigned the presidency in February 1828. Vice-President Beltranena took over, but in reality Aycinena became the principal leader against the liberals. His government drew heavily on forced loans from the clergy and local wealthy citizens, including foreign merchants, causing the latter to welcome a liberal victory. Federal troops won a bloody and costly victory in March 1828 at Chalcuapa, but thereafter the tide turned in favour of General Morazán. Completing his reconquest of Honduras and El Salvador by the end of 1828, he invaded Guatemala early in 1829, laying siege to the capital in February, when the liberals re-established a state government at Antigua. Morazán's victory at Las Charcas on 15 March was decisive, although Aycinena did not finally capitulate until 12 April.

The immediate fruits of the civil war (1826–9) were a vindictive policy toward conservative leaders and the enactment of radical liberal legislation. José F. Barrundia presided over the republic until September 1830 when elections elevated Morazán to the presidency. Morazán defeated José del Valle who, unassociated with the Arce–Aycinena government in Guatemala, was now able to return to politics, although unable to stem the liberal landslide. Juan Barrundia was reinstated briefly as governor of Guatemala, but in 1831 Mariano Gálvez won election there. Although clearly in the liberal camp, Dr Gálvez was less radical than the Barrundias, and eventually a serious split would surface between them. Morazán also had allies in office in the three central states and liberals had the upper hand in Costa Rica, but opposition in all of these states soon began to limit their effectiveness. Difficulties within El Salvador contributed to Morazán's decision to move the national capital to San Salvador in 1834.

The presidential election of 1834 reflected widespread dissatisfaction with Morazán and his programme, and José del Valle successfully challenged his bid for re-election. Unfortunately for the moderate cause, however, Valle died before taking office, and Morazán, with the second highest number of votes, constitutionally remained as president. With José del Valle, it appears, died the last hope for a moderate course. Morazán's victory under these terms left widespread bitterness and resentment among moderates and conservatives. Their frustration turned to hatred as grievances against the liberals mounted.

The case of Guatemala state best illustrates the nature of the conflicts of the 1830s and their results. Gálvez shared Morazán's belief that Central America could become a modern, progressive republic through enlightened social and economic legislation. With the leading conservatives in exile, a period of peace and order seemed assured, as, armed with extraordinary powers to deal with opposition, the Gálvez government became the pilot for Morazán's liberal programme. Convinced that Spanish colonialism was at the root of their underdevelopment, they sought to destroy Hispanic institutions and to replace them by emulating the apparent success of the United States. In practice, however, although Gálvez gained substantial acceptance of his programme among the elite, he failed to overcome widespread opposition among the lower classes of the country.

The sources of opposition were several. Liberal trade policy had damaged seriously the native weaving industry, and Gálvez's tariff modifications were too late to protect it. More serious was a new direct head tax of two pesos per capita which contributed to peasant restlessness generally. In El Salvador such a tax resulted in widespread popular rebellion in 1833, forcing suspension of the levy there, but Gálvez maintained the tax in Guatemala. Heavy demands for forced labour to build roads and other public works intensified the resentment.

Another unpopular aspect of the liberal economic programme was the policy of promoting private acquisition of public or communal lands as a means of increasing production and exports. Cochineal expansion began to increase the demand for the land and labour of Indians and *ladinos* in central and eastern Guatemala. Moreover, a number of large grants to foreigners caused considerable unrest. British commercial activity at Belize had intensified the traditional suspicion of foreigners. Spanish colonial administrations had dealt vigorously with foreign interlopers, but since independence liberal policy had welcomed them, causing apprehension among those who believed themselves to be victims of foreign competition. Foreign influence was evident in many aspects of the Gálvez programme, but the concessions made to mahogany loggers and the projects to populate the northern and eastern areas of the country with English colonists caused residents of those regions to regard the liberals as favouring foreign rather than national interests. Between March and August 1834 the Guatemalan government ceded nearly all of its public land to foreign colonization companies. As the British hold on Belize, the Miskito Shore and the Bay Islands tightened, and as Anglo-American colonizers in Texas threw off Mexican rule, many Guatemalans began to doubt the wisdom of Gálvez's colonization schemes. Ignoring or suppressing petitions from residents against the colonization contracts, however, Gálvez rejected the idea that the liberals were betraying their country to Europeans. Revolts which broke out in Chiquimula and other eastern towns in the autumn of 1835 were possibly linked to an uprising in El Salvador against Morazán. Troops suppressed the rebellion, but the inhabitants remained resentful, especially after the arrival of the first shipload of British colonists in the middle of 1836.

Another part of the liberal programme which proved offensive to the rural masses was the attack on the clergy. Anticlericalism ran especially

high since the Church had backed the conservative regime of Mariano
Aycinena from 1826 to 1829. Morazán's federal government exiled many
anti-liberal clergy, beginning with Archbishop Casáus. Following the
suppression of the regular orders and the establishment of religious
liberty, the federal government prevailed on state governments to
continue the assault on the traditional power and privilege of the clergy.
Between 1829 and 1831 Guatemala censored ecclesiastical correspondence, seized church funds and confiscated the property of religious
houses. In 1832 Gálvez stopped the collection of the tithe, ended many
religious holidays, confiscated more church property, decreed the right
of the clergy to write their wills as they pleased and legitimized the
inheritance of parents' property by children of the clergy. Later, the
Guatemalan legislature authorized civil marriage, legalized divorce and
removed education from church supervision. In Indian and *ladino* villages where parishioners were already chafing at Gálvez's policies on
other grounds, the priests railed against a government that challenged
their authority and attacked their sacred institutions, brought Protestant
foreigners into the country and threatened the very foundations of
society. These rural priests were in the vanguard of the uprisings that
rocked Guatemala in 1837.

Further opposition to Liberal government was provoked by the new
judicial system. Persuaded that the Hispanic system of private *fueros* and
multiple courts was unjust and antiquated, the liberals adopted the
Edward Livingston Codes, which went into effect on 1 January 1837.
José F. Barrundia promoted these codes, written for Louisiana in 1824,
as a modern replacement for the system they had been abolishing
piecemeal. Trial by jury was the central feature of the new system, and
almost immediately problems arose in the countryside, where illiteracy
was general and the deeply entrenched class structure made trial by jury
impracticable. The mass of the population identified the Codes more
with centralized rule from Guatemala City, with foreign influence and
with anti-clericalism than with social justice. Moreover, the authoritarian manner in which the liberals introduced these and other reforms did
little to improve relations between government and people. Military
repression in Central America had been escalating ever since the strong-
armed rule of Bustamante, but the insensitivity of both the federal and
state governments in their efforts to develop the export economy, in the
regulation of the morality of the inhabitants, in suppressing criticism of
their own policies and in persecuting their political enemies through

exile and confiscatory measures added to their unpopularity, as did the conduct of government troops.

The cholera epidemic which entered the country from Belize in 1837 turned the threatened and real grievances of the peasants in eastern Guatemala into open rebellion. In March 1837 the government quarantined infected areas and pursued other sanitary measures, undoubtedly justified but poorly understood. The peasants, already alienated from the Gálvez government, feared the vaccines and believed the priests who told them that the medicine which health officials put into the water was poison. Panic and violence resulted. Although the first major insurgency of 1837 took place at San Juan Ostuncalco, in Los Altos, where natives rioted against officials charged with effecting the Livingston Codes, the greatest trouble was in the Montaña region of eastern Guatemala. A natural leader, José Rafael Carrera, emerged who was to organize and lead the peasants to victory, and to determine the destiny of Guatemala for the next twenty-five years, until his death in 1865. Born in the capital in 1814, Carrera, a *ladino*, had served as a drummer in the conservative army during the 1826–9 civil war and later drifted into the Montaña. There he became a swineherd and gained some property after a village curate arranged a marriage with a woman of Mataquescuintla. Carrera initially commanded a patrol charged with enforcing the cholera quarantine, but he turned against the government and took his troops to the aid of peasants who were resisting a government force at Santa Rosa. Carrera's leadership turned their defeat into victory there and soon he commanded a guerrilla band that controlled much of eastern Guatemala. The cholera epidemic limited the government's ability to raise troops, but Carrera's partisans increased in numbers and effectiveness. In late June he listed his demands in a manifesto that reflected the conservative influence of the priests who advised him: 1. abolition of the Livingston Codes; 2. protection of life and property; 3. return of the archbishop and restoration of the religious orders; 4. repeal of the head tax; 5. amnesty for all exiles since 1829; and 6. respect for Carrera's orders under pain of death to violators.

Faced with popular insurgency, Gálvez formed a coalition of national unity with the conservatives, reminiscent of Arce's earlier action. He thus drove the more radical liberals led by J. F. Barrundia and Pedro Molina into an opposition faction. The divisions among the elite in the capital played into the hands of Carrera, whose ragged army extended the area of its control and terrorized the propertied classes, commerce and foreign travellers. Efforts to patch up the rift among the liberals ended in Gálvez's resignation in favour of Lieutenant Governor Pedro Valenzuela, who was more acceptable to Barrundia. But it failed to prevent Carrera's horde from over-running Guatemala City on 31 January 1838. He soon withdrew his forces from the capital and returned to his home district of Mita, but not before the beginnings of an alliance with the conservatives was born.

The economic power of the creole aristocratic class – large landowners and merchants – had been damaged but not broken by the liberal rulers. In fact, some had acquired confiscated church property and actually expanded their holdings during the 1830s. Although some members of the class remained in the liberal camp, most now supported the conservative cause. In 1833 the conservatives made a strong resurgence in the Guatemalan legislature and courted 'General' Carrera by attempting to satisfy some of his demands. The Church regained its former status; liberal military commanders were relieved of their posts; there was a move toward return to constitutional rule that allowed conservatives to gain election to office; the Livingston Codes were repealed in March. These acts reflected the popular will as voiced by the guerrilla caudillo. The preamble to a decree of 12 March, 1838, terminating all non-elected officeholders, illustrated the attention the legislature paid to this will when it acknowledged that 'a great majority of the population of the State have armed themselves to resist the administration that violated their guarantees and the fundamental pact', and justified the revolution against Gálvez, 'directed to establishing law and liberty . . . in self preservation against tyranny, [as] not only legitimate but consecrated by reason and justice'.[9]

Carrera, impatient with the slow progress of the legislature in dismantling the liberal reforms, resumed his guerrilla attacks and threatened to invade the capital once more. At the same time, conservative electoral gains and the new representative council headed by the conservative Mariano Rivera Paz put the Barrundia faction in an untenable position. In the end, Barrundia fell back on his liberal ally, Morazán, who rallied to his aid in mid-March with a thousand Salvadoran troops. Valenzuela's government had cautioned the federal caudillo against invading Guatemala, warning that it would upset the understanding with Carrera who had returned to Mita in peace. But when Carrera returned to the offensive, it forced the state to look to the federal government for help.

[9] *Boletín Oficial* (Guatemala), no. 11 (17 March 1838), 474–7.

Morazán launched an all-out campaign to track down and destroy Carrera's forces, while arresting the conservative direction of the Guatemalan government. The guerrillas responded with new ferocity. Atrocities multiplied on both sides. And by this time the federal government also faced conservative opposition in Nicaragua, Honduras and within El Salvador as well as Guatemala, while Costa Rica, now under the mildly conservative rule of Braulio Carrillo, was effectively ignoring the federation. The British consul, Frederick Chatfield, who formerly had supported Morazán, now regarded the federal cause as hopeless and sought to develop close British ties with the emerging conservative rulers. When the federal congress, recognizing and feeling these pressures, declared on 7 July 1838 that the states were 'sovereign, free and independent political bodies', Morazán returned to San Salvador to reassert his authority there.[10] He had by this time greatly weakened Carrera's influence, but had not eliminated the threat altogether.

Thus, by mid-1838 the battle lines were drawn. Carrera was the champion of the conservative cause for autonomy against Morazán and the liberals for federation. In other states the conservatives consolidated their strength and organization in alliance with the emerging popular caudillos. Thus, conservatism became closely related to local autonomy and the breakup of the Central American federation. With Morazán in San Salvador the conservatives in Guatemala quickly regained power, and on 22 July Valenzuela turned over the executive power to Rivera Paz. The new government resumed the dismantling of the liberal programme. In the country Carrera once more controlled a large area. A sudden counter-offensive in September by liberal General Carlos Salazar, however, forced Carrera to retreat into la Montaña, and when Morazán rejoined the chase, Carrera bought time by agreeing on 23 December to lay down his arms and recognize the government at Guatemala City in return for restoration of his military command in the district of Mita.

Encouraged by the apparent collapse of Carrera's guerrillas, Morazán on 30 January 1839 deposed Rivera Paz and replaced him with General Salazar. In the meantime, however, conservatives had gained power in Honduras and Nicaragua and joined forces against the liberals in El Salvador. The new liberal thrust had convinced Carrera that there could be no peace until Morazán was eliminated. On 24 March 1839 in a *pronunciamiento* from Mataquescuintla, he accused Morazán of cruelty

[10] Manuel Pineda de Mont (comp.), *Recopilación de las leyes de Guatemala* (Guatemala, 1869), I, 69.

toward the clergy and other Guatemalans, of destroying commerce, of confiscating private property and of spreading terror throughout the land. Swearing to restore Rivera Paz, he joined in alliance with the Honduran and Nicaraguan conservatives against Morazán. Within a month Rivera Paz and the conservatives once more ruled Guatemala. Carrera spent the remainder of the year mopping up in El Salvador and Honduras. Then, in January 1840, he swept into Los Altos, which in 1838 had seceded from Guatemala, and crushed the liberals there.

The inevitable showdown between Carrera and Morazán came in March 1840, when Carrera's forces routed the liberal army at Guatemala City. Morazán and a few of his officers escaped and eventually reached David in Panama, but the federation was finished. Two years later Morazán returned, reorganized his army in El Salvador with less support than he anticipated and then invaded Costa Rica, where he toppled Braulio Carrillo. Morazán's dreams of revitalizing the federation fell almost immediately before a popular insurgency that rose against him. Following a quick trial, he was executed by firing squad on 15 September 1842.

The defeat of Morazán and liberalism reflected both popular and elite disenchantment with liberal policy and a nostalgic search for a restoration of the supposed tranquillity of the Hispanic era. Also discernible is a pro-Hispanic xenophobia vaguely related to the birth of nationalism in each of the five states. The trend was most obvious in Guatemala, traditional seat of Spanish authority and tradition. However, while the conservatives had clearly strengthened their position, they were not yet dominant. In a period characterized by civil war within and between the states, the immediate masters of Central America in the 1840s were local caudillos of whom Carrera was the greatest. Carrera tried to maintain his dominance in Guatemala by playing off liberal and conservative members of the elite against each other, removing governments whenever they failed to be submissive to his bidding. The Church was the major beneficiary and his leading institutional supporter and the Jesuits and other religious orders returned to Central America. However, the liberals found that Carrera was a potential ally against the conservatives, and they were largely responsible for his accession to the presidency for the first time in 1844. Some checks on clerical privilege followed, but Carrera would never condone a full return to liberal policies, so it was inevitable that the liberals should eventually try to oust him.

New uprisings in eastern Guatemala combined with liberal opposition to force Carrera from office in 1848. The liberals were in control of Congress and Carrera's failure to end the uprising in the Montaña led him in January to offer his resignation. The conservatives persuaded him to withdraw it, but as matters worsened, he decided to accede to liberal demands for a new constituent assembly which he convened on 15 August. Addressing its opening session, he reviewed his efforts to bring peace in Guatemala, the economic growth that had occurred and his establishment of absolute Guatemalan independence in 1847. He then announced his resignation and headed for exile in Mexico, initiating at the same time the crisis that would lead to his triumphant return.

Chaos followed as Carrera watched from Chiapas. None of the series of short-term governments that followed were able to restore order or provide unified government. In mid September the conservatives regained temporary control of the Guatemalan Congress, declared Carrera a national hero and confirmed his 1847 declaration of Guatemalan independence. The liberals faced a united conservative opposition divided among themselves, as so often in this period. On 1 January 1849 Colonel Mariano Paredes took office in Guatemala City as a compromise chief of state. Closely advised by conservative statesman Luis Batres, Paredes publicly opposed Carrera's return, but privately condoned it. On 24 January Carrera announced his decision to restore peace and order in Guatemala. Liberal forces attempted to deny his return, but the Paredes government undermined their effectiveness and Carrera took Quezaltenango in April. Soon after, the government reached a peace agreement with the caudillo. Paredes remained as president, but Carrera, recommissioned a lieutenant-general, became commander-in-chief of the armed forces. Restoring order, he dealt vindictively with the liberal leaders who had opposed him. The threat of death faced those who did not flee. Thus, the liberals ceased to play a major role in Guatemalan politics for twenty years, although a few remained in the Congress and in minor offices.

After crushing rebellion in la Montaña and marching into El Salvador to assist the conservatives there (see below), Carrera once more became president of Guatemala (6 November 1851), and from 1854 president for life, a virtual monarch, with authority to designate his successor. Until his death in 1865, closely allied to the Church and the conservative aristocracy, he remained one of the most powerful caudillos in the hemisphere. He maintained friendly governments in Honduras and El

Salvador by force and also influenced the politics of Nicaragua and Costa Rica.

No Central American state escaped domination by conservative caudillos during the mid-nineteenth century, although only Guatemala had one of such durability as Carrera. In El Salvador, Honduras and Nicaragua, the turmoil among rival caudillos was especially devastating. With the liberals in disarray, some caudillos, notably Trinidad Muñoz of Nicaragua and Francisco Dueñas of El Salvador, switched parties in order to take advantage of local opportunities and circumstances.

Despite continued liberal strength in El Salvador, no leader professing Morazanista views could long escape Guatemalan intervention. Following Morazán's defeat in 1840, Carrera had placed one of his own officers, Francisco Malespín, in power. The latter's command of the military made him the dominant caudillo in El Salvador and a political force in Nicaragua and Honduras until his assassination in 1846. In addition to his ties to Carrera and the Guatemalan conservatives, Malespín worked closely with the politically active bishop of San Salvador, Jorge Viteri, and the British consul, Frederick Chatfield, so that while liberals might continue to hold political and legislative offices, conservative interests prevailed. The strength of liberalism in El Salvador, however, caused Malespín to co-operate with and use liberals (as did Carrera himself in the 1840s), which at times gave him problems with his conservative allies.

Meanwhile, Carrera's ally in Honduras, Francisco Ferrera, worked to establish conservative rule there, and he co-operated with Malespín in neutralizing the liberals in El Salvador and Nicaragua as well. Like Carrera, Ferrera came from a lower class *ladino* background and was unconnected with the leading families. As with Carrera, too, the clergy had a very great influence on his rise to power and on his way of thinking. A bitter foe of the Morazanistas, Ferrera, who had first ruled his state in 1833–5, became its first 'president' in January 1841. Although he was the leading caudillo in the country until his death in 1848, the liberals kept Honduras in a state of war much of the time. Ferrera and Malespín checked the liberals regularly. On 22 May 1845 a *coup* in Comayagua briefly gave the liberal leader, Trinidad Cabañas, control of the government for forty days. Soon back in control, Ferrera declined the presidency in 1847, but continued as minister of war under Juan Lindo, one of the more enlightened caudillos of the period and one not easily classified as liberal or conservative.

Lindo had served as first president of El Salvador (1841–2) under the protection of Malespín, where he had opposed restoration of Morazán's federation. Returning to his native Honduras he gained Ferrera's protection, although he was disliked by some of the more militaristic conservatives. Among his memorable acts as president of Honduras was his declaration of war against the United States in July 1847, in support of Mexico. In 1848 he convened a constituent assembly which established a more conservative constitution. Lindo's enlightened conservatism provided Honduras with its first real peace since independence. That peace was broken, however, when his foreign minister, General Santos Guardiola, attempted to oust him in 1850. The intervention of Trinidad Cabañas with Salvadoran liberal troops and the promise of Nicaraguan aid saved Lindo, whose conservatism was nearer that of José del Valle than that of Guardiola or Carrea. This event decidedly moved him into the liberal camp, and Lindo joined Cabañas in El Salvador in an effort to defeat Carrera in 1851. Carrera, however, won a decisive victory at San José la Arada, near Chiquimula, on 27 February 1851. In 1852 Lindo declined a third term as president and allowed the congress to elect Cabañas to succeed him. The more blatant liberalism of Cabañas and his renewed efforts to establish the Central American federation led almost immediately to an invasion from Guatemala by Guardiola, supported by Carrera, and resulted in Cabañas' defeat on 6 July 1855. Following a brief struggle for the presidency, Guardiola took possession of the office in February 1856 and held it until 1862. His unenlightened conservative rule brought some order but little progress to Honduras.

In Costa Rica, after the execution of Morazán in 1842, conservative interests generally prevailed, although the state remained politically unsettled until the strong-armed but enlightened conservative, J. Rafael Mora, seized power in 1849 and held it for a decade. By contrast Nicaragua suffered more than any of the other states from the mid-nineteenth-century civil wars between liberals and conservatives. Here the opportunistic struggles between local caudillos were more pronounced than elsewhere and the continual meddling, especially by the liberals, in the affairs of El Salvador and Honduras led to bloody and costly conflict. As conservatives consolidated their position in and around Granada, they, too, sought alliances abroad to check the persistent liberal strength of León. Nicaraguan conservatives even showed some willingness to consider reunification as a solution to the constant disorder they had experienced since independence. Fruto Chamorro, illegitimate son of an immigrant from Guatemala at the close of the colonial era, emerged as the leading conservative caudillo and established one of the most important Nicaraguan conservative clans. Liberal control of León was dealt a severe blow when José Trinidad Muñoz, renouncing his former liberal allies and supporting conservative J. L. Sandoval, took over in 1845. Sandoval and several conservative successors were almost continually besieged by liberal caudillos supported from El Salvador. In 1847 Bishop Viteri was transferred to Nicaragua where the political climate was far more favourable to him than in liberal San Salvador, and soon after Nicaragua reached a new concordat with the pope. When Muñoz returned to the liberal camp and rebelled against the government in 1851, Chamorro's forces defeated him and exiled him to El Salvador. The rise of Managua as a compromise capital between León and Granada began about this time, as several chieftains, including Chamorro in 1852, established temporary headquarters there. The conservatives generally held the upper hand during the early 1850s and followed the pattern elsewhere in Central America of emphasizing state sovereignty. They designated Nicaragua a 'republic' in 1854, changed the supreme director's title to 'president', and symbolically replaced the top stripe in the blue-white-blue liberal tricolour with a yellow stripe. Similarly symbolic was the motto of the republic's new seal: 'Liberty, Order, Labour'. A conservative constitution replaced the 1838 liberal charter. Yet the liberals refused to give up and by 1855 liberals invading from El Salvador gained control of the western part of the country and established a rival government again in León. It was at this point, as we shall see, that the filibustering expedition of William Walker arrived to play a decisive part in the conflict between liberals and conservatives in Nicaragua.

Since the independence of Central America commercial interests in North America and Europe had viewed the isthmus in terms of an interoceanic transit route. Both federal and state governments had encouraged canal schemes, but British, Dutch, American and French efforts during the first two decades after independence were ill conceived and undercapitalized. They had little effect beyond fuelling high expectations. Great Britain and the United States, however, pursued an active diplomacy designed both to insure their respective rights in any interoceanic route and to protect the interests of their subjects.

United States economic interests on the isthmus before 1850 were negligible, yet a series of U.S. agents did a remarkably good job of protecting the few Americans there, and, perhaps more importantly, they were direct carriers of the 'Jacksonian revolution' to Central America. (The French representatives had a similar ideological impact and were important noticeably in the Guatemalan revolution of 1848.)

Britain's economic and territorial interests were more substantial. British settlements at Belize and along the Miskito Shore from the Bay Islands to Costa Rica had secured for Britain a major share of Central American trade even before the close of the colonial era.[11] During the early years of independence Belize became the principal entrepot for Central American trade, while London financial houses supplied credit and loans for development to both state and federal governments. Soon after independence the English government sent George Alexander Thompson to investigate trade and canal possibilities, especially in Nicaragua. He initiated close relationships between British diplomats and Central American leaders, particularly those of the conservative party. In 1837–8 an English designer, John Baily, surveyed a canal route for the Nicaraguan government which, combined with the detailed report on canal potentials prepared by United States agent, John Lloyd Stephens, soon after, stimulated much foreign interest in the project. From 1834 to 1852 Frederick Chatfield represented the British government in Central America and worked deliberately to foster and protect British economic interests as well as trying to involve his government in more ambitious imperial schemes. Although he did not actively disrupt the Central American union, his sympathies ultimately lay with the conservatives and he became an important element in the intrigue and political manoeuvring of the 1840s as he sought guarantees for British bondholders and called in the Royal Navy when necessary to force concessions. In league with leading Guatemalan and Costa Rican conservatives, he played a significant role in the emergence of strong conservative governments in those states. Chatfield's personal secretary was Manuel F. Pavón, one of Carrera's leading advisers. Thus, as the middle states sought to restore the liberal federation, Chatfield worked to counter it with a conservative league or separate conservative sovereign states.[12]

From the outset British pretensions along the eastern coast of Central America had troubled the liberals. The Belize settlement, the ill-fated

[11] Troy S. Floyd, *The Anglo-Spanish struggle for Mosquitia* (Albuquerque, N.M., 1967).
[12] See Mario Rodríguez, *A Palmerstonian diplomat in Central America: Frederick Chatfield, Esq.* (Tucson, Ariz., 1964).

Poyais colonization adventure of Gregor MacGregor on the Honduran coast in 1823–4 and British trading posts along the Miskito coast of Nicaragua served the expansion of commerce, but they also challenged Central American sovereignty. British pursuit of fugitive slaves from Belize into Guatemalan territory was a further irritation to the liberals, who had abolished slavery immediately following independence.

In 1839 a British warship ejected Central American troops from the Bay Islands, and two years later Lord Palmerston declared that the islands were British territory, and that the British subjects who had settled there should be given some protection. This latest example of gunboat diplomacy provoked a storm of protest across Central America. The mid-century conservative governments proved more successful at resisting most British territorial ambitions and defending national independence than their liberal predecessors.

Meanwhile, close trading relations had developed between Britain and the isthmus. The Belize commercial firm headed by Marshal Bennet and John Wright took advantage of Belize's role as the principal port for Central America's exports and imports. Lacking protected deep-water ports of their own, Central Americans turned after independence to the Belize merchants to get their products to market as well as to supply them with manufactured goods. British merchants did not generally establish themselves in Central America to the extent they did in several Latin American states, but there were a few notable exceptions. Of these the most important was Bennet, who established the Guatemalan house of William Hall and Carlos Meany as a branch of his Belize firm in the 1820s. In the same decade George Skinner and Charles Klee established mercantile houses which continue to be important to the present day. Among others who served British mercantile interests during the first thirty years of independence were Thomas Manning, John Foster, Jonas Glenton and Walter Bridge in Nicaragua; William Barchard, Richard McNally, Frederick Lesperance, William Kilgour and Robert Parker, who operated with less permanent success in El Salvador; and Peter and Samuel Shepherd on the Miskito coast. The Shepherds received a massive land grant from the Miskito king in return for a few cases of whiskey and bolts of cotton chintz.

Central American imports reflected the close ties to British commerce. By 1840 nearly 60 per cent of Guatemalan imports came via the Belize settlement, while another 20 per cent came directly from Britain. Of the remaining 20 per cent, three-quarters came from Spain. The expansion of the British textile industry was important in providing markets for Salvadoran and Guatemalan indigo and cochineal. And from 1825 Britain had steadily reduced her duties on nearly all Central America's principal exports: cochineal, indigo, dyewoods, mahogany and other fine woods, hides and tortoise shells. By 1846 all Central American produce except coffee entered Britain duty free. Coffee, which had become more important than tobacco in Costa Rica after the collapse of Cuban coffee exports in the mid-1830s, soon received preferential treatment as well. Tables 2, 3 and 4 reflect the extent and expansion of British commerce during the first thirty years of independence.[13]

Belize remained the only Caribbean port of any importance, despite repeated Central American efforts to develop their own stations. Such ports as the Central Americans did maintain – Izabal, Omoa, Trujillo, San Juan del Norte, Matina – seldom harboured ships trading directly with the outside world. They served simply as transfer wharfs for the small skiffs and schooners that sailed between Belize and the Central American coast. Efforts to provide a second British entrepot at San Juan del Norte (Greytown) to serve Nicaragua and Costa Rica generally failed during the first half of the century. Most Nicaraguan and Costa Rican produce was shipped from the Pacific ports of Corinto, which gradually replaced the colonial port of Realejo in importance, or Puntarenas. Only after the completion of the Panama railway in 1855 did Central American commerce in general shift dramatically to the Pacific.

Loans added a bond of debt to that of commerce between Britain and Central America. The fiasco of the Barclay, Herring and Richardson loan of 1825 restrained investors from rushing in to Central America. Nevertheless a series of loans from British firms to the Central American states created a maze of debt problems which was not unravelled until the twentieth century. The liberals encouraged such arrangements, and

[13] Tables 2, 3 and 4 are based on data compiled from Customs records in the Public Record Office, London, by Robert A. Naylor, 'Tables of Commercial Statistics, 1821–1851', 'British commercial relations with Central America, 1821–1851' (unpublished Ph.D. thesis, Tulane University, New Orleans, 1958), 310–69. The tables are based on 'official values'. Naylor's tables in many cases also provide 'declared values' (generally lower) and volumes in tons, pounds or other units of measure as appropriate to the commodity. Tables 2, 3 and 4, of course, indicate only exports and imports between Central America and Great Britain and include produce of Belize and other British-held territory on the Central American east coast. Ciro F. S. Cardoso and Héctor Pérez Brignoli, *Centro-América y la economía occidental (1520–1930)* (San José, Costa Rica, 1977), 324–5, have compiled two statistical tables based on Naylor's data showing annual imports and exports between Britain and Central America. Unfortunately, there are some serious errors in their tables, especially in the one dealing with British exports to Central America, where Cardoso and Pérez have mistakenly included all British exports of foreign and English colonial goods to Jamaica as Central American imports. In addition, there are some mathematical or typographical errors in their totals.

Table 2 *Central American Imports from Great Britain and Jamaica,*
*1821–50*
(in thousands of £)

| Years | British Exports directly to Central America | British Exports to Belize | Jamaican Exports to Central America | Totals |
|---|---|---|---|---|
| 1821–25 | 6.7 | 1,455.9 | 0.0 | 1,462.6 |
| 1826–30 | 12.6 | 2,805.6 | 0.0 | 2,818.2 |
| 1831–35 | 112.3 | 2,937.6 | 74.0 | 3,123.9 |
| 1836–40 | 40.3 | 6,328.9 | 61.2 | 6,430.4 |
| 1841–45 | 76.0 | 4,578.1 | 56.4 | 4,710.5 |
| 1846–50 | 2,376.4 | 3,961.5 | 85.4 | 6,423.3 |

Table 3 *Central American Exports to Great Britain and Jamaica,*
*1821–50, directly and via Belize, Peru and Chile*
(in thousands of £)

| Years | British Imports from Central America | | | Jamaican Imports from C. America | Totals |
|---|---|---|---|---|---|
| | Directly from C. America | via Belize | via Peru & Chile | | |
| 1821–25 | 12.8 | 395.9 | 3.3 | 0.0 | 412.0 |
| 1826–30 | 23.9 | 402.7 | 14.2 | 0.0 | 440.8 |
| 1831–35 | 105.3 | 1,214.5 | 51.0 | 44.9 | 1,415.7 |
| 1836–40 | 368.7 | 2,719.8 | 129.7 | 41.4 | 3,259.6 |
| 1841–45 | 308.1 | 4,133.7 | 435.2 | 6.9 | 4,883.9 |
| 1846–50 | 2,631.7 | 5,526.7 | 73.0 | 2.7 | 8,234.1 |

Table 4 *Principal Central American Exports to Great Britain, 1821–50*
(As percentages of total Central American exports to Great Britain)[a]

| Years | Woods[b] % | Cochineal % | Indigo % | Coffee % |
|---|---|---|---|---|
| 1821–25 | 73.9 | 7.7 | 15.5 | 0.0 |
| 1826–30 | 66.9 | 21.6 | 8.4 | 0.0 |
| 1831–35 | 46.3 | 42.6 | 4.2 | 0.3 |
| 1836–40 | 30.7 | 63.6 | 4.3 | 0.5 |
| 1841–45 | 18.5 | 67.3 | 1.6 | 12.2 |
| 1846–50 | 20.9 | 61.2 | 0.9 | 18.8 |

[a] Total Central American exports to Great Britain based on Table 3.
[b] Mahogany, Nicaragua wood, Brazil wood, logwood, cedar, lignum vitae, fustic. Other forest products not included. Most of these woods were imported to Britain from Belize or the Miskito Shore and thus are not a major part of the trade with the Central American republics.

although conservative governments were more wary, these transactions did not end altogether. The Carrera government, for example, in negotiating a loan with the London firm of Isaac and Samuel in 1856 to pay off its earlier debt, had to pledge 50 per cent of Guatemala's customs receipts to service the debt.

As has already been mentioned, the liberals had also encouraged English colonization efforts. From Guatemala to Panama, governments designed projects to attract European immigrants. The results were disappointing. A trickle of Englishmen came, but most of them either died, returned home or drifted into urban centres. Notable were the Gálvez government's projects in Guatemala.[14] Small grants to individual foreigners were followed by a massive concession to the Eastern Coast of Central America Commercial and Agricultural Company, a group whose origins were suspiciously linked to Gregor MacGregor's Poyais enterprise. The company agreed to develop the entire eastern part of the state from Izabal and the Verapaz into the Petén. Unfortunately, the English were more interested in exploiting mahogany stands than in agricultural colonization. In the end, the project only heightened anti-British sentiment among residents of eastern Guatemala. A similar arrangement with a Belgian company to develop the port and region of Santo Tomás eventually superseded the English grant. Carrera and the conservatives had grave doubts about the wisdom of that concession, but, through bribery and intimidation, the government approved the Belgian contract and did its best to ensure its success. It had, however, collapsed by 1852 and the lowland region remained undeveloped. One by-product of these colonization projects was the improvement in shipping service from the Caribbean coast. The English company's steamer, the *Vera Paz*, linked the Golfo Dulce with Belize, thereby increasing the commercial dependence of Guatemala on the British port. The Belgian company later provided service with Belgium on an irregular basis. By 1850 there was regular, if sometimes unreliable, steamship service to Europe from the Caribbean coast.

If the British involvement in the isthmus was greater and by 1850, thanks to Chatfield, identified with the conservative cause, the United States was becoming increasingly involved in the middle of the century and usually in support of the liberals. This became more obvious after the appointment in 1849 of E. G. Squier as American envoy to Central

---

[14] William J. Griffith, *Empires in the wilderness: foreign colonization and development in Guatemala, 1834–1844* (Chapel Hill, N.C., 1965), treats this subject in detail.

America. Anglo-American rivalry intensified and came to a head over
the question of control of the transit route across the isthmus. The
discovery of gold in California in 1848 greatly accelerated United States
interest in the isthmus. As Americans streamed across Nicaragua via a
route developed by Cornelius Vanderbilt they discovered that the British
had taken control of territory on both sides of the isthmus, at San Juan
del Norte (Greytown) and Tigre Island in the Bay of Fonseca. War was
averted when cooler heads agreed, by the Clayton–Bulwer Treaty of
1850, to bilateral control and protection of any isthmian canal; Britain
and the United States pledged themselves not to 'occupy, or fortify, or
colonize, or assume or exercise any dominion over . . . any part of
Central America'. While the treaty lessened the hostile atmosphere
created by Chatfield and Squier, it hardly ended Anglo-American rivalry
in Nicaragua at the very time when the liberal–conservative showdown
was occurring there.

Among those who crossed the isthmus in 1850, probably at Panama
rather than Nicaragua, was William Walker, the son of an austere family
steeped in Protestant frontier religion and Jacksonian Democratic principles. Walker was a prodigious student; he had studied medicine at the
universities of Nashville (later Vanderbilt), Pennsylvania, Edinburgh
and Heidelberg before abandoning medicine for law in New Orleans at
the University of Louisiana (later Tulane). Almost immediately, however, he turned to journalism and became editor of the liberal and
controversial New Orleans *Crescent*. The untimely death of his fiancée,
however, led to his abandonment of New Orleans for a fresh start in
California. There he once more took up journalism, but failed either to
prosper or to satisfy his restless spirit. Through associates he involved
himself first in an abortive filibustering expedition into Mexico and then
agreed to organize an expedition to support the hard-pressed Nicaraguan
liberals.

Walker's band of 58 men landed near Realejo on 16 June 1855 and had
remarkable success in assisting the liberals to several key victories. Yet
the liberals also suffered reverses in the campaign, and the death –
through battle or disease – of several liberal leaders enabled Walker
quickly to become the dominant liberal military chieftain in Nicaragua.
Granada fell to his forces in a fierce battle, following which Walker
attempted to bring peace through the formation of a coalition with
conservative collaborationists. He assured the Church that he had no ill
will toward it and offered high office to several conservatives, including

Patricio Rivas who became president of the Republic. Some liberals, dismayed, now broke with Walker, while many conservatives refused to join the coalition. The struggle thus became one between Walker's 'democrats' and the 'legitimists'. The other Central American governments, now all under conservative rule, sent aid to the Nicaraguans opposed to Walker. Rafael Mora in Costa Rica took the lead in organizing this 'national campaign' against him. Rivas, realizing his untenable position, eventually resigned, and Walker himself succeeded him in the presidency. North Americans, mostly Mexican War veterans from the lower Mississippi Valley who had been promised land and other concessions, poured into Nicaragua to join Walker. *El Nicaragüense*, a bilingual newspaper more English than Spanish, proclaimed the liberal revolution and the establishment of a democratic regime.

The Nicaraguans and their allies – Mora's Costa Ricans, Guatemalans commanded by Mariano Paredes, Salvadorans under Gerardo Barrios and Guardiola's Hondurans – soon outnumbered Walker's forces. They first contained and then pushed back the North Americans and their remaining liberal cohorts, who suffered a cholera epidemic as well as battlefield losses. For their part the British supplied arms and other supplies to the allies through Costa Rica. The government in Washington vacillated; it never recognized Walker's regime (although the U.S. minister in Nicaragua had done so), but it was slow to take action against him. Finally a U.S. naval force arrived, in effect to rescue Walker and the few survivors of the expedition. The end came on 1 May 1857 when Walker surrendered. Returned on board a U.S. naval vessel, he received a hero's welcome in New Orleans and soon gained support for a new filibustering venture. Thwarted several times by U.S. officials, Walker finally succeeded in launching an expedition in collaboration with disgruntled British residents on Roatán who opposed Honduran sovereignty over the Bay Islands, to which Britain had agreed in 1859. Walker hoped to use Roatán as a base for a new invasion of Central America and was in touch with Trinidad Cabañas, still struggling against Guardiola in Honduras. When Walker reached Roatán, however, the British had not yet evacuated, so Walker struck directly at Trujillo. After a brief success he was captured as a result of British naval intervention, and handed over to the Honduran authorities. Following a brief trial, Walker fell before a firing squad on 12 September 1860.

The Walker episode had long-term results for Central America. The residue of anti-American and anti-British feeling remained long after to create suspicion and distrust in international relations and to encourage the xenophobia that the Conservatives had already nourished. Alliance with Walker further discredited liberals throughout Central America and allowed the conservatives to gain a stronger hold everywhere, but especially in Nicaragua. By 1860 the liberals continued to represent a serious threat only in El Salvador. Central America, although now definitively divided into five sovereign states, was solidly conservative.

In general, of course, the conservatives had better relations with Britain and Spain than with the United States or France. Spanish recognition of the Central American states and new concordats with Rome were positive achievements of conservative foreign policy. Old difficulties with the British were generally worked out amicably. The debt question was resolved through apportioning a part of it to each state, although only Costa Rica, with the smallest share, ever completed full payment. Guatemala reached apparent settlement of the Belize question in 1859, when by the Aycinena-Wyke Treaty Guatemala recognized British sovereignty there in exchange for British construction of a cart road from Guatemala City to the Caribbean. British failure to build the road eventually led to the abrogation of the treaty, as later liberal governments were unwilling to renegotiate a settlement. Honduras also settled its territorial disputes with the British by 1860, and Nicaragua made progress in the same direction, although final renunciation of British responsibility for protection of the Miskito Indians would not come until the end of the century.

Conservative domination of Central America arrested somewhat the emphasis on expanding exports and developing the country along capitalist lines which had been a feature of the liberal period. The cultural and political tone of conservative rule reflected traditional Hispanic-Catholic values, and there was a return to subsistence agriculture and a greater concern to protect Indian and *ladino* communal lands. The cities grew little, if at all, during the first half-century of independence and life remained predominantly rural. Yet the return to order after the civil wars was inevitably accompanied by an increase in agricultural production, and conservative governments could not resist the lure of increased revenue from foreign trade. Exports grew rapidly after 1840 except in Honduras which exported only livestock and foodstuffs to El Salvador and Guatemala. The dependence on natural dyestuffs of the late colonial and immediate post-independent period continued, with El Salvador and

Nicaragua the leading indigo producers and exporters. Guatemala also expanded its indigo production slightly, but depended principally on its cochineal exports. By 1845 Costa Rica's early success with coffee had begun to stimulate producers elsewhere in Central America. This became more intense after the discovery of coal-tar dyes in 1856 jeopardized the indigo and cochineal industries and eventually led to their ruin. Although dye exports continued to be the mainstay of the Salvadoran and Guatemalan export economies, coffee became increasingly important, especially in the Guatemalan highlands. By 1871, when the conservative regime finally ended there, coffee already accounted for 50 per cent of Guatemalan exports. The Civil War in the United States (1861–5) had allowed Central America to gain a larger share of the international cotton market, but only temporarily. Reliable statistics are not available for all of the states, but Tables 5, 6 and 7 (see below) illustrate the growth that occurred between 1850 and 1870.[15]

Britain remained the most important supplier of imports after 1850, even though the importance of Belize declined enormously with the development of Pacific trade after 1855. From 1850 to 1870, imports into Guatemala, as valued by customs, came from abroad in the percentages indicated in Table 8 (see below). As Table 8 also reflects, there was little trade between the Central American states. The roads were built from the capitals and producing regions to the ports, while interstate routes remained impassable. The economic interdependence that had begun to develop at the close of the colonial period was finally gone by 1870. The states were becoming more separate. Finally, while foreign involvement on the isthmus was limited when compared to other regions of Latin America, it was nevertheless highly significant from the point of view of the Central American states themselves and prepared the way for more substantial foreign domination once the liberals returned to power.

The restoration of order in most of Central America by 1860 and the emergence of coffee as a major export coincided with the resurgence of liberal efforts to control most of the Central American states. There was a restlessness among younger members of the elites, especially those

---

[15] Only fragmentary and often unreliable trade statistics have yet been compiled for most of this period in Central America. A guide to some of this material may be found in Thomas Schoonover, 'Central American commerce and maritime activity in the nineteenth century: sources for a quantitative approach', *Latin American Research Review*, 13/2 (1978), 157–69.

Table 5  *Leading Guatemalan Exports as Percentages of Total Exports,*
*1851–70*

| Years | Value of Exports (Millons of US$) | Cochineal % | Cotton % | Coffee % |
|---|---|---|---|---|
| 1851–55 | 6.2 | 78.4 | 0.0 | 0.0 |
| 1856–60 | 7.8 | 81.1 | 0.0 | 0.3 |
| 1861–65 | 7.4 | 56.4 | 8.3 | 11.3 |
| 1866–70 | 10.8 | 46.6 | 2.0 | 32.4 |

*Source:* R. L. Woodward, *Class privilege and economic development: the Consulado de Comercio of Guatemala, 1793–1871* (Chapel Hill, N.C., 1966), 58–63.

Table 6  *Leading Nicaraguan Exports as Percentages of Total Exports,*
*1841–71*

| Years | Value of Exports (Thousands of US$) | Indigo % | Precious Metals % | Hides % | Cotton % | Rubber % | Woods % | Coffee % |
|---|---|---|---|---|---|---|---|---|
| 1841 | 167.8 | 83.1 | 0.0 | 14.8 | 0.0 | 0.0 | 1.5 | 0.4 |
| 1851 | 1,010.0 | 7.9 | 39.6 | 1.2 | 0.0 | 0.0 | 15.8 | 3.0 |
| 1864 | 1,112.4 | 8.6 | 9.1 | 17.2 | 47.9 | 8.8 | 2.0 | 1.2 |
| 1865 | 1,155.0 | 16.9 | 12.3 | 8.9 | 47.1 | 4.6 | 2.5 | 2.6 |
| 1867 | 893.9 | 44.8 | 11.4 | 9.5 | 9.4 | 12.6 | 2.7 | 4.9 |
| 1870 | 930.3 | 27.0 | 17.9 | 18.0 | 1.7 | 15.7 | 9.7 | 5.4 |
| 1871 | 1,424.7 | 26.6 | 13.0 | 7.1 | 5.0 | 18.3 | 8.1 | 8.7 |

*Source:* A. Lanuza Matamoros, 'Estructuras socioeconómicas, poder y estado en Nicaragua (1821–1875)' (unpublished thesis, University of Costa Rica, 1976), 126–204.

Table 7  *Leading Salvadoran Exports, 1864–74*
(Millions of US$)

| Years | Value of Total Exports | Indigo Value | Indigo % of Total Exports | Coffee Value | Coffee % of Total Exports |
|---|---|---|---|---|---|
| 1864 | 1.7 | 1.13 | 67.4 | 0.08 | 4.8 |
| 1866 | 2.4 | 1.59 | 65.1 | 0.20 | 8.1 |
| 1870 | ? | 2.62 | ? | 0.66 | ? |
| 1874 | 3.8 | 1.70 | 44.8 | 1.33 | 35.0 |

*Sources:* Mario Flores Macal, *Orígenes de las formas de dominación en El Salvador* (San José, 1977), 147–63; David Browning, *El Salvador. Landscape and Society* (Oxford, 1971), 162.

Table 8 *Origins of Guatemalan Imports,*
*1850–70*[16]
(percentage of total)

| | |
|---|---|
| Great Britain | 61 |
| Belize | 6 |
| France | 17 |
| Germany | 5 |
| Spain & Cuba | 4 |
| U.S.A. | 3 |
| Belgium | 2 |
| Others | 2 |
| | 100 |

connected to coffee production, and a growing general awareness that, despite modest increases in exports and economic growth, Central America lagged far behind the rapidly expanding economies of western Europe and the United States. This liberal resurgence occurred first in El Salvador. Gerardo Barrios, originally a Morazanista, had served conservative governments and co-operated with Carrera and Mora against Walker, but after he gained power in El Salvador in 1859 his liberal sentiments once more surfaced, as he symbolically ordered the remains of Morazán to be brought to San Salvador for burial with state honours. Economic, political and educational reforms followed, while he carefully avoided attacking the Church and diplomatically assured Carrera in Guatemala of his continued friendship. Carrera watched suspiciously and assembled an army on the frontier. When the inevitable anticlericalism surfaced in 1863 Carrera invaded, but Barrios repulsed him at Coatepeque. Barrios then turned against Nicaragua in an effort to end Conservative domination there, but was himself defeated. A second Carrera invasion of El Salvador in October 1863 ended Barrios's regime; he was replaced by the more reliable conservative, Francisco Dueñas. An attempt by Barrios to return two years later failed, but even under Dueñas many of the liberal reforms remained.

Carrera's death in 1865 brought new hope to the liberals throughout the region. Vicente Cerna continued conservative rule in Guatemala until the *reforma* of Miguel García Granados and Justo Rufino Barrios brought him down in 1871. In the meantime, liberals in Honduras ended Conservative rule there and co-operated with Salvadoran liberals to oust Dueñas in the same year. In Nicaragua conservatives held on to

[16] Compiled from data published in the *Gaceta de Guatemala*, 1851–71.

power until 1893, but a trend toward liberal economic policy neverthe-less began soon after 1860. Costa Rica's transition to Liberal rule was somewhat more orderly, but the pattern was not significantly different. Mora was overthrown in 1859 and there followed a decade of domi-nation by the Montealegre family, moderates who had been very impor-tant in the development of coffee cultivation. Although politically conservative, certain liberal tendencies began to appear during the 1860s in their educational, ecclesiastical and economic policies. More clearly bringing the liberal *reforma* to Costa Rica, however, was General Tomás Guardia, who established a liberal dictatorship in Costa Rica in 1870.

The liberal *reforma* of the 1860s in Central America challenged the creole elites who had established neo-Hispanic regimes. After destruc-tive civil wars and political experimentation, the leading families of the late colonial period had largely succeeded in restoring their economic and social hegemony. At the same time, collaboration with popular caudillos had hastened the process of *ladino* participation in government, so that by 1870 the white elites no longer held a monopoly of high government office in Central America. Moreover, conservative rule had failed to provide the progress and expansion of the export-oriented economies at levels that significant portions of both elite and middle sectors demanded. Despite the restoration of much of the institutional framework of the colonial era, two new developments of the period were *caudillismo* and state sovereignty, both of which would survive in Central America long after the conservative party had ceased to be a force.

# 5

## VENEZUELA, COLOMBIA AND ECUADOR

Military and diplomatic necessity had made the vice-royalty of New Granada, the captaincy-general of Venezuela and the *audiencia* of Quito form one republic – the Republic of Gran Colombia – at independence. Its purpose was soon served, however, and its transience was apparent well before Bolívar's death in December 1830. The old imperial adminis-trative divisions were not always clear, not always consistent in all branches of affairs, but they were supported by both common sense and local feeling. Distances were too great, provincial identity too strong, for government from Bogotá to last for long after final victory over the Spanish forces. There were no strong economic ties between the three provinces. Already by the end of the colonial period a sense of distinct identity was felt not only by the elite, but by a far wider section of opinion. As the early federalisms of the 'Patria Boba' era showed, these loyalties were more easily felt for a smaller compass than for that of the particular republic that was to emerge in 1830, but the larger entity did have some support in opinion, as well as in imperial tradition and in the geography of possible control. The common soldiers of the Venezuelan plains showed as early as 1816 what they thought of General Santander, calling this Bogotá-educated native of Cúcuta a '*reinoso futudo*';[1] General Santander reciprocated this distrust, and both as vice-president and later in opposition to Bolívar, many of his actions and utterances looked forward to a separate New Granada. The southern frontier was more confused, but there was also a line to be drawn somewhere between Popayán and Quito. The façade of Gran Colombia had certainly been impressive – it impressed Mr Canning, it impressed the first envoys he sent out, and it impressed those who took up Colombian bond issues in the early 1820s.

[1] An accursed inhabitant of the *Nuevo Reino de Granada*.

Gran Colombia had obtained recognition; George IV had finally received 'the little yellow men', though he would sign no treaty that contained the word 'republic' in English. Yet the Foreign Office that had enthused over what was apparently destined to be the first nation of Spanish America was within five years watching its breakup with equanimity. The Royal Navy even lent a little assistance. The collapse of this political construction was accompanied by financial and economic crisis, a pattern that was to be often repeated in the subsequent history of the successor states. Not only did Gran Colombia's credit collapse in 1826. To foreigners and to natives alike – many of the inhabitants were just as vulnerable to early republican miscalcuation, and perhaps with more excuse – it became more and more apparent that economic and fiscal resources had been widely overestimated. Gran Colombia had sustained the war of liberation, had, one way or another, provided the men and the resources for Bolívar's armies in the South. The effort of unity had been made and the expense met in exceptional times and unrepeated ways. Nostalgia for union was for some time expressed by a few utopians and a larger number of Bolivarian officers, and by some federalist dissidents who opposed the new central authorities. In 1830, however, the realists of the hour were Generals Páez, Santander and Flores, who emerged as the respective rulers of Venezuela, New Granada and Ecuador.

The three successor republics had certain characteristics in common. They were sparsely populated: the total population of Gran Colombia was less than three million: New Granada may have had 1.1 million, Venezuela 0.9 million, Ecuador 0.5 million. All three were racially very diverse, diverse within themselves as well as differing one from another. The population in all three was overwhelmingly rural – no city in the region had forty thousand inhabitants – and in the nineteenth century both their total populations and their cities were to grow only slowly. As between the republics, communications within them were arduous and expensive. The predominantly upland population of New Granada and Ecuador lived in an enduring isolation; coastal and river navigation presented many problems before the coming of steam, and steam itself, no panacea, had to wait on the cargoes that made it economical. Within these national economies, which had been in varying degrees dislocated and decapitalized by the wars, few goods travelled far, and those that did for long bore the costs of the mule-train without the ability to sustain

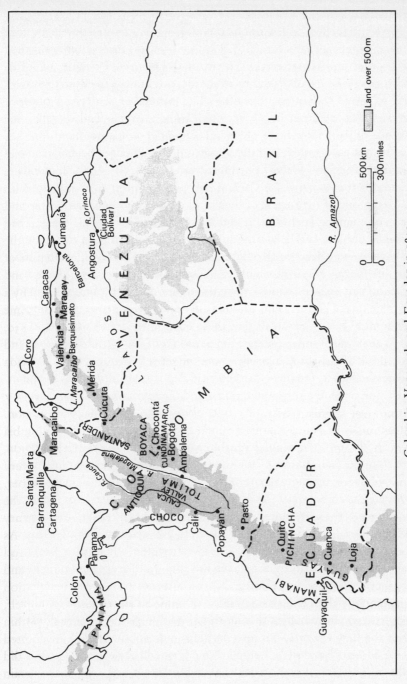

Colombia, Venezuela and Ecuador in 1830

*Note* During the nineteenth century the official names of these countries varied and boundaries changed.

dramatic advances. Wheel traffic ran for short distances, in few places. Few men travelled, as few goods travelled – the wars must have moved greater numbers than ever before but in most areas that mobility slowed with peace and the re-establishment of the restricted circuits of local interchange. Few had the means or the incentive or the freedom to move, and to move was often unhealthy. The pattern of settlement obeyed dictates that were not lightly ignored. Hardly anyone had travelled in Europe or the United States: General Santander would not have done so had he not been exiled, and the opportunity had not yet been forced on Generals Páez and Flores. Fortunes were modest. By Spanish colonial standards the *mantuanos* of Caracas had perhaps been rich, and Bolívar had been one of the richest of them. No other group in Gran Colombia had commanded such wealth and most had suffered in the wars. The colonial nobility had been tiny, and outside it few had been rich enough to have been menaced with official encouragement to buy titles. Republican life began in an atmosphere of republican austerity. There was nothing very self-conscious or puritanical about this, though some made a virtue out of poverty and provinciality and tried to turn it to political advantage. It was really all that these economies could sustain.

At the time of independence the economy of New Granada, the most populous of the three republics, was the least dynamic. New Granada possessed mines, the slave-worked gold deposits around Popayán and in the Choco, the few substantial mines and the myriad scattered placers of Antioquia, mostly worked by free labour, the investment-devouring silver mines of Santa Ana in Tolima. Indeed, precious metals were to remain the republic's most reliable export until the establishment of coffee in the last quarter of the century, and Antioquia's uninterrupted control over a substantial part of their production was an element in that province's commercial lead. Colombian mining was not severely damaged by the war, though it was naturally interrupted. All the same, it did not develop dramatically in the next half-century. Foreign investment in Tolima and Antioquía showed on the whole disappointing returns. Emancipation of the slaves and civil war disrupted mining in the southern part of the country. No new discoveries were made that substantially altered the contribution of gold and silver to the republic's exports, which remained during this period important, more constant than the new exports, but also constantly disappointing.

Besides gold and silver colonial New Granada had exported very little else. The botanical enthusiasts of Bourbon Spain had made discoveries that looked promising – cinchona bark and 'Bogotá tea' – and small quantities of cotton, tobacco and dye-wood, and even smaller quantities of other tropical products were exported from the northern coast. The infant *consulado* of Cartagena and the embryo journals of Bogotá speculated about such possible diversification in the last years of colonial rule. By 1830 little had been achieved.

Venezuela in contrast had been Spain's most successful agricultural colony. Venezuelan cacao was the finest in the world, and it was the region's leading export, to Europe and to Mexico. In the last years of the eighteenth century a shift began into coffee cultivation, which offered better returns on a smaller outlay. This change was intensified during the two decades of struggle after 1810, and though slavery had not disappeared and cacao continued to be grown, coffee and a system of sharecropping and free labour was now dominant. During this first cycle of coffee-production the crop was located in the hills of the central hinterland. Cotton and tobacco and hides were also exported, and mules and horses were sent to the islands. The Andean provinces to the west were at first relatively isolated, an isolation not overcome until coffee recovered from mid-century slump in the 1870s and 1880s. All the same, in comparison with New Granada, Venezuela had a stronger and more diversified export-sector. Coastal Ecuador also produced cacao, not as fine as Venezuelan but in greater quantity. Apart from hats, her other exports went only to her neighbours, chiefly in cloth of the highland *obrajes* and timber. Neither Venezuela nor Ecuador exploited mines of any great importance at this time.

The Swedish agent, Carl August Gosselman, travelling in 1837–8, provides figures for a succinct comparison of the value of exports from the three republics (see Table 1).

These sums are *absolutely* very small. (Ecuador's export earnings, at the conventional rate of conversion, are the equivalent of the annual income of the contemporary duke of Sutherland – £200,000.) They refer, of course, only to one sector of the economy, but that sector was the agent of growth and change, and government revenues depended more and more on the *aduana*, the support of order and stability.

It was not a reliable support. Neither Colombia, Venezuela nor Ecuador found in the nineteenth century a steady staple export. Nor were they very attractive to foreign investors. All three republics, sometimes together, sometimes individually, suffered the impact of price fluctuations and depressions, and weakened governments faced in-

Table 1 *Exports*
(in thousands of pesos)

| Date | State | Commodity | Value | |
|------|-------|-----------|-------|---|
| 1837 | Venezuela | Coffee | 1,660 | |
| | | Cacao | 875 | |
| | | Cotton | 616 | |
| | | Total | 4,944 | |
| 1836 | New Granada | Cotton | 199 | |
| | | Tobacco | 191 | |
| | | Gold Coins | 1,579 | (+ 1,000 exported clandestinely) |
| | | Total | 2,828 | |
| 1836 | Ecuador | Cacao | 690 | |
| | | Hats | 100 | |
| | | Total | 1,000 | |

creased malaise when a price went down, producers went bankrupt and merchants ceased to import. Venezuela's coffee planters, for example, borrowed at interest rates which had risen far above colonial levels. In the 1830s costs rose as they competed for labour and in the wake of the United States crisis of 1837–8 the price of coffee fell, and they were caught in the draconian provisions of the creditor's charter, the law 10 of 1834, which had removed the old colonial restrictions on freedom of contract, usury and foreclosure. The resulting outburst of polemical writing makes that particular crisis and its political repercussions in the 1840s relatively easy to follow, and similar patterns can be discerned at other times and in other places. Coffee remained all the same Venezuela's leading export for the rest of the century. She was second to Brazil and Java. The prices of her other exports were equally subject to brusque variations, particularly sharp in the late 1850s. The second cycle of coffee export, based on cultivation in the Andean states, showed production doubled in volume, but still subject to such fluctuations.

Colombia's first important agricultural export was tobacco. Under the colony a royal monopoly, it remained under government control until the late 1840s, but the government encouraged both increased private participation – the monopoly was expensive to run – and export.

Ambalema tobacco found markets, particularly in Germany, and for quarter of a century tobacco was the mainstay of Colombia's exports. Colombian merchants experimented with other commodities. *Quinas*, cinchona bark, were exported when this very unstable market was right, cotton enjoyed a brief fashion during the American civil war, money was lost in attempts to grow indigo. In the late 1870s the country's exports entered a prolonged crisis. They had been no more immune from fluctuation than Venezuela's, but this crisis was one of unprecedented completeness: tobacco failed as the scarce suitable land gave out and East Indian production took the German market; *quinas* from Colombia became unsaleable on a market glutted from Ceylon. For a while Colombia had almost nothing but the production of her mines. The country now turned to coffee which had first been planted on some scale in the 1860s, but recovery still looked very uncertain at the end of the century.

Ecuador's fortunes remained tied to cacao, which represented from a half to three-quarters of total exports. Ecuador was throughout the century the world's leading exporter, and the fluctuations in her foreign trade were less severe than those suffered by her former Gran Colombian partners. Cacao brought the coast commercial and financial preponderance and a steadily increasing demographic weight, from faster natural increase and from migration from the sierra. The coast also then produced most of the hats.

The attentive reader of the contemporary geographers and of the more patient and sympathetic travellers, of Agustín Codazzi, Felipe Pérez, Manuel Villavicencio, of Karl Appun, Isaac Holton and Friedrich Hassaurek, can soon begin to map that other economy which is not visible in the statistics of foreign trade, and to get a sense of a different sort of economic life. Much native artisan production showed itself well able to resist the more intense competition of imports that came with independence. Imports were after all nothing new. Neither Ecuadorian nor Colombian textiles were as rapidly or completely ruined as the protectionists of the 1830s argued that they would be. The finest quality local products, such as Chocontá saddles, were still traded throughout the three republics. Certainly, artisans protested at the lower fiscal tariffs of mid-century, but they were not all equally or drastically affected by them. Some activities expanded – Colombian hat-making is an example. High transport costs and peculiar market tastes remained. The variety of interacting local economies cannot be anything more than stated here, but an awareness of this variety does have important consequences: it helps one to understand how policies, or crises, varied in their local impact; it makes one aware of entrepreneurial activity and opportunity in areas that escaped consular notice, small, perhaps, in scale but often critical for later developments. It enables one to escape from the misleadingly stagnant connotations that hang around the too vague notion of subsistence, and from the conventional image of rural life as nothing but *hacendado* and *peón*, planter and slave, *cura doctrinero* and Indian community, with the wild horsemen somewhere out on the plains, generating by some telluric process the occasional caudillo.

Life for the great mass of the rural population of those three republics was not uniform, and it was by no means everywhere static. Substantial changes did occur in these years. These were directly and clearly brought by new export crops. Coffee in Venezuela had the liberating effects that it was later to have in Colombia. The colonial cacao plantation was worked with slave labour. Some coffee estates had slaves, but most were worked by systems of share-cropping and seasonal labour. Workers were attracted into new areas and escaped from old controls for the opportunities and hazards of a free labour market. For smaller numbers tobacco in Colombia performed a similar function, and beyond that its effects were far-reaching. This first substantial hot-country development brought steam navigation to the Magdalena, and gave Colombians their first experience of direct trade with Europe. Coastal cacao progressively altered the balance of Ecuador.

It would be quite anachronistic to suppose that any leader of Latin American independence had worked for an egalitarian rural order; promises of some land to the troops were not meant to amount to much, nor did they. But it cannot be said that the old order survived quite intact, apart from the effects of recruiting and of physical and fiscal ravaging. Slavery was not abolished outright, but it was undermined by the drafting of blacks into the armies, the end of the slave trade and the limited emancipation decreed by the Congress of Cúcuta. For long unimportant in Ecuador, its role in certain tasks in Venezuela and Colombia had been greater than numbers – 42,000 and 45,000 respectively around 1830 – suggest. But no new slave-based activity was begun in either republic, and in many areas the old authority was never effectively reasserted. Early Gran Colombian legislation had attempted to bring the Indian communities into the stream of republican progress, but these schemes were soon abandoned in the face of Indian resistance and much political and fiscal inconvenience. They were perhaps now less amenable to government interference, less subject to clerical control than they had been in late colonial times. The hold of the Church which had never been complete had been weakened. The Church's influence here followed the pattern of old settlement in the more temperate regions, the older upland towns and the more Indian areas. In Venezuela as a whole the Church was not strong: its dioceses were not rich, and it had little hold on the *pardos*, the slaves or the *libertos*. The missions in the east had been destroyed, and the more clerical western states carried as yet little weight in the nation's affairs. Most of rural Venezuela was not amenable to control through this institution. In New Granada too its strength was patchy: *mestizo* Colombia had given many colonial examples of hostility to the Church. Little of the hot country had been thoroughly catechized – Tolima, the Cauca valley, the Pacific and Atlantic coasts were never subject to the same degree of ecclesiastical control as the uplands of Boyacá, Cundinamarca and Pasto. Similar distinctions can be made within Ecuador, where García Moreno's theocratic authoritarianism enjoyed much less than universal acclaim. Much is usually made of the domination of rural life by *hacendado* and priest, but such rhetoric has ignored the many areas where the power of both had been weakened, had never existed, or was hedged about with many natural limitations – the *llanos* of Venezuela, the scattered populations of the Magdalena valley, the cattle plains of Tolima, the Cauca valley, the relative liberty of the Ecuadorian coast. Slavery, as has been stated, was in decline. It is now being increasingly realized that rural structures other than slavery were far too complex and varied to be summed up in any such simple word as peonage.

A picture of the rural population as one mostly made up of servile labourers not only ignores the surviving Indian communities and the areas of independent small settlement, but also much other non-agricultural activity such as artisan industry, mining, stock-raising, the breeding of horses and mules and the management of pack-trains – an essential activity that was the start of many a famous local fortune. Nor was a *peón* the same sort of person from one place to another, or necessarily engaged in one sort of activity all the year round. The nineteenth-century authors of sketches of local customs, *cuadros de costumbres*, delighted in distinguishing between one type and another, and in describing the full range of their habits and activities. Historians are beginning to do the same. The gain should be not only in the picturesque. It should help to resolve the paradox that such allegedly static and highly stratified societies should have proved so difficult to control.

For all three republics the nineteenth century was an era of government either seen to be unstable, or at best seen optimistically to be recently emerged from instability. All three suffered frequent civil wars and ended the century in war. Much contemporary local writing was a lament for these disappointing circumstances, the shame of these local struggles increased by memories of more glorious earlier fighting, of much the same pattern but against a different enemy. Much foreign comment was scathing and facetious about these *revolucioncitas*, attributing them to vainglory, an ill-defined militarism, office-seeking, the absence of constitutional monarchy, the defects of mixed races, or the incurable levity of the Latin mind. Much traditional historiography has been preoccupied with the course of these revolutions, with the failure of these nations for so long to emerge as coherent nation-states, without, however, making much progress either in analysing the causes of instability or assessing its importance and extent. The problem of order was a complex one. Few diplomats or foreign travellers examined it in detail, few native soldiers or politicians were able in their own writings to escape from partisan arguments, or from the desire to find a single cause. Notes of exaggeration creep, or even rush in. State power was limited at the best of times, and unreasoned emphasis on apparently national events over local developments has often exaggerated the catastrophic nature of these crises. Likewise, irregular fighting has been confused with barbarism and brutality, government bankruptcy with universal ruin, the participation of blacks and Indians with racial war. The criteria of judgement have been decidedly European. This is neither to say that they have not been shared by many South Americans, nor that disorder was something easily ignored.

The new governments were republican, and committed to republican notions of representative government. New Granada proclaimed universal manhood suffrage in 1853, Venezuela in 1853, Ecuador in 1861, though each maintained a literacy qualification. Moreover, these mid-century dispositions were of course neither everywhere effective nor irreversible. Elections were a source of legitimacy and cannot be dismissed as of no account because of widespread malpractices, but they were an imperfect source. Elections had to be 'made' by governments, and all three republics began their independent life under the domination of certain exclusive circles. Páez and his friends held Venezuela, to the exclusion of many a returning Bolivarian officer and of other meritorious patriot careers. General Santander, who was the first to see that assiduous electoral machine-building and sectarian journalism were the roads to power in New Granada, was a man of many enemies, lay, clerical and military, and who kept his enmities in good repair. General Flores was not even an Ecuadorian, and the colour of many of his troops did not blend with that of the sierra populace. All three had made their reputations in the wars, but these reputations were not unrivalled or uncontroverted.

Nor were they supported by imposing institutions. The Church had been weakened during the wars, both in its resources and in its hegemony. Sees fell empty and remained empty, clerical organization suffered partial collapse. All three republics remained Catholic, and sought to inherit the *patronato* of the Spanish crown, but diplomatic embarrassments held Rome back from recognizing the new states until the 1840s. And republican Catholicism was Catholicism with a difference. General Páez made it quite clear how little church support counted in Venezuela by expelling the archbishop of Caracas in 1835. General Santander's opinions and conduct were likewise hardly calculated to appeal to clerical opinion. The Church could not be left out of account by Colombian and Ecuadorian politicians: it could provide valuable support to its friends and make dangerous opposition to its enemies. As there were many sources of friction between the Church and these post-independence governments, it cannot, however, be seen as a pillar of order. Its influence varied from region to region, from the overwhelming to the negligible. Nor did the Church itself possess a strong hierarchy, which was essential for decisive national action. A bishop was still very much the sovereign in his own diocese; the religious feelings of Pasto or Medellín were not to be controlled from Bogotá.

These were not parts of the empire where the colonial bureaucracy had been very imposing. The republican replacements were likewise modest. Cabinets were usually made up of no more than three or four portfolios – *Hacienda, Guerra y Marina, Interior, Relaciones Exteriores* – and a couple of these were often combined in the hands of one person. The number of offices was not great and patronage restricted. Many offices were unattractive, and governments found it hard to find persons willing to serve as provincial judges, *alcaldes* or even provincial governors. A few careers were spectacularly or corruptly rewarded – particularly in the Venezuela of the Monagas brothers and Guzmán Blanco. Most were not. Many of these governments were notoriously honest and austere – the administrations of Páez (1831–5, 1839–43) and Soublette (1843–7) in Venezuela, of Herrán (1841–5) and Mariano Ospina (1857–61) in New Granada, of Vicente Rocafuerte (1835–9) in Ecuador were hardly touched by financial scandal. But economy and probity did not necessarily receive rewards in the shape of political support. In the early years of these republics the numbers of those directly employed by the government, or directly and immediately influenced by its actions, remained very small, even when one includes the army.

The reason was clear and common to all. Governments lacked revenue, and economized accordingly. Again, Carl August Gosselman's sober Scandinavian calculations for the mid-1830s (Table 2), years of neither euphoria nor despair, will serve for a measure and a comparison:

Table 2 *State Revenues*

| Date | State | Source | Value (in thousands of pesos) |
|------|-------|--------|-------------------------------|
| 1837 | Venezuela | Import duties | 968 |
|      |           | Export tax | 168 |
|      |           | Others (including a *contribución extraordinaria* surcharged on the customs of 221,000 pesos) | 463 |
|      |           | Total | 1,599 |
| 1836 | Colombia | Customs | 907 |
|      |          | Tobacco monopoly | 237 |
|      |          | Salt monopoly | 225 |
|      |          | Others | 654 |
|      |          | Total | 2,023 |
| 1836 | Ecuador | Customs | 202 |
|      |         | *cédulas personales* (the Indian *tributo*) | 184 |
|      |         | Others | 194 |
|      |         | Total | 580 |

The patriots had at first thought that the introduction of more advanced systems of taxation, the opening of their ports and the institution of nicely calculated fiscal tariffs would give them resources far beyond the old 'routine' of retrograde or oppressive colonial revenues. They dreamt of cadastral surveys, of the *contribución directa*. The nature of the tax-base and the unending demands of war had by the late 1820s forced them back to something very like the old system, and this could be only slowly abandoned by Gran Colombia's successor states. They were imaginative in fiscal ideas, and even capable of daring – the ending of the tobacco monopoly in Colombia was a conscious fiscal risk – but the problem was intractable. Each branch of revenue had its ceiling. Foreign credit had gone with the 1826 crash, and though efforts would be made to restore it this could not be granted much priority in most of these hard-pressed years. Neither Colombia nor Ecuador borrowed abroad again significantly in the fifty years after 1830, though Guzmán Blanco in Venezuela saw at least a personal advantage in resuming borrowing in the 1860s. Every administration had its school of financial pilot-fish, the *agiotistas*, expert in short-term loans and the manipulation of the bewildering variety of internal debt that these governments soon trailed, but the domestic money-market was rudimentary, small sums for short terms at high interest. In Venezuela Guzmán Blanco was successful in reforming and sophisticating these arrangements with the *Compañía de Crédito* in the 1870s, and the same decade saw the founding of the first Colombian banks that managed to survive, but throughout the century governments remained periodically subject to acute fiscal emergencies. All cast around for new expedients, *arbitrios*. Church wealth was sacrificed in both Venezuela and Colombia, and at the very end of the century was under Eloy Alfaro's assault in Ecuador, but the Church was not so very rich and the yield in these hard times was disappointing. The one revenue capable of rapid expansion was the customs, and all three republics came to depend on it more and more. By the 1860s it accounted for over two-thirds of Colombia's revenue, for example. Salt and alcohol monopolies, land taxes and much else were tried, and much effort and ingenuity employed in their adjustment, but strong measures could only be instituted during the very wars that greater government resources might have prevented. Even these measures hid behind their draconian exterior many compromises with victims who simply could not pay.

It is not surprising that such governments sought to keep expenses to the minimum – here European laissez-faire fashions coincided with local necessity, giving some local liberals the illusion that their microscopic administrations represented the vanguard of progress. One major item of expense which they consistently tried to cut was the armed forces. Navies were virtually abandoned. Fortresses, considered anti-republican, were allowed to decay, or even demolished. The permanent force of soldiers was everywhere after 1830 reduced to a small corps of veterans, enough to keep the arsenals and to recruit in times of emergency, but which would weigh as lightly as possible on the treasury in peacetime. The political circumstances of the dissolution of Gran Colombia favoured the reduction of armies. General Páez established his rule in Venezuela with the forces under his immediate command, and through compromise with certain locally powerful figures. The many Bolivarian officers in the armies outside Venezuela found themselves excluded. In New Granada large numbers of the officers were precisely these Venezuelans, and there were many Venezuelan troops as well. Their attempts to establish themselves locally here failed, and the Bogotá government was relieved by their departure. General Flores and forces at least part Venezuelan did establish themselves in Ecuador. Everywhere, however, by the mid-1830s numbers were small and, as few units were ever kept up to strength, smaller than those officially stated. Venezuela possessed 800 infantry and 200 cavalry. New Granada had four infantry battalions, an artillery battalion and three squadrons of cavalry, giving the comparatively heavy total of 3,300 men; however, consistent and intermittently successful efforts were made to bring this number down, and in many mid-century years the number would be less than 1,000. Ecuador officially supported 720 infantry and 360 cavalry. In all of former Gran Colombia there were therefore standing armies whose combined total was no more than 5,000 or so, often less. Even these numbers took up a large share of each republic's budget: Gosselman reported the slice as 510,000 pesos out of Ecuador's estimated revenue of 580,000; in New Granada the armed forces took 818,000 out of a budget of 2,517,000, and in Venezuela 481,000 out of 1,599,000. These high proportions should not so much be seen as signs that military considerations predominated. They derived from simple facts of political life: there was a certain minimum army required, to hold certain points. Even small armies are expensive, and troops, unlike bureaucrats, must be given pay or they will inevitably and rapidly become a menace to their surroundings and to their masters.

It was not primarily these small forces, or the regularly employed officers, who were the cause of disturbance and of that 'militarization' that many noticed *en passant* but few bothered to define. Most of these garrisons were loyal to the governments that employed them most of the time: the *cuartelazo* or barracks coup was not unknown – one started the *reformista* rebellion in Caracas in 1835, General Melo in like manner set up a rare Colombian military government in Bogotá in 1854 – but it was not characteristic of this region. Civil conflict and civil war had wider and far less simple causes – they were not what these minuscule garrisons did, but what, when circumstances grew strained, they were only too likely to fail to control.

Under the colony there had been politics of a sort – bureaucratic and *cabildo* intrigue, ecclesiastical competition – but independence brought a political life that was new in intensity, in extent, in methods and in all sorts of consequences. Republican politics were novel. To give an example, the change can be clearly seen in the Bogotano José Maria Caballero's notes and jottings in his *Diario de Santa Fé*: in 1810 a very colonial collection of observations on random occurrences and natural phenomena suddenly becomes a recognisable political diary. By 1830 all of Gran Colombia had experienced several different sorts of elections, congresses, constituent assemblies, assemblies of *padres de familia*, parties and factions with their attendant press – as well as the techniques for making elections, dissolving assemblies, overawing the press and pro-scribing political opponents. These arts were known to soldiers and civilians alike.

Participation in elections was formally restricted. There were initially limitations on the suffrage, and certain elections were indirect. There is, however, much evidence to show that informal participation was wider, and that *opinión*, the state of opinion about which governments worried, was not confined to citizens with the constitutional right to vote, or those who bothered to vote. The correspondence of the Colombian Tomás Cipriano de Mosquera, three times president (1845–9, 1863–4, 1866–7), *Gran General* and Popayán aristocrat, with his political factotum General Ramón Espina, shows much concern with the detail of working up popular opinion, and in these practices Mosquera was only following the example set by the *fons et origo* of local political practice: the British envoys to Gran Colombia were taken aback by the democratic ways of Santander, who at election times wore the popular *ruana* and drank toasts in the taverns. Timid upper-class electors often found it prudent to follow the popular opinion of their localities. Divided from the earliest days of the republic's separate existence, Colombian opinion was never easily controlled from Bogotá. Santander's energy as a correspondent and as a transparently anonymous, semi-official journalist of the *Gaceta*, his control of the administration and willingness to use it for his party's ends – these were all insufficient to secure the return of the candidate he favoured to succeed him in the election of 1836. José Ignacio de Márquez, the civilian victor, had enough support to win but not enough to govern. He had little prestige, and his support was too confined to the central uplands. He lacked sufficient national *opinión* behind him.

José Antonio Páez in Venezuela was somewhat more secure, and was able to maintain his republican reign until early 1848. But this was far from being simply based on his famous *rapport* with the *alto llano*, and it was far from being unchallenged. Many elements contributed to Páez's dominance. Military prestige and the ability to raise forces in emergency that went with that prestige were certainly important, as was seen in 1835 and 1846. But so too was Páez's skill in political manoeuvre and compromise, seen in his dealings with rivals like Generals Mariño and José Tadeo Monagas. Páez's was not the only military reputation, and others could raise troops too. Compared to his successors, Páez had a light touch: the 'conservative republic' of 1830–48 exiled some of its enemies after 1835, but the alliance of General Páez and his friends and the Caracas merchant class seemed to weigh lightly on the country while the prosperity of the 1830s lasted. Venezuela's exports recovered rapidly from the war and a mood of optimism prevailed until prices fell with the arrival of the effects of the United States crisis of 1837–8. Thereafter the extent and virulence of opposition give one a different view of this polity, a sight of the limitations of Páez's power and prestige. The heritage of colonial commerce in Caracas left merchants and landowners with more separate interests, with divisions apparently easier to exploit than elsewhere in Gran Colombia. Falling export prices exacerbated this latent conflict, and there arose against the merchant-inclined governments of these years a landowner opposition which identified with the liberal cause, and which appeared to be willing to take it to rare doctrinaire extremes. This opposition produced two journalists of genius, the ideologue Tomás Lander – in his will he was to direct that his body be mummified like Bentham's – and the versatile and well-connected demagogue, Antonio Leocadio Guzmán. The campaigns of Lander and of Guzmán can be seen to have had their effect outside as well as within the officially recognized political class. They found provincial readers, and these found listeners. The reputation of Guzmán could gather together crowds, crowds of 'artisans' and other less-definable persons. The administration could no longer control the elections to the extent that ensured a stable succession: in 1844 the Swedish diplomat, Count Adlercreutz, who himself had had first-hand experience in election-making as a mercenary Bolivarian colonel, reported to his government that the liberals had won the direct provincial elections, and that the 'oligarchic party' had only managed to bring its pressure to bear on the indirect elections for the national congress; even then, it had only been able to return mediocrities. In conditions of economic crisis, of mounting disorder, Páez lost 'the inclination and sympathies of the masses'.

Travellers from the Europe of Guizot and Louis Napoléon, Palmerston and Franz-Joseph were taken aback by the quantity of political conversation even in humble gatherings and in remote places, where these inclinations and sympathies worked themselves out, not without consequences. They were reluctant to concede much meaning to a political life lacking formal or permanent institutions, beyond a few scattered political clubs in the towns and party organizations that did not go beyond a sporadic press and a meagre network of correspondents, and in such uneducated and illiterate societies. They over-estimated the political control of landowners; power frequently brought with it land, but the reverse was much less than automatic. They underestimated the number of masterless men. Nor could they understand how local rivalries and antipathies, often of colonial origin, were caught up in new republican politics. Even had society been firmly in the control of a solidly established elite, which over much of the map was not the case, that elite would have found causes for falling out within itself. The better-known rivalries of city and city, province and province were often reproduced at less-discernible levels, down to the *veredas*, the districts of the lowly *municipio*.

The *revoluciones* and the *revolucioncitas* must be seen against this background. It is not possible in a survey of this length to give any detailed account of their causes and courses. Venezuela experienced the revolt of the *reformas*, 1835, an attempted coup by excluded Bolivarians against the prematurely civilian government of Dr José María Vargas, which placed itself under the protection of Páez; there were widespread revolts in 1846, and Páez himself fought unsuccessfully against being supplanted by his last nominee José Tadeo Monagas in 1848. The decade of rule by the Monagas family that followed was not peaceful, and culminated in the Federal War, 1859–63. Guzmán Blanco did not consolidate his power until after further fighting in 1868 and 1870. New Granada suffered an outbreak of clerical disaffection in Pasto in the south in 1839, which developed into a series of federalist declarations in other provinces, the *Guerra de los Supremos*, 1839–42. The conservative and centralist administration of Pedro Alcántara Herrán that won that war saw its men and policies progressively abandoned in the late 1840s by the succeeding government of Tomás Cipriano de Mosquera, and the conservatives lost power altogether in the elections of 1849. They revolted unsuccessfully in 1851 against the liberal government of General José Hilario López, behind whom they saw the even less reassuring figure of the popular General José María Obando. In the confused and contradictory agitation of students, artisans and Cauca valley blacks they could even discern the spectre of socialism. A brave man but a timid politician, Obando abandoned the field to the short-lived military régime of General José María Melo, which was in its turn suppressed by forces recruited and led by gentlemen of all persuasions in the short war of 1854. The conservative government that then won the elections – universal suffrage in New Granada was also counter-revolution – was then ousted by a federalist liberal rising between 1859 and 1862 led by General Mosquera. Like Venezuela, Colombia adopted an extremely federal constitution, but there the resources for a Guzmán Blanco were not to hand. Both countries saw a number of local revolts; Colombians fought major civil wars in 1876–7, and again in 1885. The long supremacy of Guzmán Blanco in Venezuela, 1870–88, seemed to indicate that certain geopolitical problems had found their solution, but the succeeding hegemony of General Joaquín Crespo, 1892–8, was not entirely peaceful. General Crespo was himself killed in battle, and like Colombia Venezuela ended the century in civil war.

In Ecuador the presence of a large Indian population in the sierra, a separate estate only intermittently concerned with white and *cholo* politics, might lead one to guess that political life was slowed by a certain passivity. This would not be a reliable conclusion. The sierra population was not always passive. Flores put down several revolts before his expulsion in 1845. Provincial rivalries were acute, all hegemonies limited in extent and capacity. The press made up for a more precarious existence and fewer readers than in Colombia or Venezuela by exceptional virulence: Ecuadorian journalism built up a tradition of violence and incitement to violence from the original massacre of those behind *El Quiteño Libre* in 1833, which reached famous heights with Gabriel García Moreno and his adversary Juan Montalvo. But the former's intense military, as well as political, activity should be stressed here. Flores did not leave Ecuador a tranquil pretorian tradition.

These wars had certain characteristics in common throughout the region, which is far from saying that they were all the same. They tended to coincide, and were more severe when they did so coincide, with periods of economic difficulty, sometimes identifiable with crises in the world economy, sometimes with particularly unfortunate local conjunctures. Economic difficulties weakened government revenue, and poor governments were less able to satisfy and enthuse their supporters and oppose their enemies. Endemic provincial dissatisfaction became more intense as needy governments kept their expenditure closer to home. In the economy at large other consequences increased the propensity for trouble. New crops, or new activities for export, such as the 1850s hide boom in the Venezuelan *llanos*, or the 1870s *quina* gathering in Santander, Colombia, brought large numbers of people into new areas and a new dependence on a fluctuating market. 'Falling back on subsistence' was not as easy as the little phrase makes it sound. For example, when the coffee price came down at the end of the 1830s it was not just the over-extended Venezuelan planter who lost, it was his now abandoned work-force, deprived of wages, now perhaps living in an unfamiliar environment, and a growing-season away from careless subsistence. Not that such people would show much initiative to revolt, but some of them would join revolts. Distress, *malestar, miseria* of this sort, not the secular poverty of the more oppressed uplands of Boyacá or Pichincha, provided a climate in which revolution could take hold. These lands were virtually unpoliced.

Another common characteristic of these wars was dictated by resources and terrain: it was hard to bring revolts to a speedy end, even when they had small beginnings. Governments had to make themselves yet more unpopular by recruiting. All three republics had militia systems, but these could not be relied on to produce troops who would serve or go long distances, and in rebellious areas they could not be relied upon at all. Recruiting was a violent and unpopular procedure. The more deferential populations would run away and hide, others would resist more dangerously, and the rebellion might appear to spread. Desertion was so common that the French traveller, Holinsky, remarked that opposing commanders in Ecuador seemed to hurry their forces into battle for fear of facing each other troopless and alone. In fact, it was not usually possible to hurry anyone anywhere. Armies could not be adequately rationed; they had to be dispersed so that they could survive, as everywhere the local surplus was limited. They had to be manoeuvred according to resources, and according to climate, not to outrun supplies and not to subject the troops to changes more brusque than they could stand. Governments occasionally enjoyed the benefit of more enthusiastic support, but on the whole relied on small forces, laboriously gathered together by their nucleus of veterans, moved with caution. Rebel systems relied more on volunteers, on the *élan* of the cause and the prospect of loot, and on the local *guerrilla*. Successful leaders had to understand the peculiarities of local warfare, both practical and psychological; what a particular region could produce or sustain in the way of resources and troops; what was the art of enthusing a particular population. The multiplication of higher ranks was not so much a reflection of a childish 'latin' delight in titles as of the need to balance local sensibilities.

It is hard to discern a standard, typical *caudillo* among these figures. Most were persons of some social standing, though the connection between property and the ability to raise troops was rarely direct – even *llaneros* like Páez and Monagas raised more men on their prestige than on their property. Even 'popular' leaders, José María Obando and Ezequiel Zamora for example, are usually found to be better connected socially than romantic admirers have made them appear; both Zamora and Obando owned a few slaves. Some had reputations made in the wars of independence; many veterans of the wars were still able and willing to take to the field in the 1860s. The range of political and military talent that appears varies in type and in origin. Zamora started life as a provincial merchant and moneylender, and found his extraordinary military ambition as a militia officer; he then indulged this penchant for combat and command in the opposition to Páez in 1846. He used guerrillas, but he was much more than a guerrilla leader – his masterpiece, the battle of Santa Inés, was an elaborate affair of entrenched ambuscades. He had perhaps a generous definition of excess, but he was a strict disciplinarian towards those who abused it; as a victor he was a model of humanity. His reputation as an egalitarian reformer rests on little more than an extraordinary *don de gente*, a gift for getting on with all classes, just as his military ascendancy came entirely from ability in the field. He was not a *llanero*, nor did he try to become one; he was not the emanation of any particular region: he won battles until he died in one: San Carlos in 1860.

José María Obando, the most popular soldier or politician Colombia produced in the last century, had bastard connections with good Popayán families, but his local reputation in the south was made first fighting for the Spanish crown and then softening the rigours of patriot occupation. He had some land in the valley of Patía, cattle country which always provided him with a hundred or so of cavalry. In the opposition to Bolívar in the late 1820s, as vice-president in 1831–2, he acquired not only notoriety as one of those accused of the assassination of Bolívar's most faithful lieutenant Antonio José de Sucre (who as the man who had ordered the sack of Pasto in 1822 was not much mourned in the south), but wider fame and popularity as one who consolidated the new republic before the return of the exiled Santander. Obando's subsequent career – the revival of the Sucre charge, civil war, exile and poverty, return and election to the presidency, failure and disgrace, alliance with his old enemy Mosquera and death in a skirmish on the eve of victory in 1861 – had a pathos which in his lifetime earned him the title of 'the American Oedipus'. With military gifts and a fine military presence Obando combined great popular attraction, heightened by the history of his persecution and exclusion by Popayán aristocrats. This appeal was not only effective in Pasto and elsewhere in Cauca, but was evident on the Caribbean coast and among the Bogotá artisans – Obando's most effective support in his brief presidency from 1853–4. But Obando was a better martyr than politician, and failed to translate this ascendancy into power. These radical reputations were matters of sentiment and affection, of prestige rather than programme.

The lives of other national military figures – not that many of them can be considered merely as soldiers – fail to conform to a common pattern. The Monagas brothers and the Sotillos were *llaneros* who kept in close touch with the *bajo llano*, the eastern Venezuelan plains. Marshal Falcón came of a landed family near Coro, in which city this kind and cultured man first became famous as an aggressive *señorito*. Guzmán Blanco was the son of the Caracas journalist Antonio Leocadio Guzmán and an aristocratic mother. The patient, worrying, commonsensical General Herrán, president of New Granada 1841–5, came from modest origins and had a long military career, some of it passed forcibly in the royalist ranks; he had, nevertheless, a very civilian mind. Gabriel García Moreno, who did a lot of fighting and who in his years of ascendancy from 1861 to 1875 was far more prone to execute opponents than the most severe general of New Granada, was the son of a Guayaquil merchant and had studied for the priesthood as far as minor orders. Tomás Cipriano de Mosquera came from a *señorial* Popayán line, and had a light-weight career as a late-independence soldier with Bolívar, a friend of his father. His appetite for power might have had something to do with this background, but it certainly cannot explain his erratic subsequent political career, or his military successes and failures; for much of the time his family looked on with alarm and disapproval.

These leaders did not make up any distinct and self-conscious caste. Not all considered themselves to be primarily soldiers, and many regarded civil war with as deep a distaste as any civilian: Falcón and Herrán were eloquent examples of the peace-loving soldier. Nor was there any greater uniformity below this level of command, as each distinct locality reacted to the breakdown of order in its own way. Some localities produced lesser commanders who gained a reputation for savagery coloured by fears of racial conflict or a repetition of past atrocities. In Venezuela there were 'el indio Rangel', 'el indio Espinosa', figures of 1846 and 1859, the Sotillo clan in the east; in Colombia, Obando's ally the 'bandit' Sarria, the *cacique* Guainas of the Páez Indians of Tierradentro, and the mulatto General David Peña of Cali, who on one famous occasion made well-born conservative ladies sweep the city streets. The Indians of the Ecuadorian sierra were not always passive victims or spectators of others' conflicts. Some of these irregulars did fight in a sanguinary way, and in some wars in some regions murderous vendettas did develop – the Barquisimeto region in the Venezuelan *Guerra Federal* is a good example. The wars confirmed and intensified local antagonisms, as the participants repeated certain inevitable patterns: what was lost in one war might be avenged in the next.

Yet it is easy to exaggerate the intensity and extent of disorder, and all too easy to exaggerate the violence of these conflicts. For logistical reasons, if for no others, as in all wars long periods passed in which nothing much happened. Armies remained relatively small, much mobilization was essentially defensive. Casualties in battle were high, and death from disease and lack of adaptation yet more common, but massacres and executions were far rarer than foreign observers deduced from the irregular nature of much of the warfare. Their conclusions seem often to be drawn from preoccupations about the violence of peoples of mixed blood, and the *frisson* produced by the sight of ragged troops with lances or *machetes*. They lumped this 'south american' fighting together with what went on in Argentina and Mexico, where conditions and practices were very different (as indeed they were in Spain). The Colombian José María Samper complained: 'Rosas is our symbol; Santa Anna, Belzú, Monagas and other terrible personages are held to be the general rule.' Of these only Monagas represented these three republics, and he was terrible only because of corruption. There are no reliable figures for the dead in these wars, and there is a strong tendency for a certain type of progressive creole writer to exaggerate the likely numbers: one suspects that Conrad's Don José Avellanos, in his *Fifty Years of Misgovernment*, painted the past of the Republic of Costaguana rather blacker and bloodier than it really was. Such authors wrote out of shame and disappointment, and often had a cosmopolitan background that did not always help them to understand the processes at work. Very few were not partisan – as always and everywhere, one side's 'energetic measures' were the other side's atrocities. One must also distinguish one conflict from another and remember that the incidence of each particular war bore harder on some provinces than others: governments might have to declare that public order was disturbed throughout their territory when that was far from being really the case.

Even short wars could be very destructive of property, particularly of cattle. The larger ones, the *Guerra Federal* in Venezuela and the contemporary Mosquera–Ospina struggle in Colombia, caused proportionately greater loss, as both governments and rebels relied on emergency exactions, armies marched from meagre surplus to meagre surplus, agriculture was abandoned and trade interrupted. The worst wars undoubtedly had severe direct economic effects. And all wars interrupted the longed-for stability: public works were abandoned, efforts to put the administration on a sound financial footing had to be forgotten, credit and reputation were lost, interest rates went higher, the speculator overshadowed the entrepreneur – where they were not combined in the same person. In such conditions governments so immediately concerned with survival could not concern themselves with much expensive continuity. The chief mourners were those who looked in these republics for the sort of government that they could not sustain.

The wars had other effects. As has been said, they confirmed and intensified, sometimes created, antagonisms that showed in more peaceful politics as well. Military mobilization was also to some extent political mobilization; those who followed a leader in war might also maintain

their attachment in peace. Wars produced heroes for parties; there was no
need to be a literate voter to admire an Obando or a Zamora. They also
decided certain important issues – a point that escapes those who are not
curious about what these wars were fought for. The *Guerra Federal* did
not have the definitively levelling effect on Venezuelan society that its
apologists hint at, but it did extinguish formal Venezuelan conservatism
– thereafter, under one colour or another, Venezuela was *liberal*. In
Colombia Mosquera's victory in the civil wars of 1859–62 was followed
by more than two decades of federal experiment, predominantly liberal-
controlled. Issues of church and state were fought out. Many involved
were deeply committed to the cause of federalism, which meant respect
for local peculiarities and needs, and escape from distant governments
unwilling or unable to perform their promises; central power is re-
established as it finds the wherewithal to have something to give.
Antonio Leocadio Guzmán's cynical assertion that his friends called
their cause federal because their opponents were centralists, and that
matters would have gone just as well the other way round, is, like much
else he said, not to be relied on. The balance of interests and regions could
sometimes only be decided by civil war. These political issues were
nowhere a simple competition for office for office's sake.

'Thank God in this well-ordered country a Diplomatic Agent can live
without taking much interest in local politics', wrote Belford Wilson,
transferred to Caracas in 1843 after some *contretemps* in Peru. He soon ran
into trouble there too, which is not surprising, for he took sides rather
clearly in the local politics he did not take much interest in. Parties were
forming, issues emerged that divided opinion, interests sought political
expression, broad liberal and conservative currents became discernible.
What decided a man, a family or a district to one current or faction or
another was not simply determined – it cannot be said that merchants
were liberals, or landowners conservatives: all such simple generalizations are too easy to disprove, and a complete account has to be built on
analysis of region, of family, of events, even of talent and inclination.
Seemingly clear-cut divisions, such as the merchant–landowner antagonism of the Venezuelan 1840s, blur on closer inspection or do not hold
for very long, as the dividing issue is resolved. Parties, however, persist,
and without denying that an analysis inspired by the methods of Sir
Lewis Namier would contribute a great deal to the understanding of
these structures too, there is much that would escape. Ownership of land
was not so easily translated into political control of the neighbourhood

or national political weight. Urban politics could be unruly, and the issues aired in the larger cities were echoed in the small towns; the artisans of Mompóx were just as concerned for their interests as the artisans of Bogotá and adopted the same democratic ideology.

Examples of the hold of liberal ideology on individual minds, and of their evolution, abound in the memoirs of the time, such as those of the increasingly sober Salvador Camacho Roldán and the always excitable aristocrat radical, Francisco de Paula Borda, who believed in Jesuit conspiracies and poisonings to the end of his days. In 1877 a moderate Colombian liberal and well-travelled merchant, Enrique Cortés, listed what he considered the lasting victories of his party: the abolition of *manos muertas* and the suppression of convents, the ending of imprisonment for debt, degrading punishments, forced labour and the death penalty; the absolute freedom of the press; municipal liberty. Less sceptical liberals would have made longer lists and would have included free trade, the expulsion of the Jesuits, the establishment of federalism and absolute separation of church and state, but Cortés was no fanatic and expressed his doubts about how long these would last. Nor did he have much illusion about the transcendental importance of the items he did record, among a population he saw as nine parts in the shadows to one part in the light. But he did see them as valuable measures achieved by his party, and he later set them against the conservative reaction of 1885.

Conservative grounds for disagreement were by no means based on archaic colonial arguments. In Colombia, the *memorias* of Mariano Ospina Rodríguez as Minister of the Interior in the early 1840s marshall conservative arguments in an impressively modern fashion. A tradition of native conservative thought not only persisted in Colombia in a way that it did not in Venezuela, where conservative argument had to re-emerge in a liberal–positivist guise, but eventually triumphed. The liberal governments of the sixties and seventies were subject to constant conservative criticism, both from the press and from the clergy, and from the example of the state of Antioquia – peaceful, relatively prosperous, strongly governed, catholic and conservative. Liberalism had to take the consequences of the collapse of the federal, free-trade radical republic between 1882 and 1885, a crisis in which 'independents' and conservatives showed themselves more pragmatic. The republic ended the century under the philosophical and political sway of Rafael Núñez, president 1880–2 and 1884–94, and Miguel Antonio Caro, president 1894–8, who together covered a wide range of conservative argument, as well as being formidable polemicists and politicians. Colombia was officially and constitutionally an island of conservatism, between the liberal confusions of Cipriano Castro in Venezuela, 1899–1908, and the radicalism of Eloy Alfaro's era in Ecuador, 1895–1912. Ideological differences were acutely felt. An *esprit fort* was needed to profess liberal beliefs in the diocese of Pasto, even under a liberal government. Conversely, Catholics in Antioquia, the Venezuelan Andes, even in the Ecuadorian sierra, did suffer from time to time from militant secularizing administrations, and responded predictably.

What was the resulting political pattern in each republic after half a century or so of independent political life? Guzmán Blanco managed to establish in Venezuela a government federal in name, increasingly centralized in practice, where the devices of the fiscal *subsidio*, the *juntas de fomento* and the *consejo federal* brought provincial rivals under increasingly tight control. Guzmán had behind him the defeat both of the conservative forces and of the leading military rivals of his own camp – and as coffee exports recovered and surpassed earlier levels, the means for such a programme. It is also hard to escape the conclusion that the experiences of the fifties and sixties had had a political and cultural effect less positive than the hypothetical levelling: there was little room for opposition, less for ideological argument. A weak Church suffered further humiliation. A tradition of adulation of the arbiter of the moment, already visible during the years of Páez, was given powerful encouragement. Páez, the Monagas brothers, Guzmán Blanco, Crespo, Castro – the successive masters of Venezuela – for all the distinct regional or class origins and tastes of each, did not *represent* those regions or classes when in power, beyond some preference for familiars. They were at the point of a civil and military balance in which, though the national government still left many aspects of regional life alone, power was still concentrated more than it was in New Granada or Ecuador. There was less correlation between social status and political power. High Caracas society never really assimilated Páez, who spent much time on his estates at Maracay and elsewhere, setting a pattern many of his successors followed. Only one of these could have claimed to be an aristocrat, and Guzmán Blanco exalted himself beyond assimilation, when he was not living far away in Paris.

New Granadan politics were not resolved in such a way. No one current extinguished the other, or came near to doing so in the entire century. Bogotá occupied a good defensive position for resisting provincial attack – it was hard for different provinces to combine against the capital and launch a simultaneous assault, and the city was situated in the midst of a dense and recruitable population – but the national government lacked the resources effective central government required. Here the 1886 constitution was a couple of decades in advance of the economy. No figure emerged from independence, which in New Granada had left the social structure relatively intact, with the political and military prestige of Páez. General Santander, perhaps Páez's equal in political skill and his superior in application, was a far more controversial figure and lacked military reputation. He could make no pretence to be above party. Colombia was to be governed by men who could put together coalitions from disparate provinces, make elections, manage congress, pay the veterans and keep everyone in a state of moderately discontented expectation. Few ascendancies lasted long – Santander was out of power by 1836, Mosquera never really established an ascendancy, the civilians Murillo Toro and Rafael Núñez only kept their influence as long as they did by making sparing use of it; both were tactful and discreet. Ideological debate was particularly keen and wide-ranging – nowhere else in Latin America did the events of 1848 in Europe find such eager followers and imitators as among the politicians, artisans, students and even soldiers of poor isolated New Granada. Nowhere else were the principles of federalism given such expression as in the Rio Negro Constitution of 1863, with its free trade in arms, its careful provisions for non-interference by the federal government in wars within the sovereign states. Reporting on Colombian political life when this period of radicalism was drawing to an end, the Chilean poet and diplomat José Antonio Soffia described how the two 'great doctrinal parties' had become more and more polarized: 'Here everything has been discussed with vehemence and passion.' To a Chilean, Colombian politics looked disorderly, over-emphatic, dangerous, lower class – the best people, with some notable exceptions, did not take part, just as the modest origins of so many army officers made the army an unattractive career for the well-born. Soffia describes a competitive atmosphere, and concedes that there were issues of principle behind these excesses. He was witnessing the decadence of mid-century liberalism, and the return of conservatism in all its renewed ideological vigour. Nuñez thought that he had a recipe for 'scientific peace' – a centralized government, rapprochement with the Church, a stronger army, a restricted suffrage. . . . Two more wars after 1885 show that again ambition had outrun resources, even if the recipe was the right one. But the solution was not sought in autocracy, but in a new coalition, now to be fortified by the support of the Church. Most features of Colombian political life – the natural federalism of so much of it, the intense use of the press, the incessant electioneering, the career open to the emergent legal–journalistic–congressional talent–did not change. It is also significant that Núñez was able to change the old sovereign states into departments, but failed in his desire to alter the administrative map of the country more fundamentally. The realities of the 1886 constitution were not as central as the appearance. The liberal party did not abandon their allegiance to the old federalism until after the end of the century.

The political beginnings of Ecuador, the 'Estado del Sur de Colombia' as it was at first officially called, were more clearly pretorian. Juan José Flores married a lady of the Quito aristocracy and had a reputation for foxy intrigue, but never abandoned his reliance on his veterans and on other Venezuelans, such as the ruthless black colonel, Juan Otamendi. Opposition to the 'odious foreigner' was not long in appearing, some of it led by the Benthamite English colonel, Francis Hall, who until his violent end was one of the leaders of the liberal intellectual group gathered around the journal *El Quiteño Libre*. Nor was military discipline easily maintained – Flores faced several mutinies, and at the end of 1833 Colonel Mena's rebellion in Guayaquil led to a long-drawn-out guerrilla war in the coastal provinces of Guayas and Manabí, the *guerra de los chihuahuas*.[2] Flores sustained militarily the succeeding government of the cosmopolitan Guayaquileño, Vicente Rocafuerte, and returned to the presidency himself until 1845, when a general movement of protest against his administration arose on his attempting to raise a three-peso poll tax. Certain subsequent presidents can be seen to have governed in the Flores mould: José María Urbina, one of his former aides-de-camp, ruled from 1852–60, in part basing his power on the *tauras*, a corps of freed slaves recruited from the region of that name; Ignacio Veintemilla, the dominant figure of the late seventies and early eighties, clearly relied heavily on his 'three thousand breachleaders'. The mutiny and the *cuartelazo* were much more common in Ecuadorean politics than in Venezuela or Colombia, where examples at the national level were rare. It was also much more usual in Ecuador to use extreme measures against opponents – soldiers and civilians. Rocafuerte as well as Flores, García

---

[2] So called because the leading figure in the opposition to Flores, Vicente Rocafuerte, had lived in Mexico; the *chihuahua* thereafter entered Ecuadorean folklore as the name of a firework figure that runs away when its backside is lit.

Moreno as well as Veintemilla, had their enemies shot or exiled; García Moreno ordered notorious whippings, and under Veintemilla's government the archbishop of Quito was poisoned with strychnine administered in the chalice during mass. One particularly arduous form of exile was to be sent to Brazil by way of the Napo river and the Amazon. These features of Ecuadorean strife perhaps derived from its origins under the domination of veterans of much independence fighting, many of whom were foreigners, and from the relatively miniature scale of political life. The Indian population of the *sierra*, not all so downtrodden as those who only observed it around Quito reported, remained an estate apart, effectively excluded from official political life in which in any case it had little desire to participate – paying the tribute usually exempted the Indian from recruitment. The mixed *montuvio* population of the coastal regions was more active, and in the last two decades of the century was effectively mobilized by the radical Alfaro.

Ideological divisions worked themselves out in the more personal politics of Ecuador; they also reflected local differences. Rocafuerte was one of the most prominent early liberals of Spanish America. Flores, related by marriage to the most prominent families, builder of an enormous and ramshackle Quito palace, became increasingly conservative. Urbina and Veintemilla were military radicals, their enemies said in imitation of New Granadan examples. García Moreno became internationally famous for his extreme clericalism, but his reforming energy did not make him popular with all the clergy. The liberal feelings of Guayaquil contrasted from the earliest days of the republic with the conservatism of Quito. For long friction was lessened by appalling communications. Ecuador also suffered far more than Colombia or Venezuela from diplomatic complications: Peru coveted the timber and ship-yards of Guayaquil, and President Castilla in 1860 attempted an invasion. Peruvian governments gave aid and comfort to Ecuadorean exiles. The northern frontier with Colombia was also complicated, as it did not match the old boundary of the *audiencia* of Quito. There were several invasions and counter-invasions, in which Ecuador usually came off worst. These preoccupations placed great strains on very scarce resources, as did the alarm caused by General Flores's plans to lead a Spanish-backed expedition of re-conquest after his departure in 1845. Ecuador did at times have cause to feel threatened in its very existence. There the very limited powers of the state are clearly seen in the career of García Moreno, so much of whose energy had to be devoted to survival against enemies within and without. Acute political despair led him to make overtures to France for the establishment of a protectorate – he was not the only beleaguered statesman of the region and the era to entertain such ideas.

But foreign observers – particularly such as the supercilious and ungrateful English mountaineer, Whymper, and the pessimistic U.S. minister Hassaurek, in Ecuador – were too prone to generalize their observations, and to present a picture of political instability and social stagnation. Significant social and economic changes occurred under these disadvantaged governments, and these are being uncovered by a local historiography not primarily concerned with national *fracasos*. Certain local economies and local regimes – the conservative government in Antioquia, Dalla Costa in Guayana, for example – can be seen to have had a measure of success, and a new scale of appreciation can be developed less concerned with such rare examples of progress as railways, capable of seeing the significance of a shorter road, an improved mule-track, an effort of local schooling, the differences in the maintenance of law and order from one region to another.

Contemporaries were aware of the importance of these differences and changes, and even made themselves at times ridiculous in their enthusiasm for what to strangers looked very small beer. They were also keenly aware of changes in customs. There was no mass immigration to any of these republics in the nineteenth-century, but there was a none the less significant immigration of a small number of foreigners, principally merchants, but, besides diplomats, also some engineers, artisans and doctors. These brought not only their specific skills but different patterns of behaviour, taste and fashion. After early rivalry with native merchants, those who survived the disappointments of the late 1820s frequently became naturalized in all but law. The Germans in Venezuela, even some few British in New Granada, married creole ladies, and, in the eyes of envoys anxious to avoid the endless labour of civil-war damage claims, became indistinguishable from the natives in their political and social involvement. More creoles travelled abroad, more were sent abroad for their education. Some of these returned not only with the prestige of the travelled and the fashionable but also with a new consciousness of their own national peculiarities, disadvantages and, occasionally, merits and good fortune. The Colombian, Medardo Rivas, discovered in himself a passionate tropical republicanism when he saw how Europeans laughed at Haitians. Most travellers, overwhelmed by the scale and wealth of London, were also appalled at the sight of urban poverty and prostitution, phenomena not yet so glaringly present in their own societies.

Foreign observers, on whom so much reliance has in the past been placed, could not have much sense of the pace of local change, however acute they were: their stays were usually short. But the changes of customs and attitudes are often to be found described in local *costumbrista* writing, and in Bogotá and its surroundings they were recorded by a historian whose memory for significant detail amounts to genius: José María Cordóvez Moure, 1835–1918, author of *Reminiscencias de Santa Fé y Bogotá*, an item of the 'traditional historiography' that puts so much subsequent writing to shame.

Neither Venezuela, Colombia nor Ecuador achieved during the nineteenth century what Don José Avellanos would have called 'a rightful place in the comity of nations'. A pioneer statistician, the Colombian priest Dr Federico C. Aguilar, in 1884 exposed the weakness of Colombia, for example, in his *Colombia en presencia de las repúblicas hispano-americanas*: low per-capita exports and imports, resulting in meagre government income; few miles of railway, expensively constructed; not much movement in the ports; few schools. The contrast with Argentina, Chile and Uruguay is all too apparent, and the distance is increasing. The only position of leadership Father Aguilar can find for Colombia is the number of newspapers. The successors of Gran Colombia had attracted little foreign investment. Guzmán Blanco's guarantees did bring some to Venezuela, but at a high cost. The comparative advantages of these 'destartaladas repúblicas del norte', in a Chilean phrase, were uncertain and unimpressive.

This made, and has made, their formal *national* histories in this first half-century or so more painful to contemplate, as years of failure by the accepted indices of progress of the time. Such a simple view must yield to the detailed study of how local disadvantages of climate and topography were overcome, of how crises turned out to be less than complete, of how each cycle left something behind. It must also be apparent that the persistent habit of stern Victorian judgement, and of regard for little but the hierarchy of international commerce, is unlikely to yield many insights into the history of these countries at this time. In his *Essayo sobre las revoluciones políticas y la condición social de las repúblicas colombianas* (1861), José María Samper complained that 'The European world has made more effort to study our volcanoes than our societies; it knows our insects better than our literature, the crocodile of our rivers better than the acts of our statesmen, and it has much more learning about how quinine bark is cut, or how hides are salted in Buenos Aires, than about the vitality of our infant democracy!' The protest is still a valid one.

# 6

## PERU AND BOLIVIA

On 28 July 1821, the Argentine general, José de San Martín, declared colonial links between Peru and Spain broken and paved the way for the political organization of the new republic. Bolívar's military campaign in 1824, which led to the destruction of the imperial army in Peru, completed the process of Peruvian independence. However, despite the wars of independence, the political, social and economic order of colonial Peru remained in many respects intact. The independence process resulted from the actions of a profoundly vulnerable Spanish and creole minority, which was intent on maintaining its former privileges under a new liberal cloak; there was a total absence of popular representation in any of the decisions taken concerning the political and economic organization of independent Peru. The very vulnerability of the dominant, though far from hegemonic, class, unable to rally behind it, on a national level, the mass of Indians and blacks, permitted the rise to power of a succession of military caudillos during the half-century after independence.

According to the *Guía de Forasteros* published in 1828, Peru had a population of one and a quarter million at the time of its independence:

| Department | Inhabitants |
|---|---|
| Arequipa | 136,812 |
| Ayacucho | 159,608 |
| Cuzco | 216,382 |
| Junín | 200,839 |
| La Libertad | 230,970 |
| Lima | 148,112 |
| Puno | 156,000 |
| Total | 1,248.723 |

[1] Translated from the Spanish by Dr Richard Southern and Dr David Brookshaw; translation revised by the Editor. The Editor wishes to thank Dr Rory Miller, Dr Luis Ortega and Dr James Dunkerley for help in the final preparation of this chapter.

The Peruvian export economy had entered a period of decline during the final years of the colonial period and the situation had worsened during the many military conflicts which had accompanied the campaign for independence. The slaves, who had constituted the basic labour force in the coastal areas, were forcibly recruited into the ranks of both the patriot and the royalist armies, with the result that the coastal sugar and cotton plantations lost one of the most important factors of production. At the same time the fall in the supply of mercury, the abolition of the *mita* (the dominant method of organizing Indian labour for the mines), the inability to deal with the permanent problem of flooding and the destruction caused by the war, all led to the marked decline of the Peruvian silver-mining industry. Output from Cerro de Pasco, which had the largest silver deposits at the time, revived during the 1830s and increased from 95,261 marks in 1830 to 219,378 marks in 1832 and to 307,213 in 1840. National silver production, however, never reached the level of the colonial period and was now exported in the form of silver coin which dramatically decreased the money supply in Peru itself. During the first two decades after independence the Peruvian economy was, therefore, mostly organized around the largely self-sufficient landed estates (haciendas) and the Indian communities *(comunidades)*. Marketable surplus was insignificant and served to supply in erratic fashion local markets. Tenuous links were maintained with international markets – mainly Britain, France, the United States and Chile – through the export of small quantities of sugar, cotton, cacao, quinine bark (which was mainly produced in Bolivia but exported through the ports of southern Peru), copper, tin and nitrates.[2] Beginning in the second half of the 1830s, in response to the growing demands of the British textile industry, significant quantities of wool, first alpaca, then sheep (and to a lesser extent vicuña and llama), began to be exported from southern Peru.[3] Given the stagnation of the export sector, at least until the late 1830s, it

[2] Shane Hunt, *Price and quantum estimates of Peruvian exports 1830–1962* (Princeton, Woodrow Wilson School, Discussion Paper no. 33, 1973) 57–8. For estimates of Peruvian exports (excluding silver) to Britain, France, the U.S. and Chile in the period 1825–40, see Hunt, *Price and quantum estimates*, 38.

[3] Wool exports reached a peak in the 1860s and 1870s by which time Islay was, after Callao, the second most important port in Peru. However, as a port Islay never managed to create its own economic life. Its growth was closely related to the economic development of the interior of the South. For this reason, the construction of the Puno–Arequipa railway and the establishment of its terminus at Mollendo in 1874 would send Islay into sudden and complete decline. Its population, which was calculated at 1,554 inhabitants in 1862, fell to 400 in 1874. From then on, Mollendo would be the main port of entry into southern Peru, and by 1878 it already had 3,000 inhabitants. See Heraclio Bonilla, *Gran Bretaña y el Perú* (Lima, 1977), 105–7.

was necessary for Peru to export vast quantities of silver coin in order to pay for its imports from Britain. In 1825 silver coin amounted to 90 per cent of all Peruvian exports. And in 1840 it still accounted for 82 per cent of exports.[4]

At the time of independence Peru had opened its ports to world, especially British, trade. Although trade routes between Europe and Peru via the port of Buenos Aires had been opened during the last thirty years of the eighteenth century, the introduction of British goods into Peru was effected for the most part via the Magellan Straits, in the far south of the continent, turning the Chilean port of Valparaíso into a strategic link in this trade. In this sense, Peruvian ports were commercially dependent on Valparaíso, although President Santa Cruz in 1836 tried to remedy the situation by rewarding ships which sailed direct to Callao. However, the overthrow of Santa Cruz and the collapse of the Peru–Bolivian Confederation in 1839 (see below) put an end to this experiment. In 1826, goods arriving at Callao via the Magellan Straits undertook a voyage lasting 102 days in all, 90 to Valparaíso and a further 12 from there to Callao. On the other hand, the old colonial route via Panama required a total of 125 days, not so much for the maritime journey as such, but because of the long delay caused by having to cross the Panamanian isthmus. After 1840, when steamships began to make their appearance in the waters of the Pacific the time of the voyage from Europe to Peru was reduced to about 45 days. At the same time lower transport costs made it more profitable to supply the urban markets of the coast with imported agricultural produce, in particular cereals and fruits, from Chile. As a result, the highlands of the interior were increasingly cut off from the economy of the Peruvian coast.

In the first half of the nineteenth century, Peru's main trading partners were, in order of importance, Great Britain, the United States and France. Britain was by far the most significant. By 1824, there were already some thirty-six British commercial houses in Peru, twenty in Lima and sixteen in Arequipa.[5] British exports to Peru steadily increased in value from £86,329 in 1821 to £559,766 in 1825, fell to £199,086 in 1826 but had reached £368,469 in 1830.[6] Between 1820 and 1830, textiles

[4] *Ibid.*, 96. For estimates of Peru's exports to Britain in the years 1825, 1839 and 1840, see William Mathew, 'Anglo-Peruvian commercial and financial relations, 1820–1865' (unpublished Ph.D. thesis, University of London, 1964), 77.

[5] R. A. Humphreys, *British consular reports on the trade and politics of Latin America, 1824–1826* (London, 1940), 126–7.

[6] Heraclio Bonilla, Lía del Rio, Pilar Ortíz de Zevallos, 'Comercio libre y crisis de la económía andina', *Histórica* (Lima), 2/1 (1978), 3.

Peru and Bolivia after Independence

accounted for approximately 95 per cent of the value of British exports to Peru. This percentage fell noticeably immediately afterwards to an average of 50 per cent of all imports for the rest of the nineteenth century. The deluge of British textiles in the ports and markets of Peru continued, in a much more extreme way, a process which had begun with the opening of the port of Buenos Aires. That is to say, the weakened and segmented domestic markets of Peru were now captured for British products on a far greater scale, virtually putting an end to native artisan production and the Indian *obrajes* (workshops), which, because of their technological obsolescence, were unable to compete successfully with imported textiles from Britain. On the other hand, the decline in the importation of textiles, which became more noticeable after 1830, indicates that these Peruvian markets were very restricted, largely because of the self-sufficient character of the family-based economy, particularly in the case of the Indian population.

'When I took office', explained Hipólito Unanue, Peru's first minister of finance:

the treasury was empty. Agricultural lands within thirty leagues of the capital were but one vast expanse of desolation. The mines were occupied by the enemy. Callao was in enemy hands, hindering all trade. The economic resources of the people had been drained as a result of the many taxes, and they had been reduced to famine because of the total siege which they had suffered. One saw nothing but misery and desolation wherever one looked.

Three years later, in 1825, the minister declared:

During the whole time that our nation struggled, with varying degrees of success, for its independence, I was called three times to serve as Minister of Finance. On the first two occasions there were still one or two ruins left with which to repair the edifice. But now even those ruins have disappeared.[7]

Yet, in addition to the servicing of a foreign debt of 26 million pesos, the new Peruvian state had to collect some 5 million pesos every year in order to finance current expenditure, mainly the cost of the civil bureaucracy and, above all, the military. (Before 1845 Peru had no proper budget, and the exact breakdown of public expenditure is unknown. But the *memorias* of Morales y Ugalde (1827) and José María de Pando (1831) provide evidence of the considerable burden of military expenditure. In 1827 it amounted to 48 per cent of total expenditure; and in 1831 its share had risen to 59 per cent.)[8] From time to time the government resorted to cuts

[7] Hipólito Unanue, *Obras científicas y literarias* (Barcelona, 1914), II, 361, 370.
[8] Emilio Romero, *Historia económica del Perú* (Buenos Aires, 1949), 318; Emilio Dancuart (ed.), *Anales de la hacienda del Perú, leyes, decretos, reglamentos y resoluciones, aranceles, presupuestos, cuentas y contratos que constituyen la legislación e historia fiscal de la República* (Lima, 1902–26), II, 154–71 (henceforth cited as *Anales*).

in the bureaucracy together with the freezing of salaries. On other occasions, temporary relief was found by resorting to voluntary or forced loans from foreign and local traders, or quite simply by confiscating various local resources. In the medium term, however, it was the revenue derived from Indian tribute, from customs and from foreign loans, which enabled the government to finance its expenditure.

On 27 August 1821, San Martín, after declaring the Indians Peruvian citizens, proceeded to the abolition of the colonial tribute. However, the insolvent Peruvian state could not afford such generosity for very long. The tribute was re-established on 11 August 1826 out of the need to sustain the finances of the Republic by taxing the Indian population, and as a result of the social policy adopted early on by the Peruvian government. 'The experience of centuries has shown that the Indian tax was established with prudence and foresight', the minister of finance, José María de Pando, declared in 1830, 'and as it is such a powerful factor in the mentality of these people, firmly rooted in custom, any new departure would be dangerous.'[9] As a consequence, the old colonial tribute once again became one of the main contributors to the exchequer and remained so until its final abolition by Ramón Castilla in 1854. As a concession to the new liberal era, however, it became known as the Indian 'contribution'.

In order to collect this 'contribution', it became necessary to divide the Indian population into three fiscal categories: (a) native Indians with access to land; (b) non-native Indians (*forasteros*) with access to lesser quantities of land; and (c) landless Indians. The first category paid between five and nine pesos per year, while the two latter paid a tax which fluctuated between 2.5 and 5 pesos per year. Finally, in addition to the Indian contribution, there was until its abolition in 1854 that of the *castas*, that is to say, taxes paid by the non-Indian sectors of society and which amounted to 5 pesos and 4 per cent of the net product of their properties. The global amount originating from the Indian contribution in 1830 came to 1,039,331 pesos, while that from the *castas* totalled 431,787 pesos.[10] In view of the political and administrative instability of Peru in this period it is no surprise to find a sizeable difference between the estimated revenue from the contribution and the amount actually collected. Nevertheless, there can be no doubt that it had a considerable impact on fiscal revenue. Whereas, for example, in 1829, according to Pando's estimates, out of revenues totalling 7,962,720 pesos, 945,468

[9] *Anales*, II, 154–71.    [10] *Anales*, II, 49–50.

pesos originated from the contribution, between 1839 and 1845 the Indian contribution produced on average 1,757,296 pesos per year, while total revenues entering the treasury averaged 4,500,000 pesos. On the other hand, the Indian contribution produced only 830,826 pesos in 1846.[11]

The imposition of the Indian tribute had been linked historically to the ownership of land, and it was this connection which was gradually, though erratically, eroded after Independence. The liberal ideology of the Independence period was, in effect, opposed to the maintenance of institutions which might hinder the unrestricted circulation of goods and people in the market. It was because of this that the very existence of the Indian community was threatened by Bolívar's decree of 8 April 1824, which declared that the Indians had the right of ownership over their lands, and by extension, the right to sell the lands to third parties. The implicit purpose of such a decision was to create a class of prosperous independent land holders. The results, however, were different. The authorities soon began to appreciate that this measure posed a serious threat to the Indian *comunidades* and delayed its application until 1850. Nevertheless, an irreparable breach had been made in the barrier which protected the Indian community from the hacienda, and thus prepared the way for the expansion of the great landed estates once new forces began to dynamize the rural economy as a whole.

As far as customs tariffs were concerned Peruvian governments were obliged to reconcile varying interests. First, there was pressure from British interests for free trade. On the other hand, there was pressure from the weak native producers, who demanded protectionist policies and measures to halt the flood of British textiles which was threatening to ruin them. Finally, there were the financial needs of the government itself, for which customs revenue represented an important source of income. Once again, the extreme political vulnerability of the Peruvian government did not allow it to follow a consistent course in this matter. Its ambivalence is visible in the many sets of regulations – six between 1821 and 1836 – governing trade.

It is clear that until 1833 the intentions of the Peruvian government were protectionist. The provisional law of 1821 imposed a duty of 40 per cent, and the law of 1826 a duty of 80 per cent on imported foreign textiles. The third law (June 1828), known as 'the law of prohibitions', prohibited the importation of goods prejudicial to native production for

[11] *Anales*, III, 54–5; IV, 36–7.

a period of ten months, although there is evidence that this prohibition could not be enforced in practice. Neither the intentions of an unstable government, nor the desires of native producers who were politically and economically weak, could have any effect in the face of the combined pressure of British interests and the government's own financial needs. With the law of 1833, the Peruvian government began to adopt a more liberal tariff policy; it reduced the tax on textile imports to 45 per cent. This tendency towards liberalization continued with the law of 1836, passed during the Peru–Bolivian Confederation (1836–9), which further reduced the tax on imported textiles to a mere 20 per cent.

This represented a victory for British merchants trading with Peru whose influence is illustrated by the fact that the 1836 legislation did no more than sanction proposals formulated by the British trading community.[12] Equally significant, a Treaty of Friendship, Commerce and Navigation between Great Britain and Peru was signed the following year. For the Peruvian government, the law of 1836 also expressed the search for direct links with Europe, which was part of its desire to undermine the hegemony of the port of Valparaíso. The substantial reduction in customs dues and the various administrative measures taken by President Santa Cruz, notably the establishment of Arica, Cobija, Callao and Paita as free ports and the imposition of supplementary dues on goods which had passed through other ports on the Pacific coast before arriving at Callao, were all aimed to this end.[13]

The defeat of Santa Cruz in 1839 and the collapse of the Confederation were regarded as a heavy blow to the commercial interests of Europe and the United States,[14] but later trading regulations maintained the tariffs established in 1836. At the same time, the process which accelerated British commercial expansion through the massive importation of cheap textiles, and turned customs revenue into one of the main supports of public spending, ended by completely wrecking native production.

With the severing of Peru's colonial links, British investors shared the enthusiasm of manufacturers and traders; they saw a chance of investing their capital in the exploitation of Peru's legendary deposits of precious metals. In the years immediately after Independence, five companies were created for this specific purpose: The Chilean and Peruvian Association; Potosí, La Paz and Peruvian Mining Association; Pasco Peruvian

12 William Mathew, 'The imperialism of free trade, Peru 1820–1870', *Economic History Review*, 2nd ser., 21 (1968), 566.
13 Jorge Basadre, *Historia de la República del Perú* (5th edn, Lima, 1962–4), II, 566.
14 Public Record Office, London, Foreign Office 61/93, Cope to Wilson, 12 October 1842.

Mining Company; Peruvian Trading and Mining Company; and the Anglo-Peruvian Mining Association. The first four had capital assets amounting to £1 million and the last one had £600,000.[15] However, illusions were very soon dispelled, and the mobilization of this capital even provoked one of the first crises in British financial capitalism in the nineteenth century. There were various reasons for this disaster, although the main one was the absence of any mechanism which might permit the mobilization of the native labour force to the mining centres. The British would have to wait until 1890 and the founding of the Peruvian Corporation for a renewed attempt at direct capital investment.

Until the war with Chile in 1879 the export of capital was normally carried out in the form of long term loans to the Peruvian government. The first loan was negotiated by San Martín in 1822. His special envoys, Juan García del Río and General Diego de Paroissien, obtained a loan of £1,200,000 from Thomas Kinder. The interest was fixed at 6 per cent, commission at 2 per cent, the cost of the bonds at 75 per cent and the repayment period at 30 years. The guarantee for this loan was to be made up of revenue from customs tariffs and silver production. Two years later, Bolívar commissioned Juan Parish to draw a new loan of £616,000 at an interest rate of 6 per cent and a cost fixed at 78 per cent. Out of this total, the sum in effect received by Peru amounted to only £200,385,[16] although she remained committed to pay back the nominal loan in full. These loans were primarily used up on maintaining the foreign army which collaborated in the Independence campaign. The stagnation of the Peruvian economy, however, did not allow the government to service the foreign debt until 1825.

Foreign sources soon dried up and the Peruvian government came to depend on internal loans for financing its expenditure not covered by the Indian contribution and customs revenue. In 1845, the internal debt was estimated at 6,846,344 pesos,[17] but included bonds contracted by the Spanish government from wealthy Lima merchants and recognized by the new regime.

The social structure of Peru in the period immediately after independence reflected the segmentation of the Peruvian economy. Rather than a national society, it is more correct to talk of regional societies, centred on the hacienda, which was the basic unit of production, with a limited

---

[15] Henry English, *A general guide to the companies formed for working foreign mines* (London, 1825), 8–51.
[16] *Anales*, I, 50.     [17] *Anales*, IV, 46.

capacity to sustain the population of the area. Politically, the *hacendado*, either directly or else in alliance with some local caudillo, exercised undisputed political power in each region, developing a whole system of typically client relationships in order to ensure the loyalty of his underlings. Despite their local power, landowners nevertheless lacked sufficient strength to generate and consolidate a system of political hegemony at the national level. The government in Lima was able to impose authority by lending its support to, or entering into alliance with, the political leaders of each region, without necessarily representing their interests. Until the presidency of Manuel Pardo in 1872, strictly speaking the source of each caudillo-president's power lay in the military capability of his followers. Here too, the problem was that these followers were numerous and divided through ties of personal loyalty to each military caudillo. As no president had the ability to establish general obedience, or to create a consensus which might permit a relatively stable government, the result was an acute and never ending rivalry for power in order to plunder the resources of the state.

After Simón Bolívar left Peru in September 1826 the country was plunged into a period of political confusion and anarchy. Despite the attempts made by conservative and liberal elements within the Peruvian aristocracy to give an institutional and political structure to the new nation, reflected in the passage of six constitutions before 1836, their efforts did not succeed in gathering enough social support, and the sources of political power remained firmly in the hands of regional caudillos. Group interests, regionalism and personal allegiance became key factors in power politics and, in that context, men of action supported by an armed following dominated the country's government for a decade. Prior to the setting up of the Peru–Bolivian Confederation in 1836, Peru had eight presidents over a period of ten years, but only one of them, the authoritarian and ruthless General Agustín Gamarra, managed to complete a full four-year term of office. However, after his departure, and for a period of almost two years, conspiracies and uprisings allowed several military leaders to take over the presidency only to be deposed within a matter of weeks by violent means. Early in 1835, a young commander of the Callao garrison, Felipe Salaverry, launched his own bid for power, which turned out to be successful. It seemed that, through Salaverry's heavy-handed rule, some degree of political stability was within reach, but exactly a year after he had seized power he was shot dead by a firing squad during a rebellion. The next challenger for power in Peru was General Andrés Santa Cruz, president of Bolivia (1829–39), an able and skilful politician, who, through alliances with some southern Peruvian caudillos, not only secured his control over most of Peru, but in October 1836 proclaimed the Peru–Bolivian Confederation.

Santa Cruz's scheme had some appeal within Peru. The southern interests, who had historic commercial links with Bolivia and resented Lima's dominance over the country, did in fact welcome the Confederation and supported it actively. However, both in Lima and La Paz it encountered firm opposition. The elite of the former strongly resented the partition of their country, as southern Peru became a separate state within the Confederation. For their part, Bolivians strongly disapproved of Santa Cruz's choice of Lima as the seat of the government of the Confederation. But the main threat to the Confederation came from abroad, especially from Chile, although Rosas, the Argentine dictator, also made his dislike evident. The Chilean government, whose leadership viewed the Confederation as a major threat to its independence and military and commercial hegemony on the Pacific, declared war in December 1836, to be followed by the Argentine government in May 1837. After an unsuccessful invasion in 1837, the Chileans made a second attempt in July 1838, this time with the active support and participation of a large contingent of Peruvian exiles, amongst whom the most prominent were Generals Agustín Gamarra and Ramón Castilla. In Peru itself a good section of the Lima elite, who had never been able to accept the loss of their country's independence, gave the expeditionary force active support. Amongst them, the liberals, who had always opposed Santa Cruz's political project and tough rule, and the followers of the ill-fated Salaverry, enthusiastically echoed the proclamation made by Gamarra and Castilla in which they announced their intention of restoring Peru's autonomy. In January 1839 the army of Santa Cruz was crushed at the battle of Yungay and the Confederation collapsed.

After the Chilean forces left Peru in October 1839, Gamarra became president once again and introduced a conservative constitution. However, soon the new president embarked on an invasion of Bolivia, where he was defeated and killed at Ingavi in November 1841. Once more Peru plunged into political chaos. As Bolivian troops invaded from the south, the Ecuadorians made clear their intention of doing the same from the north. The forces dispatched to fight the invaders ignored the authority of the Lima government and a new civil war broke out. Three generals became supreme rulers of Peru after Gamarra's constitutional successor was overthrown, and political turmoil was only brought to an end when in July 1844 Ramón Castilla defeated General Vivanco, thus becoming the country's new strong man. Castilla was to dominate Peru's political and institutional life until his death in 1868.

From the early 1840s to the beginning of the war with Chile in 1879 the economic and political evolution of Peru was dependent in one way or another on the exploitation of guano deposits on the coastal islands. The absence of rain along the Peruvian coastline meant that the guano which accumulated on the islands did not lose its chemical content. Archaeological evidence and the chronicles of José de Acosta, Pedro Cieza de León and Agustín de Zárate point to the use of guano in pre-Columbian agriculture. Equally, during the colonial period, agriculture on the coastal belt continued to make use of guano in order to increase the fertility of the soil. However, at no time did guano enter, at least to any significant degree, the colonial export trade. It was the changes in English agriculture during the nineteenth century which gave a fresh impulse to guano extraction. The growing use of fertilizers was one of the innovations in English farming techniques which was designed to increase productivity and meet the demands of industrial Britain. The use of Peruvian fertilizer, limited at first, became increasingly important until recession in Britain and Europe after 1873, the exhaustion of the best guano deposits, competition from synthetic fertilizers, and finally the capture of the deposits by the Chilean army during the War of the Pacific brought an end to the Peruvian guano boom.

Besides guano, Peru exported during this period copper, alpaca and sheep wool, cotton, sugar and nitrates as well as small quantities of tin, cacao, coffee and quinine bark. The export of precious metals, especially silver, is not recorded in the trade figures of the countries for which estimates of Peru's foreign trade are based – Britain, France, the U.S. and Chile. Silver production, however, of which the Cerro de Pasco mine accounted for more than half, remained stable at between 300,000 and half a million marks per annum throughout the period 1840–79.[18] Guano nevertheless enjoyed an absolute supremacy within Peru's export trade and was largely responsible for an average annual growth rate of exports of 4.5 per cent between 1840 and 1852, and 5.2 per cent between 1852 and 1878.[19]

[18] Hunt, *Price and quantum estimates*, 57–8.        [19] *Ibid.*, 67.

Estimates regarding the volume of guano exported and the income from its sale are fairly unreliable given the absence of coherent records of accounts, and the disorganized character of public administration. After growing steadily to almost 100,000 tons in 1849 it has been estimated that guano exports fluctuated during the period 1850 to 1878 from a little under 200,000 tons to 700,00 tons per annum.[20] J. M. Rodríguez, one of the compilers of the *Anales de la Hacienda Pública*, estimates that during the whole period, some 10,804,033 tons of guano were exported.[21] If £10 per ton is taken as an average price, then gross earnings from the sale of guano amount to something approaching £100 million. Moreover it is important to note that guano was never the private property of companies or families, whether foreign or native; from the beginning ownership was exercised by the Peruvian state. Peru therefore possessed the capital necessary to begin to rebuild her economy, diversify production and generate a more stable rate of growth. Nevertheless, although guano had an impact on certain sectors of the economy at certain times, its overall impact was negative.

Any analysis of the fluctuations in the value of returns from guano has to consider workers, local traders and the state. With regard to the former, namely the workers, their part in calculations concerning returned value is virtually irrelevant. Available estimates allow for a total of one thousand workers on the guano islands, whose maintenance represented only about 4 per cent of total costs. Between 1841 and 1849, when consignee contracts were monopolized by foreign merchant houses, notably Antony Gibbs and Sons, and when the position of the state was very weak in its ability to negotiate, the government took some 33 per cent of returned value. In subsequent contracts, this share rose to some 65 per cent. When competition by local traders in the marketing of guano became more significant, the income retained by the government and the local traders together fluctuated between 60 and 70 per cent of eventual sales. When, in 1869, Auguste Dreyfus (a French merchant with the support of the Société Générale in Paris) finally assumed monopoly control of the guano trade, the participation of the state in the income became even greater. To sum up, during the entire period 1840–80 the Peruvian government collected about 60 per cent of the income from guano, or between 381 and 432 million pesos, to which should be added

[20]  *Ibid.*, 38–9, 43–6.
[21]  J.M. Rodríguez, *Estudios económicos y financieros y ojeada sobre la Hacienda Pública del Perú y la necesidad de su reforma* (Lima, 1895), 317–19.

between 60 and 80 million pesos received by Peruvian consignees which represented a further 5–10 per cent of the income from guano. In 1846–7 income from guano accounted for approximately 5 per cent of all state revenue; in 1869 and 1875 this figure had risen to 80 per cent. However, while the resources generated by guano permitted a five-fold expansion in income between 1847 and 1872–3, expenditure increased eight times between these dates. In order to answer the question why income from guano did not have a positive effect on economic development in Peru it is important to see how revenue was spent during the guano era. More than half the income from guano was used to expand the civilian bureaucracy (29 per cent) and the military (24.5 per cent). Guano revenue was also used to expand the railway network (20 per cent), to transfer payments to foreigners and to nationals (8 per cent and 11.5 per cent) and to reduce the tax burden on the poor (7.0 per cent).[22]

One of the results of the increasing part played by guano in state revenue was the abolition of the Indian contribution during the government of Ramón Castilla. In 1854, Castilla, wishing to widen his political base, cancelled the levy to which the Indian population was subject. For the Peruvian economy as a whole, however, the abolition of the tribute led to a reduction in surplus marketable agricultural produce, which in turn led to price increases. For the majority of Indian families, the sale of this surplus was closely linked to the tribute, for only in this way were they able to find the money to bear this tax burden. Once the tribute had disappeared, there was no sense in growing and selling surplus produce, and peasant families returned to a basically self-sufficient economy. (Furthermore, with the abolition of the tribute the landowners increasingly sought to appropriate the land belonging to the Indians, as a way of maintaining access to Indian labour and control over its availability, and the state no longer had an incentive to protect the Indian community from the encroachment of the hacienda.)

Another use to which revenue from guano was put was the abolition of slavery. There were 25,505 slaves in Peru in 1854, 1.3 per cent of the total population.[23] Their manumission was carried out by means of a payment to slave-owners of 300 pesos for each freed slave. The cost of this operation involved the transfer of 7,651,500 pesos from the govern-

---

[22] Shane Hunt, *Growth and guano in nineteenth century Peru* (Princeton, Woodrow Wilson School, 1973), 64, 84, 69, 72–5, 80.

[23] Nils Jacobsen, *The development of Peru's slave population and its significance for coastal agriculture* (Berkeley, unpublished MSS. n.d.), 82.

ment to the slave-owners. The manumission of the slaves placed a considerable amount of capital in the hands of the landowners, and in some cases, as we shall see, this was used to finance the development of agriculture along the coastal belt. However, this same process of development, given the apparent impossibility of mobilizing Indian peasants from the highlands, meant that it became necessary to import vast numbers of Chinese coolies, under a system of disguised slavery, to replace the old slave labour force. Chinese immigration at the port of Callao between 1850 and 1874 amounted to 87,952; more than a quarter of that number, 25,303, arrived during the two years 1871–2.[24]

Through public expenditure guano increased internal demand and generated effects which were felt right through the Peruvian economy.[25] It has been estimated that wages increased in real terms at a rate of about 3 per cent per year during the guano period.[26] Despite these conditions, however, the structure of production did not have the capacity to respond to the incentive of demand. This failure has been attributed to the absence of an entrepreneurial class as a result of the destruction of the artisan sector, the increase in domestic costs and prices produced by guano, the choice of unfortunate projects for capital investment financed by guano and the failure of traditional institutions to create the necessary framework for strengthening production. Rather than stimulating local production, increased demand contributed to a marked increase in imports. The railways (whose construction was also financed by guano) were not completed until the end of the nineteenth century.

Another of the processes associated with the exploitation of guano was the series of loans contracted by the Peruvian government. These loans were of two types. Firstly, there were those contracted with guano traders, which were essentially mere advances to be repaid, with interest, through revenue from the sale of guano. The others were more significant, and involved a policy pursued by the Peruvian government between 1849 and 1872 of securing foreign loans guaranteed by guano sales. This policy, within reasonable limits, permitted the mobilization of foreign capital which was used to finance economic growth. However, when the servicing of the debt weakens or destroys the capacity for

[24] H. B. H. Martinet, *L'Agriculture au Pérou* (Lima, 1876), 32.
[25] Hunt, *Growth and guano, passim;* cf. Jonathan Levin, *The export economies: their pattern of development in historical perspective* (Cambridge, Mass., 1959) who explained the failure of guano to generate development in terms of the export of guano revenue in the form of profits.
[26] Hunt, *Growth and guano*, 88.

domestic capital accumulation, it can become an obstacle to growth. The Peruvian experience with its foreign debt had, in fact, disastrous consequences. It was not just a case of poor choice of financially viable projects by the government, but of a clear process of financial paralysis within the Peruvian state which led, in 1890, to the transfer of some of the country's productive resources to the control and ownership of the British creditors of Peru's foreign debt.

In 1822 and 1824, as we have seen, Peru had drawn two loans in London to the value of £1,816,000. As a result of its insolvency, it ceased paying the service on both debts two years later. In 1848, accumulated interest amounted to £2,564,532, that is to say, the total amount of the debt was now £4,380,530. When guano became Peru's main source of revenue, pressure from British bondholders and financial speculators associated with them increased in order that the service of the debt should be renewed. A final agreement was reached on 4 January 1849.[27] Repayment of the consolidated debt was to begin in 1856, for which Antony Gibbs was to deposit half of the revenue from guano sales in the Bank of England. By re-establishing the financial credibility of the Peruvian government, this operation heralded a policy of repeated foreign loans. The success of each successive loan meant the withdrawal of the bonds corresponding to the previous loan, for the exchange of which a large part of the requested loans was absorbed. In a word, they were loans to convert the debt, that is to say, to pay off previous loans.

From 1869, the railway construction programme, as we shall see, accentuated the demands of the Peruvian government for new and larger loans. Finally, in 1872 it tried to float a loan of £36.8 million, £21.8 million of which was earmarked for the conversion of the loans contracted in 1865, 1866 and 1870.

The loan of 1872 was a complete disaster. Public stock did not exceed £230,000.[28] The successive bankruptcies of Paraguay, Bolivia, and Uruguay, which were the most assiduous clients on the London market, eroded the confidence of the London lenders in the ability of Latin American countries to remain solvent, and they began to refuse fresh requests for loans. As of 1872, therefore, Peru had a foreign debt of around £35 million which carried an annual amortization charge of £2.5 million. Given the precarious nature of government finances, it was impossible to service such a large debt and, in 1876, Peru defaulted for a second time.

[27] *Parliamentary Papers* (London, 1854) LXIX, 124–6.      [28] *Anales*, IX, 35–6.

In sum, this policy of contracting huge foreign loans did nothing to finance the internal growth of the economy, but rather accustomed the state to become increasingly dependent on foreign credit, and this could only produce disastrous results when a crisis, such as that of 1872, closed off this source of foreign capital. Thus, the ground was being gradually prepared for the final collapse.

We have demonstrated the effects on the growth of internal demand which guano was able to generate through public expenditure. We have also shown the reasons why the system of production was unable to respond to this demand. A totally different picture was presented when we turn to those sectors of the economy oriented towards the overseas market, in particular to agriculture on the central and northern coastal belt. From the 1860s, the haciendas, responding to favourable international circumstances, began their process of recovery and expansion through the production of cotton and sugar. Sugar production grew at an annual rate of 28 per cent from 1862 and by 1879 sugar accounted for 32 per cent of total exports. It was produced primarily in an area situated between Trujillo and Chiclayo. In 1877 this region produced 58 per cent of sugar exports and 68 per cent a year later. The expansion of cotton production was linked to the cotton crisis in the United States. It, too, was regionally concentrated: in 1877 14 per cent of cotton exports were shipped from Piura, 38 per cent from the Department of Lima, and 42 per cent from Pisco-Ica.[29]

The expansion of export-oriented agriculture was the result of the intensive exploitation of coolie labour and a significant injection of capital. The export of cotton, for example, increased from 291 tons in 1860 to 3,609 tons in 1879, and in the same period sugar exports increased from 610 tons to 83,497 tons.[30] This would not have been possible but for the links, direct or indirect, with the benefits derived from guano. In the first place, the consolidation of the internal debt (see below) released some 50 per cent of the capital paid by the state as repayment to its internal creditors for investment in agriculture. The abolition of slavery also enabled fixed assets (the slaves) to be converted into liquid capital (the indemnity).[31] To these mechanisms one should add the credit afforded to the landowning class by the commercial and banking sectors,

---

[29] Hunt, *Growth and guano*, 55–6.   [30] Hunt, *Price and quauntum estimates*, 38–9, 43–6.
[31] Pablo Macera, 'Las plantaciones azucareras andinas, 1821–1875'. *Trabajos de Historia* (Lima, 1977),

which, in turn, owed their existence to the surplus capital generated by guano. The best example of this link between the surplus from guano and agrarian capital is the case of the Lurifico hacienda in the Jequetepeque Valley, on the northern coast of Peru.[32] However, the development of export agriculture on the coast was particularly precarious, not only because of its almost total dependence on the fluctuations of the international market, but also because of its subordination to finance capital. It has been shown that in 1875 the total debts of the sugar haciendas amounted to 30 million soles, of which 17,500,000 were owed to banking institutions.[33]

In contrast to the coast, highland agriculture was relatively little affected by the guano boom, although the increased demand for foodstuffs in Lima (as well as the mining area) did contribute in some way to the expansion of cattle raising in the Central Sierra.[34] Guano also had little impact on the industrial development of Peru. Artisan industry, as we have seen, was severely hit by the massive influx of European goods. Indeed, the streets of Lima witnessed several violent demonstrations, such as those in 1858, by artisan producers.[35] The industries which existed were concentrated mainly in Lima, and concentrated mainly on the production of beer, pasta, biscuits, chocolates, butter and other processed foodstuffs. Most factory owners were immigrants whose capital no doubt came from savings and loans. In the Sierra, the most important industrial enterprise was the textile factory established in 1859 on the Lucre hacienda in the province of Quispicanchis, where the labour force was converted from serfs into wage earners.

At the beginning of the 1870s the age of guano was coming to an end. It left Peru with a huge external debt amounting to £35 million, the servicing of which required an annual repayment of about £2.5 million. Guano had stimulated internal demand, and also raised the real wages of the urban population, while at the same time galvanizing the haciendas of the central and northern coasts into a new phase of expansion. Nevertheless, and this is the crucial point, the internal market failed to develop and expand, and local production for this market failed to increase to any real degree. If it is necessary to refer to the guano period as a period of lost opportunity, it is precisely because of the inability of the military which

[32] Manuel Burga, *De la encomienda a la hacienda capitalista* (Lima, 1976), 174–8.
[33] Hunt, *Growth and guano*, 58.
[34] Nelson Manrique, *El desarrollo del mercado interno en la sierra central* (Lima, Universidad Agraria, mimeo, 1978), 68–9.     [35] Jorge Basadre, *Historia del Perú*, III, 1291.

exercised political power throughout the period and the new dominant class which emerged during the guano age to effect an alternative programme of development, based not only on the exploitation of the country's natural wealth, but also on the eradication of the colonial character of the Peruvian economy and the establishment of the necessary institutional bases to enable the country to respond adequately to the opportunities created by the export of guano.

At the time of independence in 1821, there was no ruling class in Peru with the necessary authority and legitimacy to exercise political control over the fledgling state. It was this political vacuum which caused the military to assume control. Of all the military leaders who held power, Ramón Castilla, a *mestizo*, was the most forceful and the one who possessed the greatest political and administrative skills. Between 1844 and 1868 he held a number of senior government posts, including finance, and was twice president. In matters of practical politics, his rule reflected a highly pragmatic approach, and he was always prepared to compromise. In a country so deeply divided by civil strife, Castilla, although firm in repressing uprisings, tolerated a certain degree of criticism towards his regime, allowed Congress to meet regularly and without interference and even went as far as to appoint men of diverse political persuasions to key posts. He also devoted time and effort to the normalization of the country's finances. But law and order were his main priorities and perhaps his most remarkable achievement was his success in giving Peru its first experience of stable political rule between 1845 and 1851. Once his first term as president was over, Castilla was replaced by General José Rufino Echenique, who through lack of political and administrative experience did much to undo Castilla's political work of stabilization. It was not long before the liberals felt compelled to stage another revolution, which came in early 1854, with Castilla as its leader. In a bitter confrontation, the revolutionary forces won a considerable degree of popular support and succeeded in ousting Echenique. In July 1854 Castilla began his second term as president, which lasted until 1862. Undoubtedly the best known and more important measures taken during this administration were the already mentioned ending of the Indian tribute and the abolition of slavery, which gave Castilla the title of 'Liberator' and increased his popularity. Politically, his second term of office began with a rather heated debate about the necessity of a new constitution. The initial stages of debate were won by the liberals, who secured the passing of the 1856 charter, which reduced the powers of the executive in favour of the legislature. Castilla gave only a mild and qualified support to the new constitution, but took a moderate course of action until 1858 when he dissolved Congress and organized the election of a more conservative constituent assembly. In 1860 Peru was given yet another constitution – one which better reflected Castilla's own political convictions and reinstated the presidency as the dominant political power. The texts of these two constitutions, like the famous debate on the nature of the state between the conservative Bartolomé Herrera and the liberal Pedro Gálvez which preceded them (1846–51), are notable for their total lack of relevance to the economic and social realities of mid-nineteenth century Peru and provide interesting reading only insofar as they illustrate an enormous gap which existed between the educated elite and the nation as a whole.

In 1862 General Miguel San Román succeeded Castilla as president, but died of natural causes after a brief period in office. His successor, Vice-president General Juan Antonio Pezet, had to face the difficult years of conflict with Spain over its claim to the Chincha islands (1864–6). His conciliatory policy towards the Spanish demands was considered humiliating and caused anger and resentment within the elite and the military establishment. Finally, Colonel Mariano Ignacio Prado launched an armed revolt against the president, who was deposed in November 1865. Prado took over the presidency and led the Peruvian armed forces to a convincing military victory over the Spaniards. But he had still to consolidate his position in order to remain as chief of state, and his decision to reinstate the 1856 constitution, with liberal support, only served to provoke yet another civil war, with Castilla leading those who demanded the restoration of the constitution of 1860. The seventy year old 'Liberator' died of ill-health in the early stages of the conflict, but his second in command, General Pedro Diez Canseco, took over the leadership of the movement which achieved victory early in 1868. The victorious conservative forces reinstated the 1860 constitution, and in July appointed Colonel José Balta as president of the Republic. Balta's term of office was characterized by inefficiency and corruption, and it was during his four-year rule (1868–72) that the anti-military feeling within the Peruvian elite reached its climax with the creation of the Partido Civil and the capture of the presidency by one of its leaders, Manuel Pardo, in 1872.

When guano became the Peruvian government's most important

source of revenue, not only did external creditors redouble their efforts to obtain repayment for their loans, but internal creditors also began to struggle for the recognition of their rights. At the end of Castilla's first term in office, in 1851, the consolidated internal debt already amounted to 4,879,608 pesos.[36] According to Castilla himself, the total amount of the debt could not be more than six or seven million. However, under the government of Echenique, the recognized debt totalled 23,211,400 pesos (approximately £5 million).[37] This great increase in the recognized debt was made possible through the venality and corruption of the Peruvian bureaucracy. It was precisely this abuse which provided one of the excuses for Castilla's rebellion in 1854. The commission of inquiry set up in the following year concluded that more than 12 million pesos in consolidated debt bonds in the hands of domestic creditors – merchants and landowners – were fraudulent.[38]

In 1850 the Peruvian government had signed a ten-year contract with a group of local traders for the sale of guano to Spain, France, China, the Antilles and the U.S. These traders created the Sociedad Consignataria del Guano and set about obtaining capital through the issue of shares. The result, however, was negative. A year later they were forced to restrict their activity to the United States market alone and to limit the duration of their contracts to only five years.[39] In 1860 and 1862, however, with the capital which had been paid to them as consolidation of the internal debt, they were able to replace Antony Gibbs as consignors of guano to Britain, the most important of the European markets. The Compañía Nacional Consignataria included the most powerful Lima traders, many of them beneficiaries of the process of consolidation, who were now presented with the opportunity to increase their income not only by selling guano but also by charging heavy interest on the loans made to the Peruvian government. In this way, both speculative and commercial capital gave each other mutual sustenance.

The development of the trade in guano also necessitated institutions which might facilitate the rapid mobilization of credit. Here, too, the constitution of the first directives and, above all, the immediate subscription of shares issued, would not have been possible without the control, by local capitalists, of a large part of the income produced by guano sales. In this way, a new process of fusion occurred between commercial and

---

[36] *Anales*, IV, 5.
[37] José Echenique, *Memorias para la historia del Perú (1808–1878)* (Lima, 1952), II, 199.
[38] *Anales*, V, 46.
[39] *Anales*, V, 27–8.

financial capital. In September 1862, for example, the Banco de la Providencia was organized with capital assets of 500,000 pesos. The Banco de Perú was created in May 1863 with capital assets of 10 million pesos. It was this bank which was the most closely linked to the Compañía Nacional del Guano, for its shareholders also belonged to the Guano company. Similarly, the Banco de Lima, founded in March 1869 with capital assets of 3.2 million soles, included among its shareholders some of the period's more eminent men of fortune. Finally, the Banco de Crédito Hipotecario, specialising in the issue of mortgages and long-term credit on rural and urban property, was created in 1866 with an initial capital of 1.5 million pesos.[40]

When cotton and sugar production began to expand in the 1860s, capital from guano and from the banks found new opportunities for investment in the agrarian sector. In this way, a powerful, closely linked oligarchy became firmly established. As has been seen, its wealth was derived indiscriminately from finance, trade, and land. Consequently, there were no great internal rifts within this small circle of powerful individuals, because the capital which they controlled was committed to those sectors whose prosperity depended entirely on the excellent conditions which the international market offered.

The emergence of this oligarchy of merchants, financiers and land-owners soon manifested itself in the organization of Peru's first modern political party. The creation of the Partido Civil in 1871 gave them a vehicle through which to voice their political interests, and, as a consequence of their own power and influence, to elevate Manuel Pardo to the presidency in 1872. *Civilista* ideology was expressed through opposition to government by the military, which had controlled the country virtually without interruption since 1821, and the economic orientation of the state, in particular the use made of the resources which guano had created. The basic tenets of *civilista* ideology had begun to be expressed between 1859 and 1863 in the *Revista de Lima* and had even begun to be applied before the advent of a civilian administration. It was no coincidence that one of the main contributors to the publication was Manuel Pardo. Pardo and his friends on the *Revista de Lima* understood quite clearly that Peru's future could not continue for much longer to be linked to guano, a resource which, apart from the danger of its drying up, was likely to suffer the effects of competition from other fertilizers. Moreover, they were aware of the way in which income from guano was being

---

[40] Carlos Camprubí, *Historia de los Bancos del Perú* (Lima, 1957), I, 39–40, 61–4, 85.

squandered and used unproductively. In Pardo's opinion, it was for this reason that the economic policy of the government had to be reoriented through the channelling of the few resources still generated by guano towards the completion of the national rail network. The railways would be instrumental in fostering national production by expanding markets and bringing them closer together, and by linking the Peruvian economy more efficiently to the international market. To convert guano into railways, and attract foreign capital for any additional expense, this was the main prop of the thesis presented by Pardo and the *Revista*.

What is worth underlining here is that the equation by which railways would foster production was not envisaged in terms of fostering production for the internal market. The main railways planned by Balta, and partially built during his administration, linked coastal ports with centres for raw materials. The northern railway served cotton and sugar; the central railway, silver and copper; the southern railway, wool. Consequently, once again, it was a case of using the railways to sweep away the obstacles which hindered the relative wealth of the country from being more efficiently exploited and integrated into the international market. As far as the landowners were concerned, rugged terrain and an uncompetitive system of transport based on muleteers impeded them from taking advantage of and profiting from the increasing opportunities presented by the international market. On the other hand, the completion of the rail network would also provide access to markets in the interior for monopolistic traders to place their goods at less cost. In either case, however, the programme of *civilista* politicians did not imply any real change in the traditional model of growth adopted by the Peruvian economy. It was purely and simply a case of modernizing the system of transport in order to link the Peruvian economy more efficiently to the international market. The crucial question, in this context, is whether they could have acted differently. An alternative policy would have meant removing the props responsible for the colonial character of the Peruvian economy and society, abolishing the relations of production in force on the great estates of the coastal and highland regions, doing away with the self-sufficient character of the peasant economies in order to create the basis of a healthy internal market which might, in turn, provide internal stimulus for the growth of the country's productive sectors. However, this type of growth suggested something more than railway construction. It implied the political alteration of a system and this was too great a challenge for a group which, in spite of everything, lacked both the strength to carry it out and the conviction of its need.

When Manuel Pardo took office on 2 August 1872, after the populace of Lima had foiled an attempt by the military to remain in power, he found that the state was bankrupt. The policy of railway construction, as we have seen, had helped to increase the external debt to £35 million, the amortization of which amounted to about £2.5 million, a sum equal to the entire budget. Furthermore, the servicing of the 1870 and 1872 loans absorbed *in toto* the monthly payments which Dreyfus was committed to remit to the state by virtue of the contract of 1869, and this generated a budgetary deficit of 8.5 million soles. Unlike previous decades, the situation on the London money market prevented the Peruvian government from pursuing its previous policy of raising loans, and these circumstances were made all the worse when, in 1874, Dreyfus announced that services on previous securities would only be attended to until the end of 1875. Desperate attempts by the Peruvian government to find a replacement for Dreyfus, through commercial agreements signed with the Société Générale de Paris and Peruvian Guano Co. in 1876, eventually proved fruitless. In 1876, the Peruvian government once again entered a state of financial bankruptcy, unable to contract new foreign loans or to deal with the service on existing loans.

In such circumstances, Pardo's policies were directed primarily at reducing the budgetary deficit of 8.5 million soles. One of the measures closely examined was turning the nitrates of the desert province of Tarapacá into a new resource which might finance public expenditure. Nitrates, however, unlike guano, were a privately owned resource – by Peruvians, Chileans and other foreigners. In order to implement this policy, therefore, Pardo established a nitrate monopoly in 1873, and in 1875 expropriated the nitrate fields. Their owners received 'nitrate certificates' guaranteed by local banks. These nitrate miners thereupon transferred their operations to Chile, where they actively contributed to the war propaganda which began to rage after 1878 between Chile, Peru and Bolivia (see below).[41] Meanwhile Pardo's planned monopoly did not achieve the expected results. When foreign credit sources dried up, and guano exports began to fall, the banks and the government were forced to resort to a substantial increase in the issue of money, a process which further aggravated the crisis which had been brewing since 1872. Pardo and the civilian politicians had come to power only to be the impotent witnesses to one of Peru's greatest financial disasters, the result of a series

[41] See also ch. 7 below.

of policies adopted since the beginning of the guano boom, and a crisis which they had neither the capacity nor the opportunity to overcome.

From a political point of view, Pardo's administration was characterized by mounting confrontation and stiff opposition. His attempts to reduce public spending were met by strong opposition from civilians who had become accustomed to the generosity of previous administrations, whilst the numerous military establishment resented the effects of this policy on their institutions. The Church strongly opposed the government's policy of promoting secular education as a function of the state. It did not take very long before disaffected politicians and military men resorted once again to traditional practices, and half-way through his administration Pardo began to face military revolts, many of which were led by Nicolás de Piérola, who campaigned vigorously against what he saw as the government's anticlericalism. Neither did the poor state of the country's economy favour the consolidation of 'civilismo'. Therefore, in 1876 Pardo, believing that the only way to solve Peru's increasing political problems, especially civil and military unrest, was a strong government headed by a military man, accepted General Prado, who could have hardly been considered a *civilista,* as his successor. Soon after being inaugurated as president Prado drifted away from the *civilistas*, who had hoped to influence him and his government. He failed, however, to attract support from Piérola's followers, and his position became increasingly unstable. Several revolts organized by both groups were defeated, but not without difficulty, and, when in November 1878 Pardo was assassinated in obscure circumstances, Peru took a step nearer to chaos. The already fierce antagonism between Piérola's followers and the *civilistas*, who made the former morally responsible for Pardo's murder, intensified and acquired ominous characteristics; the likelihood of a confrontation became only too apparent. It was only avoided by more dramatic events.

In February 1879 Chile occupied the Bolivian port of Antofagasta and two months later declared war on Bolivia and on Peru, Bolivia's ally by secret, mutual defence treaty of 1873. After occupying the entire Bolivian littoral Chile successfully invaded the Peruvian province of Tarapacá late in 1879, the provinces of Tacna and Arica early in 1880 and the northern coast in September 1880. Lima fell in January 1881. The victories of the Chilean army and navy in the War of the Pacific brought to a climax in Peru both the financial and the political crises of the 1870s.[42]

[42] For a discussion of the impact of the War of the Pacific on Peru, see Heraclio Bonilla, 'The War of the Pacific and the national and colonial problem in Peru', *Past and Present*, 81, Nov. 1978, 92–118.

The present Republic of Bolivia was constituted as an independent nation on 8 August 1825, on the basis of the territory which had formed the Audiencia of Charcas. None of the new Latin American states, except perhaps Paraguay under Francia, was as isolated as Bolivia. Before the dramatic events of 1879 the country's connections with the outside world were extremely weak, amounting in effect to the continuation of two tenuous connections of colonial origin: one towards the Atlantic, the traditional route linking Potosí with Buenos Aires, lost much of its importance following the independence of the River Plate republics and the increase in transportation costs; the other towards the Pacific, probably the more important of the two, gave Bolivia access to its only port, Cobija, but only after a difficult crossing of the Atacama Desert, while trade through the Peruvian port of Arica was subject to the varying moods that governed political relations between Peru and Bolivia. In addition to this isolation from the outside world, there was a profound internal disarticulation. During the colonial period the dynamic centre of the economy of Upper Peru had been Potosí; its mineral deposits and its markets attracted the trade of entire regions like Cochabamba. With the decline of mining production, which began even before the wars of independence but which was accelerated by them, not only were these connections severed, but regions such as present-day Beni and Pando, even Santa Cruz, became internal territories practically shut in on themselves.

At the time of independence, Bolivia's population was estimated by John Barclay Pentland, the British observer, to be 1,100,000, of whom 800,000 were Indians, 200,000 whites, 100,000 *mestizos* or *cholos* (of mixed blood), 4,700 black slaves and 2,300 free blacks.[43] Probably no more than 20 per cent spoke Spanish: Quechua and Aymara were the languages of the vast majority. The largest city was La Paz with 40,000 inhabitants, followed by Cochabamba with 30,000. The economy which maintained this population was in profound crisis. In the first decades of the century Potosí had suffered a marked decline in production and population. According to Pentland, in 1827 it had scarcely 9,000 inhabitants, compared with 75,000 at the end of the eighteenth century.[44] Between 1820 and 1830 the production of the silver mines of Upper Peru fell by 30 per cent compared with 1810–20; production in the 1820s – a little under

---

[43] J. B. Pentland, *Informe sobre Bolivia, 1827* (Potosí, 1975), 40–2. This is a more complete edition in Spanish of *Report on Bolivia, 1827* (Royal Historical Society, London, 1974).   [44] *Ibid.*, 58.

200,000 marks per annum – was less than half that of the last decade of the eighteenth century. The factors impeding a recovery in mining activity were the destruction, flooding and abandonment of the mines during the wars, the lack of investment capital, a certain scarcity of labour following the abolition of the *mita* (although, it must be said, demand for labour was low and erratic) and the continuation in the post-colonial era of the state monopoly of the purchase of silver (at prices below the world market price) through the *Bancos de Rescate*, which severely reduced profits. At the time of independence – and for some time after – the production of the mines was low and largely the result of the utilization of discarded ore rather than deep workings.

In the agrarian sector where the basic units of production remained the haciendas and the *comunidades* (free Indian communities), the most important products were Peruvian bark (for the manufacture of quinine), coca, maize, wheat and potatoes; bark and coca were easily marketable outside the region, whereas the other products were mainly for local consumption. Pentland points out that in 1826 the value of the annual trade in coca in the city of La Paz reached £143,600, an amount equivalent to nearly 50 per cent of the value of exports of silver during the same year, whereas the value of the trade in maize and wheat was £60,000.[45]

The 'industrial' sector was represented by the *obrajes*, or workshops for the manufacture of textiles. However, as a result of the commercial reforms introduced by the Bourbons and the freedom of trade decreed at the time of independence, they could not compete with European cloth. Pentland estimated the value of textile production at £16,000, whereas in the past it had been as high as £200,000.[46]

As a result of the weakness of the productive structure, the contribution of the Bolivian economy to the international market was small and extremely precarious. Bolivian exports worth £722,750 in 1826 consisted primarily of silver and gold, followed at a great distance by Peruvian bark and tin. On the other hand, Bolivian imports in 1826 totalled £637,407. These goods were shipped in through Buenos Aires (a third) and, above all, through Arica (two-thirds). Of this total, about 70 per cent were imports from Britain, chiefly cloth. The balance was made up by goods from France, Germany and the Netherlands. There was also a very active local trade between Peru and Bolivia. The former exported, in particular, raw cotton and the wines and brandies produced

[45] *Ibid.*, 99.    [46] *Ibid.*, 100.

in the valleys of Moquegua and Tambo with a total value of £82,800. Bolivia, in turn, exported to Peru basically agricultural produce valued at £30,640, to satisfy the demand of the markets in southern Peru.[47] These official figures are, of course, conservative because of widespread contraband.

In these circumstances the Bolivian government encountered great financial difficulties. In 1825 and 1826 the average annual total of the state revenues was only £400,000, and in 1827 it was £350,000.[48] Around 60 per cent of this revenue was earmarked for military expenditure in the immediate aftermath of independence and continued at a level of 40–50 per cent throughout the period to 1879.[49] In addition the independent Bolivian state began its life owing £40,000 to Peru plus a further £140,000, the balance of the grant of £200,000 voted by the General Assembly in 1825 as compensation to the army of liberation.[50]

It is important to emphasize that the Bolivian government, in these early days, did not have recourse to foreign credit to finance its public expenditure. This was noticeably different from the practice established by the other governments of independent Latin America. Instead, the government of Antonio José Sucre (1825–8) attempted to attract domestic savings through the issue of bonds at a nominal value of £200,000, which were backed by assets owned by the state. These assets had been acquired as a result of the policy pursued by Sucre with the aim of destroying the power and influence of the regular clergy. In one of the most radical attacks on the Church in post-independent Spanish America Sucre closed down a large proportion of the religious houses, while the valuable urban and rural properties directly owned by the religious orders, or controlled by them through mortgages and *capellanías*, properties granted to the Church for pious works, were expropriated by the state. In the long run this policy served to strengthen the power of native landowners and merchants, who were able to acquire at rock-bottom

[47] *Ibid.*, 124, 121, 104.
[48] *Ibid.*, 139; William E. Lofstrom. 'The promise and problem of reform. Attempted social and economic change in the first years of Bolivian independence' (unpublished Ph.D. thesis, Cornell University, 1972), 456.
[49] In 1827 the army consisted of 2,291 Bolivian recruits and the 2,253 Colombian soldiers who accompanied the 'liberator', José Antonio Sucre. See Roberto Querejazu C., *Bolivia y los ingleses* (La Paz, 1973), 148–9. In 1828 Sucre maintained a force of 2,700 men, which was considered large by the standards of the day. For the size of Bolivian armies in the period before the War of the Pacific – never more than 5,000 men, more often less than half that number – and their cost – never less than 40% of national revenue and under Melgarejo as high as 70% – see James Dunkerley, 'Reassessing Caudillismo in Bolivia, 1825–79', *Bulletin of Latin American Research*, 1/1 (1981), 16–17.     [50] Pentland, *Informe sobre Bolivia*, 141.

prices the bonds originally issued to foreign soldiers and officers, when the latter had to leave Bolivia.[51] Another important source of the financing of public expenditure was the tax paid by the producers of silver in the *Bancos de Rescate*. At first the rate was equivalent to 10 per cent of the value of production, but later it was reduced successively to 8.5 per cent and to 5 per cent as a means of encouraging mining activity.[52] As in other Latin American countries, import duties and taxes on the internal movement of goods were also important sources of state revenue. However, in the case of Bolivia the collection of import duties was not so easy, because control of the Arica customs house was in the hands of Peru; even at its height only a third of Bolivia's foreign trade passed through Cobija. The Bolivian state had two other sources of revenue: the tithes and taxes levied on the minting of money.

Customs revenues, the tithes, taxes on mining production and the mint, and the confiscation of the properties of the religious orders were, however, together insufficient to meet the costs of public expenditure. For this reason, in Bolivia as in Peru, it was necessary to re-establish in 1826 the tribute (abolished by Bolívar in 1825) to which theoretically all Indian males aged 18 to 50 had been subject during the colonial period. The tribute had been replaced by the *contribución directa*, a general direct tax on urban and rural property and individual incomes. For the Indians, however, this represented only 3 pesos per annum, less than half the amount they were paying previously. Very soon the government realized the detrimental effect on state revenues. As a result, on 2 August 1826 Sucre signed the decree re-establishing the tribute, a decision which sanctioned the return to a fiscal structure which, as in the colonial period, divided the various strata of Bolivian society for tax purposes. Despite undergoing several vicissitudes, as we shall see, the tribute continued in existence until 1882.[53]

'I am convinced', Sucre prophetically wrote in a letter to Bolívar, 'the ground we are working is mud and sand, and that on such a base no building can subsist . . .'[54] The political history of Bolivia up to the war with Chile in 1879 shows an interminable series of barrack revolts, coups and counter-coups as a means of attaining power and despoiling the

[51] Lofstrom, 'Promise and problem of reform', 469–70, 259–60, 509–12.
[52] Fernando Cajías, *La Provincia de Atacama (1825–1842)* (La Paz, 1975), 218.
[53] Lofstrom, 'Promise and problem of reform', 404; Nicolás Sánchez-Albornoz, *Indios y tributos en el Alto Perú* (Lima, 1978), 191, 214.
[54] Quoted in Alcides Arguedas, *Historia general de Bolivia, 1809–1821* (La Paz, 1922), 65.

meagre resources of the state, movements undertaken by ambitious military chieftains with the complicity of some *doctores de Chuquisaca*. Against this background of political instability, even anarchy, the government of Andrés Santa Cruz (1829–39) constitutes a notable exception.

Santa Cruz, a *mestizo*, had joined the ranks of the rebels very late, but his part in the decisive battles for independence, and the favours granted to him by Bolívar, soon transformed him into one of the strong candidates to govern the destiny of independent Bolivia. It is to Santa Cruz that Bolivia owes the first attempt to achieve the efficient organization of both government and economy, and also the search for new ways to overcome the isolation of Bolivia from the outside world. The opening of the port of Cobija made it possible for the markets of southern Bolivia to be supplied with goods from abroad; these goods, transported on muleback, after a laborious crossing of the Atacama Desert, reached Potosí, Chuquisaca, Tupiza and Tarija. In view of the internal fragmentation of Bolivian territory and the almost complete absence of adequate means of internal transport, it was also essential, subsequently, to undertake the consolidation of the port of Arica as a centre for the supply of the provinces of northern Bolivia, and as a port of shipment for Bolivian exports. Despite all these achievements Santa Cruz is mainly remembered as the unsuccessful architect of Andean unity between Peru and Bolivia.

Peru and Bolivia, as we have seen, were territories with strong economic and administrative links during the colonial period. Their separation, like that of the other regions of Spanish America, was the result of the vicissitudes of the struggle for emancipation. Bolivia in the end consolidated its precarious nationhood largely through the many conflicts with its neighbours. However, this was not a clear-cut or continuous process. Ill-accustomed to an early separation which was justified neither by geography nor by economic structure, the caudillos of both countries in the post-independence era always sought to reinforce their power by utilizing the resources of the other country, and they also invoked the comradeship derived from previous military campaigns in order to obtain from the person governing the neighbouring country, in which they often found themselves exiled, the military assistance needed to reconquer power or at least to attempt to do so. This 'assistance', or the need to 'save' one of the countries from chaos, was often used as the pretext for the military expeditions undertaken from

Peru to Bolivia or vice versa. The frontier was merely an 'imaginary line', as a later president, Mariano Melgarejo, was to put it, and relations between Bolivia and Peru were inevitably conducted in a climate of mutual hostility and suspicion. When to these factors are added the difficulties involved in the shared access to the port of Arica, and the flooding of Peruvian markets with debased Bolivian currency after 1830,[55] it is not surprising that the internal politics of Peru and Bolivia should reflect the tension existing between the two countries.

Nevertheless, the threat posed by the growing economic and naval power of Chile persuaded Santa Cruz, who had briefly served as president of Peru in the 1820s, to seek a stable alliance with Peru for mutual defence and a resolution of the economic difficulties of the two nations. The pretext for the military expedition to Peru (June 1835) was, once again, the need to defend one caudillo, Orbegoso, who had been deposed by another, the turbulent Salaverry. However, the reasons for Santa Cruz's intervention were not confined to helping his fallen friend. In the justification of his acts which he wrote from exile in Ecuador, Santa Cruz argued that intervention in the affairs of Peru was a matter of life or death for Bolivia.[56]

Once victory had been attained, Santa Cruz remained in Peru to give definitive form to the new political organization which would make possible the federation of Peru and Bolivia, through the creation of three states (North Peru, South Peru and Bolivia) under his sole leadership as Protector. In this way, and in the face of the potential danger that Chile represented, the Peru–Bolivian Confederation was created on 28 October 1836 as a tardy and partial attempt to make the dreams of Bolívar come true. After the failure of this experiment, it would be 1873, once more in the face of the threat from Chile, before a similar attempt was made, this time in strictly military terms.

The fusion of Peru and Bolivia disrupted the balance of forces among the countries that had emerged from the collapse of the colonial order, and it was inevitably seen as a serious threat to their interests. This was quickly understood by Argentina and, above all, by Chile. 'United, these two States will always be more powerful than Chile in all ways and circumstances', wrote Diego Portales on 10 September 1836,[57] and on 26

---

[55] The debased coinage known as the *peso feble* was first issued by Santa Cruz in 1830; it represented 14% of issue in 1830–4 and 85% by 1850–9. See Dunkerley, 'Reassessing Caudillismo', 18.

[56] 'El General Santa Cruz explica su conducta pública y los móviles de su política en la presidencia de Bolivia en el Protectorado de la Confederación Perú-Boliviana' (Quito, 1840), in Oscar de Santa Cruz (ed.), *El General Santa Cruz* (La Paz, 1924), 74.

December he declared war on the Confederation on the grounds that it 'threatened the independence of other American nations'. Four months later, on 9th May 1837, Argentina, on the pretext of frontier disputes, took a similar decision.

The military response of Chile to the emergence of the Confederation was inspired not only by fear of the new coalition of forces, but also by concern at the measures taken by Santa Cruz to strengthen the commercial development of the ports of the Peruvian coast. Valparaíso had already acquired a very marked economic superiority by becoming the principal commercial link between the South Pacific and Europe; to counteract this development Santa Cruz declared Arica, Cobija, Callao and Paita free ports, and at the same time imposed additional duties on goods which had been unloaded at other ports. This was a measure directly aimed at Chilean commercial interests and which could only be resolved by force of arms. After an early campaign (1837) in which the troops of the Confederation gained the advantage, on 20 January 1839 at Yungay, a town in the northern highlands of Peru, the Chilean army led by Bulnes, and supported by Peruvian troops and officers, destroyed the fragile edifice of the Confederation. Santa Cruz at first took refuge in Guayaquil, and later (in 1843) went into exile to Europe.

The Peru-Bolivian Confederation (1836–9), which had only a brief existence and was throughout subject to frequent external and internal attacks, will be remembered only for its unfulfilled promise. The Confederation not only suffered the external attacks of Chile and Argentina, but it was assaulted from within from its very beginning. It was attacked by the besieged Bolivian commercial interests and many soldiers who believed that in this adventure they would inevitably lose out, and Peruvians did not, of course, like the idea of being 'protected' by a Bolivian. Northern Peruvians, in particular, did not believe that they had a destiny similar to that of the Andean inhabitants of the faraway south. At all events, for Bolivia the defeat of Santa Cruz at Yungay, followed by the defeat of Ingavi in November 1841 of Agustín Gamarra's expedition, a Peruvian attempt to impose hegemony over Bolivia, marked a definite end to all aspirations to restore the connections of the past and consolidated Bolivian independence, at the time still very much in the balance.

In the period following the collapse of the Confederation and Santa Cruz's withdrawal from the political scene, Bolivian regimes were too

---

[57] Quoted in Jorge Basadre, *Historia de la República del Perú* (5th edn, Lima, 1963), 1, 401.

precarious to maintain a consistent policy, and the differences between them depended largely on the personal style of each caudillo and his ability to attract the loyalty of his followers through the distribution of patronage. Thus, while the imagination of a man such as the aristocratic José Ballivián (1841–7) made it possible for him to encourage the exploration of eastern Bolivia, to search for a more effective outlet to the Pacific, and to reorganize the educational system with the assistance of an élite of Argentine intellectuals who had been deported by Rosas, none of these endeavours was given the time or resources to succeed. After the forced resignation of Ballivián and the fleeting return to power of the southern caudillo, José Miguel Velasco, who had been president in 1828, 1829 and 1839–41 (between Santa Cruz and Ballivián) and who often arbitrated in the clashes between northern leaders, Manuel Isidoro Belzú (1848–55) set up a government of a different character, at least in its external form. It was a government that explicitly sought to base itself on the support of the urban artisans, especially the pauperized artisans of the *obrajes*, and rural masses, and at the same time it encouraged domestic production by raising the tariffs on imported cloth and re-establishing the state monopoly of Peruvian bark. Belzú, who claimed to be a reader of Proudhon and Saint Simon, addressed to his followers such speeches as the following:

Comrades, a mad crowd of aristocrats have become the arbiters of your wealth and your destiny. They exploit you unceasingly. They shear you like sheep day and night. They distribute among themselves lands, honours, jobs and positions of authority, leaving you only misery, ignorance and hard labour. Are you not equal to the rest of the Bolivians? Is this equality not the result of the equality of the human species? Why do they alone enjoy such fat inheritances, silverware, houses and farms, and not you? Comrades, private property is the principal source of transgressions and crimes in Bolivia. It is the cause of the permanent struggle between Bolivians. It is the underlying principle of the present dominant egotism. Let there be no more property, no more proprietors. Let there be an end to the exploitation of man by man. For what reason do the Ballivianists alone occupy the highest social positions? My friends, property, in the words of a great philosopher, is the exploitation of the weak by the strong; community of goods is the exploitation of the strong by the weak. Do justice with your own hands, since the injustice of men and the times deny it you.[58]

It is, in fact, very difficult to establish to what degree his adherence to the cause of the poor reflected a sincere commitment, or to what extent it was an expression of the most crude opportunism, based on the need to broaden the bases of his personal following in response to the prolifera-

---

[58] Quoted in Querejazu, *Bolivia y los ingleses*, 285–6.

tion of his rivals. Certainly there existed as a result of the continuous deterioration of the economy a largely impoverished mass which was responsive to the demagogic appeal of any caudillo. It has been estimated that in the decade between 1840 and 1849 alone there occurred in Bolivia sixty-five attempted coups d'état. This was hardly the most favourable climate in which to attempt to resolve the urgent problems affecting the economy and society of Bolivia.

During the first half century after independence, the Bolivian economy was fundamentally based on agriculture and stockraising and agrarian structures maintained their colonial character; that is to say, haciendas and Indian communities were, as to a great extent they are still today, the units of production in which the Indians, who comprised the bulk of the rural population, worked and lived. Until 1866, the community, or at least the use of its plots of land by the Indians, was guaranteed by the Bolivian authorities as it had been by the Spanish. In contrast to the colonial period, this policy was not now aimed at ensuring the reproduction of the Indian labour force which was essential for the functioning of the mining industry, but rather at ensuring that through the tribute the state could continuously dispose of the revenues needed to defray its current expenditure – and maintain order in the countryside. The *tributario* and the *comunitario* were, in fact, one inseparable entity. And until the 1860s nearly 40 per cent of the revenue of the Republic was derived from the tribute paid by the Indians.

José María Dalence, in his *Bosquejo Estadístico de Bolivia* [Statistical Sketch of Bolivia] (1851), calculated that out of a total population of 1,381,856 in 1846, the Indian population was 710,666 (51.4 per cent). 82 per cent of the Indians lived in the departments of the altiplano, especially La Paz, Potosí and Oruro, compared with only 6 per cent in, for example, Cochabamba. The historical reasons for this disparity are well known. Whereas the poverty of the high plateau meant that the· landowners did not wish to cultivate the region and thus had no need for the Indian labour force which remained in the communities, in Cochabamba the rapid transformation of the area into the granary of Potosí caused empty lands and lands occupied by the Indians to be taken over by the landowners, who also incorporated into the estates those who were returning or escaping from the *mita*. Thus, as early as 1793 *mestizos* and whites made up 50 per cent of the population of the region. However, in addition to this regional distribution of the Indian population, estimates for 1838 show profound changes in its composition. It should be noted in the first place that the number of *tributarios* rose dramatically from 58,571 in 1770 to 124,312 in 1838 (and to 133,905 in 1858 and 143,357 in 1877). This increase took place above all in the departments of La Paz and Potosí. It is also important to emphasize that by the middle of the nineteenth century the Indian peasantry had become much more socially differentiated, a process which was reflected in an unequal access to the plots of cultivable land and also unequal participation in the payment of tribute. The number of *originarios* (original inhabitants of the community with the greatest access to land) paying tribute rose from 19,853 in 1770 to 33,308 in 1838; the numbers of tribute-paying *forasteros* ('outsiders', later arrivals with lesser landholdings) and *agregados* (like the *forasteros*, with even less or no land) together rose from 35,400 to 66,930. In addition, there was a remarkable increase in the number of tribute-paying *yanaconas* (landless Indians bound by personal service to a particular hacienda) from a total of 1,866 in 1770 to 22,227 in 1838. And a new category of *vagos*, or migrant labourers, working in the coca-plots of the Yungas, accounted for a total of 2,117 *tributarios* in 1838.[59]

It is generally held that Bolivia in the nineteenth century was the scene of a significant expansion of the big estates at the expense of the lands and people of the communities. An analysis of the register of tribute-payers, however, reveals that between 1838 and 1877 the tribute-paying population in the communities was increasing, whereas in the estates exactly the reverse was the case. In the five departments of Bolivia, the communities controlled 68 per cent of the tribute-payers in 1838, 73 per cent in 1858, and 75 per cent in 1877. Conversely, the total of tribute-payers on the estates declined continuously during this period: it was 29 per cent in 1838, 25 per cent in 1858, and 23 per cent in 1877. Furthermore, the increase in the number of *forasteros* does not appear to have affected this process. In 1838, for example, when *forasteros* and *agregados* represented 53 per cent of the total tribute-payers, 79 per cent of them lived in the communities. Finally, between 1838 and 1877, contrary to the traditional view, the estates and the communities expanded and declined together, rather than the former expanding at the expense of the latter.[60]

The reason for this remarkable stability in the agrarian structure of

---

[59] Erwin P. Grieshaber, 'Survival of Indian communities in nineteenth century Bolivia' (unpublished Ph.D. thesis, University of North Carolina, 1977), 79–80, 108, 132–7.
[60] *Ibid.*, 116, 131, 154, 291–3.

Bolivia is to be found in the economy. The decline of cities such as Potosí, Sucre and Cochabamba, combined with the small increase in the population of La Paz and Oruro, did not permit the significant increase in domestic demand needed for the more effective mobilization of the productive factors. Furthermore, the foreign market could not play a compensatory role, because during the 1840s Bolivian quinine gradually lost its access to the European market as a consequence of competition from Colombian production. It is true that in the 1860s and 1870s the renaissance of the Bolivian mining economy led to the widening of the domestic market, but demand, as will be explained below, was satisfied through other mechanisms. What happened to the Peruvian economy as a result of the expansion of cotton and sugar during the 1860s and 1870s was radically different.

This stability, however, does not mean that at various times during the nineteenth century governments did not attempt to abolish the corporate existence of the Indian communities and establish a republic of small proprietors in accordance with liberal ideology. As we have seen, such threats against the Indian communities began with Bolívar himself. In Bolivia, however, it is above all Mariano Melgarejo (1864–71) who is remembered as the author of the major assault on the property of the Indians. The growing fiscal requirements of a government constantly involved in military activity to maintain itself in power, combined with the need to reward his relations and clients, were the motives underlying Melgarejo's decision to sell the Indian community lands. The decree of 20 March 1866 declared Indians who possessed state lands to be proprietors, on condition that they paid a sum of between 25 and 100 pesos to register their individual titles. Those who did not do so within sixty days would be deprived of their property and their lands would be put up for public auction.[61] The scope of this decree was defined further in September 1868, when the National Constituent Assembly declared all community lands state property, and at the same time abolished the Indian tribute.[62]

According to Minister Lastre, in his report to the Legislative Chamber, between 20 March 1866 and 31 December 1869 the government auctioned off the lands belonging to 216 communities, or fractions of them, in the department of Mejillones (provinces of Omasuyos, Pacajes and Ingavi, Sicasica and Muñecas), 109 communities in La Paz (Yungas,

[61] Sánchez-Albornoz, *Indios y tributos,* 207.
[62] Luis Antezana, *El feudalismo de Melgarejo y la reforma agraria* (La Paz, 1970), 39.

La Unión, Larecaja, Caupolicán and Cercado), 15 in Tapacarí, Cochabamba, 12 in Yamparaes, Chuquisaca, 4 in Tarata, 3 in Oruro, and one in Potosí.[63] The total sum raised by these sales was £164,172, of which £130,144 was paid in depreciated government bonds and the balance in cash. In 1870, further sales raised a total sum of £67,637.[64] The abolition of the tribute, when combined with the dissolution of the community lands, was deprived of all significance. The Indian contribution was replaced by a personal contribution of four bolivianos and the imposition of the land tax. The former was equivalent to the five pesos that the landless Indians had always paid, while the land tax now replaced the old tribute paid by the Indians with land.[65]

The purchase of community lands with depreciated government bonds naturally did little to resolve the financial difficulties of the Bolivian state. On the contrary it was a mechanism which allowed its creditors to convert their bonds into capital, and at the same time consolidated their position within the agricultural sector. A study of Pacajes between 1866 and 1879 demonstrates that the beneficiaries of these sales were, in addition to the traditional landowners who expanded the frontiers of their estates, medium-scale proprietors, merchants, and even Indian chiefs and *mestizos*, who thus became integrated into the local and regional elites. These people, as a whole, still did not regard land as a means of production, but rather as a source of stable income and as collateral for obtaining capital for investment in medium-scale and small-scale mining undertakings.[66]

The other consequence of this process of spoilation was the massive movement of Indian protest, reflected in the risings of 1869, 1870 and 1871. The peasant population played an active part in the overthrow of Melgarejo early in 1871. Subsequently, on 31 July 1871, the Constituent Assembly declared null and void all the sales, allocations and alienations of communal lands, and at the same time promised to grant all Indians the full exercise of the rights of property. This did not mean, therefore, either the re-establishment of communal property, or the transformation of the Indian into a landless day-labourer. It has been asserted that the lands did not revert to the possession of the Indians, a view which has been challenged on the basis of the evidence obtained from four villages in

[63] Sánchez Albornoz, *Indios y tributos*, 207–8.
[64] Luis Peñaloza, *Historia económica de Bolivia* (La Paz, 1954), I, 294.
[65] Sánchez-Albornoz, *Indios y tributos*, 208–9.
[66] Silvia Rivera, 'La expansión del latifundio en el altiplano boliviano', *Avances* (La Paz), 2 (1978), 95–118.

Pacajes where the Indians did successfully reclaim their lands in 1871.[67] To what extent, however, was the case of Pacajes as a traditional centre of indigenous rebellion the exception rather than the rule? As far as the tribute was concerned, this was eliminated from the national budget, but the Indians were not exempt; its collection was entrusted to the departmental authorities until its final abolition in 1882.[68]

It is obvious that further research is needed to evaluate the results of the agrarian policy of Melgarejo and the rectification of it undertaken by Morales (1871–2). With regard to this, it should perhaps be noted that the *ley de ex-viculación* (law of disentailment) promulgated on 5 October 1874 explicitly denied the juridical existence of free Indian communities and at the same time declared that the community members would henceforth have the right of absolute ownership of the possessions of which they had hitherto had the usufruct.[69] Although we still lack the evidence necessary to measure the extent of this fresh assault on Indian communal property rights, it seems clear that this measure eliminated the legal obstacles to the expansion of the Bolivian latifundium. For this to occur, however, it was not enough to have legal authorization. What was essential was the action of what the Bolivians of the time called the forces of 'progress', that is to say mining, the international market and the railways.

The growth of the Bolivian economy from the middle of the nineteenth century was associated with the renaissance of mining activities. As in colonial times, it was the mining sector that allowed the Bolivian economy to develop a closer connection with the international market. And mining activity was at first still primarily based on the extraction and export of silver in the traditional mining zones of the altiplano. After half a century of stagnation the years between 1850 and 1873 witnessed the slow recovery of silver mining. This process was characterized by the appearance of a new group of mining entrepreneurs and later the intervention of foreign capital – and it was facilitated by new technology, especially pumping machinery worked by steam engines, and a fall in the international price of mercury. The middle and late 1870s then witnessed an impressive growth in the production of silver. Bolivia became once more one of the biggest silver producers in the world.

The resurgence of the Bolivian mining economy during the second

[67] Peñaloza, *Historia económica*, 298–9; Grieshaber, 'Survival of Indian communities', 200.
[68] Sánchez-Albornoz, *Indios y tributos*, 210–11.
[69] Ramiro Condarco Morales, *Zárate, el temible 'Willka'* (La Paz, 1965), 46.

half of the nineteenth century, unlike Potosí in the sixteenth century, was, however, unable to articulate around itself the Bolivian economy as a whole. In view of the small proportion of the labour force in mining – Huanchaca, for example, in 1877 employed only 1,567 workers[70] – as well as internal transport difficulties and the subsequent economic orientation imposed by the railways, Bolivian mining was unable (at least at that time) to contribute to the development of agriculture. On the contrary, it facilitated the expansion of Chilean exports of wheat and flour, a process which in turn transformed Cochabamba and Chayanta, which had traditionally been zones of commercial agriculture, into areas with a subsistence economy.

The inability of Bolivian mining to stimulate the development of domestic agriculture is also one explanation why the Indian population was successful for so long in maintaining its plots of land. At the same time, as happened in Peru in the case of guano, the recovery of mining undermined the importance of the Indian tribute as an instrument for financing public expenditure. Whereas between 1827 and 1866 tribute had represented an average of 37 per cent of total annual revenues, by 1886 the income derived from the collection of Indian tribute represented only 10 per cent of state revenue.[71] From the 1860s, however, the 'silver barons' were able to launch a more vigorous and more successful attack on the property and culture of the Indian population, this time in the name of progress and of the eradication of obstacles to civilization.

Around 1860 ownership of the principal mineral deposits of the altiplano was concentrated in the hands of a new elite, principally drawn from the merchants and *hacendados* of Cochabamba. For example, the Aramayo family owned the Real Socavón de Potosí, Antequera and Carguaicollo. Aniceto Arce was head of the Huanchaca company, while Gregorio Pacheco had taken over the important Guadalupe mining interests. However these proprietors, in their turn, were closely dependent on foreign capital, which exercised control over marketing and which supplied the inputs. This dependence became transformed into complete subordination in times of crisis. The case of Huanchaca, in this respect, illustrates a more general tendency.

In the 1850s the Huanchaca operations covered their costs and even generated a small profit. Nevertheless, the rate of growth was modest. The insufficient refining capacity made it impossible to derive the

[70] Grieshaber, 'Survival of Indian communities', 192–3, 222.
[71] *Ibid.*, 221.

maximum advantage from the considerable production of Pulacayo; its future development depended on the improvement of communications between the mines and the refining plants, and also on increasing the latter's capacity. For this it was necessary to have recourse to foreign capital, the influx of which was reflected in the creation of the Bolivian Huanchaca Company in 1873. This company was incorporated with a capital of £562,500 sterling, divided into three thousand shares. The control exercised by foreign capital immediately made itself evident; it was reflected in the composition of the board of directors, which was formed by the Chileans, Joaquín Dorado, Melchor Concha y Toro, Luis Warny, Hermann Fisher and the only Bolivian, Aniceto Arce, who controlled 33 per cent of the shares. At that time the participation of foreign capital was of little significance, but the reorganization of the company in 1877 facilitated the further influx of British, French and German capital. In the 1880s British capital was absolutely predominant.

British penetration into Bolivia, as elsewhere in Latin America, took two forms: first, during and immediately after independence came the export of goods and the rapid domination of markets; the second, which occurred later, consisted of the export of capital, in the form of direct investments or loans. In this connection, one factor in particular should be emphasized. The rapid saturation of the relatively small market and the precarious nature of the Bolivian economy during the first half of the nineteenth century made Bolivia a country unattractive to British interests. It was only in 1869 that the Bolivian government, through George E. Church, managed to raise a loan in London (for £1.7 million) and that transaction was rescinded shortly afterwards. Previously small loans of £187,500 and £255,549 had been raised in Peru (1865) and Chile (1868) respectively. As a result, in contrast to Peru, therefore, Bolivia in 1879 had a foreign debt of only £283,333.[72] There were few British subjects resident in Bolivia. To Stephen St John, the British envoy, Bolivia, even in November 1875, was 'one of the least interesting countries in the world.'[73] During the last third of the nineteenth century, however, the situation began to change radically. One expression of this change was the expansion of Bolivia's foreign trade. Between 1869 and 1871, for example, under Melgarejo's opening-up of the economy, British exports to Bolivia rose from £8,000 to £24,000, while Bolivian exports to Britain

[72] On these loans and Bolivia's foreign debt, see Peñaloza, *Historia económica*, 11, 344, 403, 405, 409, 416.
[73] Quoted in Querejazu, *Bolivia y los ingleses*, 362.

rose from £127,000 to £169,000 in the same period.[74] And an examination of the main products in this trade – no longer silver alone – reveals the growing penetration of foreign capital, especially British and Chilean, not only in the altiplano but also in the Pacific littoral.

From 1840 Chilean, British and French companies began the exploration and settlement of the Bolivian coast (the province of Atacama), with the aim of exploiting copper and, above all, the major deposits of guano. Between 1857 and 1866 nitrate deposits were discovered in the region of Mejillones in the southern Atacama, exploited by Chilean and British capital and exported to the expanding European market for fertilizers. From 1868 the port of Antofagasta, whose population like that of Cobija was over 90 per cent Chilean, became the chief port on the Bolivian coast.

The exploitation of nitrates by foreign capital led to the incorporation of the Bolivian littoral and vast areas of the Atacama Desert into international trade. In 1869 the most important concern operating in the area was Melbourne Clark and Co., a firm owned by the British subjects William Gibbs, George Smith and Melbourne Clark and the Chileans Agustín Edwards and Francisco Puelma. This served as a basis for the creation of the Compañía de Salitres y Ferrocarril de Antofagasta in 1872, a Chilean-British company registered in Valparaíso, which received generous concessions from the Bolivian government. In 1870 a new phase in the expansion of foreign capital in the Atacama region opened with the discovery and bringing into operation of the silver mines of Caracoles, linked to the outside world through the port of Mejillones. Investments made up to 1872 totalled around £2 million, and among the investors were the British subjects Gibbs, Smith and Simpson, and the Chileans Edwards, Concha y Toro, Napoleón Peró and Dorado, that is to say, those who already controlled the exploitation and exports of nitrates in the region.[75] The resident population of Caracoles was nearly ten thousand, of whom once again the vast majority were Chilean.

To mobilize credit and to avoid the exorbitant terms imposed by the merchant houses, the big mining concerns sponsored the establishment of banking institutions. The creation in 1871 of the National Bank of Bolivia fulfilled many of the requirements. The concession for its establishment was granted to Napoleón Peró, the founder of the

---

[74] *Ibid.*, 349.
[75] See Antonio Mitre, 'Economic and social structure of silver mining in nineteenth-century Bolivia' (unpublished Ph.D. thesis, Columbia University, 1977), 137–9.

Antofagasta Nitrate Company, while the three million pesos that formed its initial capital were subscribed by the persons who had already established an economic hegemony in the region.[76] In addition to controlling trade, nitrates, silver and banking, this group, during the 1870s, extended its control over the mining areas to the south of Potosí, first through a monopoly of marketing, and later through the supply of inputs, until finally they acquired complete ownership.

The heightened economic activity of the 1870s was abruptly interrupted when, on 14 February 1878, the Bolivian government decided to impose an additional export tax of ten centavos on every quintal of nitrate extracted since 1874 between latitudes 23°S and 24°S. The Antofagasta Nitrates and Railway Company regarded this as a clear breach of the treaty with Chile (1874) in which Bolivia had agreed not to increase taxes on Chilean companies operating in that previously disputed area in return for Chile's acceptance of 24°S as the frontier between the two countries. The authorities in Antofagasta were empowered to collect $90,000 from the Antofagasta Company; ten months later, in view of the refusal of the English manager, George Hicks, to pay this 'unjust' and 'illegal' tax, the Bolivian prefect ordered the auctioning off of the assets of the company until the amount demanded was met. Following intense lobbying by the Antofagasta Company, the Chilean response was the military occupation of Antofagasta (February 1879) and a declaration of war (April 1879) which was immediately extended to Peru, Bolivia's ally, by secret treaty, since 1873 (see above).[77] Within two months Chilean forces had occupied the Bolivian province of Atacama. By the end of the year the Bolivian army had been totally defeated. Bolivia's entire coastal territory – and a substantial part of its wealth – was permanently lost. Chile, however, had no intention of invading the altiplano; the main enemy was Peru, and Bolivia was essentially a spectator for the rest of the War of the Pacific. Politically, Bolivia's defeat led to profound changes; in particular, it brought about the end of military caudillo rule and the establishment of civilian oligarchical government, with the direct participation of the mining elite.

The reorganization of the Bolivian economy as a result of the growth of the mining sector after 1850 had transformed the class structure. The emerging group comprised those connected with the mining of silver for

[76] *Ibid.*, 139–40.
[77] For a fuller discussion of the nitrate issue and the origins of the War of the Pacific, see ch. 7 below.

export, and its policy clashed with that of the old oligarchy whose power was based on control of the land and of craft industries. However, this new economic elite had failed to achieve direct access to political control of the state or policy and was obliged to patronize various caudillos in an endeavour to gain influence over government. Belzú, with his populist style, was succeeded by José María Linares (1857–61), the first civilian president, who made some initial moves towards strengthening international trade by means of a more liberal policy. In 1858 he abolished the state monopoly of Peruvian bark, reduced by 13 per cent the duty on imported *tocuyos* (coarse cotton cloth), and began to organize guarantees for the currency although he was unable to introduce a free market in silver. His overthrow by a *coup d'état* resulted in the military again achieving political control, but in practice the military were increasingly obliged to implement measures that were in harmony with the economic policy of the new dominant group. This was to some degree evident under the government of Melgarejo and more obviously so under Agustín Morales (1871–2), who, in 1872, finally decreed the free market in bullion, Tomás Frías (1872–3, 1875–6) and, above all, Adolfo Ballivián (1873–4), the son of the former president, who expressed in a more explicit fashion the interests of the group of mining entrepreneurs to which he was linked. These governments were, however, still highly unstable, as a result of the tensions existing within a still emergent dominant class and between the new dominant class and the military, and also to some extent because of the permanent mobilization of the rural and urban lower classes, the victims of the dislocation of the traditional economy. The war provided the opportunity for the civilian elite to replace the military in government. Hilarión Daza, the strong man behind Presidents Frías and Ballivián (1872–6) and president since May 1876, who had led Bolivia, unprepared, into war and to disastrous defeat, was overthrown in December 1879. He was replaced by General Narcisco Campero, supported by the mining elites, who was committed to the establishment of stable, civilian oligarchical government. It was the beginning of a new era in Bolivian politics which was to last for more than fifty years.

Peru and Bolivia, which had shared one history from the remote past until the crisis of the colonial system, had gone their separate ways after independence from Spain. Persistent internal disturbances and disputes between their armies eventually led to the failure of attempts at reunification, and at the same time encouraged a nationalism that was somewhat narrow, but not for that reason any less powerful. However, their histories ran parallel to some extent. In both countries governments were unstable. They were based on the interests of a narrow creole group which depended on the fiscal extortion of the Indian masses, while at the same time denying them any possibility of political participation. In both countries, the economies languished until the appearance of guano in Peru and the rediscovery of silver as well as the discovery of nitrates in Bolivia. However, in both countries there was an inability to formulate a policy directed towards the utilization of these resources for the development of the economy as a whole. On account of its isolation and the fact that the renaissance of its economy occurred later, Bolivia, in contrast to Peru, did not suffer the consequences of an imprudent external indebtedness; but her markets, like those of Peru, were captured by foreign products. The common misfortune which Bolivia and Peru shared in 1879 was the price that the ruling class of both countries had to pay for failing to strengthen the economy and to give greater cohesion to society during the first half-century after independence.

# 7

## CHILE

At a banquet in Valparaíso in 1852 the Argentine publicist Juan Bautista Alberdi proposed a toast to 'the honourable exception in South America'. In one very important respect, the story of nineteenth century Chile was, it is true, a striking exception to the normal Spanish American pattern. Within fifteen years of independence Chilean politicians were constructing a system of constitutional government which was to prove remarkable (by European as well as Latin American standards) for its durability and adaptability. This successful consolidation of an effective national state excited the envious admiration of less fortunate Spanish American republics, torn and plagued as so many of them were by recurrent strife and caudillo rule. A good part of the explanation of Chile's unusual record undoubtedly lies in what can best be called the 'manageability' of the country at the time of independence, not least in terms of the basic factors of territory and population. The effective national territory of Chile in the 1820s was much smaller than it is today. Its distinctive slenderness of width – 'a sword hanging from the west side of America' – was for obvious orographical reasons no different; but lengthways no more than 700 miles or so separated the mining districts in the desert around Copiapó, at the northern limit of settlement (27°S), from the green and fertile lands along the Bío-Bío river in the south (37°S) – the area traditionally referred to as the Frontier, beyond which the Araucanian Indians stubbornly preserved their independent way of life. The peripheral clusters of population which lay still further south, at Valdivia and on the densely-forested island of Chiloé (liberated from the Spaniards only in 1826), were remote, insignificant appendages of the republic; the same could also be said slightly later on of the struggling settlement on the Straits of Magellan established in 1843 and used as a penal colony. Leaving aside the Araucanians, who numbered perhaps

200,000, the population of Chile was still fairly small: it rose slowly from an estimated 1,000,000 at the time of independence to an official (and possibly conservative) figure of 2,076,000 in 1875. The overwhelming majority of Chileans lived and worked in the country's traditional heartland, in (or very close to) the central valley extending three hundred miles southwards from Santiago. By the standards of Argentina or Mexico, of Peru or New Granada, this was a very compact territory inhabited by a compact population.

It was in many ways a homogeneous population. Both ethnically and socially the colonial past had left indelible marks. North of the Bío-Bío, few if any Indians survived in separate communities. The tiny black and mulatto trace in the community seems to have vanished within two or three decades of the abolition of slavery (1823). Republican Chile was essentially a country in which a small creole upper class (with an aristocratic elite at its core) co-existed with the huge mass of the labouring poor, who were predominantly *mestizo* and predominantly rural. The ethnic and social divisions coincided. Politically, the struggles which followed independence reflected disagreements within the fold of the upper class rather than deeper conflicts in the body social more generally. The rural poor remained passive throughout the period and, in fact, well beyond it. This relatively simple social structure was not complicated by sharp cleavages of economic interest within the upper class or by anything very much in the way of serious regional tension. Santiago and its rich hinterland dominated the republic. The remoter northern or southern provinces, whether disaffected or not, were powerless to alter the balance in their own favour, as was shown very clearly in the civil wars of 1851 and 1859. Concepción and the south underwent a frustratingly slow recovery from the wars of independence; and although Concepción, by virtue of its role as a garrison town watching over the frontier, was able in the uncertain atmosphere of the 1820s to impose its will on the capital – as it did in 1823, with the overthrow of Bernardo O'Higgins, and again in 1829 – in normal times a determined central government in control of the army (or most of it) could not easily be dislodged.

The issues which divided the upper class Chilean politicians of the 1820s into the perhaps predictable camps of Liberal and Conservative were above all ideological and personal. The dominant figure of these years, General Ramón Freire, was a well-intentioned Liberal eager to avoid the authoritarian pattern set by his immediate predecessor, the liberator O'Higgins. The new republic drifted from one makeshift political experiment to the next. The complex and ingenious constitution devised by Juan Egaña at the end of 1823 broke down within six months, its moralistic conservatism rejected by the Liberals who surrounded Freire and who wished, as they put it, 'to build the Republic on the ruins of the Colony'. The vogue for federalist ideas which overwhelmed political circles soon afterwards owed less, perhaps, to regional aspirations than to the dogmatically radical convictions of the man of the moment, José Miguel Infante; it produced a draft constitution, numerous new laws, an atmosphere of growing uncertainty, mild disorders in several towns, and a propensity to mutiny on the part of the army. The 'anarchy' of the period has often been exaggerated by Chilean historians; it was very limited in comparison with the turmoil then occurring on the other side of the Andes. Another Liberal soldier, General Francisco Antonio Pinto, president from 1827 to 1829, briefly succeeded in organizing a government which showed signs of solidity, and a new constitution (1828), the fourth since independence, duly went into effect. It proved inadequate to stem the mounting reaction against Liberal reformism, coloured as this was by anti-aristocratic verbiage and a degree of anticlericalism. In September 1829, with the vital backing of the army in Concepción, a powerful tripartite coalition of Conservatives – the traditionalist and pro-clerical *pelucones* ('big wigs'), the followers of the exiled O'Higgins, and a tough-minded group known as the *estanqueros*[1] – launched a revolt against the Liberal regime. Freire, who sprang quixotically to its defence, was defeated in April 1830 at Lircay, the battle which ended the short civil war and ushered in more than a quarter of a century of Conservative rule.

The political settlement of the 1830s was, as has been suggested, one of the more remarkable creations of nineteenth-century Latin America. The credit for its success is usually assigned to Diego Portales, the Valparaiso trader who more than anyone was the organizing genius of the Conservative reaction. Certainly Portales's ruthless tenacity was a key factor in keeping the new regime together, though his tenure of office as chief minister was fairly brief. This in itself may have impeded the crystalliza-

---

[1] In 1824 the *estanco*, or state tobacco monopoly, was leased to the Valparaiso trading house of Portales, Cea and Co., which undertook to service the £1,000,000 loan raised in London by the O'Higgins government two years earlier. The enterprise failed, and in 1826 the contract was withdrawn, occasioning much ill-feeling. The *estanquero* group was composed of men associated with this ill-starred venture; their leader was Diego Portales.

tion of a caudillo tradition in Chilean politics, for while Portales's influence was all-important, his aversion to the trappings of power was genuine enough. 'If I took up a stick and gave tranquillity to the country', he wrote, 'it was only to get the bastards and whores of Santiago to leave me in peace.'[2] Nevertheless, his actions both in government and behind the scenes, his strict emphasis on orderly management, his, at times, harsh attitude towards the defeated Liberals and, not least, his insistence on national dignity – these fixed the tone of official policy for years to come.

The work of the Conservatives in the 1830s was later described by critics of the regime as in essence a 'colonial reaction'. That it was a reaction to the ill-starred Liberal reformism of the 1820s is clear enough. But it is perhaps more accurate to see the new political system as a pragmatic fusion of the tradition of colonial authoritarianism, still very strong in Chile, with the outward forms (and something of the spirit) of nineteenth-century constitutionalism. The Constitution of 1833, whose regular operations were not interrupted until 1891 and which survived in amended form until 1925, embodied many of the principal Conservative obsessions. It was discernibly more authoritarian than its ill-fated prede-cessor of 1828, and in particular very strongly presidentialist. Two consecutive five-year terms of office were permitted, a provision which led in practice to four successive 'decennial' administrations, the first being that of Portales's nominee General Joaquín Prieto (1831–41). The president's patronage, control of the judiciary and public administration, and powers over Congress were all extensive, though the legislature was left with an ultimate check on the executive through its technical right to deny assent to the budget, taxation and military establishment. The president's emergency powers, in the form of 'extraordinary faculties' or localized states of siege, were highly conspicuous: moreover, such powers were regularly used – in one variety or another they were in force for one-third of the entire period between 1833 and 1861. The centralist spirit of the constitution was equally notable. The feeble institutional relics of the federalism of the 1820s were now swept away completely. The Intendant of each province was now defined as the president's 'natural and immediate agent' – and so it was to prove in practice: the Intendants were in some way the key officials of the regime, each Intendancy becoming in a real sense the local nexus of government. The

[2] Ernesto de la Cruz and Guillermo Feliú Cruz (eds.), *Epistolario de don Diego Portales*, 3 vols. (Santiago, 1937), I, 352.

Nineteenth-century Chile

hegemony of Santiago, already well entrenched, was thus reinforced at the expense of regional initiative.

No constitution, least of all in Spanish America, is efficacious on its own. The successful operation of the new political system depended on a number of well-tested techniques used with methodical persistence by the governments of the period. Some were more obvious than others. Repression was a recurrent tactic for three decades. By the standards of the twentieth century it did not amount to very much. The death sentence was far more often invoked than applied. The standard penalties for political dissent were incarceration, internal exile ('relegation'), or banishment abroad for a fixed period. Voluntary exile (sometimes under bond) was not uncommon, especially in the embattled decade of the 1850s. A less overt means of inculcating social discipline can be detected in the careful way in which the Conservatives restored clerical influence; until the 1850s the Church was a useful mainstay of the system. Likewise, the incipient militarism of the 1820s was curbed by a drastic purge of Liberal officers and by a comprehensive reorganization of the country's militias. By the middle of 1831 the National Guard numbered 25,000 men. It more than doubled in size later on and was a very credible counterweight to the regular army, whose peacetime establishment rarely went much above 3,000. Twice, in the mutinies of June 1837 and April 1851, the militias helped to save the regime from forcible overthrow. They also fitted very neatly into the government's control of the electoral process.

Electoral intervention runs like a constant theme through the entire period. It survived long after the repressive practices already mentioned. In fact it was a Liberal president who, when asked in 1871 by one of his ministers whether Chile would ever enjoy 'real' elections, curtly replied, 'Never!'[3] The electoral law of 1833 severely restricted the franchise, but spread the net just wide enough to include artisans and shopkeepers, many of whom formed the rank and file of the National Guard, which thus supplied a numerous voting contingent at every election. Quite apart from this invaluable support, the government resorted to any number of methods – intimidation, temporary arrest, personation, bribery – to prevent opposition voters from exercising their franchise and to secure comfortable majorities for its own candidates. The operation was co-ordinated by the Minister of the Interior, and his subaltern agents in the provinces, the Intendants, the departmental

3 Abdón Cifuentes, *Memorias*, 2 vols. (Santiago, 1936), II, 69.

*gobernadores* and the *subdelegados*, were as adept as any modern Chicago ward boss (and possibly more so) in 'delivering' the vote. It is hardly surprising that seven out of the eleven congressional elections held between 1833 and 1864 (at regular three-year intervals) were either uncontested or virtually so. Even in the more tolerant political climate of the 1860s and 1870s, an opposition stood no chance whatever of electing a majority to Congress. Not until the 1890s did the executive cease to interfere directly in elections.

In its earliest years the new Conservative system both faced and survived the ultimate test of war. The relations between Chile and Peru deteriorated sharply in the early 1830s. Commercial rivalry, a brisk tariff war, and Peru's failure to repay a Chilean loan (itself part of the £1,000,000 loan raised by O'Higgins in London in 1822, on which Chile had long since defaulted) were not in themselves a sufficient cause for aggression. This was provided in 1836, when General Andrés Santa Cruz forcibly united Peru and Bolivia into a Confederation. Portales viewed the formation of this potentially powerful state as a threat to Chilean independence; it would not be an exaggeration to say that he pushed his country into war. He was himself one of its first victims. Discontent over the war brought renewed Liberal conspiracies, and the all-powerful minister was murdered by a mutinous army battalion in June 1837, an occurrence which seems to have greatly solidified support both for the war policy and for the regime in general. Portales's death delayed but did not deflect the course of events. The second of two Chilean expeditionary forces, under the command of General Manuel Bulnes, invaded Peru and defeated Santa Cruz's army at the battle of Yungay (January 1839). The Confederation dissolved. The war of 1836–9 was an example of national assertiveness which incurred strong disapproval from Great Britain and France, but it inevitably heightened the international prestige of Chile. At home, it enabled the Prieto government to adopt a more conciliatory attitude towards the opposition, while the victorious General Bulnes became the obvious successor to the presidency. Just before the election Bulnes was betrothed to a daughter of the former Liberal president, Francisco Antonio Pinto, thus confirming the apparent trend towards political relaxation.

General Bulnes's presidency (1841–51) has often been represented as an 'era of good feelings' and for much of the time this was true. In the early 1840s, indeed, Liberalism came close to being killed by kindness. But Bulnes, for all his generous bonhomie, did nothing to undermine the authoritarian framework; in certain respects (the stiff Press Law of 1846, for instance) he added to it. The revival of Liberalism as a political force towards the end of his second term owed much to the ambitions of his chief minister, Manuel Camilo Vial, whose following, well represented in Congress, went into active parliamentary opposition when Vial was dismissed (1849). The leading Liberal intellectual of the period, José Victorino Lastarria, attempted to give direction and coherence to this new opposition. Outside the congressional arena the young idealists Francisco Bilbao and Santiago Arcos, mesmerized by the French revolution of 1848, were active in trying to mobilize support among the artisans of the capital: their Sociedad de la Igualdad, with its meetings and marches, survived for much of the year 1850, until the inevitable imposition of emergency powers by the government. The main effect of this agitation, both Liberal and *igualitario*, was to frighten the Conservative party into accepting Manuel Montt as Bulnes's successor.

President Montt (1851–61) was the first civilian to govern Chile for more than a few weeks. His oddly opaque character has defied all attempts at precise historical portraiture. His talent was undeniable; so was his austere inflexibility. ('All head and no heart' was his bluff predecessor's private opinion.) Montt's election provoked three months of full-scale civil war, in which the challenge to the regime came not only from the Liberals but also, more seriously, from the southern provinces. The leader of the revolt, General José María de la Cruz, was in fact a Conservative and the cousin of ex-president Bulnes, who defeated him in a short but bloody campaign. For the moment the regime was safe. By the mid-1850s, however, Montt's authoritarian approach was inducing strains and tensions within the Conservative governing combination itself. These finally came into the open as the result of a noisy jurisdictional conflict between the government and the Church, which was now re-emerging as an independent factor in politics. In 1857 the bulk of the Conservative party defected and joined forces with what was left of the Liberal opposition. Those Conservatives who remained loyal to Montt founded a new National party, but it lacked the wider upper class support enjoyed by the nascent Liberal-Conservative Fusion. For a second time vigorous agitation led to renewed repression and so to a further armed challenge to the regime. The civil war of 1859 is chiefly remembered for the miracles of improvisation performed by the rebel army in the mining provinces of the north – the focus of the war – but once again the government won. This time, however, military victory was followed by political defeat. Montt found it impossible to impose his own choice for the succession. This would have been Antonio Varas, Montt's closest associate and a highly talented politician. An elderly, easygoing, benevolent patrician, José Joaquín Pérez, was selected in Varas's place. It was a decisive turning point.

Under President Pérez (1861–71), the last of the four 'decennial' presidents, the Chilean political system at last began to liberalize. Pérez himself, by virtue of what was called at the time 'a supreme tolerance born of an even more supreme indifference', did as much as anybody in nineteenth-century Chile to enhance the tradition of stable constitutionalism. Repression ended, even if electoral intervention did not – Pérez's ministers saw to that. The new president, though himself nominally a National, quickly summoned the Liberal-Conservative Fusion into office (1862). This alliance between former enemies proved a remarkably workable governing combination, though it naturally attracted the opposition not only of the displaced Nationals (whose loyalty to Montt and Varas won them the name of *monttvaristas*) but also of the strongly anti-clerical 'red' or 'radical' Liberals who presently became known as the Radical party. The 1860s thus saw an increasingly diversified ideological panorama, and (except electorally) the 'new politics' was allowed to grow and thrive, although as it happened, domestic rivalries were somewhat dampened down in 1865–6, when the aggressive actions of a Spanish naval squadron cruising in Pacific waters drove Chile and three of her sister republics into a short war with their former metropolis.[4] By the close of the 1860s Liberal notions of constitutional reform were occupying the forefront of the political stage. Such ideas, centred, above all, on limiting presidential power, increasingly formed common ground between the four main parties. The first amendment to the hitherto inviolate Constitution of 1833 was passed in 1871; significantly, it prohibited the immediate re-election of the president.

It was during the government of Federico Errázuriz Zañartu (1871–6) that the final transition to Liberal-dominated politics occurred. In the early 1870s 'theological questions' (as they were called) began to be taken up as political issues. They were less concerned with theology, in fact, than with the demarcation of ecclesiastical and secular functions in the national life; they generated a good deal of feeling, both pious and

---

[4] Such fighting as there was (and there was not much) took place at sea. Before withdrawing from the Pacific, however, the Spaniards subjected Valparaíso to devastating bombardment (March 1866).

impious. A dispute about private education in 1873, pitting anticlericals against the Conservatives, who were becoming more and more identifiable as the militantly Catholic party in politics, brought about the disintegration of the Fusion. The Conservatives went into opposition, and the way was thus laid open for a new dominant coalition with a Liberal focus. The clever Errázuriz conducted the necessary manoeuvres. The Liberal Alliance (1875) was the third of the great governing combinations of the period, but the least stable, since several factions of the powerful Liberal party were invariably to be found opposing as well as supporting the government. The Errázuriz presidency also saw further constitutional reforms, all tending to limit executive influence. Important changes in electoral procedure (1874) were designed to reduce official intervention, but in 1876 Errázuriz and the Alliance had no difficulty in imposing the next president in the usual manner. Their choice fell on Aníbal Pinto, the son of the Liberal president of the later 1820s.

If the outline of the Conservative settlement of the 1830s was still very much intact, its inner workings were nonetheless altering in significant ways. Party politics had developed apace since the Pérez decade; the parties themselves were acquiring rudimentary forms of organization. The Radicals, with their network of local *asambleas*, were perhaps the first group to devise a definite (if flexible) structure. The Conservatives were the first to hold a national party conference (1878). But voting on party lines in Congress was far from automatic. When in 1876 the Radical deputy Ramón Allende (grandfather of the future president) suggested that party considerations should outweigh private principle in congressional voting, the idea was greeted with several outraged reactions. Quite apart from this, it was becoming clear by the later 1870s that Congress as a whole aspired to a much greater degree of control over the executive than had been attempted or perhaps even contemplated previously. The constitution, as we have seen, was strongly presidentialist; but it was also possible, as politicians now proved, to give it a logical 'parliamentary' interpretation. Through constant use of the *interpelación* and vote of censure, congressmen made the lives of cabinet ministers increasingly tedious and arduous. This was particularly the case during Aníbal Pinto's presidency (1876–81), which coincided, as we shall see, with several parallel crises of a very acute kind. That Chilean institutions had survived the tempests of the 1850s, that they were growing noticeably more tolerant – these things were cause for pride, certainly, but there were some politicians, including Pinto, who regarded as sterile the political squabbles now often monopolizing congressional attention to the exclusion of more urgent national business, and others who wondered whether the tension between the executive and the militant legislature might not destroy the tradition of stability. 'Gentlemen of the majority, ministers', exclaimed a Conservative deputy in 1881, 'I tell you: Don't pull the string too hard, because the thing might explode!'[5]

The connection between political stability and economic progress is never entirely clear-cut. It nevertheless seems fair to argue that the considerable commercial expansion which Chile underwent between the 1820s and the 1870s owed something, at least, to the settled conditions to be found in the country, as well as to the international demand for what Chile could produce. Expansion was not, however, completely smooth. At the close of the 1850s, with the loss of certain overseas markets for wheat and flour, coupled with two poor harvests in a row and the exhaustion of some of the silver deposits in the north, there was a brief but serious recession. At other periods (notably from the end of the 1840s to the mid-1850s, and again from the end of the 1860s into the early 1870s) the growth of trade was very rapid indeed, and Chile enjoyed boom conditions. The total value of the country's external trade rose from $7,500,000 in 1825 to $74,000,000 in 1875. Government revenues increased somewhat more slowly, from $2,000,000 in 1835 to $16,400,000 in 1875; until the 1860s they generally outran expenditure very comfortably.[6]

A highly cosmopolitan trading community established itself at Valparaíso in the years after independence, and the governments of the period saw trade with the maritime nations of the North Atlantic, especially Great Britain, as one of the main stimulants of progress. Indeed, the political settlement of the 1830s was accompanied by an 'economic settlement', largely carried through by the brilliant Manuel Rengifo, finance minister from 1830 to 1835 and again from 1841 to 1844. Rengifo blended liberalism with pragmatism in his economic measures, which included the simplification of the fiscal system and tariff laws, the consolidation of the public debt, and, not least, the establish-

[5] Cristián Zegers, *Aníbal Pinto. Historia política de su gobierno* (Santiago, 1969), 119. Ten years later, in the political crisis of 1891, the 'thing' did explode.

[6] The Chilean peso [$] maintained a more or less constant value throughout most of the period, being worth around 45*d.* in terms of sterling, or slightly less than an American dollar, except during the American civil war, when it was worth slightly more.

ment on a permanent basis of public warehouses (*almacenes fiscales*) at Valparaíso, where traders could store duty-free merchandise while awaiting favourable markets. That Valparaíso should be the dominant port on the Pacific coast was a cardinal maxim both for Rengifo and Portales.

Heavily dependent on customs duties for its revenues, the Chilean government had the strongest possible reason for wishing to augment the flow of trade, an aim which certainly reflected the view of the Chilean upper class as a whole. But broader considerations of national development were never entirely absent from the official mind. The state was active in many spheres, including the improvement of communications; and tariff policy did not ignore local interests other than those of exporters. The tariff reform of 1864, often presented by historians as a gadarene rush to free trade, was in many respects no more than a temporary aberration from the more standard nineteenth-century policy, which strove (rather ineffectively) to give at least a minimal degree of protection to certain domestic activities as well as to maximize trade. Nevertheless, it seems reasonably clear, given the extreme poverty of the new nation and the lack of a 'spirit of association' so frequently lamented by, *inter alia*, Manuel Montt, that even a much stronger dose of protectionism could hardly have done much to diversify economic activity or to develop an industrial base of any size. The country's options at this period were fairly narrow.

From the point of view of foreign trade, mining was by far the most important sector of the economy throughout the period. The miners of the north accumulated the largest individual and family fortunes of the time. The two thinly settled provinces of Atacama and Coquimbo, the area nowadays referred to by Chileans as the Norte Chico, constituted the most dynamic region of the country, with a population (about one-eighth of the nation's total in 1865) which rose much faster than was the case in the *hacienda*-dominated provinces of the central valley, thousands of whose people were lured to the ramshackle, rowdy and occasionally rebellious mining camps of the arid north; there were some 30,000 mineworkers there by the 1870s. Tough, enterprising, industrious, periodically volatile, fiercely proud – such was the distinctive culture of the mining zone. Its laboriously extracted riches had a vital impact on the rest of the nation, 'ennobling the central cities and fertilizing the fields of the south', as President Balmaceda was later to put it.[7] Of the three

[7] Roberto Hernández, *Juan Godoy o el descubrimiento de Chañarcillo*, 2 vols. (Valparaíso, 1932), II, 560.

principal metals mined in Chile in colonial times, gold did least well after independence, falling from an annual average production of 1,200 kg in the 1820s to a level of around 270 kg in the 1870s. Over the same period, by contrast, silver production rose from about 20,000 kg per annum to about 127,000 kg. (Given the persistence of smuggling, such figures are perhaps conservative). Copper, the most profitable of the three metals, was produced at an annual rate of 2,725 metric tons in the 1820s; this grew very steadily to 45,600 metric tons in the 1870s, by which time Chile regularly accounted for between one-third and one-half of the world's supply.

The allure of mineral wealth attracted numerous traders, speculators and prospectors to the northern deserts. The search for new veins of ore was incessant; the mining zone expanded slowly northwards into the Atacama desert and towards the long undefined border with Bolivia. The important early silver strikes at Agua Amarga (1811) and Arqueros (1825) were soon wholly eclipsed by the sensational discovery at Chañarcillo, south of Copiapó, in 1832. It was the single most productive mining district of the century, a veritable 'silver mountain' which yielded at least $12,000,000 in its first ten years and where by the mid-1840s there were over one hundred mines. The discovery of Tres Puntas (1848) was a further fillip to the boom, though less dramatic. The last silver rush of the period occurred in 1870, with the opening up of a major new mining district at Caracoles, across the border in Bolivia though worked almost entirely by Chileans. Copper mining depended less on new exploration than on the working of established veins of high-grade ore, but here too patient prospecting sometimes reaped a fabulous reward, as in the spectacular case of José Tomás Urmeneta, who searched for eighteen years in dire poverty before coming across, at Tamaya, his legendary deposit of copper. He was soon a millionaire, one of perhaps several dozen very rich men whose great fortunes came from the Norte Chico.

Chilean methods of mining changed only slowly and partially from the pattern established in later colonial times, which had been characterized by numerous small enterprises, individual or family entrepreneurship, simple technology and short-term marginal activity. By the 1860s, it is true, some of the larger mines – Urmeneta's at Tamaya, and José Ramón Ovalle's at Carrizal Alto, for instance – had gone in for extensive mechanization, and it is interesting that the two districts cited accounted for one-third of copper production in the 1870s. But the persistence of older practices – and a large number of small-scale operations which continued to rely, in preference to steampower, on the sturdy *barreteros* and *apires* who dug the ore and shifted it from the mine – is attested by many visitors to the north during this period. In the 1870s only some thirty-three mines in the Norte Chico used steam engines, leaving 755 which did not. Innovations in the smelting and refining of copper were a good deal more noticeable, with reverbatory furnaces (the 'English system') spreading from the 1830s onwards. Over the next two decades, in what amounted to a minor technological revolution, several large smelting plants were established on the coast, most notably at Guayacán and Tongoy in the Norte Chico and at Lirquén and Lota five hundred miles further south; these were Chile's first industrial enterprises of any size. They also processed Peruvian and Bolivian ores, and partially offset the producers' previous dependence on the smelting and refining industry of South Wales. The smelters' insatiable demand for fuel made deep inroads into the exiguous timber resources of the Norte Chico and contributed to the southward advance of the desert – that usually unremarked but basic ecological theme of Chilean history since colonial times. The main alternative to wood was coal, which was increasingly mined along the coast to the south of Concepción from the 1840s onwards. Here, domestic production was vulnerable to imports of higher-quality coal from Great Britain (or occasionally Australia), but held its own in the longer run, in part because a mixture of local and foreign coal was found to be ideal in smelting operations.

Chileans (sometimes first-generation Chileans) were outstanding among the mining entrepreneurs of this period. One or two of the copper concerns were British-owned, but these were exceptions, though foreign engineers were prominent throughout the mining zone. Men such as Urmeneta and a handful of others like him were naturally substantial capitalists in their own right, and they frequently turned their huge windfalls to good account, investing in transport and agriculture as well as in the mines, though not failing, either, to provide themselves with a suitably opulent style of life. Many of the lesser mining entrepreneurs were heavily dependent on a breed of middlemen known as *habilitadores*, who bought their ore in exchange for credit and supplies. This business was the foundation of several large fortunes, a famous example being the career of Agustín Edwards Ossandón, the son of an English doctor who settled in the Norte Chico just before independence. By the 1860s Edwards was one of the richest and most active capitalists in Chile. In 1871–2, in a well-known episode, he quietly accumulated and stockpiled vast amounts of copper, drove up the price by fifty per cent and realized a profit estimated at $1,500,000. By the time Edwards executed this audacious coup, Chile's nineteenth-century silver and copper cycle was reaching its climax. The silver mines were to maintain a high output for two more decades; but with production booming in the United States and Spain, 'Chili bars' became a decreasingly important component in the world supply of copper, no more than six per cent of which came from Chile by the 1890s. By then, of course, deserts further to the north were yielding a still greater source of wealth: nitrates.

Although mining dominated the export sector, it was agriculture which dominated most ordinary lives. Four out of five Chileans lived in the countryside in the 1860s. Here, as in so many other ways, the colonial legacy was overwhelming. Throughout the nineteenth century Chile remained a land of great estates, ownership of which conferred social status, political influence (if desired) and (less automatically before the 1850s) a comfortable income. This tradition of landownership is one of the keys to understanding Chilean history between colonial times and the mid-twentieth century. The precise number of haciendas in the mid-nineteenth century is hard to assess. The tax records of 1854 show that some 850 landowners received around two-thirds of all agricultural income in central Chile, and that of these 154 owned estates which earned in excess of $6,000 per year. (For purposes of comparison, it might be noted here that the president of the republic was paid a salary of $12,000, raised to $18,000 in 1861.) Haciendas occupied at least three-quarters of all agricultural land; most included large tracts of ground which went uncultivated from year to year. The estates were worked by a stable, resident class of *inquilinos*, or tenant-labourers, and, when necessary, by peons hired for seasonal work from outside. This type of rural labour system, as we know, was common (though with many variations) in many parts of Spanish America. When Charles Darwin rode through the Chilean countryside in the mid-1830s, he thought of it as 'feudal-like'. The Chilean *inquilino* was bound to the hacienda, allowed to cultivate his own small parcel of land in exchange for regular labour services to the landowner, by ties of custom and convenience rather than by those of law or debt. In the absence of traditional village communities of the European kind, the estate became the sole focus of his loyalty and formed his own little universe. 'Every hacienda in Chile', wrote an acute observer in 1861, 'forms a separate society, whose head is the landowner and whose subjects are the *inquilinos* . . . The landowner is an absolute monarch in his hacienda.'[8] For the tenant-labourers life was poor though not necessarily harsh; their farming methods were primitive, their diet monotonous and sometimes barely adequate and their opportunities to rise in the social scale very strictly limited. But the relative security of the hacienda could be contrasted with the plight of most of the peons outside – a destitute mass of people scraping a very precarious living by squatting on marginal land, by wandering the central valley in search of seasonal work, or in some cases by turning to cattle-rustling and banditry. From the viewpoint of the *hacendado*, there was plenty of surplus labour, as well as unused land, in the countryside. Neither was needed on a large scale before 1850 or so.

If agriculture was unproductive and unprofitable in the earlier part of this period, the reason is easy enough to identify. Local demand was quickly satisfied, while export markets were few and far between. The eighteenth-century grain trade with Peru, whose importance has probably been exaggerated by historians, was never quite re-established on the old scale following the wars of independence and the commercial rivalry of the 1830s. Between 1850 and 1880, however, the outlook for landowners improved quite radically, with haciendas responding immediately to the opening up of new markets overseas. As the only major cereal-growing country on the Pacific coast of America, Chile was well placed to take advantage of the sudden demand set up by the gold rushes in California and Australia. Exports of wheat and flour to California amounted to around 6,000 metric quintals (qqm) in 1848. Two years later no less than 277,000 qqm of wheat and 221,000 qqm of flour were shipped northwards. The boom was ephemeral – by 1855 California was self-sufficient – but it yielded high profits while it lasted, and it was responsible for consolidating a technically up-to-date milling industry in the Talca area and along Talcahuano Bay, as well as in Santiago itself slightly later on. By 1871 there were some 130 or so modern mills in Chile. (At the end of this period, further changes in the technology of milling were being pioneered in the middle west of the United States and in Europe, but these, by contrast, were slower to reach Chile.) Australia provided a second short-lived (and somewhat precarious) market for Chile in the 1850s, lucrative for a while. Landowners were well aware that geography and good luck were the causes of such windfalls, which were substantial enough: agricultural exports quintupled in value be-

---

[8] 'Atropos,' 'El inquilino en Chile', *Revista del Pacífico*, 5 (1861), 94.

tween 1844 and 1860. Nor was this by any means the end of the story. The experience gained in the Californian and Australian markets, combined with vital improvements in transport, enabled Chile in the 1860s to sell large quantities of grain (wheat and barley) to England: 2,000,000 qqm were exported in 1874, the peak year. Once again, however, Chile's competitive position in the international market place was more fragile than it appeared, and it was permanently undermined a few years later, when grain prices fell and new, more efficient cereal-growing countries were opened up.

The stimulus of these mid-century export booms brought some definite changes to the countryside. Most visible of these, perhaps, were the numerous irrigation canals now constructed, some of them remarkable feats of engineering. (The Canal de las Mercedes, sponsored by Manuel Montt and other *hacendados* in 1854, took thirty years to build and eventually extended seventy-five miles over very uneven terrain.) The quality of livestock was slowly improved, through the introduction of foreign breeds. With the growth of the towns, an expanding market for fruit and poultry greatly benefited nearby haciendas and the smaller (often specialist) farms known as *chacras*. Chileans had drunk their own wine since early colonial times; but the foundations of the great viticultural tradition which was later to produce the finest vintages in the western hemisphere were only laid in the 1850s, when pinot and cabernet grapes, brought from France, were grown locally for the first time. The government itself, as well as the Sociedad Nacional de Agricultura (in intermittent existence from 1838) tried to improve agricultural knowledge. Developments such as these, thus sketched, seem to convey an impression of vitality, but it is somewhat deceptive. Rural society and traditional farming methods were in no real way drastically disturbed, although it seems probable that monetary transactions in the countryside became more widespread than previously. There was relatively little in the way of high capital investment in agriculture (leaving aside irrigation works), and despite the enthusiasm of a number of progressive landowners, farm-machinery was never imported or employed on a large scale. (Oxen remained in universal use in Chile until the 1930s.) During the happy years of the export boom, landowners had ample reserves of both land and labour on which to draw. The acreage placed beneath the plough in these years may well have tripled or even quadrupled. New families from outside the haciendas were encouraged (and in many cases were no doubt eager) to swell the ranks of the *inquilinos*. The labour system itself was certainly tightened up, with greater demands being made on the tenant-labourers. Quite apart from *inquilinaje*, a variety of sharecropping practices, especially in the coastal range, were developed to help feed the export boom. The number of *minifundios* also seems to have risen. But in general it was the hacienda system itself, the basic underpinning of the nation's elite, which was most clearly consolidated by the changes of the mid-nineteenth century.

Such manufacturing as existed in Chile at the time of independence and for two or three decades thereafter was carried out by artisans and craftsmen in small workshops in the towns. In the countryside, the hacienda population largely clothed itself, though the growing import of British cottons probably had the effect over the years of reducing the extent of local weaving. The upper class was, on the whole, able to satisfy its demand for manufactured goods, including luxuries, from abroad, and was uninterested in promoting an industrial revolution. (Mining entrepreneurs were a partial exception here, and at the end of the period industrialism was viewed as a possible way forward for the country by a growing number of intellectuals and politicians.) There can be little doubt, however, that the expansion of national wealth after 1850 or so did provide certain opportunities for entrepreneurship in manufacturing, and such opportunities were sometimes seized – usually by foreigners, though these can better be regarded, perhaps, as first-generation Chileans. The first major industrial enterprises arose in connection with the export booms and were the copper smelters and flour mills mentioned already. In addition to these, the 1860s and 1870s saw the growth of small-scale factory production in such fields as textiles, food-processing, brick-making and glass-blowing. By the 1880s there were at least thirty breweries in the country. Furthermore, the needs of the new railways and of the mining industry itself stimulated the appearance of a number of small foundries and machine shops capable of repairing and in some instances even making equipment. In fact, what seems to have been a respectable metallurgical and engineering sector was developing with surprising speed by the early 1870s. There is growing evidence for supposing that the start of Chilean industrialization, often dated from the War of the Pacific, should be pushed back by about ten years.

It goes without saying that Chile's export-led economic expansion could hardly have taken place without improvements in transport and communications, which were also of obvious importance in consolidating the political coherence of the new nation. The number of ships

calling at Chilean ports rose more or less constantly from the 1830s
onwards, to over 4,000 per annum in the 1870s. Two 700-ton paddle
steamers were brought to Chile from England in 1840 by a very
enterprising American, William Wheelwright, the founder of the British-owned Pacific Steam Navigation Company. The outside world
began to draw closer. From the mid-1840s it became possible, with
suitable connections across the Panama isthmus, to travel to Europe in
under forty days. (Sailing ships still took three or four months.) In 1868
the now well-established P.S.N.C. (whose initials later prompted several
famous Chilean jokes) opened a direct service between Valparaíso and
Liverpool by way of the Magellan Straits. Meanwhile, inland transport
was slowly being revolutionized by the inevitable advent of the railway.
The north of Chile, indeed, installed the first substantial length of track
in Latin America. The line, built by Wheelwright and finished in 1851,
linked Copiapó with the port of Caldera fifty miles away. It was financed
by a group of wealthy miners, and it set the pattern for several later
railways in the mining zone. The vital link between Santiago and
Valparaíso had to wait somewhat longer. This was initially a mixed
venture, the government subscribing about half the capital, but in 1858,
following tiresome delays and difficulties, the state bought out most of
the private shareholders; a swashbuckling American entrepreneur,
Henry Meiggs, was entrusted with the completion of the line; and the last
sections of the wide-gauge track were laid in 1863. Another mixed
venture sponsored the third main railway, extending southwards
through the central valley, a line of particular interest to cereal-growing
*hacendados*. The Errázuriz government took this over in 1873, and only a
few years later the line joined up with a further railway which by then had
been built inland from Talcahuano and was pressing southwards into the
romantic landscapes of Araucania. In 1882 there were nearly 1,200 miles
of track in Chile, just over half state-owned. The state also subsidized and
subsequently purchased the nascent telegraph network, construction of
which began in 1852 – yet another enterprise of the indefatigable
Wheelwright, to whom, in due course, a statue was raised in Valparaíso.
Twenty years later the Chilean brothers Juan and Mateo Clark linked
Santiago to Buenos Aires; with the laying of the Brazilian submarine
cable in 1874 Chile was for the first time placed in direct touch with the
Old World.

The increasing pace of economic activity during the third quarter of
the nineteenth century left its mark on the country's financial and

commercial institutions. Up to the 1850s the main sources of credit, for instance, had been private lenders or the trading houses. This now changed, with the appearance of the first proper banks – the Banco de Ossa and the Banco de Valparaíso, founded in the mid-1850s – and banking operations were sufficiently extensive to warrant regulation in the important law of 1860. The creation in 1856 of the notable Caja de Crédito Hipotecario funnelled credit to the countryside – in practice mainly to the big landowners. Joint-stock companies now became increasingly common, though supplementing rather than replacing the individual and family concerns and partnerships which had hitherto been the standard modes of business organization. The earliest were the railway companies; by the end of the 1870s well over 150 such enterprises had been formed at one time or another, predominantly in mining, banking and insurance, and railways. Chilean capitalism showed a markedly expansionist tendency in the 1860s and 1870s, with money flowing into the nitrate business in Bolivia and Peru as well as to the silver mines at Caracoles. Unregulated stock exchanges were operating in Valparaíso and Santiago from the early 1870s, at which point 'Caracoles fever' was driving investors into a speculative frenzy without precedent in Chilean history.

Foreign trade throughout this period was largely controlled by several dozen import-export houses centred on Valparaíso and the capital; these contributed much to the building up of the new money market, and remained influential thereafter in the developing corporate sector of the economy. Foreigners, whether as permanent residents or as transient agents of overseas trading houses with branches in Chile, were particularly prominent here, with the British leading the field. The British connection was fundamental to Chile. Investment in the country by Britons was mostly confined to government bonds – to the tune of around £7,000,000 by 1880 – but Great Britain was the destination for between one-third and two-thirds of all Chile's exports and the source of between one-third and one-half of all her imports in any given year. Imports from France also ran high, reflecting upper class tastes. As in colonial times, trade with Peru continued, but this was overshadowed by the links now being forged with the North Atlantic. The steamers, railways, telegraphs, banks and joint-stock companies all played their part in cementing Chile's solidifying association with the international economy now coming into being around the world. Politicians might occasionally denounce the British traders as the 'new Carthaginians' or even (in more popular vein) as 'infidels', but by and large their presence was welcomed as a vital element in what was confidently assumed to be the progress of the nation.

Sixty years after independence Chile was an altogether more prosperous land than would have seemed likely in 1810, as well as being more integrated economically than in colonial times. Her record in this respect contrasts forcibly with the stagnation evident in several of the other Spanish American republics. But the new prosperity was not distributed proportionately (still less evenly) to all sections of the people. The wealth of the upper class increased very strikingly, and the upper class had a fairly clear idea as to what to do with it. An American visitor in the mid-1850s observed that 'the great object of life' on acquiring wealth seemed to be to 'remove to the capital, to lavish it on costly furniture, equipage and splendid living.'[9] The gradual disappearance of older, more austere, supposedly more virtuous habits of life was lamented by writers of a moralistic cast of mind; and it is probably fair to say that the adoption of more sophisticated, European styles of living – fashions across a whole range from hats to horse-racing altered visibly between the 1820s and the 1870s – may well have deepened the psychological gulf between rich and poor; it may also be one of the keys to understanding the political liberalization which set in after 1861. The elite of Chilean society was never closed to newcomers. The new magnates of mining and finance were easily assimilated, as were the children or grandchildren of success-ful immigrants – though the much remarked contingent of non-Hispanic surnames in the Chilean upper class only became really conspicuous at the end of the century. (There was only one English surname in any of the cabinets before the 1880s.) The underlying coherence of this open, flexible elite was provided by a set of economic interests – in mines, land, banks and trade – which overlapped and often interlocked. The miners or traders who in different circumstances might have formed the van-guard of a *bourgeoisie conquérante* were from the start included at the highest levels of the social hierarchy, where fundamentally aristocratic outlooks and attitudes prevailed. The supreme upper class values were those concerned with family and landownership. The importance of family connections at this period cannot easily be exaggerated. It was something which often showed up in politics. President Bulnes was the son-in-law of one of his predecessors, the nephew of another and the

[9] [Mrs. C. B. Merwin], *Three Years in Chile* (New York, 1863), 95.

brother-in-law of one of his successors. In the century after 1830, the Errázuriz family gave the republic one archbishop, three presidents, and upwards of fifty congressmen. The attraction of rural property, likewise, integrated rather than divided the elite; landownership was the highly prized badge of aristocratic status. These powerful forces for coherence clearly encouraged continuity and stability rather than change and rearrangement in the social development of Chile.

Between the landowning upper class and the labouring poor, a small, miscellaneous 'middle band' of society grew perceptibly larger as the result of economic expansion. It consisted of the owners of the smaller businesses and farms, the growing number of clerical employees in trade, the subaltern members of the bureaucracy (which even in 1880 still numbered no more than 3,000), and the artisans and craftsmen of the towns. These last were what educated Chileans of the period meant when they used the term *clase obrera*. On the upper fringe of the middle band, frustrated would-be entrants into the best circles constituted a recognizable type, well described in some of the fiction of the time. From at least the later 1850s such people were known as *siúticos* and tradition attributes the neologism, still understood if no longer widely used, to Lastarria. Chilean artisans, for their part, were never well protected by commercial policy, but the growth of the towns (and upper class wealth) created a demand for services and products which could best be met locally, and many crafts and trades seem to have flourished, at least in a modest way. In their manners and aspirations such groups evidently took their tone from high society. Referring to the 'mechanics and retail shopkeepers' of the Santiago of 1850, a sharp-eyed visitor noted:

There is an inherent want of tidiness in their domestic life; but in public, fine dress is a passion with them, and a stranger would scarcely suspect that the man he meets in a fine broad-cloth cloak, escorting a woman arrayed in silks and jewelry, occupied no higher rank in the social scale than that of tinman, carpenter or shopman whose sole stock-in-trade might be packed in a box five feet square.[10]

The spread of mutualist associations in later years provided a greater degree of security for artisans and craftsmen. The first was founded in the printing trade in 1853 and did not last long; but by 1880, thanks to the efforts of the builder and architect Fermín Vivaceta and others, there were some thirty-nine societies of this kind enjoying legal status, foreshadowing the later emergence of trade unions.

[10] Lieut. J. M. Gilliss, U.S.N., *The United States Naval Astronomical Expedition to the southern hemisphere during the years 1849–50–51–52*, vol. 1., Chile (Washington, 1855), 219.

A deep material and psychological chasm separated all the social groups so far mentioned from the great mass of the labouring poor in town and countryside, whose condition improved only marginally, if at all, over this period. Despite the higher number of families now being settled on the haciendas, the peons of the central valley were often obliged to look elsewhere for work. They migrated in their thousands to overcrowded and insalubrious districts in the main towns. Both *rotos* (urban labourers) and peons also flocked to the northern mining camps, and to the railway-building gangs, in Chile and overseas. When, at the end of the 1860s, the audacious Henry Meiggs (renowned for the remark that he would sooner employ five hundred Chilean *rotos* than a thousand Irishmen) embarked on grandiose railway-building schemes in Peru at least 25,000 Chileans answered his call. This outflow of labour provoked debates in Congress, with proposals to restrict emigration, while landowners complained of a 'shortage of hands' in the countryside. In fact, there was no real shortage, and this was appreciated by those more acute Chileans who now began to subject the labouring poor to somewhat closer scrutiny than in the past.

If emigration was (briefly) a concern of Chilean legislators, the idea of immigration from Europe, as a means of 'civilizing' the lower classes, was suggested more frequently. Traces of xenophobia may have survived among the poor, to be whipped up on occasion, as during the civil war of 1829–30, but in general foreigners were welcomed with open arms. ' "Foreigner" ', once said Antonio Varas, 'is an immoral word which should be expunged from the dictionary!' The census of 1875 counted 4,109 British, 4,033 German and 2,330 French residents in Chile, with people of other nationalities totalling nearly 15,000, a figure which included 7,000 Argentines. The role of the British in trade has already been noted; some prominent Chilean families came in due course from this quarter. The milling industry referred to earlier was largely established by Americans; Americans and British helped to build and then to operate the railway network; a high proportion of the industrial entrepreneurs of later years came from abroad. At a more modest level, foreigners also found a place in the expanding artisan class, notably in those trades which catered to the style of life favoured by the rich. European scholars and scientists such as the Frenchmen Claude Gay (author of a famous thirty-volume account of the country's natural and civil history) and Amado Pissis (who mapped the republic from 28°10′S to 41°58′S) did much to add to the store of Chilean knowledge; the government had a more or less systematic policy of employing such people. There was no mass immigration of the kind desired, but at the end of the 1840s the government encouraged the settlement of families from Germany in the thinly-populated southern territories around Valdivia and Lake Llanquihue. By 1860 there were more than 3,000 Germans in the south, hardy pioneers who cleared the forests and opened the land to cultivation, helped by migrants from Chiloé.

This new official interest in the south spelled the beginning of the end for the independent Indian enclave of Araucania, which lay inconveniently between the new areas of settlement and the country's heartland north of the Bío-Bío. The suppression of the widespread banditry which followed independence in the southern provinces, complete by the mid-1830s, had placed the Araucanians in a somewhat more vulnerable position than previously; but for the next quarter of a century they were left largely undisturbed. As in colonial times, the army patrolled the frontier while the government in Santiago cultivated (and subsidized) a number of amiably disposed caciques. The agricultural expansion of the 1850s, however, drew settlers into the area south of the Bío-Bío, causing tension with the Araucanians. The Indian attacks on frontier settlements which followed (1859–60) raised the 'Araucanian question' as a political issue, much discussed over the next few years. The policy adopted by the Pérez government was, by establishing 'lines' of forts, to enclose the Araucanians within a diminishing belt of territory. The Indians resisted the encroaching Chilean army in a further series of assaults (1868–71), but by the end of the 1870s, with settlement spilling into the frontier, the 'lines' had drawn inexorably closer together. After the War of the Pacific, troops were sent in to 'pacify' and occupy the narrow fringe of Indian territory which remained. The long, proud history of Araucania drew to its pathetic close. The Indians themselves were given, on paper, a settlement deemed generous in the eyes of Santiago, but the pattern of land transactions on the frontier over the previous twenty years was hardly a good augury. The government strove in vain to regularize land transfers in the south, but failed to prevent the formation of new latifundia, often through chicanery and intimidation. Nor could the measures taken to protect the interests of the Araucanians against predatory landowners (great and small) be described as anything but inadequate.

The most vivid contrast, in the Chile of the 1870s, was between town and country. Civilization – that term so often used to justify the 'pacification' of Araucania – was perhaps most evident in its urban setting. Nineteenth-century Chilean urbanization (modest indeed by the standards of the twentieth century) was essentially a tale of two cities – Santiago, which grew from about 70,000 in the mid-1830s to 130,000 in 1875, and Valparaíso, which by the end of our period had reached close on 100,000. Other Chilean towns lagged far behind. During the mining booms, it is true, Copiapó enjoyed a prosperous heyday; Concepción, devastated by the earthquake of 1835, flourished again with the spread of wheat-growing and milling; and among the somnolent little towns of the central valley, Talca nurtured a well-developed sense of civic pride. But none of these places had populations of more than 20,000 in 1875. The predominance of the capital and the main port, underpinned by political and commercial hegemony, was unchallengeable. As contemporary drawings and prints show clearly, Santiago retained a definitely colonial appearance until around 1850, but the mid-century export boom quickly left its mark. By 1857 the normally sober Andrés Bello could write that 'the progress made in the last five years can be called fabulous. Magnificent buildings are rising everywhere . . .; to see the Alameda on certain days of the year makes one imagine one is in one of the great cities of Europe.'[11] The year 1857, in fact, saw the inauguration of the fine Teatro Municipal and the introduction of horse-drawn trams and gas-lamps in the streets. Architectural styles altered, French (or even English) models being preferred for the new aristocratic mansions now being built. The unusually active programme carried through by Benjamín Vicuña Mackenna, the almost legendary Intendant of the early 1870s, endowed the capital with avenues, parks, squares and the superb urban folly of the Cerro Santa Lucía, which delights *santiaguinos* to this day. Valparaíso, the first Chilean town to organize a proper fire-brigade (1851), underwent similar though less flamboyantly publicized improvements. Its business district took on a faintly British atmosphere. Both capital and port (and other towns later on) soon acquired a respectable newspaper press, which flourished with particular vigour in the more liberal political climate after 1861. The doyen of the Chilean press, *El Mercurio*, founded at Valparaíso in 1827 (and a daily from 1829), is today the oldest newspaper in the Spanish-language world.

Education in this period made slower progress than many Chileans would have wished, despite the best efforts of such presidents as Montt, whose obsessive interest in the matter was shared by his great Argentine friend Sarmiento. Illiteracy fell gradually, to around seventy-seven per

[11] Domingo Amunátegui Solar, *La democracia en Chile* (Santiago, 1946), 132.

cent in 1875, at which point seventeen per cent of the school-age population was undergoing some form of primary education. By 1879, too, there were some twenty-seven public *liceos* (two for girls) and a larger number of private schools providing instruction at the secondary level, along with the prestigious Instituto Nacional, where so many of the republic's leaders received their secondary (and for many years much of their higher) education. Higher studies (and especially professional training, to which women were admitted by the decree of 1877) were greatly stimulated by the formation in 1843 of the University of Chile. Modelled on the Institut de France, it was in its early years a deliberative and supervisory body rather than a teaching institution, but its standards were high. The distinct strengthening of intellectual and cultural life which now became noticeable owed much to the first rector of the university, the eminent Venezuelan scholar, Andrés Bello, who spent the last thirty-six years of a long life in Chile. Poet, grammarian, philosopher, educationist, jurist, historian, indefatigable public servant and senator – Bello had a patient and many-sided genius which inspired a host of devoted pupils and disciples. It is impossible in the space of this chapter to survey the cultural panorama of the period; but one rather singular aspect deserves to be noted. This was the primacy accorded to history, a primacy encouraged by the university and (in a small way) by the government itself. The result, between 1850 and 1900 or so, was the fine flowering of historical narrative represented, above all, in the works of Diego Barros Arana, Miguel Luis Amunátegui, Ramón Sotomayor Valdés and Benjamín Vicuña Mackenna. Of these four, Barros Arana was the most diligent and scholarly, Vicuña Mackenna the most lyrical and vivid. All can still be read with profit.

It is possible that this Chilean preference for history both reflected and reinforced the growth of national consciousness. Patriotism, to be sure, is never easy to assess. It may be doubted whether a clear sense of *chilenidad* really penetrated very far into the countryside before the 1870s. The people of the towns, by contrast, responded ardently to the victory celebrations in 1839; the *dieciocho*, the annual national holiday, though often a pretext for prolonged alcoholic indulgence, was an undeniably popular occasion; and private as well as public initiatives saw to it that statues were raised to the heroes of independence and other national figures, starting with General Freire in 1856. (Portales and O'Higgins got their monuments in 1860 and 1872 respectively). Educated Chileans were strongly inclined to see their country as superior to others in

Spanish America – and it is hard to resist the conclusion that in certain important respects they were right. 'We saved ourselves from the general shipwreck', wrote the rising Conservative politician Carlos Walker Martínez.[12] Chile as the *república modelo*, as an example to unruly, 'tropical' lands, was a recurrent theme in speeches and editorials. 'I have such a poor idea of the . . . sister republics', observed Antonio Varas in 1864, 'that . . . I regret we have to make common cause with them.'[13] Such opinions often coincided with foreign views of Chile, especially in Europe. (In April 1880 even *The Times* used the phrase 'model republic'.) European flattery was deeply pleasing to educated Chileans, many of whom believed that Great Britain and France (in particular) were leading the world up a highway of progress which in due course Chile herself was sure to follow: 'Europe's today is our tomorrow.'[14]

This mood of confidence and optimism was severely shaken by the multiple crisis of the mid-1870s. This can effectively be dated from the collapse in 1873 of the speculative bonanza induced by the Caracoles silver boom. The economic difficulties which mounted up thereafter stemmed in part from the serious international recession which began that year (the start of the 'Great Depression' which followed the long mid-Victorian boom), but they also reflected a more fundamental problem: with the appearance in the world economy of new and more efficient producers of both wheat and copper, Chile was now being displaced in her most important export markets. The springs of prosperity were running dry. Copper prices, briefly boosted by the Franco-Prussian war (as they had earlier been by the Crimean war), went into sharp decline. The value of silver exports halved within four years, though the cause often assigned to this – the shift to the gold standard by Germany and other nations – may have been exaggerated by historians. On top of all this, an alarming and untimely cycle of both flooding and drought in the central valley brought three disastrous harvests in a row. An abrupt rise in the cost of living plunged many thousands of poorer Chileans into destitution and near-starvation. There were disturbing symptoms of social unrest. The peso, stable for so long, began to depreciate, falling from 46*d.* in 1872 to 33*d.* by 1879. (It is faintly amusing to record that in this atmosphere of desperation, official hopes were briefly raised by a

[12] C. W. Martínez, *Portales* (Paris, 1879), 452.
[13] Antonio Varas, *Correspondencia*, 5 vols. (Santiago, 1918–29), v, 48.
[14] Editorial, *El Mercurio*, 18 September 1844.

Franco-American confidence trickster who claimed to be able to convert copper into gold; he was lionized and had a polka named after him.) Fearing a catastrophic run on the now largely insolvent banks, the Pinto administration took the drastic step of declaring the inconvertibility of bank-notes (July 1878), which thus became obligatory legal tender; it was the start of a century of inflation. In its efforts to solve the acute fiscal dilemma (made still more acute by the need to service a national debt which had grown perilously fast over the previous few years), the government first resorted to cuts in public spending; the National Guard, for instance, was reduced to a mere 7,000 men. As the recession deepened, many intelligent Chileans, noting their country's heavy dependence on exports, advocated a stronger protectionist dose for the embryonic industrial sector (this was partly achieved in the tariff reform of 1878) and also the imposition of new taxes on the wealthy. This latter notion, according to the British consul-general, was well regarded 'by all but those whose pockets it would chiefly affect and who, for the misfortune of their Country, just now largely compose her Legislature'.[15] In fact, Congress in 1878–9 did agree, after much argument, to levy small taxes on inheritances and property. These had little effect on the crisis, from which Chile was saved not by fiscal improvization but by blood and iron.

The menacing international tensions of the 1870s derived from long standing border disputes with Argentina and Bolivia. Neither frontier had been precisely delineated in colonial times. The Chilean presence on the Magellan Straits after 1843 had raised the question of the ownership of Patagonia, which Argentines considered theirs. Chile, in effect, abandoned her claim to all but a fraction of this huge but desolate territory in the Fierro-Sarratea agreement of 1878, accepted by Congress despite the angry crowds outside the building and a strong speech from an irate former foreign minister, who lamented that Chile would now remain 'a poor republic' instead of becoming 'a great empire'. The agreement averted the danger of war with Argentina; there had been considerable sabre-rattling on both sides of the Andes. The problem with Bolivia was more intractable, for while few vital interests had been at stake in Patagonia this was emphatically not the case in the Atacama desert, one of the principal scenes of Chilean economic expansionism. Here in the 1860s, on the Bolivian littoral, the Chilean entrepreneurs José

---

[15] Consul-General Packenham to the Marquis of Salisbury, Santiago, 24 February 1879. Public Record Office, London: F.O.16/203.

Santos Ossa and Francisco Puelma had pioneered the extraction of nitrate, in growing demand abroad as a fertilizer. (Chilean capital was also prominent in the nitrate business in the Peruvian desert, further north; but the industry there was nationalized by the Peruvian government in 1875). In the Atacama, thanks to generous concessions by Bolivia, the powerful Compañía de Salitres y Ferrocarril de Antofagasta, a Chilean-British corporation in which a number of leading Chilean politicians held shares, was close to constituting a state within a state. Most of the population on the littoral was Chilean. Such a state of affairs is always potentially explosive. In 1874, in an attempt to settle the frontier once and for all, Chile agreed to fix it at 24°S in return for the Bolivian promise of a twenty-five-year moratorium on the further taxation of Chilean nitrate enterprises. The additional export tax of ten centavos per quintal suddenly imposed by the Bolivians in 1878 was clearly a breach of faith. (Whether the original Bolivian concessions were imprudent or not is another matter.) The refusal of the Compañía de Salitres to pay up brought threats of confiscation. In order to forestall this a small Chilean force occupied Antofagasta (February 1879) and went on to take control of the littoral. The conflict swiftly assumed graver proportions. Peru was drawn in by virtue of a secret treaty of alliance with Bolivia, concluded six years previously. Chile declared war on both countries in April 1879.

The War of the Pacific was seen at the time (by some) as a cynically premeditated exercise in plunder, with the aim of rescuing Chile from her economic plight by seizing the mineral wealth of the northern deserts. Others detected the invisible hand of more powerful nations and the foreign trading concerns so closely enmeshed with the nitrate business. The American secretary of state, the egregious James G. Blaine, even asserted later on that it was 'an English war on Peru, with Chile as the instrument', a verdict which it is difficult to sustain from the existing evidence.[16] It must, however, be said that Chilean politicians (not least those who held or had held shares in nitrate enterprises) were aware of the advantages which might accrue from control of the deserts and were equally aware of the country's dire economic position in 1879. Insofar as there had been a public 'willingness to war' over the previous months, this had mainly been directed against Argentina. Nonetheless it may well

[16] On these points, see V. G. Kiernan, 'Foreign interests in the War of the Pacific', *Hispanic American Historical Review*, 35 (1955), 14–36, and John Mayo, 'La Compañía de Salitres de Antofagasta y la Guerra del Pacífico', *Historia*, (Santiago) 14 (1979), 71–102.

be true that the eagerness with which the outbreak of hostilities was welcomed (generally, if not universally) was in some sense an outlet for the pent-up feelings of frustration which had accumulated during the years of recession. (Chile's action in February 1879 could plausibly be described as precipitate.) But neither Chile nor her enemies were prepared for war. Their armies were small and poorly equipped. Chile had cut back her military strength during the recession, while both the Peruvian and Bolivian armies were decidedly over-officered. At sea, Chile and Peru (Bolivia had no navy) were perhaps more evenly matched; and command of the sea was the key to the war. In the end, Chile's greater national coherence and traditions of settled government probably made the vital difference. At various points during this time of mortal danger, both Bolivia and Peru were afflicted by serious political upheavals. In Chile, by contrast, congressional and presidential elections were held as usual, cabinets changed without excessive drama and energetic politicking by no means ceased: neither the Conservatives nor the disaffected Liberal group led by Vicuña Mackenna (who had made an unsuccessful bid for the presidency in 1876) were invited into the cabinet, and they made up for this by mercilessly castigating the government's numerous hesitancies and failures in the conduct of the war.

The early months, taken up with a struggle for naval mastery, were a frustrating period of reverses for Chile, but also provided the single most memorable incident of the war. On 21 May 1879, off Iquique, the decrepit wooden corvette *Esmeralda* was attacked by the Peruvian ironclad *Huascar*. Although the corvette was outclassed and doomed from the outset, the Chilean commander, Captain Arturo Prat, refused to strike his colours. He himself died in an entirely hopeless boarding operation as the *Huascar* rammed his vessel, which, after further rammings, went down. Prat's heroic self-sacrifice turned him into a 'secular saint' without compare in the admiration of his countrymen. Five months later, off Cape Angamos, the Chilean fleet cornered the *Huascar* and forced her to surrender. This victory gave Chile command of the sea and enabled her to launch an offensive on land. Soon after the battle of Angamos, an expeditionary force invaded the Peruvian desert province of Tarapacá, forcing the enemy to fall back on Tacna and Arica to the north. Early in 1880 an army of 12,000 men, commanded by General Manuel Baquedano, undertook the conquest of these provinces too, in a desert campaign culminating in the ferocious battles of Campo de la Alianza and the Morro of Arica (May–June 1880). By this time, an intervention to halt the conflict had been mooted among the powers of

Europe, but the suggestion was effectively torpedoed by Bismarck. The United States, however, succeeded in arranging talks between the belligerents, aboard a cruiser off Arica, in October 1880. The conference broke down. The Chilean government, now in control of all the main nitrate-producing areas, would almost certainly have liked to make peace, but public opinion demanded the humiliation of Peru, in strident cries of 'On to Lima!' At the end of 1880 an army of more than 26,000 men, once again under Baquedano, disembarked on the central Peruvian coast. The extremely bloody battles of Chorrillos and Miraflores (January 1881) opened the gates of Lima. The war continued in the interior of Peru for two further years, with guerrilla forces resisting the army of occupation, but nothing could disguise the fact that Chile had won a total victory. A new Peruvian government eventually accepted, in the Treaty of Ancón (October 1883), most of the victor's stiff terms for peace. Tarapacá was ceded in perpetuity, and Chile was given temporary possession of Tacna and Arica – over which there developed a long diplomatic wrangle not finally resolved until 1929. The last Chilean soldiers left Peru in August 1884. A truce with Bolivia (April 1884) allowed Chile to remain in control of the Atacama until the negotiation of a full peace settlement, which only materialized in 1904.

Victory in the War of the Pacific gave Chile very substantial international prestige. For Chileans themselves there were the inevitable temptations to hubris, not entirely resisted. The optimism so seriously shattered by the crisis of the previous decade was swiftly recaptured, with the discovery that, as Vicuña Mackenna characteristically put it, 'in the Chilean soul, hidden beneath the soldier's rough tunic or coarse poncho of native weave, there throbs the sublime heroism of the age of antiquity'.[17] In every Chilean, it seemed, there was a soldier. With the conquest of the Bolivian littoral and the southern provinces of Peru, Chile enlarged her national territory by one-third. Possession of the nitrate fields meant that the country's wealth was enormously augmented overnight – and in the nick of time, given the apparent exhaustion of the sources of Chilean prosperity in the mid-1870s. As nitrate took over from copper and silver, the material progress undergone in the half-century or so before the war soon began to look modest in comparison with the boom of the 1880s. Such sudden national windfalls need to be carefully appraised and judiciously managed. For Chile, the model republic of Latin America, the victories of peace were, perhaps, to be less assured than those of war.

[17] Eugenio Orrego Vicuña, *Vicuña Mackenna, vida y trabajos*, 3rd edn (Santiago, 1951), 376.

# 8

---

## THE RIVER PLATE REPUBLICS

Argentina became independent in the second decade of the nineteenth century with few of the assets considered essential in a Latin American state. It had minerals but no mines, land but little labour, commerce but few commodities. The economy of Buenos Aires emerged from its colonial past not as a primary producer but as a pure entrepôt. The merchants of Buenos Aires made their profits not by exporting the products of the country but by importing consumer goods for a market stretching from the Atlantic to the Andes, in exchange for precious metals which had been produced or earned in Potosí. The city's rural hinterland was little developed. At the time of independence pastoral products accounted for only 20 per cent of the total exports of Buenos Aires; the other 80 per cent was silver. Until about 1815–20 land exploitation continued to be a secondary activity, and cattle estates were few in number and small in size. As for agriculture, it was confined to a few farms on the outskirts of towns, producing barely enough for the urban market.

Independence altered this primitive economy. First, the merchants of Buenos Aires were squeezed out by foreigners. With their superior resources, their capital, shipping and contacts in Europe, the British took over the entrepreneurial role previously filled by Spaniards. Unable to compete with the newcomers, local businessmen sought outlets in land and cattle. Then the province of Buenos Aires, hitherto a poor neighbour of richer cattle areas, profited from the misfortunes of its rivals. In the years after 1813 Santa Fe, Entre Ríos and Corrientes were devastated by wars of secession, while the other rich pastoral zone, the Banda Oriental, was ruined by revolution, counter-revolution and the Portuguese invasion of 1816. Buenos Aries took advantage of this opportunity, and those with capital found good returns in cattle ranching. Pasture began to expand at the expense of arable farming, the province increased its export of cattle products, and soon it came to rely upon imported grain. Finally, the trade of Buenos Aires with the interior diminished. This had always depended upon the interior's ability to earn silver from the sale of its products in the mining economies. But the competition of British imports depressed the rural and artisan industries of the interior at a time when war and secession were removing established markets in Chile and Upper Peru.

The conjuncture of British competition, the ravages of war and the decline of the interior rendered the traditional economy of Buenos Aires incapable of sustaining the ruling groups. They began, therefore, to diversify their interests, to acquire *estancias*, to establish a rural base. Land was plentiful, the soil was rich and deep, and there was normally a good supply of surface water on the pampas. The greatest danger lay on the frontier, and the frontier was uncomfortably close. The Pampa Indians, immediately to the south and west of the Río Salado, were the fiercest of all the Indians of the plains. Irredeemably savage, they lived and fought on horseback, a mobile and elusive enemy, handling the lance and the *bola* with supreme skill in their swift raids against settlements, *estancias*, personnel and property. The expansion of the *estancias* from 1815 was a disaster for the Indians. Settlers began to occupy their hunting grounds to the south of the Salado, and they retaliated by increasing their raids and enlarging their plunder. They were often joined by vagrant gauchos, deserters from the army, delinquents fleeing the justices of the peace, refugees from social or political conflicts; and their alliance was sometimes invoked in the civil wars of the time by one side or another. The new *estancieros* wanted law and order in the pampas and peace on the frontier. They also sought security of tenure.

From 1822 Bernardino Rivadavia, the modernizing minister in the provincial government of Martín Rodríguez, authorised the system of emphyteusis. Authority was given to rent public land (the sale of which was prohibited) to individuals and corporations for twenty years at fixed and extremely low rentals; the applicant simply had to measure and claim a chosen area. This simultaneously put land to productive use, especially the immense reserves of land on the expanding southern frontier, and satisfied the land hunger of prosperous families. The system favoured latifundism and land concentration. There was no limit to the area which the landowner might rent; he was then free to sell his rights and to sublet; and the commissions which determined land values and administered distribution were dominated by *estancieros*. From 1824 to 1827 a number of enormous grants were made, some individuals receiving over 10 square leagues each (66,710 acres). By 1828 almost 1,000 square leagues (over 6½ million acres) had been granted to 112 people and companies, of whom ten received more than 130,000 acres each. By the 1830s some 21 million acres of public land had been transferred to 500 individuals, many of them wealthy recruits from urban society, like the Anchorena, Santa Coloma, Alzaga and Sáenz Valiente families, the founders of Argentina's landed oligarchy.

As the pastoral economy entered a period of growth, expansion was extensive rather than intensive, for it was land, not capital, which was abundant, and there was as yet no technical innovation, no attempt to improve stock or modernize production. The number of cattle and the size of estates were all that counted. But there came a time when the pressure on grazing land and the shortage of further emphyteusis land brought the livestock sector to the limits of profitable expansion. Ranchers were pushing south once more into Indian territory in search of cheap and empty land. Government action was needed to occupy new territory and to protect it. While Rivadavia had been active in allocating land, he had done little for rural order or frontier security. Juan Manuel de Rosas, a pioneer on the southern frontier, owner of vast estates, lord of numerous peons, a militia commander who could parley with the Indians and frighten the politicians, and governor of Buenos Aires from 1829, stood for a policy of expansion and settlement and took a number of positive steps to improve the security of landholding. He organized and led the Desert Expedition of 1833 to the Río Colorado and the Río Negro, with the object of containing Indian aggression, expanding the frontier and imposing an enduring peace. His policy included diplomacy as well as force, presents as well as punishment. And it succeeded, adding to the province of Buenos Aires thousands of square miles, not desert, but land watered by great rivers. Rewards were instantaneous. The provincial government transferred large tracts of the new land to private hands in the years following 1833, especially to the senior officers of the expeditionary force itself. And as the settlers pushed southwards, they encroached once more on Indian hunting grounds. But now, in the 1840s, they were viewed by the Indians with more respect, partly because of the military reputation of Rosas, partly because of the policy of pacification by subsidy.

Rosas also introduced important and permanent modifications to the legal structure of landholding. There were three methods of land acquisition – rent, purchase and grant. Emphyteusis had now outlived its usefulness. It had facilitated land exploitation (and land concentration), but the state had profited hardly at all, for the rent was minimal. Rosas therefore decided to sell public land outright and to receive a specific revenue when he needed it. Laws of land sale in 1836–8 placed vast tracts of land on the open market. Most of it obviously went to the wealthy, the powerful, the favoured; and the names of the large purchasers were almost identical with those of the large tenants under emphyteusis, the Anchorena, Díaz Vélez, Alzaga and Arana. By 1840 3,436 square leagues (20,616,000 acres) of the province were in the possession of 293 people. Yet there was not a rush to buy land, and many would-be purchasers were deterred, either by economic recession, as during the French blockade of 1838–40, or by political insecurity. As an alternative to selling land, therefore, Rosas gave it away. Generous land grants were made to supporters of the regime, to the military who fought its wars or crushed its rebels, to bureaucrats and to favourites. Land became almost a currency and sometimes a wages and pensions fund. It was the ultimate source of patronage and, when confiscated, a terrible punishment.

By the 1840s the great plains of Buenos Aires were divided into well-stocked *estancias* and supported some 3 million head of cattle, the prime wealth of the province and the source of an export economy. They were animals of inferior grade, raised in the open range under the care of a few herdsmen; but they yielded hides and salt meat, and that was what the market demanded.

The *estancia* had to sell its products in Buenos Aires and beyond, but the infrastructure of the province was even more primitive than the estates which it served. This was a country without roads or bridges, and with tracks only on the main routes. Almost everything was done and supplied from horseback, and horses were as important a product of the *estancia* as cattle. Horses carried gauchos across the plains and armies into battle. Fishermen fished in the river on horseback; beggars even begged on horseback. But the chief method of freight transport were bullock carts, made in the workshops of Tucumán and led by hard-bitten drivers operating chiefly along the two high roads which traversed Argentina, one from Buenos Aires through San Luis and Mendoza to Chile, the other from Buenos Aires via Córdoba, Santiago, Tucumán, Salta and Jujuy to Bolivia. They travelled in trains of some fourteen carts, each drawn by six oxen with three spare, moving slowly across pampas and

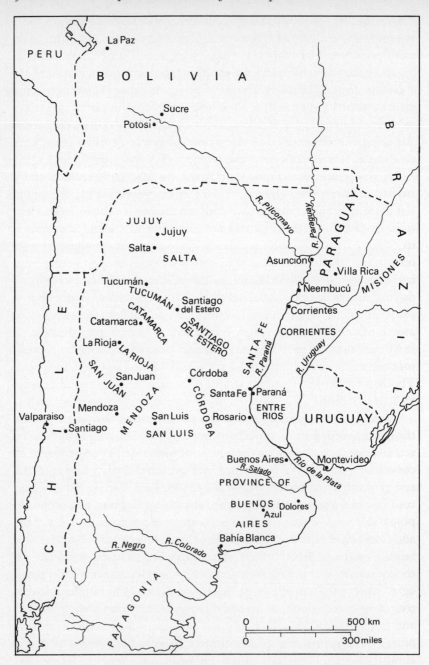

The River Plate Republics, 1820–70

hills in journeys of weeks and months. Freight charges were high, £20 a ton including provincial duties, and transport alone accounted for 40 or even 50 per cent of first cost. Cattle were much easier to move than goods, being driven rapidly by expert herdsmen from ranch to port.

The principal outlet of the *estancia* was the *saladero*. These were large establishments, where cattle were slaughtered, tallow extracted, flesh salted and dried and hides prepared for export. They opened in Buenos Aires in 1810, were closed in 1817 as the alleged cause of an urban meat shortage, but began to operate again from 1819 and to proliferate at the southern approaches to the city. By the mid-1820s there were about twenty *saladeros*; they now consumed more animals than the urban slaughter-houses, exporting their hides to Europe and their jerked beef to Brazil and Cuba. The *saladero* represented the only technical improvement in the livestock economy. By the 1840s, while the number of plants operating in and around Buenos Aires was still only twenty, their output had grown enormously and each slaughtered some 200 to 400 animals a day during the season. The *saladero* constituted a sizeable investment in plant, steaming apparatus and other equipment; most belonged to associations rather than to individuals, and many foreigners had capital in the industry. They were an integral part of the *estancia* system, managed by experts, supplied by ranchers, favoured by the government. The export of jerked beef rose from 113,404 quintals in 1835, to 198,046 in 1841, to 431,873 in 1851.

The state favoured cattle-breeders at the expense of small farmers, and the country depended ultimately on imported grain. In an age of capital scarcity, inferior technology and labour shortage, it was realistic to concentrate on pastoral farming, to realize the country's natural assets and to promote its most successful exports, even if it meant diverting resources from worthy though less profitable enterprises. The economic policy of Rivadavia was to subsidize immigration and rely on a fertile soil and market forces. But the agricultural colonization schemes of the 1820s failed through lack of capital, organization and security, in contrast to the great *estancia* expansion with its own internal dynamism. In any case agriculture was subject to particular obstacles and required special treatment. Labour was scarce and expensive, methods were primitive, and yield was low. The high cost of transport forced farmers to move nearer to cities where land prices were higher; and there was always competition from foreign grain. So agriculture needed capital and protection: at this point governments hesitated, fearful of causing dearer food and losing popular support. From independence to 1825 a low-tariff policy prevailed, in favour of consumer and export interests, and in spite of farmers' complaints. But farmers were not the only critics of free trade.

The littoral provinces and those of the interior differed from Buenos Aires in a number of ways. In the first place they were less prosperous. The wars of independence and the subsequent civil wars damaged the economies of the littoral provinces – Santa Fe, Entre Ríos and Corrientes – and retarded their development. When at last they began to recover, they found Buenos Aires dominant, resolved to monoplize trade and navigation – and the customs revenue therefrom – and to dictate a policy of free trade. The negotiations for a federal pact between the provinces, therefore, were marked by bitter debates over economic policy. In the course of 1830 Pedro Ferré, representative of Corrientes and leader of the protectionist movement in the littoral, demanded not only nationaliza-tion of the customs revenue and free navigation of the rivers, but also a revision of the tariff policies of Buenos Aires. José María Rojas y Patrón, the Buenos Aires delegate, argued in reply that protection hurt the consumer without really helping the producer; if domestic industries were not competitive, nor capable of suppling the nation's needs, no amount of protection could save them. The pastoral economy depended upon cheap land, cheap money and a constant demand for hides in foreign markets. Protection would raise prices, raise costs and damage the export trade; then the mass of the people would suffer, for the sake of a small minority outside the cattle economy. Ferré rejected these argu-ments, denounced free competition, demanded protection for native industries against more cheaply produced foreign goods and called also for the opening of other ports than Buenos Aires to direct foreign trade, thus cutting distances and transport costs for the provinces. Only in this way would the littoral and the interior develop their economies, save existing investments and reduce unemployment. Buenos Aires refused to yield and the Pact of the Littoral (1831) was concluded without Corrien-tes, though it subsequently adhered to it. The fact that Corrientes took the lead in demanding protection was not a coincidence. In addition to cattle ranches it had a vital agricultural sector producing cotton, tobacco and other subtropical products, the expansion of which needed protec-tion against Paraguayan and still more Brazilian competition. But during the first government of Rosas (1829–32) fiscal policy was designed primarily to serve the cattle industry of Buenos Aires. The changes proposed in 1831 – reduced tax on salt and on transport of cattle to the city – were only meant to protect the *saladero* industry, which claimed that it was suffering from competition from Montevideo and Rio Grande do Sul. In 1833 duties on the export of hides were reduced, and the tax on salt carried in national vessels from southern provinces was abolished. But *porteño* farming, the products of the littoral and the industries of the interior, these did not receive special treatment.

The economy of the interior – the mid-west and the west – was isolated to some degree from the direct impact of independence and suffered less than the littoral from civil wars and devastation. For a few years, it is true, the north-west frontier was a war zone, and the traditional links with the markets of Upper Peru and Chile were temporarily broken. But from 1817 the Chilean economy began to function again, stimulated now by a more active overseas trade. The Argentine west was re-incorporated into the trans-Andean market, exporting mules to the mining zone, cattle to the *saladeros* and the consumers of the towns, together with other Andean products such as fruits and wines. These outlets were opportune, for after independence the competition of European wines virtually closed the east-coast market to those of Mendoza. Salta was little more than a subsistence economy, though it still fattened mules for export outside the province. Tucumán continued to produce rice and tobacco, and to manufacture sugar, aguardiente and tanned leather. But the province was a high-cost producer and situated too far from its markets to compete, for example, with Brazilian sugar. The Andean mines, too, were outside the economy. La Rioja's gold, silver, copper and iron, San Juan's gold, silver and lead, Mendoza's gold, all were dormant assets. Rivadavia's dream of mining development through British capital was never realized. Their utter remoteness, great scarcity of labour, deficient technology and almost complete lack of transport to the coast made Argentine mines too high in cost and low in yield to warrant investment. The 'industries of the interior', therefore, consisted of little more than textiles, wine and grain, none of which, in the opinion of Buenos Aires, were worth protecting.

Yet there was a protectionist interest in Buenos Aires, sometimes voiced in the assembly, sometimes expressed in public debate, which demanded measures to safeguard national industry as well as agriculture. These opinions reflected variously the anxiety of certain manufacturing enterprises, a latent but powerful resentment of foreigners, and a kind of grass-roots federalism; but representing as they did diverse minorities and interest groups rather than a broad united front, they hardly amounted to economic nationalism. Buenos Aires had a small industrial sector consisting of textile manufacturers, silversmiths, harness-makers and blacksmiths. They supplied local and lower-class needs, and sometimes the demands of the state; indeed war kept many of them in business, for it brought orders for uniforms, equipment and hardware. In 1831 Buenos Aires contained 94 leather workshops, 83 carpenters' workshops, 47 forges and iron-works and 42 silversmiths. These were mainly artisan industries but the beginnings of a factory system could be seen, some manufacturers employing a number of workers in one place, with specialization and use of machinery; this applied to textiles, hat-making, furniture and a few other activities. Few of these enterprises could compete in price and quality with foreign imports, and they constantly pressed for state intervention in their favour. In January 1836, for example, the shoe-makers of Buenos Aires petitioned the government to prohibit the import of foreign shoes, on the grounds that they could not compete with foreign manufacturers, whose low production costs, cheaper raw materials, abundant labour and modern machinery gave them an overwhelming advantage. The *estancieros*, on the other hand, including Rosas and the Anchorena, preferred free trade to protection on grounds of economic interest and in favour of the export-orientated livestock sector. They were supported by those who opposed state intervention on principle and argued that industry would only flourish when it was qualified to do so, that national manufactures which could not compete in price and quality with foreign imports were not worth protecting. The historian and journalist, Pedro de Angelis, one of the more enlightened spokesmen for the Rosas regime, strongly attacked the idea of giving protection to the provincial wine industry and the *porteño* shoe industry, on the grounds that protection would raise prices for the mass of consumers, and divert to industry labourers who would be better employed in the agrarian sector.

Nevertheless, concern for the adverse balance of payments was sufficient to keep the protectionist lobby alive, and in due course Rosas heeded the case for intervention. In the Customs Law of December 1835 he introduced higher import duties. From a basic import duty of 17 per cent, the tariff moved upwards, giving greater protection to more vulnerable products, until it reached a point of prohibiting the import of a large number of articles such as textiles, hardware and, depending on the domestic price, wheat. Rosas thus sought to give positive assistance to arable agriculture and the manufacturing industries.

Why did he do it? Did he really believe that Argentina could become more self-sufficient in industry? Was he convinced that his regime could decrease its dependence on foreign imports, resist foreign competition, and tolerate the higher living costs? Or did he act under political constraint, a need to widen the social base of his regime? There appeared to be no reason why, in 1835–6, Rosas required the support of popular or middle groups. The regime was based firmly on the *estancieros*, who remained the dominant interest in the province and the closest allies of the government. The objectives of Rosas seem to have been to sustain the existing economic structure, while protecting those minority groups who suffered most from it. The tariff of 1835, therefore, was designed to relieve distress in the industrial and farming sectors, without subverting the livestock export economy. At the same time the law had a strong inter-provincial content; it was intended to make the federalist policy credible by giving protection to the provinces as well as to Buenos Aires.

In the event national industries, *porteño* as well as provincial, failed to respond to the protection given by the customs law and the French blockade. Even under the most favourable conditions, when they could take advantage of rising scarcity prices, local manufactures proved unable to satisfy the needs of the country. If existing industries failed to expand, there was little incentive to risk scarce capital in new enterprises. The government could not afford to continue placing undue burdens on consumers, and Rosas began to have second thoughts about protection. In 1838 import duties were reduced by one-third to minimize the effects of the French blockade (see below). Then, claiming the need to procure new revenues and pointing to the shortage of certain articles, Rosas decided (31 December 1841) to allow the entry of a large list of goods previously prohibited. The argument for free trade had been proved correct: national production had not been able to take advantage of protection, the tariff had merely caused shortages and high prices, and the principal victims were the consumers and the treasury. Rosas himself appears to have lost faith in protection, which meant in effect giving artificial respiration to the weakest sector of the economy, while strangling the stronger. Very few people would have thanked him for that. Industry therefore remained on the margin of economic life confined to workshops and artisans. When the Englishman Charles Mansfield visited the River Plate in 1852–3, he travelled like a walking advertisement for British goods: his white cotton poncho, bought in Corrientes, was made in Manchester; his electro-plated spurs, bought in Buenos Aires, were made in Birmingham. The bias towards an agropecuarian economy reflected the social structure as well as economic conditions. The upper groups preferred imported manufactures, while the rest of the population did not form a consumer market for a national industry. There were few freedoms in Buenos Aires under Rosas, but free trade was one of them.

Buenos Aires lived by foreign trade, and its expanding *estancias* depended on foreign markets. In the early years after independence there was a sizeable trade gap, as exports of precious metals fell and imports of consumer goods rose, and it took two decades for livestock exports to redress the balance. In 1829 and 1832 there was still a large excess of imports over exports, and the difference had to be met by exporting specie. The result was a shortage of currency at home and its replacement by ever larger issues of paper money. The medium of international trade was letters of credit drawn on the London exchange, and British merchants came to dominate the financial market of Buenos Aires. The essential link was the trade in textiles from Britain against hides from Argentina, a trade which underwent steady if unspectacular growth, except during the years of blockade, in 1838–9 and 1845–6, when it suffered a sharp drop. From 1822 to 1837 exports from Buenos Aires rose in value from about £700,000 to £1 million; from 1837 to 1851 they doubled in value to £2 million a year. Hides formed the bulk of these exports. There was an average annual export of 798,564 cattle hides from Buenos Aires in the 1830s; 2,303,910 in the 1840s. In 1836 hides amounted to 68.4 per cent of the total value of exports from Buenos Aires; in 1851 they amounted to 64.9 per cent. If jerked beef and other cattle products are added to hides, then the livestock industry contributed 82.8 per cent of total exports in 1836, 78 per cent in 1851. The basic cause of export growth was the incorporation of more land into the economy, especially the expansion of the southern frontier after the Desert Campaign of 1833; the province of Buenos Aires now produced about two-thirds of all hides exported from the littoral provinces. A secondary cause was the blockade of Buenos Aires by foreign powers, which helped to increase the cattle stock by temporarily stopping shipment of hides, thus leaving the cattle to multiply in the pampas.

Meanwhile imports into Buenos Aires rose from a total of £1.5 million in 1825 to £2.1 million in 1850, an increase which was probably even greater in quantity than in value, owing to the falling price of manufactured goods in Europe. There was very little saving or capital accumulation. Imports of luxury and consumer goods used up any surplus capital which might otherwise have been invested. Pianos, clocks, jewelry and precious stones comprised 10 per cent of imports. Consumer goods of a luxury kind – furniture and hardware, clothes and shoes – for the quality market amounted to 32 per cent. Thus almost half of the imports were manufactured goods for the upper end of the market. Industrial raw materials such as coal, iron and other metals accounted for only 3 per cent of imports, an indication of the small degree of industrialization, the absence of technology and the low level of artisan employment.

Argentina was already developing close economic ties with Britain. In the early years of the republic British shippers carried 60 per cent of the trade in and out of Buenos Aires; by mid-century, with competition growing, British shipping in Buenos Aires was 25 per cent of the total. Most of the trade went to Britain (322 vessels and 22.8 per cent of tonnage in 1849–51) and the United States (253 vessels and 21.6 per cent), though this still left a substantial portion of trade (33 per cent) to less developed countries, Cuba, Brazil, Italy and Spain. The value of British trade to Argentina did not rise spectacularly in the first half of the nineteenth century. The average annual exports in the period 1822–5 were between £700,000 and £800,000 sterling. In 1850 the value of British exports to Argentina was still about £900,000. Yet in spite of the growing competition, the value of British trade to the River Plate up to 1837 exceeded that of all foreign countries put together; and even in 1850 it was not far short of this. Argentina relied upon British manufactures, British shipping, British markets, but it did not yet need – could not yet use – British capital and technology, it made its own economic decisions, and its independence was never in doubt. And by mid-century it was already moving towards a better balance of trade as the British market consumed more of its raw materials.

The structure of society was simple and its scale was small. Argentina, a land full of cattle, was empty of people, and its one million square miles of territory contained in 1820 a population about one-third that of contemporary London. Yet Argentina underwent steady demographic growth in the half-century after independence, from 507,951 inhabitants in 1816, to 570,000 in 1825, 1,180,000 in 1857 and 1,736,923 in 1869. In the thirty-two years from 1825 to 1857 the population roughly doubled itself. Growth was due essentially to a fall in the mortality rate: at a time when economic conditions were improving, there was no major epidemic, and the great outbreaks of cholera and yellow fever were yet to come. There was only moderate immigration in this period, though a number of Basques, Canarians, French, Italians and British entered Buenos Aires in the 1840s, once the blockades were over. The greatest population upswing was registered in the littoral provinces, which increased their share of the total from 36 per cent in 1800 to 48.8 per cent in 1869. Buenos Aires and Córdoba had over one-third of the total. Buenos Aires was an insanitary and pestilential city, without amenities, without drainage, without even a pure water supply. But it grew in numbers from 55,416 in 1822 to 177,787 in 1869, while the total of city and province combined grew from 118,646 to 495,107 in the same period.

Society was rooted in land. It was the large *estancia* which conferred status and imposed subordination. *Estancieros* or their clients dominated the administration, the house of representatives, local government and the militia. The polarization of society was absolute. There was an upper class of landowners and their associates, and a lower class comprising the rest of the population. Some social margins, it is true, were blurred. Commerce was economically important and socially respectable, and it provided the original fortunes of some of the leading families of Argentina such as the Anchorena, the Alzaga and the Santa Coloma. But the urban elite of the early nineteenth century did not acquire a separate identity or become an independent middle class. Faced with insistent British competition in the years after independence, local businessmen began to divert their capital into land and without abandoning their urban occupations to become *estancieros* and identify themselves with a new aristocracy. Meanwhile there were no others to fill the middle ranks. The entrepreneurial function came to be exercised by foreigners: British businessmen soon dominated commercial activities, while European immigrants went into artisan occupations, supplementing the roles of local craftsmen. But whereas socially the creole merchants moved upwards into the landed aristocracy, the artisans and manufacturers merged unmistakably into the lower sectors, branded by their manual occupations which were often filled by coloured people.

If there was little prospect of a native middle sector in the towns, there was even less likelihood of finding one in the countryside, where a great gulf separated the landed proprietor from the landless peon. The homogeneity of the landed class was not absolute. While some *estancieros* were owners of truly immense properties, others possessed relatively modest estates. The former were often capitalists of urban origin with some education and aspirations to higher standards of living. The latter were more likely to come from generations of country dwellers and were little removed in culture from the gauchos around them, illiterate, indifferent to material comforts and investing nothing in improvement. Yet, in spite of differences of income, culture and social style, the *estancieros* were as one compared with the peons on their estates and the gauchos of the pampas. There was strong group cohesion and solidarity among the landed class. Rosas himself was the centre of a vast kinship group based on land. He was surrounded by a closely-knit economic and political network, linking deputies, law officers, officials and military, who were also landowners and related among themselves or with their leader. Rosas used his extensive patronage to bind this small oligarchy ever closer. The Anchorena in particular were able to extend their urban and rural properties with his direct assistance, making a profit from their alleged services to the state.

At the end of the colonial period the pampas were inhabited by wild cattle, indomitable Indians and untamed gauchos. The gaucho was a product of race mixture; the components have been disputed, but there is no doubt that there were three races in the littoral, Indians, whites and blacks. By simple definition the gaucho was a free man on horseback. But the term was used by contemporaries and by later historians in a wide sense to mean rural people in general. Greater precision would distinguish between the sedentary rural dwellers working on the land for themselves or for a *patrón* and the pure gaucho, who was nomadic and independent, tied to no estate. And further refinement of terms would identify the *gaucho malo*, who lived by violence and near-delinquency and whom the state regarded as a criminal. Whether good or bad, the classical gaucho asserted his freedom from all formal institutions; he was indifferent to government and its agents, indifferent to religion and the Church. He did not seek land; he lived by hunting, gambling and fighting. The nomadism of the gaucho had many social implications. It prevented settled work or occupation. Property, industry, habitation, these were alien concepts. So too was the gaucho family. The upper sector enjoyed great family stability and drew strength from the ties of kinship. The lower sector was much weaker institutionally. This was partly an urban-rural division between two cultures; it was also a feature of the social structure. Among the gauchos and peons unions were temporary and the resulting families were only loosely joined together. Marriage was the exception, and it was the unmarried mother who formed the nucleus of the rural family, for she was the only permanent parent. Even if the father was not prone to gaucho nomadism, he had to sell his labour where he could, or else he was recruited into armies or *montoneros*.

The ruling groups in the countryside had traditionally imposed a system of coercion upon people whom they regarded as *mozos vagos y mal entretenidos*, vagrants without employer or occupation, idlers who sat in groups singing to a guitar, drinking *mate* or liquor, gambling, but apparently not working. This class was seen as a potential labour force and it was subject to many constraints by the landed proprietors – punitive expeditions, imprisonment, conscription to the Indian frontier, corporal punishment and other penalties. Legislation sought to brand *vagos y mal entretenidos* as a criminal class by definition and vagrancy itself as a crime. Applied stringently by the justices of the peace, anti-vagrancy laws were designed to impose order and discipline in the countryside, to provide a labour pool for *hacendados* and to produce conscripts for the army. The militia became in effect an open prison, into which the most miserable part of the rural population was forcibly herded. For the gaucho the years after independence were even harsher than before. Property concentration prevented the mass of the people from acquiring land, while *estancia* expansion raised the demand for labour. During the colonial period the existence of common usages in the pampas gave the gaucho access to wild cattle on the open range. But these traditional practices came to an end when *estancias* were implanted and endowed, private property spread across the plains, and cattle was appropriated by landowners. Republican laws, those of Rivadavia as well as of Rosas, attacked vagrancy and mobilized the rural population. People were forced to carry identity cards and certificates of employment; a peon caught out of his *estancia* without permission would be conscripted into the army or assigned to public works. Thus, the gaucho was forcibly converted from a free nomad into a hired ranch-hand, a *peón de estancia*.

This primitive society was not qualified for constitutional government or political participation. The *estancia* dominated economic and social life and became the model of government. *Estancieros* ruled their domains by personal authority and demanded unqualified obedience. They were a powerful and cohesive class, unrivalled by any other. Argentina did not yet possess a middle sector of commerce or industry, and there was no great concentration of peasants. The popular classes, superior in numbers, were heterogeneous in composition and divided into disparate groups, peons on *estancias*, wage labourers, small farmers or tenants, marginal gauchos and delinquents. The subordinate condition of the lower sectors, their poor expectations and their isolation in the immense plains, combined to prevent the formation of an autonomous political movement from below. On the other hand they were ideal material for military mobilization and they were easily transformed into *montoneros*, the guerrilla forces of the plains. The causes for which they fought were not class conflicts: they were sectional struggles within the upper groups, disputes between landed proprietors or among leading families, attacks upon the existing government, or clashes with neigh-bouring provinces. In a situation of equilibrium between factions, leaders would call on their dependants and round up their reserves of manpower the better to tip the balance against their enemies. The use of popular forces, however, did not imply popular objectives. The *estancia* could mobilize its peons either for work or for war, and a regional chieftain in turn could call upon his client *estancieros*. These struggles within the oligarchy, moreover, occurred in peculiar demographic conditions, where a relatively small population was spread thinly across the plains. While ties of kinship at the top of society were close, communications between members of the popular classes, especially in the countryside, were meagre, partly because of the great distances separating rural communities, partly because peons were tied to their estates and immobilized by the rules of the *estancia*. The masses, there-fore, were ordered, recruited, manipulated, but not politicized. How was it done?

The relation of patron and client, this was the essential link. The landowner wanted labour, loyalty and service in peace and war. The peon wanted subsistence and security. The *estanciero*, therefore, was a protector, possessor of sufficient power to defend his dependants against marauding Indians, recruiting sergeants and rival hordes. He was also a provider, who developed and defended local resources and could give employment, food and shelter. By supplying what was needed and exploiting what was offered, a *hacendado* recruited a *peonada*. This primi-tive political structure, founded on individual power, raised upon personal loyalties, cemented by the authority of the patron and the dependence of the peon, was finally built into the state and became the model of *caudillismo*. For individual alliances were magnified into a social pyramid, as patrons in turn became clients to more powerful men, until the peak of power was reached and they all became clients of a super-patron. Thus, from his rural base a local caudillo, supported by his client *estancieros* and their dependents, might conquer the state, for himself, his family, his region. Then, as representative of a group, or a class, or a province, he would reproduce the personalism and patronage in which he had been nurtured and by which he had been raised. *Caudillismo* was the image of society, and the caudillos were its creatures.

The caudillo was first a warrior, a man qualified to lead and defend; during wars of liberation, civil wars, national wars, the caudillo was the strong man who could recruit troops, command resources, protect his people. The union of military power and personal authority was inherent in the caudillo. He responded, however, not only to military needs but also to civilian pressures. He was often the agent of an extended family, who constituted in effect a ruling dynasty; he was sometimes the representative of regional economic interests, which needed a defender against other regions or against the centre; and he was occasionally the man who succeeded in making a particular interest – the export-oriented *estancia*, for example – into a national one. With the resources of the state at his disposal, the caudillo then emerged as a distributor of patronage, allocating spoils to his clientage and earning yet further service from them; for in granting office and land, the caudillo, the super-patron, redeemed his promises to his followers and kept them in a state of political peonage.

The origins and the careers of the Argentine caudillos conformed to these prototypes. They came, in the majority of cases, from families which had been wealthy and powerful since colonial times, most of them owners of landed property, and many of them holders of military appointments. The caudillos themselves preserved this inheritance. Among the eighteen caudillos who ruled in the various provinces of Argentina between 1810 and 1870, thirteen were great landowers, one had landed property of medium size, one was the owner of a shipyard. They all held military appointments, either in the army or in the militia; and of the twelve who had been old enough to fight in the wars of independence, nine had done so. Wealth was an intrinsic qualification. Fifteen of the group were extremely wealthy, two were of medium wealth. Virtually all had some level of education. Political expectations were not good; nine died violently, three in exile. There was little evidence of social mobility in these careers. No doubt the revolution for independence allowed the creoles greater access to politics, the bureaucracy and commerce; but social structure based upon land, wealth, prestige and education remained essentially unchanged. According to the criterion of wealth, only two of the eighteen caudillos (Estanislao

López and Félix Aldao) showed any signs of moving upwards, from medium to great wealth. The rest followed the traditions of their family in wealth and prestige, and simply added to their patrimony. The occupational route they followed had familiar signposts, from *estanciero*, via the military, to caudillo.

The year 1820 was a year of anarchy. Independence from Spain had culminated not in national unity but in universal dismemberment. After a decade of conflict between Buenos Aires and the provinces, between central government and regional interests, between unitarians and federalists, the framework of political organization in the Río de la Plata collapsed. Independent republics proliferated throughout the interior, and when Buenos Aires sought to subdue them they fought back. Provincial caudillos – Estanislao López of Santa Fe, Francisco Ramírez of Entre Ríos – led their irregular gaucho hordes, the fearsome *montoneros*, against the capital. On 1 February 1820 they defeated the forces of Buenos Aires at the battle of Cepeda and proceeded to destroy all trace of central authority. Only the provincial government of Buenos Aires survived, and this too was harassed into anarchy, while persons and property lay at the mercy of petty caudillos, gauchos and Indians. Buenos Aires looked for protection to the countryside. While two of its leaders, Martín Rodríguez and Manuel Dorrego, desperately stemmed the tide, the *estancieros* of the south were asked to come to the rescue with their rural militias. They responded promptly, not least Rosas, appreciating the danger to their own interests from the seeping anarchy of the times. It was with the backing of the *estancieros* that Rodríguez was elected governor in September 1820 and made a negotiated peace with the caudillos.

The inspiration behind the Rodríguez administration was its chief minister, Bernardino Rivadavia, educated, liberal and bureaucratic. Rivadavia wanted to modernize Argentina. He sought economic growth through free trade, foreign investment and immigration. He applied the system of emphyteusis, the renting out of state land, to put the natural resources of Argentina to productive use. He had a vision of liberal institutions and a new infrastructure, in which the framework of modernization would be enlarged to comprise a great and unified Argentina, undivided by political and economic particularism. This was Rivadavia's plan, enlightened, developmental and unitarian. In truth it was more of a dream than a plan: some of its ideas were impractical, others were ahead of their time. But the entire model was rejected as irrelevant by Rosas and his associates, who represented a more primitive economy – cattle production for export of hides and salt meat – but one which brought immediate returns and was in harmony with the country's traditions. They were alarmed by the innovations of the new regime. On 7 February 1826 Rivadavia was appointed president of the United Provinces of the Río de la Plata; he had a unitary constitution and innumerable ideas. In March the city of Buenos Aires was declared capital of the nation and federalized. On 12 September Rivadavia sent to congress his proposal to divide the non-federalized part of the province of Buenos Aires into two, the Provincia del Paraná in the north and the Provincia del Salado in the south. These measures went to the heart of *estanciero* interests. The federalization of the city of Buenos Aires and its environs amputated the best part of the province and a large section of its population. It also involved nationalizing the revenues of the port, which amounted to 75 per cent of the provincial government's income, arousing the fear that the next step would be to raise alternative revenue by an income or land tax. To the world of the landowners, for whom Buenos Aires and its hinterland, port and province were one, these measures threatened division and disaster.

The policy of Rivadavia struck at too many interest groups to succeed. His immediate political opponents, the federalists, rejected unitary policy as undemocratic and, influenced by United States federalism, sought a federal solution to the problem of national organization. The *estancieros* saw Rivadavia as a danger to their economic and fiscal assets, an intellectual who neglected rural security and, while promoting urban progress of a European kind, allowed the savage Indians to roam the plains. Immigration they opposed as expensive, unnecessary and probably subversive, bringing competition for land and labour and raising the cost of both. The anti-clerical policy of the regime, designed primarily to curtail the temporal power of the Church, to extend religious freedom, and to bring Argentina into conformity with foreign expectations, was anathema not only to the clergy but to all those with conservative values, and served to unite federalists, *estancieros* and priests under the banner of *religión o muerte*. Rosas and the Anchorena took the lead in organizing resistance to Rivadavia's plans. Until now Rosas had not belonged to the federal party or associated with its leader Manuel Dorrego. But in the latter half of 1826, at the head of a network of friends, relations and clients, he allied himself to the party which he was eventually to absorb and destroy. He joined the federalists not for reasons of political ideology, which he did not possess, but because unitary policy threatened his plans of hegemony in the countryside.

Rivadavia yielded to the combined forces of his opponents and resigned from the presidency on 27 June 1827. In the ultimate analysis he did not have a constituency: he represented intellectuals, bureaucrats and professional politicians, groups which did not form an identifiable social sector. Rosas on the other hand had a specific power base, the *estancieros*, who possessed the principal resources of the country and considerable paramilitary force. But Rosas did not rule. It was the real federalists who came to power and Manuel Dorrego was elected governor on 12 August 1827. Dorrego's popularity, his independence and his refusal to take advice alerted Rosas and his friends: previous experience showed the danger of divergence between those who ruled in the *estancias* and those who governed in Buenos Aires. In the event Dorrego was overthrown, on 1 December 1828, not by his enemies within but by the unitarians from without, when General Juan Lavalle led a coalition of military returned from the war with Brazil, professional politicians, merchants and intellectuals. The December revolution was made in the name of liberal principles, against rural conservatism, caudillism and provincialism, and it was an attempt to restore the system of Rivadavia. But Lavalle gave a bonus to his enemies when he ordered the execution of Dorrego, a man of peace and moderation. This savage sentence caused revulsion in all sectors, especially among the populace. It branded the unitarians as political assassins and aggravated the anarchy of the times. It also left the way open for Rosas to lead the federal party. Backed by his *estanciero* allies and his rural hordes, Rosas reconquered power from Lavalle and the unitarians and was elected governor by a grateful assembly on 6 December 1829. It was no ordinary election, for the new governor was given dictatorial powers and a mandate to restore order.

The hegemony of Rosas, how can it be explained? He was in part a creature of circumstances. He represented the rise to power of a new economic interest, the *estancieros*. The classic elite of the revolution of 1810 were the merchants and bureaucrats. The struggle for independence created a group of career revolutionaries – professional politicians, state officials, a new military, men who lived by service to and income from the state. The merchants of Buenos Aires, emerging from the colony as the leading economic interest, were at first powerful allies of the new elite. From about 1820, however, many merchant families began to seek other outlets and to invest in land, cattle and meat-salting plants. These were the dominant social group of the future, a landowning oligarchy with roots in commerce and recruited from urban society. For the moment, however, they did not possess the executive power in the state, and the fact remained that those with economic power did not rule and those who ruled lacked an economic base. Inevitably the landowners began to seek direct political control. In defeating Rivadavia and Lavalle in 1827–9, they overthrew not only the unitarians but the existing ruling class, the career politicians, and took possession of the government through Rosas.

Conditions, therefore, created Rosas. He was the individual synthesis of the society and economy of the countryside, and when the interests of this sector coincided with those of the urban federalists, Rosas was at once the representative and the executive of the alliance. But he also had specific qualifications: his origins, career and control over events all made him a power in the land before he was even elected governor and narrowed the choice open to the *estancieros*. His personal career was unique and did not conform exactly to the model of merchant turned landowner which characterized so many of his supporters. He began on the *estancia*, learned the business from the working end, accumulated capital in the rural sector itself and advanced from there. He was a pioneer in the expansion of landowning and cattle-raising, starting some years before the big push southwards from 1820. He was a working, not an absentee, landlord, operating at every stage of cattle raising. Thus, he came into direct contact with the gauchos, delinquents, Indians and other denizens of the pampas, partly to hire them for his estates, partly to mobilize them for his militia. For Rosas was militia commander as well as *estanciero*, and he had more military experience than any of his peers. In the recruitment of troops, the training and control of militia, and the deployment of units not only on the frontier but in urban operations, he had no equal. It was the military dimension of Rosas's early career which gave him the edge over his rivals. This culminated in his role during the guerrilla war of 1829, when he raised, controlled and led anarchic popular forces in the irregular army which defeated Lavalle's professionals. Rosas, then, was a self-made caudillo.

Rosas divided society into those who commanded and those who obeyed. Order obsessed him, and the virtue which he most admired in a people was subordination. If there was anything more abhorrent to

Rosas than democracy, it was liberalism. The reason why he detested unitarians was not that they wanted a united Argentina but that they were liberals who believed in secular values of humanism and progress. He identified them with freemasons and intellectuals, subversives who undermined order and tradition and whom he held ultimately responsible for the political assassinations which brutalized Argentine public life from 1828 to 1835. The constitutional doctrines of the two parties did not interest him, and he was never a true federalist. He thought and ruled as a centralist, and he stood for the hegemony of Buenos Aires. Rosas destroyed the traditional division between federalists and unitarians and made these categories virtually meaningless. He substituted *rosismo* and anti-*rosismo*.

What was *rosismo*? Its power base was the *estancia*, a focus of economic resources and a system of social control. The domination of the economy by the *estancia* was continued and completed under Rosas. At the beginning of his regime much of the territory which eventually constituted the province of Buenos Aires was still controlled by Indians. And even within the frontier, north of the Salado, there were large areas unoccupied by whites. Rosas stood for a policy of territorial settlement and expansion. The Desert Campaign of 1833 added thousands of square miles south of the Río Negro to the province of Buenos Aires, together with new resources, new security and the confidence born of a great victory over the Indians. The land to the south, and the unoccupied or emphyteusis land in the north, gave the state a vast reserve of property which it could sell or give away. Rosas himself was one of the principal beneficiaries of this prodigious distribution. The law of 6 June 1834 granted him the freehold of the island of Choele-Choel in recognition of his leadership in the Desert Campaign. He was allowed to exchange this for sixty square leagues of public land wherever he chose. His followers were also rewarded. The law of 30 September 1834 made land grants up to a maximum of 50 square leagues altogether to officers who had participated in the Desert Campaign; while a law of 25 April 1835 granted land up to 16 square leagues for allocation to soldiers of the Andes Division in the same campaign. The military who took part in crushing the rebellion of the south in 1839 were rewarded by a land grant of 9 November 1839; generals received 6 square leagues, colonels 5, noncommissioned officers half a league, and privates a quarter of a league. Civilians too were recompensed for their loyalty.

The *boletos de premios en tierras*, or land certificates as rewards for military service, were one of the principal instruments of land distribution; 8,500 were issued by the government of Rosas, though not all were used by the recipients. No doubt this was a means by which an impecunious government paid salaries, grants and pensions to its servants. But there was also a political element present, for land was the richest source of patronage available, a weapon for Rosas, a welfare system for his supporters. Rosas was the great *patrón* and the *estancieros* were his *clientela*. In this sense *rosismo* was less an ideology than an interest group and a fairly exclusive one. For there was no sector outside the *estancieros* equipped to use these grants. Certificates of less than one league were virtually useless in the hands of soldiers or minor bureaucrats, when the existing agrarian structure averaged eight leagues per estate. But in the hands of those who already possessed estates or had the capital to buy them up cheaply, they were a powerful instrument for land concentration. More than 90 per cent of land certificates granted to soldiers and civilians ended up in the hands of landowners or those who were buying their way into land.

The trend of the Rosas regime, therefore, was towards greater concentration of property in the hands of a small group. In 1830 980 landowners held the 5,516 square leagues of occupied land in Buenos Aires province; of these, 60 proprietors monopolized almost 4,000 square leagues, or 76 per cent. In the period 1830–52 occupied land grew to 6,100 square leagues, with 782 proprietors. Of these 382 proprietors held 82 per cent of holdings above one square league, while 200 proprietors, or 28 per cent, held 60 per cent of holdings above ten square leagues. There were 74 holdings of over 15 square leagues (90,000 acres), and 42 holdings of over 20 square leagues (120,000 acres). Meanwhile small holdings accounted for only one per cent of the land in use. Among the eighty or so people who were members of the House of Representatives between 1835 and 1852, 60 per cent were landowners or had occupations connected with land. This was the assembly which voted Rosas into power and continued to vote for him. To some degree they could control policy making. They consistently denied Rosas permission to increase the *contribución directa*, a tax on capital and property, and they always prevented him from raising any revenue at the expense of the *estancieros*. In 1850, when total revenues reached 62 million pesos, chiefly from customs, the *contribución directa* provided only 3 per cent of the total, and most of this portion was paid by commerce rather than land. The administration too was dominated by landowners. Juan N. Terrero, economic adviser of Rosas, had 42 square leagues and left a fortune of 53 million pesos. Angel Pacheco, Rosas's principal general, had 75 square leagues. Felipe Arana, minister of foreign affairs, possessed 42 square leagues. Even Vicente López, poet, deputy and president of the high court, owned 12 square leagues. But the greatest landowners of the province were the Anchorena, cousins of Rosas and his closest political advisers; their various possessions totalled 306 square leagues (1,856,000 acres). As for Rosas himself, in 1830 in the group of about seventeen landowners with property over 50 square leagues (300,000 acres), he occupied tenth place with 70 square leagues (420,000 acres). By 1852, according to the official estimate of his property, he had accumulated 136 square leagues (816,000 acres).

The *estancia* gave Rosas the sinews of war, the alliance of fellow *estancieros* and the means of recruiting an army of peons, gauchos and vagrants. He had an instinct for manipulating the discontents of the masses and turning them against his enemies in such a way that they did not damage the basic structure of society. While Rosas identified culturally with the gauchos, he did not unite with them socially, or represent them politically. The core of his forces were his own peons and dependants, who were his servants rather than his supporters, his clients rather than his allies. When Rosas needed to make a critical push, in 1829, 1833 or 1835, he enlisted the gauchos in the countryside and the mob in the city. They were the only manpower available, and for the moment they had a value outside of the *estancia*. But the normal agrarian regime was very different: employment was obligatory, the *estancia* was a prison and conscription to the Indian frontier was an imminent alternative. And the gaucho forces lasted only as long as Rosas needed them. Once he had the apparatus of the state in his possession, from 1835, once he controlled the bureaucracy, the police and, above all, the regular army, he did not need or want the popular forces of the countryside. Rosas quickly recruited, equipped, armed and purged an army of the line, detachments of which were used against the countryside to round up conscripts. With the ultimate means of coercion in his hand, he ceased to rely on the irregular rural forces. The gaucho militias, moreover, were 'popular' forces only in the sense that they were composed of the peons of the countryside. They were not always volunteers for a cause, nor were they politicized. The fact of belonging to a military organization did not give the peons power or representation, for the rigid structure of the *estancia* was built into the militia, where the *estancieros* were the commanders, their overseers the officers and their peons the troops. These troops did not enter into direct relationship with Rosas; they were mobilized by their own particular patron, which meant that Rosas received his support not from free gaucho hordes but from *estancieros* leading their peon conscripts, a service for which the *estancieros* were paid by the state. The province was ruled by an informal alliance of *estancieros*, militia commanders and justices of the peace.

The severity of the rural regime reflected the emptiness of the pampas, the great population scarcity and the ruthless search for labour in a period of *estancia* expansion. The survival of slavery in Argentina was another indication of labour shortage. Rosas himself owned slaves and he did not question their place in the social structure. In spite of the May Revolution, the declarations of 1810 and the subsequent hope of social as well as political emancipation, slavery survived in Argentina, fed by an illegal slave trade which, until the late 1830s, the government openly tolerated. At the end of the colonial period the Río de la Plata contained over 30,000 slaves out of a population of 400,000. The incidence of slavery was greatest in the towns, especially Buenos Aires. In 1810 there were 11,837 blacks and mulattos in Buenos Aires, or 29.3 per cent, in a total population of 40,398, and most of the blacks were slaves. Slave numbers were depleted during the wars of independence, when emancipation was offered in return for military service, and military service often led to death. In 1822, of the 55,416 inhabitants of the city of Buenos Aires, 13,685, or 24.7 per cent, were blacks and mulattos; of these 6,611, or 48.3 per cent, were slaves. In 1838 non whites constituted 14,928 out of 62,957, or 23.71 per cent. Mortality rates were higher among non whites than among whites, and much higher among mulattos and free blacks than among slaves. Yet from 1822 to 1838 the number of non whites remained stationary, as their ranks were replenished from abroad. Rosas was responsible for a revival of the slave trade. His decree of 15 October 1831 allowed the sale of slaves imported as servants by foreigners; and an illegal slave trade from Brazil, Uruguay and Africa survived in the 1830s. It was not until 1839, when Rosas needed British support against the French, that a comprehensive anti-slave trade treaty was signed. By 1843, according to a British estimate, there were no more than 300 slaves in the Argentine provinces; and slaves who joined the federalist army, especially if they belonged to unitarian owners, gained freedom in return for military service. When, in the Constitution of 1853, slavery was finally abolished in the whole of Argentina, there were few slaves left. Meanwhile, Rosas had many blacks in his employment and many more in his political service. He seems to have been free of race prejudice, though he did not raise the non whites socially. They occupied the lowest situations: they were porters, carters, carriers, drivers and washerwomen, as well as domestic servants. They gave Rosas useful support in the streets and were part of his 'popular' following. They were deployed in a military role in Buenos Aires and the provinces where they formed a militia unit, the *negrada federal*, black troops in red shirts, many of them former slaves. But in the final analysis the demagogy of Rosas among the blacks and mulattos did nothing to alter their position in the society around them.

The hegemony of the landowners, the abasement of the gauchos, the dependence of the peons, all this was the heritage of Rosas. Argentina bore the imprint of extreme social stratification for many generations to come. Society became set in a rigid mould, to which economic modernization and political change had later to adapt. The Rosas state was the *estancia* writ large. Society itself was built upon the patron-peon relationship. It seemed the only alternative to anarchy.

Rosas ruled from 1829 to 1832 with absolute powers. After an interregnum during which instability in Buenos Aires and insubordination in the provinces threatened to restore anarchy, he returned to office on his own terms in March 1835 and ruled for the next seventeen years with total and unlimited power. The House of Representatives remained a creature of the governor, whom it formally 'elected'. It consisted of 44 deputies, half of whom were annually renewed by election. But only a small minority of the electorate participated, and it was the duty of the justices of the peace to deliver these votes to the regime. The assembly, lacking legislative function and financial control, was largely an exercise in public relations for the benefit of foreign and domestic audiences, and it normally responded sycophantically to the initiatives of the governor. While he controlled the legislature, Rosas also dominated the judicial power. He not only made law, he interpreted it, changed it and applied it. The machinery of justice no doubt continued to function: the justices of the peace, the judges for civil and criminal cases, the appeal judge and the supreme court, all gave institutional legitimacy to the regime. But the law did not rule. Arbitrary intervention by the executive undermined the independence of the judiciary. Rosas took many cases to himself, read the evidence, examined the police reports and, as he sat alone at his desk, gave judgement, writing on the files 'shoot him', 'fine him', 'imprison him', 'to the army'. Rosas also controlled the bureaucracy. One of his first and most uncompromising measures was to purge the old administration; this was the simplest way of removing political enemies and rewarding followers, and it was inherent in the patron-client organization of society. The new administration was not extravagantly large, and some of the early vacancies were left unfilled as part of the expenditure cuts which the government was obliged to make. But appointments of all kinds were reserved for political clients and federalists; other qualifications counted for little.

Propaganda was an essential ingredient of *rosismo*: a few simple and violent slogans took the place of ideology and these permeated the administration and were thrust relentlessly at the public. People were obliged to wear a kind of uniform and to use the federal colour, red. The symbolism was a form of coercion and conformity. To adopt the federal look and the federal language took the place of orthodoxy tests and oaths of allegiance. Federal uniformity was a measure of quasi-totalitarian pressure, by which people were forced to abandon a passive or apolitical role and to accept a specific commitment, to show their true colours. The Church was a willing ally, except for the Jesuits, who were re-admitted and re-expelled. Portraits of Rosas were carried in triumph through the streets and placed upon the altars of the principal churches. Sermons glorified the dictator and extolled the federal cause. The clergy became essential auxiliaries of the regime and preached that to resist Rosas was a sin. Political orthodoxy was conveyed by word as well as by deed, and the printing presses of Buenos Aires were kept fully employed turning out newspapers in Spanish and other languages containing official news and propaganda, for circulation at home and abroad. But the ultimate sanction was force, controlled by Rosas, applied by the military and the police.

The regime was not strictly speaking a military dictatorship: it was a civilian regime which employed a compliant military. The military establishment, consisting of the regular army and the militia, existed, however, not only to defend the country but to occupy it, not only to protect the population but to control it. Conscripted from peons, vagrants and delinquents, officered by professional soldiers, kept alive by booty and exactions from the *estancias*, the army of Rosas was a heavy burden on the rest of the population. If it was not an efficient military, it was a numerous one – perhaps 20,000 strong – and an active one, constantly engaged in foreign wars, interprovincial conflicts and internal security. But war and the economic demands of war, while they meant misery for the many, made fortunes for the few. Defence spending provided a secure market for certain industries and employment for their workers: the fairly constant demand for uniforms, arms and equipment helped to sustain a number of small workshops and artisan manufactures in an otherwise depressed industrial sector. Above all, the military market favoured several large landowners. Proprietors such as the Anchorena had long had valuable contracts for the supply of cattle to frontier forts; now the armies on other fronts became voracious consumers and regular customers. The army and its liabilities, however, increased at a time when revenue was contracting, and something had to be sacrificed. When the French blockade began to bite, from April 1838, not only were people thrown out of work and hit by rapid inflation but the regime saw its revenue from customs – its basic income – fall dramatically. Faced with heavy budget deficits, it immediately imposed severe expenditure cuts. Most of these fell on education, the social services and welfare in general. The University of Buenos Aires was virtually closed. When priorities were tested, Rosas did not even make a pretence of governing 'popularly'.

The contrast between military and social spending reflected circumstances as well as values. The enemy within, conflict with other provinces and with foreign powers, and the obligation to succour his allies in the interior, all caused Rosas to maintain a heavy defence budget. Some of these choices were forced upon him, others were preferred policy, yet others reflected a universal indifference towards welfare. In any case the consequences were socially retarding. In the 1840s the ministry of government, or home affairs, received on average between 6 and 7 per cent of the total budget, and most of this was allocated to police and political expenditure, not to social services. Defence, on the other hand, received absolute priority. The military budget varied from 4 million pesos, or 27 per cent of the total, in 1836, to 23.8 million, 49 per cent, during the French blockade in 1840, to 29.6 million, 71.11 per cent, in 1841. For the rest of the regime it never fell below 15 million, or 49 per cent.

This was the system of total government which sustained Rosas in power for over two decades. The majority of people obeyed, some with enthusiasm, others from inertia, many out of fear. But it was more than tyranny arbitrarily imposed. The government of Rosas responded to conditions inherent in Argentine society, where men had lived for too long without a common power to keep them all in awe. Rosas superseded a state of nature, in which life could be brutish and short. He offered an escape from insecurity and a promise of peace, on condition that he were granted total power, the sole antidote to total anarchy. To exercise his sovereignty Rosas used the bureaucracy, the military and the police. Even so there was some opposition. Internally there was an ideological opposition, partly from unitarians and partly from younger reformists; this came to a head in an abortive conspiracy in 1839 and continued to operate throughout the regime from its base in Montevideo. A second focus of internal opposition was formed by the landowners of the south of the province, whose resentment derived not from ideology but from economic interest. Already harassed by demands upon their manpower and resources for the Indian frontier, they were particularly hit by the French blockade, which cut off their export outlets and for which they blamed Rosas. But their rebellion of 1839 did not synchronize with the political conspiracy and they too were crushed. Finally, there was an external opposition to the regime, partly from other provinces and partly from foreign powers. If this could link with internal dissidents, Rosas would be in real danger. He therefore held in reserve another constraint, terror.

Rosas used terror as an instrument of government, to eliminate enemies, to discipline dissidents, to warn waverers and, ultimately, to control his own supporters. Terror was not simply a series of exceptional episodes, though it was regulated according to circumstances. It was an intrinsic part of the Rosas system, the distinctive style of the regime, its ultimate sanction. Rosas himself was the author of terror, ordering executions without trial by virtue of the extraordinary powers vested in him. But the special agent of terrorism was the *Sociedad Popular Restaurador*, a political club and a para-police organization. The Society had an armed wing, commonly called the *mazorca*. These were the true terrorists, recruited from the police, the militia, from professional cut-throats and delinquents, forming armed squads who went out on various missions, killing, looting and menacing. While the *mazorca* was a creature of Rosas, it was more terrorist than its creator: like many such death squads it acquired in action a semi-autonomy which its author believed he had to allow as a necessary means of government. Cruelty had its chronology. The incidence of terrorism varied according to the pressures on the regime, rising to a peak in 1839–42, when French intervention, internal rebellion, and unitarian invasion threatened to destroy the

Rosas state and inevitably produced violent counter-measures. Rosas never practised mass killing; selective assassination was enough to instil terror. And the peak of 1839–42 was not typical of the whole regime but rather an extraordinary manifestation of a general rule, namely, that terrorism existed to enforce submission to government policy in times of national emergency.

The system gave Rosas hegemony in Buenos Aires for over twenty years. But he could not apply the same strategy in the whole of Argentina. In the first place he did not govern 'Argentina'. The thirteen provinces governed themselves independently, though they were grouped in one general Confederation of the United Provinces of the Río de la Plata. Rosas accepted this and preferred inter-provincial relations to be governed by informal power rather than a written constitution. He refused to prepare an Argentine constitution, arguing that before the time was opportune for national organization the provinces must first organize themselves, that the progress of the parts must precede the ordering of the whole, and that the first task was to defeat the unitarians. Even without formal union, however, the provinces were forced to delegate certain common interests to the government of Buenos Aires, mainly defence and foreign policy, and also an element of legal jurisdiction, which enabled Rosas occasionally to reach out and arraign his enemies as federal criminals. Rosas, therefore, exercised some *de facto* control over the provinces; this he regarded as necessary, partly to prevent subversion and anarchy from seeping into Buenos Aires, partly to secure a broad base for economic and foreign policy and partly to acquire a national dimension for his regime. To impose his will he had to use some force, for the provinces did not accept him voluntarily. In the littoral and in the interior Rosas was seen as a caudillo who served the local interests of Buenos Aires; in these parts the loyalty of the *hacendados* and the service of their peons were not so easily procured. In many of the provinces of the interior the federal party had weaker economic roots and a narrower social base than in Buenos Aires; and in the remoter parts of the confederation Rosas could not instantly apply autocratic domination or regulate the use of terror. The unification of Argentina, therefore, meant the conquest of Argentina by Buenos Aires. Federalism gave way to *rosismo*, an informal system of control from the centre which Rosas achieved by patience and exercised with persistence.

The Federal Pact of 4 January 1831 between the littoral provinces, Buenos Aires, Entre Ríos, Santa Fe and later Corrientes, inaugurated a decade of relative stability in the east, though this could not disguise the hegemony of Buenos Aires, its control of customs revenue and river navigation, and its indifference to the economic interests of the other provinces. Rosas began to expand his power in the littoral in the years 1835–40. First, the governor of Entre Ríos, Pascual de Echagüe, moved away from the influence of the powerful Estanislao López and submitted himself unconditionally to Rosas. Then Corrientes, resentful of its economic subordination, declared war on its new metropolis; but the defeat and death of Governor Berón de Astrada at Pago Largo (31 March 1839) brought Corrientes too under the domination of Buenos Aires. Now there was only Santa Fe. Its governor, Estanislao López, was the most powerful of the provincial caudillos, experienced in the politics of the confederation and possessing a reputation equal to that of Rosas. But Rosas waited, and in 1838 López died. The subsequent election of Domingo Cullen, independent and anti-*rosista*, provoked a minor crisis, which was resolved by the triumph of Juan Pablo López, a protégé and now a satellite of Rosas. In each of the eastern provinces, therefore, Rosas succeeded gradually in imposing allied, dependent or weak governors. In Uruguay, an independent state since 1828, success did not come so easily, however. His ally, President Manuel Oribe, was overthrown in June 1838 by the rival caudillo, Fructuoso Rivera, backed by General Lavalle and acclaimed by the émigré unitarians. This was a serious challenge.

Rosas could not allow these local fires to remain unquenched, for there was danger of their being sucked into international conflagrations. The French government knew little about Rosas, but what it saw it did not like. Anxious to extend its trade and power in the Río de la Plata, and irritated by a dispute with Rosas over the status of its nationals under his jurisdiction, France authorized its naval forces to institute a blockade of Buenos Aires; this began on 28 March 1838 and was followed by an alliance between the French forces and Rosas's enemies in Uruguay. The French blockade, which lasted until 29 October 1840, harmed the regime in a number of ways. It caused the economy to stagnate and deprived the government of vital customs revenue; it de-stabilized the federal system and gave heart to dissidents in the littoral and the interior; and it led Rosas to rule with yet greater autocracy. But it had too little military muscle to be decisive. General Lavalle, assisted by the French and by other units from Montevideo, was expected to disembark at the port of Buenos Aires in support of the two rebel fronts within, the conspirators of the capital and the landowners of the south. In fact the various movements failed to synchronize. Lavalle led his forces not to Buenos Aires but to Entre Ríos, promising to free the Confederation from the tyrant and to give the provinces self-rule. But his association with the French, whom many considered aggressors against the Confederation, deprived him of support in Entre Ríos. He then turned aside to Corrientes, where Governor Pedro Ferré accepted him and declared against Rosas. But Corrientes was a long way from Buenos Aires, and by the time Lavalle's army reached striking distance it lacked money, arms and perhaps conviction. The French gave him naval support and arms, but could not supply military thrust. Lavalle entered the province of Buenos Aires on 5 August 1840 and finally appeared poised to attack Rosas. At this point his judgement, or his nerve, failed him. He paused to await French reinforcements, which did not come, and he lost the advantage of surprise. On 5 September, to the dismay of his associates and the bewilderment of historians, he withdrew towards Santa Fe, and his army, already demoralized by failure and desertion, began its long retreat towards the north.

The liberating expedition, humiliated in Buenos Aires, achieved a degree of success elsewhere. Its mere existence served to arouse Rosas's enemies in the interior. From April 1840 the Coalition of the North organized by Marco Avellaneda, governor of Tucumán, and including Salta, La Rioja, Catamarca and Jujuy, took the field under the command of General Aráoz de La Madrid in alliance with Lavalle, and threatened Rosas anew from the interior. Altogether, 1840 was a dangerous year for Rosas. Yet he survived, and at the beginning of 1841 the tide began to turn. The federal caudillos dominated Cuyo in the far west and began to strike back. Ex-president Oribe of Uruguay also fought bloodily for Rosas. On 28 November 1840 he defeated Lavalle's liberating army at Quebracho Herrado and completed the conquest of Córdoba. In the following year he destroyed the remnants of the Coalition of the North, first the spent forces of Lavalle at Famaillá (19 September 1841), then those of La Madrid at Rodeo del Medio (24 September 1841). These were cruel wars, and Rosas's generals wore down the enemy as much by terror as by battle. Lavalle himself was killed at Jujuy on 8 October 1841 on his way to Bolivia. The destruction of the unitarian forces in the interior, however, provoked rather than paralysed the littoral provinces. Their rebellion was eventually frustrated as much by their own disunity as by the energy of Oribe, who forced them to desist and disarm in December

1841. By February 1843 Oribe dominated the littoral. Rivera and the émigrés were enclosed within Montevideo, while Oribe and the *rosistas* were stationed at the Cerrito on the outskirts. And in the river the Buenos Aires fleet, completing the encirclement of the unitarians, destroyed the naval forces of Montevideo, imposed a blockade, and waited for victory. Yet the siege of Montevideo lasted for nine years.

British intervention was now the complicating factor. In the course of 1843 British naval forces broke the blockade of Montevideo and allowed supplies and recruits to reach the defenders. The action was crucial in saving the city, prolonging the war and pinning down Rosas to a long and painful siege. In addition to defending the independence of Uruguay, Britain also sought to open the rivers to free navigation: Rosas was branded as a threat to the first and an obstacle to the second. Anglo-French naval forces imposed a blockade on Buenos Aires from September 1845, and in November a joint expedition forced its way up the River Paraná convoying a merchant fleet to inaugurate direct trade to the interior. But the expedition encountered neither welcoming allies nor promising markets, only high customs duties, local suspicion, sluggish sales and the problem of returning down river. The blockade was no more effective than the expedition. This was a slow and clumsy weapon which hit trade rather than the enemy. Argentina's primitive economy made it virtually invulnerable to outside pressure. It could always revert to a subsistence economy and sit it out, waiting for pent-up trade to reopen while its cattle resources accumulated. As for the British, they simply blockaded their own trade. Rosas meanwhile gained great credit from the intervention of 1843–46. His defiance, determination and ultimate success placed him high in the pantheon of Argentine patriots. Argentina rallied round Rosas, and when the emergency was over and the British returned to seek peace and trade, they found the regime stronger than ever, the economy improving and a golden age beginning. But appearances were deceptive.

Rosas tamed the interior by relentless diplomacy and military force, establishing for himself an informal but enduring sovereignty. But he could not apply the same methods to the littoral provinces, where economic grievances coincided with powerful foreign interests. These provinces wanted trading rights for the river ports of the Paraná and the Uruguay, they wanted a share in customs revenue, and they wanted local autonomy. With outside assistance they could become the Achilles' heel of Rosas. The British had negotiated with the caudillos of Entre Ríos,

Corrientes and Paraguay for a coalition against Buenos Aires, but the governor of Entre Ríos, Justo José de Urquiza, was too careful to risk his future without the guarantee of powerful land forces. If the British could not supply these, Brazil could.

Brazil had its own account to settle with Rosas. Determined to prevent satellites of Buenos Aires becoming entrenched in Uruguay and the littoral, and anxious to secure free navigation of the river complex from Matto Grosso to the sea, Brazil was ready to move in opposition to the 'imperialism' of Rosas, or impelled by an imperialism of its own. An ally was at hand in Entre Ríos. Urquiza, like Rosas, was a rural caudillo, the owner of vast estates, the ruler of a personal fiefdom several hundred square miles in extent, with tens of thousands of cattle and sheep, and four *saladeros*. He made a fortune in the 1840s as a supplier to besieged Montevideo, an importer of manufactured goods and an exporter of gold to Europe. His private ambitions combined easily with provincial interests, and as a politician he was willing to supplant Rosas and initiate a constitutional reorganization of Argentina. He displayed, moreover, greater deference to education, culture and freedom than his rival and he had a superior reputation with the émigré intellectuals in Montevideo. In the person of Urquiza, therefore, the various strands of opposition came together, and he placed himself at the head of provincial interests, liberal exiles and Uruguayan patriots in' an alliance which was backed by sufficient Brazilian money and naval forces to tip the balance against Rosas. The dictator was thus confronted not from within but from without, by the Triple Alliance of Entre Ríos, Brazil and Montevideo, which went into action from May 1851.

Buenos Aires was the privileged beneficiary of *rosismo*, but here too enthusiasm waned. Rosas was expected to guarantee peace and security; this was the justification of the regime. But in the wake of so many conflicts and so much waste he was still ready to wage war, even after 1850, relentlessly pursuing his objectives in Uruguay and Paraguay, always looking for one more victory. His army was now weak and disorganized, his military commanders were not to be trusted. By his terrorist methods and his de-politicization of Buenos Aires he had destroyed whatever existed of 'popular' support. And when, in early 1852, the invading army of the Triple Alliance advanced, his troops fled and the people in town and country did not rise in his support. On 3 February, at Monte Caseros, he was defeated: he rode alone from the field of battle, took refuge in the house of the British consul, boarded a British vessel, and sailed for England and exile.

Rosas was destroyed by military defeat. But the economic structure and
the international links on which his system rested were already beginning
to shift. Cattle-raising was the preferred policy of the Rosas regime. It
required relatively low investments in land and technology, and, if
practised on an extensive scale in large units capable of dealing with
fluctuating export markets, it yielded very high profits. Investments had
to be concentrated in cattle; therefore abundant, cheap and secure land
was required. But cattle-raising gave a limited range of exports, mainly
hides and jerked beef, for which international demand was not likely to
grow. The market for hides was far from dynamic, even when continental Europe began to supplement Great Britain; and the demand for salt
beef, limited to the slave economies of Brazil and Cuba, was more likely
to contract than expand. The Rosas economy therefore faced present
stagnation and future decline. Meanwhile, by the mid-1840s, other areas
of South America were entering into competition. The *saladeros* of Rio
Grande do Sul began to undercut Buenos Aires. And within the
confederation the balance was no longer so overwhelmingly in Buenos
Aires's favour. From 1843 the littoral provinces made the most of the
peace which they enjoyed while Rosas concentrated his fighting forces
on Uruguay. Cattle resources multiplied: Entre Ríos, with six million
cattle, two million sheep and seventeen *saladeros*, was a new economic
power. Competition was not yet critical; exports of jerked beef from
Entre Ríos were still only 10 per cent of those of Buenos Aires. But there
were political implications. The *estancieros* of Entre Ríos and Corrientes,
profiting to some degree from the blockade of Buenos Aires, were not
prepared to endure for ever the stranglehold exercised by their metropolis. Why should they sustain the commercial monopoly of Buenos Aires?
Should they not by-pass its customs house and gain direct access to
outside markets? To respond to these challenges the economy of Buenos
Aires needed diversification and improvement. These came in the form
of an alternative activity. Sheep farming had already begun to threaten
the dominance of the cattle *estancia*. It was through the export of wool
that Argentina would first develop its link with the world market, its
internal productive capacity and its capital accumulation. Rosas thus
became an anachronism, a legacy from another age.

The 'merinization' of Buenos Aires, the rise of a large sheep and wool
economy, began in the 1840s and soon led to a scramble for new land.
The external stimulus was the expansion of the European textile industry, which provided a secure export market. Internal conditions were

also favourable, consisting of good soil and a local stock capable of improvement. In 1810 the province had a stock of 2–3 million sheep, but these were of poor quality and occupied marginal lands. By 1852 the number had grown to 15 million head, and in 1865 40 million. Wool exports increased from 333.7 tons in 1829, to 1,609.6 tons in 1840, to 7,681 tons in 1850; they then accelerated to 17,316.9 tons in 1860, 65,704.2 tons in 1870. In 1822 wool represented 0.94 per cent of the total value of exports from Buenos Aires, cattle hides 64.86 per cent; in 1836, 7.6 per cent and 68.4 per cent respectively; in 1851, 10.3 per cent and 64.9 per cent; in 1861, 35.9 per cent and 33.5 per cent; in 1865, 46.2 per cent and 27.2 per cent.

In the early years of independence *estancieros* showed little interest in improving breeds of sheep. It was left to a few Englishmen, John Harratt and Peter Sheridan in particular, to show the way: from the 1820s they began to purchase Spanish merinos, to preserve and refine the improved breeds and to export to Liverpool, encouraged by the almost total abolition of import duties on wool in England. The growing interest in sheep breeding was reflected in further imports of merinos from Europe and the United States in 1836–8, while the pampa sheep were also crossed with Saxony breeds. To improve the quality of sheep required not only the import of European breeds but also new forms of production – improvement of the grasses of the pampa, fencing of fields, building of sheds for shearing and storing wool, opening of wells. All this in turn raised the demand for labour. The gaucho was gradually replaced by the shepherd. Immigrant settlers arrived, either as hired labourers or as partners in profit-sharing schemes or as tenant farmers. Irish immigrants were particularly welcome as shepherds, but Basques and Galicians also came; and while this was not a massive immigration, it brought needed labour, skills and output. The new arrivals were often given a stake in the flocks of a sheep farmer through five-yearly contracts in which they became partners, receiving one-third of the increase and one-third of the wool in return for caring for the flock and paying expenses. An immigrant could earn enough in a few years to purchase an interest in half a flock and at the end of this time he had enough sheep and money to set up on his own. On the pampas between Buenos Aires and the River Salado sheep were beginning to drive cattle from the land; from the 1840s *estancia* after *estancia* passed into the hands of the sheep farmers. Cattle *estancias* survived, of course, either as mixed farms or on low and marshy lands whose reedy grasses were unsuitable for sheep. In general the lands which had been longest occupied, in the northern parts of the province, were the best adapted for sheep, while the new lands in the south were more suited to the breeding of cattle. Rosas himself had always encouraged sheep rearing, if not improvement, on his own *estancias*.

The large purchases of land by foreigners, the multiplication of sheep, the appearance of more sophisticated consumer trends, all were signs of a new Argentina. The city of Buenos Aires was growing and improving, as paved streets, horse-drawn public transport and gas supplies enhanced the environment. Near the towns the enclosure of lands for agriculture and horticulture proceeded, so that within ten years after Rosas all lands over a radius of 15–20 miles around the city of Buenos Aires were subdivided and enclosed as farms or market gardens, cultivated by Italians, Basques, French, British and German immigrants, and supplying an ever-growing urban market. Railways began to connect the interior of the province with the capital, and a fleet of steam vessels placed the various river ports in daily communication with the great entrepôt. Ocean steamers arrived and departed every two or three days. Between 1860 and 1880 the total value of imports from Europe doubled, comprising mainly textiles, hardware and machinery from Britain, and luxury goods from the continent. Meanwhile foreign trade was dominated by the customary commodities, by wool, hides and salt meat, which constituted more than 90 per cent of the total value of exports.

Economic performance differed, of course, between the three major regions. Buenos Aires maintained its dominance in spite of the obstacles to growth presented by civil and foreign wars, the exactions of the state and the raids of frontier Indians. The littoral lagged some way behind, its growth uneven but its prospects promising. Santa Fe, unlike Buenos Aires, had empty lands to fill; schemes of agricultural colonization were begun, offering a harsh life for the immigrants but a profitable one for those entrepreneurs who bought up land to re-sell to the colonists. Rosario was now an active river port, poised for further development. Entre Ríos, where Urquiza himself was the greatest proprietor, had a more established prosperity, with rich cattle *estancias* and sheep farms, and trading links with Brazil and Uruguay. Foreigners now penetrated the up-river markets more frequently. Even Corrientes, part *estancia*, part tobacco plantation, where English bottled beer was drunk on all social occasions, was emerging at last from a subsistence economy. The interior, on the other hand, was the underdeveloped region of Argentina, its production damaged by distance from the east coast and by cheap competition from Europe, its only compensating outlet being the Chilean mining market. Economic poverty and the concentration of usable land in large estates drove the poor off the soil into the hands of caudillos, who, while Buenos Aires and the littoral were moving into another age, still looked towards the past.

The defeat of Rosas did not destroy existing structures. The hegemony of the landed oligarchy survived. The dominance of Buenos Aires continued. And inter-provincial conflict simply entered another stage. The provinces conferred upon Urquiza, the victor of Caseros, the title Provisional Director of the Argentine Confederation and gave him a national role; he in turn decreed the nationalization of the customs and free navigation of the rivers Paraná and Uruguay. But Buenos Aires broke away, refused to place itself at the mercy of other provinces, some of them little more than deserts, and remained aloof from the constituent congress which Urquiza convened. The constitution, approved on 1 May 1853, reflected a number of influences – previous Argentine constitutions, the example of the United States and the bitter lessons of past conflict. But perhaps the most powerful influence was the political thought of Juan Bautista Alberdi, who advised a just balance between central power and provincial rights, and a programme of immigration, education and modernization. The constitution provided for a federal republic and incorporated the classical freedoms and civil rights. It divided power between the executive, the legislative and the judiciary. The legislature consisted of two houses, a senate to which each provincial legislature elected two members, and a chamber of deputies elected by male suffrage in public voting. While assuring local self-government to the provinces, the constitution gave countervailing authority to the federal government. The president, who was chosen by an electoral college for six years, was given strong executive powers: he could introduce his own bills, appoint and dismiss his ministers without reference to congress. The president was also empowered to intervene in any province in order to preserve republican government against internal disorder or foreign attack; to this effect he could remove local administrations and impose federal officials. The economic provisions of the constitution also addressed federal problems. Inter-provincial tariffs were abolished. The income from Buenos Aires customs house was to be nationalized and not to remain the exclusive property of the province of

Buenos Aires, which was another reason for *porteño* resistance. Urquiza was elected president for six years. But he did not preside over a nation state. A sense of national identity did not exist, or else it was not strong enough to overcome provincial and personal loyalties. While the provinces accepted the Constitution of 1853, they continued to be ruled by caudillos, even if they were called governors, and the confederation was essentially a network of personal loyalties to its president.

Argentina was now split into two states, on the one hand the city and province of Buenos Aires, ruled by its governor (from 1860 Bartolomé Mitre) and a liberal party, on the other the Argentine confederation, consisting of thirteen provinces under Urquiza and a federal party. Whereas in the past the provinces had refused to accept the domination of Buenos Aires, now Buenos Aires refused to co-operate with the provinces, or to obey a constitution which it considered a facade for *caudillismo*. And Buenos Aires could not be forced into a confederation against its wishes: it was powerful, it was rich, and its customs house was still the chief source of revenue in Argentina, the focus of foreign trade, and the property of one province. The confederation therefore established its capital at Paraná, in Entre Ríos, where Urquiza, whatever his constitutional sentiments, ruled as an old-style caudillo, though with the added role of leader of the littoral and the interior. As first president, Urquiza signed commercial treaties with Britain, France and the United States, and opened the rivers Paraná and Uruguay to free navigation for foreign trade. In normal times almost 70 per cent of imports into Buenos Aires were destined for the provinces. Now it was the policy of the confederation to free itself from Buenos Aires, trade directly with the outside world and make Rosario a new entrepôt. Urquiza was personally involved in commercial enterprises with Europe, in schemes for the establishment of import-export houses in Rosario and in the search for outside capital. But foreign shipping did not respond to the new opportunities and continued to unload at Buenos Aires: the fact remained that Rosario was not yet a sufficient market or entrepôt to justify an extra five-day journey. Further stimulus was provided in 1857 when a differential tariff was issued in the hope of tempting European trade into by-passing Buenos Aires: but even this, which only lasted until 1859, could not overcome the facts of economic life. Commercial war therefore gave way to military conflict.

By 1859 both sides were ready for a new trial by battle. Urquiza's army defeated that of Mitre at the battle of Cepeda, but Buenos Aires accepted incorporation into the confederation with great reluctance. It still had reserves of money and manpower, and in 1861 it fought back once more. The two sides met at the battle of Pavón, an encounter which was interpreted if not as a victory for Mitre at least as a defeat for the confederation, demonstrably incapable of imposing its will on the recalcitrant province. Urquiza withdrew from the battlefield, apparently convinced that if the confederation could not win quickly it would not win at all. He took his forces to Entre Ríos to guard at least his provincial interests, and left the confederation weakened and disorientated. Mitre meanwhile advanced on various fronts. He sent his military columns in support of liberal regimes in the provinces of the littoral and the interior. He negotiated with Urquiza from a position of strength and persuaded him voluntarily to dismantle the confederation. And he pressed the politicians of his own province of Buenos Aires to accept his programme of national reorganization and to proceed by negotiation rather than force.

The resultant settlement was a compromise between unitarism and federalism. Mitre accepted the constitution of 1853, with its bias towards centralism and presidential power, and was then declared national as well as provincial leader. Thus, in 1861, the idea of a federation, with Buenos Aires its centre and the interior represented there, was accepted. And Mitre, a *porteño*, a hero of the siege of Montevideo, was elected first constitutional president for the whole nation in October 1862. Now, the union of the provinces was achieved and for the first time Argentina was called Argentina and not by a clumsy circumlocution.

The opportunity for national reorganization after 1862 could have been lost had not power been held by two distinguished presidents, Bartolomé Mitre (1862–8) and Domingo F. Sarmiento (1868–74), intellectuals and men of letters as well as politicians and statesmen. Both had given many years of service towards the ideal of a greater Argentina; both now stood for three objectives, national unity, liberal institutions and modernization. In combating the confederation Mitre had fought not simply for one particular province but against fragmentation and *caudillismo*. He sought to place and keep Buenos Aires at the head of a united Argentina, and he fought on after 1862. For the caudillos did not die without a struggle. In 1863 and again in 1866–8 Mitre had to suppress rebellions in the interior. The political occasion of these insurrections was caudillo resistance to the new order. But the deeper causes were the depressed economies of the interior, the impoverishment of the provinces and their inability to sustain their populations in occupation or subsistence. Lack of work and food drove the rural peoples to the life of *montoneros*, to live in effect by banditry and booty. Forces of this kind sustained Angel Vicente Peñaloza, 'El Chacho', caudillo of wild and remote La Rioja, where one school sufficed for the entire province but where the caudillo provided personally for the welfare of his followers. When El Chacho revolted in 1863, Mitre permitted Sarmiento, governor of San Juan and a federal pro-consul in the interior, to wage a war to the death against the rebels, and the forces of Sarmiento, defending civilization with barbarism, killed their prisoners and displayed the head of El Chacho on a pole. In 1866–7 Felipe Varela, former officer of El Chacho, invaded western Argentina from Chile and raised another *montonera*, but he too was defeated and his followers mercilessly crushed by the national army. The end of the *montonera* was in sight, though it evinced further paroxysms before it was extinguished. Urquiza, reconciled now to the central state, held aloof from the provincial movements which he was supposed to patronize but now disavowed, and played his own role in supporting the new Argentina. But in the end he fell a victim to the system which he had once represented; he was assassinated in his own *estancia*, by order of a rival caudillo and former protégé, in April 1870. His killer, Ricardo López Jordán, kept alive in Entre Ríos the spirit of rebellion and the cult of *caudillismo*, until 1876. In the meantime, as president, Sarmiento, who declared that he was a *porteño* in the provinces and a provincial in Buenos Aires, had continued the work of Mitre, had defended national unity with the sword and the pen and had been even more ruthless with rebels.

In spite of provincial traditions and caudillo resistance, central power and national organization survived and took root. They were assisted by the growth of institutions with an Argentine dimension, the press, the postal service, the National Bank, the railway system. But two particular agencies promoted national identity and unity – federal justice and the national army. By law of 1862 a national judicial power was established, and in 1865–8 the Argentine Civil Code was drawn up. The supreme court and the various lower courts completed the structure of the modern state. The supreme court had power to declare unconstitutional any laws or decrees, national or provincial, in conflict with the supreme law, and thus became the interpreter of the constitution, though it was not competent to decide conflicts between the powers. The executive had the right of intervention in the provinces, a right which became more effective once it was backed by a national army. By decree of 26 January 1864 the government created a permanent army of 6,000 men distributed between artillery, infantry and cavalry. A Military Academy was established in 1869 and the formation of a professional officer corps was begun. The law of recruitment of 21 September 1872 anticipated national conscription. This was the institutional framework for the new army. But a more effective impetus was given by its operations during the rebellions of the caudillos and the War of Paraguay, when it increased its numbers and added to its experience. The army gave the president real power and enabled him to extend the executive's reach into the furthest corners of Argentina. Gradually the local oligarchies became compliant, and in return for collaboration they were offered a place in a national ruling class.

The political principles animating the presidencies of Mitre and Sarmiento were those of classical liberalism. Mitre led an identifiable Liberal Party, and after Pavón his strategy of national reorganization rested not only on the extension of federal power but also on the proliferation of liberal governments throughout the provinces, instruments of union by voluntary choice. Liberalism represented an intellectual aristocracy, survivors and heirs of the generation of 1837, now free to apply their ideas, to promote political and material progress, the rule of law, primary and secondary education, to dispel the barbarism which Sarmiento abhorred and to make the poor gaucho into a useful man. But the liberal elite held out little for the popular masses: for the gauchos and peons, who were beyond the political pale, their status to serve, their function to labour. They were represented by nothing but an epic poem, *Martín Fierro*, lamenting the departure of a noble past. The only opposition recognized by the Liberal Party was that of the federalists, who followed Urquiza and tradition and who clearly belonged to the political nation. The Liberals split into two groups during Mitre's presidency, the autonomists, who came to incorporate those federalists left leaderless by the death of Urquiza, and the nationalists, who continued to preserve pure *mitrista* principles. Meanwhile in the provinces liberalism, like federalism, was often simply another name for *caudillismo*, and political party bosses soon became known as 'caudillos'.

Modernization meant growth through exports from the rural sector, investment in a new infrastructure and immigration. Some local capital was employed in the primary sector, in cattle *estancias*, sheep farms and sugar estates. But investment depended essentially upon the import of foreign capital, mainly from Britain. Up to the early 1870s British trade to Argentina was predominantly a trade in textiles, and British investment was confined to commerce and private *estancias*. But from 1860 new trends appeared. First, several joint-stock enterprises were organized in 1861–5. These were established by British entrepreneurs with British capital and were applied to railways and banks. On 1 January 1863 the first branch of the London and River Plate Bank was opened in Buenos Aires, and in 1866 the Rosario branch went into operation. From this time iron and steel, metal manufactures and coal became more important among British exports to Argentina. The second stage comprised investment in development, encouraged by Argentina and promoted by the British who wanted to improve the market for their goods. In 1860 a loan of £2.5 million was marketed in London by Barings on behalf of the Argentine government. This was the beginning of a steady flow of capital from Britain to Argentina, much of it applied to the infrastructure, either as direct investment or as loans to the state. More substantial foreign investment had to await the period after 1870, when banks, factories and public utilities became major recipients. But one area of investment was already established, the railways, and these were essential to economic growth, bringing out agricultural exports from the vast hinterland of Buenos Aires and carrying in imported goods.

The first track was opened in 1857; this ran six miles west from Buenos Aires and was built with private local capital. During the 1860s the Northern and Southern Railways began to fan out from Buenos Aires; and in 1870 the Central Argentine Railway linked Rosario and Córdoba, and opened up the great central plains. For this line the government contracted with British capital, guaranteeing a minimum return and granting adjacent lands, necessary concessions to attract capital to an empty territory, whose value lay in future prospects rather than present performance. In twenty years 1,250 miles of track was laid in Argentina. Meanwhile communications with the outside world were improving, as steam replaced sail. The Royal Mail Company began regular service to the River Plate in 1853; Lamport and Holt in 1863; the Pacific Steam Navigation Company in 1868. The journey from England to the River Plate was cut to 22 days in a fast ship. Steamships also joined the river ports, and by 1860 a number of services were in operation. Improved docks and harbours became an urgent need, as did cable and telegraph links with Europe, and all these would soon be provided by foreign capital and technology.

The new Argentina also needed people. The growth of federal power and the hegemony of Buenos Aires in the period 1852–70 was not simply a constitutional or military process. It also represented demographic and economic forces. Argentina's population grew more rapidly after 1852, from 935,000 to 1,736,923 in 1869. The balance in favour of the coast became more pronounced. The province of Buenos Aires contained 28 per cent of the whole population in 1869; the littoral 48.8 per cent. The city of Buenos Aires increased its inhabitants from 90,076 in 1854 to 177,787 in 1869, of whom 89,661 were Argentines, 88,126 foreigners. Immigration now significantly fed population growth. After 1852 the confederation made a special effort to attract immigrants from Europe. The Constitution of 1853 gave foreigners virtually all the rights of Argentines without the obligations. In the years 1856–70 European families were brought in by the provincial government of Santa Fe to form agricultural colonies, pioneers of the 'cerealization' of the pampas. After 1862 immigration became a national policy and offices were set up in Europe, though the government did not finance the process, leaving passage and settlement to the free play of economic forces. From the late 1850s about 15,000 immigrants a year entered Argentina.

Sarmiento and others, influenced by the American model of frontier expansion, preached the virtues of agriculture and small farms, the importance of settling the immigrants in rural areas, the need to provide land for colonization and to discourage speculation and latifundism. But the actual result was different. The government viewed land as a valuable resource which could be sold or leased for fiscal purposes. Cattle and sheep raising were the basic activities of the country. The *estancieros* formed a powerful interest group, linked to the commercial leaders of the city; they regarded access to land as a vital factor for stock raising. And land speculation, either by the purchase of public land to be sold later at a profit or by subdivision and subletting of holdings, was too lucrative a business to stop. By the 1880s, therefore, most of the public land of the province of Buenos Aires, by a series of laws, had been transferred as private property to latifundists and speculators: and the pattern was repeated in other provinces. No doubt in the decades after 1850 the trend was towards smaller holdings, as the pampas became effectively occupied, land became scarce and expensive, sheep farming brought subdivision of property and new owners bought their way in and displaced the old. But this was a trend from superlatifundism to mere latifundism.

Uruguay after independence possessed a pastoral economy, an export trade, an international port and a liberal constitution. These assets were first squandered and then plundered. Uruguayans began to fight among themselves for the resources of their country. There was a fierce struggle for land, as older *estancieros* sought to secure their possessions and newcomers contended for a share. Men placed themselves under local caudillos, and these under greater caudillos, joining the *bandos*, or parties, of two rival candidates for power, the *colorados* and *blancos*. The result was the Guerra Grande, which began as a conflict between the two major caudillos, Manuel Oribe (*blanco*) and Fructuoso Rivera (*colorado*), over control of Uruguay and became, with the fall of Oribe in October 1838, an international war.

The long duration of the conflict, the presence of the *colorados* in the besieged city of Montevideo and the *blancos* in the surrounding country, brought out hitherto concealed ideological differences between the two parties. The *colorados* acquired an identity as an urban party, receptive to liberal and foreign ideas, immigrants from Europe and Brazilian support. They allied themselves with the liberal exiles from Buenos Aires against Rosas and his lieutenant Oribe, and they welcomed the intervention first of France (1838–42), then Britain and France (1843–50), when foreign interests coincided with *colorado* needs. Montevideo, therefore, was *colorado*, a European city demographically; of its 31,000 inhabitants only 11,000 were Uruguayans. European merchants dominated its trade, European loans propped up its finances (at the cost of the customs revenue), and European ideas infused its politics. But the *colorados* represented interests as well as ideas. They gained support not only from young people wanting liberty and reform, but also from immigrants hoping for land grants, from Argentine exiles using Montevideo as a base on the way back, from capitalists who owned the customs and saw the blockade of Buenos Aires as good business, and from merchants who profited from Montevideo's free access to trade and navigation of the River Plate. Rivera himself was essentially a caudillo in search of power rather than a constitutionalist. So this was an alliance of interests.

The countryside, on the other hand, was *blanco*. The *blanco* party was the party of the *estancieros*, the party of authority and tradition. It prided itself on resistance to foreign intervention, defence of 'Americanism' and alliance with the Argentina of Rosas. It was subsidized militarily and financially by Rosas, and led by a man, Oribe, who in spite of his nationalism in relation to European intervention was regarded by many as the tool of his master. The combined military forces of Rosas and Oribe were enough, if not to overcome, at least to resist the rival alliance, and the siege of Montevideo lasted from 16 February 1843 until peace was established between the Uruguayans on 8 October 1851.

In the event both parties became disillusioned with foreign intervention, Rivera with the inability of the Anglo-French allies to destroy Rosas, Oribe with Rosas's vulnerability to the rebellion led by Urquiza and both sides with the blatant exploitation of Uruguay by their respective allies. Prodded by Urquiza, the rival parties made peace in October 1851 and agreed that there was neither victor nor vanquished. Thus, they joined the rebellion against Rosas, but in a subordinate position in relation to the more powerful partners, particularly Brazil. Uruguay now made an extremely unfavourable treaty with Brazil, ceding territorial rights, granting a mortgage on the customs and allowing free (that is, untaxed) movement of cattle from Uruguay into Brazil; all this in return for a monthly subsidy, the only funds available to the Uruguayan treasury.

The Guerra Grande left Uruguay prostrate and impoverished, its livestock and *saladero* industries ruined, its government heavily in debt to national and foreign creditors, its population in decline. Private fortunes were diminished and the mass of the people destitute. And over the whole country fell the menacing shadow of Brazil. Demographically the war was a time of loss, and shortage of people was probably Uruguay's greatest problem for many years to come. The population fell from 140,000 in 1840 to 132,000 in 1852; Montevideo suffered a decline from 40,000 to 34,000. Many people, especially foreign immigrants, had abandoned the countryside to seek safety and subsistence in more prosperous parts of the Río de la Plata or Brazil, leaving a labour vacuum which retarded recuperation. Socially, while the structure of landownership had not changed, *estancias* had often changed hands. Many native landowners had been driven to seek shelter in Montevideo; their land was then neglected or plundered, it lost its cattle and its value, and the owners were forced to sell out cheaply to newcomers. From Rio Grande do Sul Brazilians surged into an empty Uruguay in the 1850s, buying their way into hundreds of *estancias*, followed by Englishmen and other Europeans. Foreigners already dominated the urban sector: in 1853, of the 2,200 merchants and artisans, 1,700 or almost 80 per cent were foreigners. Now the composition of the rural aristocracy also changed as it incorporated more and more foreigners. Secure in their titles and protected by their governments, the newcomers did not actively participat i Uruguayan politics. And the remaining native *estanciero* class was now politically homogeneous, for the *blancos*, having dominated the countryside for nine years, were now a majority, and there was no longer a struggle for land between *colorados* and *blancos*. The Guerra Grande therefore contributed to the pacification of the country-side. The rural masses, however, fared badly. The war increased their poverty and their nomadic ways, as some were conscripted and others fled from the army; now, after the war, they took reluctantly to peon status, preferring a marginal life as cowboy or rustler.

The economic consequences of war were equally grim. The basis of Uruguay's economy was the production and export of hides, jerked beef and wool. The indiscriminate slaughter of beasts, the heavy consumption of cattle by warring armies and European fleets, together with large-scale raids on *estancia* cattle by Brazilians from Rio Grande do Sul, decimated the stock of Uruguay. Cattle fell from over 6 million head in 1843 to 2 million in 1852, and many of these, wild and unimproved, were unsuitable for the export market. The *saladeros* suffered from lack of cattle and competition from Brazil for the cattle which remained; and of the twenty-four plants which functioned in 1842 no more than three or four remained in 1854. The incipient sheep industry, which in the 1830s had begun to upgrade its wool through imported stock, was stopped in its tracks. The only animals to increase during the war were the wild dogs which preyed on young cattle and became a plague of the countryside.

The cost of the war to the treasury endured long after the peace. All the resources of the state were mortgaged, either to private capitalists who had financed the *colorado* cause or to the governments of France and Brazil. In the 1850s the monthly subsidy from Brazil was virtually the only revenue of the Uruguayan government, and for this the customs remained mortgaged. Brazil became an informal metropolis and Uruguay a kind of satellite, the victim of economic penetration, financial dependence and political subordination. For Uruguay endured not only the pressure of the subsidy but also the legacy of the treaties of 1851, a Brazilian army of 5,000 (until 1855) and a Brazilian fifth column in the form of hundreds of *estancieros*, whose presence made northern Uruguay almost an appendage of Rio Grande do Sul. Uruguay was in real danger of losing its independence, at a time when Argentina, the traditional rival of Brazil in the River Plate, was pinned down by a debilitating civil war.

These were years of anarchy, isolation and nomadism in Uruguay, a time of Hobbesian insecurity. Bereft of resources and infrastructure, the state was too weak to guarantee its people their lives and possessions. As the authority of the state declined, individuals had to fend for themselves and revert to relations of personal authority and subordination characteristic of more primitive societies. The crudest *caudillismo* and clientage now prevailed.

How did Uruguay survive as a nation after the Guerra Grande and its social fabric hold together? In the end the hopelessness of their position forced *estancieros* and merchants to seek peace, to persuade the political parties to end their destructive struggle and to let economic growth take the place of conflict. From this came the policy of *fusión*, in which the parties agreed to subordinate their differences to a common object, to create a single movement animated by the ideals of peace, progress and economic recovery. And fusion was accompanied by a policy of pacts between rival caudillos to bring stability to the countryside. On 11 November 1855 Oribe made the 'Pact of Union' with Venancio Flores, the most enlightened of the *colorado* leadership. So in spite of the appearance of anarchy and the threat to fusion from periodic revolution, in fact the period after 1852 was one of relative calm in the countryside. This was the political framework in which economic recovery began, and it coincided with a decade of external peace for Uruguay and strong European demand and good prices for pastoral products during the Crimean War.

The change was seen first in demographic improvement. The population almost doubled, from 132,000 in 1852 to 221,248 in 1860. Montevideo grew from 34,000 to 57,911. Foreigners increased from 21.6 per cent of the population to 35 per cent; and in Montevideo they constituted 48 per cent. Commerce grew as internal demand for imports grew. Montevideo profited from the free navigation of the rivers and the impotence of Buenos Aires, to import and export in growing quantities, not only for itself but also for the rest of the littoral and for Rio Grande do Sul. Foreign shipping increased; foreign entrepreneurs, among them the Brazilian, Baron Mauá, extended their influence and acquired, among other assets, state bonds emanating from the war debt; foreign-controlled banks were founded.

In the countryside the cattle-breeding industry doubled its stock from 2 to 4 million in six years (1852-8), and from 4 to 8 million in 1859-62, while imported stock such as Durhams (1858), and Herefords (1864) began to upgrade the Uruguayan herds. The sheep stock, also much improved, increased from 1 million in 1852 to 3 million in 1860. A growing number of *saladeros* processed the products of the *estancia*, 160,000 head of cattle in 1858, 500,000 in 1862, and the export of hides and jerked beef surged upwards. Land prices rose by over 200 per cent in the latter half of the 1850s. But as this primitive economy rushed blindly forward it soon came up against the inevitable limits of products and purchasers.

The markets for hides and jerked beef were not dynamic, as Argentina also discovered. Jerked beef in particular had a limited outlet, the slave economies of Brazil and Cuba, and as production far exceeded demand so prices fell. Internal peace and rural abundance thus produced problems of their own and drew attention to the limitations of the economy. As boom gave way to depression, the risks involved in revolution appeared to be less daunting. The economic base was so narrow that there seemed little at stake, and the main justification for fusion and stability lost its force. Only an added dimension could make a difference, and this would come in the following decade (1860–70) with the major growth of the sheep industry. Meanwhile as Uruguay's hard-won prosperity came to an end in 1862 in a crisis of overproduction, so the fusionist assumptions were challenged and political conflict was renewed.

The state in Uruguay, as in pre-Tudor England, was weaker than its most powerful subjects. The constitution of 1830, with its president, its ministers, its congress and its civil liberties, was a facade. In the elections of 1860 Montevideo, with 60,000 inhabitants, had only 1,500 names on the civil register, and only 662 people voted. Lacking a middle or popular base, starved of revenue, without a powerful army and a modern infrastructure, the government was in no position to resist the challenge of caudillos if they had more horses, more swords and lances, and more money perhaps from foreign paymasters. Only when the state had guns and artillery, a transport system, telegraph, railways, roads and bridges (that is, from about 1875), only then could it assert itself and overcome its mighty subjects. Meanwhile, as it did not possess independent sanctions of its own, the state depended upon the good will of caudillos who had the means to sustain a government or to overthrow it. In these circumstances fusion ended and civil war was renewed. President Bernardo F. Berro (1860–4) made a brave attempt to maintain constitutionalism. But it was impossible to rule in a political vacuum, to ignore endemic *caudillismo* and factional politics. At the same time his assertion of national interests, especially against Brazil, brought a danger of intervention which he was not capable of resisting.

Brazilian settlers numbered almost 20,000 (without counting those unregistered), formed 10–15 per cent of the whole population, occupied 30 per cent of Uruguayan territory, and owned some of the best cattle property in the country. As they took root and began to spread their language and customs, they came to constitute a powerful enclave, two aspects of which were particularly worrying to the Uruguayan authorities: the concentration of their *estancias* in the frontier zone, and the tendency of the settlers to appeal to their home government against any pressure from Uruguay. The Brazilian government had reasons of its own to espouse the cause of its migrants – the search for further agricultural territory in the temperate zone, the desire to control river communications to its interior provinces, and the need to placate the immediate allies of the settlers, the magnates of Rio Grande do Sul, a peripheral province with separatist leanings. For its part, the government of President Berro attempted to control the Brazilian settlers and to impose its own law and order in the frontier territories. It took a number of positive steps to preserve Uruguayan sovereignty. It began the colonization of the frontier zone with Uruguayans, on the assumption that to populate was to defend. It sought to limit the use of slave labour on the Brazilian *estancias*. In Uruguay abolition was slow but sure, a twenty-five-year process (1825–53) comprising abolition of the slave trade, emancipation in return for military service and the gradual enactment of liberal legislation. Now the government took steps to free the slaves and semi-slaves whom Brazilian *estancieros* introduced from Rio Grande do Sul and who were thought to constitute an advantageously cheap labour supply. The Uruguayans also declined to renew the trade treaty of 1851, in order to impose duties on the passage of cattle from Uruguay to Brazil and thereby to rival *saladeros*. Finally, they placed a higher direct tax on all land and cattle in Uruguay and forced the Brazilian *estancieros* to share the tax burden of the rest of the landowning class. The cattle barons and *saladeristas* of Rio Grande do Sul opposed this campaign, for it struck at their vital interests and those of their allies and clients among the settlers in Uruguay. They demanded action from the government in Rio de Janeiro to produce a more compliant regime in Uruguay. Brazilian support for the revolution of Venancio Flores in 1863 was in part a response to the policy pursued by the Berro government.

Meanwhile Uruguay was also under pressure from Argentina. Berro remained strictly neutral in the Argentine civil war of 1861, although he and his *oribista* colleagues were politically 'federalist' and more inclined to support Urquiza than Mitre. Venancio Flores, on the other hand, fought for Mitre at Pavón and openly espoused his cause. Mitre and the *colorados* were thus bound by past alliance and present convenience. The new Argentine president would obviously prefer a Uruguayan regime which was an ally of Argentine unity to one which was a friend of federalism. Even if Argentina could not include Uruguay in its national reorganization, it might at least create a satellite Uruguay and remove a source of federalist infection.

Caught between the expansionist aims of Brazil and the menacing if uncertain intentions of Argentina, the government of Berro sought to establish a balance of power in the River Plate by forging an alliance with another nation threatened by the two giants, Paraguay, and he proposed a treaty of friendship, commerce and navigation, to save the independence of both. But Paraguay did not react positively until the end of 1864, when it was too late.

In a world of predators Berro was too honest. He did not have the power to confront Argentina and Brazil, and he did not have a strong enough base within Uruguay to resist their ally, Venancio Flores, caudillo of the *colorado* party. On 19 April 1863 Venancio Flores invaded Uruguay from Argentina. Local support was not overwhelming. Liberal *colorados* did not like assisting *caudillismo*, and Berro had a record of non-partisan government dedicated to the national interest. But Flores had other cards to play. He enjoyed the support of President Mitre, assistance from the Argentine navy in passing men and arms across the River Uruguay, and funds from sympathizers in Buenos Aires. He was backed too by the frontier *estancieros* of Rio Grande do Sul, and hoped through them to gain the support of the emperor of Brazil. The revolution of Venancio Flores had become by 1864 an episode in a wider conflict.

Brazil and Argentina were both concerned over developments among their smaller neighbours. Each had a boundary dispute with Paraguay, and each too had other interests at stake. Brazil wanted to maintain free navigation of the River Paraguay, so that Mato Grosso would have secure exit to the sea. Regional security also presupposed a compliant Uruguay, whose ports and resources could be an asset or a threat to her neighbours. Yet the more Brazil pressed on the *blanco* government of Uruguay, the more urgently this looked for support elsewhere. In 1864 Paraguay was ready to respond.

To intervene more positively in Uruguay, Brazil needed the good will of Argentina. Mitre was disposed to give this, for he too had differences with his smaller neighbours. In Argentina, to complete the victory of union and liberalism, it was thought necessary to destroy the power of Paraguay, an enduring and perhaps infectious example of the centrifugal and conservative forces which appealed to federal caudillos. Argentina also wanted a stable, friendly and preferably liberal Uruguay, and sought this through Flores. In September 1864 Brazilian forces moved into Uruguay in support of Flores. By February 1865 Montevideo had surrendered, and Flores was established in power. He was a subordinate but not a satellite, not as long as he was allied to both Argentina and Brazil, rivals as well as allies. This was a triple alliance. As for Paraguay, it had no allies and was reduced to virtual isolation.

Paraguay reverted after independence to a near-subsistence economy, trapped in an inland cul-de-sac at the end of the river system, harassed by Argentina on one side and Brazil on the other. But Paraguay was a creature of policy as well as environment. This simple society, polarized between a state ruling class and a docile peasantry, was subject to the rule of a series of dictators who imposed or inherited political and economic isolation. The first of these was Dr José Gaspar Rodríguez de Francia, a creole lawyer and philosopher, who was appointed Dictator for five years by a congress in 1814, and then Supreme Dictator for life by another in 1816, after which he ruled until his death in 1840, without a congress, a rival, or a press of any kind, but with an army to guard him and a spy system to inform him. He was accepted on his own terms because he appeared to be the only leader capable of defending Paraguay's independent identity, and to fulfil this function he demanded absolute powers. This tradition of government was continued by Carlos Antonio López, another lawyer, who ruled first as a joint consul then, from 1844, as dictator until his death in 1862. López spent much of his time establishing, promoting and rewarding his own family, reserving the ultimate prize, the succession, for his son Francisco Solano López. The relatively long reigns and the dynastic trends of these authoritarian rulers made Paraguayan government almost a monarchy in disguise.

Francia augmented the remoteness imposed by nature, and he kept Paraguay in controlled though not total isolation, sealed off from the outside world in a posture of permanent defence against the dangers which surrounded it. His policy was a response to that of Buenos Aires, which refused to accept Paraguay's independence or to treat it as other than a rebel province; Buenos Aires sought to block river traffic and strangle Paraguay's economy, denying it free navigation by its natural outlet, the Río Paraná. As a further humiliation, down-river caudillos also preyed on Paraguayan trade, harassing, confiscating and taxing. To save Paraguay from a new dependence, Francia imposed the rule of dissociation. But he admitted those foreigners who might serve the country, and he allowed a controlled trade at two river ports. Export of *yerba*, tobacco and hardwoods was conducted through Pilar to Argentina and through Ytapúa to Brazil, against imports of arms and other manufactures, the whole trade closely supervised and taxed by the state. Otherwise Paraguay had to aim at economic self-sufficiency and submit to government monopoly. The principal products were *yerba mate* and woods, though Francia also encouraged more diversified production, tobacco, sugar and hides. Farmers were assigned a production quota of grain and cotton which they had to fulfil in order to substitute for imports. The state not only controlled the activity of private *estancias* but also entered directly into production on the extensive lands at its disposal, former crown land, ex-Jesuit land, confiscations from the Church and from political opponents, and reclamations from the wilderness. These publicly owned lands were either leased out to farmers or administered directly by state overseers, who often employed slaves. Some fifty of these '*estancias* of the state' became efficient units of production, providing commodities for export, supplies for the army and reserves of food for the poor in time of need. But in the absence of great external stimulus the economy operated at little above stagnation level and living standards remained primitive.

Society assumed a peculiar formation. The old colonial aristocracy was destroyed by Francia. The Spanish entrepreneurial class was broken by taxation, isolation and persecution. The remnants took refuge in the *estanciero* class, if refuge it was. Confiscation of estates and denial of free export outlets frustrated the development of commercial agriculture and deprived Paraguay of an *estanciero* class comparable to that in the rest of the littoral. When these classes tried to fight back, in the conspiracy of 1820, Francia crushed them in a reign of terror, executing, imprisoning, banishing. The death of the ruling class did not imply the advancement of lower sectors. In effect the state and its few servants took the place of the traditional elite, rural and commercial. Francia did not come to power as the leader of a social revolution, the saviour of the Indian peasantry against the landed aristocracy. The mass of the population, the bland and docile Guaraní people – unorganized farmers and apolitical peasantry – were passive spectators of Francia's dictatorship. They continued to live and work in a subordinate position, while government agents disposed of the labour of the Indians in Misiones. Slavery endured beyond the Francia regime, and 'slaves of the state' laboured on the government *estancias* and in public works, although the law of 1842 ended the slave trade and decreed that children born to slaves after 1842 would be free on reaching the age of twenty-five (*libertos*). According to the census of 1846, in a population of 238,862 there were 17,212 *pardos* (coloureds) of whom 7,893 were slaves and 523 *libertos*.

Francia's successor modified his policy in some important aspects. A fat and bovine *mestizo*, whose neck bulged over his collar, Carlos Antonio López made a bad impression on foreigners but not on Paraguayans. He too was a dictator, though more benevolent than Francia. He too had total power, though he used it to free political prisoners, provide a minimum of education, organize a simple judicial system and establish newspapers. He too favoured state control of land and economy, though this tended to mean control by his own family. He departed from the system of Francia, however, in two fundamentals: he ended Paraguay's isolation, and he introduced the rudiments of modernization. Already in the 1840s he allowed in a number of foreign merchants and artisans, as well as a few doctors. After 1852, following the fall of Rosas and the opening of the rivers, López began to import technology on a large scale. For the skills and equipment to give Paraguay a modern infrastructure of industry, transport and arms, he looked to Europe, particularly Britain. He sent his son Francisco Solano López at the head of a mission to buy military and naval arms and to recruit technical advisers. The party visited England, France and Spain in 1853–4. In London López contracted with A. Blythe and Company of Limehouse, a shipbuilding and engineering firm, for supplies and personnel, and Paraguay soon became one of their best customers. A steam warship was ordered, equipment and arms were purchased, engineers and technicians hired, and arrangements made for the training of Paraguayan apprentices. A whole team of British contract technicians, together with military advisers and doctors, went to Paraguay, some 200 in all including a talented young engineer, William K. Whytehead, the mastermind of the first modernization programme in South America. British machinery and equipment were used to construct a shipyard with a new wharf and dry dock, capable of building and repairing steamers; this was completed by 1860. An arsenal, with capacity for producing cannons and naval gear, was founded in

1856. Factories, an iron foundry, a telegraph system, all were installed in the course of a few years. A railway was begun in 1856 to link Asunción and Villa Rica, and a state merchant marine was inaugurated with steamships built in Paraguay. The entire operation was a monument to Paraguayan determination, British ingenuity and Guaraní labour. Yet it contained some singular features. In the first place, the process did not represent a continuous flow of investment capital into Paraguay. The government bought directly from abroad, paying hard cash for equipment and high wages to personnel. Thus, it did not engender 'dependence', but at the same time it lacked permanence. Secondly, these were essentially defence contracts rather than instruments of modernization in any long-term economic sense. While they created a new infrastructure, this was for purely military purposes, not for development. Thirdly, the structure of society was not basically changed. In a sense the Paraguayan government imported an entire middle class – engineers, architects, doctors, teachers, merchants and artisans. In the 1860s foreigners held about half of all the business licences in the country. But they left hardly a mark on Paraguayan society.

Modernization depended upon, and sought to achieve, the regional security of Paraguay. López wished to establish wider trade channels than those allowed by Francia and to open Paraguay to the modern world. He permitted trade down river to all nations, if Buenos Aires or the caudillos of the littoral could be persuaded to let it through. The results were mixed. Boundaries with Argentina and Brazil were still unsettled and remained a source of friction. Moreover, López found it difficult to make headway against Rosas, who viewed Paraguay as an errant province and restricted its use of the river system. Alliance with Corrientes and with Brazil had little success. Rosas replied by blockade, and López responded with war in 1845; but this was premature, for Paraguay did not yet possess independent military power and could go to war only as a tool of Brazil. It was these humiliating experiences which moved López to modernize his country. The fall of Rosas, in which Paraguay played no part beyond a formal alliance with Brazil, enabled it to break out of isolation. The Argentine confederation declared free navigation of the rivers in 1853. American and European powers signed treaties with López between 1852 and 1860, and the river system was opened to foreign vessels. The new trade did not bring unqualified liberation to the Paraguayan economy. In some commodities it attracted competition which damaged local production hitherto protected by isolation. In the time of Francia cotton was extensively cultivated for home consumption; but after 1852 foreign manufactures penetrated up-river, and people would no longer pay seventy five cents per yard for domestic fabric when they could purchase the imported for ten. Even North American lumber (pinewood) sold in Corrientes in competition with local wood.

Congress had granted López the right to name a temporary successor, and before he died, on 10 September 1862, he nominated his own son. Hereditary *caudillismo*, this was a new phenomenon in South America, Paraguay's exhibit in the laboratory of politics. And there was nothing temporary about this succession. Francisco Solano López had been brought up as heir apparent; within the limits of his meagre and eccentric talents, he had been educated to power, and his whole formation had been designed to make him the military leader of a new Paraguay. He admired not only British technology but also the imperial ideas of Napoleon III, and he returned from his visit to Europe with a great vision. He dreamed of a South American empire, governed from Asunción and ruled by López II, and to this end he collaborated closely with his father in the construction of a military machine and its industrial base. And when he succeeded to government, he was determined to project this new strength abroad and to make Paraguay the guardian of the balance of power in the Río de la Plata. Dr Francia's army had taken a large part of the budget, but had not numbered more than 1,500 troops in Asunción and perhaps as many on the borders. Francisco Solano López raised the standing army to 28,000 and created a menacing if crude parody of a military state.

López II continued the policy of state intervention, control of the economy, and monopoly of *yerba* and its export, in contrast to the policies of economic liberalism prevailing in Buenos Aires, where he was mockingly attacked in the Argentine press. He in turn was fiercely critical of Buenos Aires, partly in self-defence, partly on ideological grounds. In his opinion, through benevolent despotism Paraguay had achieved order, material progress and military strength. In Argentina, on the other hand, the new regime was seeking to refashion the nation in a liberal mould. But the Argentine federalists and the primitive caudillos who still survived looked upon Paraguay as a last stronghold of autonomy and tradition against the centralist and liberal revolution. Two rival models therefore competed for supremacy in the Río de la Plata, in a mortal conflict of alternatives, constitutionalism against absolutism, liberalism against tradition, Mitre against López. And each side dreaded infection by the other.

While López was ready to resist the advance of liberal principles and economic domination from Argentina, he also faced the spread of Brazilian influence and power southwards towards the Río de la Plata. Paraguay's policy towards Brazil was a test of statesmanship. Although Dr Francia's dealings with the neighbouring giant had been generally friendly, and the Brazilians had supported Carlos Antonio López's stand against Rosas, relations had subsequently worsened. Frontier controversy convinced Carlos Antonio López that Brazil threatened the security of his country and that claims for free navigation and for disputed frontier territory were part of a wider initiative. Yet López refused to negotiate a settlement, either with Brazil or Argentina, on boundary or any other matters; at the same time he was reluctant to take the military initiative, which was the only alternative. Francisco Solano López, however, had more elementary convictions: he despised Brazilians, with an almost racialist intensity, and he believed that Argentina's national reorganization would fail. He was therefore willing to push his father's premises to their logical conclusion – war against both Buenos Aires and Brazil in defence of Paraguay's national interests and traditional values. The situation, he believed, was opportune. If he was menaced by alliances, he too had potential allies, the rural caudillos of Argentina and the *blancos* of Uruguay. And were his enemies united? A war against Paraguay was by no means a popular cause in Argentina. It was regarded by many as an illiberal expedient, whose results would be to magnify the power of the state, aggrandize the national army, and, while enabling some to profit from supplying the state, would lay intolerable burdens on the community. Brazil, moreover, was regarded as an obnoxious ally: to shed Argentine blood and spend Argentine money supporting a slave state in its imperialist ambitions was condemned by many as the height of folly. The war was therefore divisive. Moreover, it gave the provincial caudillos a chance to revert to a more primitive Argentina in opposition to Buenos Aires and in support of regionalist interests. López, however, with military superiority, did not have the skill to exploit these divisions within Argentina, or between Argentina and Brazil, and he recklessly wasted his assets.

Paraguay was the victim of Argentina, Brazil and its own ruler, although it was the latter who allowed himself to fulfil the role of aggressor. López's demands upon Brazil and Argentina for a statement of intent were ignored. He then sent an ultimatum to Brazil not to invade Uruguay. This was rejected. When Brazil invaded Uruguay, López broke off relations with her in November 1864, seized a Brazilian steamer in Asunción, and invaded the Mato Grosso. This was the first of many strategic mistakes: it might have been feasible to attack Brazil in Uruguay, but not in the heart of her own territory. In January 1865 López requested permission from Argentina to cross Misiones to reach Brazil. Permission was refused, and in March López declared war on Argentina and invaded Corrientes. This enabled Mitre to carry through the Brazilian alliance without political disaster at home. Mitre thus declared war on López, joining Brazil and the government of Flores in Uruguay. As for Argentina's own dissidents, they were now leaderlesss, for Urquiza committed himself to the war and became one of the army's principal suppliers. The overt object of the triple alliance was merely to secure free navigation of the rivers and to crush the tyrant López; and the war was presented as a crusade on behalf of civilization and liberty. This was propaganda. The treaty of alliance contained secret clauses providing for the annexation of disputed territory in northern Paraguay by Brazil and regions in the east and west of Paraguay by Argentina; and the war would not cease until the total destruction of the Paraguayan government. Basically the allies were determined to remove the focus of attraction which a strong Paraguay exercised on their peripheral regions.

For Paraguay, therefore, this was a war of survival. In any case a war against the two giants was bound to be debilitating and a severe test for an economy so narrowly based. López needed a swift victory, and if he could not win quickly he would probably not win at all. If he had stood on defence, Paraguay should have been virtually impregnable, except in the south-west and the line of the River Paraguay. As it was, he struck out indiscriminately and squandered his forces. His fleet was virtually destroyed in the battle of Riachuelo early in the war (June 1865), and the Brazilian naval and military forces were able to penetrate up river into the heart of Paraguay. Conditions deteriorated grimly for the Paraguayan people. Their supplies were cut off by the allied blockade. Their armed forces were slaughtered, many of them, including foreign advisers, by the crazed López himself, who believed he was surrounded by conspirators as well as by the enemy. The horror came to an end when López was killed at the battle of Cerro Corá on 1 March 1870.

The results were calamitous for Paraguay. The traditional view that she lost one million people is a gratuitous myth. The truth itself was bitter enough. She lost one half of her population, which dropped from 406,646 in 1864 to 231,000 in 1872. The majority of the survivors were women, children and old people. The country, so long isolated and intact, was torn open and devastated. There was a further irony. Although Paraguay eventually achieved an inferior version of the export-oriented growth typical of other parts of the River Plate, she failed in the end to undergo the process of modernization which she herself had pioneered and which was now monopolized by Argentina and Uruguay. Territorially Paraguay was also a loser, though the rivalry of Argentina and Brazil prevented worse dismemberment. She was forced to grant territory north-east of the River Paraguay to Brazil; and to Argentina she lost Misiones territory, between the Paraná and the Uruguay, and other land further west. Politically the country disintegrated. The age of the great dictators was over, and there was nothing to fill the vacuum; the exiled opposition returned, and Paraguay began a period of *golpes*, changing caudillos and unworkable constitutions. The Paraguayan version of development, therefore, had been a total waste of effort, money and lives. If it proved anything, it proved that it was impossible to create a Prussia in South America.

The other countries of the River Plate escaped the worst consequences of war. For Uruguay the 1860s was a period of economic growth. Politically, it is true, the prospect was not promising. The wartime government of Venancio Flores was not a stable one; it was a dictatorship which ended fusion and gave the *colorados* a monopoly of power, provoking an inevitable challenge from the *blancos* and other factions. Uruguay split into warring camps, and Flores and Berro were both assassinated on the same day, 19 February 1868. As central government disintegrated, and Uruguay slid helplessly into disorder and *caudillismo*, economy and society enjoyed an autonomy of their own and underwent great transformation. But while political anarchy did not automatically prevent economic growth, economic change did not immediately restore political equilibrium. There was in fact a prolonged time-lag between the growth of 1860–8 and the delayed stabilization of 1875.

The population of Uruguay rose from 221,000 in 1860 to 385,000 in 1868. Montevideo grew even faster, from 58,000 to 126,000. In the years 1860–8 some 50,000 immigrants came to Uruguay, principally Italians and Spaniards. Commercial expansion, a booming construction industry, the increase of ocean-going vessels and the activity of coastal and river shipping, all made Montevideo a growth point and a focus of immigration. Foreigners increased from 48 per cent of the total in 1860 to 60 per cent in 1868. Meanwhile in the countryside the growing sheep sector attracted settlers from many nations. The new population gave a boost to imports and exports. Imports increased from 8.2 million pesos in 1860 to 15 million in 1870; exports from 5.4 million pesos in 1860 to 12 million in 1870. The commerce of Montevideo was also stimulated by a new product, wool, bought up by warehouse owners from the rural producers and exported to Europe. The port was a supply base of the allied armies during the Paraguayan War, and from then became a permanent entrepôt, whose free trade regime encouraged transit trade and enabled it to rival Buenos Aires as a centre of distribution in the Río de la Plata.

There was a great and sudden transformation in wool production. Between 1860 and 1868 the number of sheep increased from 3 million head to 16/17 million head. The stimulus was in part internal, the favourable environment for sheep farming in Uruguay, the switch from cattle to sheep as prices for jerked beef went steadily down, the growth of middle-sized farms for which sheep were a more economical investment and the influence of foreign immigrants as sheep farmers and improvers; external stimulus was provided by strong demand from the textile industries of Britain, France and Belgium, and the absence of competition from cotton during the American Civil War. Sheepbreeding, especially of improved stock, demanded not only more labour but also a sedentary labour and one immune from *caudillismo* and revolutions. And sheep farming allowed the emergence, if not of a rural middle class, at least of smaller properties and farms, for immigrants could make progress in this sector more easily than in cattle, as in Argentina. It thus diversified the social structure of the countryside and introduced an alternative to the great cattle ranch. In 1862, among total exports wool accounted for 10.6 per cent, hides 32.9 per cent and jerked beef 11.5 per cent. In 1872 wool accounted for 24.4 per cent.

Uruguay now had three basic products, wool, hides and jerked beef. Markets, too, were diversified: hides went principally to Britain and the United States, jerked beef to Brazil and Cuba, wool to France and Belgium. If it was a dependent economy, it was not dependent on one product or one market. This diversification was a key to Uruguay's future prosperity. Economic conditions were propitious enough to attract foreign capital. Until now the influence of the Brazilian financier,

Baron Mauá, who had established the Banco Mauá in 1857, had been dominant. Now British capital entered. At the end of 1863 a branch of the Bank of London and the River Plate opened in Montevideo. Between 1861 and 1865 British and German capital established Liebig's extract of meat company at Fray Bentos. This was the first foreign investment in the meat industry, and it profited from excess cattle production, low prices and cheap labour, offering an escape from the limited outlets of Brazil and Cuba by producing a meat extract which European markets would accept, at least for their armies. In 1864–5 British capital began to lend to the state, and in the early 1870s British enterprise moved into railways and took them over.

These trends were momentarily halted by the crisis of 1868 and the civil war of 1870. The economic crisis was precipitated to some extent by the great drought of 1869–70, which savagely decimated livestock and sheep herds. But a number of other factors played their part, such as monetary instability, the great excess of imports over exports, the former stimulated by increase of population and conspicuous consumption of the upper classes, the latter hit by the fall of international prices and the decline of production in the *estancias*, which could not yet cope with improvement and modernization. In 1870 Uruguay imported 15 million pesos worth of goods and exported only 12 million. Between 1864 and 1869 imports exceeded exports by 18 million pesos. By 1875 the worst was over. Uruguay was now poised to move into a phase of modernization and development. With the promise of better things, merchants and *estancieros* wanted peace and strong government. The time for a powerful state and a national army was approaching.

Argentina differed from the Uruguayan version of development in three respects, its earlier start, its greater scale and its firmer political base. In Argentina, too, the transition from old to new was accompanied by crisis. In the mid 1860s the Paraguayan War coincided with monetary instability and a crisis in Europe to throw the Argentine economy out of gear. The markets for cattle products and for wool exports contracted and production declined; even sheep farming suffered depression. The internal causes of the crisis lay in the land and derived from an excessive expansion of the flocks in the relatively restricted areas of soft grasses suitable for sheep-raising. Over-stocking coincided with a severe drought, which was a further setback to owners of cattle and sheep. The policy of the state did not help. The law of November 1864 decreeing the sale of all public lands available within the frontier set prices which were too high and aggravated the rural crisis. So a period of expansion and land hunger was followed by a slump.

Recovery was rapid, but the experience caused a re-appraisal of Argentina's problems and prospects. Worried *estancieros* began to discuss the need for diversification of agrarian production, modernization of methods and greater capital investment. There was talk, too, of combining agriculture and livestock, investing urban capital in the rural sector, incorporating new land, establishing model farms. Innovatory ideas of this kind were characteristic of the group of *estancieros* who, in 1866, founded the Argentine Rural Society as a medium of debate and development. A mood of protectionism grew. One of the most notable, though abortive, projects of the Society was to establish the first textile factory in the country, in the hope that a national textile industry might develop, using Argentina's own raw materials and freeing her from dependence on foreign markets and foreign imports. Rural labour, its plight and its supply, became a matter of increasing concern. The insecurity, impoverishment and low status of the peon had often been attributed to Rosas and his military exactions, but there were few signs of improvement after 1852, and the demands of the Paraguayan War became a new scourge of the pampas. The need for more people was urgent and accepted. And mass immigration, which began as a drive to fill the desert, ended by swelling the towns. Argentina had come to the end of one age and the beginning of another.

# BIBLIOGRAPHICAL ESSAYS

ABBREVIATIONS

ESC          *Estudios Sociales Centroamericanos*
HAHR         *Hispanic American Historical Review*
JIAS         *Journal of Inter-American Studies and World Affairs*
JLAS         *Journal of Latin American Studies*
LARR         *Latin American Research Review*
TA           *The Americas*

## I.   ECONOMY AND SOCIETY

Roberto Cortés Conde and Stanley J. Stein (eds.), *Latin America. A guide to economic history 1830–1930* (Berkeley, 1977), is a comprehensive survey of existing secondary literature which concentrates on Argentina, Brazil, Chile, Colombia, Peru and Mexico. Ciro F. S. Cardoso and Héctor Pérez Brignoli, *Historia económica de América Latina* (2 vols., Barcelona, 1979), is a general economic history of Latin America which includes a valuable chapter (vol. II, chapter 4) on the post-independence period. See also Tulio Halperín Donghi, *Historia contemporánea de América Latina* (Madrid, 1969), chapters 3 and 4, and *The aftermath of revolution in Latin America* (New York, 1973), especially chapter 2.

There are a number of valuable studies of the commercial and financial relations between the new Spanish American states and Britain in the period after independence: for example, D. C. M. Platt, *Latin America and British trade, 1806–1914* (London, 1973), Leland H. Jenks, *The migration of British capital to 1875* (New York, 1927; reissued London, 1971), and J. Fred Rippy, *British investments in Latin America, 1822–1949* (Minneapolis, 1959). Sergio Villalobos R., *El comercio y la crisis colonial, un mito de la Independencia* (Santiago, 1968), examines the case of Chile, carrying to extremes Platt's scepticism about the real impact of the opening of trade which accompanied political emanicaption, from a perspective which is not exclusively Chilean.

On the whole, however, studies at the national or regional level predominate for this period. This can be partially explained by the fact that general studies inspired by the theme of dependence or reaction to dependence, so abundant over the last ten years, concentrate their attention on the colonial period or on the period after 1870. This is the case, for example, of Stanley and Barbara Stein, *The colonial heritage of Latin America* (New York, 1970), or Marcello Carmagnani, *Formación y crisis de un sistema feudal. América Latina del siglo XVI a nuestros días* (Mexico City, 1976).

A pioneering study of the impact of the Wars of Independence on the economy and society of Spanish America is Charles C. Griffin, 'Economic and social aspects of the era of Spanish American independence', *HAHR*, 29/2 (1949), 170–87, an essay revised and expanded in *Los temas sociales y económicos en la época de la Independencia* (Caracas, 1962). The impact of the political and military crisis on rural society is studied for Venezuela in Germán Carrera Damas, *Materiales para el estudio de la cuestión agraria en Venezuela (1800–1830)* (Caracas, 1964), and for Uruguay in L. S. de Touron, N. de la Torre and J. G. Rodríguez, *La revolución agraria artiguista* (Montevideo, 1969), of which there is an abridged version entitled *Artigas y su revolución agraria, 1811–1820* (Mexico, 1978). The impact on society as a whole is studied, for Mexico, by Luis Villoro in *La revolución de independencia: ensayo de interpretación histórica* (Mexico, 1953), in a more arbitrary fashion for Colombia in the relevant sections of Indalecio Lievano Aguirre, *Los grandes conflictos sociales y económicos de nuestra historia* (4 vols., Bogotá, 1966), and for Argentina, in Tulio Halperín Donghi, *Politics, economics and society in Argentina in the revolutionary period* (London, 1975). R. A. Humphreys (ed.), *British consular reports on the trade and politics of Latin America, 1824–1826* (London, 1940), covers in considerable detail the situation in the different ports, and reflects the impact on them and the new nations generally of the still recent political and military crisis. An attempt to trace the social and economic development of a nation under the twin impact of the commercial and the political/military crisis can be found in Jonathan C. Brown, *A socioeconomic history of Argentina 1776–1860* (London, 1979).

On the new economic and social order and political reconstruction after independence, once again the most important contributions concern specific countries. David Bushnell, *The Santander Regime in Gran Colombia* (Newark, Delaware, 1954), is an exemplary study of the administrative difficulties of the new state in the face of problems by no means exclusive to Colombia. Miron Burgin, *The economic aspect of Argentine federalism, 1820–52* (Cambridge, Mass., 1946), reexamines the themes studied somewhat impressionistically, but nonetheless perceptively, by Juan Alvarez in his *Estudio sobre las guerras civiles argentinas*

(Buenos Aires, 1914). An equally impressionistic but much more positive study on Chile is provided by Francisco Encina in a book which was destined to exert considerable influence both inside and outside that country: *Nuestra inferioridad económica* (Santiago, 1911). There are very few studies of social change during the second quarter of the nineteenth century. John V. Lombardi, *The decline and abolition of negro slavery in Venezuela, 1820–1854* (Westport, Conn., 1971), is worthy of mention and for Mexico, Jean Meyer, *Problemas campesinos y revueltas agrarias (1821–1910)* (Mexico, 1973). For Cuba, both Franklin W. Knight, *Slave society in Cuba during the nineteenth century* (Madison, 1970), and Manuel Moreno Fraginals, *El ingenio* (Havana, 1964; English trans., *The sugarmill*, New York, 1978), concentrate their attention on this period. The vast travel literature of the period is listed in Bernard Naylor. Worthy of special mention is H. G. Ward, *Mexico in 1827*, (2 vols., London, 1828), a systematic study by a well-informed and acutely aware, if not disinterested, observer. To this should be added the critical analyses by locally born authors: for example, José Antonio Saco's outstanding *Memoria sobre la vagancia en la isla de Cuba* (Havana, 1832), and Mariano Otero, *Ensayo sobre el verdadero estado de la cuestión social y política que se agita en la República Mexicana* (Mexico, 1842). The literature on the post-1850 period and the foundations of a new order in Spanish America is more extensive, but almost more scattered and heterogeneous. A few national studies which have implicit relevance to the whole of Latin America deserve mention. A study of the formation of a dominant group during an export boom, such as *Guano y burguesía en Perú* (Lima, 1974), by Heraclio Bonilla, is, without a doubt, an exception, as was the whole Peruvian experience at this time. The impact of the new order, as felt to the fullest by the peasantry, is the subject of T. G. Powell, *El liberalismo y el campesinado en el centro de México (1850–1876)* (Mexico, 1974), which offers a less negative view than usual of the relations between the peasantry and the first exponents of liberalism, and Arnold J. Bauer, *Chilean rural society from the Spanish Conquest to 1930* (London, 1975). Another aspect of liberal reform, the confiscation of church property, is studied in Jan Bazant, *Alienation of Church wealth in Mexico. Social and economic aspects of the liberal revolution, 1856–1875* (Cambridge, 1971). Frank Safford, *The ideal of the practical: Colombia's struggle to form a technical elite* (Austin, Texas, 1976), provides a subtle view of reformism which distances itself from the standard view of liberalism. H. S. Ferns, *Britain and Argentina in the XIXth Century* (Oxford, 1960) provides a convincing study of the transition to the age of the railway, in a country which, perhaps more than any other, would feel its impact. This period witnessed the publication of exhaustive descriptions of the geography and socio-economic characteristics of the new countries, along the lines of the pioneer study by Agostino Codazzi, published in 1842 under the title *Resúmen de la geografía de Venezuela*. In Colombia, the 'Comisión Geográfica', also directed by Codazzi, produced Manuel Ancizar's *Peregrinación de Alpha por la provincia del Norte de la Nueva Granada, en 1850 y 1851* (Bogotá, 1853). In Peru, there was the monumental work by the Italian geographer, Antonio Raimondi, *El Perú* (3 vols., Lima, 1874–80); in Chile, the even more ambitious *Historia física y política de Chile* (Paris–Santiago, 1844–71) by the French botanist Claude Gay, of which the two volumes on *La agricultura*, published in 1862 and 1865, are of particular interest; in Argentina, the *Description géographique et statistique de la Confédération Argentine* (3 vols., Paris, 1860–73), by Jean-Antoine-Victor Martin de Moussy.

On individual Spanish American countries, see *CHLA*, III, bibliographical essays 10–15.

## 2. POLITICS, IDEOLOGY AND SOCIETY

Tulio Halperín Donghi offers many imaginative insights into the post-independence period in *Historia contemporánea de América Latina* (Madrid, 1969), chapters 3 and 4, and *The aftermath of revolution in Latin America* (New York, 1973).

There is no single work on the constitutional history of all the Spanish American states. A significant work on early constitutional formation in Mexico is Nettie Lee Benson, *La diputación provincial y el federalismo mexicano* (Mexico, 1955), and a recent contribution on Central America is Mario Rodriguez, *The Cadiz experiment in Central America, 1808–1826* (Berkeley, 1978). David Bushnell's *The Santander Regime in Gran Colombia* (Newark, Delaware, 1954) is a model monograph on the early administrative and political formation of a Spanish American state.

A general view of elite ideologies in the nineteenth century may be found in Leopoldo Zea, *The Latin American mind* (Norman, Okla., 1949). Works on particular countries which shed light on Spanish America as a whole include Simon Collier, *Ideas and politics of Chilean independence, 1808–1833* (Cambridge, 1967); Jaime Jaramillo Uribe, *El pensamiento colombiano en el siglo xix* (Bogotá, 1964); Charles Hale, *Mexican liberalism in the age of Mora, 1821–1853* (New Haven, 1968). See also an interesting article by Hale, 'The reconstruction of nineteenth-century politics in Spanish America: a case for the history of ideas', *LARR*, 8/2 (1973), 53–73.

The political polarization in the middle of the nineteenth century is treated for Mexico in Hale's *Mexican liberalism* and in Moisés González Navarro, *Anatomía del poder en México, 1848–1853* (Mexico, 1977), the latter a loosely-constructed work, but one rich in suggestive detail. On Colombia, see Robert L. Gilmore, 'Nueva Granada's socialist mirage', *HAHR*, 36/2 (1956), 190–210; Germán Colmenares, *Partidos políticos y clases sociales* (Bogotá, 1968); and J. Leon Helguera, 'Antecedentes sociales de la revolución de 1851 en el sur de Colombia (1848–1851)', *Anuario Colombiano de Historia Social y de la Cultura*, 5 (1970), 53–63. On Chile, see a contemporary account, Benjamín Vicuña MacKenna, *Historia de la jornada del 20 de abril de 1851: una batalla en las calles de Santiago* (Santiago, 1878) and a recent monograph, Luis Alberto Romero, *La Sociedad de la Igualdad. Los artesanos de Santiago de Chile y sus primeras experiencias políticas, 1820–1851* (Buenos Aires, 1978).

Valuable works on social and economic aspects of political alignments are Tulio Halperín Donghi, *Politics, economics and society in Argentina in the revolutionary period* (Cambridge, 1975); Miron Burgin, *Economic aspects of Argentine Federalism, 1820–1852* (Cambridge, Mass., 1946); François Chevalier, 'Conservateurs et libéraux au Mexique: essaie de sociologie et géografie politiques de l'Independance à l'intervention française', *Cahiers d'Histoire Mondiale*, 8 (1964), 457–74; David A. Brading, *Los orígenes del nacionalismo mexicano* (Mexico, 1973). Frank Safford, 'Bases of political alignment in early republican Spanish America', in Richard Graham and Peter H. Smith (eds.), *New Approaches to Latin American history* (Austin, Texas, 1974), 71–111, offers a critical review of this topic.

On issues affecting the Church in Spanish American politics, J. Lloyd Mecham offers a country-by-country survey in *Church and state in Latin America* (Chapel Hill, N.C., 1934; 2nd edn, 1966); the first edition offers some material on the nineteenth century that is deleted in the second edition. More recent works examining the role of the Church in the economy as well as in politics are Michael P. Costeloe, *Church wealth in Mexico* (Cambridge, 1967) and Jan Bazant, *Alienation of Church wealth in Mexico. Social and economic aspects of the liberal revolution, 1856–1875* (Cambridge, 1971). Arnold Bauer's more general analysis, 'The Church and Spanish American agrarian structure 1765–1865', *The Americas*, 28/1

(1971), lucidly develops some of the ideas imbedded in Bazant's work.

There is a voluminous literature on *caudillismo*, particularly if all the biographies of caudillos are included. For many of these, see the bibliographical essays on individual countries in this period. General analyses of the phenomenon may be found in Charles E. Chapman, 'The age of the caudillos: a chapter in Hispanic American History', *HAHR*, 12/3 (1932), 281–300; Hugh M. Hamill, Jr (ed.), *Dictatorship in Spanish America* (New York, 1965); Robert L. Gilmore, *Caudillism and militarism in Venezuela, 1810–1910* (Athens, Ohio, 1964); Eric R. Wolf and Edward C. Hansen, 'Caudillo politics: a structural analysis', *Comparative Studies in Society and History*, 9/2 (1967), 168–79; Fernando Díaz Díaz, *Caudillos y caciques* (Mexico, 1972); and Malcolm Deas, 'Algunas notas sobre la historia del caciquismo en Colombia', *Revista de Occidente*, 63 (1973), 118–40. One of the most useful contributions is the analysis of a single case (Martín Güemes in the province of Salta, Argentina) by Roger Haigh, 'The creation and control of a Caudillo', *HAHR*, 44/4 (1964), 481–90. Most of the analyses of political instability in the period after independence also have something to say about *caudillismo*. Two classic works are Francisco García Calderón, *Latin America: its rise and progress* (New York, 1913) and L. Cecil Jane, *Liberty and despotism in Spanish America* (London, 1929). The most important recent contributions are two essays by Richard M. Morse, 'Toward a theory of Spanish American government', *Journal of the History of Ideas*, 15 (1954), 71–93, and 'The heritage of Latin America', in Louis Hartz (ed.), *The founding of new societies* (New York, 1964), 123–77.

On individual Spanish American countries, see *CHLA*, III, bibliographical essays 10–15.

### 3. MEXICO

Ernesto de la Torre Villar *et al.* (eds.), *Historia documental de México* (2 vols., Mexico, 1964) is an important documentary collection. F. Tena Ramírez (ed.), *Leyes fundamentales de México 1808–1973* (5th rev. edn, Mexico, 1973), reproduces all the constitutions and their drafs as well as the most important laws and decrees. For economic and social aspects of the period from around 1800 to 1852, L. Chávez Orozco (ed.), *Colección de documentos para la historia del comercio exterior de México*, in two series: series I in 7 vols. (Mexico, 1958–62); series II in 4 vols. (Mexico, 1965–67) should be consulted; it covers much more ground than the title indicates.

Documentation on the Juárez era can be found in J. L. Tamayo (ed.), *Benito Juárez, documentos, discursos y correspondencia* (14 vols., Mexico, 1964–70), and Secretaría de la Presidencia (ed.), *La administración pública en la época de Juárez* (3 vols., Mexico, 1973). For foreign relations, see L. Díaz (ed.), *Versión francesa de México. Informes diplomáticos 1853–1867* (4 vols., Mexico, 1963–7), and L. Díaz (ed.), *Versión francesa de México 1851–67. Informes económicos* (consular reports) (2 vols., Mexico, 1974).

There are a number of general works which include substantial treatment of Mexican history in the period after independence. Most notable among older works are Lucas Alamán, *Historia de México, 1808–1849* (5 vols., Mexico, 2nd edn, 1942–8), vol. v, Vicente Riva Palacio (ed.), *México a través de los siglos* (Mexico, 1889; facsimile edn, Mexico, 1958), Vols IV and v; Francisco de Paula de Arrangoiz, *México desde 1808 hasta 1867* (4 vols., Mexico, 1871–2; 2nd edn, 1974). More recently Luis González y González (ed.), *Historia general de México* (4 vols., El Colegio de México, Mexico, 1976), Vol. III (1821–1910), and Jan Bazant, *A concise history of Mexico from Hidalgo to Cárdenas* (Cambridge, 1977), chapters 2 and 3, have provided valuable syntheses. Still useful is Justo Sierra, *Evolución política del pueblo mexicano*, now available in English as *The political evolution of the Mexican people* (Austin, Texas, 1970).

On particular aspects of the period, Charles A. Hale, *Mexican liberalism in the age of Mora 1821–1853* (New Haven, 1968) is essential for the study of ideas. J. Bazant, *Historia de la deuda exterior de México 1823–1946* (Mexico, 1968), replaces the older book by Edgar Turlington, *Mexico and her foreign creditors* (New York, 1930). Michael P. Costeloe, *Church and state in independent Mexico. A study of the patronage debate 1821–1857* (London, 1978), is an excellent study of church-state relations. R. W. Randall, *Real del Monte, a British mining venture in Mexico* (Austin, Texas, 1972), is one of the few books on mining. Robert A. Potash, *El Banco de Avío de México 1821–1846* (Mexico, 1959), is essential for the history of manufacturing and government banking. For background on the Yucatán Caste War, there are three well-researched articles by Howard F. Cline: 'The "Aurora Yucateca" and the spirit of enterprise in Yucatán, 1821–1847', *HAHR*, 27 (1947), 30–60; 'The sugar episode in Yucatán. 1825–1850', *Inter-American Economic Affairs*, 1/4 (1948), 79–100; 'The Henequén episode in Yucatán', *Inter-American Economic Affairs*, 2/2 (1948), 30–51. See also Moisés González Navarro, *Raza y Tierra* (Mexico, 1970), and N. Reed, *The Caste War of Yucatán* (Stanford, 1964). On agrarian structures and the history of the hacienda, see Charles H. Harris III, *A*

*Mexican family empire. The latifundio of the Sánchez Navarros 1765–1867* (Austin, Texas, 1975); J. Bazant, *Cinco haciendas mexicanas. Tres siglos de vida rural en San Luis Potosí, 1600–1910* (Mexico, 1975), a summary of parts of which was published in English in K. Duncan and I. Rutledge, *Land and labour in Latin America. Essays on the development of agrarian capitalism in the 19th & 20th centuries* (Cambridge, 1977); Herbert J. Nickel, *Soziale Morphologie der mexikanischen Hacienda* (Wiesbaden, 1978), one of the best hacienda studies so far published; David A. Brading, *Haciendas and ranchos in the Mexican Bajío* (Cambridge, 1978). Finally, on the difficult question of church wealth and its disposal, see M. P. Costeloe, *Church wealth in Mexico* (Cambridge, 1967), and J. Bazant, *Alienation of church wealth in Mexico. Social and economic aspects of the liberal revolution 1856–1875* (Cambridge, 1971; 2nd revised edn in Spanish, *Los bienes de la iglesia en México*, Mexico, 1977). Charles R. Berry, *The reform in Oaxaca, 1856–76. A micro-history of the liberal revolution* (Lincoln, Nebraska, 1981) is a detailed regional study of the question. There are two collections of essays on aspects of the economic and social history of Mexico in the nineteenth century edited by Ciro F. S. Cardoso: *Formación y Desarrollo de la Burguesía en México. Siglo XIX* (Mexico, 1978) and *México en el siglo XIX (1821–1910). Historia económica y de la éstructura social* (Mexico, 1980).

For the period 1821–35, contemporary descriptions include J. Poinsett, *Notes on Mexico* (London, 1825) and H. G. Ward, *Mexico in 1827* (2 vols., London, 1828). Günther Kahle, *Militär und Staatsbildung in den Anfängen der Unabhängigkeit Mexikos* (Cologne, 1969), is a pioneer study of the formation of the Mexican army through the amalgamation of guerrilla fighters for independence and former royalist officers. Michael P. Costeloe, *La primera república federal de México 1824–1835* (Mexico, 1975), is a study of political parties, based on research in the press and pamphlets. Also worthy of note are R. Flores C., *Counterrevolution: the role of the Spaniards in the independence of Mexico 1804–1838* (Lincoln, Nebraska, 1974); H. D. Sims, *La expulsión de los españoles en México, 1821–1828* (Mexico, 1974), which contains valuable statistical information; and Brian R. Hamnett, *Revolución y contrarevolución en México y el Perú* (Mexico, 1978), for the difficult first years of independent Mexico.

The Texas revolution and the Mexican war have naturally received a great deal of attention from U.S. and Mexican historians, contemporary and modern. See R. S. Ripley, *The war with Mexico* (2 vols., New York, 1849, reprinted 1970); R. Alcaraz, *et al.*, *The other side: or notes for the history of the war between Mexico and the United States* (trans. and ed. by A. C.

Ramsey, New York, 1850), in which 15 prominent Mexicans describe the war; Carlos E. Castañeda (ed. and trans.), *The Mexican side of the Texan revolution 1836* (Washington, D.C., 1971) contains accounts by five chief Mexican participants, including Santa Anna; J. F. Ramírez, *Mexico during the war with the United States*, ed. by W. V. Scholes, trans. by E. B. Sherr (Columbia, Mo., 1950); G. M. Brack, *Mexico views Manifest Destiny 1821–1846, An essay on the origins of the Mexican War* (Albuquerque, N.M., 1975), a sympathetic account, well documented from Mexican newspapers and pamphlets; Charles H. Brown, *Agents of Manifest Destiny. The lives and times of the Filibusters* (Chapel Hill, N.C., 1980), a very useful study of these adventurers.

For the period after 1848 there are two studies of the later years of Santa Anna: F. Díaz D., *Caudillos y caciques* (Mexico, 1972) and M. González Navarro, *Anatomía del poder en México 1848–1853* (Mexico, 1977). On liberal politics, see W. V. Scholes, *Mexican politics during the Juárez Régime 1855–1872* (2nd edn, Columbia, Mo., 1969) and Richard N. Sinkin, *The Mexican Reform, 1855–1876. A study in liberal nation-building* (Austin, Texas, 1979); on French intervention, J. A. Dabbs, *The French Army in Mexico 1861–1867, a study in Military government* (The Hague, 1963); and on the empire, Alfred Jackson Hanna and Kathryn Abbey Hanna, *Napoleon III and Mexico. American triumph over monarchy* (Chapel Hill, N.C., 1971).

A number of political biographies are worthy of note: W. S. Robertson, *Iturbide of Mexico* (Durham, N.C., 1952) which is heavily based on archival materials (see also *Memoirs of Agustín de Iturbide* (Washington, D.C., 1971)); J. E. Rodríguez, O., *The emergence of Spanish America. Vicente Rocafuerte and Spanish Americanism 1808–1832* (Berkeley, 1975), a fine biography of an Ecuadorean liberal who took part in the struggle for the Mexican republic; Wildrid H. Callcott, *Santa Anna* (Norman, Oklahoma, 1936) and O. L. Jones Jr, *Santa Anna* (New York, 1968) which should be read together with A. F. Crawford (ed.), *The Eagle. The autobiography of Santa Anna* (Austin, Texas, 1967); Thomas E. Cotner, *The military and political career of José Joaquín de Herrera 1792–1854* (Austin, Texas, 1949); Frank A. Knapp, *The life of Sebastián Lerdo de Tejada 1823–1899* (Austin, Texas, 1951) and C. G. Blázquez, *Miguel Lerdo de Tejada* (Mexico, 1978); I. E. Cadenhead, Jr, *Benito Juárez* (New York, 1973), which to a considerable extent replaces the older and more voluminous biography by R. Roeder, *Juárez and his Mexico* (2 vols., New York, 1947); also by Cadenhead, *Jesús González Ortega and Mexican national politics*

(Texas Christian University Press, 1972); finally, Joan Haslip, *The crown of Mexico, Maximilian and his Empress Carlota* (New York, 1971), a comprehensive biography, both personal and political, of the two tragic figures.

### 4. CENTRAL AMERICA

A comparison of Lázaro Lamadrid, 'A survey of the historiography of Guatemala since 1821. Part 1 – The nineteenth century', *TA*, 8/2 (1951), 189–202; W. J. Griffith, 'The historiography of Central America since 1830', *HAHR*, 40/4 (1960), 548–69; and Griffith, 'Central America', in C. C. Griffin (ed.), *Latin America, a guide to the historical literature* (Austin, 1971), 403–21, reflects the rapid growth of historical publications in the mid-twentieth century. The following essay is concerned principally with works published since Griffin and will be most useful when employed together with the guides mentioned above and the extensive bibliographical essay in R. L. Woodward, Jr, *Central America, a nation divided* (2nd edn, New York, 1985), 278–312, as well as with appropriate sections of the *Handbook of Latin American Studies*.

While earlier general works continue to have utility, Woodward, *Central America*, and Ciro Cardoso and Héctor Pérez, *Centroamérica y la economía occidental (1520–1930)* (San José, 1977) incorporate much of the recent scholarship on the first half-century of independence, especially for the economic and social history. Edelberto Torres Rivas, *Interpretación del desarrollo social centroamericano* (San José, 1971) has provided much of the inspiration for serious recent historical research in the social sciences in Central America. Histories of individual states that reflect recent scholarship have been few, but exceptions are Alastair White, *El Salvador* (New York, 1973); Narda Dobson, *A history of Belize* (London, 1973); O. N. Bolland, *The formation of a colonial society: Belize from conquest to crown colony* (Baltimore, 1977); and David Luna, *Manual de historia económica* (San Salvador, 1971). For reference, although uneven in quality, the *Historical Dictionary* series published in Metuchen, N.J., are useful: Philip Flemion, *El Salvador* (1972); H. K. Meyer, *Nicaragua* (1972) and *Honduras* (1976); R. E. Moore, *Guatemala*, rev. edn (1973); and Theodore Creedman, *Costa Rica* (1977). Also useful are the first volumes in the World Bibliographical Series (Oxford: Clio Press): R. L. Woodward, *Belize* (1980) and *Nicaragua* (1983), and Woodman Franklin, *Guatemala* (1981).

Several recent studies deal with specific aspects of the post-independence period: D. R. Radell, *Historical geography of Western Nicaragua: the spheres of influence in León, Granada and Managua, 1519–1965* (Berkeley, 1969); David Browning, *El Salvador, landscape and society* (Oxford, 1971); Alberto Sáenz M., *Historia agrícola de Costa Rica* (San José, 1970); Carolyn Hall, *El café y el desarrollo histórico-geográfico de Costa Rica* (San José, 1976); Constantino Láscaris, *Historia de las ideas en Centroamérica* (San José, 1970); Carlos González, *Historia de la educación en Guatemala*, 2nd edn (Guatemala, 1970); Otto Olivera, *La literatura en publicaciones periódicas de Guatemala: siglo XIX* (New Orleans, 1974); Arturo Castillo, *Historia de la moneda de Honduras* (Tegucigalpa, 1974); Samuel Stone, *La dinastía de los conquistadores* (San José, 1975); Cleto González Víquez, *Capítulos de un libro sobre historia financiera de Costa Rica*, 2nd edn (San José, 1977); and R. L. Woodward, Jr, *Privilegio de clases y el desarrollo económico: el consulado de comercio de Guatemala, 1793–1871* (San José, 1981), which contains extensive documentary appendices not included in the 1966 English edition. Among the most noteworthy articles based on new research and new methodologies recently published in Central American journals are: Ciro Cardoso, 'La formación de la hacienda cafetalera en Costa Rica (siglo XIX)' *ESC*, 2/6 (1973), 22–50; Carlos Araya, 'La minería y sus relaciones con la acumulación de capital y la clase dirigente de Costa Rica, 1821–1841', *ESC*, 2/5 (1973), 31–64, and 'La minería en Costa Rica, 1821–1843', *Revista Historia* (Costa Rica), 1/2 (1976), 83–125; Héctor Pérez, 'Economía y sociedad en Honduras durante el siglo XIX. Las estructuras demográficas', *ESC*, 2/6 (1973), 51–82; Guillermo Molina, 'Estructura productiva e historia demográfica (Economía y desarrollo en Honduras)', *Anuario de Estudios Centroamericanos*, 3 (1977), 161–73; and Alberto Lanuza, 'Nicaragua: territorio y población (1821–1875)', *Revista del Pensamiento Centroamericano*, 31/151 (1976), 1–22, 'Comercio exterior de Nicaragua (1821–1875)', *ESC*, 5/14 (1976), 109–36, and 'La minería en Nicaragua (1821–1875)', *Anuario de Estudios Centroamericanos*, 3 (1977), 215–24. R. L. Woodward, Jr has reviewed the literature on the demographic history of the period in 'Crecimiento de población en Centroamérica durante la primera mitad del siglo de la independencia nacional', *Mesoamérica* 1/1 (1980), 219–31. Although he overlooks some of the work already done, Thomas Schoonover, 'Central American commerce and maritime activity in the nineteenth century: sources for a quantitative approach', *LARR*, 13/2 (1978), 157–69, provides some guidance in this area.

Among recent works dealing with the establishment of Central

American independence, clearly the most important is Mario Rodríguez, *The Cádiz Experiment in Central America, 1808–1826* (Berkeley, 1978). While Louis Bumgartner, *José del Valle of Central America* (Durham, N.C., 1963) remains the definitive work on that important political figure, Ramón López, *José Cecilio del Valle, Fouché de Centro América* (Guatemala, 1968) offers some new insights, and Rafael H. Valle, *Pensamiento vivo de José Cecilio del Valle*, 2nd edn (San José, 1971), is an excellent anthology of his writings and synthesis of his ideas. The role of the first Central American Constituent Assembly is dealt with in detail by Andrés Townsend, *Las Provincias Unidas de Centroamérica: fundación de la República* (San José, 1973) in a substantial amplification of his 1958 book of the same title. Two revisionist articles on the Federation period are Philip Flemion, 'States' rights and partisan politics: Manuel José Arce and the struggle for Central American Union', *HAHR*, 53/4 (1973), 600–18, and Mauricio Domínguez, 'El Obispado de San Salvador: foco de desavenencia político-religiosa', *Anuario de Estudios Centroamericanos*, 1 (1974), 87–133. Francisco Morazán's *Memorias*, written following his defeat in 1840 and published in Paris in 1870, were reprinted in Tegucigalpa in 1971, and a collection of his personal papers have appeared in W. J. Griffith, 'The personal archive of Francisco Morazán', *Philological and Documentary Studies*, II (Publication 12, Middle American Research Institute, Tulane University, New Orleans, 1977), 197–286. For the post-independence period, T. L. Karnes, *The failure of union: Central America, 1824–1975*, rev. edn (Center for Latin American Studies, Arizona State University, Tempe, 1976), is identical to his earlier work, and Alberto Herrarte, *El federalismo en Centroamérica* (San José, 1972), is a condensation of his *Unión de Centroamérica* (Guatemala, 1964). F. D. Parker, *Travels in Central America, 1821–1840* (Gainesville, Fla., 1970), deals with a number of the perceptive travel accounts of this period. Reflecting substantial new research are the articles on Guatemala by Mario Rodríguez, Miriam Williford, R. L. Woodward, Jr and W. J. Griffith, in *Applied Enlightenment: 19th-century liberalism* (Publication 23, Middle American Research Institute, Tulane University, New Orleans, 1972). Griffith's article in that volume, 'Attitudes toward foreign colonization: the evolution of nineteenth-century Guatemalan immigration', expands upon the ideas earlier presented in his *Empires in the wilderness* (Chapel Hill, N.C., 1966). See also Williford's 'The educational reforms of Dr. Mariano Galvez', *JIAS*, 10/3 (1968), 461–73. For the diplomatic history of the period, in addition to Mario Rodriguez's excellent

*Palmerstonian diplomat in Central America: Frederick Chatfield, Esq.* (Tucson, Arizona, 1964), see R. A. Humphreys, 'Anglo-American rivalries in Central America', in *Tradition and revolt in Latin America* (London, 1969), 154–55; David Waddell, 'Great Britain and the Bay Islands, 1821–61', *The Historical Journal*, 2/1 (1959), 59–77; C. L. Stansifer, 'Ephraim George Squier: diversos aspectos de su carrera en Centroamérica', *Revista Conservadora del Pensamiento Centroamericano*, 20/98 (1968); Cyril Allen, *France in Central America* (New York, 1966), which concentrates on canal agent Felix Belly; and Andrés Vega Bolaños, *Los atentados del superintendente de Belice* (Managua, 1971), which focuses on British activities of 1840–2. José Ramírez describes the career of an early Nicaraguan diplomat in his *José de Marcoleta: padre de la diplomacia nicaragüense* (2 vols., Managua, 1975). Chester Zelaya and L. F. Sibaja treat Costa Rican acquisition of Guanaçaste in *La anexión del partido de Nicoya* (San José, 1974). Zelaya has also elucidated the career of J. F. Osejo in *El Bachiller Osejo* (2 vols., San José, 1971). Traditional liberal condemnations of Rafael Carrera have been challenged by Luis Beltranena, *Fundación de la República de Guatemala* (Guatemala, 1971), and Keith Miceli, 'Rafael Carrera: defender and promoter of peasant interests in Guatemala, 1837–1848', *TA*, 31/1 (1974), 72–95, as well as by R. L. Woodward, 'Liberalism, conservatism and the response of the peasants of La Montaña to the government of Guatemala, 1821–1850', in *Plantation Society in the Americas*, 1/1 (1979), 109–30. See also Pedro Tobar Cruz, *Los montañeses: la facción de los Lucíos y otros acontecimientos históricos de 1846 a 1851* (Guatemala, 1971). An important memoir of the period has been republished in Francisco Ortega, *Cuarenta años (1838–1878) de historia de Nicaragua*, 2nd edn (Managua, 1974).

The Anglo-American rivalry for a transoceanic route and the William Walker episode continue to attract historical writings at all levels. Enrique Guier, *William Walker* (San José, 1971), offers nothing new but is a competent work, while Frederic Rosengarten, *Freebooters Must Die!* (Wayne, Penn., 1976) combines a lively account with many contemporary illustrations and maps. More scholarly are the works of David Folkman, *The Nicaragua route* (Salt Lake City, 1972); R. E. May, *The southern dream of a Caribbean empire, 1854–1861* (Baton Rouge, 1973); and Germán Tjarks *et al.*, 'La epidemia del cólera de 1856 en el Valle Central: análisis y consecuencias demográficas', *Revista de Historia* (Costa Rica), 2/3 (1976), 81–129. Alejandro Bolaños has begun to publish a series of works on the Walker period based on the enormous volume of materials he has been accumulating. Of the first volumes to appear, perhaps the most interesting is his *El filibustero Clinton Rollins* (Masaya, Nic., 1976), in which he exposes Rollins, supposedly an associate of Walker, as the pseudonym of H. C. Parkhurst and his accounts of Walker as fiction.

For the close of the period, Wayne Clegern, author of *British Honduras: colonial dead end* (Baton Rouge, 1967), suggests a transitional role for the Vicente Cerna administration in 'Transition from conservatism to liberalism in Guatemala, 1865–1981', in William S. Coker (ed.), *Hispanic-American essays in honor of Max Leon Moorhead* (Pensacola, Florida, 1979), also published in Spanish in *Revista del Pensamiento Centroamericano*, 31/151 (1976), 60–5. There are studies of major figures in Costa Rica and El Salvador during this period: Carlos Meléndez, *Dr. José María Montealegre* (San José, 1968), and Italo López, *Gerardo Barrios y su tiempo* (2 vols., San Salvador, 1965). Finally, valuable contemporary impressions of the period have been reprinted: Francisco Lainfiesta, *Apuntamientos para la historia de Guatemala, período de 20 años corridos del 14 de abril de 1865 al 6 de abril de 1885* (Guatemala, 1975), and Pablo Levy, *Notas geográficas y económicas sobre la República de Nicaragua*, 2nd edn (Managua, 1976).

## 5. VENEZUELA, COLOMBIA AND ECUADOR

### General

For Gran Colombia see D. Bushnell, *The Santander Régime in Gran Colombia* (Newark, N.J., 1954); J. M. Restrepo, *Historia de la revolución de la República de Colombia en la América meridional* (8 vols., Bogotá, 1942–50); R. M. Baralt and R. Díaz, *Resumen de la historia de Venezuela desde el año de 1797 hasta el de 1830* (2 vols., Bruges, 1939). Also very useful for its collapse are two volumes by C. Parra-Pérez: *Mariño y la independencia de Venezuela* (4 vols., Madrid 1954–60), vol. IV, and *La monarquía en la Gran Colombia* (Madrid, 1957). Valuable accounts of the whole area are C. A. Gosselman, *Informes sobre los estados sudamericanos en los años de 1837 y 1838* (Stockholm, 1962) and M. M. Lisboa, Barão de Japura, *Relación de un viaje a Venezuela, Nueva Granada y Ecuador* (Caracas, 1954), an account of a journey in 1852–3. A useful contemporary constitutional series of studies is J. Arosemena, *Estudios constitucionales sobre los gobiernos de la América Latina* (2nd edn, 2 vols., Paris, 1878).

*Venezuela*

J. V. Lombardi, *et al.*, *Venezuelan History: a comprehensive working bibliography* (Boston, Mass., 1977), is indispensable.

The following collections of documents also serve the period well: P. Grases and M. Pérez Vila (eds.), *Pensamiento político venezolano del siglo XIX* (15 vols., Caracas, 1960–2); T. E. Carillo Batalla, comp., *Historia de las finanzas públicas en Venezuela* (10 vols., Caracas, 1969–73); *Las fuerzas armadas de Venezuela en el siglo xix* (12 vols. to date, Caracas, 1963– ); C. Gómez R. (ed.), *Materiales para el estudio de la cuestion agraria en Venezuela (1829–1860). Enajenación y arrendamiento de tierras baldías* (Caracas, 1971); R. J. Velásquez (introd.), *Decretos del poder ejécutivo de Venezuela por el Despacho del Interior y Justicia, 1831–1842* (Caracas, 1973); A. L. Guzmán, *Causa célèbre por su iniquidad la de supuesta conspiración del redactor de 'El Venezolano' Antonio L. Guzmán en 1846* (6 vols., Caracas, 1884).

Contemporary memoirs and diaries are not as abundant as they are in Colombia, but see J. A. Páez, *Autobiografía* (2 vols., Caracas, 1973); J. M. de Rojas, *Tiempo perdido* (Caracas, 1967); W. Dupuy (ed.), *Sir Robert Kerr Porter's Caracas Diary, 1825–1842* (Caracas, 1966); L. Level de Goda, *Historia contemporánea de Venezuela política y militar, 1858–1886* (Caracas, 1976); C. Parra-Pérez (ed.), *La cartera del Coronel Conde de Adlercreutz* (Paris, 1928). There is much of interest in B. Bruni Celli (comp.), *José María Vargas – obras completas* (7 vols. in 10, Caracas, 1958–66); J. A. Cova (ed.), *Archivo del Mariscal Juan Crisóstomo Falcón* (5 vols., Caracas, 1957–60) is confused and disappointing; R. R. Castellanos V., *Guzmán Blanco íntimo* (Caracas, 1969), contains selections from a large surviving archive; see also his *Páez, proscrito y peregrino* (Caracas, 1976).

The most useful biographical studies are C. Parra-Pérez, *Mariño y las guerras civiles* (3 vols., Madrid, 1958–60); R. Díaz Sánchez, *Guzmán. Elipse de una ambición de poder* (2 vols., Caracas, 1968) – both these are well-documented 'lives and times'. F. Brito Figueroa's *Tiempo de Ezequiel Zamora* (Caracas, 1975), invited the scrupulously researched and ironically understated riposte of A. Rodríguez's *Ezequiel Zamora* (Caracas, 1977); the earlier lives of this figure by M. Landaeta Rosales and L. Villanueva (both reprinted, Caracas, 1975) are still worth reading, as is J. R. Pachano, *Biografía del Mariscal Juan C. Falcón* (2nd edn, Caracas, 1960). See also J. A. de Armas Chitty, *Fermín Toro y su época* (Caracas, 1966) R. A. Rondón Márquez, *Guzmán Blanco, 'el Autócrata Civilizador'* (2 vols., Caracas, 1944).

Of the older histories F. González Guinán, *Historia contemporánea de Venezuela* (2nd edn, 15 vols, Caracas, 1954), still contains much that is not easily found elsewhere; J. Gil Fortoul, *Historia constitucional de Venezuela* (5th edn, 3 vols., Caracas, 1967), and E. González, *Historia de Venezuela, t. III: 1830–1858* (Buenos Aires, 1944), are both lucid. J. S. Rodríguez, *Contribución al estudio de la guerra federal en Venezuela* (2nd edn, 2 vols., Caracas, 1960), and L. Alvarado, *História de la revolución federal en Venezuela* (vol. 5 of *Obras Completas*, 8 vols., Caracas, 1953–8) are both still essential. Of the 'positivists', the most rewarding is L. Vallenilla Lanz, a new edition of whose works is promised. The writings of P. M. Arcaya are also still valuable.

The evolution of Venezuelan historiography can be traced in G. Carrera Damas (comp.), *Historia de la historiografía Venezolana. Textos para su estudio* (Caracas, 1961). A recent general history is John V. Lombardi, *Venezuela* (Oxford, 1982).

An introduction to the recent historiography of nineteenth-century Venezuela is provided in the essays of M. Pérez Vila, R. P. Matthews, B. A. Frankel, M. B. Floyd and N. Harwich in M. Izard, *et al.*, *Política y economía en Venezuela, 1810–1976* (Caracas, 1976). The best short survey of the century by a single author is J. A. de Armas Chitty, *Vida política de Caracas en el siglo XIX* (Caracas, 1976). A guide to parties and factions, which include some provincial political activity, is M. V. Magallanes, *Los partidos políticos en la evolución histórica venezolana* (Caracas, 1973). M. Watters, *A history of the Church in Venezuela, 1810–1930* (New York, 1933) is likely to remain the standard survey of its subject. Among other recent monographs and articles, J. V. Lombardi, *The decline and abolition of negro slavery in Venezuela, 1820–1854* (Westport, Conn., 1971), goes well beyond its immediate subject; R. P. Matthews, *Violencia rural en Venezuela, 1840–1858, antecedentes socio-económicos de la Guerra Federal*, (Caracas, 1977), sheds more light on the Llanos than on the Federal War; R. L. Gilmore's *Caudillism and militarism in Venezuela, 1810–1910* (Athens, Ohio, 1964), seems uncertain about the precise nature of its subject. See also B. A. Frankel, *Venezuela y los Estados Unidos, 1810–1888* (Caracas, 1977); R. W. Butler, 'The origins of the Liberal Party in Venezuela, 1830–1848' (unpublished Ph.D. thesis, University of Texas, 1972); L. F. Snow Jr, 'The Páez Years – Venezuelan Economic Leglislation, 1830–1846' (unpublished Ph.D. thesis, University of North Carolina, 1970); G. E. Carl, *First among equals: Great Britain and Venezuela, 1810–1910* (Ann Arbor, 1980); J. V. Lombardi and J. A. Hanson, 'The first Venezuelan coffee cycle, 1830–1855', *Agricultural History*, 44 (1970); D. Bushnell, 'La evolución del derecho de sufragio en Venezuela', *Boletín Histórico*, 39 (1972); A. Lemmo B., *La educación en Venezuela en 1870* (Caracas, 1961).

The most famous early republican geography is A. Codazzi, *Resumen de la geografía de Venezuela (Venezuela en 1841)* (3 vols., Caracas, 1940). Outstanding travel books which described the country in this period are K. F. Appun, *En los trópicos* (Caracas, 1961); E. B. Eastwick, *Venezuela or Sketches of Life in a South American Republic* (London, 1868); P. Rosti, *Memorias de un viaje por América* (Caracas, 1968). A complete list is provided by M. L. Ganzenmuller de Blay, *Contribución a la bibliografiá de viajes y exploraciones de Venezuela* (Caracas, 1964).

The paintings of Anton Goering have been reproduced in *Venezuela de hace un siglo* (Caracas, 1969): no. 52 conveys more about an army than could be put into many words.

The following statistical compilations are available: M. Izard, *Series estadísticas para la historia de Venezuela* (Mérida, 1970); A. A. Moreno, comp., *Las estadísticas de las provincias en la época de Páez* (Caracas, 1973); M. Venezuela is provided in the essays of M. Pérez Vila, R. P. Matthews, B. A. Frankel, M. B. Floyd and N. Harwich in M. Izard, *et al.*, *Política y economía en Venezuela, 1810–1976* (Caracas, 1976). The best short survey of the century by a single author is J. A. de Armas Chitty, *Vida política de Caracas en el siglo XIX* (Caracas, 1976). A guide to parties and factions, which include some provincial political activity, is M. V. Magallanes, *Los partidos políticos en la evolución histórica venezolana* (Caracas, 1973). M. Watters, *A history of the Church in Venezuela, 1810–1930* (New York, 1933) is likely to remain the standard survey of its subject. Among other recent monographs and articles, J. V. Lombardi, *The decline and abolition of negro slavery in Venezuela, 1820–1854* (Westport, Conn., 1971), goes well beyond its immediate subject; R. P. Matthews, *Violencia rural en Venezuela, 1840–1858, antecedentes socio-económicos de la Guerra Federal*, (Caracas, 1977), sheds more light on the Llanos than on the Federal War; R. L. Gilmore's *Caudillism and militarism in Venezuela, 1810–1910* (Athens, Ohio, 1964), seems uncertain about the precise nature of its subject. See also B. A. Frankel, *Venezuela y los Estados Unidos, 1810–1888* (Caracas, 1977); R. W. Butler, 'The origins of the Liberal Party in Venezuela, 1830–1848' (unpublished Ph.D. thesis, University of Texas, 1972); L. F. Snow Jr, 'The Páez Years – Venezuelan Economic Leglislation, 1830–1846' (unpublished Ph.D. thesis, University of North Carolina, 1970); G. E. Carl, *First among equals: Great Britain and Venezuela, 1810–1910* (Ann

Arbor, 1980); J. V. Lombardi and J. A. Hanson, 'The first Venezuelan coffee cycle, 1830–1855', *Agricultural History*, 44 (1970); D. Bushnell, 'La evolución del derecho de sufragio en Venezuela', *Boletín Histórico*, 39 (1972); A. Lemmo B., *La educación en Venezuela en 1870* (Caracas, 1961).

The most famous early republican geography is A. Codazzi, *Resumen de la geografía de Venezuela (Venezuela en 1841)* (3 vols., Caracas, 1940). Outstanding travel books which described the country in this period are K. F. Appun, *En los trópicos* (Caracas, 1961); E. B. Eastwick, *Venezuela or Sketches of Life in a South American Republic* (London, 1868); P. Rosti, *Memorias de un viaje por América* (Caracas, 1968). A complete list is provided by M. L. Ganzenmuller de Blay, *Contribución a la bibliografiá de viajes y exploraciones de Venezuela* (Caracas, 1964).

The paintings of Anton Goering have been reproduced in *Venezuela de hace un siglo* (Caracas, 1969): no. 52 conveys more about an army than could be put into many words.

The following statistical compilations are available: M. Izard, *Series estadísticas para la historia de Venezuela* (Mérida, 1970); A. A. Moreno, comp., *Las estadísticas de las provincias en la época de Páez* (Caracas, 1973); M. isolated diplomatic report of great sensitivity is contained in R. Donoso, 'José Antonio Soffia en Bogotá', *Thesaurus* (Bogotá) 31/1, 1976.

For memoirs, see J. M. Restrepo, *Autobiografía* (Bogotá, 1957), and *Diario político y militar* (4 vols., Bogotá, 1954); J. M. Cordóvez Moure, *Reminiscencias de Santa Fé y Bogotá*, ed. E. Mujica (Madrid, 1962); F. de P. Borda, *Conversaciones con mis hijos* (3 vols., Bogotá, 1974); A. Parra, *Memorias* (Bogotá, 1912); S. Camacho Roldán, *Memorias* (2 vols., Bogotá, 1945); J. M. Samper, *Historia de una alma* (Bogotá, 1971); J. M. Obando, *Apuntamientos para la historia* (2 vols., Bogotá, 1945); J. Posada Gutiérrez, *Memorias histórico-políticas* (4 vols., Bogotá, 1929). For contemporary accounts of civil war see A. Cuervo, *Cómo se evapora un ejército* (Bogotá, 1953); M. Briceño, *La revolución, 1876–1877; recuerdos para la historia* (Bogotá, 1947); J. M. Vargas Valdés, *A mi paso por la tierra* (Bogotá, 1938); V. Ortiz, *Historia de la revolución del 17 de abril de 1854* (Bogotá, 1972).

Biographies: C. Cuervo Márquez, *Vida del doctor José Ignacio de Márquez* (2 vols., Bogotá, 1917); E. Posada and P. M. Ibáñez, *Vida de Herrán* (Bogotá, 1903); E. Gómez Barrientos, *Don Mariano Ospina y su época* (2 vols., Medellín, 1913–15), continued as *Veinticinco años a través del Estado de Antioquía* (2 vols., Medellín, 1918); A. and R. Cuervo, *Vida de Rufino Cuervo y noticias de su época* (2 vols., Paris, 1892); J. M. Arboleda Llorente,

*Vida del Ilmo. Señor Manuel José Mosquera, Arzobispo de Santa Fé de Bogotá* (2 vols., Bogotá, 1956); A. J. Lemos Guzmán, *Obando*, (Popayán, 1959); I. Lievano Aguirre, *Rafael Núñez* (Bogotá, 1944); G. Otero Muñoz, *La vida azarosa de Rafael Núñez* (Bogotá, 1951).

G. Arboleda, *Historia contemporánea de Colombia* (6 vols., Bogotá, 1918–35) is the most complete of older works, but unfortunately runs only to 1861. Valuable for the later years of the century is E. Rodríguez Piñeres's *El Olimpo Radical, 1864–1884* (Bogotá, 1950).

A comprehensive and magnificently documented study of its subject is J. L. Helguera, *The first Mosquera administration in New Granada, 1845–99* (unpublished Ph.D. thesis, University of North Carolina, 1958). For mid-century see G. Colmenares, *Poder político y clases sociales* (Bogotá, 1965), and for intellectual development, J. Jaramillo Uribe, *El pensamiento colombiano en el siglo XIX* (Bogotá, 1964). An introduction to party struggles is J. L. Helguera, 'Liberalism versus conservatism in Colombia, 1849–1885; in F. B. Pike (ed.), *Latin American History: Select Problems* (New York, 1969).

On economic history the fundamental work remains L. Ospina Vásquez, *Industria y protección en Colombia, 1810–1930* (Medellín, 1955), which is to be preferred to the not always reliable W. P. McGreevey, *An economic history of Colombia, 1845–1930* (Cambridge, 1971). F. Safford, *The ideal of the practical* (Austin, Texas, 1975), which explores many themes *via* a consideration of technical education, his unpublished Ph.D. thesis 'Commerce and enterprise in Central Colombia, 1821–1870' (Columbia University, 1965) and the essays in his *Aspectos del siglo XIX en Colombia* (Medellín, 1977) are all essential. So too are J. P. Harrison, 'The Colombian tobacco industry from government monopoly to free trade, 1778–1876' (unpublished Ph.D. thesis, University of California, 1951); R. C. Beyer, 'The Colombian coffee industry: origin and major trends. 1740–1940' (unpublished Ph.D. thesis, University of Minnesota, 1947); J. J. Parsons, *Antioqueño colonization in Western Colombia* (Berkeley, 1968); R. Brew, *El desarrollo económico de Antioquía desde la independencia hasta 1920*, (Bogotá, 1977). On transport see R. L. Gilmore and J. P. Harrison, 'Juan Bernardo Elbers and the introduction of steam navigation on the Magdalena River', *HAHR*, 28 (1948); H. Horna, 'Francisco Javier Cisneros: a pioneer in transportation and economic development in Colombia' (unpublished Ph.D. thesis, Vanderbilt University, 1970). J. Friede, *El indio en la lucha por la tierra* (Bogotá, 1944), and O. Fals Borda, *El hombre y la tierra en Boyacá* (Bogotá, 1975) treat aspects of highland agricultural development in the south and centre respectively. V. Restrepo, *Estudio sobre las minas de oro y de plata en Colombia* (Bogotá, 1882), is still the best source for republican mining up to the date of its publication. For Indian communities, see A. García, *Legislación indigenista de Colombia* (Mexico, 1952). For general reference, A. Pardo Pardo, *Geografía económica y humana de Colombia* (Bogotá, 1972). M. Urrutia and M. Arrubla, *Compendio de estadísticas históricas de Colombia* (Bogotá, 1970), contains series on population, wages, prices, foreign trade, tobacco, coffee and presidential elections.

For nineteenth-century geography, the reports of A. Codazzi are in Comisión Corográfica, *Geografía física y política de la provincias de la Nueva Granada* (2nd edn, 4 vols., Bogotá, 1957–8); F. Pérez, *Geografía general de los Estados Unidos de Colombia* (Bogotá, 1883), derives from the same source and M. Ancízar, *Peregrinación de Alpha* (Bogotá, 1956), from the same travels. R. Gutiérrez, *Monografías* (2 vols., Bogotá, 1920–1) contains much useful material from the 1880s.

Other valuable accounts are J. Stewart, *Bogotá in 1836–7* (New York, 1838); I. Holton, *New Granada: twenty months in the Andes* (New York, 1857): E. Rothlisberger, *El Dorado* (Bogotá, 1963); F. Von Schenk, *Viajes por Antioquia en el año 1880* (Bogotá, 1952); A. Hettner, *Viajes por los Andes Colombianos, 1882–1884* (Bogotá, 1976).

The series of watercolours reproduced in *Album de la Comisión Corográfica – suplemento de 'Hojas de cultura popular colombiana'*, are an extraordinary record of types, scenes and activities in the middle of the nineteenth century.

## Ecuador

The problems of Ecuadorian historiography are set out in A. Szászdi, 'The historiography of the Republic of Ecuador', *HAHR*, 44/4 (1964); in the short article and shorter bibliography by J. Maiguashca in E. Florescano (ed.), *La historia económica en América Latina* (2 vols., Mexico, 1972), and M. T. Hamerley, 'Quantifying the nineteenth century: the ministry reports and gazettes of Ecuador as quantitative sources', *LARR*, 13/2, 1978. C. M. Larrea's *Bibliografía científica del Ecuador* (Madrid, 1952) lists 9,300 items, but many in the historical sections are virtually unobtainable.

Three short histories provide an introduction: G. Cevallos García's textbook *Historia de Ecuador* (Cuenca, 1967); O. E. Reyes, *Breve historia general del Ecuador* (2 vols., Quito, 1942); E. Ayala, *Lucha política y origen de los partidos en Ecuador* (Quito, 1978).

I. Robalino Dávila's *Orígines del Ecuador de hoy* (collected edition, 6 vols. to date, Puebla, Mexico, 1966–) is a series of well-documented politico–biographical studies running from the ascendancy of Flores to the career of Alfaro; a conservative bias is increasingly apparent and the volume on García Moreno is much more successful than the treatment of Alfaro. The series still represents the most ambitious effort of traditional historiography, and is much less partisan than J. L. R. [J. M. Le Gouhir y Rodas], *Historia de la república del Ecuador* (3 vols., Quito, 1920–38), a Jesuit work still useful for its documentation. J. Tobar Donoso, *Monografías históricas* (Quito, 1937) and his *La iglesia ecuatoriana en el siglo XIX: de 1809 a 1845* are also valuable. *Cultura*, Vol. II, No. 6, January–April 1980, a journal published by the Banco Central del Ecuador, Quito, is entirely devoted to 'El Ecuador en 1830: ideología, economía, política'.

There is no biography of Flores and no proper study of Rocafuerte's activities in Ecuador. On García Moreno, see Vol. IV of Robalino Dávila's *Orígines*, and R. Patee, *Gabriel García Moreno y el Ecuador de su tiempo* (3rd edn, Mexico, 1962). On Montalvo, see O. E. Reyes, *Vida de Juan Montalvo* (2nd edn, Quito, 1943). Veintemilla's years produced a spirited defence from his niece Marieta: M. Veintimilla, *Páginas del Ecuador* (Lima 1890), and a reply from Flores's son Antonio: A. Flores, *Para la historia del Ecuador* (2 vols., Quito, 1891). On Alfaro, see F. Guarderas, *El viejo de Montecristi: biografía de Alfaro* (Quito, 1953); A. Pareja Diez-Canseco, *La hoguera bárbara (vida de Eloy Alfaro)* (Mexico, 1944). For the late nineteenth century church, see F. González Suárez, *Memorias íntimas* (Guayaquil–Quito, n.d.), introductory essay by H. Rodríguez Castelo.

The collections of García Moreno's writings are listed in Robalino Dávila's biography; the largest published collection of his letters is that edited by W. Loor, *Cartas de García Moreno* (4 vols., Quito, 1953–5), but it is far from complete. E. Alfaro's *Obras escogidas* provide a taste of his thinking (2 vols., Guayaquil, 1959).

There are few modern monographs. Most notable is M. T. Hamerley, *Historia social y económica de la antigua Provincia de Guayaquil, 1763–1842* (Guayaquil, 1973).

There is interesting information on the history of the sierra in Comité Inter-americano de Desarrollo Agricola (CIDA), *Tenencia de la tierra y desarrollo socio-económico del sector agrícola – Ecuador* (Washington, D.C., 1965), a study directed by R. Baraona, and in A. Rubio Orbe, *Leglislación indigenista del Ecuador* (Mexico, 1954).

C. M. Larrea's bibliography lists travellers and geographical studies. The earliest comprehensive national geography is M. Villavicencio, *Geografía de la república del Ecuador* (New York, 1858). Of foreign observers, two of the more accessible and informative are F. Hassaurek, *Four years among Spanish-Americans* (New York, 1867) and A. Holinsky, *L'Equateur – Scènes de la vie Américaine* (Paris, 1861).

## 6. PERU AND BOLIVIA

For the entire period from independence to the War of the Pacific, Jorge Basadre's great work, *Historia de la República del Perú* (5th edn, 10 vols., Lima, 1962–4), undoubtedly constitutes the most important source of reference. His earlier works, *Perú, problema y posibilidad* (Lima, 1931), and *La multitud, la ciudad y el campo* (Lima, 1947), have not only maintained their freshness but were responsible for pioneering the study of Peru's history. Apart from Basadre's classic works, another summary of this period written by Emilio Romero, *Historia económica del Perú* (Buenos Aires, 1949) contains information which is still of value. More recently, Ernesto Yepes del Castillo, *Perú 1820–1920. Un siglo de desarrollo capitalista* (Lima, 1972) has provided an overall interpretation of the nineteenth century, while Julio Cotler, in *Clases, estado y nación en el Perú* (Lima, 1978) discusses and explains the persistence of the colonial character of Peruvian society and the state after 1821. A useful general history in English is Frederick B. Pike, *The modern history of Peru* (London, 1967). Heraclio Bonilla, *Un siglo a la deriva* (Lima, 1980, chaps. I and II), and Shane Hunt, *Price and quantum estimates of Peruvian exports 1830–1962* (Princeton, Woodrow Wilson School, Discussion Paper 33, 1973) have suggested the division of the nineteenth century into economic periods, on the basis of the country's export performance.

The years between 1821 and 1840 were decisive in the process of disengagement from the colonial system and in the emergence of a new national order. However, nobody has yet undertaken a general study of this period. Heraclio Bonilla, *Gran Bretaña y el Perú. Los mecanismos de un control económico* (Lima, 1977), examines the conditions and effects of the British presence in post-independence Peru. The unique economic and social characteristics of the Andean region have been dealt with in John F. Wibel, 'The evolution of a regional community within the Spanish empire and the Peruvian nation: Arequipa, 1780–1845' (unpublished

Ph.D. thesis, Stanford University, 1975) and Alberto Flores-Galindo, *Arequipa y el Sur Andino, siglos XVIII-XX* (Lima, 1977). Relations between the communities and haciendas and the process of decomposition and recovery within the former during this period are the subject of Christine Hünefeldt, *Lucha por la tierra y protesta indígena* (Bonn, 1982). Two general works on the army and on the Church contain useful information on this period. Víctor Villanueva, *Ejército peruano: del caudillaje anárquico al militarismo reformista* (Lima, 1973) and Jeffrey Klaiber, *Religion and Revolution in Peru, 1824–1976* (Notre Dame, Ind., 1976). On the Peru-Bolivian Confederation, that is to say, the failed attempt to unite the two countries, the following are worth consulting: L. C. Kendall, 'Andrés Santa Cruz and the Peru-Bolivian Confederation', *HAHR*, 16 (1936), 29–48; Robert Burr, *By reason or force. Chile and the balancing of power in South America, 1830–1905* (Berkeley, 1965); Carlos Ortiz de Zevallos Paz Soldán, *Confederación Peru–Boliviana, 1835–1839* (2 vols, Lima, 1972–4).

Jonathan Levin, *The export economies. Their pattern of development in historical perspective* (Cambridge, Mass., 1960), inaugurated the modern debate on the impact of guano on the Peruvian economy. Levin's thesis that the guano boom produced in Peru a typical enclave economy was questioned by Hunt in *Growth and guano in nineteenth century Peru* (Princeton University, Woodrow Wilson School, 1973). On the other hand, William M. Mathew, in 'Anglo-Peruvian commercial and financial relations, 1820–1865' (unpublished Ph.D thesis, University of London, 1964), and in 'Peru and the British guano market, 1840–1870', *Economic History Review*, 2nd series, 23 (1970), has shown, by basing himself on the private papers of Antony Gibbs & Sons, the mechanics by which guano was marketed, and the considerable autonomy enjoyed by the Peruvian government. See also by W. M. Matthew, 'The imperialism of free trade, Peru 1820–1870', *Economic History Review*, 2nd series, 21 (1968); 'The first Anglo-Peruvian debt and its settlement, 1822–49', *JLAS* 2/1 (1970); 'Foreign contractors and the Peruvian government at the outset of the guano trade', *HAHR*, 52/4 (1972); 'A primitive export sector: guano production in mid-nineteenth century Peru', *JLAS*, 9/1 (1977); 'Antony Gibbs & Sons, the guano trade and the Peruvian government 1842–1861', in D. C. M. Platt (ed.), *Business imperialism 1840–1930* (Oxford, 1977); and *The House of Gibbs and the Peruvian guano monopoly* (London, 1981).

The attitude of the ruling class regarding the policy to be pursued with resources from guano, and the process by which the international crisis of 1872 affected Peruvian finances, are themes examined in Juan Maiguashca, 'A reinterpretation of the Guano age, 1840–1880' (unpublished D.Phil. thesis, University of Oxford, 1967). See also R. Miller and R. Greenhill, 'The Peruvian government and the nitrate trade, 1873–1879', *JLAS*, 41 (1973). Heraclio Bonilla *Guano y burguesía en el Perú* (Lima, 1974) examines the collapse of the Peruvian economy during the guano period in terms of the characteristics of the ruling class and the limitations of the internal market. Alfonso Quirós, in 'La consolidación de la deuda interna' (unpublished bachelor's degree dissertation, Universidad Católica de Lima, 1980), has questioned the idea that the 'consolidation of the internal debt', that is to say, the fraudulent payment of guano revenue to large numbers of the state's local creditors, was responsible for the economic recovery of the Peruvian elite. The role of guano in the growth of productive capital for export agriculture has been examined in the following: Pablo Macera, 'Las plantaciones azucareras andinas, 1821–1875', *Trabajos de Historia* (Lima) 4 (1977); Manuel Burga, *De la encomienda a la hacienda capitalista* (Lima, 1976); Juan R. Engelsen, 'Social aspects of agricultural expansion in coastal Peru, 1825–1878' (unpublished Ph.D. thesis, University of California, Los Angeles, 1977). In contrast to the direct links with agriculture on the coast, the agrarian sector of the Andean highlands grew independently of the effects of guano. The reasons for this are analysed in Florencia E. Mallon, *The defense of community in Peru's Central Highlands. Peasant struggle and capitalist transition, 1860–1940* (Princeton, 1982), Nelson Manrique, *El desarrollo del mercado interno en la sierra central* (Lima, 1978), and Martha Giraldo and Ana Lizia Franch, 'Hacienda y gamonalismo, 1850–1920' (unpublished Master's dissertation, Universidad Católica de Lima, 1979). Other changes associated with the overall effects of guano were the mobilization of capital and the creation of the banking system, the importation of Chinese workers in massive numbers and the construction of the Peruvian rail network. On the banks, Carlos Camprubí Alcazar, *Historia de los bancos del Perú, 1860–1879* (Lima, 1957) vol. 1, is still useful. On the Chinese 'coolies', Watt Stewart's pioneer work, *Chinese bondage in Peru. A history of the Chinese coolie in Peru, 1849–1874* (Durham, N.C., 1951), can be supplemented by a more recent, albeit more general study, by Arnold J. Meagher, 'The introduction of Chinese laborers to Latin America: the coolie trade, 1847–1874' (unpublished Ph.D. dissertation, University of California at Davis, 1975). A study of the railways has not yet been undertaken. The only work of any relevance is Watt Stewart's biography of the American contractor who put down the first lines: *Henry Meiggs: a Yankee Pizarro* (Durham, N.C., 1946). It is now well known that guano produced wealth and poverty at the same time. Gigantic price increases in cities like Lima in the early 1870s caused one of the first important mass uprisings. Its composition and objectives are the subject of a careful study by Margarita Giesecke, *Masas urbanas y rebelión en la historia: golpe de estado, Lima 1872* (Lima, 1978).

The demographic history of the period has been largely ignored. Although some important research is being carried out on the whole Cuzco region, the only basic work of reference currently available is George Kubler, *The Indian caste of Peru 1795–1940* (Washington, D.C., 1950).

An interesting discussion of the politics of this period and especially the role of the state can be found in Ronald H. Berg and Frederick Stirton Weaver, 'Towards a reinterpretation of political change in Peru during the first century of independence', *JIAS*, 20/1 (1978), 69–83, and Stephen M. Gorman, 'The state, elite and exports in nineteenth century Peru', *JIAS* 21/3 (1979), 395–418.

Many books of differing quality have been produced on the war with Chile. Henri Favre was the first scholar to draw attention to the need to examine the conflict from a new perspective: 'Remarques sur la lutte des classes au Pérou pendant la Guerre du Pacifique', in *Littérature et société au Pérou du XIX siècle à nos jours* (Grenoble, 1975). The war is also the starting point for analysing problems such as the issue of national identity and the colonial tradition in modern Peru. Heraclio Bonilla, 'The War of the Pacific and the national and colonial problem in Peru', *Past and Present*, 81 (1978), set out the guidelines for a re-examination of both issues. The most important work since then is Nelson Manrique, *Campesinado y nación: la sierra central durante la Guerra del Pacífico* (Lima, 1981).

The bibliography on Bolivian history between 1825 and 1879 is unfortunately still very weak. General works which offer coverage of this period include Herbert S. Klein, *Bolivia. The evolution of a multi-ethnic society* (Oxford, 1982); J. Valerie Fifer, *Bolivia: land, location and politics since 1825* (Cambridge, 1972) and Luis Peñaloza, *Historia económica de Bolivia* (2 vols., La Paz, 1946–7). *Estudios Bolivianos en homenaje a Gunner Mendoza L.* (La Paz, 1978) is an interesting collection of essays on various aspects of Bolivian history.

The transition from colony to republic is the subject of William F.

Lofstrom, 'The promise and problem of reform: attempted social and economic change in the first years of Bolivian independence', (unpublished Ph.D. thesis, Cornell University, 1972); Charles Arnade, *The emergence of the Republic of Bolivia* (Gainesville, 1957); and Alberto Crespo *et al.*, *La vida cotidiana en La Paz durante la Guerra de la Independencia* (La Paz, 1975). The state of the country's resources at the time of independence were described in J. B. Pentland, 'Report on Bolivia 1827', ed. J. Valerie Fifer, Royal Historical Society, London, *Camden Miscellany*, 35 (1974). There is a more complete version in Spanish: J. B. Pentland, *Informe sobre Bolivia, 1827* (Potosí, 1975) is a unique and indispensable collection of demographic and economic data on Bolivia in the middle of the nineteenth century. Fernando Cajías, *La provincia de Atacama, 1825–1842* (La Paz, 1975), is a valuable regional study. On the survival of the Indian tribute system, see Nicolás Sánchez-Albornoz, *Indios y tributos en el Alto Perú* (Lima, 1978). The standard work on Santa Cruz, who dominated the political life of Bolivia in the post-independence period, is Alfonso Crespo, *Santa Cruz, el cóndor indio* (Mexico, 1944). Also see Oscar de Santa Cruz (ed.), *El General Santa Cruz, Gran Mariscal de Zepita y el Gran Perú* (La Paz, 1924). Manuel Carrasco, *José Ballivián, 1805–1852* (Buenos Aires, 1960), is a biography of the third most important of the early presidents (after Sucre and Santa Cruz). An interesting discussion of Bolivian politics in this period can be found in James Dunkerley, 'Reassessing Caudillismo in Bolivia, 1825–79', *Bulletin of Latin American Research*, 1/1 (1981). The complicated relations between Great Britain and Bolivia at this time have been described, in a rather heavy-handed way, by Roberto Querejazu C., *Bolivia y los ingleses* (La Paz, 1973). An important contribution on mining in the nineteenth century has been made by Antonio Mitre in 'Economy and social structure of silver mining in nineteenth century Bolivia' (unpublished Ph.D. thesis, Columbia University, 1977), and *Los patriarcas de La Plata* (Lima, 1981). On the survival of Indian communities in the nineteenth century, Erwin P. Grieshaber, 'Survival of Indian communities in nineteenth century Bolivia' (unpublished Ph.D. thesis, University of North Carolina, 1977), and 'Survival of Indian communities in nineteenth century Bolivia: a regional comparison', *JLAS*, 12/2 (1980), 223–69 are important. A useful monograph on Melgarejo's policies is Luis Antezana, *El feudalismo de Melgarejo y la reforma agraria* (La Paz, 1970). Relations between haciendas and communities in the highlands are examined in an important article by Silvia Rivera C., 'La expansión del latifundio en el altiplano boliviano', *Avances*, 2 (1978), 95–118.

## 7. CHILE

Historical scholarship of the traditional kind in Chile tended to focus less on the post-independence period than on the colonial era and the wars of independence. While recent research has helped to fill some of the gaps in our knowledge, a good deal of basic work (not least on the economic and social side) remains to be done. Simon Collier, 'The historiography of the "Portalian" period in Chile (1830–91)', *HAHR*, 57 (1977), 660–90, provides a general discussion of the literature to the mid-1970s.

The most extensive description of the period as a whole is to be found in Francisco Antonio Encina, *Historia de Chile desde la prehistoria hasta 1891* (20 vols., Santiago, 1942–52), IX-XVII. This huge and idiosyncratically conservative work has not lacked critics. It is instructive, when using it, to consult the relevant passages of Ricardo Donoso's sustained attack, *Francisco A. Encina, simulador* (2 vols., Santiago, 1969–70). The years from independence to 1833 are covered in great detail in Diego Barros Arana, *Historia general de Chile* (16 vols., Santiago, 1884–1902), XI-XVI. Narratives of specific presidencies include Ramón Sotomayor Valdés, *Chile bajo el gobierno del general don Joaquín Prieto* (2nd edn, 4 vols., Santiago, 1900–4), Diego Barros Arana, *Un decenio de la historia de Chile 1841–1851* (2 vols., Santiago, 1905–6), Alberto Edwards, *El gobierno de don Manuel Montt* (Santiago, 1932), and, on the administrations between 1841 and 1876, Agustín Edwards, *Cuatro presidentes de Chile* (2 vols., Valparaiso, 1932). The classic account of the War of the Pacific is Gonzalo Bulnes, *La guerra del Pacífico*, (3 vols., Santiago, 1911–19). Numerous documents on the war were collected soon after it ended, as a gesture of national pride, in Pascual Ahumada Moreno (ed.), *Guerra del Pacífico: recopilación completa de todos los documentos oficiales, correspondencias y demás publicaciones referentes a la guerra* (9 vols., Valparaiso, 1884–90). This apart, there are few printed documentary collections for this period comparable to those available for colonial times and the war of independence. Congressional debates, however, were printed as *Sesiones del Congreso Nacional* from 1846 onwards. Congressional documents (and certain debates) prior to that date have been collected in Valentín Letelier (ed.), *Sesiones de los cuerpos legislativos de la República de Chile, 1811–1845* (37 vols., Santiago, 1887–1908).

On the politics of this period in general, the stimulating essay by Alberto Edwards, *La fronda aristocrática* (7th edn, Santiago, 1972), can be recommended for its many acute insights; the ideological battles of the time have been chronicled by the doyen of mid-twentieth century

Chilean historians, Ricardo Donoso, in *Las ideas políticas en Chile* (3rd edn, Buenos Aires, 1975); a promising line of inquiry has been opened up in Gabriel Marcella, 'The structure of politics in nineteenth century Spanish America: the Chilean oligarchy, 1833–1891' (unpublished Ph.D. thesis, Notre Dame University, 1973). Valuable short accounts which extend the discussion into the economic and social field include Sergio Villalobos R., Fernando Silva V., Osvaldo Silva G. and Patricio Estellé M., *Historia de Chile* (4 vols., Santiago, 1974–6), III-IV, written by Sergio Villalobos R. and Fernando Silva V.; Brian Loveman, *Chile, the legacy of Hispanic capitalism* (New York, 1979), 116–96; and Julio César Jobet, *Ensayo crítico del desarrollo económico-social de Chile* (Santiago, 1955), 31–75. Luis Vitale, *Interpretación marxista de la historia de Chile* (3 vols., Santiago, 1967–71), III, offers a further perspective on the period up to 1859.

No satisfactory study fully covers the economic history of nineteenth century Chile, and for reviews of the available literature the reader is directed to Sergio Villalobos R., 'La historiografía económica de Chile: sus comienzos', *Historia* (Santiago), 10 (1971), 7–56, and Carmen Cariola and Osvaldo Sunkel, 'Chile', in Roberto Cortés Conde and Stanley J. Stein (eds.), *Latin America. A guide to economic history 1830–1930* (Berkeley, 1977), 275–363. Markos Mamalakis, *The growth and structure of the Chilean economy* (New Haven, 1976), 3–85, deals with the period 1840–1930 in a single sweep. José Gabriel Palma, 'Growth and structure of Chilean manufacturing industry from 1830 to 1935' (unpublished D.Phil. thesis, Oxford, 1979), contains valuable insight on the economic history of the period. The long-neglected theme of agriculture has been taken up in Arnold J. Bauer's first-class study, *Chilean rural society from the Spanish Conquest to 1930* (Cambridge, 1975), which, despite the title, largely focusses on this period. Landowners' ideas have been examined in Gonzalo Izquierdo, *Un estudio de las ideologías chilenas: La Sociedad de la Agricultura en el siglo XIX* (Santiago, 1968). Much more needs to be known about copper and silver mining, but L. R. Pederson, *The mining industry of the Norte Chico, Chile* (Evanston, Ill., 1966), 160–229, is an excellent introduction. The story of nitrates to the end of the War of the Pacific can be followed in Oscar Bermúdez, *Historia del salitre desde sus orígenes hasta la Guerra del Pacífico* (Santiago, 1963), the classic work, and Thomas F. O'Brien, 'Chilean elites and foreign investors; Chilean nitrate policy 1880–82', *JLAS*, 11/1 (1979), 101–21, and *The Nitrate Industry and Chile's critical transition 1870–1891* (New York, 1982). See also his 'The Antofagasta company: a case study in peripheral capitalism', *HAHR*, 60/

1 (1980). Tariff policies in the early part of the period have been examined in John L. Rector, 'Merchants, trade and commercial policy in Chile, 1810–1840' (unpublished Ph.D. thesis, Indiana University, 1976), 88–112, and in the later part in William F. Sater, 'Economic nationalism and tax reform in late nineteenth century Chile', *TA*, 33 (1976), 311–35. The classic work on the ups-and-down of the merchant navy is Claudio Véliz, *Historia de la marina mercante de Chile* (Santiago, 1961). Railway-building and its economic context are well covered in Robert B. Oppenheimer, 'Chilean transportation development: the railroads and socio-economic change in the Central Valley' (unpublished Ph.D. thesis, University of California at Los Angeles, 1976) and, especially good on regional issues, John Whaley, 'Transportation in Chile's Bío-Bío region, 1850–1915' (unpublished Ph.D. thesis, Indiana University, 1974). The best description of monetary problems prior to 1878 is to be found in Pierre Vayssière, 'Au Chili: de l'économie coloniale à l'inflation', *Cahiers des Amériques Latines*, 5 (1970), 5–31. No detailed study of the recession of 1858–61 yet exists, but the more severe crisis of the 1870s is dealt with in William F. Sater, 'Chile and the world depression of the 1870s', *JLAS*, 11/1 (1979), 67–99, and Luis Ortega, 'Change and Crisis in Chile's economy and society, 1865–1879' (unpublished Ph.D. thesis, London University, 1979) which also presents valuable evidence on the topic of industrial growth in this period.

Social history, however broadly defined, has not been well served as yet, and some of the gaps in our knowledge here are huge. Bauer, *Chilean rural society*, contains much valuable information on the rural labouring classes. Artisans and craftsmen up to the 1850s have been studied in Luis Alberto Romero, *La Sociedad de la Igualdad. Los artesanos de Santiago de Chile y sus primeras experiencias políticas* (Instituto Torcuato di Tella, Buenos Aires, 1978). Systematic investigations of the urban lower classes, the mine-workers of the north and the upper class elite itself are urgently required. Jean-Pierre Blancpain, *Les allemands au Chili, 1816–1945* (Cologne, 1974), a magnificent piece of research, provides a fine description of the German settlements in the south after 1850. John Mayo, 'British interests in Chile and their influence, 1851–1886' (unpublished D.Phil. thesis, Oxford University, 1977) examines aspects of the British presence, so important to Chile in this period. See also, his 'Before the nitrate era: British commission houses and the Chilean economy, 1851–80', *JLAS*, 11/2 (1979), 263–303. The decline and fall of the Araucanian Indian enclave is well examined in Jacques Rossignol,

'Chiliens et Indiens Araucans au milieu du XIXe siècle', *Cahiers du Monde Hispanique et Luso-Brésilien*, 20 (1973), 69–98, as well as in the older work of Tomás Guevara, *Historia de la civilización de la Araucanía* (3 vols., Santiago, 1900–2) vol. III of which carries the story through to the 1880s. See also, Leonardo León S., 'Alianzas militares entre los indios araucanos y los grupos indios de las pampas: la rebelión araucana de 1867–1872 en Argentina y Chile', *Nueva Historia*, 1/1 (London, 1981), 3–49.

Urban histories are in general deficient for this period. On Santiago, two works by René León Echaiz, *Historia de Santiago* (2 vols., Santiago, 1975), and *Nuñohue* (Buenos Aires, 1972), the latter dealing with the eastern suburbs, can best be seen as useful introductions, but not much more. The progress of education has been usefully summarized in Fernando Campos Harriet, *Desarrollo educacional 1810–1960* (Santiago, 1960). On the 'uses of history' see Allen Woll, *A functional past. The uses of history in nineteenth century Chile* (Baton Rouge, 1982). There have been no detailed recent investigations of the role of the Catholic Church, and the study of freemasonry has not advanced since the standard account was published: Benjamín Oviedo, *La masonería en Chile* (Santiago, 1929), written from a masonic standpoint. Work on the demographic history of the nineteenth century is still in its infancy, but is likely to develop in the near future: Robert McCaa, 'Chilean social and demographic history: sources, issues and methods', *LARR*, 13/2 (1978), 104–26, gives an intelligent survey of the problems. A good case study is Ann Hagerman Johnson, 'The impact of market agriculture on family and household structure in nineteenth century Chile,' *HAHR*, 58 (1978), 625–48.

Chile's international position and the development of her diplomacy can best be followed in Robert N. Burr, *By reason or force. Chile and the balancing of power in South America, 1830–1905* (Berkeley, 1965), and in the general account, Mario Barros, *Historia diplomática de Chile, 1541–1938* (Barcelona, 1970), 63–440.

The Oficina Central de Estadística was founded as early as 1843, and the government, slightly later on, was assiduous in collecting statistical information, not least in the *Anuario estadístico* published from 1861 onwards. Commercial statistics were published from 1844, as were the censuses of 1854, 1865 and 1875. Statistical material from this period, however, has to be used with critical caution. For a detailed list of Chilean government publications, see Rosa Quintero Mesa (ed.), *Latin American serial documents. No.7, Chile* (New York, 1973). Markos Mamalakis (ed.), 'Historical statistics of Chile, 1840–1965', 4 vols. (Yale University Economic Growth Centre, mimeo) provides useful material.

In addition to the standard bibliographical aids, two Chilean sources deserve to be indicated here. The publications of the period itself are systematically listed in Ramón Briseño (ed.), *Estadística bibliográfica de la literatura chilena* (3 vols., Santiago, 1965–6). Briseño's original two volumes were published in 1862 and 1879. Vol. III contains additions and amendments by Raúl Silva Castro. Invaluable work has lately been done by the journal *Historia* (Santiago) in keeping a detailed record of all materials published on Chilean history in recent years. These are listed in the journal's regular 'Fichero bibliográfico'. The first such bibliographies were reprinted in Horacio Aránguiz Donoso (ed.), *Bibliografía histórica (1959–1967)* (Santiago, 1970). Subsequent 'ficheros' have been published in *Historia*, 10 (1971), 11 (1972–3), 12 (1974–5), 13 (1976) and 14 (1979).

## 8. THE RIVER PLATE REPUBLICS

The bibliography of nineteenth-century Argentina can be approached through Joseph R. Barager, 'The historiography of the Río de la Plata area since 1930', *HAHR*, 39 (1959), 588–642, and James R. Scobie, *Argentina. A city and a nation* (New York, 1964), 248–74. A more specialist work is Julio O. Chiappini, *Bibliografía sobre Rosas* (Rosario, 1973).

Public documents are reproduced in a number of collections. The formal policy reviews of the executive are given in H. Mabragaña, *Los Mensajes, 1810–1910* (6 vols., Buenos Aires, 1910); for the governors of Buenos Aires a better version is provided by Archivo Histórico de la Provincia de Buenos Aires, *Mensajes de los gobernadores de la provincia de Buenos Aires 1822–1849* (2 vols., La Plata, 1976). Basic legislative, constitutional and inter-provincial texts are to be found in Emilio Ravignani (ed.), *Asambleas constituyentes argentinas* (6 vols., Buenos Aires, 1937–9). The main documentation concerning Rosas is that of Adolfo Saldías (ed.), *Papeles de Rosas* (2 vols., La Plata, 1904–7), which can be supplemented by two convenient compilations of his thought and policy, Andrés M. Carretero, *El pensamiento político de Juan M. de Rosas* (Buenos Aires, 1970) and Arturo Enrique Sampay, *Las ideas políticas de Juan Manuel de Rosas* (Buenos Aires, 1972). Aspects of the opposition to Rosas are documented in Gregorio F. Rodríguez (ed.), *Contribución histórica y documental* (3 vols., Buenos Aires, 1921–2), and Archivo Histórico de la Provincia de Buenos Aires, *La campaña libertadora del general Lavalle (1838–1842)* (La Plata, 1944). Amidst other and smaller collections the monumental writings of Argentina's three most eminent figures of politics and letters stand out, beginning with Juan B. Alberdi, *Obras completas* (8 vols., Buenos Aires, 1876–86) and *Escritos póstumos* (16 vols., Buenos Aires, 1895–1901). Bartolomé Mitre, *Archivo del General Mitre: documentos y correspondencia* (28 vols., Buenos Aires, 1911–14), can be supplemented by *Correspondencia literaria, histórica y política del General Bartolomé Mitre* (3 vols., Buenos Aires, 1912) and *Correspondencia Mitre–Elizalde* (*Documentos para la historia argentina*, 26, Buenos Aires, 1960). Domingo F. Sarmiento, *Obras completas* (52 vols., Santiago, 1887–1902), is an indispensable source for Argentine history, together with *Sarmiento–Mitre: correspondencia, 1846–1868* (Buenos Aires, 1911), *Facundo* (La Plata, 1938), and *Epistolario entre Sarmiento y Posse, 1845–1888* (2 vols., Buenos Aires, 1946–7).

The subject is rich in narrative sources, and the following is no more than a brief selection. Sir Woodbine Parish, *Buenos Ayres and the Provinces of the Río de la Plata* (2nd edn, London, 1852), a work first published in 1838, is an objective and scholarly account by the former British chargé d'affaires. William MacCann, *Two thousand miles' ride through the Argentine provinces* (2 vols., London, 1853), brings the economy and the people of the pampas to life. One of the first approaches to quantification is provided by Victor Martin de Moussy, *Description géographique et statistique de la Confédération Argentine* (3 vols., Paris, 1860–4). Thomas Joseph Hutchinson, *Buenos Ayres and Argentine gleanings* (London, 1865), is a less accurate account, by the British consul at Rosario, but takes the story to 1862–3. Wilfred Latham, *The States of the River Plate* (2nd edn, London, 1868), is an amplified version of a book first published in 1866 and written from the author's 'home in the campo', a large sheep farm.

General histories are headed by the Academia Nacional de la Historia, *Historia de la nación Argentina* (2nd edn, 10 vols., Buenos Aires, 1939–50), with its sequel, *Historia argentina contemporánea, 1862–1930* (Buenos Aires, 1963– ). These are composite works, uneven in quality. Tulio Halperín Donghi, *Argentina: de la revolución de independencia a la confederación rosista* (Buenos Aires, 1972) is analytically superior, as is his masterly essay introducing *Proyecto y construcción de una nación (Argentina 1846–1880)* (Caracas, 1980), a selection of texts from major writers of Argentina's age of nation-building. Haydée Gorostegui de Torres, *Argentina: la organización nacional* (Buenos Aires, 1972), gives a balanced account of the period 1852–74.

Study of the economy can begin with Jonathan C. Brown, *A socioeconomic history of Argentina, 1776–1860* (Cambridge, 1979), which combines synthesis, original research and a sense of chronology. Miron Burgin, *The economic aspects of Argentine federalism 1820–1852* (Cambridge, Mass., 1946), is still unsurpassed for data and interpretation. Juan Carlos Nicolau, *Rosas y García (1829–35). La economía bonaerense* (Buenos Aires, 1980), concentrates on financial and fiscal policy. The basic institutional account of landowning is Miguel A. Cárcano, *Evolución histórica del régimen de la tierra pública, 1810–1916* (3rd edn, Buenos Aires, 1972), first published in 1917. The land policy of Rivadavia is identified by Emilio A. Coni, *La verdad sobre la enfiteusis de Rivadavia* (Buenos Aires, 1927). Further details on land acquisition and concentration are provided by Jacinto Oddone, *La burguesía terrateniente argentina* (3rd edn, Buenos Aires, 1956), but for more accurate data see Andrés M. Carretero, 'Contribución al conocimiento de la propiedad rural en la provincia de Buenos Aires para 1830', *Boletín del Instituto de Historia Argentina 'Doctor Emilio Ravignani'*, 2nd series, 13/22–23 (1970), 246–92, and *La propiedad de la tierra en la época de Rosas* (Buenos Aires, 1972). Cattle-raising can be studied in Horacio C. E. Giberti, *Historia económica de la ganadería argentina* (Buenos Aires, 1961), and the processing plants in Alfredo J. Montoya, *Historia de los saladeros argentinos* (Buenos Aires, 1956) and *La ganadería y la industria de salazón de carnes en el período 1810–1862* (Buenos Aires, 1971). Aspects of early industrial developments are covered in José M. Mariluz Urquijo, *Estado e industria 1810–1862* (Buenos Aires, 1969), a collection of texts; Juan Carlos Nicolau, *Antecedentes para la historia de la industria argentina* (Buenos Aires, 1968), and *Industria argentina y aduana, 1835–1854* (Buenos Aires, 1975); and Clifton Kroeber, *The growth of the shipping industry in the Río de la Plata region, 1794–1860* (Madison, 1957). Foreign trade and its participants are studied in a useful article and two important books: Juan Carlos Nicolau; 'Movimiento marítimo exterior del puerto de Buenos Aires (1810–1854)', *Nuestra Historia*, 12 (1973), 351–61; H. S. Ferns, *Britain and Argentina in the nineteenth century* (Oxford, 1960); Vera Bliss Reber, *British merchant houses in Buenos Aires, 1810–1880* (Cambridge, Mass., 1979). For the wool cycle and the economy in transition, see José Carlos Chiaramonte, *Nacionalismo y liberalismo económicos en la Argentina 1860–1880* (Buenos Aires, 1971), and the now classic H. Gibson, *The history and present state of the sheepbreeding industry in the Argentine Republic* (Buenos Aires, 1893).

Society in its demographic aspect is well described by Ernesto J. A.

Maeder, *Evolución demográfica argentina de 1810 a 1869* (Buenos Aires, 1969), while for a shorter period population change is measured by Susana R. Frías, César A. García Belsunce, *et al.*, *Buenos Aires: su gente, 1800–1830* (Buenos Aires, 1976), based on censuses of the city of Buenos Aires. These should be supplemented by George Reid Andrews, *The Afro-Argentines of Buenos Aires, 1800–1900* (Madison, 1980). On immigration, see Juan Antonio Oddone, *La emigración europea al Río de la Plata* (Montevideo, 1966). New research on the life and labour of the Irish is provided by Juan Carlos Korol and Hilda Sabato, *Cómo fue la inmigración irlandesa en la Argentina* (Buenos Aires, 1981). The most powerful social group is studied by María Sáenz Quesada, *Los estancieros* (Buenos Aires, 1980). Gauchos, peons and vagrants are placed in their historical context by Gastón Gori, *Vagos y mal entretenidos* (2nd edn, Santa Fe, 1965), and Ricardo Rodríguez Molas, *Historia social del gaucho* (Buenos Aires, 1968). Rubén H. Zorrilla, *Extracción social de los caudillos 1810–1870* (Buenos Aires, 1972), discusses the social base of *caudillismo*.

Political history can be divided into three periods, comprising Rivadavia, Rosas and national organization. On the first, Ricardo Piccirilli, *Rivadavia y su tiempo* (2nd edn, 3 vols., Buenos Aires, 1960) is a work of scholarship, and Sergio Bagú, *El plan económico del grupo Rivadaviano 1811–1827* (Rosario, 1966) a cogent interpretation with documents. The enormous bibliography on Rosas is a hindrance rather than a help to understanding. Adolfo Saldías, *Historia de la Confederación Argentina: Rosas y su época* (Buenos Aires, 9 vols., 1958), a work first published in 1881–87 from official Rosas sources, is a useful chronicle of events. Roberto Etchepareborda, *Rosas; controvertida historiografía* (Buenos Aires, 1972), is a modern survey of the 'problems'. Enrique M. Barba, *Cómo llegó Rosas al poder* (Buenos Aires, 1972), explains the conquest of power. Among the *rosista* historians, Carlos Ibarguren, *Juan Manuel de Rosas, su vida, su drama, su tiempo* (Buenos Aires, 1961), first published in 1930, provides a well-documented political biography; and Julio Irazusta, *Vida política de Juan Manuel de Rosas, a través de su correspondencia* (2nd edn, 8 vols., Buenos Aires, 1970), supplies much detail and documentation. Ernesto H. Celesia, *Rosas, aportes para su historia* (2nd edn, 2 vols., Buenos Aires, 1968), is hostile but well researched. Benito Díaz, *Juzgados de paz de campaña de la provincia de Buenos Aires (1821–1854)* (La Plata, 1959), studies a vital agency of the regime. On the foreign blockades and other forms of intervention, see John F. Cady, *Foreign intervention in the Rio de la Plata 1838–50* (Philadelphia, 1929), and Nestor S.

Colli, *La política francesa en el Río de la Plata: Rosas y el bloqueo de 1838–1840* (Buenos Aires, 1963), as well as the work by Ferns already cited. The international context of the fall of Rosas is explored by the *rosista* historian José María Rosa, *La caída de Rosas: el Imperio de Brasil y la Confederación Argentina (1843–1851)* (2nd edn, Buenos Aires, 1968). For a recent history of Rosas, his power base and his policy, see John Lynch, *Argentine dictator: Juan Manuel de Rosas 1829–1852* (Oxford, 1981).

In the period of national organization the transitional figure is Urquiza: see Beatriz Bosch, *Urquiza y su tiempo* (Buenos Aires, 1971). Older accounts of the decade after Rosas are now superseded by James R. Scobie, *La lucha por la consolidación de la nacionalidad argentina, 1852–1862* (Buenos Aires, 1964). The great constitutional statesmen have attracted a number of biographies, of which Jorge M. Mayer, *Alberdi y su tiempo* (Buenos Aires, 1963) is outstanding. Sarmiento receives scholarly attention from Ricardo Rojas, *El profeta de la pampa: vida de Sarmiento* (Buenos Aires, 1945), and José S. Campobassi, *Sarmiento y su época* (2 vols., Buenos Aires, 1975).

The history of Uruguay in the nineteenth century has an established framework of political narrative and documentation in Eduardo Acevedo, *Anales históricos del Uruguay*, vols. 2 and 3 (Montevideo, 1933), which should be supplemented for the mid-century by Juan E. Pivel Devoto, *El fin de la Guerra Grande* (Montevideo, 1953). An excellent analysis of economy, society and politics is provided by José Pedro Barrán, *Apogeo y crisis del Uruguay pastoral y caudillesco 1838–1875* (Historia Uruguaya, 4, Montevideo, 1974). On the rural structure, see José Pedro Barrán and Benjamín Nahum, *Historia rural del Uruguay moderno. Tomo I (1851–1967)* (Montevideo, 1967), a work of basic scholarship. Juan Antonio Oddone, *Economía y sociedad en el Uruguay liberal 1852–1904. Antología de textos* (Montevideo, 1967), is a collection of documents preceded by a valuable introduction. For an analysis of the social structure see Carlos M. Rama, *Historia social del pueblo uruguayo* (Montevideo, 1972).

The best approach to understanding the history of Paraguay in the nineteenth century is provided by John Hoyt Williams, *The rise and fall of the Paraguayan Republic, 1800–1870* (Austin, 1979), a work of research and interpretation. Richard Alan White, *Paraguay's autonomous revolution 1810–1840* (Albuquerque, N.M., 1978), takes a new, though partial, look at Francia. For a Paraguayan view, see Julio César Chaves, *El supremo dictador. Biografía de José Gaspar de Francia* (4th edn, Madrid, 1964). The same author has written the history of Francia's successor, *El Presidente López. Vida y gobierno de Don Carlos* (2nd edn, Buenos Aires, 1968); see also Juan F. Pérez Acosta, *Don Carlos Antonio López, 'Obrero Máximo'* (Buenos Aires, 1948). For the demographic and developmental history of the period, see John Hoyt Williams, 'Observations on the Paraguayan Census of 1846', *HAHR*, 56 (1976), 424–37, and 'Foreign Técnicos and the modernization of Paraguay, 1840–1870', *Journal of Interamerican Studies and World Affairs*, 19/2 (1977), 233–57. The latter subject is explored in further detail by Josefina Pla, *The British in Paraguay (1850–70)* (London, 1976). On the Paraguayan War, Pelham Horton Box, *The origins of the Paraguayan War* (Urbana, Ill., 1929) is still worth reading, but should be supplemented by Efraím Cardozo, *Vísperas de la guerra del Paraguay* (Buenos Aires, 1954) and *El Imperio del Brasil y el Río de la Plata* (Buenos Aires, 1962). The same author's *Hace cien años* (8 vols., Asunción, 1967–72), is a useful chronicle of events based on contemporary Paraguayan newspapers. For a history of the war in English see Charles Kolinski, *Independence or death. The story of the Paraguayan War* (Gainesville, Florida, 1965), though Ramón J. Cárcano, *Guerra del Paraguay* (3 vols., Buenos Aires, 1938–40), still has value as a work of reference. There is an expert survey of Paraguayan bibliography by John Hoyt Williams, 'Paraguayan historical resources. Part Four. A selective Paraguayan historiography', *TA*, 34 (1978), 537–52.

# INDEX

Acapulco, Mexico, 123, 152
Acosta, José de, 250
Adlercreutz, Count, 223
Agua Amarga, Chile, 295
Aguilar, Dr Federico C., 237
Agustín I, emperor of Mexico, *see* Iturbide
Alajuela, Costa Rica, 175, 177
Alamán, Lucas, 61, 82, 87, 98, 99, 100, 109,
    130, 132, 134, 135, 138, 142, 149, 151,
    152
    *Historia de México*, 105
    political career (1823–53), 130–8 *passim*,
        142, 149–52 *passim*
Alberdi, Juan Bautista, 95, 283, 351
Aldao, Félix, 331
Alfaro, Eloy, 219, 232, 235
Allende, Ramón, 292
Alvarez, Juan, 81, 152–3, 154
Alzaga family, Argentina, 316, 317, 326
Ambalema, Colombia, 213
*Amigo de la Patria, El*, 174
Amunátegui, Miguel Luis, 308
Anchorena, Tomás Manuel de, 77 n15
Anchorena family, Argentina, 316, 317, 322,
    326, 327, 332, 337, 341
Ancon, Treaty of (1883), 313
Angamos, Chile, 312
Angelis, Pedro de, 322
Angostura, Venezuela, Congress of (1819), 66
Antequera, Bolivia, 277
Antigua, Guatemala, 184
Antioquia, Colombia, 30, 31, 56, 112, 210,
    231, 232, 236
Antofagasta, Chile, 263, 279, 280, 311
Antuñano, Estevan de, 109
Appun, Karl, 213
Aramayo family, Bolivia, 277
Arana, Felipe, 337
Arana family, Argentina, 317
Araucania, Chile, 283–4, 301, 306

Arce, Aniceto, 277, 278
Arce, Manuel José de, 176, 182–3
Arcos, Santiago, 290
Arequipa, Peru, 112, 119, 239, 241
Argentina (*see also* Buenos Aires, province
    of), 61–5 *passim*, 305, 314–57, 374–5
    and Bolivia, 249, 269–70, 321
    and Brazil, 320, 325, 338, 350
    and Chile, 305, 310, 311, 321, 351
    Church, 332, 340
    Constitutions: *1826*, 62, 65; *1853*, 338,
        351–2, 353, 357
    economy (*see also* stockraising), 36–7, 42–3,
        314–25, 348–51, 355–7, 374–5
    and Great Britain, 323–6 *passim*, 338,
        346–7, 350, 352, 356–9 *passim*
    immigrants, European, 42, 325, 326, 349,
        350, 357, 375
    Indians, 43, 315, 316, 335
    landholding, 315–17, 319, 335–8, 357
    military, position of, 81, 337–8, 340–1
    and Paraguay, 320, 365–6, 368–72
    and Paraguayan War (1864–70), 371, 374–5
    and Peru–Bolivian Confederation (1836–9),
        249, 269–70
    population and social structure (*see also*
        immigrants; Indians; slavery), 24, 25, 27,
        30, 31, 81, 325–31, 333–9, 357
    railways, 33–5, 42, 356
    slavery, 24, 43, 338–9
    stockraising, 15, 16–17, 42, 43, 374
    transport and communications (*see also*
        railways), 317, 319, 350, 356
    and Uruguay, 350, 358, 363–5
Argentine Confederation (1853–61), 351–3,
    368
Arica, Chile, 246, 263–70 *passim*, 312, 313
Arista, Mariano, 149–50
Ariza y Torres, Rafael, 181
Arizona, U.S., 151

Arqueros, Chile, 295
Arriaga, Ponciano, 153
Asunción, Paraguay, 368, 369, 371
Atacama Desert, Chile, 264, 268, 279, 280,
    294, 295, 310–11, 313
Australia, 40, 42, 296, 298
Avellaneda, Marco, 345
Ayacucho, Peru, 239
Aycinena, Mariano, 183–4, 186
Aycinena faction, Central America, 174
Aycinena–Wyke Treaty (1859), 202
Ayutla, Mexico, 152

Baily, John, 195
Ballivián, Adolfo, 281
Ballivián, José, 271
Balmaceda, José Manuel, 294
Balmes, Jaime, 100
Balta, José, 39, 258, 261
Banda Oriental, *see* Uruguay
Baquedano, Manuel, 312, 313
Barchard, William, 196
Barclay, Herring and Richardson, firm of, 197
Barclay and Co., 129
Barings, firm of, 356
Barquisimeto region, Venezuela, 228
Barranquilla, Colombia, 45
Barrios, Gerardo, 201, 205
Barrios, Justo Rufino, 121, 205
Barros Arana, Diego, 308
Barrundia, José Francisco, 182–8 *passim*
Barrundia, Juan, 183, 184
Basque immigrants, in Argentina, 42, 326,
    349, 350
Batres, Luis, 191
Bay Islands, 185, 195, 196, 201
Bazant, Jan, 120
Belgium, 199, 205
Belgrano, Manuel, 61
Belize (*see also* British Honduras), 185, 187,
    195–9 *passim*, 202, 203, 205
Bello, Andrés, 307, 308
Beltranena, Mariano, 182, 183
Belzú, Manuel Isidoro, 271–2, 281
Beni region, Bolivia, 264
Bennet, Marshal, 196
Bentham, Jeremy, influence in Latin
    America, 56, 68–9, 90, 180, 234
Berón de Astrada, 344
Berro, Bernardo F., 362, 363–4, 372
Bilbao, Francisco, 93, 95, 290
Bío-Bío, river, Chile, 283
Bismarck, Otto von, 313
Blaine, James G., 311
Blancarte, José, M., 150
Blythe, A., and Co., 367

Bogotá (Santa Fé de), Colombia, 211
    1819–30, 67
    after 1830, 45, 94, 99, 110, 111, 221, 227,
    231, 232–3, 237
Bolívar, Simón
    background, 74, 210
    and Spanish American independence, 59,
    77, 245, 247; constitutions, 62, 65–7
Bolivia (formerly Upper Peru), 66, 67, 242,
    264–82
    and Argentina, 249, 269–70, 321
    banks, 279–80
    and Chile (*see also* Pacific, War of the), 249,
    269–70, 277–80 *passim*, 302, 310–11
    Church, 266
    economy (*see also* mining industry), 37,
    240, 264–7, 272–81
    foreign debts, 278
    Indians, 267, 272–6, 277
    military, position of the, 80
    mining industry, 10–14 *passim*, 41, 264–5,
    276–8, 279–80, 295, 296
    and Peru (*see also* Pacific, War of the),
    Peru–Bolivian Confederation, 249,
    264–70 *passim*, 278
    population and social structure (*see also*
    Indians), 25, 30, 264, 272–3, 280–1
Bonald, L. G. A., vicomte de, 69
Borda, Francisco de Paula, 231
Boyacá, Colombia, 215, 225
Bravo, Nicolás, 124, 128–34 *passim*, 141, 149,
    153
Brazil, 15, 17, 235, 301, 338
    and Argentina, 320, 325, 338, 350
    and Paraguay, 366, 368
    and Paraguayan War, 370–2
    and Uruguay, 347, 358–65 *passim*
Bridge, Walter, 196
British Honduras (*see also* Belize), 179
Buenos Aires, city, Argentina
    18th/early 19th cents., 338
    and struggle for independence, 331
    after independence, 46, 47, 265, 301, 314,
    319, 332, 354, 356, 357, 369
    population, 31, 45, 326, 338–9, 357
Buenos Aires, province of (*see also*
    Argentina), 55–6, 65, 83–4, 112, 314–57
    *passim*
    blockaded by European powers (1838–40,
    1845), 317, 323, 324, 341–6 *passim*, 358
    breaks away from rest of Argentina (1853–
    61), 351–3
    economy (*see also* stockraising), 42, 314–25
    *passim*, 348–51
    and Great Britain, 314, 315, 323, 324, 325,
    349, 350

population and social structure (*see also*
slavery), 315, 316, 326, 333–9, 357
railways, 33–4, 350
slavery, 43, 338–9
stockraising, 27, 42, 314–21 *passim*, 324,
348–50
and United States, 325, 349
Bulnes, Manuel, 270, 289–90, 303–4
Burgin, Miron, 119
Burke, Edmund, 69, 98
Bustamente, Anastasio, 100, 124, 133–40
*passim*
Bustamente y Guerra, José de, 172

Caballero, José Maria, 221
Cabañas, Trinidad, 192, 193, 201
Cádiz, Spain, Constitution of (1812), 62–3,
65, 172, 174, 180
Cajamarca, Peru, 112
Caldera, Chile, 301
Cali, Colombia, 99, 228
California, 40, 144, 200, 298
Callao, Peru, 241, 243, 246, 248, 253, 270
Camacho Roldán, Salvador, 231
Campeche, Mexico, 109
Campero, Narciso, 281
Campo de la Alianza, Peru, battle of (1880),
312
Canada, 40
Canarian immigrants, in Argentina, 326
Canning, George, 207
Caracas, Venezuela, 31, 45, 210, 217, 221,
222, 230, 232
Caracoles, Bolivia, 279, 295, 302
Carguaicollo, Bolivia, 277
Caro, José Eusebio, 100
Caro, Miguel Antonio, 231
Carrera, José Rafael, 187–95 *passim*, 199, 205
Carrillo, Braulio, 189, 190
Carrizal Alto, Chile, 295
Cartagena, Colombia, 110, 111, 211
Cartago, Costa Rica, 176, 177
Casáus, Archbishop Ramón, 176, 183, 186
Castes, War of the (1847), 147
Castilla, Ramón, 102, 235, 244, 249, 250, 252,
257–8, 259
Castro, Cipriano, 232
Catamarca, Argentina, 345
Cauca valley, Colombia, 30, 119, 215, 224,
227
caudillos, 72–6, 81–4, 329–31
Caupolicán, Bolivia, 275
Central America (*see also* Chiapas; Costa Rica;
Guatemala; Honduras; Nicaragua;
Salvador)
up to independence, *see* Guatemala,

kingdom of
after independence, 171–206; Church, 180,
185–6; constitution (1824), 177, 181–2;
economy, 15, 16, 45, 179, 194–9, 202–3,
204–5; and Europe (*see also* Great
Britain), 194, 195, 199, 202, 205; foreign
debts, 33, 197, 199, 202; and Great
Britain, 185, 189, 194–205 *passim*; and
Mexico, 172, 175, 176–7; political
thought, 179–80; population and social
structure, 24, 26, 45, 177–8; slavery, 24,
43; and United States, 184, 186, 194–5,
199–202, 205
Cepeda, Argentina, 331, 352
Cercado, Bolivia, 275
Cerna, Vicente, 205
Cerro Corá, battle of (1870), 371
Cerro de Pasco, Peru, 14, 240, 250
'Chacho, El' (A. V. Peñaloza), 354
Chalcuapa, El Salvador, 183
Chamorro, Fruto, 193–4
Chañarcillo, Chile, 11, 295
Chateaubriand, F. R., vicomte de, influence
in Latin America, 69
Chatenet, Maurice du, 14
Chatfield, Frederick, 189, 192, 195, 199, 200
Chayanta, Bolivia, 277
Chiapas, Mexico (*see also* Central America;
Guatemala, kingdom of), 175, 177, 191
Chiclayo, Peru, 255
Chile
struggle for independence, 58–9, 65, 75
after independence, 59–63 *passim*, 68, 70–1,
75, 94, 117, 118, 283–313; agriculture,
39–41, 297–300, 309; and Argentina,
305, 310, 311, 321, 351; banks, 302; and
Bolivia (*see also* Pacific, War of the), 249,
269–70, 277–80 *passim*, 302, 310–11;
constitutions: 1828, 62, 285, 286; 1833,
286, 288, 291; economy (*see also*
agriculture; mining industry;
stockraising), 36, 198, 293–303, 309–10;
and Great Britain, 39, 289, 293, 296,
299–305 *passim*, 309, 311; immigrants,
European, 40, 305–6; Indians, 283–4,
306; military, position of, 79, 80, 288;
mining industry, 10–14 *passim*, 39, 41,
294–7, 309; and Peru (*see also* Pacific,
War of the), 240, 241, 249, 250, 262,
263, 269–70, 289, 298, 302, 311;
population and social structure (*see also*
immigrants; Indians), 24, 31, 284, 294,
297–8, 303–7; railways, 35, 40, 301, 302;
slavery, 24, 43, 284; stockraising, 15, 16,
17; transport and communications (*see
also* railways), 299, 300–1

Chilean and Peruvian Association, 246–7
Chiloé, island, Chile, 283
Chincha islands, Peru, 258
Chinese
 in Cuba, 44
 in Peru, 44, 253, 255
Chiquimula, Guatemala, 185, 193
Chocó, province, Colombia, 108, 210
Choele-Choel, island, Argentina, 335
Chorillos, battle of (1881), 313
Chuquisaca, Bolivia, later Sucre, 268, 275
Church, George E., 278
Church (*see also under individual countries*), 49,
 52–3, 54, 57–8, 78, 89–90, 92–3, 97,
 99–103
Cieza de León, Pedro, 250
Cisplatine province, *see* Uruguay
Ciudad Real, Mexico, 175
Clark, Juan and Mateo, 301
Clark, Melbourne, 279
Clark, Melbourne, and Co., 279
Clayton–Bulwer Treaty (1850), 200
Coatepeque, El Salvador, 205
Cobija, Chile, 246, 264, 267, 268, 270, 279
Cochabamba, Bolivia, 30, 31, 264, 272–7
 *passim*
Codazzi, Agustín, 213
Colombia
 before 1819, *see* New Granada, viceroyalty
 of
 1819–30, *see* Gran Colombia
 after 1830, *see* New Granada, after 1830
 (later Colombia)
Colorado, river, Argentina, 316
Comayagua, Honduras, 175, 176, 192
Comitán, Mexico, 175
Comonfort, Ignacio, 152–5 *passim*, 158, 159,
 166
Concepción, Chile, 284, 285, 296, 307
Concha y Toro, Melchor, 278, 279
Conrad, Joseph, 229
Constant, Benjamin, influence in Latin
 America, 56, 64, 67–9
Constitución, Chile, 40
Copiapó, Chile, 39, 283, 295, 301, 307
Coquimbo, Chile, 39, 294
Córdoba, Argentina, 25, 317, 326, 345, 356
Córdoba, Mexico, Treaty of (1821), 124–5,
 126, 129
Córdovez Moure, José María, 237
Corinto, Nicaragua, 197
Coro, Venezuela, 227
Corrientes, province of, Argentina, 314, 320,
 323, 343–50 *passim*, 368, 369, 371
Cortés, Enrique, 231
Cortés y Esparza, José M., 167

Costa Rica (*see also* Central America;
 Guatemala, kingdom of)
 18th/early 19th cents., 178, 179
 struggle for independence, 175–6
 after independence, 176–7, 178, 182, 184,
 189–97 *passim*, 201, 202, 203, 206
Cottu, Charles, 68
Cousin, Victor, 69
Couto, Bernardo, 99
Crespo, General Joaquín, 224, 232
Cuba (*see also* Havana), 36, 325
 railways, 21–2
 slavery, 21–2, 43–4
 social structure, 30, 31
 sugar, 20–2, 37
 Ten Years War (1868–78), 36, 37, 44
Cúcuta, Colombia, 207
 Congress of (1821), 25, 65–6, 214
Cuevas, Luis Gonzaga, 99
Cullen, Domingo, 344
Cundinamarca, Colombia, 215
Cuyo, Argentina, 345
Cuzco, Peru, 119, 239

Dalence, José María, 272
Darwin, Charles, 297
David, Panama, 190
Daza, Hilarión, 281
Degollado, Santos, 161
Delgado, José Matías, 175, 176, 177, 182
Destutt de Tracy, Antoine Louis Claude, 69,
 90
Díaz, Porfirio, 44, 121, 169–70
Díaz Vélez family, Argentina, 317
Diez Canseco, Pedro, 258
Dorado, Joaquín, 278
Dorado Bros, firm of, 279
Dorrego, Manuel, 331, 332, 333
Dreyfus, Auguste, 39, 251, 262
Dueñas, Francisco, 192, 205
Dumont, P. E. L., 68

Echagüe, Pascual de, 344
Echenique, José Rufino, 257, 259
Echeverría, Esteban, 69, 93, 97
economy of Spanish America (*see also under
 individual countries*), 1–22, 31–47
Ecuador (*see also* Guayaquil; Quito; Gran
 Colombia), 67, 71, 209, 216–18, 221,
 224–38 *passim*
 agriculture, 18, 211–14 *passim*
 Church, 215, 217
 economy (*see also* agriculture), 208–14
 *passim*, 218–19, 225
 military, position of, 220–1, 225–6
 and Peru, 235, 249

population and social structure, 25, 26,
208, 214–16, 236–7
slavery, 214
*Editor Constitucional, El*, 174
Edwards Ossandón, Agustín, 279, 296–7
Egaña, Juan, 285
Egaña, Mariano, 70
El Salvador, *see* Salvador
England, *see* Great Britain
Entre Ríos, province of, Argentina, 314, 320,
331, 343–54 *passim*
Errázuriz family, Chile, 304
Errázuriz Zañartu, Federico, 291–2, 301, 304
Escudero y Echánove, Pedro, 167
Espina, Ramón, 221
'Espinosa, el indo', 228

Facio, José Antonio, 136
Falcón, Marshal, 227, 228
Famaillá, Argentina, 345
Ferdinand VII, king of Spain, 61
Ferré, Pedro, 320, 345
Ferrera, Francisco, 192, 193
Fierro–Sarratea Agreement (1878), 310
Filangieri, Gaetano, 68
Filísola, Vicente, 176–7
Fisher, Hermann, 278
Flores, Cirilio, 183
Flores, Juan José, 67, 208, 210, 217, 220,
224–5, 234, 235
Flores, Venancio, 361–5 *passim*, 371, 372
Forey, Marshal, 166
Foster, John, 196
France, 5, 42
and Argentina, 317, 323, 341–6 *passim*,
352, 358, 359; immigrants in, 326, 350
and Bolivia, 265, 278, 279
and Central America, 194, 195, 202, 205
and Chile, 289, 302, 305, 309
and Ecuador, 236
French Revolution (1789), 58
literature, influence of, *see* Chateaubriand;
Constant
and Mexico, 35, 138, 165–9
and Peru, 240, 241, 250, 251
politics and philosophy, influence of, 56–7,
66–9, 92–5; Enlightenment, 58, 68–9
Revolution (1848), 93–9 *passim*, 290
and Uruguay, 358, 360, 373
Francia, Dr José Gaspar Rodríguez de, 72,
365–70 *passim*
Fray Bentos, Uruguay, 356
Freire, Ramón, 284–5, 308
Frías, Tomas, 281

Gaínza, Gabino, 175, 176

Gálvez, Dr Mariano, 182–9 *passim*
Gálvez, Pedro, 258
Gálvez, brothers, 112
Gamarra, Agustín, 72, 248, 249, 270
García, Francisco, 135, 137, 140
García Calderón, Francisco, 115
García del Rio, Juan, 247
García Granados, Miguel, 205
García Moreno, Gabriel, 102, 215, 225
Gay, Claude, 305
George IV, king of Great Britain, 208
Germany, 5, 213, 374
and Argentina, immigrants in, 350
and Bolivia, 265, 278
and Chile, immigrants in, 40, 305, 306
and Venezuela, immigrants in, 236
Gibbs, Antony, and Sons, firm of, 38, 251
Gibbs, William, 279
Glenton, Jonas, 196
Goldschmitt and Co., 129
Gómez Farías, Valentín, 126, 135–7, 138,
142–3, 144, 157
Gómez Pedraza, Manuel, 110, 132–3
González, Manuel, 166
González Ortega, Jesús, 163–8 *passim*
Gosselman, Carl August, 211, 218, 220
Goyeneche y Barrera, Archbishop José
Sebastián, 102
Gran Colombia, republic of (*see also* Cúcuta,
Congress of), 24, 62, 63, 67, 207–8
Granada, Nicaragua, 175, 176–7, 182, 193,
194, 200
Great Britain, 2–8 *passim*, 33, 34
and Argentina, 314, 315, 323–6 *passim*, 338,
346–52 *passim*, 356, 358, 359
and Bolivia, 265, 278–80
and Central America, 185, 189, 194–205
*passim*
and Chile, 39, 289, 293, 296, 299–305
*passim*, 309, 311
and Gran Colombia, republic of, 207–8
and Mexico, 6–7, 129–30, 148, 163, 165
and New Granada, 236
and Paraguay, 367–8
and Peru, 38–9, 240–7 *passim*, 250, 254,
259, 262
political systems, influence of, 56–7, 66, 68,
69
and Uruguay, 346–7, 358, 359, 373, 374
Greytown (San Juan del Norte), Nicaragua,
197, 200
Guadalajara, Mexico, 140, 141, 150
Guadalupe mines, Bolivia, 277
Guainas, *cacique*, 228
Guanajuato, Mexico, 109, 147, 160
Guaraní Indians, 366–7, 368

Guardia, Tomás, 206
Guardiola, Santos, 193, 201
Guatemala (*see also* Central America;
    Guatemala, kingdom of)
    18th/early 19th cents., 178, 179
    struggle for independence, 171–5 *passim*
    after independence, 45, 176, 177, 178,
    181–205 *passim*
Guatemala, kingdom of, Central America (*see
    also* Chiapas; Costa Rica; Guatemala;
    Honduras; Nicaragua; Salvador), 171–5,
    178–9
Guatemala City, 171–5 *passim*, 186–91 *passim*,
    202
Guayacán, Chile, 296
Guayana, Venezuela, 236
Guayaquil, Ecuador, 45, 228, 234, 235, 270
Guayas, Ecuador, 234
Guerrero, Vicente, 78, 123, 124, 125, 128,
    132–4, 136, 152, 153
Guerrero, Mexico, 81, 109, 152, 153
Guizot, F. P. G., 68
Gutiérrez Estrada, José María, 138, 140, 165
Guzmán, Antonio Leocadio, 94, 222–3, 227,
    230
Guzmán Blanco, Antonio, 121, 218, 219, 224,
    227, 232, 237

Hall, Basil, 3–4
Hall, Francis, 234
Hall, William, 196
Halperín Donghi, Tulio, 78, 91, 121
Haro y Tamariz, Antonio de, 109, 150, 151
Harratt, John, 349
Hassaurek, Friedrich, 213, 236
Havana, Cuba, 20, 31, 45
Heredia, Costa Rica, 175
Hernández, José, *Martin Fierro*, 355
Herrán, Pedro Alcántara, 218, 224, 227, 228
Herrera, Bartolomé, 98–9, 100, 258
Herrera, José Joaquín, 141–2, 144, 148, 149
Herrera family, Peru, 112
Hicks, George, 280
Holnisky, A., 225
Holton, Isaac, 213
Honduras (*see also* Central America;
    Guatemala, kingdom of)
    18th/early 19th cents., 178, 179
    struggle for independence, 172, 175
    after independence, 33, 176, 178, 183,
    189–93 *passim*, 196, 201, 202, 205
Huanchaca, Bolivia, 277–8

Iglesias, José María, 156
Iglesias Law (1857), 156–7
Iguala, Plan of (1821), 123, 124, 129, 142, 169

influence in Central America, 171, 175
Indians (*see also* under *individual countries*), 25–7,
    44–5, 52, 54, 88–9
Infante, José Miguel, 285
Ingavi, Bolivia, 249, 270, 274
Iquique, Chile, 312
Ireland, immigrants and mercenaries from,
    42, 349
Isaac and Samuel, firm of, 199
Islay, Peru, 240 n3
Italy
    immigrants from: in Argentina, 325, 350;
    in Uruguay, 372
    politics, influence of, 93
Iturbide, Agustín de (Agustín I, emperor of
    Mexico), 27, 62, 123–5, 126–9, 151
    and Central American independence, 171,
    175, 176
Izabal, Guatemala, 197, 199

Jalapa, Mexico, 110, 127
Jalisco, Mexico, 108, 109
Jamaica, 198
Jane, Lionel Cecil, 115
Jesuits, 93, 101, 152, 190, 231, 340
Jiquetepeque valley, Peru, 27, 256
Juárez, Benito, 121, 153, 154, 159–70 *passim*
Juárez Law (1855), 154, 158
Jujuy, Argentina, 317, 345
Junín, Peru, 239

Kilgour, William, 196
Kinder, Thomas, 247
Klee, Charles, 196

La Cruz, José Maria de, 290
La Libertad, Peru, 239
La Madrid, Aráoz de, 345
La Paz, Bolivia, 249, 264, 265, 272–5 *passim*
La Rioja, Argentina, 321, 345, 354
La Trinidad, Honduras, 183
La Unión, Bolivia, 275
Labastida, Bishop (later Archbishop), 155,
    166
Lamennais, H. F. R. de, 93, 94
Lamport and Holt, firm of, 356
Lander, Tomás, 88, 222
Larecaja, Bolivia, 275
Laso, Benito, 112
Lastarria, José Victorino, 290, 304
Lavalle, Juan, 333, 334, 344–5
León, Nicaragua, 175, 182, 193, 194
Lerdo, Sebastián, 153, 169–70
Lerdo de Tejada, Miguel, 144, 150, 153–4,
    155–6, 159–64 *passim*
Lerdo Law (1856), 44, 155–62 *passim*

Les Charcas, Guatemala, 184
Lesperance, Frederick, 196
Liebig Co., 374
Lima, Peru
   18th/early 19th cents., 247
   after independence, 31, 112, 241, 249, 255,
     256, 259, 262, 263, 313; population, 45,
     239
Limantour, José Yves, 161, 165
Linares, José María, 281
Lindo, Juan, 192–3
Lircay, Chile, 285
Lirquén, Chile, 296
Littoral, pact of the (1831), 320
Livingston Codes, 186, 187, 188
Llanquihue, lake, Chile, 306
López, Carlos Antonio, 365–70 *passim*
López, Estanislao, 330–1, 344
López, Francisco Solano, 365–71 *passim*
López, José Hilario, 224
López, Juan Pablo, 344
López, Vicente Fidel, 337
López Jordan, Ricardo, 354
López Portillo, Jesús, 150
Los Altos, Guatemala, 187, 190
Lota, Chile, 296
Lower California, Mexico, 144
Lucre hacienda, Peru, 256
Lurifico hacienda, Peru, 256

MacGregor, Gregor, 196, 199
Machiavelli, Niccolo dei, influence of, 68
McLane–Ocampo Treaty (1859), 162
McNally, Richard, 196
Magdalena valley, Colombia, 111–12, 214,
   215
Magellan Straits, Chile, 241, 283, 301, 310
Maistre, J. M., comte de, 69
Malespín, Francisco, 192, 193
Manabí, Ecuador, 234
Managua, Nicaragua, 194
Manning, Thomas, 196
Mansfield, Charles, 323
Maracay, Venezuela, 232
Márquez, José Ignacio de, 222
Mataquescuintla, Guatemala, 187, 189
Matina, Costa Rica, 197
Mato Grosso, Brazil, 364, 371
Mauá, barão/visconde de, *see* Sousa, Irineu E.
   de
Maximilian, Archduke of Austria, emperor of
   Mexico, 61, 121, 165, 166–9
Mayas, 147, 148
Mazzini, Giuseppe, 93
Meany, Carlos, 196
Medellín, Colombia, 31, 217

Meiggs, Henry, 35, 301, 305
Mejía, General, 168–9
Mejillones, Chile, 274, 279
Melgarejo, Mariano, 269, 274–8 *passim*, 281
Melo, José María, 221, 224
Mena, Colonel, 234
Mendoza, Argentina, 317, 321
*Mercurio, El*, 307
Mexico, 63, 65, 99, 123–70
   and Central America, 172, 175, 176–7
   Church, 100–2, 125, 135–7, 143, 154–63
     *passim*
   constitutions: 1824, 62, 63, 64, 131, 143,
     151; 1836, 67, 68, 138, 140, 141; 1843,
     141, 142, 151, 155; 1857, 157–9
   declaration of independence (1821), 123–4
   economy, *see* mining industry; stockraising;
     textile industry
   empire (1821–3), 62, 123–9
   empire (1864–7), 61, 166–9
   and Europe (*see also* Great Britain), 35,
     126–7, 128, 132–3, 138, 165–9
   foreign debts, 120, 129–30, 135, 148
   and Great Britain, 6–7, 129–30, 148, 163,
     165
   Indians, 145, 147, 148
   military, position of, 79–80
   mining industry, 10–14 *passim*
   political parties or factions, 105, 108,
     109–10
   population and social structure (*see also*
     Indians; slavery), 24–30 *passim*, 44,
     145–6
   railways, 35
   slavery, 24, 43
   stockraising, 15
   textile industry, 29–30, 135
   Three Years War (1858–60), 36, 159–63
   and United States, 113–14, 131, 137,
     141–4, 148, 149, 151, 157, 162–3; war
     with (1846–8), 142–4, 157, 193
Mexico City, 45, 46, 109, 124, 143, 153, 166
   in Three Years War (1858–60), 160, 161,
     163
Michelana, Mariano José, 129
Michelet, Jules, 93
Michoacán, Mexico, 108, 109, 154, 160, 161,
   bishopric, 125
Mier, Fray Servando Teresa de, 127, 157
Miers, John, 13, 14
military, position of (*see also under individual
   countries*), 49–50, 53, 57, 78–82
Minas Gerais, Brazil, 15
Miraflores, battle of (1881), 313
Miramón, Miguel, 161, 163, 166–9 *passim*
Misiones, Argentina, 371, 372

Miskito Shore, Central America, 185, 195,
  196, 198, 202
Mitre, Bartolomé, 352–5, 364, 370, 371
Molina, Pedro, 174, 175, 187
Mollendo, Peru, 240 n3
Mompóx, Venezuela, 231
Monagas, José Tadeo, 218, 222, 223, 226,
  227, 229, 232
Monagas family, Venezuela, 218, 224, 227
Montalvo, Juan, 225
Monte Caseros, Argentina, 347
Montealegre family, Costa Rica, 206
Montesquieu, baron de 56, 68
Montevideo, Uruguay, 47, 321, 342–7 *passim*,
  358, 359, 362, 365, 373, 374
  population, 45, 358, 359, 361, 372–3
Montt, Manuel, 91, 290–1, 294, 299, 307
Moquegua valley, Peru, 266
Mora, José María Luis, 135–6, 149, 154, 157
Mora, Juan, 182
Mora, Rafael, 201, 205, 206
Morales, Agustín, 276, 281
Morales y Ugalde, José, 243
Morazán, Francisco, 183–92 *passim*, 205
Moret Law (1870), 44
Morse, Richard M., 115–18
Mosquera, Joaquín, 69, 102
Mosquera, Tomás Cipriano de, 75, 82, 221,
  224, 227–30 *passim*, 233
Munecas, Bolivia, 274
Munguía, Clemente de Jesús, bishop, 98 n27,
  102

Napoleon III, emperor of France, 61, 165,
  166, 168, 369
Negrete, General, 129
Negro, river, Argentina, 316
New Granada (*see also* Gran Colombia)
  viceroyalty of, 59
  after 1830 (later Colombia), 58–9, 62, 63,
    65, 68, 69, 75, 94, 100, 108–14 *passim*,
    209–38 *passim*
  agriculture, 18, 211–14 *passim*
  Church, 101, 102, 215, 217
  economy (*see also* agriculture; mining
    industry), 208–19 *passim*, 225
  military, position of, 79, 81, 220–1, 225–6
  mining industry, 10, 13, 210
  population and social structure (*see also*
    slavery), 25, 30–1, 208, 214–16, 236–7
  slavery, 24, 43, 214
New Mexico, U.S., 144
New Orleans, U.S., 200, 201
New Spain, *see* Mexico
Nicaragua (*see also* Central America;
  Guatemala, kingdom of)

18th/early 19th cents., 178, 179
  struggle for independence, 172, 175
  after independence, 176–7, 182, 189–97
    *passim*, 200–6 *passim*
Norte Chico, Chile, 13, 23, 35, 39, 41, 294–7
Núñez, Rafael, 121, 231, 233–4

Oaxaca, Mexico, 109, 154
Obando, José María, 75, 79, 224–8 *passim*
Ocampo, Melchor, 144, 145–6, 153–4, 157,
  160–4 *passim*, 169
O'Donojú, Juan, 123–5
O'Higgins, Bernardo, 284, 285, 289, 308
Omasuyos, Bolivia, 274
Omoa, Honduras, 197
Oribe, Manuel, 344, 345–6, 358–9, 361
Orizaba, Mexico, 109
Oruro, Bolivia, 272, 274, 275
Osorio, Alejandro, 87
Ospina Rodríguez, Mariano, 100, 114, 218,
  229, 231
Otamendi, Juan, 234
Ovalle, José Ramón, 295

Pacajes, Bolivia, 274, 275–6
Pacheco, Angel, 337
Pacheco, Gregorio, 277
Pacific, War of the (1879–83), 39, 41, 250,
  263, 280, 281, 311–13
Pacific Steam Navigation Co., 301, 356
Padilla, José, 78
Páez, José Antonio, 27, 73, 75, 79, 80, 97,
  208, 210, 217–23 *passim*, 226, 232
Pago Largo, Argentina, 344
Paita, Peru, 246, 270
Palmerston, 3rd Viscount, 196
Pampa Indians, 43, 315
Panama, 241
Pando, José María de, 69, 243, 244
Pando family, Peru, 112
Pando region, Bolivia, 264
Paraguay (*see also* Paraguayan War; Río de la
  Plata), 33, 319, 347, 365–72
  and Argentina, 320, 365–6, 368–72
  and Brazil, 366–72 *passim*
  Indians, 336–7, 368; slavery, 43, 367
Paraguay, river, 364, 371
Paraguayan War (1864–70), 36, 355, 364–5,
  371–5 *passim*
Paraná, Argentina, 332, 352
Paraná, river, 346, 351, 352, 366
Pardo, Manuel, 258–63 *passim*
Pardo family, Peru, 112
Paredes, Mariano, 191, 201
Paredes Arrillaga, Mariano, 139–43 *passim*
Parish, Juan, 247

Parker, Robert, 196
Paroissien, Diego de, 247
Paso del Norte, U.S., 168
Pasto, Colombia, 108, 215, 217, 224, 227, 232
Patagonia, Argentina, 310
Patía, valley, Colombia, 227
Pavon, Manuel F., 195
Pavón, Argentina, 353, 355, 364
Peña, David, 228
Peña y Peña, Manuel de la, 144
Peñaloza, Angel Vicente ('El Chaco'), 354
Peñalver, Fernando de, 65
Pentland, John Barclay, 264, 265
Pérez, Felipe, 213
Pérez, José Joaquín, 291, 306
Peró, Napoleón, 279–80
Peru, 62, 65, 67, 69, 94, 95, 112, 239–63, 282
    banks, 260
    and Bolivia (*see also* Pacific, War of the),
        Peru–Bolivian Confederation, 249,
        264–70 *passim*, 278
    and Central America, 198
    and Chile (*see also* Pacific, War of the), 240,
        241, 249, 250, 262, 263, 269–70, 289,
        298, 302, 311
    economy (*see also* guano trade; mining
        industry), 18, 20, 36, 240–7, 250–7,
        258–62
    and Ecuador, 235, 249
    foreign debts, 243, 253–5, 256, 262
    and Great Britain, 38–9, 240–7 *passim*, 250,
        254, 259, 262
    guano trade, 37–9, 250–62 *passim*
    Indians, 244–6, 252
    military, position of, 80–1
    mining industry, 10–14 *passim*, 240, 246–7,
        250, 296
    population and social structure (*see also*
        Indians; slavery), 24–7 *passim*, 44, 45,
        239, 247–8, 253, 255
    railways, 35, 39, 240 n3, 253, 254, 261, 305
    slavery, 24, 43, 252–3
    and United States, 240, 241, 246, 250, 259
Peru, Upper, *see* Bolivia
Peru–Bolivian Confederation (1836–9), 67,
    246, 249, 269–70, 289
Petén, the, Guatemala, 199
Pezet, Juan Antonio, 258
Piar, Manuel, 78
Pichincha, Ecuador, 225
Piérola, Nicolás de, 263
Pilar, Paraguay, 366
Pinto, Aníbal, 292–3, 310
Pinto, Francisco Antonio, 285, 289
Pisco-Ica, Peru, 255
Pissis, Amado, 305

Piura, Peru, 255
Pius IX, Pope, 101–2
Pizarro, Francisco Javier Luna, 67, 81, 112
Poinsett, Joel R., 132, 133, 145
political instability, 114–21
political parties or factions, 103–13
political systems, 56–71
politics, ideology and society, 48–56
    up to c. 1845, 56–90
    c. 1845–70, 90–122
Popayán, Colombia, 110, 111, 207, 210, 221,
    227, 228
population and social structures (*see also*
        Indians; slavery; *individual countries*),
        22–31, 43–7
Portales, Diego, 70–1, 72, 75, 79, 97, 269–70,
    285–6, 289, 294, 308
Potosí, Bolivia, 55, 264, 268, 272–7 *passim*, 314
Poyais enterprise (1823–4), 196, 199
Prado, Mariano Ignacio, 258, 263
Prat, Arturo, 312
Prieto, Guillermo, 153
Prieto, Joaquín, 75, 286, 289
Proudhon, P. J., 271
Puebla, Mexico, 30, 101, 109, 135, 143, 155,
    166, 168
Puelma, Francisco, 279, 311
Pulacayo, Bolivia, 278
Puno, Peru, 112, 239
Puntarenas, Costa Rica, 197

Quebracho Herrado, Argentina, 345
Querétaro, Mexico, 160, 168
Quezaltenango, Guatemala, 183, 191
Quinet, Edgar, 93
Quiroga, Facundo, 73
Quispicanchis, province of, Peru, 256
*Quiteño Libre, El*, 225, 234
Quito, Ecuador, 45, 207, 234, 235

railways (*see also under individual countries*), 33–5
Ramírez, Francisco, 331
Ramos Arizpe, José Miguel, 129
'Rangel, el indio', 228
Real del Monte, company of, 12
Realejo, Nicaragua, 197, 200
Rengifo, Manuel, 293–4
Riachulo, battle of (1865), 371
Rio de Janeiro, Brazil, 301
Río de la Plata, River Plate region (*see also*
        Argentina; Paraguay; Uruguay)
    social structure, 24, 25, 27, 30, 31, 81
    stockraising, 15, 16–17
Río de la Plata, United Provinces of the, *see*
        Argentina
Rio Grande do Sul, Brazil, 321, 348

Riochacha, Colombia, 108
Ripley, R. S., 148
Riva Palacio, Vicente, 27
Rivadavia, Bernardino, 315, 316, 319, 321,
    328, 331–3, 334
Rivas, Medardo, 236
Rivas, Patricio, 201
Rivera, Fructuoso, 344, 346, 358, 359
Rivera Paz, Mariano, 188, 189–90
Roatán, Central America, 201
Robertson, J. P. and W. P., 3
Rocafuerte, Vicente, 71, 218, 234, 235
Rodeo del Medio, Argentina, 345
Rodríguez, J. M., 251
Rodríguez, Martín, 315, 331
Rojas y Patrón, José María, 320
Rosario, Argentina, 350, 352, 356
Rosas, Juan Manuel de, 65, 75, 77 n15, 83,
    85, 95, 97, 112, 316–17, 320, 322–4, 328,
    331, 332–44, 350
    background and character, 72, 73, 327
    and Paraguay, 368
    and Peru–Bolivian Confederation, 249
    and Uruguay, 344–7, 358–9
Rothschild, House of, 161, 165
Rousseau, Jean-Jacques, influence of, 56, 68
Russia, 16

Sáenz Valiente family, Argentina, 316
St John, Stephen, 278
Saint-Simon, C. H., comte de, influence of,
    69, 93, 271
Salado, province of, Argentina, 332
Salado, river, Argentina, 315
Salas, José Mariano, 143
Salaverry, Felipe, 248, 249, 269
Salazar, Carlos, 189
Salta, Argentina, 317, 321, 345
Salvador, El (*see also* Central America;
    Guatemala, kingdom of)
    18th/early 19th cents., 178, 179
    struggle for independence, 172, 174, 175
    after independence, 176–7, 178, 181–5
    *passim*, 189–97 *passim*, 201–5 *passim*
Samper, José María, 229, 237–8
San Antonio, Texas, 137
San José, Costa Rica, 175, 177
San José la Arada, Guatemala, 193
San Juan, Argentina, 321, 354
San Juan de Ulúa, island, Mexico, 125, 127
San Juan del Norte, Nicaragua, 197, 200
San Juan Ostuncalco, Guatemala, 187
San Luis, Argentina, 317
San Luis Potosí, Mexico, 109, 147, 166
San Martín, José de, 244, 247
San Martín Jilotepeque, Guatemala, 183

San Román, Miguel, 258
San Salvador, El Salvador, 174–7 *passim*, 184,
    189, 194, 205
Sánchez-Albornoz, Nicolás, 30
Sandoval, J. L., 194
Santa Ana, Colombia, 210
Santa Anna, António López de, 75, 80, 82,
    100, 110, 127–8, 129, 133, 136–44 *passim*,
    149–53
Santa Coloma family, Argentina, 316, 326
Santa Cruz, Andrés, 67, 241, 246, 249, 268,
    270, 289
Santa Cruz, Bolivia, 264
Santa Fe, province of, Argentina, 42, 314,
    320, 331, 343–4, 345, 350, 357
Santa Fé de Bogotá, *see* Bogotá
Santa María, Miguel, 128
Santa Marta, Colombia, 111
Santa Rosa, Guatemala, 187
Santander, Francisco de Paula, 67, 75, 207,
    208, 210, 217, 221–2, 233
Santander, Colombia, 225
Santiago, Argentina, 317
Santiago, Chile, 31, 40, 45, 79, 284, 288, 298,
    301–6 *passim*
    building development, 307
Santiago de Guatemala, 172, 174
Santo Tomás, Guatemala, 199
Santos Ossa, José, 310–11
Sardinia, 5
Sarmiento, Domingo Faustino, 73, 95, 105,
    307, 353–7 *passim*
Sarria, 'bandit', 228
Say, J. B., 68
Shepherd, Peter, 196
Shepherd, Samuel, 196
Sheridan, Peter, 349
Sicasica, Bolivia, 274
Sierra, Justo, 119
Sierra Gorda rebellion (1840s), 147
Skinner, George, 196
slavery (*see also under individual countries*), 24,
    43–4, 88
Smith, George, 279
social structures, *see* population and social
    structures
Socorro, Colombia, 56, 108, 111–12
Soffia, José Antonio, 233
Sotillo family, Venezuela, 227, 228
Sotomayor Valdés, Ramón, 308
Soublette, Carlos, 80, 91, 218
Sousa, Irineu Evangelista de (later
    barão/visconde de Mauá), 361, 374
Spain, 5, 18
    and Argentina (*see also* Basque immigrants),
    325, 349

and Central America, 196, 202, 205
and Guatemala, kingdom of, 171–2, 174–5
and Mexico: up to independence, 123–5;
  after independence, 126–7, 128, 132–3,
  138, 165
and Peru, 258
political systems, influence of, 56–65
  *passim*, 115–18
and Uruguay, 372
Squier, E. G., 199, 200
Stephens, John Lloyd, 16, 147, 195
Sucre, Antonio José de, 227, 266–7
Sucre, Bolivia (*see also* Chuquisaca), 274

Tacna, Peru, 263, 312, 313
Talca, Chile, 298, 307
Talcahuano, Chile, 298, 301
Tamaya, Chile, 295
Tambo, valley, Peru, 266
Tampico, Mexico, 129, 133
Tapacarí, Bolivia, 275
Tarapacá, province of, Chile, 262, 263, 312
Tarata, Bolivia, 275
Tarija, Bolivia, 268
Tegucigalpa, Honduras, 175, 176
Terrero, Juan N., 336–7
Texas, U. S.
  up to 1845, 114, 137–41 *passim*, 185
  joins United States (1845), 141, 144, 157
Thompson, George Alexander, 195
Tierradentro, Colombia, 228
Tigre island, Nicaragua, 200
Tocqueville, Alexis de, 56, 68
Tolima, Colombia, 210, 215
Toluca, Mexico, 144
Tomé, Chile, 40
Tongoy, Chile, 296
Toro, Murillo, 233
Tres Puntas, Chile, 295
Trujillo, Peru, 255
Trujillo, Honduras, 197, 201
Tucumán, Argentina, 317, 321, 345
  Congress of (1816–17), 61
Tunja, Colombia, 110, 111
Tupize, Bolivia, 268
Tuxtla, Mexico, 175

Unamuno, Miguel de, 115
Unanue, Hipólito, 243
United States of America, 4–5, 40–1, 42,
  113–14
and Argentina, 325, 332, 349, 352
and Central America, 184, 186, 194–5,
  199–202, 205
and Chile, 298, 305, 313
effects of American Civil War (1861–5), 203

and Mexico, 113–14, 131, 137, 141–4, 148,
  149, 151, 157, 162–3
and Peru, 240, 241, 246, 250, 259
political and judicial systems, influence of,
  56–9 *passim*, 131, 184, 186, 332, 351
Urbina, José María, 234, 235
Urmeneta, José Tomás, 295, 296
Urquiza, Justo José de, 347, 350–5 *passim*,
  359, 364, 371
Urrutia y Montoya, Carlos, 172
Uruguay, Banda Oriental (*see also*
  Montevideo; Río de la Plata), 37, 62, 68,
  314, 319, 358–65, 372–4
and Argentina, 350, 358, 363–5
and Brazil, 347, 358–65 *passim*
Guerra Grande, 344–7, 358–9
immigrants, 358–63 *passim*, 372–3
and Paraguayan War, 364–5, 370–2, 373
slavery, 43, 338, 363
Uruguay, river, 346, 351, 352, 364

Valdivia, Chile, 283, 306
Valenzuela, Pedro, 188, 189
Valle, José Cecilio del, 174, 175, 181, 182, 184
Valparaíso, Chile, 35, 39, 40, 45, 241, 246,
  270, 279, 283, 291 n4, 293–4, 301, 302,
  307
Vanderbilt, Cornelius, 200
Varas, Antonio, 291, 305, 309
Varela, Felipe, 354
Vargas, Dr José María, 223
Veintemilla, Ignacio, 234, 235
Velasco, José Miguel, 271
Venezuela (*see also* Gran Colombia), 58–9, 62,
  65, 87, 209, 216–18, 221–32 *passim*,
  237–8
agriculture, 18–20, 211–12, 214
Church, 215, 217
economy, 36, 37, 211–12, 213–14, 218–19,
  225
military, position of, 79, 80, 81, 220–1,
  225–6
population and social structure (*see also*
  slavery), 24, 27, 30, 31, 208, 214–16,
  236–7
slavery, 24, 43, 214
Veracruz, Mexico, 110, 123, 125, 127–8, 135,
  138, 143, 160–6 *passim*
Verapaz, the, Guatemala, 199
Vial, Manuel Camilo, 290
Victoria, Guadalupe, 124, 128–33 *passim*
Vicũna Mackenna, Benjamin, 307, 308, 312,
  313
Villareal, F., 152
Villa Rica, Paraguay, 368
Villavicencio, Manuel, 213

Viteri, Bishop Jorge, 192, 194
Vivaceta, Fermín, 304
Vivanco, General, 250

Walker, William, 194, 200–2
Walker Martínez, Carlos, 309
Ward, Sir H. G., 6–7, 13
Warny, Luis, 278
Wheelwright, William, 35, 301
Whymper, Edward, 236
Whytehead, William K., 367
Wilson, Belford, 230
Wright, John, 196

Yamparaes, Bolivia, 275

Ytapúa, Paraguay, 366
Yucatán, Mexico
    rebels against Mexico (1839), 138, 140,
        146–7, 157
    after 1839, 114, 145, 147, 148, 160
Yungas, Bolivia, 273, 274
Yungay, Peru, 249, 270, 289

Zacatecas, Mexico, 11, 108, 109, 135, 136,
    137, 160, 163
Zamora, Ezequiel, 226–7
Zaragoza, General, 166
Zárate, Agustín de, 250
Zavala, Lorenzo, 86, 113–14, 133–8 *passim*
Zuloaga, Félix, 159, 160–1, 166